THE

STUDIO
STORY

THE Disney STUDIO STORY

RICHARD HOLLISS
BRIAN SIBLEY

OCTOPUS

Despite every effort on the part of the Justin Knowles Publishing Group, Richard Holliss and Brian Sibley, it is regretted that a number of motion pictures could not be illustrated because of the contractual arrangements between The Walt Disney Company and various performers.

ISBN 0 7064 3040 9

First published in 1988 by Octopus Books Limited
Michelin House, 81 Fulham Road, London SW3 6RB

Produced by the Justin Knowles Publishing Group
9 Colleton Crescent, Exeter, Devon EX2 4BY

Editor: Lydia Darbyshire
Indexer: Hazel Bell
Designer: Ron Pickless
Jacket designer: John Leach

Phototypeset by Keyspools Limited, Golborne, Lancs
Printed and bound in Hong Kong

CONTENTS

INTRODUCTION:

THE HOUSE THAT WALT BUILT . . .

It is one of America's most unusual statutes: Public Law 99–391 (08/23/86) 'A Joint Resolution To Designate December 5, 1986, as "Walt Disney Recognition Day".' The date chosen for this honour was that on which, 85 years earlier, Walter Elias Disney had been born. It was also the month that marked the 20th anniversary of his death.

What was so remarkable about this man and his work that the Senate and House of Representatives of the United States of America should set aside time to frame such a resolution? The reasons set out in the preamble to the bill provide an answer of sorts:

... The delightful characters created by Walt Disney, including Mickey Mouse and Donald Duck, have brought joy to several generations ... Walt Disney used the characters he created to promote family values and to teach civic and moral lessons ... produced nature documentaries that yielded fascinating insights into the animal kingdom and emphasized the importance of conserving the natural heritage of the Nation ... devoted an enormous amount of time and resources to improving the quality of urban life in the United States through the construction of Walt Disney World and EPCOT Center ... was an American folk hero who became famous worldwide ...

Walt Disney, showman and entrepreneur, whose films made him known and loved throughout the world.

Alone among the great movie moguls, Walt Disney became entirely and indissolubly associated with the products – films, entertainments and merchandise – that bore his name, whereas the identities of Hollywood's other movie-makers were hidden behind acronyms (MGM), partnerships (Warner Brothers) or romantic names like Universal and Paramount.

Disney's most famous creation, Mickey Mouse, with his sweetheart Minnie on an early issue of *Mickey Mouse Magazine*.

Perhaps the most important decision Walt Disney ever took was in 1925, when he changed the name of his company from Disney Brothers Studio to the Walt Disney Studio. It was a name that, as one of the speakers in the House of Representatives observed, was to become not only immortal but 'synonymous with joy, goodwill and integrity'.

It is a popular misconception that Walt Disney invented the cartoon film. He didn't; that had been done by others while he was still a child. Nor were his first attempts at making animated pictures especially unique; they were largely derivative of the films being produced by the already established animation studios of New York. However, within just a few years, he and the artists he gathered about him had elevated the cartoon medium to an art form, and his style and techniques were being copied by the rest of the industry.

Over the years there has been much debate over the exact role Walt Disney played within the multi-faceted empire that bore his name. Whenever he was asked the question – and it was often – he replied with a story:

Well, you know, I was stumped one day when a little boy asked, 'Do you draw Mickey Mouse?' I had to admit I do not draw any more. 'Then you think up all the jokes and ideas?' 'No,' I said, 'I don't do that.' Finally, he looked at me and said, 'Mr Disney, just what do you do?' 'Well,' I said, 'sometimes I think of myself as a little bee. I go from one area of the Studio to another and gather pollen and sort of stimulate everybody. I guess that's the job I do.'

In truth, there was scarcely a Disney creation that he did not motivate or to which he did not bring his own particular genius. It can be argued that without the talents of those he employed, none of his company's accomplishments would have been achieved; but without his vision and stimulation and, above all, his courage in taking risks, none of them would have been initiated or sustained.

Walt Disney's greatest attribute was his dissatisfaction with things as they are. He began animating with cut-out

The first official guide to Disneyland (using the famous pseudo-Gothic lettering) for the park's opening in 1955.

THE STORY OF
Disneyland
with a complete guide to

FANTASYLAND
TOMORROWLAND
ADVENTURELAND
FRONTIERLAND
MAIN STREET U.S.A.

© Copyright, 1955, by Disneyland, Inc.

figures but was not content until he had learned to animate by drawing and painting on celluloid. And, having mastered that, he sought every way he could to improve on the process. He was the first to add synchronized sound and, later, full colour to cartoons. The first, in the age of 'talkies', to produce a feature-length animated film. The first animator to experiment with stereo sound, 3-D, CinemaScope and Technirama. And the first and only cartoonist to make a successful break into live-action film-making.

Almost all the Studio's releases have proved to be not only timeless classics, but also an unequalled source of revenue. In 1987, the 32-year-old cartoon feature *Lady and the Tramp* sold 2 million copies on video, breaking all previous records. The same year, *Snow White and the Seven Dwarfs* celebrated its golden anniversary with a cinema rerelease that grossed a staggering $45 million in the US alone.

The characters from the Disney movies – whether animated like Mickey Mouse and Pinocchio; portrayed by actors and actresses in such roles as Long John Silver and Mary Poppins; or inanimate objects like Herbie the Volkswagen – are known throughout the world. In addition to the cinema, Walt Disney and his successors have been major producers for television. And, not content with filmed entertainment, Walt created Disneyland and the concept of the theme park, which has revolutionized the leisure industry.

Walt's business philosophy, and that of his company, is encapsulated in a phrase quoted in *The Wall Street Journal*: 'Dream, diversify – and never miss an angle.' It is a philosophy that found realization in the most successful merchandising business in the history of marketing. The company has promoted numerous commodities, as well as generating millions of books, comics, records, toys, clothes, games and watches. There is no other company whose products are so collected, and there is scarcely an item of Disneyana – from original Disney art work to ticket stubs from Disneyland – that hasn't a price and a buyer.

To what then can be ascribed the secret of The Walt Disney Company's success? In his relatively short career Walt Disney showed himself to be a survivor, and it was an aptitude he bequeathed to his heirs. With the dedicated help of his brother, Roy, and a highly creative staff, Walt built a company that overcame numerous vicissitudes: financial uncertainties, industrial unrest, economic slumps, constantly shifting market conditions and, eventually, even the death of its founder. More recently the company has weathered take-over attempts and dramatic changes in management, and finds itself, today, enjoying what the present chairman, Michael D. Eisner calls 'a Disney Renaissance', with revenues and profits standing at an all-time high.

'I feel,' Walt Disney once said, 'there is no door which, with the kind of talent we have in our organization, could not be opened.' But even he might have been astonished by the scale and ambition of the plans on the Disney drawing board six decades after the birth of Mickey Mouse.

In the annals of American film-making, there has been no other studio to compare with The Walt Disney Company. This is its story . . .

Brian Sibley

1. DISNEY IN CARTOONLAND

'Contrary to a belief prevalent among his younger fans,' wrote Phil Santora in the New York *Daily News*, 'Walt Disney wasn't born in a never-never land of enchanted dwarfs, lugubrious dragons, soft-eyed deer, impudent ducks, frisky chipmunks and dancing mushrooms. Neither did a good fairy wave her hand and summon him into this mortal world in a blaze of light.'

He was born, in fact, in Chicago in the first year of the 20th century, the fourth son of Elias and Flora Disney. His father was an optimistic but never very successful man who had worked on the Union Pacific Railroad and run a farm and later a hotel in Florida before taking his wife and their first child, Herbert, to Chicago in 1889.

Elias went into the construction business, starting by building a house for himself at 1249 Tripp Avenue. It was there that two more boys were born: Raymond Arthur in 1890 and Roy Oliver in 1893. Eight and a half years later, on 5 December 1901, Flora had another son who was named after the Reverend Walter Parr, the local congregationalist minister. Christened Walter Elias Disney, the boy was to make it one of the most famous names in the world.

The Disney brothers gained a sister in 1903, when Flora gave birth to a daughter, Ruth. Three years later, worried by growing violence in Chicago, Elias bought a 45-acre farm in Marceline, Missouri, near to a property owned by one of his brothers. The next four years made a lasting impression on the young Walt: they developed in him a fascination with nature that he never lost and that was to prove a recurrent theme in his later work; and the farm's proximity to the Atchison, Topeka & Santa Fe railroad began his lifelong love of trains. There was also Walt's first exposure to the wonders of motion pictures when he and his sister sneaked into Marceline and visited the recently opened theatre.

It was during this period too that Walt produced his first known drawings of consequence. He and Ruth discovered a barrel of tar and, dipping sticks into the black liquid, drew pictures on the whitewashed wall of the Disney homestead. Ruth's efforts were a series of zig-zags; the more ambitious Walt went in for houses and, according to some versions of the story, a portrait of a pig.

Elias Disney was a strict disciplinarian and Walt was appropriately punished for his artistic endeavours. His fondness for drawing, however, was encouraged by his Aunt Margaret, who visited the family from her home in Kansas City bringing Walt sketching pads and crayons. 'I was,' Walt later recalled, 'a little beyond the usual childhood matchstick phase of depicting the human body at that point. I was trying to draw with more form and roundness.'

All too soon, life in Marceline came to an end. The two eldest sons, rebelling against their father's authoritarian rule, ran away from home; and when, in 1909, Elias contracted typhoid fever and pneumonia, the responsibility for the farm fell to the 16-year-old Roy. Farming had been hard work for all but the youngest members of the family, and Elias, eventually giving in to pressure from his wife, agreed to sell up and move to Kansas City, where he bought a newspaper distributorship, and for the next six years Walt was an unpaid delivery boy. It was a traumatic change, and Walt retained vivid memories of his life on the farm. When, 40 years later, he built a barn on his California estate to serve as a workshop, he modelled it after the one on the Marceline farm, and his memories of the nearby small town were immortalized in dozens of his movies and as Disneyland's Main Street, U.S.A.

In 1912 Roy left home and went to work on the farm of an uncle in Kansas, while the two younger Disney children were enrolled at Benton Grammar School where Walt discovered the joy of books, avidly reading Scott, Dickens, Mark Twain and Robert Louis Stevenson. His first love remained drawing, however, although his unconventional approach to art sometimes got him into trouble, as when he was told to make a sketch of a bowl of flowers and he put faces on the blooms and gave them arms instead of leaves. Walt attended children's art classes at the Kansas City Art Institute and, at home, copied the political cartoons from Elias' socialist newspaper, *Appeal to Reason*.

Among his childhood pleasures were magic tricks and an early attempt at animation, when he made a flip-book to entertain his sister. An important friendship was made with a classmate, Walter Pfeiffer, whose parents, German immigrants, were a light-hearted couple who enjoyed sing-songs and family entertainments of the kind that, because of Elias Disney's strict, pietistic attitudes, the young Walt had never experienced before.

The Pfeiffers loved vaudeville, and the two boys made regular visits to the burlesque shows. Walt was captivated by the theatre, and he and the Pfeiffer boy were soon working up routines. These they performed at school and on amateur nights at the local theatres, appearing as 'The Two Walts', 'Hans and Mike' (Pfeiffer as a comic German and Walt as an Irishman) or as 'Charlie Chaplin and the Count'.

Young Walt Disney (right) with his friend Walt Pfeiffer in costume for one of their prize-winning comic routines.

Elias Disney found his newspaper distribution was less successful than he had expected and, in 1917, he sold up and moved to Chicago, where he bought a share in the O-Zell Jelly factory. Walt stayed in Kansas City until his graduation that summer and, after working his vacation as a candy-butcher on the railroad (selling sweets and soft drinks to passengers), he joined his parents in Chicago.

With his sights now set on a career as an artist, Walt began studying the routines of the burlesque comics and building up a file of gags for use in his cartoons. He persuaded his father to pay for a correspondence course in art, although Elias insisted that, in return, his son contribute to the family income. When he wasn't at school, McKinley High, or pursuing his artistic interests, he worked as a part-time bottle-washer at the jelly factory and as a guard on the city's elevated railway.

'As long as I can remember,' said Roy, many years later, 'Walt has been working. . . . He worked in the daytime and he worked at night. Walt didn't play much as a boy. He still can't catch a ball with any certainty.'

At night classes at the Chicago Institute of Art, Walt came under the influence of the celebrated cartoonist Carey Orr, whose comic-strip in the Chicago *Tribune* took the form of a cartoon newspaper called 'The Tiny Tribune'. Walt parodied Orr's style for the school magazine as 'The Tiny Voice – McKinley's Smallest Paper'. Roy Disney had joined the Navy in 1917, and many of his young brother's cartoons commented on the European war in which America had now become involved.

Despite being under age, Walt himself was anxious to play his part in the war and made abortive plans to run away to Canada where he would have been old enough to enlist. In 1918, he and a schoolfriend Russell Maas enlisted in the American Ambulance Corps, but the ruse collapsed when the boys needed a parental signature on their passport applications. Elias Disney refused to sign, but Flora signed the necessary document and turned a blind eye as her son changed his birth date from 1901 to 1900.

Although the Armistice was declared on 11 November 1918, there was still work for the Allies to do in Europe, and Walt left for France where he spent the next year. In his free time, he kept up his drawing – designing posters for the camp canteen, drawing cartoons on the canvas sides of the ambulances and submitting pictures to such magazines as *Judge* and *Life*.

The US forces left Paris in September 1919, and Walt was soon on his way back to America, determined to pursue his ambition to be a cartoonist. He began his search for work in Kansas City where Roy was now a teller with the First National Bank.

Walt went in search of a job as cartoonist for the *Kansas City Star*. The *Star* already had a cartoonist and turned him down. His next stop was the offices of the *Kansas City Journal*, where editor Lawrence Dickey viewed his portfolio and complimented him on its quality. However, the *Journal* didn't need a cartoonist any more than the *Star*, and all Dickey could offer Walt was a promise to keep his name on file. Roy heard of an opening at the Pesmen-Rubin Commercial Art Studio, which designed advertisements and letter-heads for local companies. Walt applied for the job, and Louis Pesmen and Bill Rubin, liking what they saw of his work, engaged him at $50 a month. His first client was the manufacturer of a particular brand of mash that, allegedly, induced hens to lay more eggs. Walt drew nests piled high with eggs and hens hatching out dollar signs.

At Pesmen-Rubin Walt made friends with a lad of his own age named Ubbe Iwwerks, the son of a Dutch immigrant. They worked on a variety of jobs, including Christmas advertisements for Kansas City stores and the cover for the weekly programme published by the Newman Theater, but they didn't realize that they had been taken on to help meet a seasonal increase in work, and as soon as the pre-Christmas rush was over, they were laid off. They immediately decided to set up in business together.

Ubbe simplified his name to Ub Iwerks and the company was called Disney-Iwerks. But Walt couldn't help feeling it sounded like a firm of opticians, and the company was re-named Iwerks-Disney Commercial Artists.

An example of artwork designed by Walt during his time at the Pesmen-Rubin Commercial Art Studio.

Ub provided lettering and illustrations while Walt contributed cartoons and acted as salesman for the company. One of their first jobs came from Walt Pfeiffer's father, who worked for the United Leatherworkers' Union and commissioned some illustrations for the Union's Journal.

Iwerks-Disney was a short-lived venture and, after only a month, in January 1920, Walt applied for a job as an artist to produce 'cartoons and wash drawings' for the Kansas City Slide Company.

Walt Disney at the drawing-board as he depicted himself on his first calling-card.

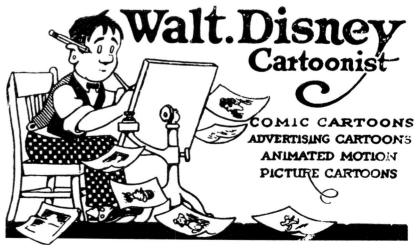

A Hollywood film mogul in the making: Walt Disney behind one of his early cameras.

(Shortly after Walt joined the staff, the company changed its name to the Kansas City Film Ad Company.) The studio produced 60-second film commercials for the picture houses using jointed paper figures photographed with a stop-motion camera, but Walt soon grew dissatisfied with this limited form of animation and began to study books on anatomy and movement and to learn how animated films such as Krazy Kat and Mutt and Jeff were made with drawings.

He had purchased his first movie camera in 1918, filming himself in Charlie Chaplin costume. Realizing the importance of being able to operate a camera effectively, he persuaded the Film Ad Company's cameraman to instruct him in its use and to let him try his hand at filming.

He also began to add gags of his own to the scripts he was given to animate. One that he fondly recalled, many years later, was an advertisement for a company that made replacement covers for automobiles. An impressed bystander asks the driver of a new-looking car, 'Hi, Old Top – new car?' to which the driver replies: 'No, old car – new top'.

While things were working out well for Walt, Ub Iwerks was in trouble. He was no salesman and, with Walt gone, less and less work came in. In March 1920, Walt persuaded A. Vern Cauger, who ran the Kansas City Film Ad Company, to take Ub onto the staff, and the two friends were together again.

Pursuing his ambition to make animated films of the kind that were produced in New York by Paul Terry, Max and Dave Fleischer and John R. Bray, Walt set up a studio in the garage of the old Disney

home where he and Roy were living with their brother Herbert and his wife. Borrowing a stop-motion camera from Cauger, Walt animated a short film about Kansas City's appalling road conditions. Though primitive, it had the unmistakable Disney touch, with drivers losing their teeth as their cars bounce over potholes. Walt showed the finished film to Milton Feld, manager of the Newman Theater Company, who was greatly amused and commissioned

Gag-shot with Walt brandishing a pistol over Carman Maxwell, Ub with megaphone and Adolph Kloepper operating the camera.

further films for which he paid 30 cents a foot. Subsequent cartoons featured jokes about political campaigns, attempts to get rid of corruption in the Kansas City Police Force and a cartoon character, Professor Whosis, who demonstrated some brutal remedies for theatre patrons who insisted on reading film captions aloud!

The series became known as Newman Laugh-O-grams, and Walt's aim was now to make a series of entertainment cartoons. Cauger didn't see any need to move out of the advertising market, and Walt realized that he would have to act on his own if he was going to achieve his ambitions. He advertised for boys who wanted to learn how to make cartoons and received three applicants. Although he couldn't afford to pay them, he undertook to teach them the rudiments of animation and promised them a share in any profits made from the series of Laugh-O-gram cartoons he was planning.

Working in the evenings Walt and his young associates produced a modernized version of *Little Red Riding Hood*. Pleased with the finished results, Walt began work on a second film, based on the folk tale *The Four Musicians of Bremen*. As with most contemporary cartoon shorts, the hallmarks of Laugh-O-grams were slapstick comedy and vaudeville gags. For example, the cat in *The Four Musicians of Bremen* gets involved in a fight with a gang of robbers and, in quick succession, loses all nine lives, which leave his body and float up to heaven; just in time, however, he catches hold of the tail of his ninth life and saves it.

With the completion of his second Laugh-O-gram, Walt was convinced that he was now in a position to leave the Film Ad Company and set up his own studio, but the Disney family was going through a difficult period. In 1920, Roy – who at the time was planning to marry his steady girlfriend, Edna Francis – contracted tuberculosis and was sent to a hospital in Santa Fe, New Mexico. Elias Disney's jelly factory failed and, together with Flora and Ruth, he returned to Kansas City, where he once again sought to earn a living from construction work. But little or no employment came his way, and when Herbert Disney, who worked for the Post Office, was transferred to Portland, Oregon, Elias, Flora and Ruth went to live with him and his wife.

The Disney home was sold and Walt moved into rooms. Quitting his job with the Film Ad Company, he rented office space on East 31st Street. In May 1922, Laugh-O-gram Films was incorporated with 300 shares of $50 apiece, put up by local investors who received company stock in exchange for supplying furniture and equipment. Walt held 70 shares and, at just 20 years of age, owned his first company.

Walt persuaded Ub Iwerks to leave the Film Ad Company and join him, and he soon had a staff of gifted young animators – Hugh Harman, Rudolf Ising, Carmen 'Max' Maxwell, Lorey Tague and Otto Walliman – together with a girl to ink and paint the celluloid animations, a salesman, business manager, secretary and a 'Technical Engineer' and cameraman, William 'Red' Lyon.

Laugh-O-gram's artists clowning around: (left to right) Walt, Ub Iwerks, Rudolf Ising and Hugh Harman.

Walt's childhood friend, Walter Pfeiffer, was engaged as 'scenario editor', and work was soon underway on a third Laugh-O-gram, *Jack and the Beanstalk*. With characteristic optimism, Walt placed an advertisement in the *Motion Picture News*, announcing a series of 12 Laugh-O-grams. Despite being well animated, the zany little cartoons could not find a distributor; so salesman Leslie Mace took *Jack and the Beanstalk* to New York where, in September 1922, he finally succeeded in signing a deal with a non-theatrical distributor, Pictorial Clubs of Tennessee, which hired films to schools and churches.

An order was placed for six Laugh-O-grams costing $11,000 to be delivered on 1 January 1924. Although this gave Walt and his colleagues a 15-month deadline, Pictorial Clubs advanced only $100: an arrangement that proved disastrous.

Two more films – *Goldie Locks and the Three Bears* and *Puss in Boots* – were produced and a sixth picture, *Cinderella*, was soon being scripted. In addition, the studio was producing a series of 'Lafflets', 300-foot long cartoon snippets. The Lafflets, with such titles as *Golf in Slow Motion*, *The Woodland Potter* and *A Pirate for a Day*, were produced in a variety of film media. Sending a sample reel to Universal Pictures, Laugh-O-gram's business manager, Adolph Kloepper, pointed out that 'two of these reels are cartoon material and the other clay modelling. In the series we will also introduce cartoons and live characters acting together in some productions...'.

Despite this industriousness, Laugh-O-grams still had no income. Walt picked up some paid work as occasional Kansas City reporter for Pathé and other newsreel studios. One unlikely source of finance was reported in the *Kansas City Star* in October 1922:

Recording the Baby's Life in Films
The Laugh-O-gram Films Co., Inc., ... has added the feature of photographing youngsters to its regular business of making animated films. An admiring parent wishing to preserve the native graces of his progeny's actions notifies 'Red Lyon', cinematographer, and 'Walt' Disney, president of the Corporation and head cartoonist for the animated cartoons ...

The following month, Laugh-O-gram found a backer in the person of Dr J. V. Cowles, a retired physician and investor, who advanced the studio $2,500 in exchange for a stock-holding. The money was desperately needed, but it was not enough. Cowles' investment helped pay-off the studio's creditors, but it was insufficient for the payment of salaries, and some of the employees began looking around for other jobs.

December 1922 brought a useful commission from a local dentist, Dr Thomas B. McCrum, who asked Laugh-O-gram to make a short educational film on dental hygiene. It is an indication of the desperate situation at Laugh-O-gram that Walt was unable to go to McCrum's office because his only pair of shoes was being repaired and he didn't have the $1.50 needed to collect them from the shoe shop. The dentist paid the shoe bill and agreed to a fee of $500 for the picture.

Tommy Tucker's Tooth tells the story of two boys, Tommy Tucker and Jimmie Jones, one of whom looks after his teeth and his personal appearance and one who does not, and how, when both boys apply for a job, it is the good Tommy Tucker who is rewarded with employment. Although a live-action film, *Tommy Tucker's Tooth* contained short animated sequences featuring the troublesome activities of tooth decay. A sequel, *Clara Cleans Her Teeth*, was made in 1926.

Financially, things were looking bad for Laugh-O-gram and in January 1923 came the first of a series of resignations when Lorey Tague quit the studio.

The following month, a local businessman advanced the company $500 and made further loans in April, May and June, in which month the studio moved to less expensive premises. The loans totalled $1,500, secured against all Laugh-O-gram's assets, including the still-to-be-paid contract with Pictorial Clubs. Walt also received regular cheques from his brother Roy, but the situation failed to improve, and several more of Laugh-O-gram's artists decided to leave.

Virginia Davis as Alice reads a fairy-tale to Julius the cat on a lobby-card for the 1924 film *Alice and the Three Bears*.

One of Walt's last attempts to raise finance was a planned live-action film series illustrating popular songs, which would be screened at theatres to an organ accompaniment or a vocal performance by a singer. Walt discussed the idea for the pictures – which he had decided to call 'Song-O-Reels' – with Carl Stalling, organist and conductor at the Isis Theater, and several possible numbers were considered. Laugh-O-gram's first and only 'Song-O-Reel' was a dramatization of Joe L. Sanders' hit 'Martha; Just a Plain Old Fashioned Name'. But *Martha* came too late upon the scene, and it was clear that the Laugh-O-gram company was finished. Roy, who had been following Walt's career from hospital, sent his brother some advice: 'Kid,' he told him, 'I think you should get out of there. I don't think you can do any more for it.'

But get out to where? Walt decided it had to be Hollywood, and in July 1923 he boarded a train bound for the movie Mecca. He had just $40 in the pocket of his threadbare jacket and his cardboard suitcase contained a shirt, a change of socks and underwear, a few drawing materials and a reel of film entitled *Alice's Wonderland*.

It had been two months earlier, in May 1923, that Walt had written to a number of New York distributors:

We have just discovered something new and clever in animated cartoons! The first subject of this distinctly different series is now in production . . . It is a new idea that will appeal to all classes, and is bound to be a winner, because it is a clever combination of live characters and cartoons, not like 'Out of the Inkwell' . . . but of an entirely different nature, using a cast of live child actors who carry on their action on cartoon scenes with cartoon characters.

The story for this innovative cartoon was vaguely inspired by Lewis Carroll's classic *Alice's Adventures in Wonderland*. Called *Alice's Wonderland*, it featured an engaging moppet with curly hair named Virginia Davis, who had been a model for the Kansas City Film Ad Company. Miss Davis played Alice, a little girl who visits an animation studio and asks to see the cartoonists 'draw some funnies'. Among those who appeared in this sequence were Walt, Ub Iwerks, Hugh Harman and Rudolf Ising. That night Alice dreams that she goes to Cartoonland and has various escapades with its inhabitants, which conclude with her being chased by lions.

On his arrival in Hollywood Walt went to live with his Uncle Robert Disney, who had retired to Los Angeles. Roy had been transferred to the Veterans Hospital in Sawtelle, west of Los Angeles, and was just a bus ride away.

Hollywood lived up to all Walt's expectations: Cecil B. De Mille was filming *The Ten Commandments* and Douglas Fairbanks was building a monumental set for *The Thief of Bagdad*. It was the year

of Lon Chaney's *The Hunchback of Notre Dame* and George Arliss' *The Green Goddess*. Hal Roach's *Our Gang* made their screen debut, Gloria Swanson was *Bluebeard's Eighth Wife*, Charlie Chaplin wrote, produced and directed *A Woman of Paris* and Harold Lloyd hung from the hands of a clock hundreds of feet above the street in *Safety Last*.

But there were no cartoon studios. The centre of the animation industry was New York. It was 17 years since James Stuart Blackton had made the first film using drawn animation, *Humorous Phases of Funny Faces*, and in that time the medium had been advanced by such pioneers as Winsor McCay, Earl Hurd, Walter Lantz and Paul Terry, and by the Fleischer brothers, with their phenomenally successful 'Out of the Inkwell' series. The top cartoon stars of the day were Mutt and Jeff and Pat Sullivan's Felix the Cat, who, animated by Otto Messmer, had made his debut in 1921 and was already a national institution.

Walt decided to offer his services to the live-action studios. Visiting the Universal Pictures studio, he handed in his card: 'Walter Disney, representing Universal News and Selznick News; Representative in Kansas City, Missouri'. He spent a fascinating day wandering around the lots and sound stages. The following morning he presented himself again and asked for employment as a director. He was shown the door. The experience at Universal was re-enacted at several other studios, and Walt began to despair of breaking into movies. With no money coming in, he had to borrow from Roy to pay the $5 a week rent due to his uncle.

Deciding that he would have to establish himself as an animation producer, he did what he had done in Kansas City and set up a temporary headquarters in Uncle Robert's garage. Securing an interview with theatre-owner Alexander Pantages, he presented ideas for a series of cartoon joke-reels of the kind he had produced for the Newman Theater.

With new stationery declaring himself 'Walt Disney Cartoonist', he wrote to Margaret J. Winkler, one of the New York distributors to whom he had sent advance information on *Alice's Wonderland*. To Walt, if not the recipient of the letter, it must have sounded like whistling in the dark:

This is to inform you that I am no longer connected with the Laugh-O-gram Films, Inc., of Kansas City, Mo., and that I am establishing a studio in Los Angeles for the purpose of producing the new and novel series of cartoons I have previously written you about.

Alice and Julius try their hand at running a railroad in the 1925 picture *Alice's Tin Pony*, which combined real and cartoon characters.

The making of these new cartoons necessitates being located in a production center that I may engage trained talent for my casts, and be within reach of the right facilities for producing. I am taking with me a select number of my former staff and will in a very short time be producing at regular intervals. It is my intention of securing working space with one of the studios that I may better study technical detail and comedy situations and combine these with my cartoons . . .

By this time, the employees of Laugh-O-gram had put the company into bankruptcy with total liabilities of over $12,000 and the creditors had to be prevailed upon to allow *Alice's Wonderland*, which was one of Laugh-O-gram's assets, to be released for Miss Winkler to view. Her response came quickly on 15 October 1923:

BELIEVE SERIES CAN BE PUT OVER BUT PHOTOGRAPHY OF ALICE SHOULD SHOW MORE DETAIL AND BE STEADIER THIS BEING NEW PRODUCT MUST SPEND LARGE AMOUNT ON EXPLOITATION AND ADVERTISING THEREFORE NEED YOUR COOPERATION WILL PAY FIFTEEN HUNDRED EACH NEGATIVE FOR FIRST SIX AND TO SHOW MY GOOD FAITH WILL PAY FULL AMOUNT ON EACH OF THESE SIX IMMEDIATELY ON DELIVERY OF NEGATIVE . . .

Walt discussed the offer with Roy, and the brothers decided to accept Miss Winkler's terms. Roy discharged himself from hospital and the deal for a series of Alice comedies was signed.

With $200 of Roy's savings and $500 borrowed from Uncle Robert, Walt rented a small office at 4651 Kingswell Avenue for $10 a month. It was a condition of Miss Winkler's offer that the same actress be used to play Alice, and Virginia Davis was given $100-a-month contract.

Work began on the first picture, animated entirely by Walt, inked and painted by two girls hired for $15 a week and photographed by Roy on a $200 second-hand camera. The completed film, *Alice's Day at Sea*, in which Alice gets shipwrecked and has a battle with an octopus, was sent to New York and deemed by Miss Winkler to be 'satisfactory'. A few days before the end of 1923, the first payment for the Alice comedies was received and work began on a second picture, *Alice Hunting in Africa*.

In January 1924, Walt hired a lot on Hollywood Boulevard for $10 a month for live-action filming, and local children were paid 50 cents a day to appear as Alice's friends in such pictures as *Alice's Spooky Adventure* and *Alice's Wild West Show*. The studio expanded when, in February, Walt hired his first animator, Rollin 'Ham' Hamilton and rented a shop adjoining his existing premises. The signwriters were called in, and the shop window was emblazoned with the words 'Disney Bros. Studio'.

Miss Winkler proved a severe critic and regularly wrote to Walt demanding improvements in timing and more laughs. Striving for perfection, Walt was soon spending more and more on the pictures and reducing – even, sometimes, eliminating – the profit margin. More finance was needed, and Walt begged loans from anyone he could: Carl Stalling provided $275, and Edna Francis, Roy's girlfriend in Kansas City, sent a cheque for $25 when, unbeknown to Roy, Walt wrote and asked for her help.

In May 1924, the sixth Alice picture, *Alice and the Dog Catcher* was completed, and Walt, realizing that he needed quality animators if the series was to survive, asked Ub Iwerks to join the studio. Ub, who had lost $1,000 with the collapse of Laugh-O-gram, was back with the Kansas City Film Ad Company and earning $50 a week. Walt offered a salary of $10 a week less, but Ub decided to accept, and he was soon contributing his considerable talents to the new Alice series with such pictures as *Alice Gets in Dutch*, *Alice and the Three Bears* and *Alice Cans the Cannibals*.

To begin with Margaret Winkler had paid promptly; now, for some reason, the cheques from New York were being delayed and were eventually reduced from the agreed $1,500 to $900 a film. There was an acrimonious correspondence between film-maker and distributor, in which Charles Mintz, who had recently married Miss Winkler and taken over her business, pleaded financial difficulties. Walt protested that he couldn't maintain the standards demanded of him if he didn't have the cash, and in December 1924 Mintz contracted for a further 18 Alice comedies at $1,800 each plus a share

in any profits. It seemed as if a more stable future for the Disney Brothers Studio was assured.

Roy Disney asked Edna Francis to come to California and be his wife. The couple were married on 7 April 1925, an event which prompted Walt to consider his own future and begin a courtship with Lillian Bounds who was employed as one of the studio's ink-and-paint girls. Two of Laugh-O-grams' best animators, Hugh Harman and Rudolf Ising, left Kansas City to join Walt, and on 6 July 1925 Walt and Roy put a $400 deposit on a lot at 2719 Hyperion Avenue where they planned to build a new studio. One week later, Walt and Lillian were married and set up home together in a minute, $40-a-month apartment.

But it wasn't long before there were new problems with Mintz, and payments were, once again, delayed. Negotiations for a new contract were fraught with hostility: Mintz proposed a reduced price of $1,500 per film and an equal share of profits after the first $300. Walt resisted but Mintz remained adamant. Eventually a deal was struck that gave Walt a share of any merchandising revenue and established the studio as owners of 'all trademarks and copyrights on *Alice* comedies'.

Virginia Davis had now left the Disney studio and, for a while, the role of Alice was played by Dawn O'Day. By the time Walt and his staff moved to Hyperion Avenue, a replacement Alice had been found in Margie Gay. The series continued with *Alice's Balloon Race*, *Alice's Little Parade* and her 30th picture, *Alice's Mysterious Mystery*, which, Mintz complained, had 'nothing in it whatever that is outstanding'.

Mintz was more complimentary of a later picture, *Alice the Fire Fighter*, which, he told Walt, was 'as good as anything you have turned out and perhaps a little better'; but Walt was beginning to tire of the series and longed for a new challenge.

This came in April 1927, when the studio was approaching its 50th Alice comedy. Carl Laemmle, head of Universal Pictures, told Charles Mintz that he was looking for a new cartoon series to feature a rabbit, and Margaret Mintz suggested Walt be offered the project. Walt jumped at the proposal, producing sketches for a black rabbit who bore something of a resemblance to Felix the Cat. Mintz named the character Oswald the Lucky Rabbit.

Walt went to work on a pilot film, *Poor Papa*, in which Oswald attempts to fight off storks who insist on delivering baby rabbits to his house. A reviewing committee was critical of the results, complaining about jerky animation, a story that was 'a succession of unrelated gags' and had too many 'dragged out' scenes and, most disastrously, describing Oswald as a far from funny character with 'no outstanding trait'. Oswald was thought too old, too fat and

A later 'Alice', Margie Gay, poses with Walt and assorted cartoon characters, including some early Disney mice.

rather too scruffy to achieve popularity with the public and Walt began transforming Oswald into a more attractive character.

A second picture but the first Oswald film to be released, *Trolley Troubles*, was seen as a great improvement and was voted a success by the movie trade press. The 56th – and last – Alice comedy, *Alice and the Beach Nut*, had been released in August 1927, and the studio was contracted to produce an Oswald picture every two weeks for a price of $2,250 a film. A run of what was to be 26 cartoons began with such titles as *Great Guns*, *The Mechanical Cow*, *Harem Scarem* and *Rickety Gin*, and won praise from *Motion Picture World* for being 'bright, speedy and genuinely amusing'.

There were many ways in which Oswald was to set the pattern for the later Mouse cartoons: he had a girlfriend, a trusty horse and an arch enemy called Peg Leg Pete; and several of his adventures were to be reworked in after years such as *The Ocean Hop*, in which Oswald uses a dachshund to power a home-made aeroplane; *Empty Socks*, which has him playing Santa Claus for a home full of mischievous orphans; and *Sky Scrappers*, in which he fights for the honour of his girl on a construction site.

Oswald also generated the first items of Disney character merchandising with Oswald badges and stencil sets, and a 5 cent chocolate bar in a wrapper with a mysterious design showing 'OSWALD The Welsh Rabbit'. 'There is something about the character of Oswald,' reported *Universal Weekly* in 1928, 'that makes people laugh. . . . He isn't just funny, he has got personality . . . he does unusual things and does them in a mighty interesting way.'

Oswald the Lucky Rabbit helps a lady friend to skate, politely raising his ears like a hat (a gag later copied by Mickey, which inspired the Mouseketeer hats).

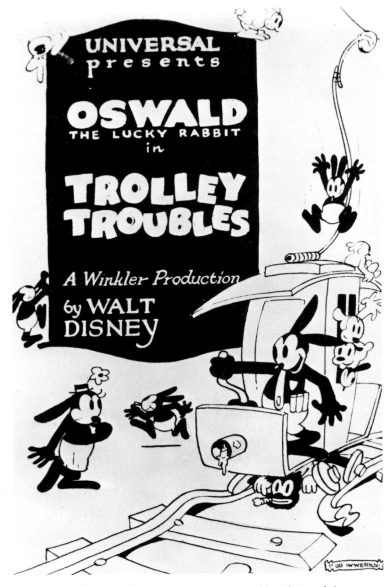

A poster for the first Oswald picture to be released, signed by 'Ub Iwwerks'.

On the strength of Oswald's success, Walt and Lilly, and Roy and Edna moved into two $7,000 prefabricated homes on Lyric Avenue. All seemed to be going well for what was now called the Walt Disney Studio. It was Ub Iwerks who first sensed something was amiss. The payments from Mintz were now being delivered in person by the distributor's brother-in-law and Hollywood agent, George Winkler, and Ub noticed that Winkler spent a great deal of time during his visits to the studio chatting to the animators.

Walt assumed that Winkler's interest was simply another indication of the distributor's satisfaction with the Oswald series and was unconcerned. In February, he and Lilly took a trip to New York to negotiate a deal for the next series of Oswald cartoons. He had intended to ask Mintz to raise the price paid for each film to $2,500, but Mintz had other plans. He offered Walt a reduced fee of $1,800 and, when Walt angrily refused, told him: 'Either you come with me at my price, or I'll take your organization away from you. I have your key men signed up.' Winkler's activities at the studio suddenly made sense. A telephone call to Roy revealed that almost all the Disney animators – Ub Iwerks being an exception – had accepted employment with Mintz.

Walt was frantically looking for an alternative distributor when Charles Mintz delivered the death blow: under the terms of his contract Oswald was the sole property of Universal Pictures and Walt had no rights in the character his studio had created. 'Never again,' he told Lilly, 'will I work for somebody else.'

There was nothing left to do, but take the train back to Hollywood.

2. ENTER THE MOUSE

When Walt Disney looked back on the many achievements of his company, he would often remark to his employees: 'I hope we never lose sight of one fact . . . that this was all started by a Mouse.'

As good an example as any of the simple, homespun Disney philosophy that proved so irresistible to journalists, the statement was, nevertheless, true. Walt identified more closely with Mickey Mouse than with any other character created by his Studio. After all, the perky little tike in white gloves and button-pants was a permanent reminder of the humble origins of his company and just how remarkable had been the accomplishments of the organization founded on the movie exploits of so unlikely a hero.

Mickey Mouse, Walt recalled in 1948, had popped out of his mind onto a drawing pad 'at a time when disaster seemed just around the corner.' Certainly, things couldn't have been more disastrous than they were on that day, in March 1928, when Walt and Lilly left New York for Hollywood. He had lost his film distributor, his cartoon star and most of his animators.

'DON'T WORRY,' he cabled Roy before leaving for home, 'EVERYTHING OK WILL GIVE DETAILS WHEN ARRIVE.' Everything, of course, was very far from OK, but, with the irrepressible optimism that was one of his strongest attributes he clung to a belief that 'whatever does happen is for the best'.

Walt viewed the blow that fate had dealt him as a positive opportunity: a chance to create a *new* cartoon character that might prove even more successful than Oswald the not-so-lucky Rabbit.

Exactly how that character was created has been the subject of so much myth – often of Walt's own devising – that it is difficult to be certain of the facts. According to some, Mickey Mouse was devised at a crisis conference with Roy and Ub, after Walt's return. But the most frequently told version tells how, as the train chugged its way on the long journey westward, Walt sat doodling characters on a sketch-pad, hoping for inspiration and a solution to his problems. In one of his many accounts of that journey, Walt recalled:

Out of the trouble and confusion stood a mocking, merry little figure. Vague and indefinable at first. But it grew and grew. And finally arrived – a mouse. A romping, rollicking little mouse. The idea completely engulfed me. The wheels turned to the tune of it. '*Chug, chug, mouse, chug, chug, mouse*', the train seemed to say. The whistle screeched it. '*A m-m-m-owa-ouse*', it wailed.

And why a mouse? Years before, so runs the tale, when Walt was a struggling young artist, he had befriended a family of mice that took up residence in a waste-paper basket. One particular mouse had, reputedly, become so tame it would climb up onto Walt's drawing board to be fed on scraps of food.

Not everyone believed this anecdote, among them Louis B. Mayer, production head of MGM, who commented in his characteristically blunt manner: 'That's a hokey story. Mickey Mouse was created in the imaginative mind of Walt Disney. Walt didn't need any help from a dirty little pesty animal.'

In truth, there were probably quite prosaic reasons for choosing a mouse. Among household animals the choice of potential characters was fairly restricted: cats and dogs were out of the question for Felix the Cat and Krazy Kat were already established cartoon stars and animator Walter Lantz had produced a successful series, 'Hot Dog

Cartoons', featuring Pete the Pup, and had also created Weakheart, the canine companion of his popular child character Dinky Doodle.

Cartoon mice, however, tended to be employed only in supporting roles. With the exception of Krazy Kat's rodent side-kick, Ignatz, mice had never been given screen personalities, although the cartoon mouse-shape was well established and their characteristic raffishness and quickness of movement obviously offered considerable opportunities for gags.

Whatever the reasons, Walt decided that his new character was to be a mouse. He also decided to call him Mortimer. It is one of Hollywood's best-known behind-the-screen stories that Lilly Disney disliked the name and persuaded her husband to change it to Mickey. Maybe Mickey Mouse didn't sound quite as onomatopoeic as Mortimer Mouse, but it was a friendlier, more informal name, suggesting an affinity with the common man.

Back in Hollywood, Walt had to break the bad news about the loss of Oswald to Roy and Ub. He was able to temper it, however, with the positive news that he had an idea for a new series of cartoons.

Since the defecting animators would not be leaving for another three months, Walt and Ub were forced to work in secret. The scenario they devised was inspired by the exploits of Charles Lindbergh who, in 1927, had made the first solo, non-stop flight across the Atlantic. In the film, which was to be called *Plane Crazy*, Mickey reads about 'Lindy' the 'Ace of Aces' and, assisted by his farmyard friends, builds an airplane in which he takes off, with his girlfriend Minnie, for a rickety flight into the bright blue yonder.

Plane Crazy not only set the trend for many of Mickey's earliest escapades, it also showed that while Mickey was described as a Mouse, there was little to justify the description beyond the vaguest facial resemblance. Large enough to consort with horses, cows and dogs, Mickey was neither mouse nor man but rather a symbol of youth, optimism and adventure.

Mickey emulated Charles Lindbergh when, together with Minnie, he took to the air in *Plane Crazy*.

The rest of the Studio was working on *Sleigh Bells*, the 24th Oswald cartoon and one of three titles still to be delivered under the terms of Walt's contract with Mintz. But while these were being completed, Ub Iwerks was busy animating *Plane Crazy* single-handed. If any of the other animators happened to wander into Ub's room he quickly hid his Mickey Mouse drawings under pictures of Oswald the Rabbit.

Ub worked at a phenomenal rate, producing 700 drawings a day, and each evening Walt took Ub's animation drawings home where they were inked and painted onto celluloid by Lilly Disney, Roy's wife Edna and Walt's sister-in-law, Hazel Sewell. Then Walt would return to the Studio with other completed animation cels to be photographed by cameraman Mike Marcus who had remained loyal to the Disneys.

Despite the problems, *Plane Crazy* was completed, at a cost of $1,772.89. It was previewed, with an organ accompaniment, at a theatre on Sunset Boulevard on 15 May 1928 and favourably – if not ecstatically – received. By the time work began on a second Mickey Mouse film, *Gallopin' Gaucho*, the rebel animators had left the Studio so there was no longer any need for secrecy, and the young assistant animators – Johnny Cannon, Wilfred Jackson and Les Clark – who were not part of the defection, could help.

Ub Iwerks, however, remained the key to Mickey Mouse's potential success, and how highly his contribution was rated can be seen from the fact that he was paid $90 a week compared with the $60 Walt gave himself or the $35 earned by Roy.

Although *Gallopin' Gaucho* was nearing completion, Walt was still looking for a distributor for the series. MGM viewed *Plane Crazy* but offered compliments rather than a contract, so Walt engaged E. J. Denison, a New York film dealer, to sell Mickey to one of the East Coast distributors.

Walt needed an advance of $3,000 a cartoon for supplying 26 films a year, but although he was convinced that 'with good pictures and a good release' they could 'make the name of "Mickey Mouse" as well-known as any cartoon on the market', Denison failed to interest any of the distributors. The trouble was that, while Mickey's movies were lively and well animated, there was nothing particularly original about them.

It was then that Walt and Ub decided that they would make their cartoons unique by giving them what no other animated series had – synchronized sound. Surely no one would ignore Mickey Mouse if he was the first cartoon character to talk.

There had been numerous earlier attempts at synchronizing sound and pictures, beginning in 1887 when Thomas Edison conceived an idea for adding sound accompaniment to his Kinetoscope. Then came a variety of contraptions such as the Synchroscope, the Cameraphone, the Phonofilm and the Photokinema with which, in 1921, D. W. Griffith showed *Dream Street*, an historic film that had sequences with dialogue.

But it was the development of Vitaphone by the Bell Laboratories that sounded the death knell for the silent movie. In April 1926, Western Electric licensed Warner Brothers to produce talking pictures. Their first experiment using the Vitaphone disc process was to add a synchronized orchestral score to John Barrymore's silent picture, *Don Juan*. Then, on 6 October 1927, came *The Jazz Singer* and, in July 1928, Warner Brothers released the first all-talking picture, *Lights of New York*.

'Audiences are saying it *everywhere* –,' ran an early advertisement for Vitaphone. 'At last – "*Pictures* that *talk* like *living people*!"' Although many film-makers refused at first to believe that sound movies were anything more than a nine-day wonder, by the autumn of 1929 almost 5,000 theatres in America were equipped for sound, while the studios of Hollywood worked flat out to meet the public demand for 'talkies'.

Walt and Ub Iwerks were quick to realize the potential sound offered to the cartoon film and, although they had not yet sold the first two films, they decided to give Mickey a voice.

Plane Crazy and *Gallopin' Gaucho* had been conceived and made as silent pictures with sounds represented by the appearance on screen of such words as 'crash!', 'bang!', 'ha-ha!' and so forth. It was

Loosely based on Douglas Fairbanks' film *The Gaucho*, Mickey's second screen adventure was entitled *Gallopin' Gaucho*.

not enough simply to add sound to these films. They would have to produce a new film designed to exploit sound to the full.

For inspiration they looked to the movies – to Buster Keaton's 1928 hit, *Steamboat Bill Jr* – and came up with *Steamboat Willie*, in which Mickey was cast as the mate on a riverboat, skippered by the cat Pete, who later became Peg Leg Pete.

The film's score was of vital importance, and Walt chose two popular songs. The opening sequence featured Mickey whistling 'Steamboat Bill' as he spun the steering-wheel with a reckless disregard for the rules of navigation; 'Turkey in the Straw' was chosen for a later sequence in which Mickey put on an impromptu concert, using the cargo of livestock as musical instruments.

However, Walt had little idea how to synchronize sound and pictures. Fortunately, animator Wilfred Jackson had some knowledge of musical timing and suggested using a metronome to time the tunes. This they did, Jackson playing a harmonica and Walt calculating the ratio of musical notes per foot of film and logging the information on an exposure sheet.

As soon as animation on *Steamboat Willie* was completed, Walt and his colleagues made their first attempt at improvising a soundtrack. One July evening they set up the projector outside the studio window (to minimize noise from the machine), and Roy projected *Steamboat Willie* onto a bed sheet while Walt, Ub, Wilfred Jackson and Johnny Cannon provided music, voices and sound effects. 'It was terrible,' Walt later recalled, 'but it was wonderful! And it was something new!' Reputedly the wives who formed *Steamboat Willie*'s first audience were more interested in discussing babies and recipes than their husbands' creative efforts; but, whatever the reception, Walt had confirmation that the antics of his cartoon mouse were going to be immeasurably enhanced by the addition of sound. What they needed now was a professional sound system.

One of the first people Walt approached was Sam Goldwyn. Although he apparently failed to convince Goldwyn of the inevitability of the sound cartoon, for he received no practical assistance from MGM, Walt must have made a great impression on the mogul. Asked by another visitor who the young man was, Goldwyn is said to have replied 'That's young Disney. He's going to rewrite nature and make it talk. It's a mute point though, a mute point.'

Eventually Walt decided to go to New York, where he hoped it might be easier to find available recording systems than in sound-crazy Hollywood. On the way, he stopped in Kansas City to get advice from Carl Stalling, the theatre organist and orchestra leader who had earlier loaned him $275. Walt showed Stalling the primitive 'score' that he and Wilfred Jackson had devised and left him with prints of *Plane Crazy* and *Gallopin' Gaucho*, for which he agreed to compose music.

In New York Walt began his search for an efficient, and affordable, sound system. The Recording Company of America (RCA) agreed to provide the required soundtrack and, as an example of their work, showed Walt an experimental recording for one of Paul Terry's 'Aesop's Fables'. Walt was very unimpressed, cabling Roy and Ub: '*My gosh – terrible.*' But while *Steamboat Willie* might be superior to the pictures being produced by other studios, Walt could not afford RCA's proposed charges. He found this particularly frustrating since, as he wrote to Roy and Ub, he was convinced that sound pictures were 'here to stay and in time will develop into a wonderful thing. The ones that get in on the ground floor are the ones that will more likely profit by its future development.' First, however, he had to get *in* on the ground floor.

Then he met Pat Powers, a slick Irishman whom he described in a letter home as being 'a very big and influential guy'. What Walt didn't know was that P. A. Powers was also one of the most unscrupulous operators in New York. A self-made man, Powers had a dubious record in business affairs including an attempt, in 1912, to wrest control of Universal Pictures from his partner, Carl Laemmle. A former blacksmith from Buffalo, Powers had begun his career in movies by trading in pirated camera equipment. By the time the somewhat naïve Walt met him in 1928, he was peddling a sound system called Powers Cinephone, which was actually based on the patented inventions of others.

Powers was quick to recognize the value in being associated with the first sound cartoon series, and he offered to record a soundtrack for *Steamboat Willie* for $1,000 and to help Walt find a distributor. Since it was the best offer he had so far received, Walt agreed and paid a deposit of $500. Powers also introduced Walt to Carl Edouarde – conductor of the Strand Theater orchestra and one of New York's most successful and highly paid musicians – who offered to conduct the recording session for *Steamboat Willie*, assuring Walt that he would require only a few musicians.

At last, everything seemed to be working out. But Walt's problems were far from over. When he arrived for the recording session he found that the promised orchestra of five or six musicians had grown to 17 plus three drummers and sound effects men. To make matters worse, Edouarde declined to use Walt's system for synchronizing sound and picture, believing he could do it by eye and ear alone. The results were disastrous, and Walt had to make the costly decision to attempt another recording.

Writing home to Roy he put a brave face on things: 'I am very optimistic about results, and our future looks bright.' Roy, however, was having a hard time raising the necessary cash for a second recording session. It was the shape of things to come: Roy was to devote the rest of his career to raising money for Walt to spend.

Although Walt admitted to being almost too worried to eat or sleep, he maintained a positive outlook in his correspondence with Roy and Ub. Getting the best soundtrack possible for *Steamboat Willie* was, he told them, their guarantee of future success. 'This may mean the making of a big organization out of our little Dump,' he wrote prophetically. He authorized Roy to 'slap as big a mortgage on everything we got' and to sell Walt's car to raise enough money.

It was with considerable trepidation that Walt faced the next recording session. However, Edouarde agreed to work with a small orchestra and to follow marks on the frames of film indicating the beat of the music; and with Walt himself providing the limited vocalizations of Mickey, Minnie and the ship's parrot, the recording was a success. Pictures and sounds were perfectly synchronized.

With *Steamboat Willie* in the can, Walt pushed ahead with the series. While Ub Iwerks was hard at work in Hollywood, completing a fourth mouse cartoon, *The Barn Dance*, Walt was cabling Carl Stalling in Kansas City, asking him to come to New York with the scores for *Plane Crazy* and *Gallopin' Gaucho*.

Despite all this confident activity, Walt had yet to find a distributor. Pat Powers showed *Steamboat Willie* to many of the major companies but, much to Walt's frustration, none of them showed any interest in Mickey's antics. 'We will all just have to have patience and confidence,' he wrote to Lilly. 'I am very optimistic about everything and want you all to feel the same way.' But days passed into weeks and there was still no buyer.

'This made me mad,' Walt recalled some years later, 'and I said "To hell with the whole bunch of them," and I went out and peddled

The first sound cartoon, *Steamboat Willie*, was a triumph; 'Clever is a mild word to use,' said a critic, 'It is a Wow!'

it myself on the open market.' As a result, Walt received an offer from Harry Reichenbach, manager of Universal Pictures' Colony Theater in New York and a man experienced in promotion and publicity, who convinced Walt that a Broadway screening would in no way prejudice the film's chances of finding a distributor. What's more, Reichenbach offered to pay Walt $250 a week for the film – a fee greater than had ever previously been paid for a cartoon.

The main feature at the Colony Theater on Sunday, 18 November 1928 was *Gang War*, an early talkie starring Olive Borden and Jack Pickford, but it was completely upstaged by a seven-minute cartoon. A title-card featuring Mickey and Minnie flickered onto the screen: 'Disney Cartoons present a *Mickey Mouse* sound cartoon – *Steamboat Willie* – A Walt Disney Comic by Ub Iwerks – Recorded by Powers Cinephone system.'

At the back of the auditorium, Walt, accompanied by Stalling, nervously awaited the audience reaction. 'We sat on almost the last row,' Stalling later recalled, 'and heard laughs and snickers all around us.' Confirmation of success came with the reviews. *Variety* described it as 'a peach of a synchronization job all the way, bright, snappy and fitting the situation perfectly ... Giggles came so fast at the Colony they were stumbling over each other.' *Weekly Film Review* enthused that the cartoon 'kept the audience laughing and chuckling from the moment the lead titles came on the screen and left them applauding'.

Although Mickey's debut had been nothing short of a triumph, Walt was still without a distributor. Several companies made attractive offers, but all wanted control of the character and, after his experiences with Charles Mintz, that was something Walt wasn't prepared to consider. Just as he was, once again, beginning to despair, Powers offered to help Walt retain his independence by advancing the $2,500 required to make more Mickey Mouse pictures while undertaking to handle all distribution expenses. The cost to Walt was to be 10 per cent of the gross takings.

There was, however, nothing altruistic about Powers' offer. *Steamboat Willie* had proved an excellent vehicle to introduce Powers Cinephone to the industry and several of the reviews had spoken as enthusiastically of the sound system as of the cartoon itself. Though Walt didn't realize it, Powers needed him and Mickey Mouse as much as they needed him.

Walt and Carl Stalling had now added soundtracks to the next three Mickey Mouse pictures and Powers – getting two of the titles slightly wrong – announced that 'Steamboat Willie', 'The Barn Dance', 'Galloping Gaucho' and 'Plain Crazy' were 'now ready for Pre-Release Bookings and Territorial Rights'. Proof that *Steamboat Willie's* success was no mere fluke came when Powers succeeded in placing a second picture with the prestigious Roxy Theater. And when Roxy (Samuel L. Rothafel) saw the rapturous reception Mickey received from his patrons, he immediately ordered the film to be held over for two more weeks.

Studio group (1929), standing: Johnny Cannon, Walt, Bert Gillett, Ub, Wilfred Jackson; seated: Carl Stalling, Jack King.

For several months, Walt's one obsession had been to give Mickey sound and find a distributor. Those goals had now been achieved, but Walt faced another problem: even though Ub Iwerks was a prolific draughtsman, he couldn't hope to meet the demand for new pictures single-handed. He therefore began recruiting among the established animators and cartoonists of New York, many of whom showed interest in joining Disney.

Walt finally headed back to Hollywood in December 1928. Stalling had agreed to become the Studio's musical director, and Walt, who had been through so many difficulties, now thought that everything was more than satisfactory – after all, he had Powers' contract in his pocket and $2,500 in cash.

If Walt had expected Roy to be equally delighted about the deal with Powers he was in for a rude awakening. Roy was far from pleased to find his brother had signed an agreement without consulting him, particularly since it undertook to pay Powers $26,000 per annum for 10 years for the use of Powers Cinephone.

Walt reasoned that they had to have a sound system and, so long as Mickey sustained his initial popularity, the Studio stood to earn a lot of money from the series; certainly they would have no difficulty in meeting the payments to Powers. In any event, discussion was academic since the contract was signed and the equipment already on its way from New York.

Walt realized that he had not only to maintain but to improve the quality of his films, for although the first few Mickey Mouse pictures were an unrivalled novelty, Walt's competitors were now adding sound to their cartoons. Walter Lantz was the first off the mark in January 1929 with an Oswald the Rabbit picture called *Ozzie of the Circus*. Then came Paul Terry's first 'Aesop's Fable' with sound, and the first of a series of 'Screen Songs' animated by Dave Fleischer. Later in 1929, Fleischer launched his 'Talkatoon' series, and Columbia Pictures released a Krazy Kat picture with a synchronized soundtrack.

Since it was clear to Walt that, with the growing popularity of sound cartoons, Mickey Mouse would have to compete with many more rivals, he began looking for a means of taking animation beyond 'the cut and dried little stock type of character'. It was Carl Stalling who suggested that Walt should diversify with a series that would make specific use of music to tell a story. 'For a name or title for the series,' Stalling later recalled, 'I suggested *not* using the word "music" or "musical" . . . but to use the word "symphony" together

with a humorous word. At the next gag meeting, I don't know who suggested it, but Walt asked me: "Carl, how would 'Silly Symphony' sound to you?" I said, "Perfect!" ' It was an idea that was to bring about a radical change in the nature of the cartoon film, enabling it to develop from a comic-strip with movement to an art form capable of conveying the subtle nuances of drama.

The theme of the first Silly Symphony was suggested by Stalling who, as a boy, had owned a toy skeleton made of jointed cardboard, which danced on a string; and he had once seen a vaudeville act featuring skeletal dancers that had left a lasting impression on him.

'The Spook Dance', as the picture was first called, was set in a graveyard where a troupe of skeletons gather for a musical frolic. Walt and Ub devised a storyline that was about as loosely-constructed as the characters it contained, and Stalling composed a score featuring some boney xylophone music and part of 'The March of the Dwarfs' from Grieg's *Peer Gynt Suite*.

But production costs were high, since, with the exception of one short sequence, *The Skeleton Dance*, as the film was finally called, was animated solely by Ub. Walt thought this was an unnecessary extravagance and tried to convince Ub to concentrate on the key drawings and leave the junior animators to produce the drawings in-between. Ub was adamant that he must do the entire film himself.

It was not the first time there had been friction between Walt and Ub. On an earlier occasion, Ub had become angry when he found that, after he'd left for the night, Walt was going over his work and re-timing the exposure sheets for his animation. Everyone who remembers Ub recalls him as a gentle, courteous man, but he deeply resented Walt's interference and made that absolutely clear.

Walt, who recognized that he needed Ub's skills and was genuinely appreciative of his talent, avoided further confrontation until the clash over *The Skeleton Dance*. Although neither man realized it, it was a disagreement that was to have far-reaching effects.

The Skeleton Dance was despatched to New York, but Powers' response was disappointing: 'They don't want this,' ran the terse cable, 'MORE MICE'. A similarly negative reaction came from a Los Angeles theatre manager who viewed the film: 'Can't recommend it,' he told Walt. 'Too gruesome.' Undaunted, Walt got someone to screen *The Skeleton Dance* for Fred Miller, manager of the celebrated Carthay Circle Theater. Luckily, it appealed to Miller, and he booked the picture. Public and critics alike gave their unhesitating approval, and Powers persuaded Rothafel to show the picture at his New York Roxy Theater where it was an instant hit.

However, although the public had demonstrated that there was an audience for further Silly Symphonies, that audience – and the theatre managers – were still demanding more mice. To meet that demand the Studio was already expanding. The first influx of New York artists had begun in the spring of 1929 with Burton 'Bert' Gillett (who had worked on the 'Krazy Kat' and 'The Katzenjammer Kids' series at Hearst's International Studios) and Ben Sharpsteen (who had begun his artistic career in 1916 with Raoul Barré, the French-Canadian animator of Mutt and Jeff). They were joined a few months later, by Jack King and Norman 'Fergy' Ferguson, who had begun his career as a book-keeper at the Paul Terry Studio, before deciding to try his hand at animation.

The New Yorkers brought experience and freshness to the Studio and were well paid for their services. Although Walt and Roy were taking only $50 and $35 a week respectively, and Ub was still being paid $90, Gillett and Ferguson received $100 and Sharpsteen and King $125 a week.

The Studio also began to attract youngsters just out of art school: Bill Cottrell, Jack Cutting, Dick Lundy and Roy Williams began learning the art of animation in the ink-and-paint department for a weekly salary of just $18–$20; in later years, all were to make a significant contribution to the Studio.

This expansion, however, did nothing to diminish Ub's importance. As well as being an officer of the company with a 20 per cent share in its ownership, he often acted as an intermediary between Walt and the animators who respected Ub both for his draughtsmanship and for his role in developing the style that was already recognized as uniquely 'Disney'.

The stucco buildings of the Disney studio on Hyperion Avenue as it looked during the years of the Silly Symphonies and Mickey Mouse's greatest fame. The triumphant rodent adorned the Studio sign.

By the summer of 1929, Ub, together with Wilfred Jackson and Les Clark began work on a second Silly Symphony, *Springtime*, while the rest of the animators, under the general supervision of Bert Gillett, maintained the output of Mickey Mouse cartoons with such titles as *Barnyard Battle*, *The Karnival Kid* and *Mickey's Follies*.

Mickey and Minnie Mouse were already as popular as many flesh-and-blood movie stars and it wasn't long before people began cashing-in on Mickey's growing fame. While in New York in 1929, Walt was repeatedly pestered by a man offering him $300 for the right to use Mickey's image on children's notebooks. As usual, the Disneys were hard up for cash, so Walt took the money. Within a year hundreds of manufacturers were producing thousands of items of officially licensed Mickey Mouse merchandise.

Another manifestation of Mickey's popularity came in the autumn of 1929, when Walt was approached by Harry W. Woodin, Manager of the Fox Dome Theater, with an idea for starting a Mickey Mouse Club at his cinema. Walt gave the scheme his blessing, and, on 14 September, 'Mickey Mouse's "Daddy"' made a personal appearance. 'Assisted by Carl Stalling, at the piano, and U. B. Iwerk, cartoonist', in order to 'Show You How They Do It'.

King Features – the company responsible for syndicating the work of many of America's most popular cartoonists – asked Walt for a Mickey Mouse comic-strip for the daily newspapers. Despite the Studio's heavy commitments, Walt characteristically agreed, and the first strip – written by Walt, drawn by Ub and jointly credited – appeared on 13 January 1930 in *The New York Mirror*.

Despite large numbers of poor, the US seemed during the summer of 1929 to be on the crest of a wave, with record investments being made on the stock market. But on 24 October 1929 the crash came. Some 13 million shares changed hands for absurd prices, businesses collapsed and careers were destroyed. In the days that followed, the value of shares continued to fall, until many were sold for any price that was offered.

It was the beginning of a decade of depression. But scampering through the gloom, like a spark of light, was Mickey Mouse. 'Oddly,' comments animation historian, Mike Barrier, 'Mickey's vagueness as a character became an asset – a source of his popularity. However difficult he might be to describe, he was undeniably an active, positive character and this was very important at a time when the world was sliding into the worst days of the Great Depression. Audiences could read into him an optimistic affirmation of their own values.'

Mickey may have been optimistic but at the Studio known as 'The Mouse Factory' things were looking black. Walt's insistence on perfection meant that expenditure kept rising until his pictures were costing $5,500 apiece, and the income due from Pat Powers simply never materialized, although the distributor was collecting rentals on

each film of nearly $17,000. Roy went to New York to confront the Irishman, who bluffed his way through the meeting, and Roy returned with nothing more than a conviction that their genial distributor was a crook.

Deciding they needed sound legal advice, the Disneys hired attorney Gunther Lessing, who had once advised Pancho Villa, the Mexican revolutionary. Lessing accompanied Walt and Lilly on yet another trip to New York. First, Walt met with Powers alone and asked to see a record of the receipts earned by the Disney cartoons. Powers showed him something else instead: a telegram stating that Ub Iwerks had signed a contract with Powers to produce a new series of cartoons for a salary of $300 a week.

Walt couldn't believe it. How could Ub possibly have betrayed him? But Powers assured him it was true and that by now Ub would have told Roy Disney he was leaving. On 21 January 1930 Ub informed Roy that he wished to withdraw from the partnership. He said nothing, however, about having signed with Powers, only that he had decided to quit because of his recent differences with Walt.

Meanwhile in New York, Powers told Walt he would give Ub back to the Studio and pay Walt a personal weekly salary of $2,500 if he signed over the rights in Disney cartoons. Walt unhesitatingly refused, saying that, under the circumstances, he wouldn't want to work with Ub again. Lessing drew up a document releasing Ub from the partnership, and 'all of his right, title and interest' was purchased for $2,920. Today his share in the company would have been worth several hundred million dollars. There's little doubt that Ub had been duped by Powers, but although Roy tried to change his mind, he clearly felt unable to go back on his decision. The crisis was compounded when Carl Stalling, learning that Ub was leaving – and believing that, as a result, the Studio was finished – also resigned.

Walt was left with no alternative but to bring an action against Powers or to write off the loss and try and find another distributor. He decided on the latter course. But finding a company willing to handle Disney films was not easy, particularly since Powers was threatening to sue anyone who signed up with the Studio. Rescue, however, was at hand when Harry Cohn of Columbia Pictures – acting on the advice of one of his finest young directors, Frank Capra – offered Walt an advance of $7,000 for each cartoon. Cohn also set aside $25,000 to defray any legal costs that might result from action by Powers. But Powers, realizing he was beaten, suggested a settlement of $100,000 to end their association. Offsetting the $50,000 that Powers admitted was due to the Studio, this left Walt owing $50,000. Columbia advanced a loan for this amount and on 7 February 1930 Walt cabled to Roy: 'HAVE DEFINITELY BROKE WITH POWERS STOP WILL DELIVER NO MORE PICTURES STOP PLAN TO TEMPORARILY SUSPEND PRODUCTION MICKEYS AND CONCENTRATE ON SYMPHONIES WHICH WE WILL DELIVER TO COLUMBIA.'

Once again, Walt and Lilly set off for Hollywood with many uncertainties still facing the Disney Studio and the hopeful, ever-smiling little mouse, that was its star.

3. THE SYMPHONY WORKS

'Mickey and I are firm friends,' Walt Disney once said, 'we have weathered the storms together.' And, indeed, for many years life was anything but plain sailing.

As far as the Studio was concerned, the departure of Ub Iwerks and Carl Stalling was regrettable but not devastating. The fact that two of the most senior personnel appeared to lack confidence in Walt was unsettling to the more junior animators; but, with so many good artists on the payroll, the success of Mickey Mouse no longer depended on Ub, and other composers and musical arrangers could be hired to replace Stalling.

More than anything, the events of January 1930 came as a personal blow to Walt: the treachery of Pat Powers, someone in whom Walt had placed such trust, was bad enough; but to be let down by Iwerks and Stalling – men whom he considered friends and partners – was something he found very difficult to understand.

Stalling went to work for Paul Terry, who offered him three times what he'd been paid at Disney to compose and arrange music for the 'Aesop's Fables' series. However, the studio already had a resident musical director, and when several months passed without his being given a film to work on Stalling quit, believing that his engagement had been 'just a trick to break Walt'.

Walt was particularly saddened by the split with Ub who had made such a vital contribution to the creation of Mickey Mouse as Walt had readily acknowledged by his willingness to give Ub a share of the credit and financial rewards from the series. But Ub wanted his independence. Apart from his occasional disagreements with Walt, the growth of the Studio meant that he became only one of a number of skilled animators and he was, understandably, attracted by the prospect of seeing his own name above the titles of films he animated. He established his own studio on Western Avenue and began producing films with a new cartoon star, Flip the Frog. Distributed by Pat Powers Celebrity Productions, Flip made his debut in a short entitled *Fiddlesticks*, during which he played a piano to accompany a mouse violinist who bore a striking resemblance to Mickey.

Not that Mickey needed to fear competition from other mice: his place in the public's affection was by now unrivalled. Songwriters, including the great Cole Porter, sang his praises; poets and novelists, among them John Betjeman and E. M. Forster, applauded him; film-makers such as Sergei Eisenstein acknowledged his contribution to cinema; while among the philosophers who contemplated the enigma of the Mouse's appeal was Carl Jung, who viewed the trinity of circles comprising Mickey's head as symbolizing 'the single most vital aspect of life – its ultimate wholeness'.

It was estimated that, in just one year, no fewer than 468 million cinema-goers saw a Mickey Mouse movie, and that didn't include such celebrated devotees as King George V and Queen Mary, President Roosevelt, Benito Mussolini, Mahomet Zahir Khan the Nizam of Hyderabad and Field Marshall Jan Christian Smuts. Mickey's younger admirers included the boy King of Siam, Princess Elizabeth Alexandra Mary – the future Queen of England – and millions of ordinary kids the world over.

In 1930, following the success of the Mickey Mouse Club run by Harry Woodin, Walt had the idea of extending the club to other cinemas. He invited Woodin to join the Studio as General Manager of Mickey Mouse Clubs and, within months, he had convinced hundreds of cinema managers that Mickey offered 'an easily arranged and inexpensive method of getting and holding the patronage of youngsters'. The Mickey Mouse Club eventually had a million members.

The success of the Mickey Mouse Clubs proved that Mickey's appeal was a saleable commodity. This was confirmed in 1930, when Walt entered into a merchandising contract with the George Borgfeldt Corporation of New York, which issued its first Disney licence to Waldburger, Tanner and Company of St Gall, Switzerland, for the manufacture of Mickey and Minnie Mouse handkerchiefs.

Walt had also appointed William Banks Levy (formerly Powers' Cinephone manager in England) as his London representative for merchandising, and it wasn't long before Levy had a staggering range of British manufacturers offering everything from Mickey Mouse eggcups and toothbrushes to designs for dress fabrics and wallpaper.

Someone else who saw the potential of Mickey was an American manufacturer of soft toys and novelties named Charlotte Clark. Deciding to make a Mickey Mouse doll, she asked her young nephew, Bob Clampett (an enthusiastic amateur artist who later became a successful animation director with Warner Brothers) to draw up a design. From Clampett's sketches, Charlotte Clark produced the first stuffed Mickey Mouse doll. When Mrs Clark contacted Walt and Roy for permission to manufacture the toy, she received not only encouragement but practical assistance in the form of a house near the Studio where she could work. Mrs Clark produced dozens of Mickey Mouse dolls, which were given away to visitors and business associates. Then, when a photograph of Walt with one of the toys appeared in *Screen Play Secrets* magazine, there was such an enormous public demand for the dolls that, by November 1930, Mrs Clark was making up to 400 Mickeys a week.

By that time a rival toy was being produced by Borgfeldt. However, it failed to meet the brothers' rigorous standards – its feet were too small, its legs were too thick, the gloves were too big and the mouth was, according to Roy, 'crooked and not as we like it'.

In 1932, Walt's concern that Disney toys should be true to the original characters led to McCall being allowed to publish the Charlotte Clark pattern so that people could make the dolls for themselves. When, two years later, Mrs Clark went to work as a designer for the Knickerbocker Toy Company in New York, she began creating a range of toys based on Mickey and his friends that, although mass produced, were of the finest quality.

Nevertheless, Walt remained dissatisfied with much of the other merchandise that was being produced. He was looking for a way of controlling what was done with his characters when he received a telephone call from Herman 'Kay' Kamen, founder of the Kansas City advertising agency, Kamen-Blair. Kamen offered to manage the licensing of Disney characters on the understanding that he would become sole agent when the contracts with Borgfeldt and Levy expired. Since Kamen was generally acknowledged as one of the finest promotional men in America, Walt was quick to sign with him.

One of Kamen's first deals was to license National Dairy Products to produce 30,000,000 Mickey Mouse ice-cream cones. By the end of 1934 he had negotiated $35-million worth of merchandise, ranging from Mickey Mouse cookie-cutters, lunch tins and hot-water bottles to a Minnie Mouse car-mascot. Among Kamen's many marketing triumphs was his decision to license Ingersoll-Waterbury to produce a Mickey Mouse watch. At the time, Ingersoll was on the brink of

Mickey sees his lady love being menaced by the dastardly Peg Leg Pete in a 1934 western adventure, *Two-Gun Mickey*.

bankruptcy, but the $3.75 wristwatch proved a phenomenal success. Macy's department store sold a staggering 11,000 Mickey Mouse watches in one day, Ingersoll was saved and over the next five years sold a total of $4,771,490.96 of Disney character merchandise – almost a quarter of a million dollars in royalty payments to Disney.

Mickey Mouse found his way not just onto toys and games, but onto virtually every item of clothing and household goods. The first Mickey Mouse books were instant best-sellers, *Mickey Mouse Weekly* became one of the most popular children's comics in Britain, and being associated with Disney characters proved good for a diversity of firms from Cartier, who produced a $12,000 diamond-studded Mickey Mouse pin, to the English confectioners E. Sharp & Sons, which, in one week, sold 150 tons of Mickey Mouse toffees.

Kay Kamen – who managed Disney's character merchandise until his tragic death in 1949 – laid the foundations for what was to prove a major source of continuing income for the Studio, until, by 1986, it was contributing over $130 million to the company's annual revenue.

One of the many successful by-products of Mickey's popularity was the newspaper strip Ub Iwerks and Walt had begun in January 1930. On Ub's resignation, the strip was taken over by Win Smith, an artist who had been employed to ink-in Ub's pencil drawings. It wasn't long, however, before Walt found he hadn't time to write the stories and Smith was asked to take on the writing as well. When he refused and quit, Walt approached Floyd Gottfredson, who was working as an in-betweener in the animation department.

Gottfredson had been engaged as a back-up artist for the comic strip but was just getting interested in animation when Walt asked him to take on the newspaper strip. Because Gottfredson said he now wanted to stay in animation, Walt asked him to write and draw the daily strip for two weeks only, until he could find another artist. 'After a month,' Floyd Gottfredson later recalled, 'I began to wonder if he was looking for anyone. After two months I was worrying for

fear that he would find someone.' When he finally retired, in 1975, Gottfredson had been drawing Mickey's adventures for 45 years. By the mid-30s the strip was read by an estimated 28 million people, and over the years that followed it was joined by strips featuring the Silly Symphony stories and other Disney characters.

Gottfredson often drew inspiration from Mickey's movies, which, during these early years, featured an extraordinary diversity of plots. Many shorts were little more than artfully choreographed dance numbers with occasional gags; others were action-packed adventures. There was, as a result, a freshness and an element of surprise about each new Mickey. There was also a growing company of supporting players, whose varied personalities complemented that of the Mouse. In almost every picture, Mickey was partnered by Minnie, whom he was invariably called upon to rescue from some desperate situation – often involving the villainous Peg Leg Pete. In his more rustic escapades Mickey was supported by Horace Horse-collar and Clarabelle Cow, as well as several minor characters such as the gargantuan Peter and Patricia Pigg. Another important character made his debut in *The Chain Gang* (1930), as one of a pair of unnamed bloodhounds; later the same year, he reappeared as Minnie's dog, Rover, in *The Picnic*; by 1931 he was established as belonging to Mickey and answering to the name Pluto.

One reason for the success of Mickey's pictures was the unspoken premise that he and his friends were movie actors who might be cast in westerns such as *The Cactus Kid* (1930), spook-films like *The Haunted House* (1929), rural entertainments, as in *The Barnyard Concert* (1930), or costume dramas, of which *Pioneer Days* (1930) is an early example.

Equally varied were the Silly Symphonies, although those still largely comprised music and simple visual effects on a theme – *Cannibal Capers*, *Monkey Melodies*, *Arctic Antics* – rather than complexities of plot and characterization. It was probably not until *The Ugly Duckling* (1931), that the Disney animators showed that they could successfully convey a wide range of emotions, including pathos, without resorting to melodrama.

A poster for *Barnyard Olympics* (1932), one of many Mickey Mouse pictures with a sporting theme.

Although Ub Iwerks' departure had been a loss, the continued success of the Mickey Mouse and Silly Symphony cartoons during 1930 and 1931, proved that the Disney characters were of greater importance than their creators. And, despite their best endeavours, the cartoon stars of other studios – including Iwerks' Flip the Frog – failed to challenge the extraordinary popular appeal of Mickey and his chums.

New buildings were added to the Hyperion Avenue Studio to accommodate a growing personnel. Among the new artists and writers were Ted Sears, Jack King, Webb Smith, Tom Palmer and Dave Hand, who had an established reputation as an animator and director with the Fleischer studio. This expansion was accompanied by improved standards of storytelling and animation and by streamlined methods of organization of which two innovations were particularly significant. To enable detailed discussion of each sequence in a film, the 'storyboard' was introduced. Story sketches and lines of dialogue were pinned onto this, which allowed changes and refinements to be made long before the costly process of animation began.

The other development was the filming of animators' pencil drawings before they were inked and painted. The artists then viewed these 'pencil tests' to assess how the completed footage would look. The fact that these screenings were held in a small room with no air-conditioning led to them being known as 'sweatbox sessions'. It was an apt phrase: apart from the room's humidity, the animators also had to justify their work to Walt and gain his approval. 'They used to dread comin' in,' Walt later recalled, 'I'd just tear hell out of them.' And certainly, the sweatbox became a test not only of an animator's drawings but of his personal stamina.

Before this period, the direction had been organized on an *ad hoc* basis, with particular artists, such as Bert Gillett, supervising specific sequences rather than an entire film. Walt himself generally oversaw all the productions, but with so many diverse matters requiring his attention, he realized he was going to have to delegate much more authority.

The first of the Studio's artists to be given directorial responsibility was Wilfred Jackson, who had joined Disney in 1928 and had made an important contribution to Mickey's first movie soundtrack. In 1931, Jackson asked Walt if he might be allowed to handle a film on his own, by which he meant that he wanted to animate an entire cartoon; but Walt interpreted the request somewhat differently. There were various odds and ends which had been cut out of earlier Mickey Mouse films, and Walt asked Jackson to work these up into a new story. Jackson was not at all enamoured with this assignment but produced *The Castaway*, a gem of a film in which Mickey is shipwrecked on a tropical island and has a series of hilarious encounters with seals, crocodiles, lions and a piano-playing gorilla.

In a somewhat similar position was Ben Sharpsteen who, like Jackson, was made a director and given the additional responsibility of training new recruits in the techniques and technicalities of animation as part of Walt's programme to refine the animator's art. The in-house training under Sharpsteen, however, was only a beginning, and in 1931 Walt decided to send his animators to art evening classes. He approached various schools, but the fees were all too high and none of the colleges was willing to offer him any concessions. Finally he went to the Chouinard School of Art.

Founded in the summer of 1921 by Mrs Nelbert Chouinard, out of over-crowded classes from the Otis Arts Institute, Chouinard began with just 35 students. Within 18 months, that number had grown to 180. Walt was impressed by Chouinard's reputation and by the character of its bespectacled, rather schoolmarmish, founder, who ran her college in much the same way as Walt ran his Studio, borrowing money against her house and car, when necessary, to keep things going.

Walt received a sympathetic reception from Nelbert Chouinard: 'Mr Disney, I admire very much what you're doing,' she told him, 'Just send your boys down and we'll worry about the price later.'

Walt was given concessionary rates for the tuition and he ferried the 15 or so students to the school each Friday night, and, after spending the evening working at the Studio, returned to collect them when classes ended.

The young animators learned a number of lessons at Chouinard, the most important of which was the necessity of rooting the techniques of cartooning and caricature in an understanding of the physical laws of human dynamics. The classes in life study were taken by Don Graham, himself a former Chouinard student, who used some of Nelbert Chouinard's own teaching methods, particularly those of her 'Memory Sketch' sessions, in which students were required to make 'quick sketches and memory drawings from the model in action' – a process that had 'specific importance in stimulating quick observation and rapid expression.'

Although this was a seminal period in the Studio's development, it was also one of problems and anxieties. The years of worrying about producing quality work, finding distributors, building up – and keeping – a competent team of artists as well as finding the finance to achieve all he wanted to do, eventually took their toll, and in 1931 Walt had a nervous breakdown.

A vacation, which began in Washington and took Walt and Lilly to Cuba and back by ship, via the Panama Canal, to Los Angeles, enabled Walt to make a complete recovery, and he soon regained his impetus to push on with his plans to raise animation to an accepted art form. The financial headaches, however, remained as great.

The agreement with Columbia Pictures provided the Studio with an advance of $7,000 for each film and a half share of the profits after Columbia had deducted the 35 per cent payable to them for distribution costs. However, Walt and Roy still had to repay the $50,000 that Columbia had loaned them to pay off Pat Powers; and, by the time that was paid, there were little or no profits left.

This presented the Studio with an enormous difficulty, since production costs of a single film had risen from $5,400 to $13,500, a sum no longer covered by the advances from Columbia. Roy often found it hard to meet the animators' salaries. One week the pay packets contained nothing more than a $10 gold piece, and other weeks they received no wages at all. In desperation, the brothers asked Columbia to increase the advance to $15,000 a film, but the request was denied, and Walt realized he would have to find another distributor.

Walt met with Carl Laemmle, President of Universal Pictures, who offered to distribute Disney's films providing the copyright in them was made over to Universal. It was not an offer Walt had to consider for long. Then a producer friend, Sol Lesser, introduced the brothers to Joseph Schenck, President of United Artists, a company owned and run by film-makers Douglas Fairbanks, Mary Pickford, Samuel Goldwyn and Charlie Chaplin.

There were several advantages to signing with United Artists: first, the Disney cartoons would be the only ones distributed by the

'All for one! One for all! If we stick together we can't fall!' The diminutive heroes of *Three Blind Mousketeers* (1936).

company so, for the first time, they would not be offered alongside shorts from other studios. Second, the financial arrangements gave the Studio a sliding-scale percentage – reckoned at not less than 60 per cent – of the gross receipts. Since the Disney cartoons grossed most in their first year of release (and about 50 per cent of those takings during their second year), it meant that the Studio could expect to recoup its investment within 12 months and, a year later, to make a respectable profit.

With the growth in the number of artists employed at the Studio, the weekly trips to Chouinard became increasingly impractical and, towards the end of 1932, Walt asked Don Graham to lecture at the Studio instead. The Disney Art Class – of 25 animators – first met on the Studio soundstage on the night of 15 November. The numbers attending Graham's twice-weekly lectures quickly grew – helped along, it has been suggested, by the introduction of life classes using nude female models.

It was also during 1932 that Walt took the major – and very costly – decision to produce cartoons in colour. There had been limited experimentation with the use of red, blue and green and Walter Lantz had produced a two-colour animated sequence for the 1930 feature *King of Jazz*; but the development of a three-colour process by Technicolor in 1930 promised the most revolutionary innovation since the coming of sound. While most of the movie industry viewed the prospect of colour with scepticism, Walt Disney could see its potential. Although the Technicolor process could not, in 1932, be applied to live-action movies, it was possible to use it for cartoons. Walt was convinced that colour would add a new dimension to his films and signed an exclusive deal with Technicolor under which his was the only animation studio to be able to use the process for two years.

Roy was far from happy that Walt had a new incentive for spending more money, arguing that, as they had just signed with United Artists, they could not obtain an additional advance to cover the costs of using colour. Walt, on the other hand, argued that colour would give a novelty value to Disney cartoons that would ensure longer bookings by theatres and, as a result, greater revenues. Unable to convince Roy, Walt – as he so often did – went ahead regardless, adding colour to a Silly Symphony entitled *Flowers and Trees*, which was already in production as a black and white film.

The process of animating in colour was not without its problems. One of the dire predictions that Roy had made was that the paints would not adhere to the celluloids and, sure enough, no sooner was the paint dry than it began to chip. In addition, the colours quickly faded as soon as they were subjected to the strong lights used under the camera.

Undaunted, Walt and his technicians developed new paints, and the results, as they appeared in the first test scenes of *Flowers and Trees*, were satisfactory. Although the picture was incomplete, Walt screened the footage for his friend Rob Wagner – editor of the literary magazine, *Script* – who recommended it to theatre-owner, Sid Grauman. As a result, Grauman asked Walt to complete the film in time to accompany the opening, at Grauman's Chinese Theater, of the new MGM movie of Eugene O'Neill's *Strange Interlude*.

After long hours of overtime, director Bert Gillett and the animators completed *Flowers and Trees* on time. The sylvan idyll proved an appropriate subject for the introduction of colour, which gave the film a vibrant – if somewhat primitive – beauty.

Flowers and Trees was an immediate success, not merely because it was something new, but because it was so well done. Mickey Mouse had a serious rival at last – not the films of Flip the Frog, Betty Boop or Oswald, but Disney's own Silly Symphonies. Walt decided that all future Silly Symphonies should be made in colour, and among those released over the next few months – and which, mostly under the direction of Bert Gillett, showed an increasing deftness of style – were *King Neptune*, *Babes in the Woods* and *Santa's Workshop*, with its elaborately detailed and gag-filled scenes of Santa and his elves making toys on Christmas Eve.

Walt and Roy pose with the special Oscar that was awarded to them in 1932 for the creation of Mickey Mouse.

Adapted from a popular folk-tale, Disney's 1933 Silly Symphony *Three Little Pigs* was an Academy Award-winning hit.

Movieland's formal acknowledgement of the Studio's success came in November 1932, at the fifth annual awards ceremony of the Academy of Motion Picture Arts and Sciences, when Academy President, Conrad Nagel, presented Walt with his first Oscar – a Special Award 'for the creation of Mickey Mouse'. Walt collected a second Academy Award when *Flowers and Trees* won in the newly-introduced category of Best Cartoon Short Subject.

A month after winning his awards, Walt put a new Silly Symphony into production – *Three Little Pigs*. In a memo to his staff, Walt asked that the animals be 'more like human characters' and expressed the hope that the film would tell a story that had 'depth and feelings' and 'would teach a moral'. The primary emphasis, however, was on entertainment through the potential 'cuteness' of the pigs and the opportunity 'for a lot of good gags'.

The successful and experienced Bert Gillett directed, but the task of drawing the roly-poly pigs was entrusted to Fred Moore, a young artist with an astonishing and intuitive gift for animation. Chosen to give leering, salivating life to the Big Bad Wolf was Norm Ferguson, already established as the talented animator of Pluto.

The story offered scope for characterization and also for the imaginative use of music and song, and it was decided that the two foolish pigs would play a fiddle and a fife. The pigs' lively song, 'Who's Afraid of the Big Bad Wolf?', was composed by the Studio's musical arranger, Frank Churchill, with help from storyman, Ted Sears, and vocal performer Pinto Colvig. A former clown and a clarinetist, Colvig also spoke for the sensible Practical Pig (and, later,

for Goofy). Practical Pig's piano-playing was provided by the now freelance Carl Stalling.

Walt was justifiably elated by the finished film: 'At last,' he told Roy, 'we have achieved true personality in a whole picture.' But it failed, at first, to receive much critical acclaim, and most reviewers didn't even note its opening at New York's Radio City Music Hall. Nevertheless, Hal Horne, who was responsible for United Artists' publicity, declared *Three Little Pigs* was 'the greatest picture Walt's ever made'; and that view was soon borne out by the film's reception in the ordinary movie houses of New York.

Three Little Pigs was a sensation: often billed on theatre marquees above the main attraction, it ran for weeks in many theatres – one manager attaching beards on pigs displayed outside his cinema, which he lengthened each time the film was held over for another week. The film's success was partly due to its appearing to present an allegory of survival in the dark days of the Depression, while the Practical Pig's exhortations to work hard seemed to echo the positive politics of the newly-elected President Roosevelt who, in presenting his 'New Deal', had reassured his fellow Americans that they had nothing to fear but fear itself.

Walt watches Frank Churchill rehearse 'Who's Afraid of the Big Bad Wolf?' with Mary Moder, Pinto Colvig and Dorothy Compton.

Animator Art Babbitt, who worked on the Practical Pig, says there 'were absolutely no political connotations intended, none whatsoever.' But intentional or not, audiences saw those connotations and, as film historian Lewis Jacobs has observed: 'The film became by force of circumstance and the time spirit a heartening call to the people of a troubled country.'

It had cost $22,000 to make (slightly more than the average cost of a Silly Symphony), but within 12 months the film earned $125,000 and went on to make as much again before the end of its first release. The film also generated a great deal of money through character merchandise, which included alarm clocks, porcelain figurines, nursery ware, jigsaw puzzles and race games.

Faced with such a block-buster, United Artists demanded 'more pigs', just as Disney's previous distributors had wanted 'more mice' and 'more skeletons'. But Walt was reluctant to make a sequel, believing that 'you can't top pigs with pigs'. Eventually, however, three more pig films were made – *The Big Bad Wolf* (1934), *Three Little Wolves* (1936) and *The Practical Pig* (1939) – but they served only to prove Walt's theory and are now all but forgotten.

In March 1934, *Three Little Pigs* won the Academy Award for Best Cartoon Short subject; but, once more, Walt had to pay the price of success when Bert Gillett was hired by RKO-Radio Pictures to supervise a series of musical fables entitled *Rainbow Parades*.

Competing with *Three Little Pigs* for the Oscar was a Mickey Mouse cartoon, *Building a Building*; but, although beaten again by a Silly Symphony, the Mouse pictures had themselves gone from strength to strength, and, under the direction of Gillett, Wilfred Jackson and Dave Hand, they showed a marked maturity of style and characterization. Few movie-goers were aware of just how much work went into making a seven-minute Mickey Mouse short, and yet

Orphan's Benefit (1934), featuring Horace Horsecollar, Clarabelle Cow and Goofy, was remade in colour in 1941.

Milkman Clarence Nash entertained children with bird impressions before getting the job of quacking for Donald Duck.

the animators discussed every nuance of each new creation; and, under the tutelage of Don Graham, were encouraged to analyse character and action. Mickey – speaking, as he had since birth, in a hesitant falsetto supplied by Walt – remained central to the appeal of Disney cartoons, and although he was far less anarchic than in his first films, he was still cast in some wild adventures such as *The Klondike Kid* (1932), a drama set in the days of the gold-rush; *The Mad Doctor* (1933), inspired by the popular genre of Old Dark House movies; and *Shanghaied* (1934), in which Mickey rescues Minnie from a piratical Peg Leg Pete and a gang of cut-throats.

Increasingly, however, Mickey was sharing the acting laurels with a growing company of players. His early co-stars Minnie, Pete, Horace Horsecollar, Clarabelle Cow and the ingenuous hound Pluto, were now joined by Clara Cluck, the big-bosomed hen with a

coloratura voice and two performers who, eventually, upstaged them all: the accident-prone Dippy Dawg, who developed into Goofy, and the perpetually irascible Donald Duck.

Donald made his debut in a cameo role in *The Wise Little Hen* (1934). Cast as an idle wastrel wearing a sailor suit and living on a broken-down boat, he belligerently declines to help the Wise Little Hen plant her corn. His unique voice was supplied by Clarence Nash, who had auditioned at the Studio while working for a milk company.

Donald was quickly teamed with Mickey and the gang for the 1934 movie *Orphan's Benefit*, in which he made several unsuccessful attempts at reciting 'Mary Had a Little Lamb' to an audience of unruly mouselings. Later the same year, in *The Dognapper*, Donald and Mickey became policemen, who rescue Minnie's pekinese from Peg Leg Pete. Then, in 1935 Donald made a scene-stealing appearance in *The Band Concert*, as a piccolo-playing peanut-vendor who constantly interrupts conductor Mickey Mouse and his musicians. Despite various distractions – troublesome insects, the unstoppable Donald and, finally, a full-blown tornado – the band somehow succeeds in completing a spirited performance of 'The William Tell Overture'. *The Band Concert* was the first Mickey Mouse picture to be made in Technicolor, and it is a miniature masterpiece.

The lively stories and engaging characters of Silly Symphonies such as *Funny Little Bunnies* (1934) reached an even wider child audience through colourful picture books.

Despite the success of *The Band Concert* and the colour Mickey Mouse pictures that followed, it was the Silly Symphony series that, under the direction of Wilfred Jackson, remained the showcase for Disney animation. After *Three Little Pigs* came a variety of films that showed the Studio's animators as capable of not simply filling their pictures with wit and invention but of using illustrative techniques in storytelling that were richer and more elaborate than anything previously seen in a cartoon.

The Silly Symphony series produced many classics: *Lullaby Land* (1933) about a baby who dreams he and his toy dog are exploring the land of the counterpane where trees are made of rattles and flowers are powder-puffs; *The Grasshopper and the Ants* (1934), a lively reworking of Aesop's fable featuring an army of ants and a happy-go-lucky grasshopper (voiced by Pinto Colvig) who performs another snappy Disney hit, 'The World Owes Me a Living'; and *Funny Little Bunnies* (1934), a riotously colourful picture about the ingenious ways in which Easter eggs are manufactured and decorated by playful Easter bunnies.

These, and such other Silly Symphonies were clearly portents of greater things to come. For Walt Disney had an ambitious scheme in mind: he had decided he was going to produce a feature-length animated picture that would be based on Grimm's popular fairy-tale about Snow White.

4. DISNEY'S FOLLY

The story of the little princess who runs away from her wicked stepmother and seeks refuge with seven little men in a woodland cottage is one of the world's best-loved fairy-tales. It is an old story and one that, through hundreds of retellings, has become a part of the nursery mythology of Britain and America.

Early film-makers were quick to capitalize on Snow White's popularity, and several silent movie versions were made including an hour-long production in 1916. As a newsboy in Kansas City, Walt had been given a ticket to a special screening of this film. Shown simultaneously on four large screens, of which Walt was able to see two at once, the film made a lasting impression on him.

It was not *Snow White*, however, but *Alice in Wonderland* that Walt first chose as a subject when he decided to make what was referred to in rumour as 'a Mickey Mouse feature'.

Lewis Carroll's famous fantasy had considerable cinematic potential, and as early as 1931 Walt was talking about making a film of the book. That year, unfortunately, the Commonwealth Pictures Corporation released the first talking movie of Alice's adventures and Walt had to shelve his plans. Two years later he again considered an Alice feature, financed by Mary Pickford who was also to play Alice as a real character in a cartoon Wonderland. But again the project had to be abandoned when Paramount Pictures announced they were making a movie version with a star-studded cast including Gary Cooper, Cary Grant and W.C. Fields.

There was also talk of a picture based on Washington Irving's *Rip Van Winkle*, with Will Rogers as the Dutch colonist who mislays 20 years of his life after drinking with the strange little men of the Catskill Mountains. For a second time, however, a project was aborted when Paramount, which owned the rights to the story, refused to grant Disney permission. Discussions then took place with Merian C. Cooper (the producer of *King Kong*) about making an animated film of the popular Victor Herbert operetta, *Babes in Toyland*. But RKO, which owned the rights, had plans of its own to use the play as a film vehicle for Laurel and Hardy, and turned Disney down.

Finally, Walt considered Snow White, a story he had been thinking about for some time as a Silly Symphony. Undaunted by the release in 1933 of a Max Fleischer short, *Snow White* (somewhat incongruously starring Betty Boop), Walt decided that this was the subject for what he now called his 'Feature Symphony'. It had, Walt observed, a 'perfect plot' containing humour, romance and pathos. If the story were good it would inevitably make a good picture.

Disney cartoons had never been more popular and, with hindsight, it is easy to see just how well-timed was Walt's decision to make an animated feature. When the news broke, however, the movie industry shook its corporate head and dubbed the project 'Disney's folly', Roy Disney was similarly pessimistic about the idea but that didn't deter Walt. Like Charlie Chaplin, Laurel and Hardy and Buster Keaton, Walt was convinced that the only real future in movies was for feature films. However good the short cartoons, they could only ever bring in limited returns, particularly since they had begun to be crowded out of movie programmes by the 'double-bill'. Walt felt sure that investing in a feature offered a promise of generous dividends.

What worried Roy, and what the critics doubted, was whether an audience would sit through a 90-minute cartoon. But Walt had confidence in the team of artists he had built up, a team that included

Mickey dons a deerstalker and goes spook-hunting in the classic 1937 short, *Lonesome Ghosts*.

many of those who, for the next 40 years or more, would be responsible for establishing and maintaining the Disney style.

Among those who joined the Studio in 1933 were Dick Huemer, who began his career with the Raoul Barré studio in 1916 and became interested in Disney through his friend Ben Sharpsteen; and Joe Grant, who had worked as a caricaturist on the *Los Angeles Record*. Grant was hired during the making of *Mickey's Gala Premiere* to provide caricatured likenesses of the celebrities who attended Mickey's big night. After the film was completed, Walt invited Grant to stay on, and he became one of the leading story artists for the Silly Symphonies and, later, the features.

Also recruited in 1933 were Eric Larson and Wolfgang 'Woolie' Reitherman who, some 30 years later, became the Studio's senior animation producer. Together with veteran Les Clark, Larson and Reitherman formed the nucleus of a group affectionately known, in after years, as the 'Nine Old Men', which also included Milt Kahl, Frank Thomas and Ward Kimball, who joined in 1934, and Marc Davis, Ollie Johnston and John Lounsbery, who were recruited the following year. Others who joined the Studio during this period were Hamilton Luske, Perce Pearce, Ken Anderson, Jim Algar, Claude Coats, Fred Spencer, Grim Natwick, Art Babbitt, effects animators Cy Young and Josh Meador and the man who earned the nickname 'the Michaelangelo of animation', Vladimir Tytla.

In the mid-1930s, of course, the careers of all these men were still ahead of them, but they quickly demonstrated their potential for advancing the quality of animation. Walt was so encouraged that he invited Don Graham to join the Studio on a full-time basis in 1934 to help achieve even higher standards of screen-writing and draughtsmanship.

Graham's art classes soon transformed the Studio into a place which animator John Hubley (who later helped create UPA's Mr Magoo) described as being 'like a marvellous big Renaissance craft hall'. Trips were organized to the Griffith Park Zoo, where artists could study and draw animals, and there were life-classes, seminars

Marie Dressler, Wallace Beery and Lionel Barrymore (in his Rasputin make-up) attend *Mickey's Gala Premiere* (1933).

and study sessions in which films – animated and live-action – were screened and discussed. And, in addition to those activities, which took place during working hours, evening classes were held five nights a week. One or two of the older, more experienced animators at first somewhat resented having to go back to school, but they quickly discovered that there was much they could learn and apply to their art, and they soon became as enthusiastic as the younger artists who eagerly joined the Studio, despite the low wages paid to beginners, for the valuable training they would receive.

At the centre of this devoted, energetic group was Walt himself whose personality, in the words of one of his earliest employees Jack Cutting, was 'like a drop of mercury rolling around on a slab of marble'. Describing Walt's methods of working, Cutting says: 'He could grasp your ideas and interpret your thoughts rapidly. You didn't have to give Walt a five-page memo or talk to him for hours about an idea. He understood right away and would start quarter-backing and running with the ball if he liked the idea.'

The first the artists heard about *Snow White and the Seven Dwarfs* was on an evening early in 1934. Animator Ken Anderson remembers that Walt gave each of them 65 cents so they could have dinner at a café on Hyperion Avenue and then return to the Studio. That evening, recalls Anderson, Walt sat them down in a circle on the sound stage and 'proceeded to intrigue us from eight o'clock until early midnight acting and telling [the scenario of *Snow White*] ... even anticipating the songs and the kind of music, and he so thrilled us with the complete recitation of all the characters that he had created that we were just carried away ... we had no concept that we were ever going to do anything else. We wanted to do what he had just told us!'

While most of the animators continued producing Mickeys and Silly Symphonies, a small group began work on *Snow White* in a room alongside Walt's office so that he could maintain close involvement with the project.

Walt was probably responsible for the first written outline

A picture book of the Silly Symphony *The Tortoise and the Hare* (1935), a film that proved that slow and steady can win not only the race but an Academy Award.

prepared for the movie in August, 1934. Closely following the version told by the Grimm brothers in 1812, the outline also established the principle that each of the dwarfs would have an individual person-ality, characterized by his name.

The task of designing the characters was assigned to Joe Grant and Albert Hurter. Like Grant, Hurter had begun in animation, but Walt soon realized that his talent 'lay in humorous exaggeration and the humanizing of inanimate objects'. Released from animation, Hurter set to work drawing thousands of inspirational sketches. Described by Walt as 'a master creator of fantasy' in whose 'whimsical imagination all things were possible', he designed many of the ornate

Animator's model-sheet for *The Goddess of Spring* (1934), in which the heroine served as an experimental figure for Snow White.

furnishings and fittings to the dwarfs' cottage, such as the pipe-organ elaborately carved with birds and animals.

As drawn by Hurter and Grant, the dwarfs had an earthy, warty appearance, which not everyone, including Lilly Disney, found attractive. However, the dwarfs were to change considerably before reaching the screen as a bunch of engaging eccentrics.

The dwarfs were not the only characters to undergo transformation during the making of the film: Snow White began as a cherubic blonde and, to start with there was some indecision as to how the Queen was to be played. Eventually the choice was for a character with cold regality, and by October 1934 the Queen was being described as 'a mixture of Lady Macbeth and the Big Bad Wolf'. In the same outline, Snow White was described as a 14-year-old 'Janet Gaynor type' and her Prince as a 'Doug Fairbanks type – 18 years old', which was easy enough to express in words, but considerably harder to draw.

Walt knew all too well that, while the dwarfs presented few problems – their kind having already appeared in such Silly Symphonies as *The Merry Dwarfs*, *Babes in the Woods* and *The Night Before Christmas* – the artists had no real experience in animating realistic human figures.

In order to gain that experience, Walt put into production a Silly Symphony entitled *The Goddess of Spring*, based on the Greek legend of Persephone. Although a mythical character, Persephone was required to move and perform as a live actress would, conveying wide-ranging subtleties of emotion. This onerous task fell to Ham Luske, who based Persephone on sketches of his wife; Pluto, who was depicted as a Mephistophelian character, was acted out and animated by Dick Huemer. The final results, however, were disappointing: the heroine and villain, as Huemer later admitted, 'came out pretty terrible'.

Walt might easily have been discouraged by this failure, but it only strengthened his resolve to improve the standard of figure animation. The 'Feature Symphony' was now involving more and more of the Studio's artists, who were still producing the increasingly sophisticated Silly Symphonies and such memorable Mickey Mouse pictures as *Mickey's Garden*, *Mickey's Fire Brigade* and *On Ice*.

Walt, who remained in personal control of the project, was assisted by Dave Hand as Supervising Director and five directors who

were responsible for individual sequences of the film: Perce Pearce, Larry Morey, who also wrote the film's songs with Frank Churchill, and veterans Wilfred Jackson and Ben Sharpsteen. The fifth director was Bill Cottrell, later to marry Walt's sister-in-law, Hazel Sewell, who had worked as an inker on *Plane Crazy* and was now one of the art directors for *Snow White*. Others who contributed to the film's art direction were Charlie Philippi, Hugh Hennesy, Tom Codrick, Ken Anderson and children's book illustrator, Gustaf Tenggren.

Thousands of sketches and watercolours were produced as the artists refined characters, and the writers – including Ted Sears, Earl Hurd and Otto Englander – honed the plot. Every aspect of the story, from the characters' motivations to the settings in which they were to perform, were discussed in the minutest detail. Through hours of discussions, plot, character and dialogue were shaped and refined. Everyone felt free to put forward ideas: sometimes they were seized upon, sometimes they were shot down in flames. But no one had more ideas than Walt who bubbled over with them. No limits were placed on the potential development of the story, and several sequences were planned that, for various reasons, never made the final film. There was, for example, a scene in which the Queen holds the Prince prisoner in her dungeons, and uses magic to make the skeletons of previous prisoners dance for his entertainment.

Other episodes that were eventually abandoned included a fantasy sequence to accompany Snow White's song 'Some Day My Prince

Disney's madcap triumvirate – Mickey, Goofy and Donald – in one of many frenetic exploits as *Mickey's Fire Brigade* (1935).

Will Come' in which the heroine imagined herself dancing among the clouds with her dream prince, attended by an entourage of stars; and a scene in which the dwarfs build an elaborate bed for Snow White with help from the woodland birds and animals. Much of the bed-building sequence never progressed beyond the storyboard stage, much to the chagrin of several of the young artists, including Ward Kimball, who worked on the scene. However, a passage in which the dwarfs eat the soup Snow White has made them and sing a comic song, 'Music in your Soup', was completed in pencil animation and only cut, because it slowed down the pace of the story, shortly before being inked and painted.

The critics had dubbed *Snow White and the Seven Dwarfs* 'Disney's folly', and, as Walt poured more and more resources into making the film, his actions seemed to confirm their judgement. Even though the number of artists and technicians employed at the Studio had grown from a mere handful to over two hundred, Walt knew that he needed still more. 'He came to me one day,' recalled Don Graham, 'and said, "I need 300 artists – get them".'

So began a major quest for new talent: Graham went to New York and opened a recruiting office in the RCA Building in Manhattan.

There was also a major campaign of press advertisements, first on the West Coast, then in national papers and periodicals. One of these was included in the Chouinard catalogue to emphasize the role the school was playing in aiding the animation industry. Of those who joined the Studio, some stayed for only a few years before pursuing other careers in comic art: among them were Virgil Partch, later 'VIP' of *The New Yorker*; Hardie Gramatky, author and illustrator of the children's book about a mischievous New York tug-boat, *Little Toot*; Hank Ketcham, creator of the well-meaning, but accident-prone cartoon child Dennis the Menace and Walt Kelly whose satirical comic-strip featuring Pogo the possum is now as much an American institution as Mickey Mouse.

Among those who made their careers at the Studio were Bill Justice, Dick Kelsey, Al Dempster, Jack Kinney, Bill Peet, Erdman Penner, Art Riley, Al Zinnen, John Hench and T. Hee.

In a long memo to Graham in 1935, Walt had listed what he believed to be the essential qualities of a good animator:

1. Good draftsmanship.
2. Knowledge of caricature, of action as well as features.
3. Knowledge and appreciation of acting.
4. Ability to think up gags and put over gags.
5. Knowledge of story construction and audience values.
6. Knowledge and understanding of all the mechanical and detailed routine involved in his work, in order that he may be able to apply his other abilities without becoming tied in a knot by lack of technique along these lines.

To achieve these aims there were lectures by Graham and by established Studio artists such as Norm Ferguson, Fred Moore, Ham Luske, Fred Spencer and Bill Tytla. And everyone was encouraged to gain an appreciation of the widest possible spectrum of the arts. 'We saw every ballet,' recalls animator Marc Davis, 'we saw every film. If a film was good we would go and see it five times . . . Anything that might produce growth, that might be stimulating – the cutting of scenes, the staging, how a group of scenes was put together. Everybody was studying constantly . . . it was a perfect time of many things coming together in one orbit. Walt was that lodestone.'

There were always new lessons to be learned, obstacles to be surmounted and pitfalls to be avoided. After seeing an over-colourful Harman-Ising cartoon, *Spring*, Walt warned against the use of 'comic supplement coloring':

We want to imagine it as rich as we can without spashing color all over the place . . . We have to strive for a certain depth and realism . . . the subduing of colors at the right time and for the right effect.

And there were still many problems to be overcome in the animation itself. The dwarfs were in the capable hands of Fred Moore (who

Layout sketch for the sequence in which Snow White is entertained by Sleepy, Grumpy, Bashful, Doc, Sneezy, Happy and Dopey.

brought to the characters the same appealing roundness of design he had given the Three Little Pigs), Bill Tytla, Fred Spencer and Frank Thomas. The woodland creatures who befriend Snow White were entrusted to three of the younger animators: Eric Larson, Milt Kahl and Jim Algar (who later directed many of the True-Life Adventures). Wolfgang Reitherman animated the Magic Mirror, Art Babbitt drew the Queen before her transformation and Norm Ferguson after she became a Witch. Grim Natwick took on the thankless task of animating the Prince. Natwick later recalled: 'Disney had only one rule: whatever we did had to be better than anybody else could do it, even if you had to animate it nine times, as I once did.'

It was Ham Luske who had, perhaps, the hardest job of all in drawing Snow White herself. 'What he did,' Dick Huemer later observed, 'was really a sensational advance in the history of animation for serious human characters.' The problems in animating Persephone in *The Goddess of Spring* had convinced Walt that the animators needed living models from which to draw. A young actress and dancer, Marjorie Belcher (later one half of the famous dance partnership Marge and Gower Champion) posed, in a Snow White costume, for the live-action camera. This film footage was then transformed by Luske into a convincing animated character. Live-action footage was also shot of Lewis Hightower to help in animating the Prince; and three real dwarfs were filmed so the animators could study the way in which small people move.

The wicked Queen prepares to drink the magic draught that will transform her beauty into ugliness.

Like all animated films, *Snow White and the Seven Dwarfs* was cast twice: with the animators, who were to give physical form to the characters, and with the voices, which were to bring them to life.

For the dwarfs (apart from Dopey who remained silent), Walt cast radio and vaudeville performers: Otis Harlan as Happy, Scotty Mattraw as Bashful and Pinto Colvig in the dual roles of Sleepy and Grumpy. Radio comic Roy Atwell, whose act included monstrously muddled sentences, was signed to play the befuddled Doc. Another dwarf was cast when veteran screen comedian Billy Gilbert – who specialized in a violent sneezing routine – read in *Variety* that one of the dwarfs was named Sneezy and telephoned for an audition.

Movie heavy Moroni Olsen was cast as the voice of the Magic Mirror; Harry Stockwell was given the largely-singing role of the Prince: studio employee Stuart Buchanan became the Huntsman, and actress Lucille La Verne – who had played a variety of hags and crones in such pictures as *Orphans of the Storm* and *A Tale of Two Cities* – was cast as the Witch and, when no one more suitable could be found, the Queen as well.

The most difficult task was finding a voice for Snow White herself. A hundred or more girls auditioned for the part, singing 'I'm Wishing', 'Whistle While You Work' and the other delightful Morey-

Preliminary sketch by Joe Grant of the evil Witch who has terrorized several generations of young movie-goers.

Churchill songs that were such an integral part of the story. Walt had a sound system wired up to his office so he could listen in on the auditions without being unduly influenced by the girls' appearances. One performer, rejected by Walt as being 'too mature', turned out to be young Hollywood star, Deanna Durbin.

The solution came unexpectedly when Walt's casting director, Roy Scott, telephoned to ask the advice of Guido Caselotti, a Los Angeles singing coach who was married to a prima donna of the Royal Opera House in Rome. Evesdropping on an extension telephone was Caselotti's 19-year-old daughter, Adriana, who herself had some opera training. When Adriana interrupted the conversation, asking in a child's voice if she could try out for the part, her father told her to get off the line, but Scott was intrigued by the voice and invited her to audition. As soon as Walt heard Adriana singing in her distinctive bell-like coloratura, he cried: 'That's the girl! That's Snow White!' The recording took 48 days to complete, and Adriana Caselotti received $970 and a place in movie history.

Story, characters and voices were now firmly established, although there were still various technical problems to be solved. Previously animation drawings were made on sheets of paper and celluloid measuring $9\frac{1}{2} \times 12$in (240×300mm). The camera could then be used either to photograph the drawing complete or to select part of it – known as the 'field' – for a close-up shot. It was soon realized that the maximum area of this size paper, referred to as 'five field', would be inadequate for the complexities of some of the work in *Snow White*. A system was devised which would provide a 'six-and-a-half field' using an increased paper and cell size of $12\frac{1}{2} \times 16$in (318×406mm), but it was a costly innovation since the camera equipment had to be modified, and all the animation boards used by the artists, inkers and painters had to be redesigned, built and installed.

There were other problems too: for the camera to zoom in from a long shot to a close-up of distant figures required the drawings to be made on an impossibly small scale – a difficulty finally solved by the introduction of a system of photographically reducing the animators' drawings to the appropriate size.

Then there was the perennial difficulty of conveying 'depth', something that hadn't mattered in the early comic cartoons but that was of vital importance in creating the realistic mood Walt wanted for *Snow White*. An illusion of depth was eventually achieved by

William Garity, head of the camera department, who devised the huge but extremely versatile 'multiplane camera', which was first tried out on the 1937 Silly Symphony, *The Old Mill*.

The biggest problem of all was, not unexpectedly, money. Walt's original estimate for making *Snow White* was $250,000, but that figure quickly doubled to $500,000 once work began. Roy had never been very happy about the idea of a feature-length cartoon, but when costs kept spiralling upwards and more money had to be borrowed – and yet the film got no nearer completion – he began having confrontations with Walt. Given the slightest opportunity, Roy would voice his concerns about what he saw as Walt's disregard for financial prudence. When some trial scenes from the film were screened and employees' opinions sought, the responses included a note that simply said: 'Stick to shorts.' Many believed it came from Roy.

Eventually matters came to a head when Joseph Rosenberg, who handled the Disney loans at the Bank of America, baulked at advancing still more money. He told Roy that he had to see what was already on film. Walt thought the idea of showing the incomplete film was a dangerous one, but Roy was adamant. 'The only way we're going to get more money,' he told his brother, 'is to show them what they're lending the money for.'

Walt and the artists therefore set about cobbling together a rough version of the film, which was a far from easy task since some of the picture existed only in pencil animation while even more of it didn't exist at all. However, by filming storyboard sketches and layout designs to cover some of the gaps, Walt was able to produce a show reel, which he screened for Rosenberg. Since the soundtrack was no more complete than the film, Walt had to improvise the missing dialogue and lyrics. Rosenberg offered Walt little encouragement, simply watching and listening and occasionally saying 'Yes, yes . . .' to Walt's increasingly manic explanations and excuses.

Finally, the film ran out and the lights came up. Rosenberg rose to leave and Walt escorted him to his car, but the banker still made no comment about the picture. As Rosenberg politely chatted about the weather, Walt was convinced he wasn't going to get the money. Only when the banker was about to drive away, did he remark: 'That thing is going to make you a hatful of money!'

The complex and costly multiplane camera, which gave an illusion of depth to the animated film.

The Old Mill (1937) made spectacular use of the multiplane camera to distinguish between background and foreground detail.

What was irritating, in view of the progress being made on the film, was that it was still being referred to as 'Disney's folly'. Walt asked Hal Horne of United Artists whether 'all the bad talk' could damage the picture's chances. 'Let 'em call it "Disney's folly", ' Horne told him, 'or any other damn thing, as long as they keep talking about it. That thing is going to pay off, and the more suspense you build up, the more it will pay off.'

As it happened, Walt didn't actually need to do anything – others kept the suspense building for him: like the film critic of *Esquire* who reported having viewed 10 Disney shorts one after the other to see if it was possible to watch cartoons for as long as an hour and a half and decided that you could, despite 'moments of extreme physical exhaustion if you abandoned yourself to laughter'; or the correspondent in *Life* who speculated on whether the film's advance publicity had reached 'such proportions that Mr Disney may well worry lest the public expect too much!'

With, as he later recalled 'the family fortune wrapped up in it', Walt had far more important things to worry about: 'I am afraid one department will fall down when all the rest of us have done the work,' he told Dave Hand and, indeed, there was greater chance of something going wrong now the animators were going flat out to complete the film. For six months teams of animators, working in shifts – 24 hours a day, 7 days a week – frantically animated, inked, painted and photographed sequence after sequence, snatching a few hours of sleep by their drawing boards whenever they could. It was a unique demonstration of loyalty and artistic cooperation, which would never be seen at the Studio to the same degree again.

It was towards the end of 1937 that the film was completed at a cost of $1,488,423 – six times the original budget.

The picture was to be the first Disney movie distributed by RKO, to which Disney had transferred when United Artists insisted the Studio relinquish the tv rights in its films. 'I don't know what television is,' Walt had responded, 'and I'm not going to sign away anything I don't know about.'

The glittering premiere at Los Angeles' Carthay Circle Theater on 21 December 1937 brought to mind scenes from *Mickey's Gala Premiere*, as the stars of Hollywood – including Marlene Dietrich, Judy Garland, and Charles Laughton – made their way along the red carpet to honour a cartoon film. For 83 minutes the glamorous guests – among whom were more than a few movie-world cynics – laughed and cried; and as the picture came to an end, the audience – cheering and applauding – rose to its feet.

The critics were uniformly euphoric. Speaking for many, Howard Barnes wrote in the *New York Herald Tribune*:

> It is one of those rare works of inspired artistry that weaves an irresistible spell around the beholder ... *Snow White and the Seven Dwarfs* is more than a completely satisfying entertainment, more than a perfect moving picture, in the full sense of that term. It offers one a memorable and deeply enriching experience.

'Disney's folly' had turned out to be an enchanted castle. *Snow White and the Seven Dwarfs* was proof, beyond any doubt, of the genius of Walt Disney and his artists. Later in a radio interview, Cecil B. de Mille asked Walt to explain the secret of *Snow White's* appeal. He replied:

> Over at our place we're sure of just one thing – everybody in the world was once a child. We grow up, our personalities change, but within every one of us something remains of our childhood. It knows nothing of sophistication and distinction, it's where all of us are simple and naive, without prejudice and bias, we're friendly and trusting ... So, in planning a new picture, we don't think of grown-ups and we don't think of children, but just of that fine, clean, unspoiled spot down deep in every one of us, that the world has maybe made us forget and maybe our pictures can help recall.

It was a philosophy that was to provide the Studio with a formula that would earn it success after success for 50 years to come.

5. THE GOLDEN AGE

The success of *Snow White and the Seven Dwarfs* was immediate and international. Walt Disney had achieved his ambition: his Studio had made an animated movie that audiences believed in as much as if it had been filmed with flesh-and-blood players, perhaps even more so, for to see *Snow White and the Seven Dwarfs* was, as one critic put it, 'to see into Fairyland'.

The film went on general release on 4 February 1938, attended by an exhaustive range of character merchandise. Not only were there the predictable dolls, toys, books, records, nurseryware and children's jewellery but such oddities as 'Smarties' corsets with 'Walt Disney's fairytale princess woven or printed on the fabric'; Snow White Flower Seeds (including 'The Wicked Queen Prize-Winning Fantasy Zinnia'); and Snow White 'Latexeen' Baby Pants: 'The most comfortable I've ever worn – says Mickey Mouse!' There were also special promotional campaigns tied-in with the film and advertising the products of, among others, Colgate-Palmolive, National Dairies, Super Suds, Armour's Star Ham, Royal Typewriters and Indian

Head Sheets, which were advertised as being as 'white as Snow White's forehead fair, and closely woven for longer wear'.

And in addition to promotions and merchandise featuring Snow White, there were thousands of other items capitalizing on the continued appeal of Mickey Mouse's gang and of characters from the Silly Symphonies. 'Demand for this merchandise,' reported Disney's Character Merchandise catalogue for 1938–9, 'has grown to such an extent that it has become of signal importance, not only to retail institutions everywhere, but to American industry as a whole. During every month of the current year, many of our licensees have been working to capacity. All volume records for Disney character merchandise have been broken.'

Walt Disney, it seemed, could do no wrong. *Snow White and the Seven Dwarfs* had come as a crowning achievement to two years of quite exceptional film entertainment with such Silly Symphonies as *Elmer Elephant, Little Hiawatha, Woodland Cafe* and another Oscar-winner, *The Country Cousin*.

Equally successful was the Mickey Mouse series, although Mickey himself made fewer solo appearances and, with one or two notable exceptions – like *Thru the Mirror* (1936) – shared the acting honours

One of the many fine Silly Symphony cartoons was *Woodland Cafe*, with its Lionel Barrymore-inspired heavy.

Spoofing Lewis Carroll's *Alice* fantasies, *Thru the Mirror* (1936) was one of Mickey's greatest solo pictures.

with the far more versatile Donald and Goofy in wildly inventive pictures such as *Moving Day* and *Alpine Climbers* (1936), *Moose Hunters*, *Clock Cleaners* and *Lonesome Ghosts* (1937).

In preparation, for release in 1938, were five more Silly Symphonies: *Wynken, Blynken and Nod* and *The Moth and the Flame* (two of the Studio's most technically perfect shorts), and *Merbabies*, *Farmyard Symphony* and *Mother Goose Goes Hollywood*, featuring wickedly funny caricatures of movie stars cast in the roles of nursery-rhyme characters. *Mother Goose Goes Hollywood* earned an Oscar nomination along with no fewer than three other Disney shorts: Mickey Mouse's *Brave Little Tailor*, in which Mickey turned giant-killer; Donald Duck's *Good Scouts* and *Ferdinand the Bull*, a special based on Munro Leaf's engaging story of the bull who preferred sniffing flowers to fighting in the bull-ring.

At the Academy Awards ceremony in February 1939, Ferdinand took the Oscar. And later the same evening, Shirley Temple climbed onto a chair to present Walt with a special award recognizing *Snow White and the Seven Dwarfs* 'as a significant screen innovation which

As the *Brave Little Tailor* (1938), Mickey vanquished the giant, won Minnie's hand and earned an Oscar nomination.

has charmed millions and pioneered a great new entertainment field for the motion picture cartoon'. The award comprised one regular Oscar and seven miniatures. 'Isn't it bright and shiny Mr Disney?' cooed Shirley Temple. 'Yes,' replied Walt, 'I'm so proud of it, I'm going to burst!' At which Hollywood's favourite child-star exclaimed: 'Oh, don't do that, Mr Disney!'

The film industry had acknowledged *Snow White* as a movie milestone, and Hollywood soon began capitalizing on the Disney-made market for fantasy. Among the live-action pictures owing a debt to *Snow White* were *The Wizard of Oz* and *The Blue Bird*, and in the output of rival animation studios the influence was even more marked. A great many non-Disney shorts had strikingly familiar titles – *Skeleton Frolic*, *Poor Elmer* and *Little Moth's Big Flame* (all animated by Ub Iwerks for Color Rhapsodies), *Jolly Little Elves*, *Candyland* and *Baby Kittens* by Walter Lantz and others such as *The Little Dutch Mill*, *Somewhere In Dreamland*, *The Little Match Girl* and *The Blue Danube* – and sought to imitate the style of the Silly Symphonies. Max Fleischer, creator of Popeye, who had dismissed *Snow White* as 'too arty', was soon producing, at Paramount's request, an animated feature based on *Gulliver's Travels*; while Universal's Walter Lantz began (but never completed) a full-length cartoon film of *Aladdin and his Wonderful Lamp* with the acquired talents of Disney's leading musician Frank Churchill.

No sooner had *Snow White and the Seven Dwarfs* been declared a success than, as Walt later recalled, 'the shout went up for more dwarfs'. His response was simple: 'Top dwarfs with dwarfs? Why

Shirley Temple presents Walt Disney with a special Academy Award for *Snow White and the Seven Dwarfs*.

try?' In an interview, only a few days after *Snow White* was premiered, Walt announced that he was planning three new animated features: *Pinocchio*, *Bambi* and that film project he just wouldn't let die, *Alice in Wonderland*. What Walt didn't reveal in 1937 was that three further potential features were being researched: *Cinderella* (an obvious successor to *Snow White*) and two more English classics, Kenneth Grahame's *The Wind in the Willows* and J.M. Barrie's *Peter Pan*.

Early work on Barrie's play included some imaginative designs for the Never Land with lush jungles and subterranean caverns full of pirate gold guarded by skeletal buccaneers. One of the artists who worked, briefly, on *Peter Pan* was David S. Hall, a remarkable draughtsman who had joined the Studio in 1937. Hall also produced hundreds of sketches and watercolours to establish a style for

One of David Hall's evocative sketches for an imaginative version of *Alice in Wonderland* that was never made.

been established during the early 1930s to handle such things as Disney real estate and merchandising. Of the new issue of 150,000 shares, Walt and Lilly received 45,000 apiece, with 30,000 each going to Roy and his wife Edna.

With so many projects in hand and a rapidly growing staff, an attempt was also made to rationalize company procedure. In May 1938, a huge document was drawn up, together with a complex 'Organization Diagram: Showing Responsibilities for Inter-Studio Creative and Managerial Operations'. Everybody's function within the company was set down in legalistic language that was a far cry from the *ad-hoc* system that had been operating for years.

Walt's responsibility, as Executive Producer, was now described as 'authorizing the function of all story work according to his judgement of the advisability of the production of suggested story ideas, dictating the course which those stories are to follow, exercising complete jurisdiction over them throughout all stages of production, indicating to the General Production Manager the creative personnel to be assigned to the production.' For the next two years, Walt exercised those functions on four major animated films, the first of which was *Pinocchio*.

The movie was inspired by the stories of the 19th-century writer, Carlo Collodi. Not surprisingly, in view of the picaresque nature of Collodi's book, *Pinocchio* proved a challenging – often difficult – project. The story was rich with incident, but it lacked the conciseness and simplicity of *Snow White,* and it took a long time to establish a workable scenario. The main difficulty, however, was Pinocchio himself, whom Collodi had portrayed as a wilful, disobedient brat. This made for an unsympathetic hero, particularly as the artists originally depicted him as a grotesque. Attempts to draw Pinocchio in a cuter, more appealing style only rendered the character insipid and ineffectual, particularly in confrontations with the story's outrageous villains.

To make Pinocchio more assertive, the storymen wrote dialogue scenes in which the puppet argued out the rights and wrongs of the various situations in which he found himself; this device, while making Pinocchio more sympathetic, proved tedious and cumbersome.

After six months of work, Walt halted production to reassess the story. The search for a device led them back to an episode in the original book in which Pinocchio encounters a Talking Cricket who warns the puppet that his ambition to do nothing but 'eat, drink, and sleep, and have a good time from morning till night' will only lead to trouble. Pinocchio, who dislikes the advice, gets angry with the cricket and squashes him with a mallet.

From this incident emerged an idea: keep the insect alive, give him a personality, call him Jiminy Cricket and make him act as Pinocchio's conscience. 'At first,' said Walt, 'we made Jiminy a sort of pompous little old fellow – kind of a windbag,' but the character changed when the puckish entertainer Cliff Edwards was cast to speak for the cricket and sing the two unforgettable songs – 'Give a

Disney's version of *Alice in Wonderland* that was individualistic and full of surrealist imagery. But the film was once again postponed, and *Alice* was shortly joined on the shelf by *The Wind in the Willows, Cinderella* and *Peter Pan*.

Pinocchio and *Bambi*, however, were soon in production, although it was clear to Walt that, with such an ambitious schedule, they could not continue at the old studio on Hyperion Avenue. During the years in which *Snow White* was being made, they had added various new buildings including a feature unit, a paint lab, a sound shop, film vaults and a projection room. Several adjacent bungalows were purchased and utilized, but conditions were still hopelessly crowded.

Walt and Roy eventually decided that they needed new premises, and they decided to build a studio suited to the particular needs of animation. A site was found, costing $100,000, on Buena Vista Street in Burbank, and on 31 August 1938 a deposit of $10,000 was paid and planning and building began. The money for this expansion was provided by *Snow White*, which, within six months, grossed $2,000,000 and by the time it had concluded its first run, had taken $8,500,000.

As a result, Roy decided the time had come to restructure the company. Begun as a partnership, the company had been incorporated in 1929 with assets of $85,852 and liabilities of $32,813. The 10,000 shares had been divided within the family, with 3,000 held each by Walt and Lilly, and 4,000 by Roy. In 1938 Walt Disney Productions was reorganized to include other companies that had

At planning meetings Walt would give animated performances as he put forward his ideas to the artists and writers. Here, at a preproduction meeting for *Pinocchio* (1940), he enthusiastically demonstrates a key scene in the story.

Mickey and the gang survey the new custom-built Disney Studio in Burbank.

The Blue Fairy teaches the imprisoned Pinocchio that a lie keeps growing until it is as plain as the nose on your face.

Little Whistle' and 'When You Wish Upon a Star' – written for him by Leigh Harline and Ned Washington. Cliff Edwards had, said Walt, a vocal performance with 'so much life and fun in it that we altered the character to conform with the voice. Thus Jiminy comes to the screen younger and not pompous at all, but just merry and lively and full of funny quips.'

Despite a tendency to preach, Jiminy Cricket was, as one writer put it, 'one hell of a guy at heart'.

Those quips, which lighten Jiminy's moralistic character, comprise snappy American colloquialisms such as his indignant outburst when, rapping with his umbrella on the teeth of Monstro the Whale, he shouts 'C'mon, Blubbermouth, open up!'; or, when the Blue Fairy brings Pinocchio to life and he whistles incredulously: 'Gee, what they can do these days!'

Pictorially, Jiminy developed from a character similar in appearance to the hero of *The Grasshopper and the Ants* into what the animators referred to as 'the little green man', lacking almost all resemblance to an insect other than a diminutive stature.

Jiminy proved a perfect foil for Pinocchio, able to lecture on good and evil when required, but with sufficient spunk to tackle anyone who sought to lead Pinocchio astray.

The responsibility for animating Jiminy Cricket went to Wolfgang Reitherman, Don Towsley and Ward Kimball who – upset that his work on the bed-building sequence in *Snow White* had not been used – was on the point of handing in his notice when Walt called him into his office and sold him the idea of bringing Jiminy to life. Much imaginative animation went into the cricket sequences, emphasizing his smallness by the use of shadows and low-level perspectives.

As with *Snow White*, the characters in *Pinocchio* were one of the picture's strongest assets. Particularly memorable performances were those of J. Worthington Foulfellow ('Honest John' to the unsuspecting Pinocchio), the foxy confidence-trickster, animated with Dickensian flair by Norm Ferguson and John Lounsbery and voiced by Walter Catlett; and Stromboli, the puppet-master who constantly explodes into indecipherable Italian (supplied by Charles Judels) while his entire physique, masterfully animated by Bill Tytla, quivers with Latin rage. There were also Lampwick, the Brooklyn-esque tough-guy; the demonic Coachman, who carried the disobedient boys to their doom on Pleasure Island; the ethereal Blue Fairy, voiced by Evelyn Venable and modelled by Marge Belcher; the addled old wood carver Geppetto, animated by Art Babbitt and based on Austrian character actor, Christian Rub; Gideon, Honest John's feline side-kick, who resembled Harpo Marx at his most anarchic; and Geppetto's pets: Figaro the mischievous kitten and Cleo the coquettish goldfish.

The settings for *Pinocchio* surpassed even those in *Snow White*, drawing their inspiration from a series of exquisite watercolours by Gustaf Tenggren, and were full of the ingenious embellishments of Albert Hurter, such as Geppetto's huge collection of elaborately carved clocks that take on animated life in the film. The Studio went to great lengths to research *Pinocchio* with groups of artists filming and sketching seascapes on the Pacific coast, collecting sea shells and studying the marine gardens at Catalina Island from glass-bottomed boats. Many of the props used in the picture – clocks, toys and fire-dogs – were made for the animators to study, as were a marionette of Pinocchio and a working model of the stagecoach.

Pinocchio contained much pioneering animation with effects ranging from violent storms to flickering candles. The underwater episodes were given an evocative rippling atmosphere through the use of specially ground distorting-glass, and there were several striking scenes using the multiplane camera: notably the sequence showing the awakening village, which begins among the roof-tops and then moves down among the narrow, winding streets bustling with people. That one shot cost $48,000, almost twice the cost of an entire short cartoon.

A number of elaborate sequences were planned for *Pinocchio* only to be abandoned. The visit to Pleasure Island, for example, was originally conceived as a much longer sequence, and consideration was given to an episode in which Geppetto tells Pinocchio about the puppet's grandfather, an old pine tree. The 'Grandfather Tree' sequence was never used, but the woodland storm and forest fire, which it featured, were later included in the other major film project being planned at this time, *Bambi*.

Based on a book by the German novelist and playwright Felix Salten, *Bambi* told the story of a wild fawn from birth to maturity, a plot that had obvious attractions for an animation studio that had already produced many popular animal characters. *Bambi*, however, demanded a far greater degree of naturalism than had been attempted in any Disney cartoon, and the artists working on the project studied animal movement and anatomy under the celebrated California artist and Chouinard lecturer, Rico Le Brun. Cameraman Maurice Day shot live-action footage in the woods of Maine so that the artists could study the different moods created by the elements and the changing seasons; and two real fawns were supplied by the Maine Development Commission, which, along with rabbits, skunks, mice and other creatures, provided life-study subjects for the artists headed by Milt Kahl and Eric Larson (who had animated *Snow White*'s forest friends), Frank Thomas and Ollie Johnston.

Artist and Chouinard lecturer, Rico Le Brun, pets a live deer modelling for the animators working on *Bambi*.

But this naturalistic approach to Bambi presented numerous animation problems: the shape of a deer's head, with widely separated eyes, a mouth not designed for making speech patterns, made it difficult to convey the range of expressions necessary for an effective animated character; and the detail required – such as the spots on a young fawn's coat – meant that it took anything up to an hour for an animator to make just one drawing. Instead of the usual daily average of 10 feet of film, the *Bambi* artists produced little more than six inches a day.

Further problems arose in attempting to translate to the screen the serious tone of Salten's book. *Bambi* was originally written for adult readers and the Disney version was criticized for the heart-rending scene in which Bambi's mother is shot by hunters. But the book contains many more such chilling episodes: within just three paragraphs, for example, a baby hare is killed by crows, a pheasant is torn to pieces by a fox, and a squirrel is mortally wounded by a ferret.

In an attempt to lighten the mood, the book's adaptor, Larry Morey, and his colleagues invented two companions for Bambi – Thumper the rabbit and Flower the skunk – who provided much-needed humorous relief, as in the scene when Thumper takes the inexperienced Bambi sliding on a frozen pond. But there was no opportunity for using the conventional gags found in the shorts or even the anthropomorphic clowning of the animals in *Snow White*. The film's appeal rests almost entirely on stunning visual beauty and its unrelenting – often cloying – sentimentality, only heightened by the use of American moppet-voices.

There were, however, animation sequences of consummate brilliance, such as the forest fire – with the terrified animals silhouetted against a raging furnace of flame – and the fight of the stags, which Walt wanted to see animated 'black on black' and which was achieved by highlighting the stags in purple, ochre and silver as they clashed in brooding shadows.

Progress on *Bambi* was slow, and Walt realized there was no way it could be hurried if it was to succeed. Besides, he was now deeply involved in a third major project.

It had begun in 1937 when Walt had chanced upon Paul Dukas' fantasy scherzo *L'Apprenti-Sorcier* (*The Sorcerer's Apprentice*). The music depicted an ancient tale about a lad with ambitions to become a great magician who experiments with his master's magic and gives life to a broomstick which he sets to work, carrying buckets of water. The enchantment, however, gets out of control, the broomstick proves unstoppable, and chaos ensues.

Clearly *The Sorcerer's Apprentice* was an ideal subject for a Silly Symphony, and who better for the title-part than Mickey Mouse, whose screen popularity – compared with Goofy and Donald Duck – was in something of a decline?

There were some who thought the recently created Dopey would be better in the part, but Walt was adamant: 'I feel that to separate Dopey from the other dwarfs, to take him away from his surroundings, to place him in a strange world to fend for himself, would be wrong.' Besides, Walt owed too much to Mickey Mouse to let his stardom fade. So in May 1937, Walt began negotiating for the rights to Dukas' music.

A few months later Walt was dining alone at Chasen's restaurant in Beverly Hills when he noticed Leopold Stokowski at a nearby table. The idiosyncratic conductor of the Philadelphia Orchestra was becoming something of a Hollywood personality with film appearances in *One Hundred Men and a Girl* and *The Big Broadcast of 1937*. Walt invited Stokowski to join him, and in the course of a lively, three-hour conversation, mentioned his plan for filming *The Sorcerer's Apprentice*, which Stokowski immediately offered to conduct.

Stokowski, however, had one reservation about the project: 'May I make a suggestion which perhaps is impractical?' he wrote to Walt, 'What would you think of creating an entirely new personality for this film instead of Mickey? A personality which could represent *you and me* . . . You may have strong reasons for wishing Mickey to be the hero . . . this is merely a suggestion, which . . . discard immediately if it does not interest you.'

Walt *had* and he *did*. Stokowski recorded the soundtrack in January 1938, with an orchestra of hand-picked musicians, while at the Studio work began on the film. The animators assigned to the picture included Les Clark and Fred Moore, and Moore took the opportunity to restyle Mickey's appearance and increase his expressiveness by giving him, for the first time, eyes with pupils.

The completed picture had cost $125,000, three or four times the amount spent on an average Silly Symphony; also, at 10½ minutes, it was longer than a normal cartoon short. One option, obviously, was to cut it, but Walt had other ideas. What the Studio had done with Dukas' music it could surely do with the work of other composers, and Walt decided that *The Sorcerer's Apprentice* would become one episode in a much longer film.

Stokowski responded enthusiastically to the idea and suggested involving Deems Taylor, a noted composer and musical commentator who regularly introduced the radio broadcasts of the New York Symphony Orchestra. Since the film was to combine music and pictures, Walt chose Joe Grant, head of the Character Model Department, and Dick Huemer to join him, Taylor and Stokowski in choosing the compositions to be used and devising stories. The five-man team met together for the first time in September 1938 and began listening to, and discussing, hundreds of pieces of music.

Gradually the choice of pieces was narrowed down, sometimes as a result of the images suggested by the music: Moussorgsky's *Night on Bald Mountain* and Schubert's *Ave Maria* were chosen to provide dramatically contrasting themes symbolic of the profane and the spiritual, while the choice of Stravinsky's *The Rite of Spring* grew out of a search for a composition to depict a very specific theme of prehistoric life.

In addition to these works and *The Sorcerer's Apprentice*, the film was to contain Tchaikovsky's *The Nutcracker Suite*, an entertainment with 'flowers, butterflies, glow-worms and fairies'; Stokowski's orchestration of Bach's *Toccata and Fugue in D Minor*, which was to be accompanied by 'abstractions, geometrical and color patterns'; and 'The Dance of the Hours' ballet from Ponchielli's opera *La Gioconda* with 'a troupe of elephants, hippos, giraffes and other dainty jungle ballerinas', all of which compositions appeared, in some shape or form, in the final film.

Also listed were Pierne's *Cydalese* to accompany a romp with 'Fauns, Pans, Centaurs, Winged Horses and Nymphs'; and an evocation of 'a world painted silver by the moon' in illustration of Debussy's *Clair de Lune*, which would contain 'no story thread, very little animation, merely the mood of the music visualized'.

The scenario for the 'Cydalese' sequence was later used, against Stokowski's wishes, to accompany Beethoven's 6th Symphony, 'The Pastoral', and the moonlight sequence eventually found its way into *Make Mine Music* (1946) set to the popular melody 'Blue Bayou'.

It was an exciting period for those involved in the project with a fair amount of wild talk – such as filming 'The Concert Feature', as the project was then known, in 3-D – and a suggestion that they might use Debussy's 'Perfumes of the Night' led to a discussion about the feasibility of spraying fragrances into the theatre during screenings. Another proposal was for the use of wide-screen when, in the 'Ave Maria' sequence, the camera moved through the interior of a vast cathedral towards a stained glass window depicting the Virgin and Child; but both the wide-screen technique and the Madonna image were subsequently scrapped.

Clearly the sound quality of the picture was of paramount importance, and Stokowski worked closely with William E. Garity, head of the Studio's sound department, on devising a revolutionary sound system. With the exception of *The Sorcerer's Apprentice*, which was already recorded, the music was performed by Stokowski and the Philadelphia Orchestra and recorded by Garity, one section of the orchestra at a time. Stokowski then mixed these recordings into four tracks, highlighting various parts of the performance to tie-in with the images being created for the screen.

Planning for 'The Concert Feature' was at its most intense when, in 1939, the Studio moved to its new premises. Designed by a group of architects and engineers working under the personal supervision of Walt, the new Studio in Burbank had to achieve two, seemingly conflicting aims: a building where production could be carried out as efficiently as possible and an environment that would not only allow but encourage the creativity of the individual artist.

Writing in 1942, R.D. Feild described the new premises, which had cost $3,000,000, as 'a modern industrial plant laid out with all the precision necessary for the most up-to-date factory,' although he later qualified this remark by adding: 'It may be a factory, but in this 20th century, by so becoming, it has dignified the artist's calling.'

Dominating the site was the animation building, three storeys high with four wings arranged to provide the maximum available daylight for the artists. Like the rest of the Studio, the building was air conditioned – the name 'sweatbox' was used only now through habit – and was equipped with such features as external sunblinds that could be operated by a handle inside each office.

The building housed everyone involved in the creative process from Walt (who had a suite of offices and a bed for late nights) and his Production Manager, through the Story Department, the Supervising Animators and their Assistants and In-betweeners, to the 'Checkers', responsible for ensuring the accuracy of drawings sent for inking and painting. The building also housed a library and a 'morgue' where animation drawings that had been finished with were filed away for future reference. Other buildings nearby were designated to the camera, cutting and ink-and-paint departments, a music sound-stage, a dialogue and effects building and a theatre.

Among the creations of this period were Goofy's first solo short, *Goofy and Wilbur*, and several hilarious Donald Duck pictures, including *Donald's Lucky Day, Sea Scouts* and *The Autograph Hound*. There was also one of Mickey's now infrequent appearances in *The Pointer*, which was nominated for an Academy Award, but which lost to the last Silly Symphony, a colour remake of *The Ugly Duckling*.

Work was also progressing on *Pinocchio, Bambi* and 'The Concert Feature', in which Walt continued to take a lively interest, and which gradually engaged the skills of almost all the artists. Albert Hurter produced more of his fanciful sketches showing a variety of strange mythological beings for 'The Pastoral Symphony' sequence, a section of the film that also inspired a series of Art Deco pastels and watercolours of a beauty and delicacy, which, sadly, proved somewhat elusive when the animation process began.

Walt also engaged talent from outside the Studio, such as the Danish artist Kay Nielsen, who had illustrated *East of the Sun and West of the Moon* and *A Thousand and One Nights*. Nielsen created the ghouls, ghosts and goblins for *The Night on Bald Mountain* sequence and the gothic-arched forests for *Ave Maria*. Like Gustaf Tenggren, Nielsen was one of the few inspirational artists whose style was clearly discernible in the finished film, but his association with Disney was short-lived. Writing in her *Treasury of the Great Children's Illustrators*, Susan E. Mayer records that 'Nielsen, who was proud and obstinate, didn't care for the dogmatic Disney and

Clarence Nash and Pinto Colvig, the voices of Donald Duck and Goofy, pose together at the microphone.

what began as a leave of absence ... eventually resulted in a permanently severed relationship.' Another casualty was the German experimental animator Oskar Fischinger who had produced several innovative films animating abstract forms. Fischinger was engaged to work with Cy Young, head of the Studio's effects department, on the 'Toccata and Fugue' but quit 'in disgust and despair' before the sequence was completed.

For those who stayed the course, there was much research to be done: sketching flowers and fossils, watching the amusing antics of a well-built actor posing as the rear-end of a centaur or studying film footage of Marge Belcher dancing for the bestial ballerinas in 'The Dance of the Hours'. One young artist, John Hench, who was somewhat contemptuous of ballet, was dispatched by Walt to watch and draw the performers of the Ballet Russe; while others grappled with a problem for which there were no living models – the animation of dinosaurs: 'Just draw a 12-storey building in perspective,' advised Bill Roberts, co-director of the Stravinsky sequence, 'then convert it into a dinosaur and animate it.'

To begin with, Dick Huemer recalls, there hadn't been 'any great excitement' about the project, but that soon changed, and a succession of celebrated visitors to the Studio found themselves posing for the camera with Walt beside the storyboard of pterodactyls in flight or being asked to scrutinize plaster figurines of hippo

Experimenting with the Sorcerer's magic hat was the beginning of Mickey's troubles and the origin of *Fantasia*.

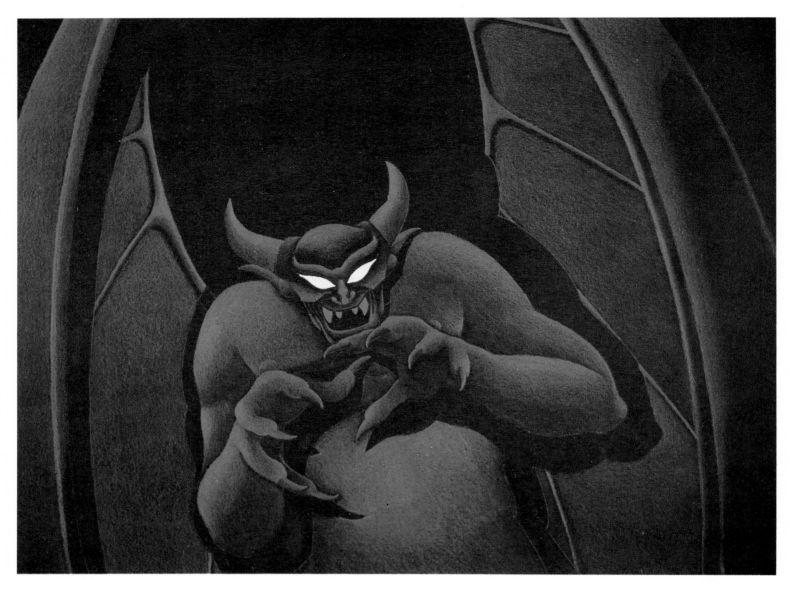

A film of contrasting images, *Fantasia* depicts terror with the demon of Bald Mountain (above) and beauty with the graceful Pegasus family featured in the 'Pastoral Symphony'.

ballerinas. Among those to whom Walt proudly displayed the work on 'The Concert Feature' were choreographer George Balanchine, novelist Thomas Mann, actresses Katharine Cornell and Maude Adams (America's first Peter Pan) and Kirsten Flagstad, with whom Walt may have discussed an idea he had for animating 'The Ride of the Valkyrie' from *The Ring of the Nibelung* as one of a number of

pieces – including Sibelius' *Swan of Tuonela* and Rimsky-Korsakov's *The Flight of the Bumble Bee* – with which he intended to vary the programme of 'The Concert Feature' from time to time.

Many of Disney's visitors agreed to address the artists, among them the writer and critic Alexander Woollcott, who enthused about having seen a rough pencil test for *The Sorcerer's Apprentice*. Rather less enthusiastic was the architect Frank Lloyd Wright, who dismissed Disney animation as 'trying to be symphonic or too damned artistic'.

Two other visitors were astronomer Dr Edwin P. Hubble of California's Mount Wilson Observatory and biologist Sir Julian Huxley who gave their enthusiastic approval of the evolutionary pageant developed for *The Rite of Spring*, while the composer, Igor Stravinsky, posed for a photograph in which he was shown studying a copy of the score with Walt. Some years later, however, Stravinsky was to denounce Stokowski's performance as 'execrable', adding: 'I will say nothing about the visual compliment, as I do not wish to criticize an unresisting imbecility.'

'The Concert Feature', which was now to be formally introduced by Deems Taylor in white tie and tails, still required a title. 'When it was nearly completed,' remembered Dick Huemer, 'Walt decided on the name *Fantasia*, which had been lurking almost unnoticed in the background right from the beginning.'

'In a profession that has been an unending voyage of discovery in the realms of color, sound and motion,' said Walt, '*Fantasia* represents our most exciting adventure.' But before that adventure – or even those of Pinocchio – reached the screen, a turn in world events was to have far-reaching effects on the Studio and all but eclipse the stunning achievements of Disney's Golden Age.

6. DISNEY AND THE DRAGON SLAYERS

On 1 September 1939 Germany invaded Poland. Two days later Britain's Prime Minister, Neville Chamberlain, declared war on Germany. America's response to these events came in a statement from President Franklin D. Roosevelt: 'This nation will remain a neutral nation ... As long as it remains within my power to prevent, there will be no blackout of peace in the United States.'

At the time the Studio looked to be in a healthy financial position with a surplus of $1,250,000; but with *Pinocchio*, *Bambi* and *Fantasia* still on the drawing boards and proving costly, the prospect of a full-scale war in Europe posed alarming questions for the future.

Mousebrow and highbrow: Mickey meets Stokowski in *Fantasia*.

No less than 45 per cent of Disney income came from overseas markets, and the war quickly closed Germany, Italy, Poland and Czechoslovakia to the movie-makers of Hollywood while the governments of Britain and France ordered the freezing of American revenue earned in their countries.

As income to the Studio diminished so costs escalated, particularly on *Fantasia*. The bill for Stokowski's recordings alone had run to $400,000, and by the time the film was completed it had cost a staggering $2,280,000, plus considerable additional costs for the sophisticated sound system – called 'Fantasound' – which required three speakers placed behind the screen and 65 others specially installed in each auditorium.

Even more costly than *Fantasia* was *Pinocchio* on which $2,600,000 had been spent by the time of its release in February 1940. Writing in *The New York Times*, Frank S. Nugent described *Pinocchio* as 'a blithe, chucklesome, witty, fresh and beautifully

drawn fantasy ... the best thing Mr Disney has done and therefore the best cartoon ever made.' In particular, Nugent praised the film for its technical superiority over *Snow White and the Seven Dwarfs*. Some critics cavilled that the score was much inferior to that of *Snow White*, but at the Academy Award ceremony, *Pinocchio* took the Oscar for best song with Leigh Harline and Ned Washington's haunting ballad 'When You Wish Upon a Star' – that was, ever after, Disney's unofficial signature tune – while Harline and Washington, together with Paul J. Smith, won another Oscar for best film score.

Describing the characters in *Pinocchio* as 'vivid, rounded personalities', the film critic of London's *Daily Express* wrote: 'To be funny and beautiful and moving and exciting – that is probably the synthesis of every film-maker's ambition. Disney, without human aid, does it with such wonderful ease.'

In truth, of course, Walt Disney had a great deal of human aid: the Studio currently employed 1000 people, a crucial factor contributing to the serious financial position in which they now found themselves. A hefty payroll, the expensive new premises, the cost of *Pinocchio* – which, despite the plaudits, failed to do well at the box-office – and the mounting expenditure on *Bambi* and *Fantasia* all quickly demolished the profits earned by *Snow White and the Seven Dwarfs*.

In the spring of 1940, Roy Disney confronted his brother with the alarming news that the Studio was in debt to the extent of $4½ million. Walt's first reaction was to burst out laughing, a response triggered by the memory of a time when they couldn't borrow so much as a thousand dollars, let alone several million. The situation, however, was far from amusing since there was insufficient money to complete and distribute *Fantasia*. Roy's solution was one the brothers had long resisted: an issue of stock on the public market. In April 1940, Walt

Jiminy Cricket comes eye to eye with Monstro the Whale in *Pinocchio*.

Disney Productions – President and Executive Production Manager, Walter E. Disney, and Executive Vice-President and Business Manager, Roy O. Disney – offered 155,000 shares of 6 per cent cumulative convertible preferred stock at $25 par value and 600,000 shares of common stock at $5 a share.

Years in the making, *Bambi* contains many delightful scenes such as the young deer's meeting with Thumper.

To prevent too much Disney stock leaving the organization, Walt announced that of the shares reserved for Roy and himself, 20 per cent would be distributed among employees; and the exercise, while marking the end of an era, was a profitable one, raising $3,500,000 of much-needed capital.

The additional finance raised enabled the completion of *Fantasia* which was premiered on 13 November 1940 at New York's Broadway Theater. 'At last,' wrote Walt Disney in the film's souvenir programme, 'we have found a way to use in our medium the great music of all times and the flood of new ideas which it inspires. Perhaps Bach and Beethoven are strange bedfellows for Mickey Mouse, but it's all been a lot of fun . . .'

The critics, however, were divided: Dorothy Thompson of the *New York Herald Tribune* reported leaving the theatre 'in a condition bordering on nervous breakdown' and accused Disney and Stokowski of a 'brutalization of sensibility in this remarkable nightmare'. The reviewer in *Look* magazine hailed *Fantasia* as a 'masterpiece', and Pare Lorentz, writing in *McCall's*, declared that Disney had taken art 'out of the temple, put it in carpet slippers, and an old sweater, and made it work to surround, support, and synchronize a brilliantly-drawn series of animated color sketches'.

Walt had intended to open the film in 76 theatres across America, but there were major problems over the 'Fantasound' system. Apart from costing $30,000 a unit, RCA had produced only 12 sets of speakers when national defence priorities caused production to be suspended.

Fantasia received special roadshow screenings in Boston, Cleveland, Chicago, Detroit and other cities as well as in New York, but the average movie-goer – expecting, perhaps, another fairy-tale in the tradition of *Snow White* and *Pinocchio* – was somewhat confused by Disney's brush with culture. Critic Howard Barnes might call it 'a courageous and distinguished production', but all they knew was that it didn't seem to contain much of what they understood as traditional Disney.

Walt was forced to allow *Fantasia* to have a normal release with an ordinary soundtrack. His distributor, RKO, asked that the film be cut from two hours to the length of an average feature, and Walt had no choice but to agree, although he left the task of editing the picture to 82 minutes to someone else. An emasculated version of *Fantasia* finally went on general release on a double-bill with a Western.

It is curious then that *Fantasia* as it was originally conceived should have won two special Academy Awards: one to Walt Disney, William E. Garity, John N.A. Hawkins and the RCA Manufacturing Company 'for their outstanding contribution to the advancement of the use of sound in motion pictures'; and the other to Leopold Stokowski and his associates 'for their unique achievement in the creation of a new form of visualized music'. *Fantasia* was also voted one of The Ten Best pictures of 1940 by the National Board of Review. Sadly none of this helped its performance at the box-office.

In consequence, Walt abandoned plans for making new programme items for *Fantasia*, but he remained convinced that the film would, one day, be a success. Although a subsequent reissue in 1946 failed to take the film into profit, Walt eventually decided it should be shown as he originally intended and almost all the cut footage was restored in 1956. Today – with a new soundtrack in digital stereo – it remains, of all Disney films, the one that most powerfully demonstrates both the range and the limitations of the Studio's art.

In 1940, however, *Fantasia*'s failure was a catastrophic blow, and, with the 1939 surplus of $1,250,000 transformed into a deficit of $120,000, drastic action had to be taken. Although, as Walt Disney Productions' first Annual Report announced, the number of pictures in production was the largest in the company's history, a 20 per cent scale-down in operations was begun. The number of short subjects to be made was reduced (Silly Symphonies were discontinued altogether), and, while work was resumed on *Peter Pan* and *The Wind in the Willows*, two relatively small-budget pictures were put into production. One was an animated film about a baby elephant named *Dumbo*, the other was a live-action movie with animated sequences entitled *The Reluctant Dragon*.

Budgeted at a mere $600,000, *The Reluctant Dragon* was intended to be a low-cost picture that would give a quick – and, hopefully,

'What the world needs,' wrote Robert Benchley, 'are more Reluctant Dragons. Then we could all have a chance to cultivate our gardens, read our poetry, eat our green vegetables and get somewhere.'

substantial – return. It was also aimed at capitalizing on Walt's enormous popularity and answering the public's frequent request to know how the Disney cartoons were made.

The Reluctant Dragon was conceived as a vehicle for Robert Benchley, the popular American humorist and film personality, who had won an Oscar for his 'How To' series of comic shorts. Benchley visits the Studio with the aim of interesting Walt in the idea of filming a story from Kenneth Grahame's book *Dream Days*. *En route* to his interview, Benchley discovers the behind-the-screen secrets of cartoon film-making. When he finally meets Walt he is whisked into a

Walt's encounter with Robert Benchley (holding an animator's bust of himself) as seen by *Punch* cartoonist J. H. Dowd. (Reproduced by permission of *Punch*)

viewing theatre to see the Studio's latest picture, which turns out, of course, to be *The Reluctant Dragon*.

The Studio's first foray into live-action movies was directed by veteran Hollywood director Alfred Werker, and the animation personnel included Ham Luske, Ken Anderson, Fred Moore, Wolfgang Reitherman and Ub Iwerks, who had recently returned to the Studio to work in the area of special effects and camera development. Among the members of staff who were seen in front of the camera were Ward Kimball and Norm Ferguson, although a number of actors, including the young Alan Ladd, were engaged to play Disney staff members.

The film contained some fascinating footage: artists drawing an elephant from life for *Dumbo*, Clarence Nash and Florence Gill recording a duet for Donald Duck and Clara Cluck, and sound men creating thunderstorms and talking railway trains. The animated sequences included Goofy in a Benchleyesque short 'How to Ride a Horse', and the story of a juvenile genius, 'Baby Weems', which was told in an innovative form using still drawings and limited animation and which was one of several Disney experiments to predate the highly stylized work of UPA Studio in the 1950s.

The Studio's other film title, *Dumbo*, began as a modest project based on a slight children's story by Helen Aberson and Harold Pearl. Walt read the tale when it was in the galley-proof stage, and decided to make a 30-minute 'Special'. After some initial work had been done, in which the original story had been expanded and Dumbo's character developed, Walt abandoned the picture. A short time later, however, Joe Grant and Dick Huemer took the work that had already been done in order, as Huemer later recalled, 'to see if we could rekindle Walt's enthusiasm for *Dumbo*'.

Grant and Huemer worked quickly and enthusiastically on what they saw as a 'nearly flawless story'. This they set down on paper 'straightening out what appeared to be stumbling blocks, adding new material, submitting this a chapter at a time for Walt to read as a sort of continued novel'. Walt immediately responded to their treatment, and *Dumbo* was put back into production. The animation was eventually completed within a year for just $812,000.

The film which emerged has many charms: the gay circus-poster colours; the bright carnival tunes by Oliver Wallace, Frank Churchill and Ned Washington; the picture-book animation with its humanized animals and an anthropomorphic train chugging across a cartoon map of America; the special effects such as the raising of the big top at night in a thunderstorm; the surreal imagination of the sequence in which Dumbo gets drunk and dreams of pink elephants; and the two central characters – the guileless, silent Dumbo who begins life as a freak but who turns the handicap of his monstrous ears to unique advantage, and Timothy Mouse, the tough-talking little guy with a heart of gold who makes himself Dumbo's spokesman and protector.

Once again there was some intuitive vocal casting: Ed Brophy, portrayer of numerous movie tough guys, as Timothy Mouse; Sterling Holloway as the bird-brained Stork in charge of baby Dumbo's delivery; Verna Felton as the vitriolic matriarch of the elephant herd, and Cliff Edwards as Jim Crow, leader of the raucous quintet who aid Dumbo's aeronautical ambitions and sing the film's hit number 'When I See An Elephant Fly'.

Despite the efficiency with which work progressed on *Dumbo* and *The Reluctant Dragon*, everything at the Studio was far from well. There was not only the ever-present problem of money – weekly operation costs were $90,000 of which $70,000 (or $2000 an hour) went on salaries – but there was also a growing unrest among the employees.

It had begun, in a sense, with the move from the old Hyperion Avenue studio, where a remarkable atmosphere of cameraderie and freedom of expression had grown up. The new buildings, despite all the thought and money that went into their planning, seemed, to some of the animators, to diminish that atmosphere.

Robert Benchley was seen in *The Reluctant Dragon*, wandering from one happy-go-lucky department to another; in reality, the animators worked in units each of which had a 'control desk' with 'control girl' to supervise movement between departments.

The expansion that had followed the release of *Snow White*, the onerous financial burdens that demanded a high degree of business efficiency and the rapidly growing personnel, made such controls inevitable, as had the detailed Organization Outline, drawn up in 1938, which specified the responsibilities of each employee:

> The Unit Director is directly responsible to the Unit Director Supervisor for all the creative results of production from completion of story to the final screen results ... He is responsible for delivering to the Animator the correct conception of all footage handed out by him, so that the successive efforts of the Layout Man and the Animator, and other functions, may produce the desired result. He must maintain a complete knowledge of the movement of the Animators with whom he is concerned, so that his production may move through its successive phases of production with a minimum of cost ...

Many of the artists who had previously been used to involving themselves in each stage of a film's production felt isolated from their colleagues and working in a creative vacuum. Worse than that, they felt cut off from Walt, who, though they didn't realize it, disliked the necessity for titles, job-descriptions and increasing regimentation as much as anyone.

There were, however, compensations. As soon as the Studio's financial position had improved, Walt – who had long paid above-average wages – shared the prosperity with his staff. 'He became very liberal with his employees,' said Dick Huemer, 'Almost paternalistic. For instance, he established a savings and loan plan where anyone could get a loan at very small interest, far below the current rate. He instituted a generous bonus system. This had never before been done in the cartoon industry. He gave *paid* vacations, something I had never enjoyed in all my twenty-odd previous years of labor over the light board. He also presented stock to deserving employees.'

There was a high price to pay for this liberality: in a period of seven years, almost half a million dollars had been distributed to the staff in bonuses and adjustments; paid vacations cost $140,000 a year, plus another $70,000 for the six legal holidays; while sick benefits amounted to an annual bill of some $28,000.

Walt's own salary was now $500 a week but, as he later pointed out, 'As long as we have been in business, I have never received the salary that was credited to me. When the reorganization and the issue of preferred stock came out, all the back salary credited to my account was wiped out and turned into common stock.'

Nevertheless, once the Studio was again under financial pressure, rumours and complaints about management began to proliferate among some of the staff. It was believed that Walt was preparing for wholesale lay-offs by training up women artists and second-rate animators who would be cheaper to employ; and criticism was made of what was seen as needless expenditure on such items as the large number of waitresses employed in the cafeteria or the planting of grass in certain parts of the studio grounds.

There were also charges that Walt had an 'inner ring' of close associates who were given privileges not accorded to the mass of employees and who, alone, were recognized for their value to the company.

As a result of this disharmony, when the value of Disney stock began to fall, many animators chose to cash in their shares. Dispirited though Walt was at seeing the share value drop first from $25 to $14 and then to $12, $10 and finally $3, he demonstrated his own belief in the company by buying back the shares of those who decided to sell.

With their uncertainty about the future and frustration at the regulations that had been imposed to protect the Studio's interests, Disney animators became a prime target for Hollywood's union activists.

Unrest was everywhere, and few movie moguls could afford to ignore the growth of unionism, which many of them associated, rightly or wrongly, with communism. One of Disney's main rivals, Max Fleischer, had set up a new studio in Miami, Florida, after his New York studio was hit by a labour dispute in 1937. And, in Hollywood, labour racketeer Willie Bioff, together with George E. Brown, had been blackmailing studio heads into paying large sums of money to buy off strikes and wage demands.

Disney already operated closed shop agreements with musicians, electricians, make-up artists, costume and prop men. The only group of people who were, as yet, not unionized were the animators, and because of the Studio's pre-eminence in the field, it was important to the unions to establish a credible powerbase there.

Two separate unions were canvassing the animators: the independent Federation of Screen Cartoonists and the Screen Cartoonists Guild, which was affiliated to the International Brotherhood of Painters, Paperhangers and Decorators of America and was led by the tough labour tactician, Herbert K. Sorrell.

For the most part, the animators were politically innocent and indecisive: several of them joined both unions, while many of them joined neither. Sorrell tried to get Walt to sign up with the Screen Cartoonists Guild, claiming that the majority of the Disney artists had already joined the Guild. Walt, who didn't believe Sorrell had anything even approaching a majority, told him he wanted the matter put to a ballot organized by the National Labor Relations Board. But Sorrell, who had once lost just such a ballot by only one vote, refused.

'He said he would strike,' Walt later recalled in giving evidence to the House Committee on Un-American Activities. 'He said, "I have all the tools of the trade sharpened," that I couldn't stand the ridicule or the smear of a strike. I told him that it was a matter of principle with me, that I couldn't go on working with my boys feeling that I had sold them down the river on his say-so, and he laughed at me and told me I was naive and foolish. He said, "You can't stand this strike, I will smear you, and I will make a dust bowl out of your plant." I told him ... that he might be able to do all that, but I would have to stand on that ...'

The Disney-Sorrell confrontation was a reflection of the divisions that now existed between the animators and that threatened to destroy the Studio. In February 1941, deciding that there had been too little communication between himself and his staff, Walt addressed all employees in an attempt to end the rumours, answer the criticisms and generate new cooperation.

Speaking of the crisis the company was facing, Walt talked from the heart:

> Everything you're going to hear here is entirely from me. There was no gag meeting or anything to write this thing. It's all me, and that will probably account for some of the poor grammatical construction and the numerous two-syllable words ...

Nevertheless, the speech, which ran to 26 pages in transcript, was read from a prepared text, and the address was recorded on discs, the authenticity of which was verified by 'three impartial witnesses', one of whom was a notary public, who all signed the recordings.

Outlining the major events in the Studio's history, Walt spoke of the risks and chances he had taken to keep the Studio together, his struggles with bankers and distributors and his 'stubborn, blind confidence' in animation as 'one of the greatest mediums of fantasy and entertainment yet developed'. He answered the various charges of negligence, explaining that the number of waitresses employed was essential to ensuring the efficient control of lunch breaks, and the planting of grass had been undertaken to cut down the amount of dust – always a danger to animation – that had been getting into the Studio buildings. He defended the right of less experienced animators to try and prove themselves and justified the training of women both because the Studio needed to be prepared in the event of men being enlisted into the forces as well as because of their 'right to expect the same chances for advancement as men'.

Describing animation as 'a pioneering venture', Walt reiterated that he had 'never been interested in personal gain or profit'. Regardless of what the animators thought of conditions, he said, 'I honestly believe that instead of complaining, we should count our blessings.' He concluded with a passionate plea:

> This business is ready to go ahead. If you want to go ahead with it ... you've got to be ready for some hard work ...
>
> If the business is to survive the many storms that are ahead of it, it must be made strong; and that strength comes from the individual strength of the employees.

Animators picket the Disney Studio in 1941. 'To me,' said Walt, 'the entire situation is a catastrophe.' *Insert*: An anonymous Disney artist catches the Boss in disenchanted mood.

Don't forget this – it's the law of the universe that the strong shall survive and the weak must fall by the way; and I don't give a damn what idealistic plan is cooked up, nothing can change that.

But the unrest continued and came to a head with the dismissal of Goofy's chief animator Art Babbitt, who had been critical of what he saw as the inequality of a system that paid him $300 a week, while his assistant was receiving only $50, and who, as a result, had become an active supporter of the Cartoonists Guild. Claiming that Babbitt had been sacked for his union activities, Sorrell finally called the threatened strike on 29 May 1941.

Of the 293 employees who went on strike, some were militant activists, some were settling personal differences with Walt and others genuinely believed that, with the growth in the industry, unionization was a necessary safeguard. Although 60 per cent of the staff crossed the picket lines and went into work, there were some, like Bill Tytla, who while not necessarily sympathizing with the strike, stayed out through loyalty to their colleagues.

Tensions between strikers and nonstrikers mounted and tempers flared. Arriving at the Studio one day, Walt was harangued by Babbitt on a loudspeaker from a picket line carrying placards with such slogans as 'The Reluctant Disney', 'Are We Mice or Men?' and, adapting a song from *Pinocchio*, 'There Are No Strings on Me!' Walt leapt from his car and studio guards had to restrain him and Babbitt from coming to blows.

'At the time,' Disney later recalled, 'I took photographs of those picket lines and studied those photos. I'd never seen half of those faces. They'd never been near my Studio. When I showed them to the FBI and to the investigators for the California Un-American Activities Committee, I was told, "The fellows in those photos have been in every strike Sorrell has called".'

Several of those who continued to work have spoken of the threats of violence and the verbal and physical attacks they received, although neither side, as Walt was to admit, were exactly 'gentlemen of the old school' and, on one occasion, an anti-Sorrell group spilled gasoline in a ring around the pickets, lit a cigarette and threatened to set light to the gas if the strikers' spokesman were to repeat a particularly abusive remark that he had made.

It is ironic that just when the strike was at its height, in June 1941, *The Reluctant Dragon* went on release. The depiction of the Disney Studio as a place of harmony, fun and creativity could scarcely have been further from the truth.

Although the critics were kind to *The Reluctant Dragon*, they were quick to point out that it was really little more than 'a super de luxe

The precocious Baby Weems gives instruction to Albert Einstein in *The Reluctant Dragon* (1941).

commercial film showing Disney's sumptuous new diggings out in San Fernando Valley'; or, as another put it, coining a new – and prophetic – word, 'a glorified travelogue about Colorful Disneyland'.

Nevertheless, *The New York Times* dipped into what it called Disney's 'grab-bag of whimsical cartoon sketches' and voted the characters 'the most delightful company of the season'. Special praise was accorded to the title cartoon and its central characters: Sir Giles 'an emaciated English blighter with the wits of a Philadelphia lawyer' and the dragon who, in a case of mistaken gender, the critic described as a 'dizzy dowager'. In conclusion, however, the writer expressed a regret that Disney had 'confused a skylarking fable with a lot of shop talk'.

For the most part, audiences tended to agree, and, as the war in Europe escalated, perhaps found the fight-shy dragon with his outrageously camp mannerisms and frivolous versifying an inappropriate hero for the age.

Introducing the book-of-the-film, Robert Benchley wrote: 'I do wish that a lot of people I knew (or know of) would take a look at the Reluctant Dragon and, whenever they feel the old urge coming on to get red-blooded and lash out, would remember that putting two heads together is better in the long run than kicking them around on the ground, and nowhere near so messy . . .'

Benchley's pacifist injunction might profitably have been addressed to the warring factions at the Studio, where the dispute was heightened when Sorrell organized a secondary boycott by workers at Technicolor and instigated a bitter press campaign to discredit Walt and depict the Studio as a sweatshop.

Among the newspapers reporting the strike was *The Times* of London – a publication rarely given to flights of fancy – which speculated on whether the real trouble-makers might not be the Big Bad Wolf, the Wicked Queen and Mr J. Worthington Foulfellow. *The Times*' correspondent concluded by remarking that 'it would be welcome news that both outside and inside the Studio, the dispute had been amicably made up'; but while, as the summer of 1941 dragged on, there were discussions and negotiations, a resolution to the strike still seemed far off.

Recalling the effects on Walt Disney of the strike, Joe Grant says: 'It hurt him deeply. He felt betrayed, felt that everyone who had formerly been behind him, had now left him. It also marred his relationships and made him feel that he would never depend on other people again.'

But, just when, along with his loyal animators, Walt was suffering from what he called 'a case of the DD's – disillusionment and discouragement', an unexpected opportunity came their way in the form of an invitation to take a trip to South America.

Gunther Lessing, Studio Vice-President and legal adviser, was at that time serving on the Short Subject Committee of the motion picture division of the Coordinator of Inter-American Affairs, an organization set up under Nelson Rockefeller to counteract the influence of Nazism and Fascism that had begun to take a hold in South America following an influx of Germans and Italians.

Through Lessing, Walt was introduced to the director of the CIAA's Motion Picture Division, John Hay Whitney, who proposed that Walt should make a goodwill tour of Latin America. At first Walt was reticent; as he told John Hay Whitney: 'I'm no glad-hander. I wouldn't know what to do on such a tour.' To which Whitney suggested Walt should take some animators with him and gather material for a film series on the different South American countries. 'That's more like it,' Walt responded, 'I'm not so hot at just shaking hands and showing my teeth. But I *do* make movies.'

It wasn't, of course, quite as easy as that: there was the situation at the Studio to be considered and the usual money problems. The Bank of America was currently advancing the Studio credit on demand, in return for which it received all earnings from RKO releases of Disney pictures. By 1941, Walt had borrowed $3,400,000, and the war and the strike were dramatically affecting film revenues. What concerned the Bank of America was whether any films that Walt might make as a result of this proposed trip were likely to earn any money. However, the government agreed to underwrite the project with an expense budget of $70,000 and a guarantee of $50,000 a film for up to

Film-making down Mexico way offered Walt an escape from the tense situation at his beleaguered Studio.

five pictures, providing that money was repaid in the event of a profit being made.

Walt carefully selected a team to accompany him from those not involved in completing *Bambi* and *Dumbo*. Norm Ferguson was appointed producer-director for all the pictures resulting from the trip, with Frank Thomas giving assistance with animation. The rest of the party comprised storymen Bill Cottrell, Ted Sears and Webb Smith; story-sketch artists Jack Miller, James Bodrero, and husband and wife Lee and Mary Blair. Larry Lansburgh, a member of Ferguson's animation unit at the Studio, and his wife Janet were to work on animals and characterizations; while Herb Ryman, a talented artist who had joined the Studio from MGM, was to study landscapes and architecture. Charles Wolcott was to represent the music department, and Jack Cutting, who had already visited South America and had supervised the foreign language versions of earlier Disney films, was to act as an adviser. Also in the group were business manager, John Rose and publicist, Janet Martin, as well as Lilly Disney and Hazell Cottrell.

Following extensive research into South American culture, folk-lore and traditions the company left Los Angeles on 17 August 1941. After a lengthy flight, Walt and his colleagues arrived at Belem on the mouth of the Amazon where they visited a local zoo to make their first introduction to the wildlife of South America.

The next day, they travelled to Rio de Janeiro where they were met by John Hay Whitney from the CIAA, dined by President Vargas and attended the Brazilian premiere of *Fantasia*, at the beginning of what was to be a three-week stay crammed with a variety of cultural events that were to provide the artists from Hollywood – who were quickly nicknamed *El Groupo* – with much colourful inspiration.

From Rio they flew on to Buenos Aires where, amid considerable publicity, a temporary studio was established at the Alvear Palace Hotel. After a month – during which time there was talk of establishing a permanent branch of the Studio in Argentina – the team left Buenos Aires for various destinations: Herb Ryman, John Miller, Lee and Mary Blair went to La Paz in Bolivia and explored the region around Lake Titicaca, 12,000 feet above sea level in the Andes. Frank Thomas, Jim Bodrero and Larry and Janet Lansburgh travelled to the gaucho heartland of northern Argentina; while Walt, Norm Ferguson, Bill Cottrell and Ted Sears flew to Mendoza and the rest of the party left for the Chilean city of Santiago.

At the end of the trip, *El Groupo* headed for home, taking a 17-day sea voyage from Valparaiso to New York City, during which time they worked on a variety of story ideas based on their experiences. One of these was a tale about a baby mail plane, Pedro, which makes his first solo flight across the Andes from Santiago to Mendoza and braves the thunderstorms and freak air currents around the glowering mountain Aconcagua.

Other stories were to feature members of the Disney stock company, with Pluto encountering a playful armadillo; Goofy, cast as a North American cowboy, whisked down south to learn about the ways of the gaucho; and Donald Duck as a typical American tourist having problems with the papyrus boats on Lake Titicaca, taking an hilariously dangerous climb in the Andes with a supercilious llama, and learning how to dance the samba from a loquacious parrot, José Carioca.

Returning to California in October, Disney found the strike settled and Herb Sorrell claiming a victory for the unions. 'The method used to settle it,' said Walt 15 years later, 'was simplicity itself. The negotiators gave Sorrell practically everything he wanted.' The settlement terms included the reinstatement of Art Babbitt, and a formula guaranteeing that, in the event of cutbacks in production, layoffs would include an equal number of strikers and non-strikers.

But the animosities and ugly confrontations were not easily forgotten by either side and within two years, many of the strikers, including Babbitt, had left the Studio. Subsequently many harsh things were said about the strike, including several sustained and bitter personal attacks on Walt, who responded with his characteristic bluntness:

> It was probably the best thing that ever happened to me. It eventually cleaned house at the Studio a lot more thoroughly than I could have done ... An elimination process took place I couldn't have forced if I'd wanted to. Our organization sifted down to the steady, dependable people. The others had gone.

A flying elephant, hailed as 'The ninth wonder of the universe', hits the headlines in *Dumbo* (1941).

Dumbo's friends and foes ride the circus train pulled by Casey Jnr in this poster-art for the film's reissue.

Gone too, however, were some of his best talent in men like Babbitt, Walt Kelly, Virgil Partch and Sam Cobean, and the Studio's unique spirit of united enterprise, which was replaced by the time-clock.

A change was noted in Walt's attitudes: wary of further trouble, he insisted that every employee, even the gardeners, join the appropriate unions; moreover, in his relationships, he became more cautious and, for a time at least, more remote. He took every opportunity to fight communism, accepting the position of first Vice-President of the Motion Picture Alliance for the Preservation of American Ideals. Walt also testified to the House Committee on Un-American Activities in 1947, expressing the view that the communists in the movie industry 'really ought to be smoked out and shown up for what they are, so that all the good, free causes in this country, all the liberalisms that really are American, can go out without the taint of communism.'

The strike also left its mark on *Dumbo*, which was completed while Walt and his colleagues were in South America and which contains in one sequence, it is said, caricatures of the Studio strikers among the circus clowns seen talking about 'hitting the boss for a raise'.

Dumbo was premiered at the Broadway Theater on 23 October 1941, to great acclaim. The critics were unanimous in their praise. Particularly enthusiastic was Bosley Crowther in *The New York Times*, who commended the brevity of the film and crowed, in the style of a circus ringmaster:

> Ladeez and gentlemen, step right this way ... and see the most genial, the most endearing, the most completely precious cartoon feature film ever to emerge from the ... brushes of Walt Disney's wonder-working artists!

But Disney and his artists had little chance to savour *Dumbo*'s success. The flying pachyderm was to have been given the distinction of appearing on a cover of *Time* magazine for Christmas 1941, but the design was dropped following the bombing of Pearl Harbor on 7 December 1941: an event that dramatically changed the fortunes of the United States and brought the American people, and the Walt Disney Studio, into World War II.

A storyboard sketch by Joe Grant of Dumbo and the gossipy elephants who make his little life a misery. (Courtesy of the artist)

7. VICTORY THROUGH ANIMATION

The effect on Walt Disney Productions of America's entry into the war was immediate: on the very day of the Pearl Harbor bombing, the Army moved into the Studio. It was late afternoon, and Walt was at home when he received a telephone call from a member of his security staff who anxiously reported that the Army was commandeering the soundstage for the repair of military vehicles and anti-aircraft guns; an action prompted by a fear that the nearby Lockheed Aircraft plant would become a prime target for enemy bombing. The Studio was placed under guard, the Disney personnel – including Walt and Roy – were fingerprinted and issued with identity cards, and 3,000,000 rounds of ammunition was stored in the parking lot.

Within 24 hours however, the Studio was given a somewhat less passive role to play in the war effort; Walt was commissioned by the Navy Bureau of Aeronautics to produce 20 short training films.

The pen may be mightier than the sword, but Donald uses both in leading a battalion of Disney characters to war.

Earlier in 1941, looking for new ways of exploiting animation, Walt had made *Four Methods of Flush Riveting*, an experimental training film for Lockheed Aircraft Corporation employees. The film contained no humour and none of the Disney characters, yet it successfully used animation as a teaching aid, and Walt began trying to interest others in the medium's educational potential.

In April, only weeks before the strike, Walt had shown examples of Disney animation to a number of distinguished guests including John Grierson, Commissioner of the National Film Board of Canada. Grierson purchased the Canadian rights to *Four Methods of Flush Riveting* and commissioned another training film, *Stop That Tank* (on the handling of the Boys Mk1 Anti-Tank Rifle), and four brief commercials promoting the purchase of Canadian War Bonds.

Directed by Ub Iwerks, *Stop That Tank* contained one or two comic episodes, but it was essentially a serious instructional film using some live action and, for the most part, limited animation.

The bond-selling films, however, which were designed to have a

more popular appeal, featured well-known Disney stars. *The Thrifty Pig* was a reworking of *Three Little Pigs* with the Big Bad Wolf, turned Nazi, trying – but failing – to blow down the house that Practical Pig had built out of Canadian War Bonds. Next came *The Seven Wise Dwarfs*, in which – after a day's work at their diamond mine – the dwarfs march off with sacks of gems with which to buy their savings certificates. *Donald's Decision* depicted the struggle between the angelic and demonic sides of Donald's character as he considers whether to buy war bonds with his savings or spend them on having a good time. The last film, *All Together*, featured a parade of Disney characters – Mickey, Donald and his nephews, Pinocchio, Geppetto and the Seven Dwarfs – marching past the Canadian Parliament Building with placards announcing the 'Get 5 for 4' incentive then on offer to savers.

The Navy immediately recognized the huge potential of animation and, in December 1941, ordered a series of films on aircraft and warship identification. Each of the 20 films was to cost $4,500 and run 1,000 feet; the first of them had to be ready within 90 days and all of them completed within six months. It was a demanding schedule for a studio used to taking anything up to three years to produce a 7,000-foot feature, apart from the added difficulties of coping with the Army's presence on the Studio site and the gradual drafting of key employees into the services.

In addition to the identification films, the Studio produced short pictures on a diverse range of subjects including, *Protection Against Chemical Warfare, Rules of the Nautical Road* and 'A Few Quick Facts' about the dangers of venereal disease.

But there was neither the time nor the money for the previous technical quality. Wherever possible, economies were made – often through the use of models, still drawings and cutouts rather than full animation. Even so, the Studio found it difficult to meet the demands of its employers in Washington, and the Camera Department was forced to operate 20 hours a day (the other four being used for repair and maintenance), six days a week.

Within a year of America's involvement in the war, Government contracts worth $2,600,000 accounted for the major part of the Studio's production programme. 'The work being done for the various Government agencies,' wrote Walt in the company's Annual Report, 'is developing new techniques and is providing an experience in the educational and commercial field that we believe will lead to more diversification of our product in post-war years.'

However, films with such functional titles as *Aircraft Carrier Landing Signals* and *British Torpedo Plane Tactics* offered little opportunity for imaginative animation; even if, once in a while there were, what Ward Kimball calls, 'small oases of humour' among the deserts of seriousness.

The Studio's comic tradition was to find freer reign in some of the theatrical shorts produced during the war years. Mickey, whose happy-go-lucky antics now seemed ill-suited to the times, was all but forgotten, but other members of the Gang were soon actively involved in the war effort: Goofy with *Victory Vehicles*; Pluto with *Army Mascot, Dog Watch* and *Private Pluto*; and the ever-feisty Donald Duck in a series of shorts – including *Donald Gets Drafted, The Vanishing Private, Fall Out—Fall In* and *Commando Duck* – in several of which he waged a simultaneous private war against his Sergeant, formerly Peg Leg Pete.

Donald's patriotism, however, was never in doubt, particularly after his sterling work on an earlier 'civilian' project. Towards the end of 1941, Walt was summoned to Washington for a meeting with Secretary Henry J. Morganthau of the Treasury Department. Walt supposed the meeting was in connection with the Government's campaign for selling war bonds, but in Washington he found not only Secretary Morganthau but also Guy Helvering, Commissioner of Internal Revenue.

Helvering explained that the Government's recently-passed tax bill gave them access to some 15 million new taxpayers and they wanted a film designed to promote the idea of paying taxes. There was, however, an uncomfortable degree of urgency to the project: Helvering insisted on a deadline of the end of February 1942 so that the film could be in the theatres before the final tax date of 15 March.

It was then 18 December, and Walt warned Secretary Morganthau that his short subjects were costing, at that time, in the region of $43,000, but that this particular project would probably cost considerably more because it had to be produced so quickly. No contracts were signed and all Walt received was a 'letter of intent' that later was to prove the cause of much aggravation.

Returning to California, Walt found Joe Grant and Dick Huemer had already sketched out a story featuring Donald Duck as the average citizen who tries to avoid paying his taxes – until it is explained to him what that money means to his country's war effort.

When the storyboards for the picture, entitled *The New Spirit*, were complete, Walt, accompanied by Grant and Huemer, flew to Washington to show Secretary Morganthau how the project was developing. The hour of the meeting arrived but only Walt was admitted to Morganthau's office. With the help of the storyboards, he acted out the short, explaining how Donald would equip himself with calculators, ready reckoners and headache pills, only to find they were unnecessary with the new, simplified tax forms that Washington was introducing.

Once convinced of the importance of paying his taxes, Donald did his duty with eager enthusiasm: entering his earnings on the form, calculating his tax and deducting the allowance for his dependents, Huey, Dewey and Louie. Told that the vital thing he had then to do was post his return, Donald saluted – two star-spangled banners in his eyes – and went one better by running all the way from California to Washington to deliver his tax to the Treasury in person.

The official audience was unimpressed. Morganthau said that he had hoped Walt would have created a Mr Taxpayer for the film rather than use one of the Studio's characters, and Morganthau's

Hitler gets one in the eye from Donald Duck on this cover (drawn by T. Hee) of a magazine for Disney personnel in the forces.

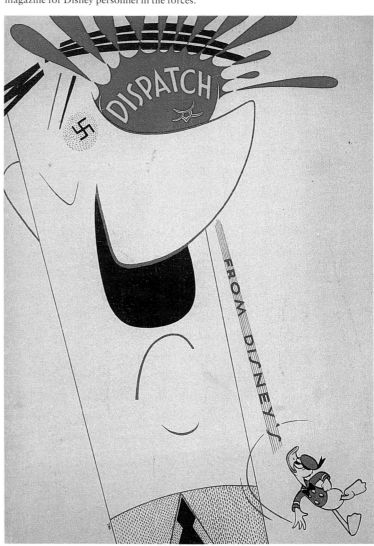

secretary added that she didn't like Donald Duck anyway.

'I'm sorry you don't,' Walt replied, 'but there are a lot of people who do ... I've given you Donald. At our Studio that's like MGM giving you Clark Gable.' Walt also pointed out that by using Donald he stood to lose revenue from every cinema that would have otherwise booked a conventional Donald Duck short.

Morganthau had no choice but to agree, since if the film had to be started anew it could not possibly be completed in time. Animation on *The New Spirit* was begun under the direction of Wilfred Jackson, who later recalled 'the absolutely ridiculous, completely *impossible* deadline'. Eventually, by eliminating various stages in the animation process, *The New Spirit* was completed on time and proved as successful as Walt had predicted. A Gallup poll credited the film with inducing 37 per cent of Americans who saw it to pay their taxes immediately. In consequence, the Studio was commissioned to produce a sequel, *The Spirit of '43*, the following year.

As Walt had feared, however, *The New Spirit* had a drastic effect on Studio revenue because most of the cinemas who showed the film dropped the Donald Duck cartoon they had already booked.

Not only did the Treasury picture lose Walt money, he found it far from easy to get paid. The bill for $83,000 was submitted to Congress for approval on the same day as several dubious wartime projects and, quite unfairly, Walt was accused of being an 'unpatriotic war profiteer'. He finally received only $43,000 for the highly successful use of Hollywood's greatest cartoon star.

Undaunted, Walt continued to produce instructional and educational films for the Army and Navy and a variety of other government agencies, including the US Department of Agriculture, for which he made *Food Will Win the War* (1942), and the

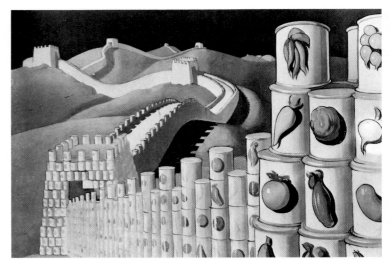

A Great Wall of China made out of canned food provides a strong visual image for *Food Will Win the War* (1942).

Conservation Division of the War Production Board, which used the talents of Minnie Mouse in *Out of the Frying Pan Into the Firing Line* (1942) to advocate the saving of valuable cooking fats.

The same year Minnie was portraying the all-American hostess in the theatrical short, *Mickey's Birthday Party* while the rest of the Gang kept wartime audiences laughing with largely nostalgic pictures like *Orphans' Benefit*, *The Nifty Nineties*, *Symphony Hour* and the Academy Award-winning *Lend a Paw*.

Goofy, now under the direction of Jack Kinney, pursued his chaotic career as recreational instructor with *The Art of Skiing, The Art of Self-Defense, How To Play Baseball, How To Swim* and *How To Fish*; while the misadventures of Donald Duck, directed by Jack King, continued with *Chef Donald, Donald's Snow Fight, Donald's Gold Mine* and *Bellboy Donald*.

A rather more gentle star made his debut in 1942 when, after four and a half years, *Bambi* finally went on release. For the first time the critical response to a Disney feature was decidedly uneven: one critic spoke of the film's 'cheap vulgarity'; another described it as having 'qualities which belong to the older arts of poetry and painting'. Several reviewers commented on the film's allegorical form, while Archer Winston of *The New York Post* asked whether young audiences would accept such a 'serious and elemental' picture. The British critic C. A. Lejeune assured readers that Disney had 'sought after no new forms, pursued no social allegory ... He is happy and relaxed with the things he does best – sketches of wildlife; studies of young animals and their endearing ways.' The reviewer of *The New York Times*, although finding much praise, was critical of Disney's 'discouraging tendency to trespass beyond the bounds of cartoon fantasy into the tight naturalism of magazine illustration'.

The tide of critical opinion, it seemed, was turning against the Studio: in January 1942, *The New Republic* had published cartoonist David Low's glowing appraisal of Disney as 'the most significant figure in graphic art since Leonardo', but within a few months the magazine carried Manny Farber's attack on *Bambi* as a 'Saccharine Symphony' that was Disney's first 'entirely unpleasant' cartoon.

Bambi, which had cost $1,741,000, performed disappointingly at the box-office, audiences preferring, perhaps, the escapism offered by more robust movies such as *The Talk of the Town, Road to Morocco* and *Holiday Inn*.

Unlikely though it may seem, even the innocent woodland creatures in *Bambi* became involved in the war effort. Not long after the mobilization of American forces, various units wrote to the Studio requesting specially designed insignia featuring the popular Disney characters and among some 1,200 designs which were produced, at no charge (although they cost the Studio in the region of $30,000), were ones depicting Thumper as a flying instructor in a mortarboard, Flower, suitably equipped with a gas mask, and Friend Owl as a machine gunner. The Studio's natural troublemakers –

A REMINDER –
Mr Ground Observer

Remember
PEARL
HARBOR

KEEP AWAKE!

© WALT DISNEY

In one of many wartime posters, the peace-loving Mickey Mouse warns against the perils of civilian complacency.

South American tourist Donald Duck sight-seeing at Lake Titicaca in the first South American film, *Saludos Amigos* (1942).

before, stalking wild fantasy in its own wonderland; it is a fairly sophisticated young man of the Western world, exchanging bright and pointed pleasantries with our Latin-American friends, bringing our viewpoints into accord like a witty ambassador ... The great redeeming hope is that the child is not grown up for good, but only for the duration.

One of the particularly grown-up pursuits with which Walt Disney and his artists were concerned for the duration was film propaganda. Their involvement had begun in 1942, with the government's 'Why We Fight' series, supervised by Frank Capra. Although Capra's documentaries were compiled from stock newsreel footage, they were written, directed and narrated by some of Hollywood's top talent, including Anatole Litvak, Anthony Veiller, Ben Hecht, Irving Wallace, Ernst Lubitsch, Walter Huston and Dana Andrews. When, therefore, Capra decided to use animated maps and diagrams, it was natural for him to turn to Disney for assistance.

The series, which began with *Prelude to War*, contained, on average, 25 per cent animated footage, drawn in the most sparing of styles and filmed in black and white. Capra proved a demanding producer with no concept of the time required to create the simplest animated sequences and, as a result, the artists had few opportunities to demonstrate their imaginative flair. There were, nevertheless, several striking images created for the pictures such as that of Nazi insects eating away at the foundations of a castle representing France, and a mailed Nazi fist stamping a Swastika seal on the island of Crete. The 'Why We Fight' series proved the propagandist power of animation and paved the way for what was, for Walt, an even more important project.

In the spring of 1942 a remarkable book had been published by Major Alexander de Seversky of the US Air Corps Reserve, entitled *Victory Through Air Power*. When, with America's entry into World War II, the military leaders virtually ignored aviation and concentrated their efforts on naval offensives, de Seversky put all his energies into promoting the importance of strategic air power to an Allied victory. Dismissed as a crank by most of Washington's top brass, de Seversky presented his arguments in a book that quickly became a bestseller. Walt, who had been considering the idea of an aviation picture, approached de Seversky and, by July 1942, had purchased the film rights to *Victory Through Air Power* and signed de Seversky as consultant, a role later expanded into that of on-screen presenter.

The prospect of filming *Victory Through Air Power* was a daunting one, particularly since the Studio, not the government, would be financing the project, and since, in all likelihood, the picture would greatly displease the military departments whose commissions were keeping the Studio in business. There was also concern about how such a picture would sell, especially when a poll of movie-goers showed that they were beginning to tire of war films. The greatest difficulty, however, was finding a way of presenting the serious content of de Seversky's book in an entertaining form that would, to some extent, meet the public expectations for a Disney picture.

Nevertheless, Walt put *Victory Through Air Power* into production, sugaring the pill with an extended opening sequence showing a light-hearted history of aviation.

The team of animators, working under the supervision of David Hand, included Ward Kimball, John Lounsbery and Bill Tytla; while Walt imported the services of H. C. Potter – director of *Hellzapoppin* – to direct the live-action sequences featuring Seversky. The Major threw himself into the project with unbounded enthusiasm declaring that the film would help America 'come closer to leadership in the aeronautical era which humankind is now entering'.

It was around this time that Walt began work on another – more whimsical – aeronautical feature inspired by *Gremlin Lore*, an unpublished story about those mischievous sprites allegedly responsible for wartime air disasters.

The tale was the work of Roald Dahl, at that time an airman serving with the British Embassy in Washington. The story was based on talk Dahl had heard while serving in the Middle East. Friends in Washington sent the story to Walt who bought it, after considerable negotiations with the British Air Ministry, with Dahl agreeing to give all his proceeds to the RAF Benevolent Fund.

Donald Duck, Big Bad Wolf, Lampwick, Honest John and Gideon – were all shown dropping bombs, as was Chernabog, the demon of Bald Mountain.

Among the newer creations to be used was José Carioca, the nattily-dressed parrot from Brazil, who was depicted igniting a bomb with his cigar, and whose film career had been launched with the release of a short theatrical feature resulting from the South American tour.

The original plan had been to make a series of 12 short subjects, although Walt had been careful to keep his options open. It was not until later in 1942 that the Studio released *South of the Border With Disney*, a 30-minute educational film aimed at fostering the hemispheric unity extolled in President Roosevelt's Good Neighbor Policy.

The decision, in 1942, to compile some of the South American shorts into a feature resulted from a suggestion by David O. Selznick, who advised Walt and John Hay Whitney of the Coordinator of Inter-American Affairs office that such a format would give greater credibility to the government's policy for encouraging unity.

Entitled *Saludos Amigos*, the film ran for just 43 minutes and featured El Gaucho Goofy and the story of Pedro the mailplane as well as Donald's antics in the Andes and his musical encounter with José Carioca. The animation was linked by Walt's personal 16mm live-action footage of the tour.

Saludos Amigos opened first in South America towards the end of 1942 and in the United States the following February. South of the border the film played to capacity audiences, grossing $1.3 million and confirming the judgment of critic Howard Barnes who found it 'singularly beautiful and diverting as well as a striking bit of propaganda for Pan-American unity'.

James Agee, on the other hand, dismissed the film as 'a few infallible bits of slapstick and one or two kitschy ingenuities with color'; while John T. McManus, writing in *PM*, perceived a change in the Disney style:

I think most of us will experience ... mingled pride and sadness over the growing up of a beloved something we all foolishly hoped could stay young forever. For *Saludos* ... is not the fable-minded Disney child of

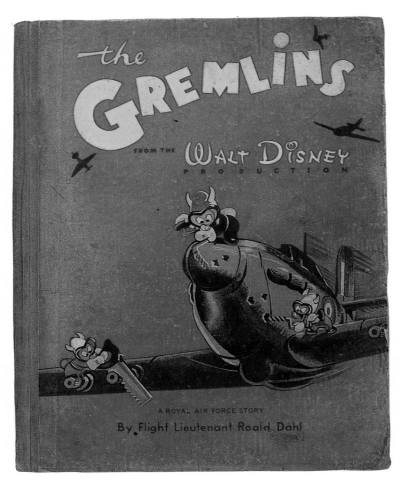

In *The Gremlins* Roald Dahl invented a race of creatures with suction boots (for wing walking) and drills for sabotage.

There were, however, problems with the project from the outset since the Air Ministry insisted that the RAF should have 'the power to say no to anything being done', and sent Dahl's superior to check how the material was being used.

Despite such restrictions, Walt remained enthusiastic about the picture, which he decided to film as a combination of live action and animation. But while the air imps held obvious attractions as a story with humour and wartime appeal, the Gremlin phenomenon, at the time, was scarcely known outside Britain. The Studio immediately embarked on an intensive Gremlin-familiarization campaign, and articles on the subject by Dahl, accompanied by preliminary Disney artwork, began to appear in American newspapers and magazines, and a range of Gremlin character dolls was also designed.

Dahl's story of *The Gremlins*, with Disney illustrations, was published in Britain and America in 1943. It told how the Gremlins had been peace-loving woodland creatures until men ripped up their forest to build an aircraft factory. As a result the Gremlins took a solemn oath:

'We will follow those big tin birds wherever they go,' vowed the leader, and he spoke for them all, 'to get revenge for the loss of our homes. We will make mischief for them, and we will harry and tease the men who fly them, until we obtain some satisfaction for all the harm that has been done to us.'

As the months went by it seemed to some that the Gremlins were becoming rather too real. Jim Bodrero reported in a staff magazine that 'complaints are heard that the Gremlins have moved into Disney's – reports of movieola Gremlins, sound Gremlins, splice-cutting Gremlins and Monday-morning-stomach Gremlins have filtered down the corridors...'. And Walt's plans for the picture itself eventually came under attack from a particularly irksome species of Hollywood gremlin, when MGM, Universal, Columbia and Warner Brothers studios all registered film titles with a gremlin theme.

Thanks to the persuasive powers of Roy Disney, MGM and Universal both abandoned their pictures, as did Columbia. Only Warner Brothers, which was well advanced on two film projects, was unable to cancel them.

This competition, together with the realization that gremlins had become a fad and could, therefore, lose their popularity as quickly as they had acquired it, led Walt to rethink the project. And in October 1943 he abandoned the Gremlin feature. The *Gremlins* had proved an expensive experiment, with advance work on the project costing $50,000 at a time when the Studio could ill afford it.

At the end of 1942, the Studio had a loss of $191,000, which resulted in a total deficit of $1,216,909, a figure that included a half million dollars required just to keep the Studio functioning. *Dumbo* had done well at the box office earning $658,783, but the government projects lost nearly $13,000 in the first year.

Disney characters were featured on hundreds of wartime insignia such as this one for Livermore Naval Air Station, California.

In 1943 those losses were temporarily transformed into a surplus of over $72,000, a sum that was retained by the Studio in case more losses were sustained in future years. It was a precarious time for Walt, not least because of the depletion of his personnel for war service. Of the employees who served with the forces, several – such as Ted Berman, Lee Blair, Tom Codrick, Dick Kelsey, Woolie Reitherman and Frank Thomas – volunteered, but many of the most promising in-betweeners were automatically drafted because they weren't sufficiently trained or experienced to merit exemption.

Walt had to fight hard to prevent the loss of more of his animators, even inviting members of the Draft Board to visit the Studio and see for themselves the importance of the war-work being done.

Writing in the Studio's staff magazine, *Dispatch from Disney's*, Joe Grant and Dick Huemer described the animated cartoon as the 'smash-Hitler weapon' with which humour and fantasy were endeavouring to help fight the war:

No other weapon of propaganda can ridicule the Axis, expose its absurdities, as deftly. How else could inanimate objects and animals take on such unbelievable personalities and fight on our side? And then again there is the vividness of our form of presentation which we arrive at by the use of caricature and symbolism.

Symbolism such as was used in *Chicken Little*, in which the nursery fable of the foolish chicken who persuaded its peers that the sky was falling was retold as an allegory on the dangers of war-time gossip-mongering; or in *Reason and Emotion*, which showed the struggle between two characters who wish to sit in the driving seat of the human brain: Reason 'a sober, intellectual-looking figure' and Emotion 'a swarthy, low-browed caveman sort of fellow'.

An equally blatant piece of propaganda was found in *Education for Death*, which opens with what appears to be a traditional Disneyesque treatment of 'The Sleeping Beauty'. Almost immediately, however, the mood is transformed into caricature when the sleeping princess is revealed as an overweight, flaxen-haired maiden representing slumbering Germany before the awakening kiss of her dream prince Adolf Hitler. *Education for Death* contains some of the Studio's most dramatic use of imagery: the wild-eyed Hitler youth, chanting and saluting; the sinister silhouetted figures of Nazi storm-troopers; and the transformation of the Bible into a copy of *Mein Kampf* and a crucifix into a Nazi sword.

But the most successful of these films was undoubtedly the Academy Award-winning *Der Fuehrer's Face*, in which Donald

The gentleman expressing one objective of Disney films is a combination of Joe Grant and Dick Huemer.

A symbolic demonstration of the power of the cartoonist over the forces of Nazism, drawn for the staff magazine *Dispatch from Disney's*.

dreamt he was a worker in a 'Nutziland' munitions factory, struggling to keep up with the impossible demands of the Fuehrer. The film not only contains broad comedy – as when Donald eats his breakfast of sawdust bread sprayed with 'Aroma de Bacon and Eggs' and coffee made from one bean on a piece of string dipped in a cup of water – but also moments of wild surrealism as Donald finds himself on a conveyer belt being fixed by talking, singing, goose-stepping shells. For the theme song, Walt had told Oliver Wallace: 'I want a serious song, *but it's got to be funny*.' Wallace composed a vulgar parody of German band music, which concluded with a loud Bronx cheer as a rotten tomato was seen being thrown at Hitler's face:

> Ven Der Fuehrer says, 'Ve iss der Master race',
> Ve Heil! Heil! Right in Der Fuehrer's Face!

A few months after the release of Donald's Nazi nightmare came the premiere of *Victory Through Air Power* with its own striking imagery such as the climactic battle between an American eagle and a gross Japanese octopus, which holds the world in its tentacled grasp. 'With typical ingenuity,' read one press release, attempting to establish the widest possible appeal for the film, 'the animation sequences have been woven in such a way that laughs, thrills, stark drama and sheer beauty are all vividly portrayed ... Gorgeous vistas of sea and sky suddenly become maelstroms of death and destruction as air and naval units clash in mortal combat.'

Such scenes alarmed some critics. Howard Barnes, writing in the *New York Herald Tribune*, acknowledged that 'from a technical standpoint, it is difficult to quarrel with the production' but added

that 'it is the ideological content of the offering which is likely to give one pause'.

In *The New York Times*, however, Thomas M. Pryor described the film as 'an extraordinary accomplishment, marking as it were a new milestone in the screen's recently accelerated march towards maturity'; but James Agee noted, with some unease, 'that there were no suffering and dying enemy civilians under all those proud promises of bombs'.

If the moral dilemmas of the strategic bombing theory posed problems for the Studio in making *Victory Through Air Power*, they were nothing compared with the difficulties in marketing the film. Exhibitors were candidly advised to promote the film by 'avoiding as much as possible the war angle and concentrating on the name of Walt Disney, in order to show that the picture is entertainment *not* documentary'.

Although Mickey and the Gang did not appear in *Victory Through Air Power*, the characters were used to decorate the campaign books issued to cinemas exhibiting the film.

When *Victory Through Air Power* was in the planning stage there had been some talk of involving Mickey Mouse and Donald Duck, but although this idea was abandoned, exhibitors' campaign books for the film contained cartoons showing Donald pleading with de Seversky for a part in the picture, eavesdropping with Mickey outside the Major's office and finally being evicted on the toe of the Major's boot.

Donald and Mickey attempt to find out what's going on at a Studio planning conference for *Victory Through Air Power*.

'The Same Old Wish, but never more sincerely said . . .' Disney's 1942 Christmas card reflects hopes of victory.

Despite the attempts of José Carioca to pull him away, Donald Duck is smitten by Aurora Miranda (left) and a quartet of Mexican beauties, in this 1945 publicity still for Disney's second South American picture *The Three Caballeros*.

The film was given an intensive publicity campaign, but it did only moderately well at the box-office, grossing just $11,000 more than its cost of $788,000. Having personally financed the film, Walt was forced to sell *Victory Through Air Power* in the same way as any one of his other features, but his objective in making the picture had always been to help de Seversky's theory become a reality and this, to an extent, it did.

At the Quebec Conference of August 1943, Winston Churchill commented approvingly about *Victory Through Air Power* to Franklin D. Roosevelt and on finding the President had not seen the film, had a print brought to the Conference by fighter plane. As a result, Roosevelt ordered the picture to be shown to the Joint Chiefs of Staff; and it is likely that the film helped to influence the air strategy employed by the Allies on 6 June 1944.

So that the Studio might complete *Victory Through Air Power*, the production of a second South American feature, provisionally titled *Surprise Package*, had had to be postponed. Scheduled for a Christmas 1944 release, the film was further delayed by difficulties in getting prints from Technicolor. Retitled *The Three Caballeros*, it

Major Alexander P. de Seversky, author of the best-seller *Victory Through Air Power* and presenter of Disney's film version.

eventually opened in February 1945. Containing material, mostly about Brazil and Mexico, not incorporated in *Saludos Amigos*, the film also featured specially filmed live-action footage of South American stars Aurora Miranda, Dora Luz and Carmen Molina.

Considerably more time and money was spent on *The Three Caballeros* than on its predecessor and, as a result, the picture has a greater semblance of continuity: Donald Duck receives a birthday present from his South American friends which contains a movie

The Seven Dwarfs protect themselves against the malaria-carrying anopheles mosquito in *The Winged Scourge* (1943), an educational film for the Coordinator of Inter-American Affairs.

projector and films, picture books, a flying serape and a toy-filled *piñata* from Mexico, all of which provide links between the sequences.

The Three Caballeros, nevertheless, contains an often uneasy blend of graphic and storytelling styles. There is the conventional short subject material such as the stories about a young Mexican gaucho with a flying burro and Pablo the cold-blooded penguin who leaves the South Pole in search of warmer climes; but there are also musical travelogue sequences combining the film's live and animated stars, and episodes of animated anarchy such as Donald's encounter with the crazy aracuan bird and his adventures in company with José Carioca and a new character Panchito, the roistering, gun-toting rooster.

Many of the critics condemned the film for what they saw as its 'atrocious taste', especially in allowing Donald Duck to repeatedly express his physical attraction towards the South American beauties who were his co-stars and, in one episode, a beachful of bathing belles at Acapulco.

Despite some hostile reviews, *The Three Caballeros* had a successful release and grossed $3.4 million, although many filmgoers would probably have agreed with Bosley Crowther's assessment of the picture as 'a firecracker show which dazzles and numbs the senses without making any tangible sense'.

In retrospect, however, *The Three Caballeros* can be seen for its true worth: as the first Disney feature to be uninhibitedly 'modern' in its energetic and iconoclastic use of animation; and as the picture that pioneered the effective combination of cartoon and live-action film, employed in several later Disney classics.

Two other South American subjects – *Pluto and the Armadillo* and *The Pelican and the Snipe* – appeared as shorts and Donald had a rumbustious reunion with José Carioca and the Aracuan Bird in the 1948 feature *Melody Time*.

The Studio also produced several more health education films for the CIAA on such subjects as ways of getting rid of the body louse and how to build and where to locate a privy so as not to pollute the drinking water. Looking back on the war years, Walt said: 'We didn't come out of the war smelling like a rose – but we had acquired a wonderful education and a determination to diversify our entertainment product.'

Unlike Frank Capra, who was awarded the Distinguished Service Medal, Walt Disney received no recognition of his contribution to the war effort. But he did have the satisfaction of having survived the war with his Studio intact and in a stronger financial position than it had been for many years. The million dollar deficit that had existed since before Pearl Harbor had at last been reduced to a mere $300,000.

Addressing his employees in the company report for 1944, Walt had answered the rhetorical question 'What of the future of our company?' by saying:

I often wonder if many of us realize the possibilities and potentialities of our medium of expression. In addition to its many other advantages, ours is a medium in which abstract ideas can be visualized clearly and understood with equal clarity by people of every language. These potentialities are a challenge to us all. This is our future.

But for all Walt's optimism, it was several years before the Studio could fully respond to the challenges of the post-war era. That they eventually did so, and with such success, was due in no small measure to the lessons of adaptability they had learned during the war.

8. MASHED POTATO AND GRAVY

'We're through with caviar,' Walt Disney is said to have remarked at the end of the war. 'From now on it's mashed potato and gravy.' When, however, he came to write a 'Message from Walt' for the 1945 Annual Report for Employees, he weighed his words more carefully: 'The end of the war,' he wrote, 'has given us the chance to go ahead with plans which until now we could only think about. It has also confronted us with a number of problems.'

Those problems included the reorganization of the staff to employ the experienced men who were beginning to return from the forces and the effective training of new talent needed to meet an increase in production that was essential to the Studio's future. After so many years of making training and propaganda films, there was also a need for a convincing schedule of good entertainment projects. Several ideas had already been progressed to various stages of development, and these were valued at $4,236,363. Among them were *Beauty and the Beast*; Hans Andersen's *The Little Fir Tree* and *The Emperor's New Clothes*; Hugh Lofting's *Doctor Dolittle*; Beatrix Potter's *The Tale of Peter Rabbit* and Don Marquis' *Archy and Mehitabel*, a tale of a literary cockroach and a fallen feline.

Other possibilities included *The Return of Snow White* and several left-overs from the planned sequel to *Fantasia* such as Ravel's *Bolero*, Saint-Saëns' *Carnival of the Animals* and extracts from Wagner's *Ring* with Grumpy and Dopey as two of the *Nibelungen*. There were also a number of original animal tales written by Joe Grant, Dick Huemer, Bill Cottrell and Otto Englander: *The Camel Camellia*, whose attempts to make the desert bloom are thwarted by the Sandman; *Hootsie the Owl*, about an owl hypnotized by a snake into stealing owl eggs; and *Inspector Bones*, in which a dog detective investigates the case of a missing flea circus.

There was also a highly experimental venture, *Destino*, a further legacy from the South American tour. *Destino* was intended as an animated adaptation of a romantic ballad, performed by singer Dora Luz who had starred in *The Three Caballeros*, and designed by the Spanish surrealist painter Salvador Dali.

Walt had met Dali in 1945, shortly after the painter had designed the dream sequence for Alfred Hitchcock's *Spellbound*. When he was invited to create the style and storyline for *Destino*, Dali was delighted, expressing the view that 'animation enhances art', and confidently declaring that 'Dali and Disney will produce the first motion picture of the Never Seen Before'.

Dali moved into the Studio and began making sketches and water-colour paintings for *Destino*, which Walt described as 'just a simple story about a young girl in search of her real love'. Dali's approach, however, was anything but simple and utilized much of his popular surreal imagery such as shells, statues and desert landscapes as well as a swan which metamorphosed into an elephant. 'I have been given absolute freedom,' he remarked. 'That is paradise for the artist.'

John Hench and Bob Cormack were assigned to work with Dali, and for a while the film seemed to be progressing well. Eventually, however, it became clear that Dali and Disney had differing views of *Destino*, and the project was abandoned with only 15 seconds of the picture on film.

Later there was talk of another collaboration, this time on an animated version of *Don Quixote*, but this too failed to materialize.

Walt's insistence that the Studio had to return to the production of pictures animated in the elaborate style of the pre-war features demonstrated itself not only in projects such as *Destino*, but in his decision to recommence work on the long-planned features *The Wind in the Willows, Cinderella, Alice in Wonderland* and *Peter Pan*.

It was a decision that brought about another of Walt's spasmodic fights with Roy, who was particularly doubtful about the earning potential of *Peter Pan* and *Alice*. Roy had good cause for concern: net income for 1945 was down on the previous year by over $130,000, and the amount currently on loan from the Bank of America was $1,027,226, compared with $528,311 in 1944.

Roy eventually convinced Walt that the Studio needed to pursue a careful course if it was to survive, and the planned features were postponed in favour of more economic productions. *Fantasia* and the two South American features had proved that a variety of material that might otherwise have been released as short subjects, could be successfully strung together into a feature-length film. It was decided to utilize some of the projects currently on the drawing board in this way. As a result, the Studio's output of short subject cartoons remained at its war-time level of some 12 pictures a year, half the number produced during some years before the war.

This decision, combined with the rise of energetic new cartoon stars at other studios such as MGM's Tom and Jerry and the Warner Brothers' menagerie (all of whose adventures were more concerned with action than character), resulted in Disney losing its pre-eminence in the field of short cartoons. Whereas the Studio had taken the Academy Award for best cartoon every year, with one exception, from 1932 to 1943, MGM's Hanna and Barbera began an Oscar-winning run in 1944 with *Yankee Doodle Mouse* and it was 10 years before Disney won another award in the cartoon category.

The first of the Studio's compilation features was *Make Mine Music* in 1944. Following the release of *Fantasia* a number of people had urged Walt to make a similar film based on popular rather than classical music, although when he did, it was a film that contained a wide range of musical styles; one virtue of this approach being that a considerable amount of work already put in on some of the classical pieces planned for *Fantasia*'s changing repertoire could be used.

'Casey, the pride of them all': the saga of a great American sporting legend was featured in one of the sequences in *Make Mine Music* (1944).

Willie the operatic Whale in *Make Mine Music* imagines himself singing the role of Mephistopheles in *Faust*. Willie's vocal performance was supplied by Nelson Eddy.

Make Mine Music proved an uneven production, however, largely because of the diversity of material, which ranged from classical music and jazz numbers, to stickily sentimental ballads and vaudeville recitations. There was an equally motley display of animation styles: some sequences, such as 'Johnny Fedora and Alice Blue Bonnet', are bland and insipid; others, like the story of the perennially-feuding families 'The Martins and the Coys', are little more than a succession of tired slapstick gags. The least memorable are those in which the Studio made self-conscious attempts at

Sonia the Duck meets her doom in 'Peter and the Wolf', which Sergei Prokofiev composed with Disney in mind.

'artiness', such as 'Two Silhouettes' in which a sugary love song is unhappily married with a rotoscoped *pas de deux* by ballet dancers, vulgarly aped by a pair of plump-limbed cartoon cherubs.

On the other hand, genuine – and quite breathtaking – beauty is achieved in 'Blue Bayou', an exquisite piece of animation set in the moonlit everglades and originally designed to accompany *Clair de Lune*. For sheer inventiveness, the animation plaudits go to two Benny Goodman numbers: 'All the Cats Join In' and 'After You've Gone'. *Make Mine Music*'s other highlights are the melancholy tale of Willie 'The Whale Who Wanted to Sing at the Met' and the almost-faultless presentation of Prokofiev's 'Peter and the Wolf'.

The critics were severe with the picture: Bosley Crowther in *The New York Times* described its contents as 'vivid, motley, ornamental and just a bit questionable in spots'. More generously, Otis L. Guernsey in the *Herald Tribune* observed that 'those who do not insist on the rare experience of a Disney masterpiece will have the delightful experience of a Disney pot-boiler, whose comedy, artistry, and fantasy make most of the live actor entertainments look drab and pedestrian by comparison.'

Reassessing the film 40 years later, Robin Allan described it as demonstrating a new mood at the Studio: 'The eclecticism, the nervous tension, the uncertainty, the experimentation, the satire and wit, the lack of sentimentality – and of taste – the sadness, melancholy and sense of loss, are all here in *Make Mine Music*.'

But in 1946, it seemed to many that Walt Disney has lost his way. In truth, Walt – who was personally dissatisfied with *Make Mine Music* – had not so much lost his way as changed directions, although the movie-going public had still to discover the fact. As he later recalled: 'I knew that I must diversify . . . I tried that in the beginning . . . Now I wanted . . . to go beyond the cartoon . . . I needed to diversify further and that meant live action.'

The Studio had only limited experience with live-action filmmaking – *The Reluctant Dragon*, *Victory Through Air Power* and the

Brer Rabbit falls foul of the sticky Tar Baby in one of the animated sequences to
Song of the South (1946).

South American features – but it had much to recommend it, not least
its relative cheapness compared with animation. Nevertheless, Walt
bore in mind the expectations of his audience and decided to make a
picture that would contain animated sequences. He turned to the
tales of Brer Rabbit from the Uncle Remus stories of Joel Chandler
Harris and commissioned Dalton Raymond to write a screenstory set
on the kind of plantation in the South where Uncle Remus might have
lived. This provided the framework for a series of cartoon adventures
of the cunning rabbit and his arch-enemies Brer Fox and Brer Bear.

Entitled *Song of the South*, the picture boasted some remarkable
talents, including Oscar-winning cinematographer Gregg Toland
and the cream of the Disney animation unit: Milt Kahl, Eric Larson,
Les Clark, Marc Davis and John Lounsbery under the direction of
Wilfred Jackson.

The human cast featured stars Ruth Warrick, Lucille Watson and
Hattie McDaniel, while the children were played by newcomers
Luana Patten, Glenn Leedy and the already-established child star
Bobby Driscoll, a wide-eyed, nine-year-old innocent, who provided
the perfect audience for Uncle Remus' tales. Uncle Remus was
portrayed with gentle, roguish charm by James Baskett, who also
provided the frenetic chatter of Brer Fox, while Johnny Lee and
Nicodemus Stewart spoke for Brer Rabbit and Brer Bear.

Only 30 per cent of the film was animation, but it sparkled with
more wit and energy than any Disney cartoon for a long time and had
a warm, rich atmosphere, which owed much to the colour styling of
Claude Coats and Mary Blair. The remaining 70 per cent live-action
footage was a highly competent piece of storytelling, even if it was a
little melodramatic and sentimental. The highlight of the film was
undoubtedly the sequence combining live action and animation in
which James Baskett sang 'Zip-A-Dee-Doo-Dah' accompanied by
assorted cartoon birds and animals, including the top-hatted 'Mr
Bluebird on my shoulder' of the lyric.

Song of the South opened in November 1946 and the following
March, at the Academy Award ceremony, Dinah Shore presented
Allie Wrubel and Ray Gilbert with an Oscar for 'Zip-A-Dee-Doo-
Dah' as Best Song, and Ingrid Bergman gave James Baskett a Special

Award 'for his able and heart-warming characterization of Uncle
Remus, friend and storyteller to the children of the world'.

On its release, however, the movie generated considerable criticism of the portrayal of Uncle Remus. *Time* magazine commented
that it would 'enrage all educated Negroes, and a number of damn
yankees', and the National Urban League condemned the film for
perpetuating 'the stereotype casting of the Negro in the servant role'.
Notwithstanding, the critic of the Black newspaper *The Pittsburgh
Courier*, expressed the view that *Song of the South* would 'prove of
inestimable good in the furthering of interracial relations'.

Other critics were less impressed: 'The Disney wonder workers,'
wrote Bosley Crowther, 'are just a lot of conventional hacks when it
comes to telling a story with live actors instead of cartoons.' Walt
could have well done without such criticisms; by the end of 1946, the
Studio's indebtedness to the Bank of America had risen to $4,276,764
and renewed confrontations ensued with Roy and with the bank.
Nevertheless, Walt announced that he would be producing at least
one feature combining animation and live action every year.

The Studio's financial problems had already led to the company's
original shareholders approving a stock-conversion scheme, which
resulted in capitalization of $1,364,200 and raised the number of
shareholders to 1900. Writing in the company's Annual Report, Walt
told his shareholders and employees:

> The flush days of wartime, when almost any motion picture found
> profitable reception at the box office, are gone. A seller's market has
> suddenly turned into a buyer's market. Shopping for motion pictures will
> be the rule and not the exception . . . More than ever, teamwork must be
> the order of the day throughout 1947.

In an attempt to find new sources of revenue, the Studio undertook a
number of commercial projects, under the supervision of Ben
Sharpsteen, for such corporations as Firestone and General Motors.
But haunted, perhaps, by the spectre of those tedious war years
making training films, Walt eventually abandoned these projects,
telling Sharpsteen that they needed to find a way of combining
documentary material with what they knew how to do best –
entertainment.

The first experiment in what Walt called 'sugar-coated education'
was an idea he had for making a film about America's 'last frontier',

Alaska. Alfred and Elma Milotte who had already made several travelogues, were commissioned to shoot the footage, but when Al Milotte asked Walt what kind of pictures he was looking for, Walt replied vaguely: 'I don't know – just pictures. Movies. You know – mining, fishing, building roads, the development of Alaska. I guess it will be a documentary or something – you know.'

The Milottes set to and filmed, as they later put it, 'everything that moved'. The footage was shipped to Walt, who wired them: 'Too many mines. Too many roads. More animals. More Eskimos.' In response, the Milottes spent a year living with the Eskimos and filming in the Pribilof Islands. More footage poured into the Studio, much to the alarm of Roy, who was concerned at the rising costs of this ill-defined project. Walt, however, started to see the beginning of a film shape and wired for 'more seals'.

In August 1947, Walt visited Alaska and returned with a plan. 'Why don't we ... build a story around the life cycle of the seals? Focus on them – don't show any humans. We'll plan this for a theatrical release, but don't worry about the length.' When the miles of film had finally been edited, the picture, *Seal Island*, ran for just 27 minutes, which caused a good deal of unease with distributor, RKO, which told Walt the film would have to run at feature length if it was to secure a theatrical release.

Walt decided to approach various theatre managers personally and succeeded in convincing Albert Leroy to show *Seal Island* at the Crown Theater, Pasadena, as a supporting feature. It was an immediate hit with the public and was quickly booked for one of Loew's New York theatres to accompany *The Barkleys of Broadway*.

The critics were euphoric, one describing it as having 'all the fascination of a fairy story, with the added appeal of actuality', and at the Oscar ceremony, a few months later, *Seal Island* won the Award for Best Two-Reel Short Subject and further films were planned.

But although the success of *Seal Island* may have opened a profitable new market for the Studio, its financial position was still perilous, with almost $4,000,000 owing to the bank and to RKO, which had advanced a loan in return for an extension of its distribution rights.

There were some successes: *Snow White and the Seven Dwarfs* was dubbed for audiences in Japan, China, Java and Malaya; while *Bambi* did record business in various countries: running 31 weeks in Copenhagen and showing in Helsinki, Finland, in three theatres consecutively, as well as being the first American-made film to be dubbed into Hindustani.

Rather less successful, however, was the spate of packaged features, which had continued, in the autumn of 1947, with *Fun and Fancy Free*, comprising two totally unrelated stories – 'Bongo' and 'Mickey and the Beanstalk' – linked, somewhat inexplicably, by Jiminy Cricket. *Fun and Fancy Free* is an uneven film with occasional flashes of brilliance such as the hilarious, wildly kitsch, sequence in which Bongo, the runaway circus bear, woos his girlfriend Lulubelle among pink candyfloss clouds manufactured by little cupid bears with flit guns, and that in which the beanstalk grows, twisting and writhing in the moonlight.

Writing in *The New York Times* in a mood of indulgence, Bosley Crowther, declared that Disney had 'knocked out a gay and colorful show – nothing brave and inspired but just plain happy'.

The following year, the same critic was – rather less indulgently – describing the new Disney offering, *Melody Time*, as 'a gaudy grab-bag show in which a couple of items are delightful and the rest are just adequate fillers-in'. Opening in the spring of 1948, the film returned to the format of *Make Mine Music*, with Roy Rogers, Dennis Day, Ethel Smith, Francis Langford and others performing seven ill-assorted sequences. The story material drew heavily on old-world American culture with legends and folk tales such as 'Pecos Bill' and 'Johnny Appleseed', a sentimental setting of Joyce Kilmer's famous poem 'Trees' and an adaptation of the popular children's story about a mischievous tugboat, 'Little Toot', by former Disney animator Hardie Gramatky.

Although one critic considered the cartoons in *Melody Time* to be nothing more than 'characteristic Disney productions', the film did contain moments of extraordinarily surreal animation in 'Blame it on

Walt with Cliff Edwards ('Ukelele Ike'), who spoke for Jiminy Cricket in *Pinocchio* and *Fun and Fancy Free* (1947).

the Samba', a heady cocktail reuniting Donald Duck and José Carioca, and 'Bumble Boogie', which presented a jazz rendition of Rimsky-Korsakov's *The Flight of the Bumble Bee*.

The animation in *Melody Time* is, at times, startlingly 'modern', drawing its inspiration from the stylized preliminary sketches made for the film by Mary Blair, Claude Coats and Dick Kelsey. 'Johnny Appleseed', for example, has an impressionistic, rather than realistic, appearance, and 'Once Upon a Wintertime' is drawn with an economy of line that was to be a feature of many 1950s cartoons and the development of which is generally, but erroneously, credited to the studios of UPA.

One further compilation, provisionally entitled *Two Fabulous Characters*, was in production, but Walt was hankering after something more demanding. Everyone who worked with Walt knew that *Make Mine Music* and its successors were nothing more than a way of getting back into feature-length animation. It could only be a matter of time before Walt would begin work on a single-story feature, and the 1948 Annual Report announced that *Cinderella* would be the first post-war all-cartoon picture 'on a grand scale'.

The film went into production with Wilfred Jackson, Ham Luske and Clyde Geronimi as directors and an experienced animation team, which included Larson, Ferguson, Kimball, Johnston, Thomas, Lounsbery, Reitherman, Davis, Kahl and Clark. Among those who worked on the adaptation of the fairy-tale were Ken Anderson, Bill Peet, Ted Sears and Winston Hibler, with Walt himself making a more enthusiastic contribution to story conferences than he had for some years.

Animator Ward Kimball drawing Pecos Bill, the cowboy hero, whose yarn is one of the tales told in *Melody Time* (1948).

The Studio acknowledged fan letters with cards such as this one showing characters from *Melody Time*.

While *Cinderella* was on the drawing boards, two more movies emerged. The first was *So Dear to My Heart*, a largely live-action picture with a few animated sequences. Based on Sterling North's novel, *Midnight and Jeremiah*, the film tells the story of a young boy, Jeremiah Kincaid, who lives on an Indiana farm in 1903 with his grandmother and Danny, a havoc-wreaking pet ram. Although *So Dear to My Heart* was obviously conceived as a successor to *Song of the South*, it is a much better movie.

John Tucker Battle's tightly constructed screenplay retains all the wistful sentiment of the original book as well as the strong protestant ethics represented by Granny Kincaid who 'laid down more commandments than Jehovah'. Not surprisingly, the story appealed to Walt, whose memories of his own childhood on the farm in Missouri gave him a special affection for the project. The cast included Beulah Bondi, Harry Carey and Burl Ives, and Disney's popular child duo Bobby Driscoll and Luana Patten. The animation was directed by Ham Luske and designed by John Hench, Mary Blair and Dick Kelsey, in the elaborate illustrative style of the calendars, greetings cards and Sunday School tracts of the early 1900s.

Unlike *Song of the South*, the animation in *So Dear to My Heart* is purely an embellishment – albeit a delightful one. A pedagogic owl from a series of 'Wise Words' postcards lectures Jeremiah and Danny on the lessons to be learned from the careers of Christopher Columbus, Robert the Bruce and such Biblical characters as David and Joshua, who all possessed that Disneyesque attribute 'Stick-to-it-ivity'.

The second movie to appear at this time was *The Adventures of*

Ichabod and Mr Toad (formerly *Two Fabulous Characters*). The Disney version of Kenneth Grahame's *The Wind in the Willows* had been originally conceived as a feature, and its shortened running time was merely an economic expediency as was its being linked with an adaptation of Washington Irving's *The Legend of Sleepy Hollow*. The uncomfortable union was highlighted by the choice of Basil Rathbone to tell the story of Toad and of Bing Crosby to sing of Ichabod Crane and his encounter with the Headless Horseman.

Of the two sequences, 'The Wind in the Willows' was by far the more successful. Although it took many liberties with the book and ignored all the magic and mystery in Grahame's story in favour of the broad comedy of Toad's adventures, the adaptation captured much of the wit and robust energy of the original. In addition to Basil Rathbone's clipped, no-nonsense, narration, the sequence featured the voices of a clutch of eccentric English comics: Claud Allister as Ratty, Colin Campbell as Mole, Eric Blore as the mercurial Mr Toad and J. Pat O'Malley as the Lancashire caravan horse, Cyril, who is 'a bit of a trotter, a bit of a rotter'.

The Wise Owl teaches Danny the lamb a lesson in one of the animated sequences to the 1949 film *So Dear to My Heart*.

In contrast to the largely animal cast of *The Wind in the Willows*, the human characters in the *Sleepy Hollow* sequence – with the exception of Ichabod Crane himself – appear wooden and unenchanting. And, unlike the story of Toad, which benefited from the considerable preliminary work that had been put into the sequence over the years, it looked as if it had been hastily scamped together.

A figurine by Leonardi of Bongo and Lulubelle whose love story was sung by Dinah Shore in *Fun and Fancy Free* (1947).

A fan-card for *The Adventures of Ichabod and Mr Toad*, showing the characters in a wild race with the Headless Horseman.

Nevertheless, the story of the itinerant schoolmaster who is afraid of ghosts, is redeemed by Bing Crosby's spirited vocal performance and by one or two ingenious episodes: notably the rival courtship of the beautiful Katrina by Ichabod and the local bully boy, Brom Bones, and the climactic sequence in which Ichabod takes his fateful ride through the benighted Hollow.

C. A. Lejeune writing in *The Observer* found the conclusion unsatisfactory and dismissed Ichabod's exploits as 'sometimes gruesome and on the whole rather commonplace', likening Walt Disney to Mr Toad and claiming he had 'gone lusting after strange contraptions, and neglected the homely things he used to know'.

For Walt it was a depressing end to another difficult year. In 1948, the Studio had made a loss of $39,038; but the Annual Report for 1949 had to announce the even worse loss of $93,899. The cover of the report was decorated with dozens of smiling Mickey Mice, but there was little to smile about.

Drastic economies had to be made, and staff were urged to adopt 'a constructive attitude towards every dollar which goes into developing, producing and selling the scheduled pictures'. As a result, a 34 per cent reduction was made to the payroll accounts and strict guidelines were laid down about future expenditure.

From now on, Walt advised his employees, there would be a production schedule that would be adhered to; money spent on pictures would be limited to projected budgets; stories would be more thoroughly prepared so as to minimize change and all departments would be policed in order to prevent unnecessary expenses.

'Ever since *Snow White and the Seven Dwarfs*,' said Walt, 'I have been eager to make a feature which would possess all of that picture's entertainment qualities and have the same worldwide appeal . . .' Released in 1950, that picture was *Cinderella*, a richly stylized film with elaborate settings (below) and memorable characters such as (right) the courageous mice, Jaq and Gus.

Walt also stressed the necessity of selling and exploiting the Studio's pictures to the fullest, the importance of which came home to the company with the death in a plane crash on 28 October 1949 of Kay Kamen, who had been the Studio's licensing representative for 17 years and whom Walt described as 'a valued business associate as well as a close and fine friend'.

Following Kamen's death, the licensing operations were integrated into Walt Disney Productions under the management of company director, O. B. Johnston, and by the spring of 1950, the shops were full of figurines, clockwork toys, jewellery, jigsaws, books and musical boxes featuring characters from *Cinderella*.

'This,' said Roy Disney in retrospect, 'was our Cinderella year',

and the film – the first true full-length feature since *Bambi* – grossed over \$4 million on its first release. The success of *Cinderella* was due to a combination of factors: the emotional strength of the original story, the dramatic styling of the picture, and the supporting characters, who made believable and sympathetic the somewhat unbelievable lovers.

The film also contained a lively score, blithe numbers by Mack David, Jerry Livingston and Al Hoffman and the voices of Ilene Woods as Cinderella, Eleanor Audley as the sadistic stepmother and Verna Felton as the Fairy Godmother. Studio sound effects man Jimmy Macdonald (who had taken over as the voice of Mickey Mouse from Walt) spoke for the mice Jaq and Gus, whose running battle with the cat, Lucifer, provides a dramatic counterpoint to the struggles of Cinderella.

Cinderella began what might be described as a Disney 'Renaissance' demonstrating that the Studio was still capable of sustaining a feature-length animated story and creating vivid new characterizations. Freed from the shackles imposed by the piecemeal films of the past few years, the Disney artists produced some astonishing sequences of animation such as the night-time scene in which the dainty pumpkin coach, with tendril wheels, races through the town towards the castle.

The film's most enduring delights, however, are undoubtedly those episodes featuring the mice and birds: waking Cinderella from her dream-filled sleep and helping her to wash and dress, or working together in chaotic harmony to make her an elegant ballgown. And the frenzied attempt by Jaq and Gus, during the film's climax, to carry a key twice their size up a dizzying flight of stairs is a masterpiece of comic drama.

For all *Cinderella*'s charms the critics were only partially appreciative: gone were the days when a new Disney was greeted with universal acclaim. *The New York Times*' reviewer regretted the film's tendency to lean 'rather heavily towards a glamorous style of illustration', while others condemned its 'cheap and stereotyped cartoon' characters, 'vulgar patches of colour' and 'slushy songs'. Nevertheless, the public liked it, and the film's excellent performance at the box-office helped to turn the financial loss of 1949 into a profit for 1950 of \$717,542.

The success of *Cinderella* was quickly followed by another triumph when, in July 1950, the Studio released its first entirely live-action movie, *Treasure Island*.

At the end of 1948, the amount of blocked funds in foreign countries, including Britain, had reached over \$850,000 and Walt, having decided to make use of some of this resource by producing a film in England, formed Walt Disney British Films Ltd. For a subject he chose Robert Louis Stevenson's popular romance of buccaneers and buried gold, and the production was put in the capable hands of Perce Pearce. For a director, Walt chose Byron Haskin, a former cameraman and special effects expert and director of the successful 1948 gangster picture *I Walk Alone*.

Among the British talents used on *Treasure Island* were the distinguished cinematographer F.A. Young, matte artist Peter Ellenshaw and composer Clifton Parker, whose dramatic score was performed by the Royal Philharmonic Orchestra. In the role of Jim Hawkins, Walt cast Bobby Driscoll who, while *Treasure Island* was in production, won a Special Academy Award 'as outstanding juvenile actor of 1949' for his roles in *So Dear to My Heart* and RKO's *The Window*. Supporting Driscoll was a cast of English, Irish and Scottish players including Basil Sydney, Walter Fitzgerald, Denis O'Dea, Finley Currie and John Laurie, and, in a moment of inspired casting, Walt engaged Robert Newton to play the sea-cook, Long John Silver. Newton had already created an unforgettable screen gallery of rogues and villains, and his performance in *Treasure Island* was the film's chief, but by no means only, delight.

On seeing the partially completed film in the autumn of 1949, Phil Reisman, head of RKO's Foreign Sales department, cabled the distributor's Sales Manager, Robert Mochne: 'It is my honest considered opinion that we have one of the great RKO pictures of all times.' And, for the most part, the critics agreed.

Treasure Island convinced Walt that live action was to play a

Treasure Island stars Robert Newton and Bobby Driscoll as seen by *Punch* cartoonist R. S. Sherriffs. (Reproduced by permission of *Punch*)

major role in the future success of the Studio. He visited the film crew during production and, returning to Burbank, he half-jestingly remarked to his animators: 'Those actors over there in England, they're great. You give 'em the lines and they rehearse it a couple of times, and you've got it on film – it's finished. You guys take six months to draw a scene.'

The supporting picture with *Treasure Island* was a second True-Life Adventure, *Beaver Valley*: a double-bill format that was to set the trend for many Disney programmes to come. Not too surprisingly, perhaps, there were those among the Studio artists who believed, as one of them put it, that 'as soon as Walt rode on a camera crane, we were going to lose him'. But Walt was still fervently committed to animation, even more so since the success of *Cinderella*, and in the Annual Report for 1950 he announced that the next feature cartoon would be *Alice in Wonderland*.

Alice in Wonderland was to receive a considerable boost to its advance publicity when, in December 1950, Walt Disney and his cartoon characters made their debut on television. Walt had long been fascinated by the medium's potential. As early as 1937 he had changed his distributor when United Artists wanted him to sign away the tv rights to his films; and in 1945, he had told his shareholders and employees that television was going to have 'a tremendous impact on the world of entertainment, motion pictures included'.

In 1945 the Studio applied for permission 'to build and operate a television station in Los Angeles'. Although nothing came of that proposal, Walt continued to look for a suitable opening into television. This came in 1950. At three o'clock on Christmas Day afternoon, viewers to NBC received the following invitation:

Everyday, millions of friendly Americans, young and old, in millions of American homes, large and small, pause and refresh themselves with the wholesome, delicious goodness of ice-cold Coca-Cola. And today, Christmas Day, the Coca-Cola Company and your friendly neighbour who bottles Coca-Cola invite you to pause and be refreshed by an hour of wholesome entertainment, delightful entertainment. We now bring you Walt Disney and his beloved characters in their world television premiere.

One Hour in Wonderland, as the programme was called, featured ventriloquist Edgar Bergen and his dummies Charlie McCarthy and Mortimer Snerd entertaining Walt Disney and an audience of children – including Walt's daughters Diane and Sharon – at a party in the Studio. Also taking part were Kathryn Beaumont, the young English actress who had been cast as the voice of Alice, Bobby Driscoll currently working on recording the title role in *Peter Pan* and Hans Conried, who portrayed the Slave of the Magic Mirror from *Snow White* and who conjured up extracts from Disney classics including the still-to-be-released *Alice in Wonderland*.

One reviewer speculated: 'That telecast should be worth \$1,000,000 at the box-office to *Alice in Wonderland*. That, as it happens, proved not to be the case, but as a prelude to over 30 years of Disney tv shows, *One Hour in Wonderland* was, perhaps, the Studio's most significant venture in a decade.

9. WONDERLAND, NEVER LAND AND DISNEYLAND

About two-thirds of the way through a 161-page chapter-by-chapter analysis of Lewis Carroll's *Alice's Adventures in Wonderland*, a Disney storyman came to the conclusion that 'we are going to have to change it radically all the way through ... and forget almost all of Carroll's stuff'.

Without doubt, Alice was the Studio's problem child: Walt had been toying with the project since 1933 and several treatments and a variety of different approaches had already been considered and abandoned. His interest in the story surfaced again towards the end of the war, and he assigned Bill Cottrell and T. Hee to produce fresh reports on the classic that many people kept saying was a natural choice for the Studio.

As a result of their research Cottrell and Hee found themselves having serious reservations about the idea. 'It is a fallacious argument,' they told Walt, 'to say that a picture should be made from a book just on the grounds that it is a literary classic.' Undeterred, Walt decided to enlist the help of the English novelist Aldous Huxley, who had worked on the screenplays for Hollywood's versions of *Pride and Prejudice* and *Jane Eyre*.

Huxley, who appeared to have had little understanding of the animated film, attended a series of frustrating story conferences and,

Comics Jerry Colonna and Ed Wynn join Kathryn Beaumont at a recording session for the mad tea-party in *Alice in Wonderland* (1951).

Aldous Huxley (by Joe Grant) presents a perplexing *Alice* script to Dick Heumer, Grant, Walt Disney, Bill Cottrell and Ham Luske. (Courtesy of the artist)

in December 1945, delivered a draft script for a live-action film incorporating animated sequences of the kind being planned for *Song of the South*. The Huxley treatment was high on literacy but low on humour. It featured C. L. Dodgson ('Lewis Carroll') and the real Alice, and a cast of Victorian eccentrics who were to have counterparts among the strange creatures of Wonderland. But the script failed to find favour and, once again, the project went into limbo.

A few years later, despite Roy's doubts, *Alice* surfaced again as one of the cartoon subjects with which Walt intended to return to feature-length animated film-making.

Walt decided to cast 11-year-old English actress, Kathryn

Beaumont as Alice, and, to support her, Walt not only cast some well-known performers as the Wonderland characters, but also broke with long Studio tradition and gave them billing on posters and publicity. The vaudeville and radio star Ed Wynn was signed to play the Mad Hatter and teamed with comic Jerry Colonna as the March Hare. English actor Richard Haydn was cast as the Caterpillar, while Sterling Holloway was given the role of the constantly disappearing Cheshire Cat. Other voices included Verna Felton as the Queen of Hearts; Bill Thompson as the White Rabbit and the Dodo; Jimmy Macdonald as the Dormouse and J.Pat O'Malley as Tweedledum and Tweedledee, the Walrus and the Carpenter and their ill-fated dinner companions, the Oysters.

With Ben Sharpsteen as production supervisor and virtually the same team of directors and animators as had been responsible for *Cinderella*, work began on *Alice in Wonderland* in the autumn of 1949. Among the 13 storymen scripting the film – which was also to include material from *Through the Looking Glass* – were Joe Grant and Dick Huemer, contributing to their last Disney feature together. To assist the animators, a full-length live-action film of the story was shot on the sound stage, something which hadn't been done for almost a decade, with Kathryn Beaumont and a group of actors in character costumes performing the script and using simple props.

Colour stylists John Hench, Mary Blair, Claude Coats and Ken Anderson gave the film a haunting, dream-like atmosphere through the use of shapes and colours which verged on the surreal, while the animators vied with one another to produce wildly comic sequences, which owed more to the Studio's short subjects and compilation movies than to any of its conventional features. As a result, the picture had, what Walt himself called 'the tempo of a three-ring circus', and animator Ward Kimball later felt that one of the film's problems was its unrelenting mood of zaniness.

After some 50,000 man hours and some 700,000 drawings, *Alice in Wonderland* was completed, at a cost of almost $4 million, and premiered at London's Leicester Square Theatre on 26 July 1951.

A studio fan-card for *Alice in Wonderland*, which Walt Disney optimistically described as 'one of the world's great motion picture properties'.

almost a million dollars and profits dropped from over $700,000 in 1950 to $429,840.

The one compensation was the warm critical reception given to *Alice*'s supporting programme, *Nature's Half Acre*, the third of the True-Life Adventures. Associate producer for the series was Ben Sharpsteen, who had left the animation unit to work full time on researching new True-Life Adventure projects, and who later developed the equally successful People and Places series, beginning, in 1953, with *The Alaskan Eskimo*. Also involved were director Jim Algar and experienced writers Ted Sears and Winston Hibler, who, with his warm mid-West accent, narrated the films.

Nature red in tooth and claw: a ferocious bobcat in the 1953 True-Life Adventure, *The Living Desert*.

'When you deal with such a popular classic,' Walt had remarked in 1946, 'you're laying yourself wide open to the critics.' It is doubtful, however, whether even he was prepared for the savaging that *Alice in Wonderland* received at the hands of the British critics.

The views of William Whitebait in *The New Statesman* were typical of many: 'This million-pound ineptitude deserves nothing but boos, and I wish cinema audiences were in the habit of according them.' And, despite the best endeavours of the publicity men, the reception wasn't any more favourable in America, where *The New Yorker* complained about 'the introduction of shiny little tunes, and touches more suited to a flea circus than to a major imaginative effort'.

To make matters worse, *another* film version of *Alice in Wonderland*, produced by French film-maker Lou Bunin, pre-empted Disney's American release by just two days. Disney sought a court injuction to stop the Bunin film being distributed, claiming that two pictures with the same title would confuse the public. However, the judge ruled that anyone had a right to film *Alice in Wonderland*, a verdict that prompted one critic to remark that the judge would have served the public better if he had stopped *both* producers from getting anywhere near Lewis Carroll's book!

Recalling the film, some years later, Walt blamed its failure on the fact that it was 'filled with weird characters you couldn't get with', and had a heroine who 'wasn't very sympathetic': a curious response when one remembers his dogged persistence, over many years, in making the film.

In writing his Annual Report for 1951, however, Walt was rather more circumspect: 'Due to generally poorer attendance at motion picture theatres during the period of its release, *Alice* has not performed as well at the box-office as did *Cinderella*... However, it is a classic property which should be a valuable asset to the company indefinitely.' Indeed, on subsequent reissues, *Alice* fared rather better and when, during the 1970s, it was screened in America as a double-bill with *Fantasia* it achieved something of a cult following.

But its initial failure was both a disappointment and a matter for considerable concern, since the company's gross income fell by

The True-Life Adventures proved popular with the public, and four of the shorts – *Beaver Valley*, *Nature's Half Acre*, *Water Birds* and *Bear Country* – won Academy Awards. This success eventually led Walt to the conclusion that the winning formula of these two-reel subjects could be extended to feature-length films and the first such picture, *The Living Desert*, was released in 1953 by the new Disney distribution company, Buena Vista, which had been formed as a result of Roy's increasing dissatisfaction with the way RKO were handling Disney films.

The Living Desert, which won the Oscar for Best Documentary Feature, contained some remarkable footage, particularly of insect life, photographed by N. Paul Kenworthy, who worked on several subsequent nature films including *The Vanishing Prairie* (1954). Other photographers on the series included John Nash Ott, who specialized in time-lapse photography, and the husband and wife team of Alfred and Elma Milotte who, in 1952, set off for Africa with

'Alas! my poor brother,' *Punch* artist Sherriffs speculates on Mickey Mouse's view of *The Living Desert*. (Reproduced by permission of *Punch*)

another of Walt's somewhat vague commissions, this time to discover Africa from a lion's viewpoint. The resulting picture, *The African Lion* (1955), is an exceptionally beautiful and dramatic film that – despite its failure to win an Academy Award – is, perhaps, the finest in the series.

For *The African Lion* Walt sent Alfred and Elma Milotte to find and film 'what the animals do when nobody's trying to kill 'em'.

The nature films were part of a continuing diversification that Roy Disney saw as offering the company some protection 'against the ups and downs of economic conditions'. In 1952, for example, the True-Life Adventure *Water Birds* had shared the bill with a short whimsical cartoon, *The Little House*, and the Studio's latest live-action movie filmed in England, *The Story of Robin Hood*.

Produced by Perce Pearce and with a screenplay by Lawrence E. Watkin, *The Story of Robin Hood* featured a relative newcomer, Richard Todd, as the outlaw of Sherwood Forest, Joan Rice as Maid Marian and a solid supporting cast of British character actors, among them Peter Finch as the Sheriff of Nottingham, James Hayter as Friar Tuck and James Robertson Justice as Little John. The film was a Disney debut for the British director Ken Annakin, who produced a handsome, energetic movie, which critic A. H. Weiler found 'as pretty as its Technicolor hues and as lively as a sturdy Western'.

Annakin subsequently directed Richard Todd in two more competent historical dramas, *The Sword and the Rose* (1953) and *Rob Roy, the Highland Rogue* (1954). With some $1,100,000-worth of revenue still blocked in 18 foreign countries, these films made a significant contribution to the company's income and, by the end of 1953, gross income had risen by a further million dollars to $8,365,861 resulting in a profit of $510,426.

A year later, revenues topped $11 million, despite expenditure of over $4 million on the next live-action picture, *20,000 Leagues Under the Sea*. Premiered in December 1954, Disney's film of Jules Verne's fantasy about Captain Nemo and his submarine *The Nautilus*, had sprung from a very different project.

In 1952, Walt assigned Studio designer Harper Goff to work on a True-Life Adventure with an underwater theme, and a storyboard was drawn up that incorporated scenes with deep-sea divers, inspired by Universal's 1916 silent-film version of *20,000 Leagues*. The treatment so captured Walt's imagination, that he decided to acquire the film rights to Verne's novel as a possible vehicle for an animated film. However, a few months later, Walt abandoned the concept of an animated film and put *20,000 Leagues Under the Sea* into production as a live-action movie.

The film was sold as 'The Mightiest Motion Picture of Them All', and, despite the publicity men's hyperbole, *20,000 Leagues* proved a masterpiece of sci-fi film-making and inspired a spate of Hollywood romances based on the works of Jules Verne. To direct the film, which was to be shot in CinemaScope, Walt chose Richard Fleischer (whose father, Max, had been the Studio's long-time cartoon rival),

and the production team included Hollywood cameraman Franz Planer, pioneer effects photographer Ralph Hammeras, matte artist Peter Ellenshaw and mechanical effects operator Robert A. Mattey.

To realize Goff's preliminary designs, Walt engaged the Oscar-winning team of art director John Meehan and set decorator Emile Kuri, who fitted out *The Nautilus*' claustrophobic interior with sumptuous furnishings in red velvet and gleaming brass, rococo decorations and a magnificent pipe organ. The film's cast was headed by Kirk Douglas, Paul Lucas and Peter Lorre, who are taken prisoner by the enigmatic Captain Nemo, played with relish by James Mason.

20,000 Leagues contains some stunning effects ranging from the minute – such as animations of fish and bubbles by Ub Iwerks, John Hench and Josh Meador – to Robert Mattey's articulated model of the giant squid, which attacks and wrestles with *The Nautilus*. This particular sequence caused Fleischer considerable problems. Shot in a tank, with a calm sea and daylight setting, the control wires operating the creature were clearly visible, so the entire scene was then reshot as if at night with a simulated storm that not only disguised the mechanics but greatly heightened the dramatic tension.

The completed picture proved both an artistic and a critical success, winning two Academy Awards for Best Art Direction/Set Decoration and Best Special Effects and garnering a clutch of enthusiastic reviews. For Bosley Crowther, Disney's new picture was 'as fabulous and fantastic as anything he has ever done in cartoons – which seemed to reinforce a view expressed by Roy Disney a year earlier when he had written in the Annual Report that the broad variety of pictures currently being produced were 'a long step ahead of the time not so many years ago when the company's security largely rested on a few high-cost, all-cartoon features'.

Walt saw *The Nautilus* as being sleek and futuristic, but Harper Goff designed it to look like a creature of the deep.

But, despite Roy's mistrust of Walt's animated film projects, 1953 had seen the release of another high-cost cartoon feature. *Peter Pan* had been on and off the drawing-boards almost as many times as *Alice in Wonderland* since 1939, when Walt obtained the animated film rights for a fee of £5,000. Character models were made and a good deal of preliminary artwork was created during the two years following the acquisition of the play; but with the bombing of Pearl Harbor, the project – along with others – went into abeyance.

Work resumed in 1949 with the now regular team of Disney directors and animators. As with *Alice*, a live-action film was made for the artists' guidance in which the part of Peter was enacted by dancer Roland Dupree. The character's voice, however, was provided by Bobby Driscoll, giving his last performance in a Disney movie and making history by being the first male to portray the boy who wouldn't grow up.

The voice and actions of both Captain Hook and Mr Darling were supplied by Hans Conried. Kathryn Beaumont was given her second voice-role as Wendy, and radio comic Candy Candido was cast as the Indian Chief and given one of Sammy Cahn and Sammy Fain's best songs for the film, 'What Makes the Red Man Red?'

On stage, an actress had always played Peter Pan, but animation gave Disney the freedom to portray him as a real boy.

After some initial work, a rough treatment for the picture was screened at the Studio – along with one based on T. H. White's novel *The Sword in the Stone* – to gauge audience reaction. In a lengthy inter-office communication Card Walker advised Walt of the response, which was mixed. The audience was particularly critical of the film's storyline, which involved a contemporary Wendy, John and Michael Darling (possibly to be filmed in live-action) reading Barrie's book from which animated characters would come to life.

In the event, the story was simplified while remaining remarkably close, at least in spirit, to the original play. Posters for *Peter Pan* invited movie-goers to '*See* The Land Beyond Imagination Where Adventure Never Ends', and the film's romantic visualization of the Never Land with its jumble of forests, prairies, mountains, caverns and lagoons was vividly rendered in splashes of vibrant colour by artists Ray Huffine, Art Riley, Al Dempster, Thelma Witmer and others who produced a record 934 backgrounds for the film.

Similarly evocative is the depiction of Edwardian London, and the film's undeniable *tour de force* is the Darling children's night-time flight to Never Land over the roofs of the Houses of Parliament, beneath Tower Bridge and away down river towards the Second Star to the Right. In addition to the breathtaking flying sequences, *Peter Pan* contains some exceptional effects animation, notably the shimmering pixiedust, which is liberally sprinkled over everybody and everything including the pirate galleon for the film's magical climax.

The characterizations are among the most successful since those in *Pinocchio*: Peter, Wendy and the other children are convincing and sympathetic, and there is much humour in the comic business with Captain Hook, Mr Smee and the tick-tocking crocodile.

Perhaps the only character about whom there remains a question is Tinker Bell the fairy who, since the play's first production in 1904, had only ever been represented by a spotlight and a peal of tiny bells. Now, in the hands of the Disney artists, she became a curvaceous little blonde minx modelled on Margaret Kerry. 'Tinker Bell is just terrible,' a member of the 1948 preview audience had commented. 'She should be sweet and dainty – more like the fairies in *Fantasia*. She looks like a little nite club dame.'

In Britain, criticisms of the film were almost as harsh as those received by Walt's last animated feature: 'Having mutilated *Alice in Wonderland*', wrote one critic, 'he now murders *Peter Pan*, and I hate the assumed innocence with which he does it.' Paul Holt, in *The*

Daily Herald, complained that 'in place of childhood dreaming there is strip-cartoon violence and constant hints at sex'; while Richard Mallett in *Punch* dismissed *Peter Pan* as 'a monument to misguided ingenuity'.

In America, where the original play was almost as popular as in Britain, the reception was scarcely less critical: 'Mr Disney,' wrote Bosley Crowther, 'has completely eliminated from his film, the spirit of guileless credulity in fairy magic that prevails in the play … However, that's not to say it isn't a wholly amusing and engaging piece of work within the defined limitations of the "Disney style".'

An early sketch for Tinker Bell, complete with bells, before she developed into a Monroesque minx.

If there were limitations to the prevailing Disney style then they were most clearly seen, not in the features, which are full of fresh ingenuities, but in the Studio's output of short cartoons. Although there was no doubt that the quality of the animation in Disney short subjects was still far superior to that of many rival studios, the Disney stars were now being outshone by more adaptable cartoon characters such as Bugs Bunny and Daffy Duck.

The least successful of the once-great Disney triumvirate was Mickey Mouse, whose now-rare film appearances were almost entirely dependent on Pluto for their humour and who made his last short for 30 years, *The Simple Things*, in 1953, the year in which he celebrated his 25th anniversary. Goofy continued, for a while, with his disastrous sporting lectures and was then gradually transformed into a more human – and far less appealing – character representing middle-class American man in films like *Father's Day Off* and *Father's Weekend* (1953); Donald Duck, of course, continued his eternal struggle with the fates, represented by a variety of insects and animals, but most frequently by the troublesome chipmunks, Chip an' Dale, who had made their screen debut in 1943. But even at his most explosive, Donald's antics paled into insignificance beside the violently anarchic characters created by Tex Avery, Chuck Jones and others.

Further rivalry emerged with the rise of United Pictures of America (UPA), whose personnel included former Disney artists Stephen Bosustow and John Hubley and which had gained a reputation as the new creative force in cartoon film-making. With highly stylized pictures such as *Robin Hoodlum*, *The Magic Fluke* and the 1951

Oscar-winner, *Gerald McBoing Boing*, UPA won unstinting critical praise: 'The positive virtues of UPA,' wrote Gilbert Seldes in *The Saturday Review*, 'are their impudent and intelligent approach to subject matter . . . the use of color and line always to suggest, never to render completely, a great deal of warmth, and an unfailing wit.'

To Seldes and others it seemed that UPA, and not Disney, was now the true pioneer of the animation industry: an ironic conclusion, since UPA's techniques owed much to the Disney innovation of the 1940s that had been dismissed by critics at the time as nothing more than 'a passing novelty'. As a result the attempts to reintroduce stylization into Disney cartoons was seen, by some, as an attempt to ape the UPA approach. It was not, as it happened, a form of animation particularly suited to the Disney characters so long established in the fully-rounded style of the last 20 years, and pictures such as *Rugged Bear* (1953) and *Donald's Diary* (1954) were unattractive experiments.

The Disney short subject unit went into decline, with several key artists and directors leaving for other studios and fewer and fewer cartoons being made before it was finally closed down in 1956. The number of annual releases remained constant only because sequences from the package features were now being re-issued as shorts and because occasional one-off 'Specials' were produced such as *The Brave Engineer* (1950), *Susie the Little Blue Coupe* (1952) and *Social Lion* (1954).

A contemporary equivalent of the Silly Symphonies, these 'Specials' provided a better opportunity for the creative use of contemporary animation styles, which were used to particular effect in *Pigs is Pigs* (1954), *Jack and Old Mac* and *A Cowboy Needs a Horse* (both 1956). The best of these were undoubtedly two 1953 pictures: *Melody*, the Studio's first 3-D cartoon, and *Toot, Whistle, Plunk and Boom*, which won Walt his first Academy Award for a cartoon in 10 years. Tracing the history of musical instruments, *Toot, Whistle, Plunk and Boom* was directed by Ward Kimball and made imaginative use of the newly devised wide-screen process of CinemaScope. Several shorts – among them *Grand Canyonscope* (1954), *Bearly Asleep* (1955) and *Chips Ahoy* (1956) – were subsequently filmed in CinemaScope, as was the Studio's next animated feature, *Lady and the Tramp*.

Like so many of the Studio's projects this one had been around since 1937, when Joe Grant had written a witty little tale based on the character of Lady, the cocker spaniel owned by Joe and his wife, Jennie. Models and preliminary art work were made for Lady and the two troublesome Siamese cats who come into her life, and a version of Grant's story was published in a 1944 Disney picturebook.

While searching for a storyline that would fill out Lady's private doggy life, Walt came across another dog story by Ward Greene, *Happy Dan, the Whistling Dog*, which concerned a somewhat raffish mutt who came from the wrong side of the tracks. Walt suggested to Greene that their two dogs should 'get together', and Joe Grant (who had already done considerable work on the picture with Dick Huemer) made all his material available. Greene, who subsequently received sole credit for the story, wrote a draft script entitled *Happy Dan, the Whistling Dog, and Miss Patsy, the Beautiful Spaniel*. He was also commissioned to write a novelization which Walt was anxious to publish in advance of the movie's release in order to make the public aware of the story and so strengthen its box-office potential.

The picture was finally put into production as *Lady and the Tramp*, a title that both Greene and Disney's then distributor, RKO, felt suggested a somewhat different kind of movie and that might even be confused with the song 'The Lady is a Tramp'. But Walt remained adamant: 'That's what it's about,' he told his critics, 'a lady and a tramp'; and that's what the title remained.

The screenplay was written by experienced Disney storymen Erdman Penner, Joe Rinaldi, Ralph Wright and Don Da Gradi, who added a supporting cast of canine characters: Trusty, the ancient bloodhound, who had lost the sense of smell; Jock, the feisty Scottish terrier, and a motley collection of waifs and strays living in the local Dog Pound; including Dachsie, a neurotic dachshund; Boris, a melancholic Russian wolfhound given to quoting Gorki; and Peg, a

Donald's Diary shows the '50s look to animation; the names of Daisy's former lovers carved on the tree trunk are those of Disney personnel!

blonde, dewy-eyed, Pekinese vamp with a Mae West walk and the seductive voice of Peggy Lee, after whom she was named.

Peggy Lee also provided the voice for Lady's mistress, Darling, and the wicked Siamese cats Si and Am as well as writing the film's songs with Sonny Burke which included the melodious ballad 'Bella Notte', the 'Siamese Cat Song' and Peg's torch song 'He's a Tramp'. Television actress Barbara Luddy provided the voice for Lady, Larry

Toot, Whistle, Plunk and Boom (1953), presented a zany history of music. The bespectacled whistler is a caricature of director Ward Kimball.

Roberts for the Tramp, with other parts played by Bill Thompson, Verna Felton, and comics Alan Reed and Stan Freberg.

Directed by Ham Luske, Clyde Geronimi and Wilfred Jackson, *Lady and the Tramp* was set in the small-town America of 1910, a period with which Walt strongly identified. This, plus the freedom of not having to work with 'classic' material, resulted in Walt giving the project his keen attention.

An elegant, warmly nostalgic picture, *Lady and the Tramp* opened in the summer of 1955 and, somewhat surprisingly, received a number of critical brickbats. Richard Mallett in *Punch*, for example, carped at Disney's 'calculated passages of twittering-birdie "charm", which is here once or twice laid on with what amounts to a steam-shovel'; and Bosley Crowther complained that 'the sentimentality is mighty, and the use of the CinemaScope size does not make for any less awareness of the thickness of the goo'.

The cocker spaniel puppy, Lady, makes an engaging entry in *Lady and the Tramp*, the first cartoon in CinemaScope.

Writing in *The Spectator*, Virginia Graham was almost the lone voice of praise when she declared that in 'returning to the animal kingdom, Mr Disney has recaptured the magic he was in danger of losing, and all the small ridiculous touches are here again to charm one into a state of cooing idiocy'.

Walt had little need to worry about the film's critical reception: it proved an immensely popular family movie and did good business at the box-office. And, as it happened, he had very little time to worry about anything other than his latest major venture – Disneyland.

The idea for building an amusement park grew out of Walt's experiences as a father. Looking back in 1960, he recalled: 'I was always trying to think of a place to take my two small daughters on a Saturday or Sunday afternoon – a place where *I* could have fun too.' The more Walt thought about his idea for a park 'where the parents and children could have fun together', the more he wanted to develop it. When the Studio moved to new premises in Burbank in 1939, he had begun to formulate his first plan. This was for a 'magical little park', about eight acres in size, on an adjacent site that would serve as

An early sketch by Joe Grant of Lady and her wolfish inner-nature that never appeared in the final film version. (Courtesy of the artist)

an attraction for visitors and a place for the weekend recreation of employees and their families. Early ideas for the 'magical little park' included statues of Mickey Mouse and other Disney characters, as well as 'Singing Waterfalls' and a working vintage locomotive.

This initial concept developed into an elaborate plan based on the theme of the American old West with a homestead, an Indian encampment, a sternwheel paddlesteamer and 'Old Town' complete with Main Street buildings and railroad station. Then came the war, and Walt had neither the leisure nor the money to pursue his plans. After the war, however, his interest was rekindled when first he built a scale railroad in the grounds of his home, and then took up model-making as a hobby. Walt paid Studio artist Ken Anderson to paint him a series of Americana scenes, which he could then construct. The first of these was a miniature replica of Granny Kincaid's cabin from *So Dear To My Heart*, and Walt talked enthusiastically about making a travelling exhibit of such models. It wasn't long, however, before this idea gave way to new plans for an amusement park.

'Walt does a lot of talking about an amusement park,' Roy Disney wrote to a correspondent in 1951, 'but really, I don't know how deep his interest really is. I think he's more interested in ideas that would be good in an amusement park than in actually running one himself.' Roy couldn't have been more wrong. Walt was already doing a great deal of research into the subject, visiting zoos, fairs, circuses, exhibitions and museums to see how they were planned and run.

In 1952, Walt formed a new company to develop his ideas for a 'family park', which he had now decided would be called Disneyland, with himself as President and his brother-in-law, Bill Cottrell, as Vice-President. Initially called Walt Disney Incorporated the name was later changed to WED (for Walter Elias Disney) Enterprises to avoid any objections that might be raised by stockholders in Walt Disney Productions. WED Enterprises employed three of the Studio's most creative artists, John Hench, Ken Anderson and, later, Marc Davis; as well as Harper Goff, who had contributed to the success of 20,000 *Leagues Under the Sea*; and two Twentieth Century-Fox artists, Richard Irvine (who had earlier worked on *Victory Through Air Power*) and Marvin Davis.

'Almost everyone warned us,' Walt later recalled, 'that Disneyland would be a Hollywood spectacular – a spectacular failure.' There was negative response from various members of the Disney board; but, as was always the case with Walt, these objections served only to strengthen his resolve. 'There's nothing like it in the whole world,' he told them, 'I know, because I've looked. That's why it can be great: because it will be unique. A new concept in entertainment, and I think – I *know* – it can be a success.'

Persuading prospective investors proved difficult, especially since the company was already heavily indebted to the Bank of America. As he had done on several previous occasions, Walt decided to back his ideas with his own money, selling his second home in Palm Springs and borrowing $100,000 against his life insurance. A number of the Studio's employees formed themselves into an investment group called the Backers and Boosters, and one or two far-sighted bankers decided to ignore the gloomy predictions of most of their profession and put up finance.

In 1953, Walt commissioned the Stanford Research Institute to advise on the best possible siting for Disneyland and, after a comprehensive study of the Southern California area, they recommended a 160-acre site in Anaheim, Orange County, just 25 miles from Los Angeles. In addition to an equable climate, the site – chiefly given over to the cultivation of oranges – was situated near the planned Santa Ana Freeway, which would give Californians easy access to Disneyland. The Institute also produced an estimated annual attendance figure of between 2,500,000 and 3,000,000. While intentionally conservative, the findings were extremely encouraging.

An imaginative topography of Disneyland was emerging from the plans being made at WED Enterprises, but the initial cost of this conversion was placed at around $7,000,000, which required a considerable investment to be made at a point when the existing finances on the project had all but run out.

The solution, Walt decided, was television. The Studio had already produced two Christmas 'specials', and several broadcasting

When purchased, the Disneyland site was, Walt later recalled, 'all flat – no rivers, no mountains, no castles, no rocketships – just orange groves and a few acres of walnut trees.' To show potential backers how it *could* look, Walt engaged artist Herb Ryman to visualize all his exciting ideas. The two men worked over a weekend, and the aerial painting which resulted helped Roy Disney sell the dream to the businessmen of New York.

networks had expressed an interest in the idea of a regular Disney television series. It was an idea which Walt had so far resisted, believing that although it might prove beneficial to the Disney film product it would, in itself, be costly and time consuming to produce. If, however, it were to help finance and promote Disneyland, it could be the answer to his problems.

Roy Disney, who had at last come to accept the viability of the project, decided to go to New York and meet with the television companies. His concern, however, was how to present Disneyland to the prospective investors when so many aspects of the idea existed only in the imaginations of Walt and his associates. All that was on paper was a preliminary ground plan of the roughly triangular-shaped site. This showed Main Street leading to a hub from which radiated various 'lands': Fantasy Land with a fairy-tale castle within the walls of which would be found Pinocchio Square, King Arthur's Carousel and attractions based on *Snow White, Alice* and *Peter Pan*; Frontier Land with trains, stagecoaches, riverboats, a western town and a recreation of Granny Kincaid's Farm; The World of Tomorrow, where visitors would travel by Moving Sidewalk to visit various scientific and industrial exhibits and a Rocket Space Ship trip to the Moon. Also envisaged were Holiday Land, with seasonal attractions including circuses, flower festivals, carnivals and winter sports; a Lilliputian Land, 'a miniature American village inhabited by mechanical people nine inches high'; a Recreation Land park with a bandstand and picnic area; and True-Life Adventure Land, 'a beautiful botanical garden of tropical flora and fauna'.

Such a plan, however, was not enough. Roy needed a pictorial rendering that would capture the magical atmosphere conveyed by Disneyland's architecture and landscaping. Walt turned for help to a former Studio artist, Herb Ryman, a gifted landscape artist who had been on the South American tour and had recently done work for

Twentieth Century-Fox. For a whole weekend in September 1953, with Walt at his side, Ryman worked at the drawing board. By the Monday morning he had completed a picturesque aerial view of Disneyland, and copies were hurriedly made and coloured in by Dick Irvine and Marvin Davis for Roy to take with him to New York.

Roy also carried with him a publicity brochure, which announced that: '*Walt Disney* sometime – in 1955 – will present for the people of the world – and to children of all ages – a new experience in entertainment ... DISNEYLAND.' There followed a detailed description of the park's attractions and the first attempt to put Walt's Disneyland philosophy into words:

> The idea of Disneyland is a simple one. It will be a place for people to find happiness and knowledge. .... It will be filled with the accomplishments, the joys and hopes of the world we live in. And it will remind us and show us how to make these wonders part of our own lives.

The initial response in New York was mixed, with the Columbia Broadcasting System turning down his proposal for a tv series and other companies asking to see pilot programmes before making a decision. There was, however, considerable interest on the part of both the National Broadcasting Company and the American Broadcasting Company. Roy favoured NBC, because it had already televised a Disney Christmas television programme and had the substantial backing of the Radio Corporation of America. There were several rounds of negotiations, but NBC repeatedly stopped short of a commitment. Finally, in frustration, Roy telephoned Leonard Goldensen, President of ABC.

The smaller of the two networks, ABC had much to gain from the prestige of a Disney television series, and Goldensen was quick to agree a deal with Roy. In exchange for a $500,000 investment in Disneyland and guaranteed loans of up to $4,500,000, ABC became a 35 per cent owner of the park and would receive a television series.

At last, the money – or, at least, a good deal of it – was available for Walt's dream of a place that was 'something of a fair, an exhibition, a playground, a community center, a museum of living facts, and a show-place of beauty and magic'.

10. TRUE-LIFE FANTASIES

'Disneyland,' says Ray Bradbury, 'causes you to care all over again. You feel it is that first day in the spring of that special year when you discovered you were really alive.'

In 1951, however, when Walt established Disneyland Incorporated, the place was little more than a dream. Three years later the company was reconstituted, with ABC and Walt Disney Productions each having a $500,000 investment, a $200,000 stake held by Western Printing and Lithographing and Walt with a personal investment of $250,000. 'I don't want the public to see the world they live in while they're in Disneyland,' Walt said, 'I want them to feel they're in another world.' So, when excavation began in August 1954, one of the first tasks was the moving of 35,000 cubic yards of earth to form a 20-foot high embankment around the park.

The original conception had now undergone several major changes: two of the themed areas: Holiday Land and Lilliputian Land were dropped (although the latter was subsequently developed as a model Disney village for Fantasyland called Storybook Land), and Walt was advised that his plans for True-Life Adventureland were not really feasible. In theory it had sounded delightful: colourful Explorer Boats cruising down 'the River of Romance' through Everglades where 'alligators lurk along the banks, and otters and turtles play in the water about you', and 'monkeys chatter in the orchid-flowered trees'; but, in practice, as zoologists explained to Walt, the creatures were more likely to be asleep or in hiding. The area was resited and renamed Adventureland, and the Disney designers – or, as Walt called them, Imagineers – began creating a

The completed Disneyland with some of the original surrounding orange groves still in existence.

cast of mechanically-operated animal figures for the jungles and waterways, which were guaranteed to 'perform' on cue for every boatload of 'explorers'.

The futuristic section of Disneyland, which had been called either the Land or the World of Tomorrow, was now named Tomorrowland, and, together with Adventureland, Frontierland and Fantasyland, it became one of the park's four themed 'lands' and gave rise to the term 'theme park'.

The 'lands' also provided the four themes to the Disneyland television series, which ABC premiered on 27 October 1954, when viewers saw for the first time one of television's most famous title sequences: Tinker Bell flying over a fairy-tale castle and showering the screen with pixiedust. The series was produced by Bill Walsh, who had once worked in the Studio's press and publicity department and to whom Walt had already entrusted the production of the first television specials. Walsh was never quite sure why Walt selected him, but the choice was a fortuitous one, and Walsh made vital contributions to the Studio before his untimely death in 1975.

The first programme, entitled 'The Disneyland Story', was simply a preview of the series. The show, like the series, was hosted by Walt, whose weekly appearances turned the previously publicity-shy film-maker into a popular television personality. Although Walt found the presentation of his television series a nerve-wracking business, his easy, avuncular style on camera won him an Emmy nomination from the Television Academy. The first series also produced an Emmy-winning programme with 'Operation Undersea', on the making of *20,000 Leagues Under the Sea*.

Other editions of the *Disneyland* series were devoted to a diversity of cartoon, live-action and nature subjects, with screenings of *Alice in Wonderland* (the first Disney feature to appear on tv), *So Dear to My Heart, Treasure Island* and *Beaver Valley*, as well as 'The Donald Duck Story', 'Cameras in Africa' (on the filming of *The African Lion*) and the first of several imaginative, and prophetic, scientific subjects, *Man in Space*, which combined the light-hearted animation talents of Ward Kimball and others with the serious predictions of such authorities as Willy Ley, Heinz Haber and Wernher von Braun.

The programme also had an enormous, and quite unexpected,

The first layout design for Disneyland shows various themed areas, such as Lilliputian Land, that were later abandoned.

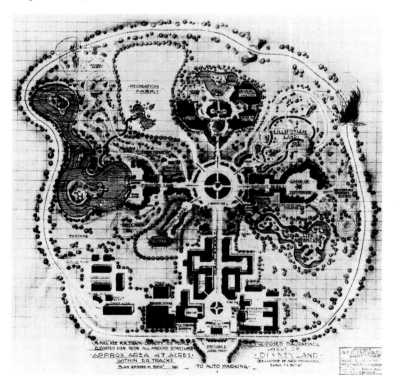

Heinz Haber offers some prognostications about space travel in the Disneyland tv show 'Man in Space'.

phenomenal income from the sale of Davy Crockett outfits, rifles, tents, guitars, lunch boxes, pocket knives and no fewer than 10 million coonskin hats.

Just two months after Davy Crockett's tv death at the Alamo, the three episodes were edited into a feature, *Davy Crockett, King of the Wild Frontier*. Astonishingly, the film version drew huge audiences and made over $2½ million. A second feature, *Davy Crockett and the River Pirates*, followed in 1956, and Fess Parker went on to star in several other Disney western-type adventures including *The Great Locomotive Chase* and *Westward Ho. The Wagons!* (both 1956).

The first season of the *Disneyland* programme was a great success – reaching second place in the national ratings within four months – and won a Sylvania Television Award. It ended with a 'Further Report on Disneyland', aired only four days before the park was due to open, but the programme did not reveal the mounting tension within the organization or the extent of the work still to be done.

For 11 months, Walt and his colleagues had been frantically working on the site and its attractions. More than 3,000 men were employed on the construction, which used 20,000 feet of timber, 5,000 cubic yards of concrete and a million square feet of asphalt. The Disneyland railroad and its locomotives were constructed by Roger Broggie in the Studio's machine shop to a scale of five-eighths normal size, as was the superstructure of the Mark Twain paddlesteamer. Other vehicles, including surreys, covered wagons and horse-drawn trams, were specially constructed by outside craftsmen to Disney specifications.

Scale was of pre-eminent importance to the Disney illusion. The buildings, for example, were nine-tenths true scale on the ground floor and eight-tenths on the second storey. Although this added considerably to the costs, Walt felt that it gave the buildings – particularly those on Main Street – a toylike appearance. To decorate

success with three films on the life of Davy Crockett. 'Davy Crockett, Indian Fighter', 'Davy Crockett Goes to Congress' and 'Davy Crockett at the Alamo' made a star of Fess Parker, helped to re-establish the career of Buddy Ebsen (who played Crockett's side-kick, George Russel) and created a nationwide 'Crockett Craze'. The theme song, 'The Ballad of Davy Crockett', was written by the film's scriptwriter Tom Blackburn and composer George Bruns only because the first episode underran by several minutes. Opening with the lines, 'Born on a mountain top in Tennessee . . . killed him a bear when he was only three . . .', it became the subject of hundreds of juvenile parodies and was in the hit parade for 13 weeks.

Although the Davy Crockett films cost considerably more than the sum budgeted for each episode of the tv series, the Studio derived a

By the time Davy Crockett was 'one of the biggest overnight hits in tv history' his demise at the Alamo had been filmed.

'The way I see it,' Walt said, 'my park will never be finished. It's something I can keep on developing and adding to.'

Main Street, WED acquired a number of genuine period relics, including 100-year-old gas lamps from Philadelphia, grill work from the plantations of Nashville and park benches from San Francisco.

Since nothing like Disneyland had ever been built before, any number of unexpected problems arose: the first prototypes for Fantasyland's flying Dumbo ride, which weighed 700 pounds each, refused to be hoisted into the air; and the meandering Rivers of America had scarcely been filled before the water seeped away.

By 1 January 1955, building work was so far behind schedule that it was decided to postpone work on Tomorrowland until after the park had opened; but, after serious thought, Walt reverted to his original plans, believing that all Disneyland's themed areas had to be in existence on opening day, which was now set for 17 July. But, as the deadline approached, it seemed less and less likely that they would have Disneyland ready for visitors.

At midnight on 16 July 1955 – with a total investment of $17 million now at stake – painters were still at work by the light of arc-lamps; and, when opening day dawned, plumbers were still installing washrooms and carpenters were busily at work among the tv crews, who were setting up their equipment to record the event. Tomorrowland was desperately incomplete, and Walt gave instructions to cover up its deficiencies 'with balloons and pennants'.

From first light on 17 July, the Santa Ana Freeway was blocked with a 7-mile traffic jam and there was similar chaos on many other roads within a 10-mile radius of Disneyland. Admittance to the Opening Gala was by invitation, of which 22,000 had been issued to local dignitaries, the press, WED and Studio employees and a host of movie stars. What the Disneyland staff didn't know was that thousands of counterfeit invitations had been printed, so that by mid-morning some 30,000 people had passed through the turnstiles. It was the beginning of what Walt later called 'Black Sunday'.

The ceremonies – in the presence of California Governor Goodwin Knight – opened with prayers and a dedication by Walt based on the philosophy that had sold the Disneyland project to ABC:

> To all who come to this happy place: welcome. Disneyland is your land. Here age relives fond memories of the past . . . and here youth may savour the challenge and promise of the future. Disneyland is dedicated to the ideals, dreams and the hard facts which have created America . . . with the hope that it will be a source of joy and inspiration to all the world.

But Disneyland was not a happy place for long: many of the staff had been hired from agencies and treated the lengthening queues of visitors with the same belligerence they used for dealing with crowds at baseball parks and racetracks. Several rides broke down, and other attractions became dangerously overcrowded, among them the *Mark Twain*, which set off on its maiden voyage with its lower deck awash with water.

The food and drink ran out, and the number of water fountains proved hopelessly inadequate; the park was littered with trash, and as the day got hotter, the stiletto heels worn by many of the women sank into the asphalt on Main Street.

Walt, however, was quite unaware of the disaster. He was rushing from one location to another for the live 90-minute tv show, 'Dateline Disneyland'. The tv coverage – hosted by Art Linkletter, Bob Cummings and Ronald Reagan – was itself very nearly a fiasco, with microphones going dead, Walt getting tangled up with cables and cameras picking up wrong shots so that a commentary on the parade described Cinderella's magical coach while viewers were looking at Fess Parker and Buddy Ebsen on horseback.

The following morning, a generous reporter for *The Minneapolis Tribune* enthusiastically informed his readers: 'If it's an amusement park, it's the gosh-darnedest, most happily-inspired, most carefully-planned, most adventure-filled park ever conceived. No ride or concession in it is like anything in any other amusement park anywhere.' Others, less inclined to overlook the short-comings of opening day, showed their disgust with such headlines as 'Disneyland opens amid traffic jams', 'Park can't handle opening day crush' and, most devastatingly, 'Walt's dream a nightmare'.

Hollywood columnist Sheila Graham tried to put things in context: 'Don't be discouraged, boys and girls, Walt Disney has

Vaguely inspired by *The African Queen*, the Jungle Cruise is one of Disneyland's most popular attractions.

always been a smart trader and I'm sure there'll be some changes made.' In fact, changes were already underway. For two frantic weeks, Walt spent 24 hours a day in Disneyland, living in the apartment he had made for himself over the Main Street Fire Station and working to overcome the park's problems.

An army of young men was employed to clear litter, standards for staff courtesy and efficiency were established and ways of speeding up the waiting time for rides were found. Despite the headaches, Disneyland offered Walt a potential not found in movie-making: an opportunity continually to improve. By early September, just seven weeks after opening, Disneyland welcomed its one-millionth visitor and within a year the figure reached 5 million. Disneyland was a turning point in the fortunes of the Studio: gross income for 1955 was over $24½ million (against $8 and $11 millions is in 1953 and 1954) and profits were approaching $1½ million. Twelve months later, Roy Disney was able to report that net profits, at $2,623,541, were the highest in the company's history.

The development of Disneyland began at once, and 1956 saw the addition of Storybook Land and Tom Sawyer Island, a project personally designed by Walt, which featured, as he put it, 'all the things I wanted to do as a kid – and couldn't. Including getting into something without a ticket'. Disneyland's first large expansion since its opening came in 1959 when $7.3 million worth of additional attractions included a fanciful submarine voyage, the Disneyland-Alweg Monorail System (the first complete monorail operating daily in America) and the 14-storey high Matterhorn Mountain with two bobsled runs hurtling through its interior. Built to one-hundredth actual size, the Matterhorn was (and still is) climbed by Disney mountaineers and planted with pines and edelweiss that are constantly pruned to maintain the illusion of scale.

An impressive roll-call of visitors began with President Sukarno of Indonesia, and included King Hussein of Jordan, the Aga Khan, Jawaharlal Nehru, King Mohammad V of Morocco, Harry S. Truman, General Eisenhower, Lord Louis Mountbatten, the Emperor Haile Selassie, Sir Edmund Hilary and a galaxy of stars, among them Bob Hope, Sophia Loren, Betty Hutton and Charles Laughton, who first introduced fantasy writer Ray Bradbury to the marvels of Disneyland. Initially a reluctant visitor, Bradbury quickly succumbed and found himself, along with hundreds of others, riding the Mark Twain riverboat, 'hands sticky . . . coats snowed with popcorn salt, smiles hammer-tacked to our faces by one explosion of delight and surprise after another'.

Among those who had taken part in Disneyland's opening-day parade were a group of 24 youngsters who were, as yet, unknown but who were to have an astonishing impact on American popular culture of the 1950s. Known as the Mouseketeers, they were the founder members of Walt Disney's *Mickey Mouse Club*.

When King Baudouin of Belgium asked why the Matterhorn had holes, Walt replied: 'Because it's a Swiss mountain!'

Disney's 1956 Christmas card showed Donald's nephews – like millions of other kids – watching the Mickey Mouse Club.

The idea for a daily children's television show had come from ABC, and with it came the promise of a further $1.5 million investment in Disneyland. Walt's earliest ideas for a 'kid show' appear in rough notes made during the summer of 1954. There was to be a club house in Disneyland, with viewers entering 'thru cave – up hollow tree to tree house'. Other random jottings included: 'Famous events in history with club members enacting roles . . . Contest Prizes . . . Club song . . . Tour country with club show . . .'

Clearly the idea derived some of its inspiration from the first Mickey Mouse Clubs that Harry W. Woodin had organized in cinemas during the 1930s with the philosophy of 'inspirational, patriotic and character-building activities . . . to aid children in learning good citizenship'. One of the features of those original Mickey Mouse Clubs was the election, every eight weeks, of a Chief Mickey Mouse from among the children. This seemed to have been in Walt's mind when, on 8 December 1954, he came up with some more ideas for the programme:

Mouse party: audience participation . . . Children selected to be Mickey, Donald, etc (with costumes), others play the part of Pluto, cat, etc . . . Children from audience visit with characters from history . . . Presents to kids in audience with birthdays, also unbirthday presents . . . Drawing lessons . . . Gadget band: kids participate . . . Story of children around the world, children in sports (honor Sunday school teachers?) . . . Everyone Can Sing-song slides . . .

Some of these suggestions were eventually incorporated into the *Mickey Mouse Club* tv show, but the format for the series was developed by a process of trial and error, since children's programmes at the time consisted either of animal series such as *My Friend Flicka* and *Fury*, western adventures with, among others, *Hopalong Cassidy* and *Wild Bill Hickok* or frenetic audience-shows like the long-running 'Howdy Doody' and 'Pinky Lee Show', against which the *Mickey Mouse Club* was eventually scheduled.

In planning the show, Walt enlisted the services of Bill Walsh, Hal Adelquist, head of the Studio's story department, and gag-man Roy Williams, who had worked at the Studio for over 20 years. Walsh devised a preliminary format for the show, which would be divided into four 15-minute segments featuring Disney cartoons (few of which would have been seen by young audiences), guest stars and stunts, contests and quizzes. He felt that each programme should have a feeling of just 'happening' rather than a sense of being planned beforehand and suggested a different theme for each evening's show.

Then, in March 1955, an important decision was arrived at, communicated in a simply-worded memo: 'Call kids Mouseketeers – get costumes, sweaters, little hats.' Walt and Bill Walsh began looking around for someone to host the show, and they chose Jimmie Dodd, a lively, red-headed, composer-cum-singer, actor and dancer who had been put on the Studio staff after writing a number for the *Disneyland* show. Although 45, Jimmie Dodd had youthful looks, a sunny personality and a strong Christian faith, which Walt found appealing and which eventually inspired the show's improving 'Mousethoughts' and songs such as 'Good Samaritan' and 'Do What the Good Book Says', which Dodd composed with his wife, Ruth.

In the meanwhile, Roy Williams had been working on drawings for sets and costumes, and had come up with a design for the Mouse-keteers' 'little hats'. Inspired by a gag in 1929's *The Karnival Kid* – in which Mickey raised the top of his head as if it were a hat – Williams sketched a skull-cap with round Mickey Mouse ears. It was a stroke of genius, but he soon found himself with an altogether unexpected job. 'Walt was in my office one day,' Williams later recalled. 'Suddenly he looked up at me and said, "Say, you're fat and funny-looking. I'm going to put you on the show and call you the 'Big Mooseketeer'." . . . I said, "What?" The next thing I knew I was acting . . .'

The teaming of Jimmie Dodd and Roy Williams proved a happy combination of personalities and one that not only won the affection of the Mouseketeers but of millions of youngsters all over America.

Both men joined Walt and Bill Walsh in the search for the kids who were to be featured on the *Mickey Mouse Club*. It was no easy matter since Walt was adamant about what he *didn't* want: 'I don't want those kids that . . . blow trumpets while they're tap dancing or skip rope or have curly hair like Shirley Temple or nutty mothers and things like that. I just want ordinary kids.'

The word went out, and hundreds of 'ordinary kids' arrived at the Studio to do their party pieces for Bill Walsh, Jimmie Dodd and Walt, while Roy Williams sat at an easel making lightning sketches of the children doing their turns. Eventually 24 youngsters were chosen, including Darlene, Bobby, Sharon, Tommy, Johnny, Bonnie, Lonnie, Sherry, Cubby and Karen and the girl who was to become the pin-up of millions of American boys, Annette Funicello.

'M-I-C-K-E-Y M-O-U-S-E!' Former child-star Sid Miller (seated left) directs Jimmie Dodd, Roy Williams and the Mouseketeers watched by Walt and Bill Walsh.

On becoming a Mouseketeer, Annette asked if she could change her Italian surname to Turner, but Walt told her she could not: 'Once people learn how to pronounce it,' he told her, 'they'll never forget it.' He was right, and Annette was soon receiving a fan mail of over 6,000 letters a month and went on to have a successful career as a movie actress and recording star long after she hung up her Mickey Mouse ears.

A third adult, Bob Amsberry, joined the team and became, as he described it, the Club's 'utility man', performing in a variety of guises on the shows until his death in a car accident during the second series.

The format for the show was finalized and opened with the 'Mickey Mouse Club March' and a title-sequence animated by Bill Justice and others, featuring Mickey and members of the gang (including Donald Duck who was forever trying to sabotage the proceedings), followed by an introduction from Mickey. Monday was Fun with Music Day; Tuesday, Guest Star Day; Wednesday, Anything Can Happen Day; Thursday, Circus Day; and Friday, Talent Round-up Day. These general headings covered a variety of material, including newsreels about children around the world ('Hawaiian Adventure', 'Youth Takes Over the Atom'); drawing lessons from Roy Williams; fun and games with the English glove-puppet, Sooty, and educational items presented by Jiminy Cricket, among which were lectures on safety, wildlife and biology.

Another regular feature was the serial, which included 'The Adventures of Spin and Marty', with Tim Considine and David Stollery as two boys who meet at a summer camp. Considine also appeared, with Tommy Kirk, in two series based on Franklin W. Dixon's Hardy Boys mysteries, while the most popular of the girl Mouseketeers, Annette Funicello and Darlene Gillespie, were given their own serials as well as being teamed with Considine and Stollery for an adolescent sequel to 'Spin and Marty'.

Premiering on 3 October 1955, the *Club* was an instant success,

becoming – as ABC happily announced – the highest rated television programme 'of all time'. It ran for four years, first as an hour show (1955–7) and then in a half-hour format (1957–9). Later it was re-issued in syndication and shown in many foreign countries including Japan, Mexico, Finland and Switzerland. And, three decades after its debut, the show became a daily feature of The Disney Channel.

ABC had arranged for the Studio to have a revolving credit line of a million dollars, and, over four years, the series cost more than $14 million. Almost 200 people worked on the shows, including writers, artists, designers, cameramen and 14 composers, who wrote virtually a song a day for three years. Recalling the frenzy of sustaining the output of shows, Bill Walsh said: 'It was like a Chinese firedrill. But it was fun ...' And it was that fun that communicated itself to youngsters and made the *Mickey Mouse Club* one of the unforgettable memories of a whole generation of Americans.

The Studio scored another television hit with *Zorro*, a weekly series of half-hour shows based on Johnston McCulley's tales of the masked avenger of Spanish California. The project had begun in the early 1950s, when Walt purchased the rights in the stories with the intention of producing a tv series through WED Enterprises.

Fourteen episodes were scripted and some pre-production planning was done, but when Walt failed to interest any of the television companies – all of which wanted to see a pilot for the series – he postponed further work on the project to concentrate on Disneyland.

He returned to *Zorro* in 1957, making the first of 78 episodes televised by ABC over the next two years. Cast in the role of the effete Don Diego and his swashbuckling alter-ego was Guy Williams who became a major tv star as a result. The *Zorro* series achieved record ratings – 35 million viewers a week – and captured the imagination of boys all over the world, who eagerly purchased Zorro hats, masks, capes, swords, whips, lariats and signet rings, not to mention a 49 cent Zorro Water Pistol 'shooting 250 shots or more'.

Zorro's adventures were later featured on ABC's *Walt Disney Presents* (the new title for the *Disneyland* tv series), and California's Scarlet Pimpernel made his final appearance – with Disney at least –

Walt with artwork and models for the tv series about Zorro, whose aim was 'to aid the oppressed and punish the unjust'.

Planned for tv, but released as a feature, *The Shaggy Dog* told the unlikely tale of a boy (Tommy Kirk) who turns into a sheepdog. In his first Disney film, Fred MacMurray starred as the boy's bemused father.

in the feature-length films *The Sign of Zorro* (1958) and *Zorro the Avenger* (1959), both compiled from the series.

Many of the Studio's live-action movies during the late 1950s were based on stories with western and pioneering themes; these included *The Light in the Forest*, *Tonka* and *Johnny Tremain*, a tale of the American Revolution distinguished for being the first Disney picture directed by British-born Robert Stevenson.

Reviewing *Johnny Tremain* in *The New York Times*, Howard Thompson found it 'pretty good' but complained that 'under Robert Stevenson's tentative, genteel direction, the Boston Tea Party seems more like a musical-comedy frolic'. The same critic was more generously disposed towards Stevenson's next picture, *Old Yeller* (1957), which he complimented for the 'straightforward honesty' of its direction. A rustic tear-jerker, the film is chiefly memorable for the performance of its juveniles: Tommy Kirk and Kevin Corcoran, and for its tragic, un-Disneylike ending in which the young hero has to shoot his dog because the animal had been infected with rabies. Some of Walt's colleagues suggested a less traumatic conclusion, but Walt was determined to remain faithful to the book.

Old Yeller, which one reviewer described as 'sentimental ... but also sturdy as a hickory stick', made more money than any previous live-action film and was the first of a long line of children-and-animal pictures such as *Big Red* (1962), *Savage Sam* (1963) and *Rascal* (1969).

A somewhat different dog-tale was to be found in a low-budget picture of this period called *The Shaggy Dog*. Walt's first live-action comedy, it established a formula for family movies filled with crazy capers and disastrous misunderstandings that were to become a staple part of the Studio's output.

Eighteenth-century Boston at night: one of Peter Ellenshaw's stunning matte-paintings for *Johnny Tremain* (1957).

Critical response to *The Shaggy Dog* was, at best, luke-warm: the reviewer for *Time* magazine complained: 'Disney tells his shaggy-dog story so doggedly that he soon runs it into the pound.' Nevertheless, the film proved a tremendous success – especially with the young – and grossed $8 million.

The Shaggy Dog was 'suggested' by a novel by Felix Salten, the author of *Bambi* and of *Perri* (1957). Although made by part of the team responsible for the True-Life Adventures – which had continued with *Secrets of Life* (1956) – *Perri*, the story of a red squirrel, marked a significant departure from the style of those films. Written by Ralph Wright and Winston Hibler, *Perri* represented the ultimate blurring of fact and fiction, using evocative nature-film photography (edited from over 200,000 feet of film) to tell a story that is semi-fantasy. Perhaps because Salten's story of *Perri* is essentially a fable, the film has a close affinity with the Studio's animated traditions. Nowhere is this more evident than in the surreal winter-dream sequence in which animals and birds materialize from animated snowflakes and perform a survival ballet within a shimmering moonlit snowscape.

The Studio's first 'True-Life Fantasy', as it was enigmatically advertised, received rough handling from many critics, who damned it for its 'cloying and cheapening coyness' and its elements 'of baby-food mush', although Howard Thompson acknowledged: 'Technically, in the stunning color photography and in the extremely adroit easing of actual incidents into the story flow, the result is admirable.'

Two further True-Life Adventures were made – the Academy Award-winning *White Wilderness* (1958) and *Jungle Cat* (1960) – but it was *Perri* that was to provide the format for the Studio's later nature films such as *Nikki, Wild Dog of the North* (1961), *The Legend of Lobo* (1962) and *The Incredible Journey* (1963).

One of the Studio's finest achievements in this period was the live-action fantasy, *Darby O'Gill and the Little People*, which earned Robert Stevenson many future directing assignments for the Studio.

Perri was praised for its 'vignettes of forest creatures in repose, on the prowl and, most forcibly, in intramural warfare.'

The story had been through various stages of development since the early 1940s, when Walt had come across the delightful yarns of H. T. Kavanagh and decided they would make a fitting subject for an animated feature. As with many of the Studio's projects, the war intervened and it was not until 1945 that *The Little People*, as it was then called, was listed as a forthcoming feature, now to be made as a live-action film. Although there were further lengthy delays, Walt discovered the actor whom he wanted for the role of Darby O'Gill when he saw Albert Sharpe in the Broadway production of *Finian's Rainbow*.

The cast also included Janet Munro, Sean Connery, Walter Fitzgerald, Estelle Winwood, and Irish character comedian Jimmy O'Dea as the 5,000-year-old, 21-inch high King Brian of Knocknasheega: *Darby O'Gill and the Little People* is the sum of many talents: Lawrence E. Watkin's whimsical screenplay, Winston C. Hoch's haunting photography, and the exceptional special effects photography of Peter Ellenshaw and Eustace Lycett.

Although given a grand premiere in Dublin, *Darby O'Gill and the Little People* proved anything but a crock of gold. The critics were full of praise for Albert Sharpe, but the film itself was dismissed as an 'overpoweringly charming concoction of standard Gaelic tall stories, fantasy and romance'.

Despite the response to *Darby O'Gill*, Walt Disney Productions seemed – as the 1950s drew to a close – to be set on a remarkably

Despite great elegance, *Sleeping Beauty* was to contribute to a $7 million nose-dive in Disney motion picture returns.

successful course. Gross income had risen annually by almost $10 million since 1956; and, by 1958, profits reached a record $3,865,473. But the following year they were to fall by $400,000 and, in 1960, the company had to report a staggering loss of $1.3 million.

One reason for this sudden decline was the extraordinary failure of what, in 1956, Walt had proudly called the Studio's 'biggest and finest animated feature', *Sleeping Beauty*.

One of the problems with *Sleeping Beauty*, which went into production in 1956 as the first cartoon ever to be filmed in 70mm, was Walt's lack of involvement with the project. With Disneyland and the tv shows making increasing demands on his time, Walt delegated most of the responsibility for *Sleeping Beauty* to others, chiefly Ken Peterson, Clyde Geronimi, Eric Larson, Wolfgang Reitherman and Les Clark. The animation team included such stalwarts as Milt Kahl, Marc Davis, Frank Thomas, Ollie Johnston and John Lounsbery.

The task of adapting the fairy-tale was assigned to Erdman Penner, but, for all the skill with which he undertook the work, it relied almost exclusively on human characters. There was, admittedly, a charming collection of woodland creatures, but they had none of the personality of the talking mice and birds in *Cinderella* nor enough of the comic business that had been given to Snow White's animal friends.

Apart from the young lovers, the rest of the cast was decidedly middle-aged and characterized – especially in the case of the meddling fairies Flora, Fauna and Merryweather – more by good-humoured, bumbling ineptitude than the richly inventive comedy that had made the seven dwarfs so memorable. Only Maleficent emerges as a dynamic creation whose ruthless wickedness elicits sympathy for Aurora and gives credence to the heroism of Prince Phillip.

The film's style was undoubtedly more classical than popular with a lush score, adapted by George Bruns from Tchaikovsky's 'Sleeping Beauty' ballet, the sophisticated singing voices of soprano Mary Costa and baritone Bill Shirley as Aurora and Phillip, and a near absence of hummable songs.

Equally unconventional were the film's minutely-detailed settings, executed in an angular, geometric style designed by Eyvind Earle. Despite their considerable beauty, these impressionistic backgrounds provided a curious environment for the characters, which were an assortment of realistic, rotoscoped, figures and rounded Disneyesque caricatures. But for all its failings, *Sleeping Beauty* contains moments of rare animation brilliance that rival anything which the Studio ever produced, such as the film's dramatic climax with Maleficent transformed into a terrifying, fire-breathing dragon.

Completed at a record cost of $6 million, *Sleeping Beauty* was given a show-case screening with stereophonic sound in 45 selected theatres. An inkling of disaster came with the reviews. *Sleeping Beauty*, said *The New York Herald Tribune* was 'Disney imitating Disney'; C. A. Lejeune in *The Observer*, compared the film – as many critics did – with *Snow White*, and asked: 'Has Disney's work developed from that time to this? So far as techniques are concerned, yes, undoubtedly. In all that affects the imagination, regrettably but definitely no.' The public response to *Sleeping Beauty* fell far short of what was expected or needed at a time when financial problems seemed, once again, to be conspiring against the Studio.

In addition to a decline in Disney movie revenues, which Walt blamed on 'a considerable leaning on the part of the public towards pictures involving violence, sex, and other such subjects', lack of advertising commitment among ABC's sponsors resulted in the dropping of *Zorro* and the *Mickey Mouse Club*. Ironically, the only increasingly prosperous venture was Disneyland, the one so many critics had predicted would end in failure.

Sleeping Beauty, which eventually grossed an inadequate $5.3 million on its first release, proved to be Walt Disney's last great fling, his final baroque masterpiece, that – because of its undoubted flaws and a change in the tastes of movie-goers – might easily have brought about the end of the Disney animated feature, but that, instead, ushered in a new era in animation.

11. RIDING THE CAROUSEL OF PROGRESS

Announcing the Studio's next animated feature film, in 1960, Walt Disney wrote: 'The cartoon will introduce some technical advancements which, I believe, enhance the work of our fine staff of animators.'

The cartoon in question was *One Hundred and One Dalmatians* and, in truth, Walt was less than enthusiastic about the 'technical advancement' that it employed. He realized, however, that it was an innovation that might enable the Studio to continue making animated features after the expensive débâcle of *Sleeping Beauty*.

One of the most costly and time-consuming stages in the animation process was the meticulous task of tracing onto celluloid the animators' pencil drawings. At first this had been done using black ink, but with the advent of colour and the greater sophistication developed with the Silly Symphonies, the Studio began using inks ranging from flesh tones for faces to appropriate colours for hair, clothing, fur or feathers. In some sequences requiring the interaction of a number of characters, as many as a dozen or more different inks might be used, making the whole exercise a slow and expensive one.

The villainous Cruella de Vil contemplates a dalmatian-skin coat on this German lobby-card for *One Hundred and One Dalmatians*.

Then, in the late 1950s, Ub Iwerks developed a new technique using an adapted Xerox process to transfer drawings onto celluloid mechanically. This facility not only eliminated one of the stages in cartoon film-making, it also resulted in a freer, more fluid, form of animation that was closer to the animators' original drawings. Its chief drawback, and one which Walt found difficult to accept after years of striving for perfection, was the heavy black line that now delineated the characters and that was incapable of reproducing the finer detail of an animation drawing.

It was essential, therefore, that the graphic style of any film using the new technique should match the boldness of the character animation. Designed by Ken Anderson, *One Hundred and One Dalmatians* used impressionistic backgrounds created by areas of flat pastel colours, overlaid with linear sketches in black. Although the results could scarcely have been more different from the picturesque fussiness of *Sleeping Beauty*, they had a simple illustrative appeal and one that was well suited to a story about black-and-white dogs.

Using sharply observed caricatures to blur the distinctions between people and canines, *One Hundred and One Dalmatians* was one of the first Disney films in which human characters were essentially unrealistic and yet, at the same time, convincing.

As for the animals, the directing animators created a cast of memorable characters including the Dalmatian hero and heroine, Pongo and Perdita, whose puppies are dognapped by the wicked Cruella de Vil; Colonel, the old sheepdog with defective hearing, and his assistant Sergeant Tibs; and the various members of the newsnetwork, known as the Twilight Bark, such as the Great Dane of Hampstead and his excitable little friend the Terrier, who first receive Pongo's all-dog alert.

The film's masterpiece of characterization, however, is Marc Davis' rendition of the villainess, Cruella de Vil, voiced by Martha Wentworth and bearing more than a passing resemblance to Tallulah Bankhead as she flounces around, smoking cigarettes which leave trails of lurid green smoke.

Few of the critics, who gave an enthusiastic welcome to the movie on its release in February 1961, realized quite how revolutionary was

One of the many visual joys of *One Hundred and One Dalmatians* (1961) were the cunning caricatures of dogs and humans.

Among the splendid characters in *The Sword in the Stone* (1963), are Merlin and Madam Mim, whose wizards' duel involves them changing into a succession of creatures great and small.

its style. *Punch* described the drawings as 'far more interesting than usual' and the *Monthly Film Bulletin* commented on its 'strong and simple lines', but for the most part it was enough that the film seemed to many to be what *Time* magazine called 'the wittiest, most charming, least pretentious cartoon feature Walt Disney has ever made'.

Dodie Smith, on whose novel the picture was based, described herself as 'delighted' with the film, perhaps because, despite the changes from her book, it relied on sophisticated humour rather than comic gags and melodious sentimentality. In fact, for the first time in a Disney cartoon feature, songs (of which there were just three) were less important than its other, considerable, attractions.

The film, which had been modestly budgeted at $3.6 million, did excellent business and contributed to a financially successful year in which the 1960 deficit of $1.3 million was transformed into a handsome profit of $4,465,486. This was also the year in which the company's 22-year-old liability to the Bank of America was finally paid off.

The success of *One Hundred and One Dalmatians* prompted Walt to begin work on filming another modern British classic, *The Sword in the Stone*. The rights to T. H. White's novel about the boyhood of King Arthur had been purchased in 1939, the year after the book's publication, but Walt was slow to put the story into production, feeling that the book's reputation was not widely enough established – especially within the USA – to be the basis of a Disney feature.

The Sword in the Stone was again considered briefly in the early 1950s, and Walt's interest in the story was revived when, in 1959, Lerner and Loewe decided to write *Camelot*, a musical based on White's complete cycle of Arthurian romances, *The Once and Future King*. Although the story of how Merlin educates the young Arthur by translating him into birds, beasts and fish was not particularly suited to the stage, it was a natural subject for Disney.

Less suitable, however, was the style of animation that had seemed so appropriate to *One Hundred and One Dalmatians*. Ironically, the medieval tapestry of White's book would have benefited from the more elaborate techniques lavished on *Sleeping Beauty*. As it was,

The Sword in the Stone had to make do with a style dictated more by economic than aesthetic values. White's idiosyncratic story with its curious anachronisms presented a difficult challenge to adaptor Bill Peet, and much of the book's original magic was lost in the process. Nevertheless, under the direction of Woolie Reitherman (the first to direct a Disney feature single-handed), *The Sword in the Stone* contained some delightful characterizations and many entertaining and imaginative episodes. On its release, *The Sword in the Stone* received a mixed critical reception. Howard Thompson found it 'a warm, wise and amusing film', and Judith Crist in *The New York Herald Tribune* described the film as 'a thorough delight'. Others were less entertained, among them *The New Republic's* Stanley Kauffmann who described the film as a 'huge coast-to-coast malted milk made of pasteurized Arthurian ingredients'. In a particularly virulent attack, one British reviewer condemned the movie for 'a lack of exhuberance and a fatal lack of imagination', and concluded that 'as Disney has concentrated more and more on nature films and on children's live-action films, bringing the latter to a very high standard, his cartoons have degenerated almost beyond repair'.

The public response to *The Sword in the Stone* shows it to have been anything but a failure, yet it is true that the increasing output of high-quality live-action movies made the Studio far less dependent on animation.

Kevin Corcoran and friend in *Toby Tyler* (1960), described by one critic as 'a minor classic among children's movies'.

The last film of the 1950s, *The Third Man on the Mountain* marked a significant departure in that, while Walt remained Executive Producer, it was the first picture to credit another producer – William H. ('Bill') Anderson. Directed by Ken Annakin, *The Third Man on the Mountain* contained some stunning location photography and powerful performances from Michael Rennie, Janet Munro, Herbert Lom and James MacArthur. The following year, James MacArthur co-starred with Peter Finch in a remarkably faithful, but somewhat dull, adaptation of Robert Louis Stevenson's *Kidnapped*; while another of the Studio's juvenile talents, Kevin Corcoran received his first major screen role in *Toby Tyler, or Ten Weeks with a Circus*.

Under the direction of Charles Barton, the undemanding plot of *Toby Tyler* was embellished by a cast of larger-than-life characters, a spattering of circus thrills and spills and a scene-stealing performance from a chimpanzee called Mr Stubbs, who begat a string of 'monkey movies' including *Moon Pilot* (1962), *The Monkey's Uncle* (1965) and *Monkeys, Go Home!* (1967).

Kevin Corcoran and James MacArthur also appeared, together with Disney regulars Janet Munro and Tommy Kirk, in the 1960 Panavision spectacular *Swiss Family Robinson*, which began filming in Tobago after five months' planning and set-building. Since the island had little in the way of animal and bird life, arrangements were made for elephants, tigers, monkeys, zebras, ostriches, parrots and a colony of flamingos to be specially shipped in.

Numerous problems with the livestock and the elements resulted in a lengthy and expensive shoot. One particular sequence, in which

The ingenuous Hayley Mills in her first Disney role as the wide-eyed, optimistic heroine of *Pollyanna* (1960).

the family come ashore from the wrecked ship with their domestic animals lashed to remnants of the vessel, took 10 days to film; and the final total of 22 weeks' filming contributed substantially to an expenditure of $4 million.

Released on Christmas Eve 1960, the film divided the reviewers between those who found it 'a fast, furious humdinger' and those who considered it 'a regular Donald Duck comedy in live action' and criticized the film's occasional tendency towards slapstick humour especially in the fight with the pirates. Most, however, were in agreement about the central performances of Dorothy McGuire and John Mills as the parents. Mills was particularly successful as the firm, but kindly and adventurous, father, although *Swiss Family Robinson* was to be his only picture for the Studio. A member of his real-life family, however, was to become a major Disney star.

Walt first saw the 13-year-old Hayley Mills in her film debut, *Tiger Bay*. At the time, he was looking for a youngster to play the title role in a screen version of Eleanor H. Porter's quaint novel *Pollyanna*. Pollyanna and her philosophy of being 'glad' are quintessentially American, whereas Hayley Mills had a decidedly English accent; but Walt, who was never particularly bothered by such details, cast her in the part formerly played on screen by Mary Pickford. He also engaged a strong supporting cast including Jane Wyman, Karl Malden, Nancy Olson and movie veterans Donald Crisp, Adolphe Menjou (in his last film) and Agnes Moorehead, in top form as the acid-tongued hypochondriac, Mrs Snow, who – like everyone else in the film – is relentlessly cheered up by Pollyanna.

Running at 134 minutes, *Pollyanna* turned out to be something of a marathon of gladness, although the richness of its settings and the strength of its performances made it an altogether charming piece of entertainment. So, indeed, thought most of the critics who tended towards the view that it was Walt's best live-action feature, being full of what *The Saturday Review* called 'the feeling for Americana, the nostalgic glow of a simpler, gentler way of life'. *Time*, on the other hand, called it 'a Niagara of drivel'; and, at the box-office, the film took only $3,750,000 – over $2 million short of expectations.

As for Hayley Mills – who was a perfect example of the then Hollywood adage: 'Disney gets them on the way up or the way down' – *Pollyanna* established her as a star, won her an honorary Academy Award, and earned her a series of new roles with the Studio, beginning, in 1961, with *The Parent Trap*. Also starring Maureen O'Hara and Brian Keith (making his Disney debut), it was voted 'a surprisingly sufferable film' by Bosley Crowther in *The New York Times*, who described Hayley Mills' performances (as twin sisters) as having 'delightful insouciance, dexterity and charm'.

The following year Hayley Mills starred in an eccentric romp entitled *In Search of the Castaways* along with Maurice Chevalier, George Sanders, Wilfred Hyde White and Michael Anderson, Jr. Based on *Captain Grant's Children* by Jules Verne, the film – which one critic called 'more gimmicky than imaginative' – was part of the current obsession with the great French fantasist that had been started by *20,000 Leagues Under the Sea*.

Hayley was next teamed with Burl Ives and Dorothy McGuire in *Summer Magic* (1963), based on Kate Douglas Wiggins' popular novel *Mother Carey's Chickens*. The film featured seven songs by Richard and Robert Sherman, one of which, 'The Ugly Bug Ball', achieved considerable popularity. Reviewing *Summer Magic* in *The New York Times*, Eugene Archer complained that 'the girlish Miss Mills, whose acting ability is not improving with adolescence ... is reaching the ominous stage of puppy love'.

It was not, however, until *The Moon-Spinners* (1964), a romantic thriller set on Crete, that what the publicity writers called 'a new, vivacious, svelte Hayley Mills' received 'her first in-earnest screen kiss' from Peter McEnery.

The Moon-Spinners was directed by former American war photographer James Neilson, one of a group of new Disney directors including Britisher Don Chaffey, responsible for two of Disney's most wistful live-action pictures: *Greyfriars Bobby* (1961), the story of a little dog that keeps a nightly vigil by its dead master's grave; and *The Three Lives of Thomasina* (1964) based on Paul Gallico's book about a cat who transforms the loveless life of a widowed vet.

As well as introducing two bright young newcomers, Karen Dotrice and Matthew Garber, *Thomasina* starred Patrick McGoohan, Susan Hampshire and Laurence Naismith who had also co-starred in *Greyfriars Bobby* with Donald Crisp. These were just a few of the distinguished performers who were now appearing in Disney films; others included Edmund O'Brien, Robert Taylor, Lilli Palmer, Curt Jurgens, Eddie Albert, Leo G. Carroll, Joan Greenwood, silent screen star Pola Negri (for whom *The Moon-Spinners* was her first film in 20 years) and Walter Pidgeon who starred in the beautifully understated dog drama, *Big Red* (1962).

Among numerous other animal pictures was *The Incredible Journey* (1963), based on Sheila Burnford's best-seller about a labrador, a bull terrier and a Siamese cat who cross Canada in search of their human family. Scripted and co-produced by James Algar, and photographed by Jack Couffer and Lloyd Beebe (who, in 1962, had filmed *The Legend of Lobo*), *The Incredible Journey* contained, what *The New York Times* called, 'some of the most disarming, four-footed trouping ever filmed'.

Among the more curious of the Studio's productions were a sophisticated satire on the US space programme, *Moon Pilot* (1962), with Tom Tryon; a film about the Vienna Boys Choir, *Almost Angels* (1962); and a wartime drama-cum-horse-picture, *Miracle of the White Stallions* (1963). There was also a laborious comedy, *Bon Voyage* (1962), with Fred MacMurray, Jane Wyman, Tommy Kirk, Deborah Walley and Kevin Corcoran as a family of American tourists on an accident-prone, cliché-ridden trip to Paris; which, despite damning reviews, made $5 million on its domestic release.

Fred MacMurray fared rather better in what was the Studio's biggest hit of the early 1960s, *The Absent-Minded Professor*, a farce in the same mould as the successful *The Shaggy Dog*. The screenplay by Bill Walsh tells how Professor Ned Brainard accidentally discovers an anti-gravity substance called 'Flubber', with which he turns his Model T Ford into a flying car and makes aerodynamic sneakers for his college basketball team.

In 1963, two years after the release of *The Absent-Minded Professor*, Fred MacMurray and co-stars Nancy Olson, Keenan and Ed Wynn and Tommy Kirk were reunited in *Son of Flubber*. Although critics found it a somewhat synthetic sequel, Professor Brainard's later exploits – including the invention of 'dry rain' – grossed over $9 million, and inspired subsequent gimmick movies such as the Tommy Kirk vehicles *The Misadventures of Merlin Jones* (1964) and *The Monkey's Uncle* (1965).

Starring opposite Tommy Kirk, as Merlin Jones' co-ed girlfriend was the former Mouseketeer, Annette Funicello, who had starred as Mary Contrary in Disney's first live-action musical, *Babes in Toyland*. Based on the popular Victor Herbert operetta, *Babes in Toyland* was scripted by Lowell S. Hawley and animators Joe Rinaldi and Ward Kimball. The picture was directed by Jack Donohue, responsible for several MGM musicals, and had 12 tuneful numbers and bright storybook sets and colourful costumes, reminiscent of *The Wizard of Oz*.

The cast was headed by two celebrated players: Ray Bolger as Barnaby the evil villain, and 75-year-old radio star Ed Wynn as the addled toymaker. There were also the ubiquitous Tommy Kirk and Kevin Corcoran, and popular singing star Tommy Sands as Annette's sweetheart, Tom Piper.

The most popular of the Mouseketeers, Annette Funicello, was teamed with Tommy Sands – star of tv's *The Singing Idol* – in an extravaganza based on the operetta *Babes in Toyland* (1961). Despite excellent special effects and a good deal of charm, it was not a great success, having as one critic put it 'the character of frosting without any cake underneath'.

It was Walt's first experiment with the film musical, and it was only partially successful, grossing just $4.6 million despite considerable publicity and merchandising campaigns and an hour-long television show, 'Backstage Party', aired in December 1961 to promote the picture.

The Disney television programmes had recently gone through a difficult phase as a result of relationships with ABC. *The Mickey Mouse Club* had been discontinued, following its fourth season, because, according to ABC, sponsorship was not forthcoming. Walt, however, believed the show's excessive number of commercials had resulted in a decline in public interest. The *Zorro* series, although still popular, had also been dropped as an unnecessary expense for a network that already owned enough shows without buying-in from

Walt signs up the doggy star of a new movie based on the true story of *Greyfriars Bobby* (1961). (Courtesy of Mail Newspapers plc)

independent producers, and *Walt Disney Presents* had been forced to become little more than a series of western subjects, as ABC fought for audiences with NBC's *Wagon Train*, the show that had finally dislodged the Disney show from its number one spot in the tv ratings.

Walt had responded to ABC's demand for 'more westerns' with *Tales of Texas John Slaughter, The Nine Lives of Elfego Baca, The Saga of Andy Burnett*, and a series on the life of Daniel Boone. But the success of these shows was, as Walt saw it, something of a disadvantage. 'They made so much money for ABC,' he said, 'that before long *I* found myself in a straightjacket . . . when I came up with a fresh idea in another field, the network executives would say no.'

Matters came to a head when ABC refused to allow the Studio to screen either the *Mickey Mouse Club* or *Zorro* on any other network, even though ABC no longer wanted them. Disney began legal proceedings against ABC and, after lengthy negotiations, settlement was reached with the Studio recovering the rights to its programmes and gaining the freedom to offer *Walt Disney Presents* to an alternative network, on the understanding it bought out ABC's one-third stake in Disneyland. Walt Disney Productions had already purchased the interests owned by Western Printing and that personally held by Walt, so the $7.5 million settlement with ABC not only gave the Studio the opportunity of negotiating with other companies for tv rights but also the sole ownership of Disneyland.

For some time, Walt had been encouraging and promoting a team of younger men to positions of responsibility within the company, delegating a great deal of production work to colleagues such as Bill Walsh, James Algar and Bill Anderson who, as a Vice-President and a member of the Board of Directors, was now in charge of the day-to-day running of the Studio. Creative contributions were being made by both Walt's son-in-law, Ron Miller, and nephew, Roy E. Disney; while, in the animation unit, Woolie Reitherman and others found themselves enjoying a greater degree of autonomy than ever before.

Two young men who had risen through the company to senior positions were E. Cardon 'Card' Walker and Donn B. Tatum. As vice-presidents in charge of, respectively, Advertising and Television Sales, Walker and Tatum accompanied Walt and Roy when they went to New York to talk with NBC. Walt had long anticipated television's transition into colour and, although most of his recent programmes had been shown in black-and-white, they had been filmed in colour. Since RCA, owners of NBC, were currently promoting the sale of its colour tv sets, they were an obvious candidate for a Disney colour series.

A deal was clinched with NBC, and 24 September 1961 saw the debut of *Walt Disney's Wonderful World of Color* with Ludwig Von Drake (allegedly an uncle of Donald Duck) presenting 'An Adventure in Color', which included a brief look at Disney films from silent black-and-white to sound and colour.

Ludwig Von Drake introduced numerous editions of the *Wonderful World of Color* such as 'The Hunting Instinct', 'Inside Donald Duck' and 'Kids is Kids'. Most of the shows, however, featured live-action subjects, among them tv versions of such movies as *Toby Tyler, Pollyanna, Summer Magic* and *Moon Pilot* as well as new two-and three-part films, many of which were given theatrical release in Europe, including *The Magnificent Rebel, The Horsemasters, Escapade in Florence, The Legend of Young Dick Turpin, Ballerina* and *The Scarecrow of Romney Marsh*.

Walt continued to use the television series to promote Disneyland with programmes like 'Disneyland After Dark', in which Annette appeared with another former Mouseketeer, Bobby Burgess, and with Louis Armstrong and the Osmond Brothers, and 'The Golden Horseshoe Revue', filmed on the stage of the celebrated Frontierland show with one of its stars, Wally Boag, and guests Ed Wynn, Gene Sheldon and, yet again, Annette.

In January 1965, the *Wonderful World of Color* televised 'Disneyland's 10th Anniversary', marking the park's first decade; and that year saw the total number of visitors to Disneyland reach 52 million. There had been consistent developments at Disneyland over the past few years including, in 1960, a Mine Train ride through Nature's Wonderland and a new 360° Circarama film *America the Beautiful*.

Ludwig Von Drake, host of *Walt Disney's Wonderful World of Color*, delivering one of his tv lectures in an eccentric European accent.

In 1961 the monorail system was extended to connect the park with the then non-Disney-owned Disneyland Hotel; and the following year saw the installation of a 70-foot high replica of the Swiss Family Robinson's Tree House. The total investment in Disneyland, in 1962, stood at $42 million.

During the 1960s the ever-rising fortunes of the Disney empire were the subject of many articles in the world's top journals.

In June 1963 Disneyland opened the Enchanted Tiki Room employing 'a new medium of three-dimensional entertainment'. It had begun many years before when, on a visit to New Orleans, Walt had bought an antique automaton of a bird in a gilded cage. Walt was fascinated by this 100-year-old toy, and began looking for ways to refine and use such mechanical entertainments. His first idea was to add sound and movement to some of the miniature models he had begun designing following the war, and the scale replica of Granny Kincaid's cabin was planned to contain a moving figure of the old lady in her rocking chair imparting words of wisdom in the voice of actress Beulah Bondi.

Then in 1951, Walt and the technicians at WED Enterprises constructed a 9-inch Dancing Man modelled on Buddy Ebsen, which was followed by a more complex Barbershop Quartet using metal cams to make the figures move and appear to sing.

With Disneyland under construction, Walt was forced to shelve any future plans for his automata, although simplified figures of birds and animals were designed for the park's jungle river ride and, later, Nature's Wonderland. The possibility of achieving three-dimensional animation fascinated Walt and encouraged him to strive for greater sophistication.

This came as a result of plans for a Polynesian Tea Room in Disneyland. WED artist John Hench produced some renditions showing flowers, ferns and bamboo and birds in cages. Walt liked the designs but objected to the birds on grounds of hygiene, so Hench suggested they use stuffed birds instead: 'Well, we just can't have static stuffed birds sitting up there,' he said, 'that's not too good.' Regretting having included the birds, John Hench suggested that they should forget them. Walt thought a moment and then said: 'Maybe make them chirp . . .'

Hench set to work with Marc Davis and Rollie Crump who designed a series of sculptures of Polynesian gods and a driftwood mobile with birds. Detailed research was undertaken into Polynesian folk art, specimens of tropical birds were collected, at considerable expense, by a South American bird expert and models designed and made. These were operated by a system called 'Audio-Animatronics' using standard optical soundtrack tape sending signals to solenoid coils in the figures. The mechanical birds were then 'feathered' with chicken and turkey feathers.

Richard and Robert Sherman devised a catchy calypso, and Wally Boag and Fulton Burley from 'The Golden Horseshoe Revue' provided the voices. But as the attraction developed, Walt began to worry about how efficiently it could be run as a restaurant, since the entertainment would make it difficult to get patrons to eat up and leave. Eventually the idea of serving food was abandoned, the tables were replaced by more chairs and it became a show presentation.

At this time also on the drawing boards for Disneyland was a new themed area to be called Liberty Square, and it was there that Walt decided he would build a Hall of Presidents for a show on American history. called 'One Nation Under God', it would feature Abraham Lincoln addressing an assembly comprising every one of the nation's Chief Executives. For the time being, however, visitors to Disneyland had to make do with the talking birds, flowers and gods of the Tiki Room.

Disneyland continued to draw the crowds, and there was, it seemed, no limit to its fame. When, in 1960, the then Soviet Premier Nikita Khrushchev visited America, he was disconsolate to find that security arrangements made it impossible for him to go to Disneyland.

There were numerous requests for Walt to build other parks in America but he repeatedly declined. Approaches from overseas, however, were seriously considered, and British circus owner Billy Smart flew to Burbank to discuss an English Disneyland for the northern seaside resort of Blackpool. A site was negotiated for, at an annual rental of £10,000, but the plan failed due to a reluctance on the part of British businessmen to sponsor the project.

A more feasible opportunity to use some of the skills developed for Disneyland arose in 1959, when it was announced that a World's Fair would be held in New York in five years' time. Walt decided to approach a number of leading corporations and offer to design their

'Audio-Animatronics' cavemen awaiting installation in the Ford Motor Company's 'Magic Skyway' at the New York World's Fair in 1964.

attractions. It was a decision that was to have far-reaching consequences.

The Ford Motor Company welcomed the suggestion and bought Walt's designs for a car-ride through history from caveman to spaceman. A second client was acquired when Walt made a presentation to General Electric using design ideas that had been developed for a proposed Edison Square in Disneyland. Both companies agreed to a fee of one million dollars for the use of the Walt Disney name.

During 1963, while Disney was working on the exhibits for Ford and General Electric, Robert Moses, President of the New York World's Fair, visited WED where he saw designs for the Hall of Presidents and a prototype of the Abraham Lincoln figure. Moses wanted the attraction for the Fair, and although it was not possible to complete the entire Hall of Presidents, Walt undertook to try and have Abraham Lincoln ready in time.

The staff of WED researched every aspect of Lincoln's life: recreating the President's head from a death mask and combining elements of several patriotic speeches to be spoken by actor Royal Dano. The WED technicians had made enormous strides with the 'Audio-Animatronics' system, not least the discovery of Duraflex, a plastisol substance that had the flexibility and texture of human skin and, unlike rubber, was not prone to disintegration.

Just nine months before the opening, Pepsi Cola approached the Studio to commission a pavilion, the profits from which would be donated to UNICEF (the United Nations International Children's Education Fund). The artists began sketching ideas from which grew 'It's a Small World', a boatride around a miniature world inhabited by figures of children dressed in national costume and singing and dancing together in peace and harmony. The concept was a perfect one, not just as a symbol for UNICEF and the World's Fair, but as an image-enhancing exhibit for Pepsi Cola and one ideally suited to carry the Walt Disney name. The overall theme of the World's Fair was 'Man's Achievement in an Expanding Universe', a concept that was strongly reflected in WED's attractions for Ford and General Electric and that later became the keynote of Disney's EPCOT.

A week before the Fair opened, the figure of Abraham Lincoln was shipped to New York. The show was entitled 'Great Moments with Mr Lincoln', but, for a while, it seemed as if there were not actually going to be any. First, there was trouble with the wiring; then there were problems with the power supply. On 20 April, when 200 invited guests arrived for the premiere of Lincoln's performance, the President – who was capable of 48 separate body actions and 15 facial movements – was still not functioning properly, and Walt refused to let the show go ahead. There was a tense week of long hours and frustrating attempts to make the 'Audio-Animatronics' figure work before the problems were solved and Lincoln could rise from his chair and speak of mankind as having been 'made for immortality'. Just as

It's A Small World's 120-foot high 'Tower of the Four Winds' kinetic mobile became a landmark of the World's Fair.

Walt had intended, audiences experienced 'the sensation of being in the crowd the day Lincoln himself made the speech', and the show became one of the Fair's major attractions.

The Fair closed for the winter of 1964, and, when it re-opened in 1965, a new, improved Lincoln was in operation; and, as the Fair came to an end, a third figure was installed in the Opera House on Main Street, Disneyland.

The four Disney-designed exhibits at the World's Fair received 46,871,236 visitors, which represented 91 per cent of everyone who attended the Fair. 'It's a Small World' alone was visited by over 10 million guests and, when the Fair closed, what was called 'The Happiest Cruise That Ever Sailed' was taken to Disneyland. The 'Carousel of Progress', with its revolving view of ever-improving family life, was also transferred to the park, under the continued sponsorship of General Electric; and the dinosaurs that had featured in the Ford display were incorporated into a prehistoric panorama for the Disneyland Railroad ride, where an 'Audio-Animatronics' Tyranosaurus Rex and a Stegosaurus are locked in mortal combat to this day.

The art of 'Audio Animatronics', which the World's Fair helped to foster, was applied to another, more modest, project: a lifelike figure of a robin, which, in a 1964 Disney movie, perched on the finger of a magical English nanny as she sang of her philosophy that 'a spoonful of sugar helps the medicine go down'.

'It's a world of laughter, a world of tears, It's a world of hopes and a world of fears, It's a small world after all . . .'

12. PRACTICALLY PERFECT IN EVERY WAY

'Mary Poppins,' said the *Times Literary Supplement* on the publication of her first book of adventures in 1934, 'is the embodiment of authority, protection, and cynical common sense; her powers are magical. Basically, she is the Good Fairy whom we are all seeking.'

Walt Disney first became aware of *Mary Poppins* and its sequel, *Mary Poppins Comes Back*, in the early 1940s, when one of his daughters was reading them. Quick to recognize their cinematic potential, Walt began to try and acquire the film rights.

Learning that their author P. L. Travers was living in New York to avoid the London Blitz, Walt asked Roy to call on her when he visited the city in 1944 and discuss the possibility of a *Mary Poppins* film. Mrs Travers, who had recently published her third book of the series, *Mary Poppins Opens the Door*, was reticent about relinquishing her rights.

Following Roy's visit, Walt invited Mrs Travers to visit the Studio and discuss the idea more fully; but the author remained hesitant and nothing further happened until Walt called on her during one of his visits to London in the 1950s. Author and film-maker got on well together, and Mrs Travers was particularly struck by Walt's charismatic personality, but it was to be another 10 years before she began to give serious consideration to Walt's continuing requests to film the books. One of her terms was that she should be consultant to any film project, and the fact that Walt made the unprecedented decision to agree to such an arrangement shows how eager he was to obtain the rights.

Walt suggested that Mrs Travers should visit the Studio to view some preliminary treatments for the film, and, on his return to America, he sent for Richard and Robert Sherman and handed them a copy of the one-volume edition of the first two Mary Poppins books, with a request that they read it and give him their views. The Shermans quickly discovered that the books were a series of short stories without any connecting plot. Selecting what they considered the six best episodes from the books, the Sherman brothers produced a rough storyline and drafted some preliminary song sketches. When, at their next meeting with Walt, they presented their ideas, he responded enthusiastically. Only when they had finished did he show them his personal copy of the book – with the same six chapters marked for development.

Bill Walsh and Don da Gradi were assigned the task of writing the screenplay and the Sherman brothers began composing the first of some 37 possible songs for the picture.

P. L. Travers' visit to the Studio in 1961 proved a difficult experience for both parties: she was unprepared for the considerable changes and compressions that Walt was proposing to make, and he was unprepared for dealing with an author who not only held strong convictions about how her books should be dramatized but who expressed them so unequivocably.

Amendments and revisions were made to the script and agreement was finally reached, and, despite their differences, P. L. Travers and Walt parted amicably, with the author giving him a copy of her fourth book, *Mary Poppins in the Park*, inscribed: 'To Walt Disney, hoping that your association with Mary Poppins will bring you joy and satisfaction and be as she herself *has* so often put it – a Pleasure and a Treat!'

Work progressed on the storyline, which included several sequences later abandoned including a trip round the world with Mary Poppins' magic compass and an elaborate underwater episode (later revised and incorporated into *Bedknobs and Broomsticks*).

Bette Davis and Mary Martin were both considered for the role of Mary Poppins, but Walt eventually signed Julie Andrews after seeing her in the stage version of *Camelot*. Walt also engaged Dick Van Dyke, whose tv comedy show was then at the height of its popularity, and a cast of British and American veterans, among them Hermione Baddeley and Reginald Owen. Ed Wynn was cast as Mary Poppins 'laughaholic' Uncle Albert, and David Tomlinson secured one of the best roles of his later career as the punctilious Mr Banks, whose troubled household is visited by Mary Poppins.

To play the children, Jane and Michael Banks, Walt signed two engaging British youngsters, Karen Dotrice and Matthew Garber, who had both previously appeared in *The Three Lives of Thomasina*. The film also featured 83-year-old actress Jane Darwell in the cameo role of the Bird Woman.

At the suggestion of P. L. Travers, the story had been set in the Edwardian England of 1910, and the scriptwriters had decided to make the abstracted Mrs Banks into a zealous suffragette. Walt invited Glynis Johns, who had appeared in several of the Studio's historical dramas, to read for the part, but found that the actress had hoped to be considered for the role of Mary Poppins.

In an attempt to persuade Glynis Johns that the part of Mrs Banks was a desirable one, Walt told her that the Sherman brothers were writing a special number for the film. Robert and Richard Sherman, who had heard nothing about such a song before, worked frantically to revise a number they had sketched for Mary Poppins, entitled 'Practically Perfect in Every Way', into a new one called 'Sister Suffragette', which won Glynis Johns' approval and gave Mrs Banks a lively character routine.

The film was co-produced by Bill Walsh, and among the experienced team of technicians and creative talent, headed by director Robert Stevenson, were art director Carroll Clark, set

Mary Poppins (Julie Andrews) and Bert (Dick Van Dyke) enjoy a 'Jolly Holiday' in one of Bert's chalk pavement pictures.

One critic described *Mary Poppins* (1964) as 'sparkling with originality, melody and magical performances'.

decorator Emile Kuri, musical arranger and conductor Irwin Kostal, and animation director Hamilton Luske. Long-serving Disney special effects men Peter Ellenshaw, Eustace Lycett and Robert A. Mattey enabled Mary Poppins to float over London on a cloud, slide up bannisters, hold a tea party on the ceiling, dispense different coloured medicines from one bottle and go inside a chalk pavement picture.

The only technical hitch during filming was when one of the flying sequences went wrong and Julie Andrews crashed onto the sound stage. 'Is Miss Andrews down yet?' enquired the winch-operator. 'Down?' bellowed Julie, momentarily forgetting her Poppins decorum, 'I'm bloody nearly through the floor!'

But for the most part the Studio atmosphere was relaxed and happy. 'As the original *Mary Poppins* budget of $5 million continued to grow,' Walt later recalled, 'I never saw a sad face around the entire Studio and this made me nervous. I knew the picture would have to gross $10 million for us to break even. But still there was no negative

Having been passed over by Jack Warner for the film of *My Fair Lady*, Julie Andrews rose to movie stardom with *Mary Poppins*.

head-shaking. No prophets of doom. Even Roy was happy. He didn't even ask me to show the unfinished picture to a banker. The horrible thought struck me – suppose the staff had finally conceded that I knew what I was doing?'

Walt began worrying in case the picture was too long (it eventually ran for 139 minutes plus an intermission), and he contemplated cutting the lullaby 'Stay Awake' and the episode in which Mary Poppins takes the children to visit her Uncle Albert and they become infected with laughing gas, but Walt eventually relented and decided to let the film run to its completed length. However, he continued to fuss about the film. 'The suspense,' Walt later said, 'was too much.' He decided to consult an old friend, exhibitor David Wallerstein of Balaban and Katz, who could 'smell a hit – or a flop – through a six-foot wall'. After seeing a screening of part of the film, Wallerstein told him: 'You can relax, Walt. The picture will be a tremendous success'. Only then did Walt start 'smiling right back at the staff'.

For P. L. Travers, however, Mary Poppins' excursion to Hollywood was not an altogether happy one. 'Books,' she says, 'have to undergo some sort of sea-change when they are translated to the screen. Magic, conveyed in a book by words and the silences between words, inevitably, in a film, become trick. The film of *Mary Poppins*, with all its glamour and splendours and the devoted energy of its cast, has been a tremendous success. But if we are comparing book and film, the sea-change has also been tremendous.'

It is true that the film failed to capture the poetry and mystery of the original books, but it had a literate script incorporating subtle wit, vaudeville humour and a touch of social satire. And, considering the Studio's only other attempt at a full-scale film musical was the mediocre *Babes in Toyland*, *Mary Poppins* was little short of miraculous.

Sumptuously dressed, set and photographed, the film moved lightly and effortlessly through its fantastic theme, carried along by more than a dozen unforgettable songs and several nimble dance routines choreographed by Marc Breaux and Dee Dee Woods. Although Julie Andrews was somewhat prettier than P. L. Travers' description of Mary Poppins, she was, at 27 years old, the same age as the literary character and captured much of that unique personality which the author calls 'a mixture of arrogance and poetry and, underlying both, a certain invincible integrity'. Somewhat less successful is Bert, the pavement-artist-cum-chimney-sweep portrayed by Dick Van Dyke with a strongly Americanized cockney accent. Despite this and the fact that, towards the end of the film, his character is allowed to usurp Mary Poppins' central position in the story, Van Dyke sings and dances with an irrepressible energy.

While *Mary Poppins* was in production, Walt was also deeply involved with many other projects, one of which was an idea for a new kind of art school that brought together the different artistic disciplines. The idea had grown out of an increasing involvement with the Chouinard Art Institute. The years had not been kind to the Institute: its founder, Mrs Nelbert Chouinard, was now in her seventies, and the school had suffered from bad management and the machinations of an embezzler.

By the mid-1950s, the Institute was in grave difficulty, and Mrs Chouinard met with Walt and told him about the Institute's problems. As a result, Walt sponsored two foundation scholarships and began making a series of financial gifts to the school. Nelbert Chouinard invited Walt to join the Institute's Board and, in May 1956, bestowed on him an honorary Doctor of Fine Arts Degree.

Towards the end of the 1950s, Chouinard was, despite injections of Disney cash, close to insolvency. Walt sent in two businessmen to run the Institute's affairs and commissioned Economics Research Associates to take a long-term view on Chouinard's future. Various suggestions were put forward, including one for a City of the Arts that would embrace art, music, theatre, dance and film. The proposal appealed to Walt: 'I like the workshop idea,' he said, 'with students being able to drop in and learn all kinds of arts. You know, a kid might start out in art and end up as a talented musician. A school should . . . develop the best in its students.'

Chouinard was not alone in its problems: similar difficulties were besetting the Los Angeles Conservatory of Music. Founded in 1883, the Conservatory had fallen on hard times and had now only one patron, Mrs Lula Von Hagen, wife of a Los Angeles lawyer and businessman. Walt met with Mrs Von Hagen, and a scheme emerged for bringing together Chouinard and the Conservatory as part of a California Institute of the Arts modelled along the lines of Caltech, the California Institute of Technology. As Walt saw it, the CalArts project would not only help to foster the artistic skills of young California artists; it would, eventually, help to supply new talent for his own and other Hollywood studios.

In 1962 the Chouinard Art Institute officially merged with the Los Angeles Conservatory of Music. With the kind of thoroughness he had shown in planning Disneyland, Walt began researching the running of schools and colleges and looking for a suitable site for CalArts. Various locations were mooted, but eventually Walt and Roy donated 38 acres of Walt Disney Productions' 2,728 acre Golden Oak Ranch, in Placerita Canyon, north of the San Fernando Valley, which had been bought in 1959 as a location for filming and had been used for, among other movies, *Toby Tyler*.

Among those who joined the CalArts Board of Trustees were Disney artists Marc Davis and John Hench, animator Chuck Jones, musicians Henry Mancini and Nelson Riddle, costume designer Edith Head and singer Mary Costa.

Walt decided to use the premiere of *Mary Poppins* to promote CalArts and produced a 15-minute film about the project with which to open the evening. On 27 August 1964, some 3,000 fans began congregating outside Grauman's Chinese Theater in Hollywood. Several hours later they were treated to an elaborate street parade with Pearlie-bands and a train-load of cartoon characters. Sweeps and penguins danced down Hollywood Boulevard, thousands of balloons were released, and a succession of Cadillacs delivered stars to the theatre.

Inside, Walt took the stage with Lula Von Hagen, Chairman of the CalArts Trustees, and introduced *The CalArts Story*, after which came the screening of what was soon being called 'Walt Disney's Greatest Achievement'. It was exactly 20 years since Walt had first tried to secure the film rights to the Mary Poppins books.

The enthusiastic response that the picture received from the audience that night was confirmed by the reviews which followed. *Mary Poppins*, said Hollis Alpert in *The Saturday Review*, was 'one of the most magnificent pieces of entertainment ever to come from Hollywood'. There were a few negative criticisms: one writer complained that Walt Disney's *Mary Poppins* was nothing more than a 'great marshmallow covered cream-puff', and another suggested the film would be 'better renamed *Lollipoppins*'. But, for the most part, the film received the kind of adulation that hadn't been accorded a Disney movie in almost thirty years.

Mary Poppins was backed by the biggest exploitation budget for any Disney movie to date. Advertising campaigns were arranged with dozens of companies on both sides of the Atlantic including Nabisco

and G. N. Coughlan Company (producers of Chimney Sweep Fireplace Powder), and there were major 'Spoonful of Sugar' promotions with America's National Sugar Company and Britain's Tate & Lyle Limited. World-renowned rose grower Harry Wheatcroft produced a Mary Poppins rose described as 'Practically Perfect in Every Way', and in America alone, 46 manufacturers were licensed to sell Mary Poppins kites, umbrellas, hats, handbags, bedspreads, bubble-bath, dolls, toys, tea-sets and tins of Scuffy Shoe Polish.

King Features syndicated a strip-cartoon version of the film. Picture books, comics and colouring books rolled off the presses in their millions and, in addition to soundtrack recordings, the *Mary Poppins* numbers were recorded by Duke Ellington, Louis Prima, Burl Ives and the singer once considered for the film's title-role, Mary Martin.

On its first release, *Mary Poppins* was seen by an estimated audience of 200 million and took $45,000,000 in worldwide rentals, resulting in a $4 million increase in the company's profits during 1965 and a rise in share dividends to $6.08 from $3.96 the previous year.

In February 1965 Julie Andrews – in this her first movie role – took the Hollywood Foreign Press Association's Golden Globe for best actress in a musical or comedy film. Later the same month, Julie, who had been passed over for the film of *My Fair Lady*, was nominated for an Academy Award as Best Actress, one of 13 nominations for the film, among them Robert Stevenson for Director, Tony Walton for Costume Design, Irwin Kostal for Musical Arrangement and Bill Walsh and Don da Gradi for Screenplay.

Although Stevenson, Walton and Kostal lost out to *My Fair Lady*'s George Cukor, Cecil Beaton and André Previn and the Best Screenplay Award went to Edward Anhalt for *Becket*, the Sherman brothers won Best Song with 'Chim Chim Cher-ee' and Best Score, while Academy Awards went to Cotton Warburton for Film Editing and to Peter Ellenshaw, Hamilton Luske and Eustace Lycett for Special Visual Effects. Then, Sidney Poitier announced that the Best Actress was Julie Andrews. 'I know where to start,' she began her speech, 'Mr Walt Disney gets the biggest thanks...'

The 1964 Academy Awards concluded with *My Fair Lady* beating *Mary Poppins* to the Oscar for Best Picture. It was the first and only time (to date) that a Disney picture had been nominated in that category, and had it not been running against *My Fair Lady* it would almost certainly have won.

'If he had made no other film in his lifetime,' wrote Leonard Maltin, '*Mary Poppins* would earn Walt Disney the gratitude of the world. As it happens, it was instead the pinnacle of an already fantastic career.' It was also a hard act to follow, and none of the movies released over the next few years fulfilled the promise of *Poppins*.

There was a capable, but desperately slow, adaptation of Erich Kastner's *Emil and the Detectives*; Tommy Kirk monkeying around with Annette and a chimp in *The Monkey's Uncle*, the first film to be co-produced by Walt's son-in-law, Ron Miller; Dick Van Dyke (and another chimp) as castaways on a tropical island in *Lt Robin Crusoe, U.S.N.*; and Peter McEnery and Susan Hampshire in the swashbuckling adventure *The Fighting Prince of Donegal*.

One of the best of the post-*Poppins* movies was an atmospheric rural drama *Those Calloways*, about a New England family who build a bird sanctuary for migrating geese. Directed by Norman Tokar, with a screenplay by Louis Pelletier, the film had many attributes: breathtaking scenery, photographed by Edward Colman, a strong supporting cast and a richly romantic score by Max Steiner.

But, alas, *Those Calloways* was not in the same box-office league as *Mary Poppins* – or even *That Darn Cat*, a sprightly comedy thriller, directed by Robert Stevenson, about a Siamese cat called DC, who joins forces with the FBI to track down a couple of desperate bank robbers. Grossing $9½ million on its domestic run alone, *That Darn Cat* was followed by another success, when Dean Jones teamed up with Suzanne Pleshette for *The Ugly Dachshund*. Despite being described by one critic as 'a thin, contrived, one-joke comedy' it earned $6 million. For many, however, the Great Dane who thought he was a dachshund was eclipsed by the star of the supporting programme, *Winnie the Pooh and the Honey Tree*.

Donald, Mickey and Pluto join the pearly band from *Mary Poppins* on Disney's 1964 Christmas card.

WALT DISNEY THE MONKEY'S UNCLE

Poster-art for *The Monkey's Uncle*, a screwball comedy with a theme-song sung by Annette and the Beach Boys.

Although Walt had for some years known of A. A. Milne's popular stories about Christopher Robin and his teddy bear, it was not until the early 1960s that he became interested in filming the books. Sensing that the adventures of Pooh and his companions Piglet, Eeyore, Tigger, Kanga and Roo would lend themselves to animation, Walt approached Milne's widow and obtained the film rights.

The project, which began as a feature-length film, was entrusted to Woolie Reitherman, who decided that the picture should take its style from E. H. Shepard's distinctive illustrations to the stories; and that the books themselves should be used as a device, with characters moving from one page to another and even, on occasions, reacting to the printed words.

Since one of the strengths of the books is their narrative line, Reitherman engaged the vocal talents of British character actor Sebastian Cabot to act as storyteller. Veteran Disney voice, Sterling Holloway, got the best vocal role of his long career as Winnie the Pooh, Junius C. Matthews, who had played Rabbit on the radio, reprised the role for the film, Studio writers Hal Smith and Ralph Wright spoke for Owl and Eeyore and the director's 9-year-old son, Bruce Reitherman, gave what, for British audiences, was to be a controversial performance as Christopher Robin.

As work progressed on the picture, various problems emerged. Some of the Studio personnel thought the film too juvenile, and it proved difficult to keep the original Milne style and make it understandable to the American audience while not upsetting the British. It was, perhaps, anxiety over the 'Britishness' of the subject matter that resulted in the project being reduced from feature length to a 20-minute 'featurette'. Certainly, it resulted in the Hums of Pooh being rewritten by the Sherman brothers and the introduction of a character not found in any story by A. A. Milne.

A gopher, possessing what Woolie Reitherman called a 'folksy all-American, grass-roots image' not only set up an excavation business in the 100 Acre Wood, he ousted Pooh's devoted companion, Piglet. 'It appears,' wrote the *Daily Mail* in outrage, 'that in the Very Unenchanted Forest of film commerce, a gopher is *worth more* than a Piglet.'

The journalists of Fleet Street had a field day with what they termed Disney's 'extraordinary attack on one of the last proud remnants of the British Empire'.

Film critic of London's *Evening News*, Felix Barker, learning that *Winnie the Pooh and the Honey Tree* was to be screened at a Royal Film Performance, cabled the Studio:

REGRET EXCERPTS FROM CHRISTOPHER ROBIN SHORT SHOWN HERE GIVE HIM AMERICAN ACCENT STOP BEG TO POINT OUT THIS CHARACTER VIRTUALLY ENGLISH FOLK-HERO STOP SUCH TREATMENT BOUND TO CAUSE CRITICISM STOP PLEASE CONSIDER REDUBBING BEFORE ROYAL FILM SHOW STOP

Barker continued his campaign by pointing out that *The House at Pooh Corner* was not the work of Damon Runyon and asking if Walt would have dared give Johnny Appleseed an English accent. Eventually, after several weeks' silence on the part of the Studio, it emerged that the only print of the picture in Britain had been recalled to Hollywood. 'Disney is going to redub the voice!' Barker announced triumphantly.

Reflecting on this minor *cause célèbre*, one of the screenwriters said: 'It's the old story of trying to please everyone and failing to do so.' The books' illustrator, E. H. Shepard, called it 'a complete travesty', but Mrs Milne declared herself delighted with it as, indeed, were most movie-goers and a good many critics.

Work was soon in hand on a sequel, provisionally entitled *Winnie the Pooh and the Heffalumps* but released in 1968 as *Winnie the Pooh and the Blustery Day*. To pacify the critics, the second film – which won an Academy Award – featured Piglet as well as introducing Tigger (voiced by Paul Winchell) whose popularity came to rival that of Pooh and who reappeared in *Winnie the Pooh and Tigger Too* (1974). The three films were eventually compiled into a feature, *The Many Adventures of Winnie the Pooh*, and a fourth film, *Winnie the Pooh and a Day for Eeyore*, was produced in 1983.

One of the critics of Walt's expedition to Pooh Corner commented that to the Studio 'Winnie the Pooh is not really all that different from Mickey Mouse'. And certainly, in terms of merchandising, Pooh proved one of the most successful characters since the Mouse. Tied in with the release of *Winnie the Pooh and the Honey Tree* were 168 items from 49 licensees that surpassed even the *Mary Poppins* bonanza. In addition to soft toys, children's fashions, games and puzzles, there were no fewer than 19 different publications, and as part of the Studio's 'total marketing' approach, the characters were featured in Disneyland's 1965 Christmas attraction 'Fantasy on Parade'.

Keeping his promise that 'Disneyland will never be completed', Walt had continued to add new attractions and improve existing ones. In July 1966 came the opening of New Orleans Square, a themed area with courtyards and winding streets of buildings decorated with traditional fretted ironwork and stained glass. The following month Disneyland's attendance exceeded 57 million people and the total investment in the park reached $75 million.

Among the ambitious schemes for Disneyland's future were two major attractions utilizing 'Audio-Animatronics': an 'eerie but humorous' Haunted Mansion and 'Pirates of the Caribbean', a spectacular boat ride back to the days when buccaneers looted, burned and pillaged the sea ports of the Spanish Main. There were also elaborate plans for a $20 million face-lift for Tomorrowland making the area twice the size of 'yesterday's Tomorrowland' backed by sponsorship from American corporations Monsanto, McDonnell-Douglas, General Electric and the Bell System.

Winnie the Pooh made his movie debut in 1966; two years later saw the arrival of his irrepressible friend Tigger.

During the 1960s it became increasingly clear that the area of Walt Disney Productions' operations most open to development was its leisure activities, and the fact that the increasing success of Disneyland was soon contributing a third or more of the company's annual income prompted various diversifications.

In 1960 Walt had personally invested in the Celebrity Sports Center in Denver, Colorado, along with George Burns, Art Linkletter, Spike Jones and other celebrities. The Sports Center had 80 10-pin bowling lanes, an indoor 50-metre swimming pool and a 13,500 square feet model car racing track. Two years later, Walt Disney Productions bought out the various interests in the Celebrity Sports Center and ran it as a going concern until 1979, during which time it provided a valuable training facility for Disneyland personnel.

Another sports project had its beginnings in 1958 when Walt visited Switzerland for the filming of *The Third Man on the Mountain*. He conceived a plan for a ski resort in Southern california and spent a good deal of his time finding out about the expectations and requirements of tourists and instructors.

Two years later, he commissioned Economics Research Associates to survey various possible sites in southern California. The same year, 1960, that he was asked to stage the ceremonies for the Winter Olympics to be held in Squaw Valley. It was a recognition of the

Disney showmanship skills, and Walt planned nightly entertainments, a 100-piece band for the opening ceremonial and elaborate ice sculptures to decorate the valley.

During the Olympics, Walt met and struck up a friendship with Willy Schaeffler, a ski-expert who was coaching at Denver University. Schaeffler was hired to advise on the ski-resort project and a site was selected at Mineral King, an area of great natural beauty in the High Sierra and near Sequoia National Park.

In 1965 the US Forest Service accepted an offer of $35 million from Walt Disney Productions to develop its plans providing agreement could be reached with the federal government for a state highway to Mineral King. Disney received a 30-year operating lease, and plans began for constructing eight ski-lifts to serve four ski bowls that would handle initially up to 7,000 skiers – eventually increasing to 20,000 – and an Alpine-style village complex for 1,500 overnight guests.

Weather studies were carried out in the valley and the surrounding 12,000-foot high peaks, and Economics Research Associates estimated that Mineral King would attract 2.5 million visitors annually by 1976, resulting in a billion-dollar addition to California's economy and creating some 2,400 jobs. By 1966, the federal government agreed to build a $25,000,000 all-weather highway, and all was now ready for the Mineral King development. But Walt had his sights set on something even more ambitious ...

Although Walt had said there would never be another Disneyland, he eventually began to consider the possibility as a way of developing ideas he was beginning to formulate for a Futuristic City development. In 1958 Economics Research Associates had undertaken a study to find a suitable location for a second Disney attraction and had recommended Florida because its weather offered the potential for all-year round operation. The following year the company had discussions with RCA about a possible joint venture in the Palm Beach area, but negotiations fell through.

A further study in 1961 narrowed down the best locations for what was being referred to as 'Disneyland East' to two areas of Florida: Ocala and Orlando. However, the company's extensive commitment to the New York World's Fair prevented further planning until 1963, when a fresh survey showed that a proposed freeway route in Central Florida made Orlando the more attractive choice.

In addition to his key personnel, Donn Tatum and Card Walker, Walt enlisted the help of William E. ('Joe') Potter, a retired general who was serving as aide to Robert Moses, president of the New York World's Fair. A visit to Central Florida confirmed the suitability of the area, but also convinced Walt that he would need to acquire sufficient land to avoid the problems he had encountered with Disneyland. The Anaheim park was surrounded, even overlooked, by other people's developments, and this was something Walt was determined would not be repeated in Florida.

Walt poses with a rogue's gallery of buccaneer heads designed for Disneyland's Pirates of the Caribbean.

Disneyland's secretary, Robert Foster, was assigned the difficult task of acquiring the necessary land. Since any hint that Walt Disney was a possible purchaser would have sent land prices soaring, the landowners involved were approached with great secrecy. Walt himself did not dare be seen in the area, and whenever Roy or other company executives went to Florida they stayed in hotels under assumed names.

Eventually 27,443 acres had been purchased for $5 million, but there was speculation in Florida about who was behind such a massive land deal. Was it the Ford Motor Company? Or Boeing? Or McDonnell-Douglas? On a visit to the Disney Studio, a reporter from the *Orlando Sentinel* asked Walt if he were buying up land in Central Florida, to which Walt replied: 'I'd rather not say.' The next day, the *Sentinel* carried the headline: 'We say it's Disney.'

The news was out. Land prices rocketed from $183 to $1,000 an acre. Statements were made by Disney and Florida's Governor Haydon Burns and a press conference was called for 15 September 1965. 'It gives me great pride,' said Governor Burns, 'to introduce to you ... the man of the decade ... who will bring a new world of entertainment, pleasure and economic development to ... Florida.'

Walt was careful to avoid committing himself before he had a chance to develop his plans. He did, however, talk of a $100 million investment and made it clear that what he had in mind was much more than another Disneyland: 'Something that is unique ... a new concept ...' An intuitive member of the press asked if it was possible that Walt was planning a city of the future. 'Well,' replied Walt, 'that's the thing that's been going around in our mind for a long time ... I would like to be a part of building a model community, a City of Tomorrow as you might say ...'

The significance of Walt's reply, however, was lost among more immediately tangible news: the fact that what was now called 'Project Florida' would require the granting of certain municipality rights by the Florida legislature so that Disney could operate in the areas of drainage, sewage disposal and fire and police protection. It was also estimated that the development would employ 4,000 people and result in a 100 per cent increase in tourism. The *Orlando Sentinel* ran a new headline: 'It's Official: This is Disney's Land!'

At the same time Walt was deeply involved with many new film projects including an animated version of Rudyard Kipling's *The Jungle Book*; a California goldrush spoof, *The Adventures of Bullwhip Griffin* starring Roddy McDowall; another chimp comedy, *Monkeys, Go Home!* with Maurice Chevalier and Dean Jones; a boy-scout saga, *Follow Me, Boys!* with Fred MacMurray, Vera Miles and Lillian Gish; an adaptation of Upton Sinclair's *The Gnome-Mobile* with Walter Brennan and 'The *Mary Poppins* Kids' Matthew Garber and Karen Dotrice; and a musical version of *The Happiest Millionaire*, the true story of Anthony J. Drexel Biddle, a Philadelphia millionaire who kept alligators, taught boxing and ran a Bible-class.

Walt (with map), Roy, Card Walker and Joe Fowler on a Disney World site meeting in Florida during 1966.

At the 1965 press conference, one of the journalists asked Walt if the Florida project was going to be called 'Disney World' and, by the following year that had, indeed, become its name. In September 1966, Walt recorded the commentary for a promotional film about Disney World and what he considered 'the most exciting – by far the most important – part of our Florida Project, in fact the very heart of everything we'll be doing in Disney World', EPCOT: an Experimental Prototype Community of Tomorrow for some 30,000 inhabitants. The same day, he shared his dream with a reporter from *The Chicago Tribune*:

> It's like the city of tomorrow ought to be ... It will be a controlled community, a showcase for American industry and research, schools, cultural and educational opportunities.
>
> In EPCOT there will be no slum areas because we won't let them develop. There's be no landowners ... People will rent homes instead of buying them ... Everyone must be employed. One of our requirements is that the people who live in EPCOT must help keep it alive.

There was also a hint of a second prototype city, 'built specifically as an experimental laboratory for administering municipal governments'. The estimated investment in Disney World was now talked about as a staggering $500 million.

Walt with his plans for EPCOT in the promotional film he made on Disney World in 1966, shortly before his death.

The following month, Walt received another of the thousands of awards made to him over the years, when the National Association of Theater Owners bestowed upon him a singular distinction, calling him The Showman of the World. But, unbeknown to any except those closest to him, he was unwell. On 2 November he was admitted to hospital for tests and X-rays showed a spot on the left lung. The lung was cancerous and was removed; but, after two weeks in hospital, Walt seemed to be recovering. Back at work, he involved himself in the many projects requiring his attention: attending a Trustee meeting for CalArts; viewing rushes of *The Gnome-Mobile*; testing a rocket-to-the-moon ride for Tomorrowland; going over sketches for an 'Audio-Animatronics' country bear band designed for Mineral King; and visiting the set where Robert Stevenson was directing *Blackbeard's Ghost*.

But his health deteriorated again and, on 30 November, he was readmitted to hospital. His 65th birthday, on 5 December, went uncelebrated but, the following week, he seemed to rally, and on the evening of 14 December he talked to Roy about more of his plans for Disney World and EPCOT. Then at 9.35 am on 15 December 1966, Walt Disney died of acute circulatory collapse.

Disneyland opened for business as usual and it was only when the American flag had been lowered in Town Square that evening that an announcer told visitors that 'Walt Disney, the creator and chief architect of Disneyland, died today'. The Disneyland band played 'When You Wish Upon a Star' ...

13. LIFE AFTER WALT

Speaking on *CBS Evening News* on 15 December 1966, Eric Sevareid said: 'It would take more time than anybody has around the daily news shops to think of the right thing to say about Walt Disney.' That, however, did not stop them from trying.

Among the thousands of eulogies hyperbole ran riot and clichés were two a penny. 'All the children in the world,' said a Parisian newspaper, 'are in mourning. And we have never felt so close to them . . .'; the *National Review* reported, 'Hollywood is holding its heart today. One of its truly great is gone . . .'. The headline writers dubbed him 'The Dream Merchant', 'The Joymaker', 'Fairy-Tale Magician', 'King of Cartoons', 'Bringer of Laughter', 'Master of Fantasy' and 'Mr Imagination'. *The Los Angeles Times* described Walt Disney as 'Aesop with a magic brush, Andersen with a color camera'.

Virtually every American newspaper cartoonist attempted a pictorial comment on the event, many of which were in gross bad taste: Mickey Mouse and friends were shown mourning their creator's death, holding wreaths, even acting as pallbearers. More appropriate tributes were to be found in the pages of *Variety* from, among others, Julie Andrews, Fess Parker, Fred MacMurray, Sam Goldwyn, Jack Warner and Richard Zanuck who said: 'No eulogy will be read or monument built to equal the memorial Walt Disney has left in the hearts and minds and imaginations of the world's peoples.'

Letters of sympathy poured into the Studio from all over the world: former President Dwight D. Eisenhower said: 'His appeal and influence were universal . . . for he touched a common chord in all humanity.' A little girl wrote: 'Mrs Disney, I would like to tell you how much we thought of Mr Disney. I thought all of his ideas were so realistic.'

The employees of Walt Disney Productions were as devastated as everyone else and nobody more so than Roy Disney. As soon as the news broke of Walt's death, Roy's office began receiving requests for a statement: What will happen to the company? Who will run it? What about the plans for Disney World? Roy asked Marty Sklar, a young man who had helped Walt with his script for the EPCOT film, to draft a statement for him:

> . . . As President and Chairman of the Board of Walt Disney Productions, I want to assure the public, our stockholders and each of our more than 4000 employees that we will continue to operate Walt Disney's company in the way he has established and guided it . . . All of the plans for the future that Walt had begun – new motion pictures, the expansion of Disneyland, television production, and our Florida and Mineral King projects – will continue to move ahead. That is the way Walt wanted it to be.

Interviewing Walt in 1963, *National Geographic* had asked, 'What happens when there is no more Walt Disney?' He replied: 'I think about that. Every day I'm throwing more responsibility to other men. Every day I'm trying to organize them more strongly.' He may indeed have anticipated what would happen to the company when he died, but for those closest to Walt, who had been used to discussing with him every aspect of the projects they were working on, it was a difficult time. Not unnaturally, they approached every problem by asking 'What would Walt have done?', and they measured their plans and ideas for the future against what could only ever be a yardstick from the past.

Before they could do anything, of course, they had first to complete the various projects that Walt had put in hand. In some areas it was business as usual: Disneyland had opened on the day Walt died because, said Roy, 'a lot of people had come from a lot of different places that day to see Disneyland'; now work pushed ahead on the new attractions Walt had planned for 1967.

On television, Walt Disney's *Wonderful World of Color* – currently reaching an estimated weekly audience of 50 million on NBC – continued with its scheduled programmes, including those in which Walt appeared, and filming was in progress on the usual assortment of comedies, westerns, animal stories and cartoons.

Writing in the company's Annual Report, shortly before his death, Walt said: 'Many people have asked, "Why don't you make another *Mary Poppins*?" Well, by nature I'm a born experimenter. To this day I don't believe in sequels. I can't follow popular cycles. I have to move on to new things . . . And so we're always looking for new ideas and new stories, hoping that somehow we'll come up with a different kind of *Mary Poppins* . . .'

Unfortunately none of the live-action movies released during 1967 were quite touched with the *Poppins* magic, although several fared better at the box-office than they did in the review columns. A case in point was *Follow Me, Boys!*, released a few weeks before Walt died. Directed by Norman Tokar, the film starred Fred MacMurray as a retired sax-player who starts a Scout troup in a typical Disney small-town of the 1930s. Judith Crist in *The New York World Journal Tribune* dismissed the movie as a 'two-hour commercial for the Boy Scouts of America' and an 'ecstatic eulogy to The Cliches of Pure-Hearted Simple-Minded Americana'.

Nevertheless, *Follow Me, Boys!* was playing to packed audiences at New York's Radio City Music Hall on the day Walt died, and did well enough on release to earn $5.5 million.

There were two other pictures with considerable style – bearing Walt's unmistakable imprint – that, because they were released in the immediate post-Disney era were underrated and, subsequently, largely forgotten.

The Adventures of Bullwhip Griffin was a pastiche of life out west in the gold rush days, and of the movies made about them. It had a spirited cast: Roddy McDowall, Suzanne Pleshette, Karl Malden, Hermione Baddeley, Cecil Kellaway and Richard Haydn (who, after problems on set, replaced British comedian Tony Hancock). There were also 'titles and things' by Ward Kimball who produced cartoon links in the style of 19th-century saloon posters.

In a different vein, *The Gnome-Mobile* was the Studio's first fantasy film since *Mary Poppins*; and like it, and the earlier *Darby O'Gill and the Little People*, the picture shows Disney special effects magic at its best. Reviewers criticized *The Gnome-Mobile* for its 'criss cross jumble of slapstick and broadly handled locomotion' and condemned it as 'shrill and bumpy'; but Matthew Garber and Karen Dotrice are at their most winsome and Walter Brennan doubly delightful as both the lumber mogul D. J. Mulrooney and Knobby, the 943-year-old gnome whose beloved California redwoods are being put to the axe.

Despite its very real charms, *The Gnome-Mobile* turned out not to be the 'different kind of *Mary Poppins*' Walt was hoping for. However, there were other possibilities. 'Perhaps,' he wrote in 1966, 'it will be a motion picture like *The Happiest Millionaire*'.

Given that *The Happiest Millionaire* received a glittering premiere at the Pantages Theater (once again to promote and benefit the California Institute of the Arts) and that it employed the talents of many of the *Mary Poppins* team, including songwriters Richard and Robert Sherman and choreographers Marc Breaux and Dee Dee Wood, it was seen by many as an attempt to repeat – or even top – a winning formula. It wasn't.

Where it failed was first in the choice of subject – the story of an outlandish millionaire with alligators in the conservatory provided only a handful of opportunities for good old Disney fun and absolutely none for fantasy – and second in the decision to make the story as a full-blown musical.

The starry cast headed by Fred MacMurray, had Greer Garson in Mrs Miniver mood, Hermione Baddeley in one of her numerous roles as put-upon Cook and Tommy Steele as the butler newly-emigrated from Ireland. The choice of Tommy Steele not only inspired the Shermans to compose some snappy song-and-dance numbers, it encouraged them and screenwriter A. J. Carothers to develop his part until the character came close to stealing the show. By the time shooting was complete, the film was running at almost three hours. The slightness of the plot scarcely justified such indulgence and several scenes were cut, the finished film running at 159 minutes.

The Happiest Millionaire performed disappointingly, perhaps because since *My Fair Lady* and *Mary Poppins* the public had been subjected to a spate of lavish film musicals including *The Sound of Music* and, in 1967 alone, *Dr Dolittle*, *Camelot* and *Thoroughly Modern Millie*. The reviews were mixed: *Variety* thought it 'outstanding', but more representative was *The New York Times*' verdict that it was 'an over-decorated, over-fluffed, over-sentimentalized endeavour to pretend the lace-curtain millionaires are – or were – every bit as folksy as the old prize-fighters and the Irish brawlers in the saloon'.

The Disney reputation was redeemed when, a few days before Christmas 1967, the Studio's first cartoon feature in four years, *The Jungle Book*, was released. It was, said the critics, 'thoroughly delightful', 'perfectly dandy' and 'Disney at his most imaginative'.

Describing the animals in Rudyard Kipling's books, literary critic Margery Fisher has written that they are 'as near to human characters as they are to animal behaviour', and it was this anthropomorphic quality that suited them so well to the Disney treatment and that was enhanced by the cast of voices, which included Sebastian Cabot as the prim and proper panther, Bagheera; George Sanders as the suave, sneering tiger, Shere Khan; Sterling Holloway as Kaa, the sibilant snake with sinus trouble; jazzman Louis Prima as the syncopated ape, King Louie; Pat O'Malley as the pompous commander of the jungle's pachyderm patrol, Colonel Hathi and comedian Phil Harris as Baloo, the happy-go-lucky bear.

Wolfgang Reitherman who, following Walt Disney's death, assumed responsibility for the Studio's animated films.

Describing the process of recording the film's soundtrack, director Woolie Reitherman said: 'When Phil Harris did the voice of Baloo, he gave it a bubble of life. We didn't coach him, just let it happen. All the rest of the characters evolved in the same way. And as they grew in dimension, the story was altered as they interacted with each other. We always leave the plot loose enough so that the personalities meshing together enhance it by their natural action.'

It was, however, to be the last occasion on which quite so much latitude in development was allowed, since experimentation proved costly. In fact, an entire sequence featuring a rhinoceros eventually seemed not to fit with the rest of the story and had to be abandoned. Running at just 78 minutes, *The Jungle Book* was one of the Studio's most economic examples of storytelling since *Dumbo*, a film with which it was compared by several critics.

The Jungle Book was a hit; released 30 years after the premiere of *Snow White and the Seven Dwarfs*, it proved the company's most successful animated feature to date, grossing almost $26 million. Its success undoubtedly guaranteed the future of Disney animated features which, with Walt's passing, had by no means been assured.

There was, Reitherman later recalled, a feeling among some of the Studio's executives that Disney had enough cartoons in its library without making more. Similar memories are held by Bill Anderson, who was Vice-President in charge of production – and, with Ron Miller, Winston Hibler, James Algar, Bill Walsh and others, part of a committee set up by Roy to deal with future film production. Not long after Walt's death, Roy Disney sent for Anderson and told him that he wanted the animation unit wound down. Nobody other than Walt, Roy argued, had ever produced a successful animated feature. Anderson pointed out that now *The Jungle Book* was nearing completion the animators were already working on the storyboards for another feature – about kidnapped kittens – that had been fully discussed with Walt before his death.

Roy, who doubtless knew that even Walt had sometimes doubted whether the animation department could survive his death, persisted with the view that once *The Jungle Book* was finished the animation unit should be disbanded. Anderson said he would do such a thing only if Roy personally communicated it to him by official memo as he needed to be able to tell the animators exactly why they were being laid off. He left Roy's office and waited: the memo never came.

Despite *The Jungle Book*'s success, revenue from motion pictures in 1967 was down by $11.5 million, and was exceeded by income from Disneyland that year by over $8 million.

It had been a record year at Disneyland with some 8 million visitors (almost as many people as were then living in New York). This dramatic increase in attendance – more than 18 per cent up on 1966 –

Mowgli and Bagheera in *The Jungle Book* (1967), described by one critic as 'simple, uncluttered, straightforward fun'.

Giving his writers Kipling's *The Jungle Book*, Walt told them: 'The first thing I want you to do is not read it!'

was largely due to the opening of the park's new Tomorrowland and Pirates of the Caribbean which, during its first six months, carried 4 million aspirant buccaneers through its waterways and caverns.

More records were broken in 1969 with the opening of The

Ay, th' dreadful duds
what pirates wore,
Were ten times frightful
than their roar.

One of the desperate swashbucklers designed by Marc Davis for the Pirates of the Caribbean, which opened in 1967.

Haunted Mansion and a new $2.3 million fleet of monorail trains. With 53 major attractions and representing a total investment of $126 million, Disneyland welcomed over 1½ million visitors in August alone; and, on one particular day that month, no fewer than 82,516 people passed through the turnstiles. Two years later Disneyland welcomed its 100 millionth visitor and created a new themed area, Bear Country, centered around the 'Audio-Animatronics' Country Bear Jamboree which had originally been designed for Mineral King.

As well as the expansion at Disneyland, Roy Disney pushed ahead with Walt's other plans. Now in his 70s, Roy wanted to see as many as possible of his younger brother's dreams realized during his own lifetime: it was, he felt, his duty to Walt. One of those dreams was the California Institute of the Arts.

When he died, Walt left CalArts 45 per cent of his estate, which, after tax, amounted to $15 million. He was not able, however, to leave anything more than the vaguest idea of how he might have built

his City of the Arts, and the Board of Trustees was left to do its best. The company agreed to buy back the land at Golden Oak Ranch that Disney had donated, and the money was used to purchase a larger site in Valencia, although it was to be several more years before the Institute was officially opened.

Some progress was made on the Mineral King project when, in 1967, the California Highway Commission approved seven-year

Roy Disney with some of the characters made famous by his brother.

Walt Disney World was to boast an advanced monorail system that would pass right inside the Contemporary Hotel.

A sketch by Herb Ryman for Liberty Square, a themed area designed as a home for the Hall of Presidents attraction.

In 1968, work began on water control and conservation and the organizing of plans for a 'total integrated communications system' that would eventually handle everything from telephones and security monitoring to computerized hotel bookings.

The same year, Walt Disney was awarded two posthumous honours: a gold medal presented by Congress to Lilly Disney in recognition of Walt's 'distinguished public service and outstanding contributions to the United States and to the world'; and an official commemorative postage stamp, which depicted Walt's portrait surrounded by children from the Small World show, which was now one of Disneyland's most popular attractions.

The *Disney on Parade* stage show was seen by more than two million people in 27 American cities.

financing for road construction. The following year, the Department of the Interior (responsible for the administration of Sequoia National Park) approved the routing for the road and the development was planned to be open by winter 1973. Planning came to a halt, however, when in 1969 a conservationist group sought an injunction to prevent the government issuing permits to construct and operate the necessary facilities. It was the beginning of 10 years of litigation (to which Disney was not a party) that eventually resulted in Mineral King becoming part of Sequoia National Park and Disney abandoning its plans.

The company had better fortune with Project Florida. Walt had referred to it simply as 'Disney World'; but Roy, determined that it should be remembered as a personal, rather than merely a corporate, achievement, decided to call it 'Walt Disney World'.

On 12 May 1967, Florida's Governor Claude Kirk signed the legislation required for Walt Disney Productions to operate its new venture, and Roy announced plans for what was called 'Phase One: The Entertainment Vacation Complex'. Scheduled for opening in 1971, this was to provide the core of what quickly became known as a 'Vacation Kingdom' containing a 'new Disneyland', a transportation system and resort-hotels. Plans for EPCOT were put in abeyance.

On site in Florida, aerial mapping and soil analysis were being carried out to determine the exact location of the 'new Disneyland' and subsequent themed areas; while WED's Vice-Presidents Dick Irvine and John Hench were heading the team that was creating the plans, layouts and models for Walt Disney World's buildings and the attractions for the Magic Kingdom, several of which – such as a rollercoaster dark-ride, Space Mountain – were entirely new. Among other projects that would shortly be under construction was an 'Audio-Animatronics' show, featuring all the American presidents, based on Walt's 'One Nation Under God' concept originally planned for Disneyland.

Elsa Lanchester and Peter Ustinov in *Blackbeard's Ghost*, about an 18th-century pirate conjured into the 20th century.

Other Disney film productions for cinema and television were cast very much in the traditional mould. There were animal movies: *Charlie the Lonesome Cougar* (1967), *Rascal* (1969), *King of the Grizzlies* (1970) and *Napoleon and Samantha* (1971); and pioneering, homesteading, western adventures such as *Smith!* (1969), *The Wild Country* (1971), *Scandalous John* (1971) and *One Little Indian* (1973).

There were also more examples of the well-established Disney format for live-action cartoons: *Never a Dull Moment* (1968) with Dick Van Dyke as an actor who plays a gangster getting involved with a gang of real hoods led by Edward G. Robinson; *The Boatniks* (1970) with Phil Silvers, Robert Morse, Stefanie Powers and lots of messing about in boats; and *$1,000,000 Duck* (1971), once again starring the long-suffering Dean Jones who, the following year, appeared in another domestic comedy, *Snowball Express* about an accountant who tries to run a ski-resort in the Rockies.

Fred MacMurray returned to Disney in 1973 in a small-town fantasy, *Charley and the Angel*, about an angelic ambassador – played by Disney regular Harry Morgan – who transforms life for the miserable MacMurray.

Charley and the Angel featured the Studio's prolific juvenile lead, Kurt Russell, who also starred in *The Barefoot Executive* (1971) – along with yet another of those Disney chimpanzees – and a series of college-kid inventor pictures, beginning with *The Computer Wore Tennis Shoes* (1970) and followed by *Now You See Him, Now You Don't* (1972) and *The Strongest Man in the World* (1973).

The Computer Wore Tennis Shoes was made for less than a million dollars but grossed, on its domestic release alone, over $5,500,000. It was, said *Variety*, 'delightful Disney fare', although the reviewer saved most of its praise for the 'wide-spectrum humour' of the supporting programme: a 22-minute, largely animated short, *It's Tough to be a Bird*, directed with zany flair by Ward Kimball.

In terms of the company Walt left behind him, income was showing signs of recovering, with profits up by $2 million to over $13 million. Roy Disney had also taken what he called 'a further step in preparing our organization to better handle our rather widespread and fast-moving business'. While remaining Chairman of the Board and Chief Executive Officer, he had relinquished the post of President. One of the company's former Vice-Presidents, Donn Tatum, moved up to the Presidency, and Card Walker was appointed to the newly-created post of Executive Vice-President.

With so much major building work being planned, an Engineering and Construction Division was set up in the charge of Joe Fowler; and Ron Miller was made Executive Producer in charge of all the Studio's motion picture and television products.

While Ron Miller began planning the future programme, the company was releasing the last of the films instigated by his late father-in-law. Produced by Bill Walsh and directed by Robert Stevenson, *Blackbeard's Ghost* (1968) featured Disney regulars Dean Jones, Suzanne Pleshette and Elsa Lanchester, although the film was stolen from under all their noses by some cunning special effects and what one reviewer called Peter Ustinov's 'Falstaffian fairy godfather'.

The following year, Walsh and Stevenson had another hit (and Dean Jones was again upstaged – this time by a car) when the Studio released *The Love Bug*, in which the Volkswagen with a mind of its own not only defeated David Tomlinson's dastardly screen villain but also won the hearts of even the most cynical critics. *The Love Bug* became the year's top box-office hit in America and the Studio's second largest grossing picture after *Mary Poppins*, with a total revenue of $33,600,000. Herbie became a 'star' and was featured, along with Mickey Mouse, Dumbo and Alice in Wonderland in a touring $2 million spectacular entitled *Disney on Parade*. In a subsequent show, Herbie returned in company with a shocking-pink 'girl-sized' VW called Gloria; and, in the movies, went on to make a string of sequels: *Herbie Rides Again* (1974), *Herbie Goes to Monte Carlo* (1977) and *Herbie Goes Bananas* (1980).

M. C. Bird, the feathered anti-hero of the Academy Award-winning short *It's Tough to be a Bird* (1969).

In addition to conventional animation, *It's Tough to be a Bird* used live-action footage and montage techniques of the kind later made popular by *Monty Python's Flying Circus*. A more traditional approach, however, was adopted for the Studio's next feature-length cartoon, *The Aristocats*.

Based on a story by Tom McGowan and Tom Rowe, *The Aristocats* (1970) was pre-planned with meticulous care in order to avoid costly edits of the kind made to *The Jungle Book*, which could have easily reopened discussions on the merits of making new Disney animated features.

As a result, *The Aristocats* is a safe, unadventurous movie, which suffers from economies in production that Walt might well have resisted. The story of the avaricious butler who cat-naps the beautiful Duchess and her three kittens when he learns they are to be the

Phil Harris, who voiced *The Jungle Book*'s Baloo, also provided the voice of Thomas O'Malley the alley cat in *The Aristocats*, here courting Eva Gabor's upper-class feline, Duchess.

inheritors of his mistress' estate was directed by Woolie Reitherman, who also co-produced the picture with Winston Hibler.

'I think,' said Reitherman at the time, 'that a little of Walt rubbed off on all of us' and *The Aristocats* is as good an example as any of the Studio's attempts to create something in the way it was thought Walt would have done. With Ken Anderson as production designer and veteran animators Milt Kahl, Ollie Johnston, Frank Thomas, John Lounsbery, Hal King and Eric Larson working on the picture, it wasn't far off target and certainly bore a passable likeness to what audiences expected of a Disney cartoon.

The songs were by *The Jungle Book*'s composers Terry Gilkyson and the Shermans, although they proved a lot less memorable, the film's real hit being Floyd Huddleston and Al Rinker's jazz number 'Ev'rybody Wants to be a Cat' performed, *à la* King Louie, by a hip feline called Scat Cat (voiced by Scatman Crothers) and a band of ethnic stereotyped cats. Other voices included Phil Harris, Eva Gabor, Sterling Holloway, Hermione Baddeley, Pat Buttram and George Lindsey as well as tv personalities Roddy Maude-Roxby, Nancy Kulp, Monica Evans and Carole Shelley. The title song was sung by Maurice Chevalier, who came out of retirement to pay tribute to Walt Disney.

The Aristocats had taken four years to make and cost $4 million and when it opened, at Christmas 1970, *Variety* praised its 'outstanding animation' while criticizing the story as 'a series of well-plotted vignettes, bracketed by establishing sequences which suggest but don't deliver a sturdy plot line, and finished by a limp run-out'. Nevertheless, the magazine predicted *The Aristocats* would have 'very good potential with the holiday trade'. And, despite some critical reviews, the picture achieved a domestic gross of $10.1 million and a further $16 million on its first release overseas. If nothing else, its success removed all further doubt about the future of Disney animation; an animation apprenticeship programme was established, and it was soon announced that work was now underway on a new picture, based on the legends of Robin Hood.

There was more animation the following year with a funny cartoon sequence, directed by Ward Kimball for what was the Studio's most costly movie to date, *Bedknobs and Broomsticks*. Quickly dubbed 'Mary Poppins Mark II', it was based – very loosely – on a children's book by British writer Mary Norton, which Walt had bought long before the *Poppins* books and which he considered making instead of *Mary Poppins* when he ran into difficulties with P. L. Travers.

Adapted for the screen by Bill Walsh and Don da Gradi, *Bedknobs and Broomsticks* was made into a wartime musical comedy-drama with a Nazi invasion of England being thwarted by amateur witchcraft and an insular spinster being humanized by a trio of cockney evacuees. With Robert Stevenson as director, Richard and Robert Sherman responsible for the words and music, comparisons with *Mary Poppins* were inevitable, even though few people realized that the film contained sequences and songs originally planned for the 1964 blockbuster.

Not surprisingly, Julie Andrews had been considered for the role of trainee witch, Eglantine Price, as had Lynn Redgrave, Leslie Caron and Judy Carne. The part finally went to Angela Lansbury, who had recently enjoyed a Broadway hit as *Mame*. Ron Moody was spoken of for the film's male lead but was eventually replaced by David Tomlinson, thereby reinforcing the *Mary Poppins* connection.

In an attempt to stop *Bedknobs and Broomsticks* reaching the tedious length of its disastrous predecessor, *The Happiest Millionaire*, the picture was ruthlessly edited – so much so that Roddy McDowall's performance, as an unctuous curate after Miss Lansbury's hand, was largely left on the cutting-room floor. Also lost were several key songs and most of the characters' motivation. It is perhaps surprising, therefore, that what remained was as good as it was.

Reviews of what the Disney publicity men called a 'bewitching, bedazzling, magical musical!', were mixed; *Films Illustrated* dismissed it as 'a computer-built entertainment designed to pick up where *Mary Poppins* wisely left off'. Others, like John Russell Taylor in *The Times* went so far as to say that 'the same as before is better than before'. One critic hazarded that *Bedknobs and Broomsticks*

Bedknobs and Broomsticks (1971): David Tomlinson, Angela Lansbury and kids 'bobbing along on the bottom of the beautiful briny sea'.

would 'take a mint of money'. On its initial release, it in fact took $17,500,000, a respectable sum had the film not cost almost $20 million. Whatever its similarities to *Mary Poppins*, they stopped short at the box-office.

Despite the disappointing returns from *Bedknobs*, film revenue was up by $2 million and Walt Disney Productions had profits of almost $27 million – more than twice what they were in the year of Walt's death. It was the most successful year in the company's history, but even greater success was in store with the opening, in October 1971, of Walt Disney World.

During the preceding five years, preparations had been forging ahead for what was to become the world's largest private building venture. Artists and technicians were working on scale replicas of Captain Nemo's *The Nautilus* and creating the fish, mermaids and monsters that would be seen by travellers on the submarines; façades were designed for African bazaars, colonial mansions, western saloons and turn-of-the-century dime stores. 'Audio-Animatronics' elephants, presidents and singing bears, together with an orchestra of 85 cartoon characters under the baton of Mickey Mouse, were being constructed, costumed and wired-up.

On site, a 4000-strong work force dredged sand from the natural Bay Lake to make attractive white beaches, while on the 107-acre area chosen for the Magic Kingdom, waterways were cut and tropical jungles created. In one 16-hour day, some 2000 truck-loads of earth were moved: just a fraction of the 7 million cubic yards that were shifted during construction.

A 15th-century castle, 176 feet high, began to rise at the heart of the Magic Kingdom, while elsewhere thousands of trees and plants were being grown, including cartoon-shaped topiary animals; an 18-hole golf course was being contoured and grassed; a 4.7 mile four-lane road was being built and the steel superstructures for the Contemporary Resort Hotel were being erected and fitted with their 1057 modular room units. A 7,500-acre conservation area was set aside for the protection of natural beauty and wildlife and an island sanctuary was created in Bay Lake, a short boat ride from the Magic Kingdom.

After 52 months of construction work, and representing an investment of $400 million, Walt Disney World opened on schedule on 1 October 1971. The world's press scrambled to report on the wonders. Some were hypercritical: Joseph Morgenstern, in a *Newsweek* article entitled 'What Hath Disney Wrought!', called the place 'a programed paradise' which demonstrated America's 'manifest destiny to become Disneyland to the world'.

Other visitors, however, were impressed by the technology and captivated by the magic: 'Incredible,' raved Wayne Warga of *The Los Angeles Times*, 'Absolutely incredible. It seems to go on forever, a limitless land of fantasy and sport.' Architect, Robert Venturi was quoted, in *The New York Times Magazine*, as saying: 'Disney World is nearer to what people really want than anything architects have ever given them ... It's a symbolic American utopia.'

The fact that the public flocked to Walt Disney World in such numbers seemed to endorse that view: initial estimates in 1965 had been for annual attendance figures of 6.8 million, but that figure was subsequently revised first to 8 and then 10 million. Within its first year, the Vacation Kingdom welcomed 10,712,991 visitors and grossed over $139 million in revenue. 'I believe our company,' wrote Roy Disney in his Annual Report, 'is in excellent financial condition and has a long, productive and profitable period ahead.'

For Roy, however, time was limited. In November 1971 he attended the opening of the California Institute of the Arts and a month later, on 20 December, died of a cerebral haemorrhage. He was 78 years old.

Writing to Roy's widow, Edna, President Richard M. Nixon paid tribute to 'Roy's tremendous and enduring contributions to our society' and his 'long and rewarding life'. The tributes and obituaries to Roy fill only one volume compared with the 20 devoted to his brother, but that was how he would have wanted it: at the opening of Walt Disney World he had conspicuously avoided personal publicity; asked why, he had simply answered: 'Let this be Walt's day . . .'

In a sense, Roy probably felt his work was done but had he lived another year he would have seen Walt Disney Productions total income increase by 87.2 per cent to $328,830,000 and its profits rise $13.5 million to $40,293,000. Donn Tatum, who succeeded Roy as Chairman of the Board, told Disney shareholders:

It is now clear, in the sharpest of focus, that the new opportunities, which had been foreseen to stem from the accomplishment of the goals which have been attained this year, do now exist ... With confidence and optimism, leavened by the proper amount of prudence, there is no reason to doubt that we can and will proceed to new levels of achievement.

A country-and-western minstrel tells the legend of *Robin Hood* 'like it is . . . or was . . . or whatever!'

The following year, more than $63 million-worth of developments were begun in Walt Disney World, and these helped increase attendances by over 8 per cent and income by 21 per cent. Those who doubted the company would survive Walt's death had been confounded: gross revenue, since 1966, had increased 230 per cent to more than $385 million.

The company's golden anniversary was celebrated with television specials; a retrospective film festival at New York's Lincoln Center; the opening of The Walt Disney Story exhibit in Disneyland and Walt Disney World; the publication of a lavishly illustrated art book on the Studio; and a major programme of film releases and reissues. *Mary Poppins* returned and grossed another $9 million; *That Darn Cat, Fantasia* and *The Sword in the Stone* were also reprised, but the major event of the year was the release of what was billed as the Studio's 'most ambitious cartoon feature ever' – *Robin Hood*.

The story was written by Larry Clemmons, based on 'character and story conceptions' by Ken Anderson that translated the heroes and villains of the old legends into animals. Both men received credit on posters and press advertisements, along with director Woolie Reitherman and animators Milt Kahl, Ollie Johnston, Frank Thomas and John Lounsbery. While such acknowledgements marked a significant departure from Disney tradition, *Robin Hood* turned out to be an extremely traditional cartoon. It was, noted *Variety*, 'a return to a phantasmagoria of sight gags of the type that helped make the late producer famous as a master of animation production'.

Other critics pointed out that the film was also something of a return to *The Jungle Book* in that several of the animals were familiar: a Baloo-type bear for Little John (with a Baloo-type vocal performance from Phil Harris); a snake for Prince John's adviser, Sir

Hiss, with a penchant for hypnosis recalling the insidious Kaa; an elephant or two from Colonel Hathi's dawn patrol and a couple of vultures, which, in addition to *The Jungle Book* had appeared in *Bedknobs and Broomsticks*. There were even sequences that were nothing more than reworked animation cycles from not just *The Jungle Book* but also *The Aristocats* and even *Snow White and the Seven Dwarfs*.

The voices included, in addition to Phil Harris, Brian Bedford as Robin Hood (a part originally intended for Tommy Steele); Pat Buttram as a Sheriff of Nottingham in wolf's clothing; Andy Devine as Friar Tuck, a badger; Roger Miller as Alan-a-Dale, a cockerel balladeer; Terry-Thomas as the gap-toothed Sir Hiss; and Peter Ustinov as Prince John, a scrawny lion with a mother fixation.

'The voices,' wrote Alexander Walker, 'come over with such a rich rasp of wit and inventiveness that the mere drawings which accompany them seem too often uninspired – an example of how economy and mass production has brought the once incomparable draughtsmanship of the Disney studios down to the level of the merely competent.'

Some critics clearly enjoyed the film – *The New York Daily News* gave it a four-star rating – but its reception, rather like *The Aristocats*, was luke-warm to cold, and there were those who found Disney animation too safe and predictable when compared with the innovative style of Ralph Bakshi's X-rated cartoons *Fritz the Cat* and *Heavy Traffic*. At the box office, however, the film did exceptionally good business, taking more than $260,000 at New York's Radio City Music Hall during the Thanksgiving holiday week. In Britain alone, *Robin Hood* took $2,600,000, an all-time record for an animated film, and by 1974 the picture had a domestic gross of $9.5 million.

As Walt Disney Productions began its 51st year in the entertainment business, the United States was experiencing difficult times: the aftermath of the Watergate scandal had brought about a crisis of confidence in government, which coupled with spiralling inflation and anxiety over the availability of gasoline, left many industries depressed. Although Disney was not exempt from these problems, it nevertheless enjoyed its seventh consecutive year with record revenues.

With a gross income of almost $430 million, Donn Tatum and Card Walker could announce with some confidence: 'We are stronger financially, creatively and organizationally than we have ever been . . . We shall continue to progress and will emerge from the current period uniquely prepared for further success in the years ahead'. Although it was now almost eight years since Walt's death, the company had remained true to his philosophy and, perhaps, remembered one of his many sayings: 'Recession doesn't deserve the right to exist. There are just too many things to be done . . . to be bogged down by temporary economic dislocations.'

But the recession of 1974 was nothing compared with the ups and downs of the decade that lay ahead . . .

A trio of villains from *Robin Hood* (1973); the inept Prince John, his slithery servant, Sir Hiss, and the Sheriff of Nottingham.

14. WALTOPIA INC

'To those who have followed the progress of Walt Disney Productions through the decades,' said Card Walker, '1975 will be remembered with satisfaction as a milestone in our company's history.'

Disney revenue stood at a new all-time high of $520,006,000; Disneyland celebrated its 20th anniversary with its total number of visitors topping 145 million, and Phase 1 of Walt Disney World was completed just 10 years after Walt and Roy had announced their plans at a press conference in Florida. Most importantly, it was the year in which Card Walker, Donn Tatum and their colleagues announced their intention to proceed with Walt's Experimental Prototype Community of Tomorrow.

EPCOT had presented the Disney management with something of a headache. Walt's original announcement of the project had been unequivocal: 'A community of tomorrow that will never be completed . . . a living blueprint of the future, where people actually live a life they can't find anywhere else today.' The problem was he hadn't lived long enough to explain how that was to be achieved and, apart from a few vague sketches by Walt – some of them doodled on paper napkins from the studio commissary – the company had little to work on.

One thing became clear early on, EPCOT would not literally be a city of the future. 'We believe,' Card Walker told shareholders, 'that in order to attain Walt Disney's goals for EPCOT, we must avoid building a huge, traditional "bricks and mortar" community which might possibly become obsolete, in EPCOT terms, as soon as it is completed. We believe we must develop a community system oriented to the communication of new ideas, rather than serving the day-to-day needs of a limited number of permanent residents.'

The original EPCOT artwork had shown a vast radial city with towering buildings; the revised concepts for an 'EPCOT Future World Theme Center', comprising a series of pavilions devoted to 'Community', 'Science and Technology' and 'Communications and

Advance brochure on EPCOT Center with evocative artwork by Herb Ryman showing the dominant structure of Spaceship Earth.

the Arts', were now shown centred upon not a real city, but a 'World City Model', representing a 'community of the future in the process of growth and adaptation'.

In addition to the EPCOT developments, Disney was researching two other recreation attractions: an outdoor resort at Independence Lake in Northern California to accommodate some of the plans that had been devised for the frustrated project at Mineral King; and an Oriental Disneyland for Tokyo Bay in Japan.

At the two Magic Kingdoms already in existence, new entertainments were staged – such as a spectacular parade marking the American Bicentennial in 1975 – and several new attractions were opened, among them Space Mountain and Big Thunder Mountain Railroad, which, during its first six weeks of operation at Disneyland, carried half a million visitors.

Walt Disney World increased its recreation facilities with the opening in 1976 of River Country: a six-acre attraction themed around the rustic American institution, the ol' swimmin' hole; and, that year, the theme parks brought in more than three times what was being earned by films.

'I have every confidence,' Walt once said, 'that so long as our film presentations toughen the minds and warm the heart with the best the motion picture industry can offer in art and craftsmanship and

Scale model of EPCOT built by WED Imagineering shows Future World with Spaceship Earth and, beyond, World Showcase.

Highly detailed backgrounds and meticulous attention to scale contributed to *The Rescuers'* strong visual appeal.

The *Rescuers* was produced by Woolie Reitherman and co-directed with John Lounsbery and Art Stevens. Directing animators on the picture were Ollie Johnston, Frank Thomas and Milt Kahl – who distinguished this, his last film before retirement, with his brilliant animation of the comic villainess Madame Medusa (portrayed with great vocal relish by Geraldine Page). The fourth member of the team was a talented newcomer, Don Bluth, who had first worked at Disney in 1958, as an inbetweener to John Lounsbery on *Sleeping Beauty* and, after several years with the Filmation studio, returned, in 1971, to work on *Robin Hood*.

'A new classic of Disney animation,' wrote a critic of *The Rescuers*. 'The best work by Disney animators in many years.'

genuine human warmth, so long may we expect prosperous support and a long life.'

By the mid-1970s – despite annual increases in film revenue – some people in the movie industry were beginning to ask how long Disney could go on expecting that prosperous support to continue. There were indications of that as early as 1974, when *The Island at the Top of the World* – a Jules Vernesque adventure about a lost civilization of Vikings at the North Pole – grossed only $10 million on its domestic release, after being four years in development.

Despite attracting an impressive line-up of talent – such as James Garner, Elliott Gould, David Niven, Helen Hayes, Bette Davis, Eddie Albert, Leo McKern and Christopher Lee – the tenor of the movies in which they starred appeared to have changed little in a decade. There was the usual budget of adventures with kids and/or animals: *Ride a Wild Pony* (1975); *No Deposit, No Return* (1976), *The Littlest Horse Thieves* (1977) and *Treasure of Matecumbe* (1976), which, with a gross of little more than $4 million, earned less than half what was taken by a re-issue of *Snow White and the Seven Dwarfs*.

To many observers it seemed that the Studio was at its most predictable with its comedies. Spoof westerns like the two 'Apple Dumpling Gang' movies (1975 and 1979) and *Hot Lead and Cold Feet* (1978), while relatively successful, were seen as blatantly chasing the success of Mel Brooks' 1974 hit, *Blazing Saddles*; and the public appeared to be losing its appetite for the Disney-style in whacky comedy typified by movies such as *One of Our Dinosaurs is Missing* (1975); a sequel to *The Shaggy Dog*, entitled *The Shaggy D.A.* (1976) with Dean Jones as a grown-up version of the hairy character played by Tommy Kirk in 1959; *Gus* (1976), about a mule that joins a football team; and *Freaky Friday* (1977), a better-than-average movie based on a *Vice-Versa*-type story about a harassed mother and a wild teenager who swap bodies for a day.

By 1977, an already unsatisfactory situation seemed to be getting worse with a fall in film revenue of more than a million dollars.

Then came an appropriately-named animated feature *The Rescuers*, which grossed $16,300,000 on its first domestic run. Loosely based on Margery Sharp's charming series of books, *The Rescuers* brought together the talents of Disney's Old Guard writers and animators with some of the newer men who had been attracted to the Studio through its training programme.

The charm of *The Rescuers* was in its story, which captured the delightful personalities of the feminine Miss Bianca and her heroic friend Bernard (perfectly voiced by Eva Gabor and Bob Newhart) and their adventure in rescuing an orphan girl from the evil clutches of Medusa. The plot was entirely the work of a talented group which included such veterans as Larry Clemmons, Ken Anderson, Vance Gerry and Frank Thomas, as well as writers Ted Berman, Dave Michener and Burny Mattinson.

The Rescuers proved phenomenally successful: with domestic earnings of $16.3 million and a record foreign take of $31.2 million. As a result, Disney film revenues rose by 29 per cent to a new high of $152,135,000.

Animation was also a feature of the 1977 live-action musical *Pete's Dragon*, the story of another of Disney's winsome orphans (Sean Marshall) and Elliott, a huge green dragon with pink wings, created by Ken Anderson and animated under the direction of Don Bluth.

Describing the lack-lustre *Pete's Dragon* in one of its memorable headlines, *Variety* declared: 'Dragon puts zip into draggin' tale.'

Preliminary artwork for *The Black Hole*, a project surrounded by secrecy 'to rival anything the Pentagon could design'.

The live cast, headed by Helen Reddy, Jim Dale, Mickey Rooney, Red Buttons and Shelley Winters, worked hard at what was at times an implausible overly-sentimental story, but the plaudits undoubtedly went to Elliott. 'He's gorgeous,' wrote *Time*'s reviewer 'in a ghastly sort of way ...'; and Tom Hutchinson in the *Sunday Telegraph* called him 'as sly, ingratiating and endearing a monster as was ever dreamed up by Disney in the golden days'.

The following year there was more cause for looking back to Disney's 'golden days' when Mickey Mouse celebrated his 50th birthday with parades and parties in Disneyland and Walt Disney World's Magic Kingdom and a 90-minute all-star tv special on NBC. The Mouse also became the first animated figure to be given a star on Hollywood Boulevard's Walk of Fame.

Commenting on Mickey's birthday, Card Walker remarked that 'clearly Mickey is fifty years *young*, with all the vigor he has always enjoyed. And there could be no better present for him than the solid proof ... that Walt Disney Productions continues to maintain the same kind of youthful vigor ... We have already begun to raise the curtain on a new generation of Disney entertainment.'

Certainly there was a need for a new type of Disney entertainment. Although the Studio's traditional pictures were doing good business in Europe, they were far less successful in America. Whereas in 1974 foreign film revenues had been approximately half domestic earnings, by 1979 they exceeded them by almost $8 million.

The expectations of young American movie-goers had dramatically changed with the release, in 1977, of George Lucas' *Star Wars* and Steven Spielberg's *Close Encounters of the Third Kind*. One of the most important things about *Star Wars* was 20th Century-Fox's decision to accept the PG (Parental Guidance) rating given the picture rather than make the kind of edits that would have ensured it of a G (General) rating. Not only did the PG label win *Star Wars* a far greater family audience, it made the film acceptable to teenagers and particularly attractive to those youngsters who thought G-rated films beneath them.

At Disney, however, every film since the rating system had been introduced had been made with a view to being rated G. Now the question that was being asked was could – or would – Disney ever produce a PG picture? There were those who argued it would break faith with Walt's well-known views about family entertainment and could result in adverse publicity that might affect other Disney enterprises; others held that Walt, had he been alive, would have had the courage to adapt to the trends within the industry.

Disney management perhaps recalled that Walt had once said: 'The motion picture has long been a chance-taking business. This doesn't mean timidity in planning an operation.' At any rate, in 1976 (before the release of *Star Wars*) it had announced it was going to make its 'most ambitious motion picture': a science-fiction picture entitled *Space Station One*, scheduled for Christmas 1978. A year later the film was being called *Space Probe* and had been rescheduled for 1979. It eventually went into production towards the end of 1978 with a new title, *The Black Hole*, and a record budget of $17 million.

Apart from a few fantasy films about flying cars, disappearing college kids and the like, Disney had very little experience in the science-fiction genre and none in making space pictures. It had made *Escape to Witch Mountain* (1975) about alien children with strange powers and was planning two sci-fi comedies – *The Cat from Outer Space* (1978) and *Unidentified Flying Oddball* (1979) – but *The Black Hole* was in an altogether different league.

Under the direction of Gary Nelson, the picture began a 14-month filming schedule with an amazingly starry cast: Maximilian Schell, Anthony Perkins, Robert Forster, Joseph Bottoms, Yvette Mimieux and Ernest Borgnine. In addition to the acting talent, *The Black Hole* boasted an impressive line-up of technicians, including four Oscarwinners: production designer Peter Ellenshaw, Eustace Lycett, Art Cruickshank and Danny Lee. In some scenes as many as 12 different photographic processes would be combined on screen at one time, through the use of a computerized camera system, ACES (Automated Camera Effects System), pioneered specially for *The Black Hole*.

'Nearly everything about this mammoth undertaking,' said the Studio's publicity 'sets it apart from our efforts of the past.' For this reason, extreme secrecy was adopted with security precautions for those entering and leaving sets. So secret was the project that no one – not even the stars – knew how the picture would end: various possible concluding scenes were shot, and the final choice was made shortly before the film's premiere in December 1979.

The Black Hole, announced the film posters, is 'A Journey that Begins Where Everything Ends'; but it had the misfortune to begin in the same year as *Alien* and the week after *Star Trek – The Movie*. Unlike *Star Trek*, Disney's space odyssey had been rated PG (and given an A certificate in Britain), a fact that left several commentators unimpressed and prompted one writer to suggest that the space travellers might simply find Mickey Mouse waiting for them inside the black hole. The actual conclusion to the film, was for most audiences, baffling and disappointing, being a stylized vision of heaven and hell *à la* finale to *Fantasia*.

Despite the publicity copy-line '$20,000,000 to make, and like no other Disney film ever made', there were those who pointed to similarities with Disney's *20,000 Leagues Under the Sea*, and with *Star Wars*. Like the Lucas movie, *The Black Hole* had two comic robots, V.I.N.CENT and Old Bob (humorously voiced by Roddy McDowall and Slim Pickens), and an army of plastic-armoured stormtroopers.

Some critics found words of praise for the film: '*The Black Hole*,' said one, was 'light years ahead of its rivals.' But others were less complimentary, one suggesting that the first appearance of the black hole on the computer-screen was really 'a great yawn in outer space, which due to the bending of time, the computer has picked up from the audience 95 minutes later'.

A plethora of merchandise – books, jigsaws, watches, sneakers, lunch-boxes and toiletries (or 'Black Hole Decontamination Kits') – was produced, but the film did poor business at the box-office. Foreign movie revenues were only marginally down on 1978 takings, but domestic earnings dropped $20 million, and total film revenues were now less than a quarter of the sum earned by the recreation division.

The Black Hole didn't even have the consolation of winning any awards: it was nominated for Oscars in two categories, but at the Academy Awards ceremony in 1980 it lost out to *Apocalypse Now* for Best Cinematography and to *Alien* for Best Visual Effects.

The Black Hole's production designer, Peter Ellenshaw, who had earlier worked on *Mary Poppins* and other pictures.

Animator Andy Gaskill (left) with three artists who, in 1979, quit the studio: John Pomeroy, Don Bluth and Gary Goldman.

Troubles seldom come singly, and 1979 was a bad year for Disney. On 13 September three leading figures from the Studio's group of younger animators – Don Bluth, Gary Goldman and John Pomeroy – handed in their notice. The following day, 11 other animators joined them. Don Bluth had been growing increasingly discontented since he had seen the results of the animation unit's work on *Robin Hood*. To him and some of his colleagues, it seemed that the new Disney films lacked the commitment to quality and attention to detail that had previously been hallmarks of Disney animation. More importantly, in Bluth's view, *Robin Hood* lacked 'soul'.

As a reaction, Bluth and some of his colleagues began producing a film of their own, financed from their savings and animated in their spare time. Despite having a story too-closely modelled on *The Aristocats*, Bluth's short, *Banjo the Woodpile Cat*, attempted to reinstate some of the qualities the young animators felt were missing from the productions on which they were currently working, such as *Winnie the Pooh and Tigger Too*, *The Small One* and *The Fox and the Hound*. *Banjo* took seven years to complete and when Disney showed no particular interest in the project, it was screened for other producers. The result was that Bluth was offered $6.5 million to direct his own feature and with a subject already in mind – Robert C. O'Brien's book *Mrs Frisby and the Rats of NIMH* – he and his associates quit Disney to go it alone.

Thus it was that in 1979 – with *The Fox and the Hound* part-completed – the Studio suddenly found itself with an animation department that had been utterly decimated.

The following year, Walt Disney Productions attempted to put a brave face on what had been a difficult period. For the 13th consecutive year, total revenues and profits were up and the beginnings of a gentle transference of power was to be seen. In June, the Board of Directors approved a restructuring of management 'to maximize future potential and to allow for executive growth and experience to insure an orderly transfer of responsibility to future management'.

Card Walker, while retaining the title Chief Executive Officer, relinquished the role of President to Ron Miller and became Chairman instead. Former Chairman, Donn Tatum, now headed up an Executive Committee (composed of himself, Walker and Miller).

Tom Wilhite, a 27-year-old former publicity executive with the Studio, was promoted to Vice-President of Creative Affairs, and began assembling what was optimistically referred to as 'the freshest and most diverse line-up of films in the company's history'.

The aim of the motion picture unit was to broaden the Studio's appeal 'to reach a greater share of the young adult market', and the first of its new releases in 1980, *Midnight Madness*, was the second Disney picture to receive a PG rating.

Over the next two years an assortment of films emerged, ranging from another Love Bug movie, *Herbie Goes Bananas*, and *Amy*, a sentimental film about a deaf girl, to *The Devil and Max Devlin*, a PG-rated update on the Faust legend with Elliott Gould making

To PG or not to PG ... Disney joined the ratings game in 1980 with the release of the adult comedy *Midnight Madness*.

dubious deals with a Satanic henchman, played by Bill Cosby. There was also *Condorman*, an inept comedy about a comic-book artist who gets involved with spies and the CIA, and two pictures co-produced with Paramount, the first of which was *Popeye*, an ill-begotten attempt to make a live-action musical based on the famous cartoon anti-hero, with Robin Williams as Popeye and Shelley Duvall as Olive Oyl.

Films with real actors playing cartoon characters was nothing new – a long and successful series featuring Blondie and Dagwood had begun in 1938, and the first *Superman* film had been released in 1978 – but director Robert Altman aimed for what *The New Yorker* called 'the two-dimensional look and the jumbled congested Krazy Kat feeling of some of the early strips'. Despite a few good songs and quantities of spinach, *Popeye* was a less than successful experiment.

The second Paramount co-production, *Dragonslayer*, possessed two formidable attractions: one was the magnificent dragon (built by George Lucas' effects company, Industrial Light and Magic and the Disney Studio); the other was Sir Ralph Richardson's performance as Ulric, the eccentric sorcerer. Although *Dragonslayer* had an excellent score by Alex North and breathtaking photography by Derek Vanlint, it suffered from competing with two other sword-and-sorcery epics, *Excalibur* and *Conan the Barbarian*, and Spielberg's *Raiders of the Lost Ark*.

Disney's least dignified disaster was *The Watcher in the Woods*, which opened at the Ziegfeld Theater in New York at Easter 1980 and was immediately assaulted by the critics who were particularly harsh about the ending which, allegedly, featured an alien manifesting itself as 'a giant seaweed-covered lobster'. Disney withdrew *Watcher* and, at a cost of £375,000, reshot the final scenes at Britain's Pinewood Studios. Despite the additional effort and expense, *The Watcher in the Woods* was indifferently received and marketed in Britain with the slogan: 'It is not a fairy tale'. It, and the situation at Disney, was more like a nightmare.

One bright spot was provided by *The Fox and the Hound*, finally released in 1981, although the mood of the picture was decidedly sombre. Based on Daniel P. Mannix' book about a fox cub and hound pup who grow up as friends only to find themselves eventually confronting one another as enemies, it was a return to some of the themes and emotions that had run through *Bambi*.

The animal voices – provided by Mickey Rooney as Tod, the fox; Kurt Russell as Copper, the hound; and Pearl Bailey as Big Mama, the wise old owl – are unconvincing, but the naturalistic settings and animation are almost as beautiful and evocative as those in *Bambi*. 'The darkish, subdued backgrounds,' wrote *Variety*, 'probably represent the picture's artistic highlight'; and several critics were of the opinion that it was 'one of the loveliest pictures to come out of Disney in many years.'

It was also seen as establishing the reputation of a new school of Disney animators. Co-produced by Woolie Reitherman with Art Stevens, who also served as director, *The Fox and the Hound* contained Frank Thomas and Ollie Johnston's last animation for Disney, as well as dynamic work by young artists such as Glen Keane, whose climactic battle between Tod and a ferocious bear is a scene of consummate brilliance.

What *The Fox and the Hound* was not, as *Variety* pointed out, was a movie with 'the razzle dazzle that will pop kids' eyes'. What it was, wrote Richard Corliss in *Time*, was 'a movie that confronts the Dostoyevskian terrors of the heart'. Even the film's lighter moments are a comic motif reflecting the larger drama of Tod and Copper.

It had been another year of variable fortunes for Disney, and although movie income in 1981 was up by $25 million (as a result of home video sales) and although the company's total revenues exceeded the billion dollar mark, profits were down in 1980 by more than $13 million.

The Studio began 1982 with only three movies scheduled for release. All were to be PG-rated, but none of them was to provide Disney with a box-office bonanza in a year when they were competing with block-busters such as *Poltergeist*, *Blade Runner*, *The Thing* and, most sensationally, *ET: The Extraterrestrial*.

From Disney came *Night Crossing*, Disney's first 'political' movie about an escape attempt from East Germany by hot-air balloon. Then *Tex*, which Janet Maslin in *The New York Times* confidently announced would 'forever alter the way movie-goers think about Walt Disney pictures'. Directed by Tim Hunter from the book by S. E. Hinton, *Tex* examines the growing pains of a parentless 15-year-old learning about life and death. Despite some strong language and one or two violent scenes, *Tex* proved that Disney could approach its perennial topic of adolescence with a maturity and contemporary realism *and* gain praise from the critics. 'This is a film,' Janet Maslin concluded her fulsome review, 'that accomplishes everything that it attempts, and does so expertly.'

Tex was one of several projects brought to Disney by its new Vice President of Creative Affairs, Tom Wilhite, who was also responsible for *TRON*, a picture aimed at capitalizing on the current youthful obsession with electronic games. The first feature-length film using computer animation, *TRON* proved one of the Studio's most innovative, but sadly flawed movies.

An electronic fairy-tale, which uses imagery borrowed wholesale from such pre-computer-age stories as *The Wizard of Oz*, *Alice in Wonderland* and *Journey to the Centre of the Earth*, *TRON* presents a stylized fantasy-cum-morality play full of reflections and distortions: each person in the real world having his or her computerized counterpart inside a video game. The computer graphics are stunningly beautiful and might have made it Disney's most significant film since *Fantasia* but for several major omissions. 'Its technical wizardry,' wrote Janet Maslin in *The New York Times*, 'isn't accompanied by any of the old-fashioned virtues – plot, drama, clarity and emotion – for which Disney movies ... are best remembered. It is beautiful – spectacularly so, at times – but dumb.'

Praising the illusions created in the film, Peter Ackroyd wrote in *The Spectator*: 'The stomach churns as it would on a roller-coaster, as the screen shifts and moves so that it seems to hover on two or three planes at once; the camera swoops through whirlpools of light

The Fox and the Hound (1981) was, as one critic put it, 'a return to primal Disney, to the glory days of the early features'.

and emerges within a network of dots and bleeps ...' He went on, however, to condemn 'the fantasy of technology' that inspired the picture and that, he reported second hand, was also to be found in Disney's recently opened Experimental Prototype Community of Tomorrow, now named EPCOT Center.

'We have waited a long time for this day,' said Card Walker at EPCOT Center's dedication ceremony on 24 October 1982, 'but the wait – and the results – were well worth the effort.'

Ground breaking on the project had taken place in 1979, and for three years the WED Imagineers and the teams of construction workers had laboured to give concrete reality to what was generally

referred to as 'Walt Disney's greatest dream'. The concept had changed considerably since Walt's death and by 1978 had taken the form of a 260-acre site, two miles south-east of the Magic Kingdom, to combine what had at first been called the Future World Theme Center with the idea of a World Showcase. These two thematic areas were designed as interlocking parks: one centered upon a 160-foot high geosphere; the other gathered around a lagoon and represented by pavilions built in the classic architectural styles of the different participating countries.

A myriad projects were begun on the first of the themed pavilions for Future World, which were to be devoted to Energy, Communications, Transportation, Imagination and the Land. Many of the concepts were new, like an experimental future farm where plants would be grown without soil; others – such as a journey back in time to the age of the dinosaurs and a history of transport from foot to rocket-power – owed inspiration to Disney movies and the attractions created for the 1964 New York World's Fair.

TRON (1982) told the story of a computer programmer who gets zapped into the exotic world of one of his games.

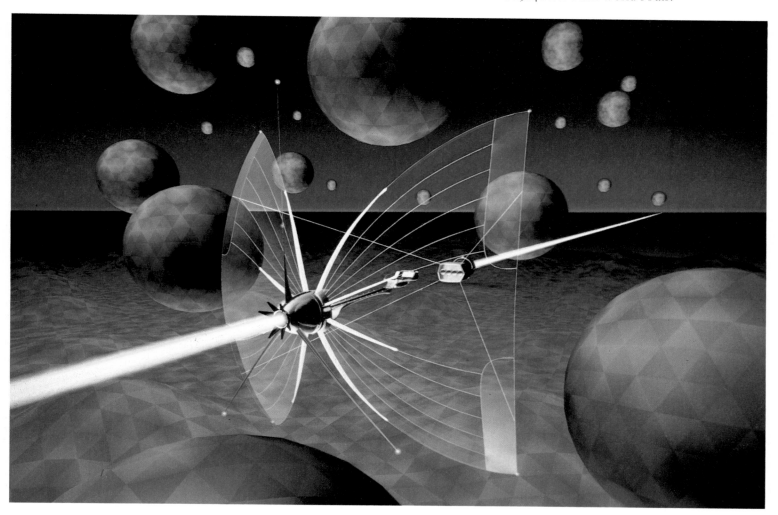

Experts were brought in for consultation from the different spheres of science, technology and the arts: botanists, paleontologists, historians, astronomers, astronauts, artists, sculptors and writers among them Ray Bradbury, who designed the concept for a ride through the history of human communication that was to spiral through EPCOT Center's geosphere, called Spaceship Earth.

By 1981, with the major Future World structures nearing completion and work beginning on a variety of exotic building projects, the Annual Report announced:

> EPCOT Center, a monument to man's progress – and, more importantly, his promise – is dramatically moving towards completion. The 21st Century will indeed begin on October 1st 1982, when the first guests enter Spaceship Earth for the initial leg of their journey through the most spectacular and extraordinary complex ever conceived for the entertainment and education of people the world over.

It was a bold claim, but one justified by EPCOT Center's many developments and innovations – including a computerized information service, an entire building partially powered by a solar-panelled roof and new sophistications in entertainment attractions using stunning *Circle-Vision* 360° films of Canada and China, and hundreds of highly advanced 'Audio-Animatronics' figures from Benjamin Franklin and Mark Twain charting the course of America's history, to a rampaging Tyranosaurus Rex and a kitchen full of singing fruit and vegetables.

What seemed to some a considerable gamble was EPCOT Center's accent on education. In movies such as the True-Life Adventures and the People and Places series, Disney had sought to educate as well as entertain, believing that 'Pictures can make both teaching and learning a pleasure. Now Disney was building a theme park where every attraction and ride would offer a learning experience. There would, of course, be one or two opportunities for almost pure entertainment such as Journey into Imagination with its extraordinary 70mm 3-D film *Magic Journeys*, but most of the films and shows

would have rather a more serious intent: powerful movie presentations such as *Symbiosis*, reflecting the partnership between man and the land; the history of earth's fuel resources in Universe of Energy; and, within World Showcase, an international kaleidoscope of cultures as diverse as the Calgary stampede and the Noh theatre of Japan.

Commemorative tickets for the opening of EPCOT Center, on 1 October 1982, were selling long before the project was completed. It was clear that Disney's new venture, despite the high level of investment, would prove a success with the public.

Walt Disney had talked about EPCOT as 'a showcase for American industry and research', taking 'its cue from the new ideas and technologies that are now emerging ... introducing and testing and demonstrating new materials and systems', and – however far EPCOT Center had become removed from the concept of a real city of the future – those intentions were still avowedly part of the package.

While the publicity men were referring to EPCOT Center as 'The Dawn of a New Disney Era', there were undoubtedly those who wondered if the public would buy – and *keep* buying – tickets to what had become a permanent World's Fair. If not, it might easily prove the onset of a Disney twilight.

After what was reckoned at 25 million man-hours and a total investment of $1 billion, EPCOT Center opened its gates to the public. Three weeks and 1 million visitors later, in the presence of Lillian Disney, it was officially dedicated in words that recalled Walt's dedication speech at Disneyland, 27 years earlier:

> To all who come to this place of joy, hope and friendship, welcome.
> EPCOT Center is inspired by Walt Disney's creative genius. Here, human achievements are celebrated through imagination, the wonders of enterprise, and the concepts of a future that promises new and exciting benefits for all.
> May EPCOT Center entertain, inform and inspire. And, above all, may it instill a new sense of belief and pride in man's ability to shape a world that offers hope to people everywhere.

Many years before, when WED official Marty Sklar had been working on the early plans for EPCOT, he had irreverently suggested a possible title for the project: 'Waltopia'. Though it had undergone, in the intervening years, a considerable sea-change, EPCOT Center was still very much a 'Waltopian' concept. In his dedication address, Card Walker said:

> EPCOT Center is a cross-roads of people, culture, and technology.
> From the shining structures of Future World to the architectural landmarks of World Showcase, the heritage of the past and the realities of the present, merge ... with the hopes and possibilities for the future.

With corporate profits down 18 per cent on the previous year, the dismal performance of Disney movies at the box-office and huge sums invested, not only in EPCOT Center but in the creation of a new Fantasyland for the Magic Kingdom in California and in the planning of Tokyo Disneyland now approaching completion in Japan, it was the hopes and possibilities not so much of the world but of Walt Disney Productions that were really on the line.

Under construction: the world's largest geosphere, Spaceship Earth, with a diameter of 165 feet, nears completion at EPCOT Center in 1982.

15. TOUCHSTONE OF SUCCESS

'Mickey Mouse has seen the future – and has made it work,' declared *Omni* magazine. 'The EPCOT vision is so clean and error-free that even steel-hard realists may not be able to resist its allure.'

There were some detractors: one journalist complained about EPCOT Center's 'sugary rhetoric and glorified educational values', but by 1983, with the projected attendance figure of 20 million visitors exceeded, there was little doubt that EPCOT would succeed.

A new attraction, Horizons, opening there that year, presented a depiction of future life-styles and prompted Ron Miller – who had succeeded to the title of Chief Executive Officer – to speculate on the future of Disney. 'We know,' he said, 'that as long as our vision is measured in terms of generations rather than months or even years, we will always be on the threshold of new horizons.'

There were, however, those who were not so willing to take a long-term view of a company with profits that had fallen to $93 million – their lowest ebb in five years.

Tokyo Disneyland had opened in April 1983, operated by the Oriental Land Company under licence from Disney and, *Harper's Magazine* reported: 'From the Emperor down, Japan is presently in the grip of mouse fever.' On one day alone, Tokyo Disneyland received 94,378 visitors, breaking all records for Disney theme parks.

In Anaheim, the drawbridge to Sleeping Beauty Castle was lowered for the first time since Disneyland's opening day and hundreds of children streamed across it into the new Fantasyland with its attractive village of carefully 'aged' buildings in a jumble of architectural styles, from German Gothic to English Tudor.

Aside from the theme parks, where revenues increased by $305.5 million (against increased operational costs of $241.3 million), Disney's other major development in 1983 was the launch of The Disney Channel, a cable television network offering a range of diversions from Disney classics and new feature productions to a kids' aerobic show, 'Mousercise' and gently moral tales from 'Welcome to Pooh Corner' and 'Dumbo's Circus'.

The Disney Channel was endorsed by the National PTA, recommended by the National Education Association and described by President Reagan as an opportunity 'for millions of American cable subscribers to enjoy the informative, entertaining and wholesome family entertainment for which Walt Disney and the organization he founded are so justly famous'. Within a year The Channel had almost $1\frac{1}{4}$ million subscribers.

Disney Home Video was providing a successful marketing strategy for utilizing the extensive library of Disney movies. Even pictures that had not performed especially well at the cinema proved successful sellers with *Alice in Wonderland* and *TRON* bringing in over a million dollars each; although the true potential of Disney video was only realized several years later with such astonishing sales as the $60 million earned by *Lady and the Tramp*.

The area of Disney's various enterprises that presented the most concern was that on which the company had been founded: motion pictures. In 1983 the Disney board had created a new corporate division, Walt Disney Pictures, under the presidency of Richard Berger, to tackle the problems by 'developing a boldly diversified program of films aimed at significantly broadening the Disney audience'. The first film to be initiated by the new company was *Country*, a contemporary drama on that age-old Disney theme of life-on-the-farm. A gloomy, down-beat picture, *Country* arrived in the movie-theatres in the wake of the similarly themed *Places of the Heart* and *The River*, and did poor business.

Long before the fate of *Country* was known, however, Walt Disney Pictures released the residue of projects that had been instigated by Tom Wilhite and his colleagues. The first of these, a mystery thriller, *Trenchcoat*, was quietly unsuccessful. Not so, the next production, *Something Wicked This Way Comes*, which suffered the undeserved indignity of a very public death. Based on Ray Bradbury's bestseller about a sinister carnival that descends on a small American town bringing unimaginable terrors into its midst, *Something Wicked This Way Comes* was a story uniquely suited to be filmed and that Disney was well-equipped to translate into a powerful motion-picture experience.

The film's producer, Peter Vincent Douglas (son of Kirk) cast Jonathan Pryce in the role of the demonic showman, Mr Dark, and Jason Robards as the gentle-mannered town librarian who pits his wits against the forces of evil represented by the freaks and monsters of Dark's carnival. With a screenplay by Ray Bradbury himself and direction by Jack Clayton, *Something Wicked* looked set for success. The problems began during filming and were so numerous as to become the subject of lengthy soul-baring articles in film magazines.

Moody poster-art promoting the sinister – but unsuccessful – film of Ray Bradbury's *Something Wicked This Way Comes* (1983).

Poster-art for Carroll Ballard's beautifully filmed *Never Cry Wolf*, which, unaccountably, failed at the box-office.

There were major disagreements over Clayton's direction and difficulties with special effects because of the number of Disney technicians involved on *TRON*; and, once filming had been completed, extensive – and not entirely creative – post-production work was nervously undertaken. New scenes were shot, old scenes enhanced by additional effects while pseudo-Bradbury rewrites to the narration were undertaken by considerably less gifted writers.

The critical response to *Something Wicked* was mixed: 'a stylish and intelligent answer to most comic-strip sci-fi extravaganzas' wrote one reviewer, another praising it as 'an allegory and an imaginative, supernatural spine-chiller'. But Richard Cook, writing in *New Musical Express*, voiced what was the disappointment of many: 'A film that should spin and glitter and deceive has ended up as

cautiously artificial, labouring the magic of Bradbury's excellent story and making it mere illusion.'

With *Something Wicked* having cost an estimated $20 million, it was a reception Walt Disney Productions needed like the assassination of Mickey Mouse. Nor did it need the financial failure of its next picture: Carroll Ballard's film, *Never Cry Wolf*. The success of Ballard's 1979 film *The Black Stallion* had prompted some commentators to observe that it was exactly the kind of movie that Disney could have produced, so it was not surprising that the company should have looked for a film project on which to work with Ballard. Farley Mowat's autobiography, *Never Cry Wolf*, the story of his experiences as a biologist working among the wolves and caribou of 'the desolate wastes of the subarctic Barren Lands', seemed ideal.

The movie was fairly rapturously received – 'a film of humanity and constant wonder' and 'breathtakingly beautiful' were not untypical – and Charles Martin Smith's virtually solo performance as the biologist was described as 'childlike, touching, funny and modestly heroic'. However, the Disney connection was generally only sneered at: 'It is,' said Phillip Bergson, 'a very watchable and intelligent heir to those rather twee nature films that Disney used to make'; while Alexander Walker commented that, 'Disney had a hand in this marvellous movie: but fortunately, perhaps, it doesn't seem to have done more than write the cheque that made it all possible in the first place.'

Disney, it seemed, was in a no-win situation. To make matters worse, *Never Cry Wolf* performed badly at the box-office. Realizing that Walt Disney Pictures required a hit, and badly, Ron Miller bought *Splash!* – an unlikely love story about a man and a mermaid – from producer Brian Grazer. He then established a new distribution name – Touchstone Pictures – to handle a film that could not be

A goofy-looking Ghost of Jacob Marley returns to haunt Ebenezer Scrooge (alias McDuck) in *Mickey's Christmas Carol* (1983).

released bearing a Disney tag. With Ron Howard as director, the cute tale of a tail and the extremely sexy mermaid to whom it belonged went into production.

After a troublesome year, 1983 drew to a close with Disney's Christmas offering, *Mickey's Christmas Carol*, a 24-minute animated version of Charles Dickens' classic with Mickey Mouse making a comeback to movies after 30 years as Bob Cratchit. Directed by Burny Mattinson, *Mickey's Christmas Carol* also featured Minnie Mouse, Goofy, Jiminy Cricket as well as Donald Duck and his uncle Scrooge McDuck who, after years as a comic book character, achieved wider notoriety in the role of the stoney-hearted skinflint who is taught to love Christmas and his fellow men.

Despite the success of *Mickey's Christmas Carol*, the mood within Walt Disney Productions was not exactly one of peace and goodwill to all men; and by the following spring, the company was facing the worst crisis of its corporate life.

The rumours began in March 1984, following Roy E. Disney's decision to resign from the board of directors. Dissatisfied at the company's recent performance, he began increasing his shareholding in Walt Disney Productions and looking for a way to bring about management changes. Among those with whom Roy and his financial adviser, Stanley Gold, had discussions, was Frank Wells, a former lawyer who was now Vice Chairman of Warner Brothers. Wells suggested the Disney management needed the creative inspiration of someone like Michael D. Eisner, President of Paramount Pictures, whose successes, over an eight-year period, included *Saturday Night Fever*, *Grease*, *Raiders of the Lost Ark*, *Terms of Endearment* and *An Officer and a Gentleman*. Before Paramount, Michael Eisner had worked for ABC and, as Vice-President of daytime television, took his network to the number one position in that field.

The rumours that were now spreading through the motion picture industry, however, concerned someone rather different – Saul Steinberg, a shadowy New York financier whose Reliance Insurance Company was expressing an interest in Disney. Steinberg's business activities, which had already worried a number of corporations, consisted of acquiring controlling stock in companies whose fortunes were in decline and either splitting up and disposing of the various assets, or selling his shares back to management at a profit, in a form of dealing that has become known as 'greenmailing'.

Towards the end of March 1984, Steinberg announced that he held 6.3 per cent of Disney stock. A few weeks later he had raised that figure to 8.3 per cent and had filed notice that it was his intention to acquire up to 25 per cent of the issued shares in Disney. By 1 May, he was almost half-way to his goal with a 12.1 per cent holding.

Disney's President and Chairman, Ron Miller and Ray Watson, had taken the precaution of increasing the company's credit line with the Bank of America and others from $400 to $1.3 billion, a sum that would allow the expansion of Walt Disney Productions and, in consequence, reduce the significance of any major shareholding such as that being acquired by Steinberg.

This effectively happened when Disney decided to purchase the Arvida Corporation, a Florida development company. The acquisition was achieved by 3.3 million Disney shares being exchanged for Arvida's outstanding stock.

The merger with Arvida – whose resort and community developments were a potential asset to a company with Disney's real-estate holdings – threatened Steinberg's plans by weakening his stock-holding. Nevertheless, offering $67.50 a share, Steinberg made a bid for 49 per cent of Walt Disney Productions and stated his intention to remove the existing board of directors.

Disney responded by making it known that it would pay $80 a share for the remaining 51 per cent of stock, which it would then retire. Such a move would have left Steinberg in control of a company with $2 billion of debts. Faced with this situation, Steinberg agreed to sell back his shares to the Disney management. After considerable bartering, a figure of $77.50 a share was agreed, and Steinberg's 4.2 million shares were repurchased for a total cost of $328 million.

The purchase of Arvida, however, had not only reduced the value of Steinberg's holding in Disney but also that of Roy Disney and others. Stockholders' equity dropped from 59 per cent to 42 per cent of the company's assets. This situation led to negotiations between the two branches of the Disney family and, as a result, an offer to Roy Disney of three seats on the board. He was joined by his financial adviser, Stanley Gold and advertising executive, Peter Dailey.

Steinberg's departure from the scene did not signal the end of Disney's problems. With the repurchase of Steinberg's shares a public outcry had ensued with financiers, politicians and the world's business press decrying the principle of greenmailing that had given Steinberg such an extraordinary profit.

A new threat now came from Irwin Jacobs, a sometime associate of Steinberg (known in business circles as 'Irv the Liquidator') and already a major Disney shareholder. Believing Disney stock to be undervalued in the wake of the Steinberg deal, Jacobs tried to increase his 6 per cent stockholding. Jacobs' assault on Disney just happened to coincide with an exceptional box-office performance by Touchstone Pictures' first film. On its opening weekend, *Splash!* grossed $6,174,059, the highest take yet recorded in Disney history. Company stock rose almost four points in three days, and within four and a half weeks the film had earned over $50 million.

Splash!, a contemporary romance, starred Tom Hanks as the fruit wholesaler who falls, literally, for a mermaid off Cape Cod. The mermaid is played – with and without fins – by Daryl Hannah who had achieved stardom in *Blade Runner*. Perhaps, as one newspaper speculated, Ms Hannah had won the role 'because her blonde mane would ensure that at all times she could go topless and remain decent.'

At least one reviewer speculated on how 'the puritanical grand old man of family entertainment' would have reacted to *Splash!*, but most agreed with *Time*'s recommendation to 'take a plunge on *Splash!*' and wondered whether perhaps Disney wasn't on the way up out of the doldrums at long last.

The success of *Splash!* fuelled financier Irwin Jacobs' ambition to seize control of Disney. Then came what seemed an opportunity to discredit and replace the company's management. Disney had begun negotiations for the acquisition of Gibson Greetings, Inc, a Cincinnati-based card manufacturer, which had been one of the companies considered as an expansion investment before the purchase of Arvida.

The price set on obtaining Gibson – which offered diversification into an area that would enhance Disney marketing potential – was $337.5 million, a sum to be raised by a new issue of Disney stock. Such a stock issue, however, would further reduce shareholders'

Walt's nephew Roy E. Disney, once a film editor on True-Life Adventures, is now Vice-Chairman of The Walt Disney Company.

Michael D. Eisner, Chairman and Chief Executive of The Walt Disney Company since 1984, has projects planned into the next century.

A successful lawyer, Frank G. Wells joined The Walt Disney Company in 1984 as President and Chief Operating Officer.

equity and, when dissenting voices on the Disney board were heard claiming that the price of the Gibson deal was too high, Jacobs made a move.

Threatening legal action to stop the deal, Jacobs gave the Disney board 72 hours in which either to abandon the acquisition or at least to put it to the vote of shareholders. When Disney failed to respond to Jacobs' demands, he and four associates instituted proceedings in the Los Angeles superior court, claiming a breach of fiduciary duty and waste of corporate assets.

On 17 August Disney decided to abrogate the deal, with an agreed payment to Gibson of $7.5 million. The following month, the Bass family (who owned a 70 per cent controlling share in Arvida) bought out Jacobs' 7.7 per cent share in Disney and so became the major stockholders in Walt Disney Productions, with 28.83 per cent of the company's shares.

The final act in this seven-month drama was played out in September when a special committee was appointed by the board to review recent management performance and, as a result, Ron Miller tendered his resignation. On 22 September 1984 Michael D. Eisner replaced Ray Watson as Chairman and Chief Executive Officer, and Frank Wells became President and Chief Operating Officer.

In their first letter to Disney shareholders, Eisner and Wells set the tone for their administration:

> We clearly recognize the legacy of a true creative genius of the twentieth century, Walt Disney. We also acknowledge that we cannot rely on the Disney name and reputation alone to satisfy all the entertainment tastes of a new generation. Our objectives are to not only manage and aggressively market existing values and ideas, but to take our company to a leading position in today's entertainment industry . . .

This they set about doing in a variety of ways: new personnel was drafted into the company, including Gary Wilson, who left the Marriott Corporation to become Disney's chief financial officer, Jeffrey Katzenberg and Richard H. Frank as Chairman and President of the Walt Disney Studios. To lessen financial risks to shareholders, an agreement was signed with Silver Screen Partners II, a public limited partnership of 28,000 members investing in Disney and Touchstone Pictures.

In an attempt to open up new television markets, Disney launched *The Golden Girls*, a sophisticated half-hour comedy series on NBC. Written by Susan Harris, the series starred Beatrice Arthur, Betty White, Rue McClanahan and Estelle Getty. Disney also produced two cartoon series for young viewers – *The Wuzzles* and *Disney's Adventures of the Gummi Bears* – which, while not quite of the same standard as classic Disney animation, were the most superior Saturday morning cartoon shows to be televised in years.

For the first time, vintage Disney material was made available for television syndication, and the limited video release of such celebrated features as *Pinocchio* provided a valuable new source of income.

Disneyland, in an attempt to attract teenage visitors to the park, opened Videopolis, a night-time dance club, while in 1985, as part of the celebrations to mark three decades of Disneyland, every 30th visitor through the turnstiles received a gift which might be a tub of popcorn or a brand new Cadillac from General Motors. And while such famous Disneyland fans as Ray Bradbury and Annette Funicello were reminiscing about the park's opening for the benefit of the nostalgia-hungry media, Michael Eisner was having discussions with George Lucas and Steven Spielberg – seen by many as Walt Disney's true spiritual heirs – about possible future attractions for the Magic Kingdom.

December 1985 saw another significant development for Disney when Eisner signed a letter of intent confirming the company's plans for a Disneyland in France. The site selected for Euro Disneyland (a project begun under the previous administration) was Marne-la-Vallée, a new town 20 miles east of Paris.

As a result of a corporate study, it was discovered that the name 'Walt Disney Productions' was seen as suggesting an organization primarily concerned with films and television. Disney had so significantly diversified, in the 47 years since the title had been adopted, it was now proposed that the name be changed to 'The Walt Disney Company', something which the shareholders approved at their Annual General Meeting in February 1986.

In terms of revenue, filmed entertainment in 1985 brought The Walt Disney Company just a little over a quarter of the income generated by entertainment and recreation projects. As a share of the company's total annual revenue – which for the first time exceeded $2 billion – movies and television together only represented approx-

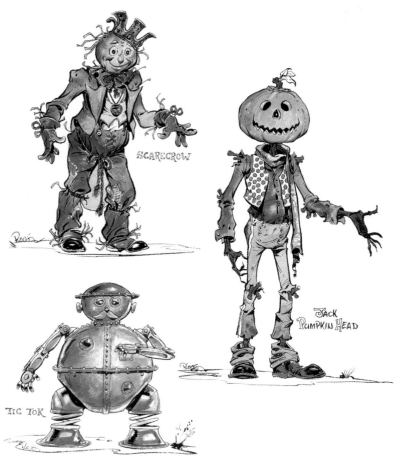

Costume designs for *Return to Oz* (1985) capture the feeling of the illustrations to L. Frank Baum's original books.

imately one-sixth of Disney earnings. One cause of this was a depression affecting the movie industry in general; another was the poor performance of such pictures as *Country*, *Baby: Secret of the Lost Legend* and *My Science Project*. There was also *Return to Oz*, a dark, often sinister picture that, while faithful to the books of L. Frank Baum, lacked the spangled glitter and vaudeville knock-about of MGM's *The Wizard of Oz*.

Two films that fared better were *The Journey of Natty Gann*, a 'girl-who-befriends-a-wolf' movie given real substance by convincing characters and an emotive plot set during the American Depression; and *One Magic Christmas*, a Santa Claus story that earned almost $8 million in its first 10 days.

The biggest disappointment of 1985 was undoubtedly *The Black Cauldron*, which had been on and off the boil for 10 years. Based on Lloyd Alexander's 'Chronicles of Prydain', a cycle of fantasy novels set in medieval Wales, *The Black Cauldron* had passed through many hands before reaching completion under the aegis of Roy E. Disney, now Vice-Chairman and head of animation.

Although costing $25 million, *The Black Cauldron* proved a desperately flawed production, with inconsistent draughtsmanship and a poorly-structured plot. Lloyd Alexander's story of Taran, the assistant pig-keeper who is responsible for looking after a pig with oracular powers and who finds himself caught up in an adventure of sword-and-sorcery, contained many elements suited to the animator's art, including a grisly army of skeletal warriors in the thrall of the grotesque Horned King.

Under the direction of Ted Berman and Richard Rich the animators produced several sequences of pyrotechnical artistry. These, however, were insufficient compensation for a muddled film. The critics were generally unkind. 'Instead of well-defined characters,' wrote Jane Ehrlich in *Films and Filming*, 'we get interchangeably-faced hero and heroine, with enough wide eyes to make even Bambi nauseous ... Taran and the Princess become caricatures of themselves, which is pretty strange, considering they are already cartoons.'

The Black Cauldron was described as 'the most ambitious animated production since *Pinocchio*'. Ironically that film was also reissued in 1985, becoming the Studio's most successful re-release, with a record box-office performance for one day and one week and a total gross in excess of $24 million.

The film fortunes of The Walt Disney Company began a startling recovery in 1986 with *Down and Out in Beverly Hills*, a remarkably liberated choice of movie, even for Touchstone Pictures. It was the Studio's first R-rated production.

Freely adapted – and Americanized – from Jean Renoir's classic French comedy, *Boudu Saved from Drowning*, Paul Mazursky's *Down and Out in Beverly Hills* translates the story of the tramp taken in by the wealthy but unhappy family into a satire on California high-life. Despite excellent central performances from Nick Nolte as the hobo, Richard Dreyfuss as the wealthy coat-hanger tycoon and Bette Midler as his busty, loveless wife, not everyone found the movie to their liking. British critic, Nigel Andrew called it 'disappointingly clumsy ... oafish, over-anxious stuff'. The critic of *The New York Times*, Vincent Canby, pointed out that despite the film's licence in permitting Nick Nolte's down-and-out to seduce Miss Midler's spoilt socialite as well as her daughter and the maid, the character

Despite some structural weaknesses, *The Black Cauldron* (1985) contained stunning special effects and moments of genuine terror.

significantly draws the line at seducing the family's androgenous son. '*Down and Out in Beverly Hills*,' the reviewer concluded, 'also draws the line. After establishing – with all too much conviction – the monstrously foolish nature of its conspicuously consuming characters, as well as the utterly fatuous lives they lead, Mr Mazursky draws back, as if afraid to acknowledge the truth of his own observations.'

Nevertheless, *Down and Out* was a box-office hit on a scale the company hadn't enjoyed for years, taking over $60 million. Even this success, however, was eclipsed by the $70 million grossed the following year by *Ruthless People*, the story of a rich and very unpleasant businessman (Danny deVito) who plans to kill his wife (Bette Midler) and then, when she is unexpectedly kidnapped, just refuses to pay the ransom money.

In 1986 Disney filmed entertainment revenue was up by almost $200 million to $511 million, helped by the success of another Touchstone Picture, *The Color of Money* starring Paul Newman in a sequel to his 1961 movie about a young pool player, *The Hustler*. Although *The Hustler* has acquired the stature of a classic, *The Color of Money* received rave reviews for the staging of the pool games, described by one critic as having 'a fascinating choreography', and for the film's central performances.

Not every Touchstone Picture was quite so successful, but the level of output, for a Studio so recently in despair, was remarkable and the strike-rate astonishingly high. Other films included *Off-Beat*, *Tough Guys*, *Tin Men* and *Ernest Goes to Camp*. In the midst of the raunchy, street-wise Touchstone comedies, a more traditional Disney picture was released: the Studio's first animated feature since the expensive disaster of *The Black Cauldron*. Loosely based on Eve Titus' children's book *Basil of Baker Street* – about a mouse sleuth who lives behind the skirting-boards of Sherlock Holmes' residence at 221b Baker Street – *The Great Mouse Detective* showed that Disney was back on form in the medium it had dominated for so many years but which recently appeared to be slipping from its grasp.

Produced and co-directed by Burny Mattinson, *The Great Mouse Detective* had, as supervising animators, a group of four young men – Mark Henn, Glen Keane, Robert Minkoff and Hendel Butoy – who re-established the animation values so long cherished by Disney's Nine Old Men. Although only one year in the making, the story of

Basil's arch-enemy, Professor Ratigan (succulently voiced by Vincent Price) plots with his repulsive friend Fidget the Bat.

Basil's adventures in the mouse underworld of Victorian London was four years in the planning, and that pre-production work resulted in a tightly-paced story and a well-developed plot structure, embellished with imaginatively conceived settings that place the worlds of mice and men in witty juxtaposition.

'The animation is rich,' wrote *Variety*, 'the characters memorable and the story equally as entertaining for adults as for children. Box-office should be healthy.' It was, taking $18 million in its first month.

Movies were not the only success enjoyed by Disney during 1986 – a year in which total revenue reached almost $2¼ billion. TV's *Golden Girls* received 15 Emmy nominations and won the awards for Best Comedy Actress (Betty White) and Best Comedy Series. The Disney Channel increased the number of its subscribers to almost 3 million. Disney videos provided record sales, with the Studio's one-time box-office failure, *Sleeping Beauty*, selling over a million copies.

In January 1986, EPCOT Center opened its latest attraction, The Living Seas, with its 5.7 million-gallon aquarium and a combination of films and exhibits that typify the EPCOT philosophy of entertainment and education. Later that year, Walt Disney World celebrated its 15th anniversary with parades, concerts, stage shows and what the *Washington Post* described as 'the kind of extravaganza only Hollywood could mastermind'.

Tokyo Disneyland welcomed its 30 millionth visitor, while in the original theme park in California, a gala premiere was given to a

'Basil,' said a reviewer, 'is a truly Great Mouse Detective, and *The Great Mouse Detective* is a great little movie.'

The Disney Channel introduced DTV, pop music videos with skillfully edited images from Disney animated classics.

Housed in a wave-shaped building, the Living Seas joined EPCOT's Future World complex in 1986.

Tokyo Disneyland, the first Disney theme park outside America, opened in Japan in April 1983 and brought the country 'close to Mouse madness'.

The enigmatic Michael Jackson and Fuzzball in Disneyland's 3-D musical adventure, *Captain EO*.

multi-million dollar movie with a running-time of just 17 minutes. Produced by George Lucas and directed by Francis Ford Coppola, *Captain EO* is a 3-D musical space fantasy starring Michael Jackson as an inter-galactic hero who brings music, dance and light to a drab, colourless world, ruled by a menacing Black Queen. To accommodate the vast numbers who wanted to see *Captain EO*, Disneyland remained open round the clock for 60 hours and had 157,000 visitors.

USA Today called the picture an 'extraterrestrial "Thriller", a song-and-dance *Star Wars*'. An interesting analogy, since George Lucas' famous space movie provided the inspiration for another new Disneyland attraction which opened in January 1987.

Star Tours, devised by Walt Disney Imagineering (as WED was now known) and George Lucas' Industrial Light and Magic, uses flight-simulator technology to take visitors on a hair-raising cinematic rollercoaster adventure to that famous galaxy far, far away. At

a spectacular weekend-long opening party, Mickey Mouse welcomed the celebrated Lucas droids C-3PO and R2-D2 to Tomorrowland: the first non-Disney film characters to find a home in the Magic Kingdom.

At the movies, hits for 1987 included *Adventures in Babysitting*, *Benji the Hunted*, *Stakeout* and, at the beginning of the year, *Outrageous Fortune*, which brought together the comedic talents of Bette Midler and Shelley Long as an ill-assorted couple fighting one another to win the affections of a handsome, two-timing, con-man.

A somewhat different heroine was the re-issued Snow White, who celebrated her golden anniversary by grossing $45 million at the US box-office. Despite being 50 years old, *Snow White and the Seven Dwarfs* is, it seems, still 'the fairest one of all'.

In beginning his 1986 Chairman's letter to shareholders and employees, Michael Eisner remarked: 'Our prospects look uncommonly bright, now and for the future. The fundamentals are in place. . . . The strength of the company as a whole stands behind each of our individual enterprises. The opportunities remain boundless.'

With so many ambitious, potentially far-reaching plans on the drawing boards and in construction, it would seem a safe prediction. These plans include the Disney/MGM Studios and Studio Tour as a third major attraction for Walt Disney World, scheduled to open in 1988 and 1989 along with a new 900-room Grand Floridian Beach Resort, a 6-acre night-time entertainment venue, Pleasure Island, and a new recreation attraction, Typhoon Lagoon.

There are also plans for a major new ride for Disneyland, Splash Mountain, inspired by *Song of the South*; a Wonders of Life Pavilion

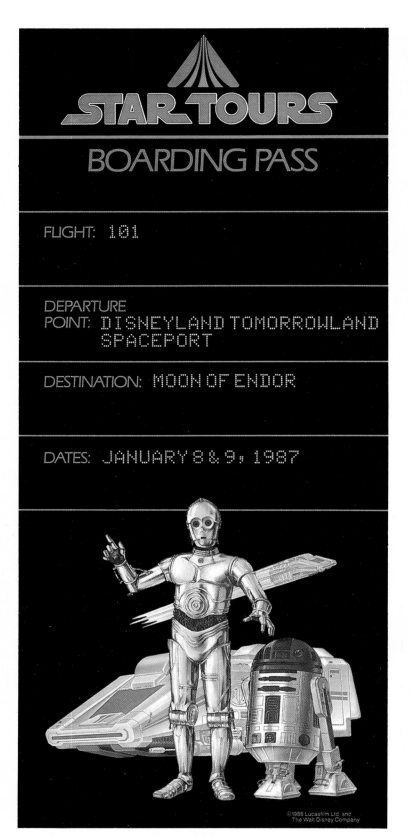

A pass for the opening of Star Tours, which brought together the wizardry of Lucasfilm and Disney Imagineering.

Pleasure Island, the latest entertainment complex for Walt Disney World, with restaurants, shows and discotheques.

In what must be seen as a development of major significance, Disney began to work with Steven Spielberg's Amblin Entertainment to produce *Who Framed Roger Rabbit?*, a comedy fantasy combining live-action and animation. Directed by Robert Zemeckis and animated by the Oscar-winning animator Richard Williams, *Who Framed Roger Rabbit?* will star Bob Hoskins and a cast of legendary cartoon stars from Disney and some of its long-time rivals.

EPCOT's newest planned attraction, a Wonders of Life exhibit; clearly very much in the spirit of Walt's original vision for a 'community of tomorrow'.

for EPCOT Center, housed in a 100,000 square foot golden dome; a 40-acre Disney/MGM Studio Backlot attraction for Burbank, California; and the possibility of further overseas developments to follow Euro Disneyland.

Plans for Disney and Touchstone Pictures include sequels to *The Rescuers* and *Splash!*, as well as another mermaid picture, this time an animated version of Andersen's fairy tale, *The Little Mermaid*; and *Oliver and Company*, a musical cartoon based on Charles Dickens' *Oliver Twist* with a cast of animal characters and a contemporary New York setting.

Speaking of the company's achievements, Michael Eisner says:

We believe in taking risks, for the worst risk of all is not to take any. We believe in trying the new without abandoning the old ... Most of all, we believe in ourselves building on the foundation of a daring and treasured past, constantly renewing the magic that has made us what we are.

While Walt Disney could never have envisaged such a diversity of projects being done in his name, he would undoubtedly have understood the motivation for them. 'In this volatile business of ours,' he once said, 'we can ill afford to rest on our laurels, even to pause in retrospect. Times and conditions change so rapidly that we must keep our aim constantly focused on the future ...'

ACADEMY AWARDS:
WINNERS AND NOMINEES

(★ denotes winners)

1931/32

Short Subjects (Cartoon)
★ *Flowers and Trees*
Mickey's Orphans

Special Award
★ Walt Disney for the creation of Mickey Mouse (statuette)

1932/33

Short Subjects (Cartoon)
★ *Three Little Pigs*
Building a Building

1934

Short Subjects (Cartoon)
★ *The Tortoise and the Hare*

1935

Short Subjects (Cartoon)
★ *Three Orphan Kittens*
Who Killed Cock Robin?

1936

Short Subjects (Cartoon)
★ *The Country Cousin*

1937

Score
Snow White and the Seven Dwarfs Walt Disney Studio Music Department, Leigh Harline, Frank Churchill and Paul J. Smith

Short Subjects (Cartoon)
★ *The Old Mill*

Scientific or Technical Class II (plaque)
★ Walt Disney Productions, Ltd., for the design and application to production of the multi-plane camera

1938

Short Subjects (Cartoon)
★ *Ferdinand the Bull*

Brave Little Tailor
Mother Goose Goes Hollywood
Good Scouts

Special Award
★ Walt Disney for *Snow White and the Seven Dwarfs*, recognized as a significant screen innovation, which has charmed millions and pioneered a great new entertainment field for the motion picture cartoon (one statuette and seven miniature statuettes on a single base)

1939

Short Subjects (Cartoon)
★ *The Ugly Duckling*
The Pointer

1940

Song
★ Leigh Harline (music), Ned Washington (lyrics) 'When You Wish Upon a Star' in *Pinocchio*

Original Score
★ Leigh Harline, Paul J. Smith and Ned Washington *Pinocchio*

1941

Song
Frank Churchill (music), Ned Washington (lyrics) 'Baby Mine' in *Dumbo*

Scoring of a Musical Picture
★ Frank Churchill and Oliver Wallace *Dumbo*

Short Subjects (Cartoon)
★ *Lend a Paw*
Truant Officer Donald

Irving G. Thalberg Memorial Award
★ Walt Disney

Special Awards
★ Leopold Stokowski and his associates for their unique achievement in the creation of a new form of visualized music in Walt Disney's production *Fantasia*, thereby widening the scope of the motion picture as entertainment and as an art form (certificate)
★ Walt Disney, William Garity, John N. A. Hawkins and the RCA Manufacturing Company for their outstanding contribution to the advancement of the use of sound in motion pictures through the production of *Fantasia* (certificates)

1942

Sound
C.O. Slyfield *Bambi*

Song
Frank Churchill (music), Larry Morey (lyrics) 'Love is a Song' in *Bambi*

Scoring of a Dramatic or Comedy Picture
Frank Churchill and Edward Plumb *Bambi*

Short Subjects (Cartoon)
★ *Der Fuehrer's Face*

Documentary
The Grain That Built a Hemisphere
The New Spirit

1943

Sound
C.O. Slyfield *Saludos Amigos*

Song
Charles Wolcott (music), Ned Washington (lyrics) 'Saludos Amigos' in *Saludos Amigos*

Scoring of a Dramatic or Comedy Picture
Edward H. Plumb, Paul J. Smith and Oliver Wallace *Victory Through Air Power*

Scoring of a Musical Picture
Edward H. Plumb, Paul J. Smith and Charles Wolcott *Saludos Amigos*

Short Subjects (Cartoon)
Reason and Emotion

1944

Short Subjects (Cartoon)
How To Play Football

1945

Sound
C.O. Slyfield *The Three Caballeros*

Scoring of a Musical Picture
Edward H. Plumb, Paul J. Smith and Charles Wolcott *The Three Caballeros*

Short Subjects (Cartoon)
Donald's Crime

1946

Short Subjects (Cartoon)
Squatter's Rights

Scientific or Technical Class III (citation)
★ Arthur F. Blinn, Robert O. Cook, C.O. Slyfield and the Walt Disney Studio Sound Department for the design and development of an audio finder and track viewer for checking and locating noise in sound tracks

1947

Song
★ Allie Wrubel (music), Ray Gilbert (lyrics) 'Zip-A-Dee-Doo-Dah' in *Song Of The South*

Scoring of a Musical Picture
Daniel Amfitheatrof, Paul J. Smith and Charles Wolcott *Song Of The South*

Short Subjects (Cartoon)
Chip an' Dale
Pluto's Blue Note

Special Award
★ James Baskett for his able and heartwarming characterization of Uncle Remus, friend and storyteller to the children of the world (statuette)

1948

Short Subjects (Cartoon)
Mickey and the Seal
Tea For Two Hundred

Short Subjects (Two-Reel)
★ *Seal Island* (True-Life Adventure)

1949

Song
Eliot Daniel (music), Larry Morey (lyrics) 'Lavender Blue' in *So Dear To My Heart*

Short Subjects (Cartoon)
Toy Tinkers

Special Award
★ Bobby Driscoll as the outstanding juvenile actor of 1949 (miniature statuette)

1950

Sound
Walt Disney Studio Sound Department *Cinderella*

Song
Mack David, Al Hoffman and Jerry Livingston (music and lyrics) 'Bibbidi-Bobbidi-Boo' in *Cinderella*

Scoring of a Musical Picture
Oliver Wallace and Paul J. Smith *Cinderella*

Short Subjects (Two-Reel)
★ *In Beaver Valley* (True-Life Adventure)

1951

Scoring of a Musical Picture
Oliver Wallace *Alice in Wonderland*

Short Subjects (Cartoon)
Lambert the Sheepish Lion

Short Subjects (Two-Reel)
★ *Nature's Half Acre* (True-Life Adventure)

1952

Short Subjects (Two-Reel)
★ *Water Birds* (True-Life Adventure)

1953

Short Subjects (Cartoon)
★ *Toot, Whistle, Plunk, and Boom*
Rugged Bear

Short Subjects (Two-Reel)
★ *Bear Country* (True-Life Adventure)
Ben and Me

Short Subjects (Documentary)
★ *The Alaskan Eskimo* (People and Places)

Features (Documentary)
★ *The Living Desert* (True-Life Adventure)

1954

Art Direction/Set Decoration (colour)
★ John Meehan and Emile Kuri *20,000 Leagues Under the Sea*

Film Editing
Elmo Williams *20,000 Leagues Under the Sea*

Special Effects
★ Walt Disney Studio Special Effects Department *20,000 Leagues Under the Sea*

Short Subjects (Cartoon)
Pigs Is Pigs

Short Subjects (Two-Reel)
Siam (People and Places)

Features (Documentary)
★ *The Vanishing Prairie* (True-Life Adventure)

1955

Short Subjects (Cartoon)
No Hunting

Short Subjects (Two-Reel)
Switzerland (People and Places)

Short Subjects (Documentary)
★ *Men Against the Arctic* (People and Places)

1956

Short Subjects (Two-Reel)
Larry Lansburgh (Producer) *Cow Dog*
Samoa (People and Places)

Short Subjects (Documentary)
Ward Kimball (Producer) *Man in Space*

1957

Score
Paul J. Smith *Perri*

Short Subjects (Cartoon)
The Truth About Mother Goose

Short Subjects (Live-Action)
★ Ben Sharpsteen (Producer) *The Wetback Hound*
Larry Lansburgh (Producer) *Portugal* (People and Places)

1958

Scoring of a Dramatic or Comedy Picture
Oliver Wallace *White Wilderness* (True-Life Adventure)

Short Subjects (Cartoon)
Paul Bunyan

Short Subjects (Live-Action)
★ *Grand Canyon*

Short Subjects (Documentary)
★ Ben Sharpsteen (Producer) *The Ama Girls*

Features (Documentary)
★ Ben Sharpsteen (Producer) *White Wilderness* (True-Life Adventure)

1959

Scoring of a Musical Picture
George Bruns *Sleeping Beauty*

Short Subjects (Cartoon)
Noah's Ark

Short Subjects (Live-Action)
Mysteries of the Deep

Short Subjects (Documentary)
Donald in Mathmagic Land

Scientific or Technical Class III (citation)
★ Ub Iwerks of Walt Disney Productions for the design of an improved optical printer for special effects and matte shots

1960

Short Subjects (Cartoon)
Goliath II

Short Subjects (Live-Action)
Islands of the Sea

Features (Documentary)
★ Larry Lansburgh (Producer) *The Horse with the Flying Tail*

Honorary Award (statuette)
★ Hayley Mills for *Pollyanna*, the most outstanding juvenile performance during 1960

1961

Cinematography (black and white)
Edward Colman *The Absent Minded Professor*

Art Direction/Set Decoration (black and white)
Carroll Clark (art), Emile Kuri and Hal Gausman (set) *The Absent Minded Professor*

Sound
Robert O. Cook *The Parent Trap*

Scoring of a Musical Picture
George Bruns *Babes in Toyland*

Film Editing
Philip W. Anderson *The Parent Trap*

Costume Design (colour)
Bill Thomas *Babes in Toyland*

Special Effects
Robert A. Mattey and Eustace Lycett *The Absent Minded Professor*

Short Subjects (Cartoon)
Aquamania

1962

Sound
Robert O. Cook *Bon Voyage*

Costume Design (colour)
Bill Thomas *Bon Voyage*

Short Subjects (Cartoon)
A Symposium on Popular Songs

1963

Scoring of Music (adaptation or treatment)
George Bruns *The Sword in the Stone*

1964

Best Picture
Walt Disney and Bill Walsh (Producers) *Mary Poppins*

Best Actress
★ Julie Andrews *Mary Poppins*

Best Director
Robert Stevenson *Mary Poppins*

Writing (screenplay based on material from another medium)
Bill Walsh and Don da Gradi *Mary Poppins*

Cinematography (colour)
Edward Colman *Mary Poppins*

Art Direction/Set Decoration
Carroll Clark and William H. Tuntke (art), Emile Kuri and Hal Gausman (set) *Mary Poppins*

Sound
Robert O. Cook *Mary Poppins*

Song
★ Richard M. and Robert B. Sherman 'Chim-Chim-Cher-ee' in *Mary Poppins*

Music Score (substantially original)
★ Richard and Robert Sherman *Mary Poppins*

Scoring of Music (adaptation or treatment)
Irwin Kostal *Mary Poppins*

Film Editing
★ Cotton Warburton *Mary Poppins*

Costume Design (colour)
Tony Walton *Mary Poppins*

Special Visual Effects
★ Peter Ellenshaw, Eustace Lycett and Hamilton Luske *Mary Poppins*

Scientific or Technical Class I (statuette)
★ Petro Vlahos, Wadsworth E. Pohl and Ub Iwerks for the conception and perfection of techniques for Colour Traveling Matte Composite Cinematography

1967

Costume Design
Bill Thomas *The Happiest Millionaire*

Song
Terry Gilkyson 'The Bare Necessities' in *The Jungle Book*

1968

Short Subjects (Cartoon)
★ *Winnie the Pooh and the Blustery Day*

1969

Short Subjects (Cartoon)
★ Ward Kimball (Producer) *It's Tough To Be A Bird*

1971

Art Direction/Set Decoration
John B. Mansbridge and Peter Ellenshaw (art), Emile Kuri and Hal Gausman (set) *Bedknobs and Broomsticks*

Song
Richard M. and Robert B. Sherman (music and lyrics) 'The Age of not Believing' in *Bedknobs and Broomsticks*

Scoring: Adaptation and Original Song Score
Song score by Richard M. and Robert B. Sherman adapted by Irwin Kostal *Bedknobs and Broomsticks*

Costume Design
Bill Thomas *Bedknobs and Broomsticks*

Special Visual Effects
★ Alan Maley, Eustace Lycett and Danny Lee *Bedknobs and Broomsticks*

1972

Original Dramatic Score
Buddy Baker *Napoleon and Samantha*

1973

Song
George Bruns (music), Floyd Huddleston (lyrics) 'Love' in *Robin Hood*

1974

Art Direction/Set Decoration
Peter Ellenshaw, John B. Mansbridge, Walter Tyler and Al Roelofs (art) and Hal Gausman (set) *The Island at the Top of the World*

Short Films (Animated)
Wolfgang Reitherman (Producer) *Winnie the Pooh and Tigger Too*

1977

Original Song
Al Kasha and Joel Hirschhorn 'Candle on the Water' in *Pete's Dragon*
Sammy Fain, Carol Connors and Ayn Robbins 'Someone's Waiting For You' in *The Rescuers*

Original Song Score (and its adaptation or adaptation score)
Al Kasha, Joel Hirschhorn and Irwin Kostal *Pete's Dragon*

1979

Cinematography
Frank Phillips *The Black Hole*

Visual Effects
Peter Ellenshaw, Art Cruickshank, Eustace Lycett, Danny Lee, Harrison Ellenshaw and Joe Hale *The Black Hole*

1981

Original Score
Alex North *Dragonslayer*

Visual Effects
Dennis Muren, Phil Tippett, Ken Ralston and Brian Johnson *Dragonslayer*

1982

Sound
Michael Minkler, Bob Minkler, Lee Minkler and Jim La Rue *TRON*

Costume Design
Elois Jenssen and Rosanna Norton *TRON*

1983

Sound
Alan R. Splet, Todd Boekelheide, Randy Thom and David Parker *Never Cry Wolf*

Short Films
Burny Mattinson (Producer) *Mickey's Christmas Carol*

1984

Screenplay written directly for the screen
Lowell Ganz, Babaloo Mandel and Bruce Jay Friedman *Splash!*; screen story by Bruce Jay Friedman based on a story by Brian Grazer

Best Actress
Jessica Lange *Country*

1985

Costume Design
Albert Wolsky *The Journey of Natty Gann*

Visual Effects
Will Vinton, Ian Wingrove, Zoran Perisic and Michael Lloyd *Return To Oz*

Scientific or Technical
★ David W. Spencer for the development of an animation photo transfer process.

1987

Best Actor
★ Paul Newman *The Color of Money*

Best Actress in a Supporting Role
Mary Elizabeth Mastrantonio *The Color of Money*

Art Direction/Set Decoration
Boris Leven (art), Karen A. O'Hara (set) *The Color of Money*

Screenplay (based on material from another medium)
Richard Price *The Color of Money*

INTRODUCTION

Worldwide during 1986 Disney film rentals exceeded $146 million. This success was due, in part, to the new movies being released by Walt Disney Pictures – *The Great Mouse Detective* and *Flight of the Navigator*, for example – and by the company's new adult entertainment division, Touchstone Pictures – with movies like *Down and Out in Beverly Hills*, *Ruthless People*, *The Color of Money* and *Tough Guys*. However, some of that revenue can also be attributed to the highly successful re-issue of classic films such as *One Hundred and One Dalmatians*, *Sleeping Beauty*, *Song of the South* and *Lady and the Tramp*.

Following this Introduction is a chronological listing of Disney film releases. The only titles excluded are non-Disney educational releases, videos, original television material and 8mm home movies. All films made after 1932 are in Technicolor unless otherwise stated.

Shorts
Walt Disney's early silent films, including the *Alice Comedies* and *Oswald the Lucky Rabbit* (1924–8) are indexed by title only, since detailed synopses are no longer available. After the release of the first Mickey Mouse cartoon, *Steamboat Willie* (1928), all Disney shorts were produced with sound, and they

are listed with a brief synopsis. Where possible, all titles carry a director credit.

During World War II, Disney produced an extensive number of military training films for the armed forces. These, like the early silent films, are listed by title only; widely distributed propaganda and educational shorts are, however, dealt with in greater detail, as are later educational specials leased to schools and colleges.

Motion pictures made by the Studio for inclusion in international exhibitions and the company's theme parks – Disneyland, Walt Disney World and Tokyo Disneyland – are also listed.

Each entry is accompanied by an abbreviation to indicate the type of film. The abbreviations are:

CD	Chip an' Dale
Com	Commercial or public-service cartoon
DD	Donald Duck
Ed	Educational titles
F	Feature/featurette
Fi	Figaro
G	Goofy
MM	Mickey Mouse
P	Pluto
P&P	People and Places
Sp	Specials (films that do not belong in any specific series)
SS	Silly Symphonies
TLA	True-Life Adventures
TP	Films made for viewing at the theme parks

A film such as the 1958 release *Our Friend the Atom*, for instance, began life as a Disney television programme and was later released as an educational featurette. It therefore carries the letters Ed.

16 millimetre (16mm)

In 1965 the company's Annual Report announced that:

an estimated 55,000 different 16mm prints of Disney films (ranging from *Donald Duck in Mathmagic Land* to *Bear Country*, *You the Human Animal* and *Man in Space*) are currently in circulation around the world. More than 2,000 clients rent or lease these films each year, including school systems, public libraries, auto clubs, universities, health departments, forestry and park groups, financial institutions, industries and nearly 1,000 organizations. Disney 16mm films have been translated into 14 languages and shown in 56 countries.

The Report then gave three examples of overseas clients – Turkey's Ministry of Education (*Secrets of the Bee World*), Esso Oil Company of Germany (*Mars and Beyond*) and various electric utility companies in Latin America (Spanish and Portuguese versions of *Our Friend the Atom*).

All 16mm (educational and entertainment) films are included in the Filmography. Extracts released to schools that are edited-down versions of a major Disney feature (*Small Animals of the Plains* from the 1954 theatrical production *The Vanishing Prairie*, for instance) are listed by title only, with the relevant source indicated. All titles are fully indexed, for quick reference, at the end of the Filmography.

Features/featurettes

All feature-length productions, whether animated or live action, are included, even if the title was not distributed theatrically in the US. Some European releases were originally filmed for the Disney television shows – *Disneyland*, *Walt Disney Presents* and *The Wonderful World of Color* – and are recorded as such.

Until the release of *Snow White and the Seven Dwarfs* in 1937, all Disney films were shorts, ranging from seven to eight minutes in length. Although running times are not included, the letter F next to a title denotes those films considered by the Studio as being in the featurette or feature length category.

Awards

Some feature films, such as *The Absent-Minded Professor* and *The Ugly Dachshund* won SCMPC Awards (Southern California Motion Picture Council); others, like *Make Mine Music* and *The African Lion*, were awarded A-1 Legion of Decency citations. Although numerous other national and international, religious and educational awards were bestowed on countless Disney films, it would be impracticable to attempt a complete listing of them in the Filmography. However, major awards, in particular those given by the Academy of Motion Picture Arts and Sciences (Oscars) are included. Films that won an Academy Award are marked ★; films that were nominated are marked ☆. Certain films, although not the recipient of such a prestigious accolade may be cited, however, if the award is considered particularly relevant to the film in question. Some of the more recent 16mm educational titles fall into this category.

Distribution

It is important to note that, prior to setting up an independent distributor (Buena Vista) for his films in 1953, Walt Disney released his products through the following companies: M. J. Winkler (1924–7); Universal (1927–8); Columbia (1928–32); United Artists (1932–7) and RKO Radio Pictures (1937–56).

Richard Holliss

© WALT DISNEY PRODUCTIONS

1920

NEWMAN LAUGH-O-GRAMS Short cartoons made for screening at the Newman Theater, Kansas City. Lasting less than a minute, they dealt with topical local issues.

1922

TOMMY TUCKER'S TOOTH A dental training film about Tommy who cares for his teeth and Jimmie Jones who is neglectful of his. It was made for Dr Thomas B. McCrum in Kansas City.

LAUGH-O-GRAMS A series of six fairy stories: *The Four Musicians of Bremen, Little Red Riding Hood, Puss in Boots, Jack and the Beanstalk, Goldie Locks and the Three Bears* and *Cinderella*.

1923

MARTHA (Song-O-Reel) A filmed story accompanying a vocalist's rendition of the song 'Martha; Just a Plain Old Fashioned Name' by Joe L. Sanders.

ALICE'S WONDERLAND A film, combining cartoons and live action, that was never released; it may be regarded as a 'pilot' for the Alice Comedies.

1924

ALICE COMEDIES *Alice's Day at Sea, Alice Hunting in Africa, Alice's Spooky Adventure, Alice's Wild West Show, Alice's Fishy Story, Alice and the Dog Catcher, Alice the Peacemaker, Alice Gets in Dutch, Alice and the Three Bears* and *Alice the Piper*.

1925

ALICE COMEDIES *Alice Cans the Cannibals, Alice the Toreador, Alice Gets Stung, Alice Solves the Puzzle, Alice's Egg Plant, Alice Loses Out, Alice Stage Struck, Alice Wins the Derby, Alice Picks the Champ, Alice's Tin Pony, Alice Chops the Suey, Alice the Jail Bird, Alice Plays Cupid, Alice Rattled by Rats* and *Alice in the Jungle*.

1926

ALICE COMEDIES (below) *Alice on the Farm, Alice's Balloon Race, Alice's Ornery Orphan, Alice's Little Parade, Alice's Mysterious Mystery, Alice in the Wooly West, Alice's Monkey Business, Alice Charms the Fish, Alice the Fire Fighter, Alice Cuts the Ice, Alice Helps the Romance, Alice's Spanish Guitar, Alice's Brown Derby* and *Alice the Lumber Jack*.

CLARA CLEANS HER TEETH A second dental short for Dr Thomas B. McCrum.

1927

ALICE COMEDIES *Alice the Golf Bug, Alice Foils the Pirates, Alice at the Carnival, Alice's Rodeo* (also titled *Alice at the Rodeo*), *Alice the Collegiate, Alice in the Alps, Alice's Auto Race, Alice's Circus Daze, Alice's Knaughty Knight, Alice's Three Bad Eggs, Alice in the Klondike, Alice's Picnic, Alice's Channel Swim, Alice's Medicine Show, Alice the Whaler, Alice in the Big League* and *Alice the Beach Nut*.

OSWALD THE LUCKY RABBIT SERIES (above) *Trolley Troubles, Oh, Teacher, Great Guns, The Mechanical Cow, All Wet, The Ocean Hop, The Banker's Daughter, Rickety Gin* and *Empty Socks*.

1928

OSWALD THE LUCKY RABBIT SERIES *Harem Scarem, Neck 'n' Neck, The Ol' Swimmin' 'Ole, Africa Before Dark, Rival Romeos, Bright Lights, Sagebrush Sadie, Ride 'Em Plow Boy, Ozzie of the Mounted, hungry Hoboes, Oh, What a Knight, Sky Scrappers, Poor Papa, The Fox Chase, Tall Timber, Sleigh Bells* and *Hot Dog*.

STEAMBOAT WILLIE (MM) Director Walt Disney. The most famous Mickey Mouse cartoon ever made – and possibly the most famous cartoon ever made. Although Walt had originally planned the film as the third short featuring his new character, the advent of sound in Hollywood with Warner Brothers' release *The Jazz Singer* temporarily halted production. Cancelling the attempts at distribution of the two already completed Mickey shorts, *Plane Crazy* and *Gallopin' Gaucho*, a sophisticated soundtrack of noises, squeaks and bumps was hurriedly synchronized to *Steamboat Willie*, which was released to enthusiastic audiences on 18 November 1928 at the Colony Theater, New York. Mickey is a deck hand on Captain Pete's paddle-steamer (right). After upsetting the captain, Mickey enters into a spirited rendition of 'Turkey in the Straw' with his sweetheart Minnie Mouse. Although it has a simple tale, the ingenious film is crammed full of highly inventive gags. Mickey uses the ship's onboard animal menagerie as musical instruments (a practice he followed in later shorts) and utilizes all manner of props and gadgets to create a

musical interlude. Animated by Ub Iwerks, the film has been featured in numerous retrospectives on Disney, and it formed part of the 1973 16mm release *Milestones in Animation*.

GALLOPIN' GAUCHO (MM) Director Walt Disney. Argentina premiered a number of cartoon compilations in the 1960s and 1970s, but as early as 1928 Mickey Mouse starred in a South American adventure. As the infamous hero El Gaucho, Mickey sees Minnie dancing at the *Cantino Argentino* (a rough bar with a side-door bearing the sign 'Family Entrance'), and he falls in love with her. Wicked Pete kidnaps her (starting a trend that was to be followed in countless cartoons), but, after a fierce swordfight, Mickey is victorious. Crudely drawn, as were all the early black and white shorts, the combination of clever gags and ingenious techniques gives the film a unique place in cinema history.

PLANE CRAZY (MM) Director Walt Disney. When Walt returned to Hollywood from New York in 1928 he brought with him an idea for a new cartoon character. In this, his first film, Mickey Mouse imitates the great aviation pioneer Charles Lindbergh (right). Having built an aircraft in his backyard, Mickey enlists the help of the other barnyard inhabitants to get it off the ground. Minnie joins him on his maiden flight, but they are interrupted by an unwilling passenger in the form of a cow. Ingenious gags, drawn by Ub Iwerks, include a wonderfully anthropomorphic plane and some amazing aerial stunts.

When sound came to Hollywood, Disney decided to hold back distribution of this film (as well as Mickey's second adventure, *Gallopin' Gaucho*) until after the release of *Steamboat Willie*, and then release them with a soundtrack. *Plane Crazy* appeared on the first *Disneyland* television programme in 1954 and in the 16mm compilation *Milestones for Mickey* (1974).

THE BARN DANCE (MM) Director Walt Disney. Mickey cannot dance, and Minnie finds herself the unwilling partner of the villainous Pete.

1929

THE OPRY HOUSE (MM) Director Walt Disney. Mickey Mouse puts on his first vaudeville show, and one of the highlights of the programme is Mickey's ability to play the piano – so much so that the exhausted instrument finally retaliates.

WHEN THE CAT'S AWAY (MM) Director Walt Disney. Mickey and Minnie tap dance on a piano keyboard, accompanied by a number of popular tunes. This was one of the few occasions when Mickey was depicted as being the size of a real mouse and not, as animator Ward Kimball later remarked, as 'a three foot high mouse'.

THE SKELETON DANCE (SS) Director Walt Disney. Carl Stalling, the Studio's resident musician in the late 1920s, suggested to Walt that he experiment with a short film combining classical music and an original story. The first of these Silly Symphonies, which was drawn primarily by Ub Iwerks, concerned a troupe of gyrating skeletons, who scuttle back to their graves when the cock crows. Plans to use Saint-Saëns' *Danse Macabre* were shelved, and instead, a bizarre musical accompaniment adds to the sinister goings-on. Considered a Disney classic in the same mould as *Steamboat Willie* and *The Old Mill*, the film was later featured as part of the 16mm release *Milestones in Animation* (1973).

THE BARNYARD BATTLE (MM) Director Walt Disney. Mickey is one of the first mice to enlist so that he may defend his homestead from a bunch of cats. Single-handedly, he conquers the enemy and returns a hero.

THE PLOW BOY (MM) Director Walt Disney. Mickey tries to show Minnie how to milk a cow. Clarabelle and Horace Horsecollar star in this early cartoon, and both became stars in their own right, appearing in a number of early shorts. When Horace plays a trick on Mickey, he enlists the help of a small bee to enact his revenge.

THE KARNIVAL KID (MM) Director Walt Disney. Hot-dog seller Mickey Mouse offers Minnie, who is playing the part of a 'shimmy dancer', some lunch and finally gets the opportunity to serenade her with the help of some unusual friends.

MICKEY'S FOLLIES (MM) Director Wilfred Jackson. Two chickens perform an Apache dance, and a pig soprano finds it difficult to stop singing. Mickey saves the day by singing and dancing on top of a piano until the entire barnyard joins in with the musical festivities. The film is notable for the first appearance of Mickey's theme song, 'Minnie's Yoo Hoo'.

EL TERRIBLE TOREADOR (SS) Director Walt Disney. Most of the early Silly Symphonies burlesqued musical sequences featured in other films. This engaging story is no exception, although the action takes place in the bull-fighting arena.

MICKEY'S CHOO-CHOO (MM) Director Walt Disney. Mickey encounters some hair-raising situations as a train engineer. His anthropomorphic locomotive with its smiling face predates some of the Studio's other animated trains in such films as *The Reluctant Dragon* (1941), *Dumbo* (1941), *Saludos Amigos* (1943) and *The Brave Engineer* (1950).

SPRINGTIME (SS) Director Ub Iwerks. The first of a short series of stories about the lives of the woodland creatures through the changing seasons.

THE JAZZ FOOL (MM) Director Walt Disney. Mickey Mouse always showed a natural flair when it came to playing musical instruments. Here, he performs on the calliope (steam whistles) and is accompanied by a troupe of dancing animals.

HELL'S BELLS (SS) Director Ub Iwerks. The Devil and all his works (below) featured in a number of Disney films, but in this black and white Silly Symphony satanic goings-on are burlesqued by a group of cavorting creatures and skeletons.

JUNGLE RHYTHM (MM) Director Walt Disney. Many early Mickey Mouse cartoons contained extensive musical numbers because cinema audiences still found it fascinating to watch drawings synchronized to sound. Mickey encounters some fierce wild animals, but his musical ability soon has all the animals dancing away.

THE MERRY DWARFS (SS) Director Walt Disney. There's a certain similarity in the formats of some of the early Silly Symphonies. *The Merry Dwarfs*, for example, consists of a very long dance routine performed by small bearded men with pointed hats (below) – their movements are not so very different from those of the boney stars of *The Skeleton Dance* (1929).

THE HAUNTED HOUSE (MM) Director Walt Disney. Mickey seeks refuge from a storm and soon finds himself an unwilling organist for the spookiest party of ghosts and ghouls he has ever seen.

WILD WAVES (MM) Director Bert Gillett. Mickey and his friends are having a wonderful day at the seaside, and Mickey is overjoyed when Minnie arrives dressed in a snappy-looking bathing costume. However, he is soon called upon to rescue his sweetheart when she is swept out to sea.

1930

SUMMER (SS) Director Ub Iwerks. The second in a short series of films featured a cast of insects, woodland animals and plants, who celebrate the passing of the seasons.

AUTUMN (SS) Director Ub Iwerks. The forest animals, preparing to hibernate, build up stocks of winter food.

JUST MICKEY (MM) Director Walt Disney. Mickey wears an outrageous wig in order to play the part of a sophisticated violinist, occasionally interrupting his energetic performance to address the cinema audience. (Copyrighted as *Fiddlin' Around*.)

CANNIBAL CAPERS (SS) Director Bert Gillett. A native tribe in a far-off jungle is enjoying a 'swinging' party. The festivities are brought to an abrupt end when a lion appears on the scene and captures one of them.

THE BARNYARD CONCERT (MM) Director Walt Disney. Mickey is the conductor at a musical revue involving all the farm animals. But, just as he will be plagued by interruptions in *The Band Concert* (1935), he has a difficult time trying to keep his musicians together.

NIGHT (SS) Director Walt Disney. Based on an idea that was later expanded in the Award-winning Silly Symphony *The Old Mill*, *Night* is a musical fantasy with a cast of owls, frogs and fireflies.

THE CACTUS KID (MM) Director Walt Disney. Mickey, in his first western-type adventure, stars as caballero Don Mickey, who rescues señorita Minnie from kidnapper Peg Leg Pedro. Mickey and Minnie feel no remorse when the villain falls over a cliff at the climax of the film.

FROLICKING FISH (SS) Director Bert Gillett. An underwater fantasy in which all manner of sea creatures amuse themselves by singing and dancing.

THE FIRE FIGHTERS (MM) Director Bert Gillett. By the time fire chief Mickey Mouse has answered an emergency call (above), a skyscraper is ablaze. Poor Minnie is trapped on the top floor, so Mickey bravely winches himself across on a clothesline to rescue her.

ARCTIC ANTICS (SS) Director Ub Iwerks. Another *tour de force* from animator and director Ub Iwerks, this time illustrating the carefree lifestyle of polar bears, seals and penguins in the frozen north.

THE SHINDIG (MM) Director Bert Gillett. A small dancing dachshund is joined by all manner of farm animals in a spectacular dance routine.

MIDNIGHT IN A TOY SHOP (SS) Director Wilfred Jackson. A small spider has a frightening experience when all the toys come to life. The tiny arachnid beats a hasty retreat when some firecrackers are accidentally ignited by a lighted candle.

THE CHAIN GANG (MM) Director Bert Gillett. Some of the classic one-reel comedies of the 1930s, whether starring Chaplin, Keaton or Laurel and Hardy, involved stories in which the heroes found themselves in prison. Gillett worked a number of amusing gags into a saga of captivity and escape. This time it's Mickey who breaks gaol and is pursued by the wardens and a familiar-looking dog, who was later to become Pluto.

MONKEY MELODIES (SS) Director Bert Gillett. A blossoming romance between a girl and boy monkey adds to the fun. When their island turns out to be the back of an alligator, they manage to escape by swinging through the trees.

THE GORILLA MYSTERY (MM) Director Bert Gillett. The gorilla, who seems to be of a similar build to Mickey Mouse's nemesis Peg Leg Pete, threatens Minnie. Hearing that a huge ape has escaped from the city zoo, Mickey races over to rescue his sweetheart.

THE PICNIC (MM) Director Bert Gillett. Before Pluto appeared on the scene, Minnie's own pet dog (above right) could be relied upon to wreak havoc. When it starts to rain, Mickey and Minnie head for home, the dog proving its worth as it uses its tail as a windscreen wiper.

WINTER (SS) Director Bert Gillett. When the snow comes, the animals have fun skating and dancing on the ice, but they scamper back to their shelters when dark clouds cover the sun.

PIONEER DAYS (MM) Director Bert Gillett. Mickey Mouse and Minnie are hardy travellers heading west in a covered wagon. Minnie is captured by Indians, and Mickey bravely sets out to rescue her. Pretending to be an army of soldiers, they return to the wagon train and frighten the rest of the Indians away.

PLAYFUL PAN (SS) Director Bert Gillett. When a fire threatens the forest animals, Pan (below) lures the flames into a lake where they are extinguished. In order to escape the inferno, the animals swim to the safety of a tiny island, a scene reminiscent of one in *Bambi* (1942).

1931

THE BIRTHDAY PARTY (MM) Director Bert Gillett. The then-resident gang of Disney stock players surprise Mickey with a party at Minnie's house. Among the guests are Horace Horsecollar, Clarabelle Cow, a duck (not Donald, because he hadn't yet made his screen debut) and a whole barnyard of animal friends. Mickey is given a piano as a present, and a high-spirited dance routine follows.

BIRDS OF A FEATHER (SS) Director Bert Gillett. A flock of birds launches an attack on a hawk who has kidnapped a little chick.

TRAFFIC TROUBLES (MM) Director Bert Gillett. In the best tradition of a Laurel and Hardy short, Mickey recklessly drives his taxi through the streets to pick up Minnie. Disaster strikes when the cab gets a flat tyre. Encounters with a strange medicine man, a cow and the inhabitants of a barnyard lead to a furiously funny climax.

THE CASTAWAY (MM) Director Wilfred Jackson. Mickey is shipwrecked on a desert island, in a

plot loosely based on the story of Robinson Crusoe. After a musical interlude, he encounters an unfriendly gorilla (first seen in 1930's *The Gorilla Mystery*), an angry lion and an extremely hungry crocodile. Mickey eventually escapes by hitching a ride on the back of a turtle.

MOTHER GOOSE MELODIES (SS) Director Bert Gillett. Although the short *Mother Goose Goes Hollywood* (1938), with its spoofs of some of the Hollywood 'greats', was an enormous success, the black and white inhabitants of *Mother Goose Melodies* are just as entertaining. Each page of the classic Mother Goose volume releases its own nursery-rhyme character in an amazing musical extravaganza. Unlike the work of some of the other animation studios in the early 1930s, every frame of this Disney film (above) is packed to overflowing with new ideas and ingenious gags.

THE MOOSE HUNT (MM) Director Bert Gillett. Pluto, Mickey's lifelong canine companion, put in an anonymous appearance in *The Chain Gang* (1930), but it wasn't until *The Moose Hunt* that he was referred to by name. Pluto speaks for the first and only time in his entire career, after Mickey accidentally shoots him, and this was also the only occasion on which Pluto was seen to flap his ears and fly.

THE CHINA PLATE (SS) Director Wilfred Jackson. The characters painted on the surface of a plate come to life, but the plate's sudden submersion in a dishpan brings this highly inventive and un-usual short to an end.

THE DELIVERY BOY (MM) Director Bert Gillett. Gillett achieves an extraordinary degree of fluidity with Mickey and Minnie as they play a variety of musical instruments and perform for their barnyard friends. After a song-and-dance extravaganza, the writers introduce Peg Leg Pete in a cameo performance as a workman blasting away rocks for a new road. Pluto retrieves a stick of the dynamite, and the party comes to an explosive end, leaving Mickey to hammer out the tunes on the ribcage of his donkey.

THE BUSY BEAVERS (SS) Director Wilfred Jackson. When their dam breaks a colony of beavers is saved by a brave little beaver, who blocks the gap by gnawing through a large tree.

MICKEY STEPS OUT (MM) Director Bert Gillett. Spruced up and happily on his way to meet Minnie, Mickey falls in some mud. When he eventually arrives at Minnie's house, Mickey does some amusing juggling and dance routines

while Minnie accompanies him on the piano. Pluto chases a cat into the house and in the resulting mayhem, both dancer and musician get covered in soot from the stove.

THE CAT'S OUT (SS) Director Wilfred Jackson. A feline chasing his feathered friends is knocked unconscious and dreams he is being tried for his crimes by a jury of birds and bats, in a short that anticipates *Pluto's Judgment Day* (1935). (Copyrighted as *The Cat's Nightmare*.)

BLUE RHYTHM (MM) Director Bert Gillett. Orchestra leader Mickey imitates Ted Lewis; Minnie sings while Mickey accompanies her on the piano.

EGYPTIAN MELODIES (SS) Director Wilfred Jackson. Although they never became members of the Disney 'Hall of Fame', some of the personalities in the early Silly Symphonies were distinctly intriguing. One of these, a little spider,

appeared in *Egyptian Melodies*, as well as in *Midnight in a Toyshop* (1930) and *The Spider and the Fly* (1931). This time the spider has some adventures among the sphinx and pyramids, until some mummies come to life and scare him away.

FISHIN' AROUND (MM) Director Bert Gillett. In his early film career, Mickey Mouse was more mischievous than the Studio later allowed. When he and Pluto deliberately fish where they're not supposed to, they are forced to beat a hasty retreat when a police officer tries to arrest them.

THE CLOCK STORE (SS) Director Wilfred Jackson. Most of the early animation studios produced animated shorts about stores full of inanimate objects that suddenly spring to life. Toys and books were always favourite subjects, but tobacco products, confectionery and even bottles were used to good effect. In *The Clock Store* a wall clock is the referee between pugilist alarm

clocks, while two tiny figures dance to the swinging pendulum of a grandfather clock. (Copyrighted as *In A Clock Store*.)

THE BARNYARD BROADCAST (MM) Director Bert Gillett. Mickey is enjoying an opportunity to be a radio announcer when the transmission is brought to an abrupt end by a gang of alley cats who eventually wreck the makeshift studio.

THE SPIDER AND THE FLY (SS) Director Wilfred Jackson. Tiny flies join forces to battle against a voracious spider who tries to capture them in its web. There are some hilarious gags involving *horse*-flies and *dragon*-flies.

THE BEACH PARTY (MM) Director Bert Gillett. Clarabelle Cow falls into the sea and is rescued by an inner-tube inflated by Pluto. Later, a mischievous octopus invades the beach and chases Mickey and the gang away.

THE FOX HUNT (SS) Director Wilfred Jackson. When a fox is cornered by hunters, a skunk comes to the rescue and chases them off. A Technicolor remake starring Donald Duck and Goofy appeared in 1938.

MICKEY CUTS UP (MM) Director Bert Gillett. Mickey has problems with a belligerent tornado when he tries to clear up Minnie's backyard in *The Little Whirlwind* (1941). But a similar task proves just as difficult when Pluto gets entangled with a runaway lawn mower.

☆MICKEY'S ORPHANS (MM) Director Bert Gillett. Cats constantly plagued Mickey's carefree existence. Sometimes they were in the shape of the villainous Pete, but in *Mickey's Orphans* they took the form of a basketful of kittens, which were left on his doorstep (opposite above). The kittens take over the household and strip the Christmas tree of gifts and candy.

THE UGLY DUCKLING (SS) Director Wilfred Jackson. This version of Hans Christian

Andersen's story is now almost completely overshadowed by the 1939 colour remake, which won an Academy Award. Although much cruder in design, this engaging film contains some delightful gags and an appealing cast of characters (opposite below).

1932

THE BIRD STORE (SS) Director Wilfred Jackson. A baby canary is threatened by a voracious cat. Tricked by some other birds into entering a cage, the cat ends up suspended on a pole above the local dog pound.

THE DUCK HUNT (MM) Director Bert Gillett. Just as Mickey and Pluto were plagued by seagulls in *The Simple Things* (1953), they find themselves the victims of some angry ducks when they go on a hunting expedition.

THE GROCERY BOY (MM) Director Wilfred Jackson. Mickey Mouse is thrilled when he has an opportunity to deliver Minnie's groceries. But while he and Minnie prepare dinner, Pluto steals the turkey. After a furious chase, Mickey ends up covered in chocolate cake.

THE MAD DOG (MM) Director Bert Gillett. Pluto's refusal to take a bath results in a tug of war with Mickey. Pluto swallows the soap, is labelled a mad dog and only just escapes from Pete the dog-catcher before humbly agreeing to be bathed.

BARNYARD OLYMPICS (MM) Director Wilfred Jackson. Mickey and the gang are involved in a bicycle race that concludes with a burlesque on athletic events.

MICKEY'S REVUE (MM) Director Wilfred Jackson. The entertainment is brought to a premature close by Pluto, who chases some cats on stage. In the ensuing riot Horace Horsecollar drops the curtain on top of the performers. The film is notable for marking Goofy's debut (above).

MUSICAL FARMER (MM) Director Wilfred Jackson. Another barnyard extravaganza, this one has some gags with egg-laying hens. When Mickey decides to photograph the cast of his rural show, the flashlight causes an explosion.

THE BEARS AND THE BEES (SS) Director Wilfred Jackson. Some bear cubs are chased from their lunch of berries and honey by a large grizzly. When the bees turn the tables on the gate-crasher, the cubs are left in peace to enjoy their meal.

MICKEY IN ARABIA (MM) Director Wilfred Jackson. Mickey and Minnie are tourists. After some problems with a drunken camel, Minnie is kidnapped by a sheik, but Mickey, true to form, sets off to the rescue.

JUST DOGS (SS) Director Bert Gillett. A puppy in the city pound releases all the other dogs. After a free for all, the little dog befriends a large mongrel. This was the last black and white Silly Symphony.

MICKEY'S NIGHTMARE (MM) Director Bert Gillett. Mickey dreams of marrying Minnie, but scenes of their blissful relationship in a heart-shaped home, accompanied by the ever-faithful Pluto, come to an abrupt end when a flock of storks brings lots of baby mice (left).

★FLOWERS AND TREES (SS) Director Bert Gillett. The 29th Silly Symphony began life as a black and

TOUCHDOWN MICKEY (MM) Director Wilfred Jackson. Mickey Mouse is proclaimed the hero when he manages to win, almost single-handedly, a game of football against a team of alley cats.

THE WAYWARD CANARY (MM) Director Bert Gillett. Minnie's pet bird escapes and causes mischief by bathing in ink. Fortunately, Pluto is on hand to rescue the runaway from the clutches of a wily cat.

THE KLONDIKE KID (MM) Director Wilfred Jackson. Mickey Mouse again finds himself hot on the heels of Peg Leg Pierre (played by his old enemy Pete). Mickey rescues his sweetheart and watches as the villain falls over a cliff and is buried beneath his own runaway log cabin.

BABES IN THE WOODS (SS) Director Bert Gillett. Almost as a forerunner to Snow White's rescue by the Seven Dwarfs, the Babes in the Woods are saved from the wicked witch by an army of little men. Although this Silly Symphony begins with the usual revelry – dancing, drinking and playing – it becomes rather nightmarish once the action moves inside the witch's gingerbread house.

SANTA'S WORKSHOP (SS) Director Wilfred Jackson. Helped by hundreds of gnomes, Santa prepares the presents for Christmas at his home

white short, but Walt was fascinated by experiments with the new three-strip Technicolor process and saw the potential of releasing the film in colour. The animation was reshot, and the results won an Academy Award. The story concerns the love between two young saplings. When one is kidnapped by a villainous old tree she has to be rescued. In retaliation the evil tree starts a forest fire in which it is itself consumed by the flames. Apart from the rich texture of the colour – Walt had signed a short-term agreement giving him sole rights to the Technicolor process for making animated shorts – the film includes an appropriate musical soundtrack. Excerpts from Schubert's chilling 'Erl King', Rossini's 'William Tell' overture and Mendelssohn's 'Wedding March', were all successfully synchronized with the story (above). The film was re-released in two 'Academy Award Specials' (1937 and 1967) and as part of the film *Milestones in Animation* (1973).

TRADER MICKEY (MM) Director Dave Hand. While exploring dense jungle, Mickey and Pluto are captured by cannibals. The tribe finds some musical instruments in Mickey's canoe, and he gives an impromptu jam session, in which the cannibals join and forget all about eating their captives.

KING NEPTUNE (SS) Director Bert Gillett. When a group of pirates captures a lovely mermaid princess the other sea creatures launch an attack on their ship. Much needed assistance is finally provided by King Neptune himself (centre). The ship is sunk, and the mermaid claims ownership of the pirates' treasure for her undersea friends.

THE WHOOPEE PARTY (MM) Director Wilfred Jackson. Minnie plays the piano while Mickey taps out the rhythm on a variety of household objects – including milk bottles, mousetraps and a window blind – in a crazy performance of 'Running Wild'. By the time the police arrive, the party is in full swing with everybody, including some of the furniture, joining in the dancing.

BUGS IN LOVE (SS) Director Bert Gillett. A little boy bug rescues his sweetheart who has been kidnapped by a crow.

at the North Pole (opposite below). A sequel entitled *The Night Before Christmas*, also directed by Jackson, was released in 1933.

MICKEY'S GOOD DEED (MM) Director Bert Gillett. Street musician Mickey sells Pluto to a rich family at Christmastime to raise money for the poor. But Pluto, with a turkey tied to his tail, is thrown out, and the two pals are reunited.

1933

☆ BUILDING A BUILDING (MM) Director Dave Hand. Yet again Mickey rescues Minnie from the evil Pete. This time the location is a building site, and there are plenty of opportunities for Mickey to indulge in Harold Lloyd-type gags high up on the steel frame of a skyscraper.

THE MAD DOCTOR (MM) Director Dave Hand. A number of Mickey Mouse shorts involved dreams – sometimes Mickey dreams that he is married to Minnie, that he visits Wonderland and even that he receives praise from his Hollywood peers at a special celebratory party. In *The Mad Doctor*, however, he dreams that Pluto has been kidnapped by a mad scientist and sets off to rescue him. The wonderfully spooky setting – a dreary, ghost-infested castle – and the terrible experiments of the crazy scientist add up to one of Mickey's most chilling adventures (below). Spoofing the highly successful horror film series from Universal, this tale was considered by the British film censor as too frightening for some audiences. Years later the 16mm release was still categorized as 'unsuitable for young children'.

MICKEY'S PAL PLUTO (MM) Director Bert Gillett. Mickey and Minnie find some kittens, which makes Pluto jealous. When the cats fall into a deep well, Pluto wrestles with his good and bad consciences to decide if he should attempt a rescue. A colour remake, *Lend A Paw* (1941), won an Academy Award.

BIRDS IN THE SPRING (SS) Director Dave Hand. Otto, a baby bird, gets lost in the forest. After various misadventures, including being hypnotized by a rattlesnake, Otto is rescued – and soundly spanked – by his father.

MICKEY'S MELLERDRAMMER (MM) Director Wilfred Jackson. Horace Horsecollar stars as the

melodramatic figure of Simon Legree while Mickey plays Uncle Tom (above). Unfortunately the curtain is brought down rather prematurely on this adaptation of the classic *Uncle Tom's Cabin* by a pack of unruly bloodhounds.

YE OLDEN DAYS (MM) Director Bert Gillett. Medieval minstrel Mickey frees Minnie, who has been imprisoned by her father. Then he has to joust with Prince Dippy (who later became Goofy) to win Minnie's hand in marriage.

FATHER NOAH'S ARK (SS) Director Wilfred Jackson. The Studio's first version of the Biblical tale of Noah, his family and an ark full of animals who escape the great flood. In 1959 a stop-motion version of the story was made.

THE MAIL PILOT (MM) Director Dave Hand. Mickey has to elude the bandit Pete in his bat-shaped plane and deliver the mail safely. The short is full of delightful invention, as Mickey, struggling to keep his plane in the air, uses all manner of objects, including the sails of a windmill, as a propeller.

★ THREE LITTLE PIGS (SS) Director Bert Gillett. Released at the height of the Depression, this

famous Silly Symphony, with its catchy song 'Who's Afraid of the Big Bad Wolf?' (written by Frank Churchill) proved to be a great morale booster. Having destroyed the houses of sticks and straw, the wolf is unable to blow down Practical Pig's house because it is built from bricks (above). Animated in part by Fred Moore, the film won an Academy Award for 1932–3, and it was so popular that during its initial run one cinema manager stuck facial hair on the drawings of the pigs outside his theatre, adding the words, 'You've kept us here so long we've grown beards'. The public response caused the distributors, United Artists, to plead, 'Send us more pigs!' Two sequels followed: *The Big Bad Wolf* (1934) and *Three Little Wolves* (1936). Disney released a third film, *The Practical Pig*, through RKO Radio Pictures in 1939, although Walt had commented 'You can't top pigs with pigs!' He was proved right – none of the sequels made as much impact on the movie-going public as the original. It was released in 1973 on 16mm as part of the compilation film *Milestones in Animation*.

MICKEY'S MECHANICAL MAN (MM) Director Wilfred Jackson. Inventor Mickey Mouse is rather proud of his robot. When the hairy star of *The Gorilla Mystery* challenges him to a boxing match, Mickey brings his robot to life in time to win the fight.

MICKEY'S GALA PREMIERE (MM) Director Bert Gillett. From the first moment Mickey Mouse cavorted across the screen, Walt dreamt of a time when his new star would be recognized alongside the other Hollywood greats. The Disney ani-

mators paid affectionate homage to the stars of the silver screen when Mickey is guest of honour at the premiere of his latest film at Grauman's Chinese Theater. The centre of attraction, he is idolized by delightful caricatures of Clark Gable, Mae West, Harold Lloyd, Marlene Dietrich, Laurel and Hardy, Charlie Chaplin and many others (opposite below). Sadly, Mickey awakes to find it's only a dream.

OLD KING COLE (SS) Director Dave Hand. In a story that is reminiscent of the short *Mother Goose Melodies* (1931), nursery-rhyme characters are invited to a ball at King Cole's castle. Highlights of this brilliantly inventive film are when the various characters emerge from the pages of a large book (above). A similar device was used to great effect in the finale of *Mother Goose Goes Hollywood* and in the 'Baia' sequence of *The Three Caballeros* (1945).

LULLABY LAND (SS) Director Wilfred Jackson. A small baby and a toy dog find themselves in a strange land of patchwork-quilt fields, where rattles grow on trees and nursery crockery, safety pins and bottles of castor oil take on a life of their own. In a Forbidden Garden with the sign 'Baby Stay Away', are penknives, scissors and boxes of matches. Fortunately Mr Sandman arrives before the baby gets into too much trouble and sends him back to sleep. A strikingly animated film, the backgrounds are among the most fascinating of all the Silly Symphony cartoons, while the story has some similarities to the adventures of *Wynken, Blynken and Nod* (1938).

PUPPY LOVE (MM) Director Wilfred Jackson. Pluto swaps a box of candy for one of his bones. Pluto wants the gift for Fifi, the dog next door, with whom he is in love; Mickey had intended the candy to be a gift for Minnie. Minnie forgives Mickey when she finds out the truth.

THE PIED PIPER (SS) Director Wilfred Jackson. As in the classic story, the piper (centre) lures the rats out of Hamelin, but instead of drowning, the rats disappear forever into a giant Swiss cheese. When the townspeople refuse to pay for his services, the piper leads the children away into a huge mountain wherein lies the Garden of Happiness.

THE STEEPLE CHASE (MM) Director Bert Gillett. Mickey Mouse is a proud jockey. Unfortunately his horse gets drunk before the big race, so Mickey puts two stable boys into a pantomime horse costume, hoping that no one will notice the difference. Problems with a swarm of hornets help Mickey and his ersatz steed to win, but the ruse is uncovered.

THE PET STORE (MM) Director Wilfred Jackson. Mickey enlists the help of some caged animals when a large gorilla captures Minnie. In a sequence reminiscent of the climax to *King Kong* (released the same year), the ape climbs to the top of a pile of packing cases, which resembles New York's Empire State Building. It is interesting to note the contrast between the simple features of Mickey and Minnie and the artists' experiments with the human figure of Tony, the pet store owner.

GIANTLAND (MM) Director Bert Gillett. Loosely based on the story of Jack and the Beanstalk, Mickey tells his nephews how he climbed the famous beanstalk and defeated a ferocious giant.

THE NIGHT BEFORE CHRISTMAS (SS) Director Wilfred Jackson. A sequel to the Silly Symphony *Santa's Workshop* (1932), the short relates what happens when Santa Claus enlists the aid of all his toys to decorate the Christmas tree. The gags allow for the occasional spoof on Hollywood personalities like Chaplin, and the film was later released on 16mm under the title *Santa's Toys*.

1934

THE CHINA SHOP (SS) Director Wilfred Jackson. Like a scene from a Fred Astaire and Ginger Rogers film, two delicate china figures dance together after the shop owner has gone home for the night. A china figure of a horned satyr comes to life and kidnaps the girl, but so much china is broken when the boy rescues her that the next morning the owner changes the sign in the window from 'Fine China' to 'Antiques'.

SHANGHAIED (MM) Director Bert Gillett. Mickey comes to the daring rescue of his sweetheart Minnie, but first he has to do battle with the villainous Peg Leg Pete and his band of cutthroats.

GRASSHOPPER AND THE ANTS (SS) Director Wilfred Jackson. Pinto Colvig voices a lazy grasshopper who prefers to sing and dance instead of work (below). He soon realizes how foolish he's been when winter comes and he has to beg for help from the hard-working ants. The grasshopper's song, 'The World Owes Me a Living', was sung by Colvig, the voice of Goofy, in a number of other cartoons.

CAMPING OUT (MM) Director David Hand. Mickey, Minnie, Clarabelle and Horace are enjoying a peaceful summer's day in the country when the rural calm is brought to a swift end by an army of mosquitoes. Quick-thinking Mickey traps the swarm in a pair of Clarabelle's bloomers.

PLAYFUL PLUTO (MM) Director Bert Gillett. In one of his classic routines, Pluto, helping Mickey to spring-clean the house, becomes entangled in a piece of flypaper. The sequence, devised by Webb Smith and animated by Norm Ferguson, is considered an epic of animation and comic timing.

FUNNY LITTLE BUNNIES (SS) Director Wilfred Jackson. Wolfgang Reitherman's first assignment at the Studio was animating Easter eggs. As he recalled in later years: 'I always remember having trouble with the eggs. In animation, they tended to look as if they were going backwards instead of forwards.' The film shows rabbits, at rainbow's end, making Easter eggs, which are beribboned by birds.

THE BIG BAD WOLF (SS) Director Bert Gillett. The Studio disguised the follow-up to *Three Little Pigs* by giving the villain the leading role. *The Big Bad Wolf* was based on the story of Red Riding Hood and her Grandmother, and the pigs were actually relegated to having guest-star roles. As in the first film, however, everyone is saved by Practical Pig, who scares off the wolf with a combination of hot coals and popping corn.

GULLIVER MICKEY (MM) Director Bert Gillett. Mickey finds himself tied up by the Lilliputians. He escapes, is attacked by their miniature navy, but saves the day by rescuing the town from a large spider.

THE WISE LITTLE HEN (SS) Director Wilfred Jackson. A mother hen fails to find anyone who will help her plant her corn: this deceptively simple story formed the basis of a very important Silly Symphony – it was the occasion of the movie debut of the Studio's most successful star, Donald Duck. Deceitful from the very beginning, this cameo performance was just the start of a burgeoning screen career, while the mother hen (below), her chicks and Donald's friend Peter Pig were never seen or heard of again.

MICKEY'S STEAM ROLLER (MM) Director Dave Hand. The vehicle in question is driven by his nephews but runs out of control and smashes a hotel (above). The film underlines how Mickey's affection for Minnie usually meant he forgot the job he was supposed to be doing.

THE FLYING MOUSE (SS) Director Dave Hand. A mouse rescues a butterfly fairy from a spider's web and is granted a wish. He chooses a pair of wings so that he can fly, only to regret his choice when his family fails to recognize him and thinks he's a bat instead. Fortunately the fairy is on hand to restore him to his former self.

ORPHAN'S BENEFIT (MM) Director Bert Gillett. In this short, the first to feature Donald and Goofy together, Mickey puts on a show. Donald's rendition of 'Mary had a Little Lamb' is ridiculed by the audience, which tries to sabotage his act. Such was the popularity of the short, it was remade in Technicolor in 1941.

PECULIAR PENGUINS (SS) Director Wilfred Jackson. Unlike Pablo in the feature *The Three Caballeros* (1945), who escaped from his wintry climate, Peter and Polly Penguin enjoy life in the Arctic. When Polly is chased by a shark, Peter comes to the rescue.

MICKEY PLAYS PAPA (MM) Director Bert Gillett. Mickey finds an abandoned baby on his doorstep and gets the opportunity to imitate screen greats like Charlie Chaplin and Jimmy Durante in his attempts to stop the baby from crying.

THE GODDESS OF SPRING (SS) Director Wilfred Jackson. Animator Eric Larson recalled once how Walt Disney asked him to dance for the artists who were planning the choreography of Persephone in this Silly Symphony. 'It came out as one of the worst pictures we ever did,' he said. 'Not because of my dancing, but because it was one of the first efforts to do a human girl.' In fact, there is a lot of colour and ingenuity in the film,

especially in the scene in which the goddess (opposite below) is captured by the devil (Pluto) and taken to Hades to be his bride. Although Persephone does move like Mickey did in the earlier films, the Studio quickly progressed with the animation of human characters until it achieved the perfection of *Snow White and the Seven Dwarfs*.

THE DOGNAPPER (MM) Director Dave Hand. Mickey and Donald rescue Minnie's Pekinese from the evil clutches of Peg Leg Pete, who is keeping the dog prisoner in a deserted sawmill.

TWO-GUN MICKEY (MM) Director Ben Sharpsteen. Mickey (left) bravely comes to Minnie's rescue, but first he has to dispatch a whole group of bandits led by the infamous Pete.

1935

★THE TORTOISE AND THE HARE (SS) Director Wilfred Jackson. Max Hare is so confident that he will win the race against slowcoach Toby Tortoise that he stops *en route* to entertain some pretty female rabbits with a display of his tennis-playing prowess. Unfortunately he mis-times the delay, and, through his own stupidity, loses to the persistently plodding tortoise (below).

MICKEY'S MAN FRIDAY (MM) Director Dave Hand. Mickey befriends a native who helps him escape from the cannibals. One of Mickey's last black and white adventures, the film is loosely based on the story of Robinson Crusoe.

THE BAND CONCERT (MM) Director Wilfred Jackson. Walt had established Jackson as one of his leading directors as early as 1931 and placed him at the helm of Mickey Mouse's first Technicolor short. Wearing a bright red uniform, Mickey attempts to conduct a spirited version of the 'William Tell' overture between interruptions from peanut vendor and flute player Donald Duck, who tries to persuade the musicians to play 'Turkey in the Straw' instead. A real cyclone accompanies 'the storm' section of the music and hurls the entire ensemble into the air. The film could almost be described as a Silly Symphony with Mickey as the star (above). Donald was already establishing his role as a nuisance-maker, and the frantic energy of the short leaves the viewer quite breathless. The short was later released in *Milestones for Mickey* in 1974.

MICKEY'S SERVICE STATION (MM) Director Ben Sharpsteen. Big-time mobster Peg Leg Pete takes his car to the garage so that Mickey, Donald and Goofy can locate a strange squealing sound in the engine. The gang totally wrecks the villain's car in order to find the trouble, which turns out to be a cricket. Included in the 1974 16mm compilation *Milestones for Mickey*, the short was directed with great flair.

THE GOLDEN TOUCH (SS) Director Walt Disney. Based on the story of greedy King Midas, the film relates how the King is granted his wish to turn everything he touches to gold. Unfortunately, all food turns to gold before he can eat it, juice squirting from a grapefruit becoming a shower of gold coins. The dejected King sees an evil spectre delighting in his plight. 'My kingdom for a hamburger,' he cries and is promptly restored to normal.

MICKEY'S KANGAROO (MM) Director Dave Hand. An unusual present from Australia arrives on Mickey's doorstep. Pluto is upset when the visitor, a marsupial with boxing gloves, challenges his owner to a contest. Fortunately all

three soon become firm friends, in this, the last Mickey Mouse cartoon to be released in black and white.

THE ROBBER KITTEN (SS) Director Dave Hand. A kitten runs away to become a bandit, but the tables are turned when he is robbed himself. Frightened out of his wits, he quickly returns to the safety of his home.

WATER BABIES (SS) Director Wilfred Jackson. Loosely based on Charles Kingsley's classic story, the Silly Symphony follows the escapades of the fairy folk who inhabit a quiet lagoon. Awakening from their sleep, these aquatic infants pretend to be rodeo riders on the backs of frogs, fly with birds or frolic in tiny leaf boats. Such was the popularity of these characters that the Studio

decided to bring them back in a sequel, *Merbabies* (1938).

THE COOKIE CARNIVAL (SS) Director Ben Sharpsteen. Pinto Colvig voices a gingerbread boy who helps a confectionery Cinderella to attend the Cookie Queen Carnival. With the aid of cakes, cream, fudge, toffee and chocolate éclairs, the boy makes her beautiful in a song routine reminiscent of a Dick Powell and Ruby Keeler number. Winning the title of Cookie Queen, she chooses the gingerbread boy as King.

☆ WHO KILLED COCK ROBIN? (SS) Director Dave Hand. In this brilliant retelling of the classic rhyme, Robin's sweetheart Jenny Wren is a sharply accurate caricature of Hollywood star Mae West (below). Jenny revives Robin with a kiss.

MICKEY'S GARDEN (MM) Director Wilfred Jackson. Mickey is upset when he sees the bugs eating his plants. In retaliation, he mixes an extremely potent insecticide but accidentally sprays it on himself. In a wonderfully surreal sequence, he finds himself in a giant garden populated by angry bugs.

MICKEY'S FIRE BRIGADE (MM) Director Ben Sharpsteen. Mickey was cast in the role of firefighter twice during his career – once he rescued Minnie in the film *The Fire Fighters* and, with Donald and Goofy, he saved Clarabelle Cow. Completely unaware of the impending danger, Clarabelle is relaxing in her bathtub when Mickey, Donald and Goofy break down the bathroom door. This was one of Clarabelle's last appearances in a Mickey Mouse short.

PLUTO'S JUDGMENT DAY (MM) Director Dave Hand. Pluto has a terrible nightmare in which he dreams he is on trial for chasing cats. Sentenced to a grisly end by the feline jury, he awakes determined to make amends with a kitten.

ON ICE (MM) Director Ben Sharpsteen. Goofy tries, without much success, to catch fish, while Donald, who can't resist a prank or two, plays a

COCK O' THE WALK (SS) Director Ben Sharpsteen. All the hens are excited when the champion boxer comes to town. The tough, cigar-smoking bird steals the affections of a young rooster's girlfriend. The film uses the theme of the *Carioca* to pay homage to some of Busby Berkeley's stunning dance routines, here performed by peacocks, ducks and chickens.

BROKEN TOYS (SS) Director Ben Sharpsteen. Caricatures of Hollywood stars (below left) tell how a sailor doll, discarded on the city dump, performs a delicate operation to restore the sight of a small doll.

1936

MICKEY'S POLO TEAM (MM) Director Dave Hand. Having wowed the stars of Hollywood at *Mickey's Gala Premiere* (1933), Mickey and the gang challenge other screen stars to a polo match (below right). Donald Duck certainly meets his match when he tries to get the ball from a brilliantly caricatured Harpo Marx. Walt enjoyed playing polo with other celebrities, including Spencer Tracy, at the time short was made.

ORPHAN'S PICNIC (MM) Director Ben Sharpsteen. Donald has problems with the youngsters who plagued him in both the original and the remake of *Orphan's Benefit*. This time they tease and torment the poor Duck until he has trouble with a beehive and inadvertently swallows one of its inhabitants.

ELMER ELEPHANT (SS) Director Wilfred Jackson. Although an endearing character who became a popular comic-book hero, Elmer made only one screen appearance. He is ridiculed by the other jungle animals for having a trunk, but he proves what an advantage it is when he rescues Tillie Tiger from her burning tree house.

THREE LITTLE WOLVES (SS) Director Dave Hand. In this second sequel to the highly successful *Three Little Pigs* (1933), the Big Bad Wolf disguises himself as Bo-Peep in order to lure the

trick on Pluto. Mickey eventually comes to Donald's rescue when he is swept away on an ice floe.

MUSIC LAND (SS) Director Wilfred Jackson. Although some of the Mickey and Donald cartoons had predictable storylines, the same could not be said for the Silly Symphonies. This colourful saga is a musical retelling of the story of Romeo and Juliet set on the Isle of Jazz and the Land of Symphony. All the characters are designed to resemble instruments from the orchestra. Queen Cello is angry when King Sax's son, Crown Prince Max, sneaks into the Land of Symphony to woo her daughter, Princess Fiddle Dee Dee. The film was a perfect vehicle for the

series as all the characters 'speak' with musical notes. At the climax, both lands wage war to the strains of Wagner's 'Ride of the Valkyries', which adds to the medley of music used as weapons. Finally all is resolved, and a Bridge of Harmony is built between the two enemies. (Copyrighted as *Musicland*.)

★THREE ORPHAN KITTENS (SS) Director Dave Hand. Recently much has been said of the need to use computer animation to simulate moving backgrounds, yet long before such devices were available, Disney animators were achieving remarkable results in shorts such as this. The film follows the exploits of three kittens (above), in a world of giant chairs, tables and a grand piano.

THREE BLIND MOUSEKETEERS (SS) Director Dave Hand. Captain Katt, who bears a striking resemblance to Peg Leg Pete, sets some mouse traps. The mice outwit him, however, and turn the tables on their feline adversary.

MICKEY'S ELEPHANT (MM) Director Dave Hand. Pluto is jealous when Mickey builds a new house for his pet pachyderm, Bobo. Bobo has problems with sneezing when Pluto puts pepper in his trunk, a gag repeated (with soap) in *The Big Wash* (1948).

★ THE COUNTRY COUSIN (SS) Director Wilfred Jackson. This beautifully animated short relates how Abner, a small country mouse from the town of Podunk, goes to visit his cousin Monty who lives in the big city. Monty's lifestyle is splendid beyond belief, but poor Abner gets drunk, is chased by a cat and sees just how terrifying the hustle and bustle of city life can be (right). A popular story with animators, it was also used in an MGM Tom and Jerry short, *Mouse In Manhattan*, and in an outrageous Tex Avery production, *Little Rural Riding Hood*.

MOTHER PLUTO (SS) Director Dave Hand. Some baby chicks are hatched inside Pluto's kennel,

two frivolous pigs into a trap. Fortunately their sensible brother, Practical Pig, is on hand to rescue them with the aid of an amazing invention called a 'Wolf Pacifier'.

MICKEY'S GRAND OPERA (MM) Director Wilfred Jackson. Clarence Nash, the voice of Donald Duck, and Florence Gill, who spoke for the lesser known character Clara Cluck, sing a duet: Mickey is the conductor, but Pluto brings the house down when he tampers with the bizarre inhabitants of a magician's hat (above).

THRU THE MIRROR (MM) Director Dave Hand. Mickey Mouse dreams he is acting out the part of Lewis Carroll's Alice in this ingenious film, which demonstrates several of Mickey's talents as he sings and dances with a pack of cards in true Busby Berkeley style, performs a solo routine and fights off some extraordinary adversaries in a strange world on the other side of his bedroom mirror. This popular short was featured in the 16mm release *Milestones for Mickey* (1974).

MICKEY'S RIVAL (MM) Director Wilfred Jackson. Sly and despicable rodent Mortimer Mouse woos Minnie away from Mickey. This fast-talking villain plays practical jokes on Mickey, while his sports car terrifies the life out of Mickey's old car. When a ferocious bull escapes from a field, Mortimer leaves Minnie helpless, and Mickey bravely comes to the rescue. Mortimer was, in fact, one of the first names suggested by Walt for Mickey Mouse, when he was trying to create a character to replace Oswald the Lucky Rabbit in 1928.

MOVING DAY (MM) Director Ben Sharpsteen. Landlord Pete evicts Mickey and Donald (right), and, as a favour, Goofy the iceman attempts to move their furniture for them, although he reckons without the antics of a piano that refuses to leave home.

ALPINE CLIMBERS (MM) Director Dave Hand. Donald has problems with a mountain goat, Pluto and a friendly St Bernard become inebriated while Mickey falls foul of a mother eagle and her offspring. Donald saves the day.

MICKEY'S CIRCUS (MM) Director Ben Sharpsteen. Characters like Donald Duck and Pluto were becoming the real stars of the Mickey

Mouse shorts. Here, Captain Donald and his performing sea lions turn the circus into a riot, as all kinds of acrobatics take place on the highwire.

TOBY TORTOISE RETURNS (SS) Director Wilfred Jackson. This time Toby, who won the race against smart-aleck Max Hare in *The Tortoise and the Hare* (1935), finds himself prize-fighting with his old adversary. Surprise, surprise – Toby wins (right).

DONALD AND PLUTO (MM) Director Ben Sharpsteen. When Donald drops a magnet in his attempts at D-I-Y home plumbing, Pluto accidentally swallows it. Donald's frustration as he tries to repair broken water pipes grows when Pluto mysteriously magnetizes everything within his reach. Sharpsteen, who was later promoted to animated features, shows in this classic that he was the master of the short subject.

and Pluto feels duty-bound to keep them out of harm's way. But it's a case of 'easier barked than done'.

MORE KITTENS (SS) Director Dave Hand. Turned out of their house, the stars of *Three Orphan Kittens* (1935) seek refuge with a friendly St Bernard.

1937

THE WORM TURNS (MM) Director Ben Sharpsteen. Mickey concocts a magic fluid that increases the size of animals. A fly turns the tables on a spider and a cat chases poor Pluto, who is rescued in the nick of time from the dog-catcher.

DON DONALD (MM) Director Ben Sharpsteen. Donald stars in his first solo role as a romantic

troubadour who, much to the disgust of his sweetheart Donna Duck, has a very unromantic sense of humour. Trading in his faithful burro for a motor car, Donald wrecks the desert landscape all in the name of love.

MAGICIAN MICKEY (MM) Director Dave Hand. Donald Duck, himself a victim of a bad audience in *Orphan's Benefit*, takes a great delight in heckling Mickey's stage performance. Finally, an exasperated Mickey calls Donald up to the stage and proceeds to show his critic some amazing magic tricks (above right).

MOOSE HUNTERS (MM) Director Ben Sharpsteen. Mickey is again out hunting, this time accompanied by Donald and Goofy who disguise themselves as an alluring female moose to décoy the real moose to where Mickey lies in wait.

☆ SNOW WHITE AND THE SEVEN DWARFS (F) Supervising director Dave Hand. When this landmark (below) in cinema history opened, the Disney publicity machine went into full swing with an advertising campaign worthy of any Hollywood epic. 'As many as 750 artists worked on the production,' it announced to an eager public. 'These consisted of 32 animators, 102 assistants, 167 in betweeners, 20 layout artists, 25 artists doing water colour backgrounds, 65 effects animators (those who draw smoke, water, clouds, etc.) and 159 young women adept at inking and painting the Disney figures on transparent celluloid sheets.' Yet, unbeknown to the majority of cinema-goers who were about to be enthralled, entertained and delighted beyond their wildest imagination, Hollywood had been referring to this vast undertaking as 'Disney's folly', convinced that the film would bankrupt

the Studio and bring to an abrupt end the career of Mickey and the gang. They couldn't have been more wrong. The film received a glittering premiere at the Carthay Circle Theater in Los Angeles in December 1937 and was released worldwide the following year. Costing $1¼ million to produce (well over budget), it grossed over $8 million. Even the Academy of Motion Picture Arts and Sciences honoured Disney with a special statuette at the 1939 awards ceremony, although it failed to acknowledge any of the film's wonderful songs – 'Heigh Ho', 'Someday My Prince will Come', 'Whistle While you Work' and 'With a Smile and a Song'. The voice talents, although not recognized on the film's original credits, include a young singer, Adriana Caselotti, as Snow White, Harry Stockwell (father of Dean) as the Prince, Lucille La Verne as the Wicked Stepmother, and a number of radio and screen personalities including Otis Harlan, Scotty Mattraw, Roy Atwell, Billy Gilbert and Pinto (Goofy) Colvig as the voices of six of the dwarfs (the seventh dwarf, Dopey, doesn't actually speak in the film not because he can't but, as Doc explains to Snow White, because he's never tried). The story was adapted from the classic fairy-tale by Ted Sears, Otto Englander and Earl Hurd, and was four years in production. It makes excellent use of characterization, editing, sound and delicate Technicolor photography, and the thrilling climax subtly blends the powers of good and evil with tremendous impact. Re-issued six times up until 1983, it has earned in the region of $47 million at the American box office. The 50th anniversary re-issue in 1987 garnered an additional $40 million in under eight weeks – an indication that, when the majority of early Hollywood films are restricted to television, Disney's 'crown jewels' continue to achieve phenomenal success at the box-office. One advertising campaign even hinted that the film would still be the number one hit in 2037. In 1978, a 16mm release, *Snow White: A Lesson in Cooperation*, was released for schools.

WOODLAND CAFÉ (SS) Director Wilfred Jackson. The bugs and insects who frequent a popular nightclub mirror their human counterparts in numerous Hollywood dramas. Ingenious routines involving all types of caterpillars, spiders and fireflies include a brilliant caricature of actor John Barrymore. Animator Max Fleischer's second feature film, *Mr Bug Goes to Town,* has sequences that are very reminiscent of this entertaining short.

MICKEY'S AMATEURS (MM) Directors Pinto Colvig, Walt Pfeiffer and Ed Penner. Mickey makes a radio broadcast from a local barnyard, and guest stars Donald Duck, Clara Cluck, Clarabelle (above) and Goofy are invited to go through their paces. Goofy's one-man-band rendition of 'In the Good Ol' Summertime' is the highspot of the entertainment.

LITTLE HIAWATHA (SS) Director Dave Hand. A young Indian brave goes hunting in the forest. Meeting up with a ferocious grizzly bear, he is rescued in the nick of time by some friendly woodland creatures.

ACADEMY AWARD REVIEW OF WALT DISNEY CARTOONS With the imminent release of the Studio's first feature-length animated film *Snow White and the Seven Dwarfs*, Walt compiled a featurette celebrating previous Academy Award-winning Silly Symphonies, each of which was introduced by a narrator.

MODERN INVENTIONS (MM) Director Jack King. Wonderful art deco designs appear as the backdrop against which Donald Duck experiments with sophisticated devices in a museum of modern marvels. In a running gag, a robot butler keeps taking Donald's hat, while a robotized barber's chair succeeds in giving Donald's face a wonderful shine and his tail a stylish trim.

HAWAIIAN HOLIDAY (MM) Director Ben Sharpsteen. This was the first of the Studio's cartoons to be distributed by RKO Radio Pictures. In the tranquil setting of an Hawaiian island, Mickey, Minnie, Donald, Goofy and Pluto are enjoying a well-deserved vacation. Unfortunately, the serenity of the scene is disturbed when Pluto comes across a mischievous starfish and surf-boarding Goofy falls victim to some waves with minds of their own.

CLOCK CLEANERS (MM) Director Ben Sharpsteen. In one of the best shorts to star Mickey, Donald and Goofy, the trio attempt to restore a clock tower to its former glory. Donald has trouble with the mainspring, Mickey finds a stork living in the works, and Goofy has problems with the mechanical figures that ring the hourly bell. Excellent backgrounds accentuate the dizzy heights of the tower and look most impressive on the cinema screen.

★ THE OLD MILL (SS) Director Wilfred Jackson. In the year that Disney won the Scientific and Technical Class II plaque for the design and application of the multi-plane camera, he also won an Academy Award for the Silly Symphony that had used this sophisticated equipment. The film tells the simple story of animal and bird life living within the confines of a ramshackle mill (right). The tranquillity of the setting is broken by a remarkable thunderstorm that tosses the ancient structure back and forth. Effective editing and the careful use of music and three-dimensional animation create some stark and terrifying realism. The short proved to Disney that his special effects department was capable of handling anything that might be required of it to perfect the feature films then in progress. Re-issued countless times, it was included as one of the shorts in *Milestones in Animation*, released on 16mm in 1973.

PLUTO'S QUIN-PUPLETS (P) Director Ben Sharpsteen. When Fifi goes out Pluto is left in charge of five pups. Unfortunately, he gets drunk and the puppies get covered in paint spray. Fifi is so disgusted that she disowns them all, and a bedraggled Pluto sleeps in a barrel with the pups (opposite below).

DONALD'S OSTRICH (DD) Director Jack King. An ostrich escapes from its crate, swallows a radio and gives Donald a serious bout of hiccoughs.

LONESOME GHOSTS (MM) Director Bert Gillett. Made at the height of the Disney characters' popularity with audiences, the film follows the adventures of Donald and Goofy when they join Mickey's team of Ghost Exterminators. They are invited to a spooky mansion to rid it of a gang of ghosts, little realizing that the ghosts, bored with having no one to scare, extended the invitation themselves. Vivid colour and hilarious routines contribute to a highly entertaining film, as Mickey and the gang finally turn the tables on their spectral hosts.

1938

SELF CONTROL (DD) Director Jack King. Smiling Uncle Smiley philosophizes on the radio about the importance of controlling one's anger. But, although Donald tries, the combination of a hammock, a bluebottle, a caterpillar, a wood-pecker and hundreds of apples only succeeds in giving him a raging temper.

BOAT BUILDERS (MM) Director Ben Sharpsteen. Mickey, Donald and Goofy buy a do-it-yourself ship. All goes well until Minnie breaks a bottle of champagne across the ship's bows and, as it slides down the slipway, it totally disintegrates.

DONALD'S BETTER SELF (DD) Director Jack King. In this moralistic tale Donald's good- and bad-selves discuss the difference between right and wrong. Surprisingly, perhaps, the better-self wins. Animation from this short was used in a bond-selling film, *Donald's Decision* (1942).

MOTH AND THE FLAME (SS) Director Bert Gillett. The Silly Symphonies provided a showcase for experimentation, and the special effects depart-ment was called upon to create an amazingly realistic flame, which threatens the life of a little girl moth in an old costume shop. Effects anima-tion of this type had progressed in leaps and bounds since the days of the forest fire in *Flowers and Trees* (1932), and this short was further proof of how much closer Disney had come to perfect-ing the art of animation.

DONALD'S NEPHEWS (DD) Director Jack King. Huey, Dewey and Louie first came to the screen in 1938, and, like cousin Gus and other visitors who found themselves on Donald's doorstep, they prove a constant irritation to the hot-headed Duck. However, as Donald's sister Dumbella never seems to want them back, the nephews have stayed with Donald throughout numerous film and comic-strip adventures.

MICKEY'S TRAILER (MM) Director Ben Sharpsteen. In one of the highlights of his career, Mickey teams up with Donald and Goofy in a runaway trailer. Overcoming all obstacles, in-cluding a precipitous mountain path and a fast-moving express train, the three are re-united when the trailer re-hitches itself to the back of Goofy's car (below).

★ FERDINAND THE BULL (Sp) Director Dick Rickard. Occasionally a picture book's original illustrations were adapted for use in a cartoon short. *Little Toot*, for example, the story of a tugboat in the film *Melody Time*, closely re-sembles the work of artist Hardie Gramatky. In *Ferdinand the Bull* the designs were adapted from Robert Lawson's illustrations in the book by Munro Leaf. The film tells the marvellous story

outwitted by a large walrus, while Donald uses the 'Pied Piper' technique to round up a group of penguins.

☆GOOD SCOUTS (DD) Director Jack King. Huey, Dewey and Louie go camping with Donald, but the expedition ends in disaster when Donald falls victim to a geyser called Old Faithful and an angry bear.

THE FOX HUNT (DD) Director Ben Sharpsteen. Although Disney didn't care much for sequels, some of the stories used in the early black and white shorts were refilmed in colour. Donald Duck and Goofy star in this remake of the 1931 Silly Symphony. When Donald corners the poor fox, a friendly skunk comes to the rescue and chases the hunters away.

THE WHALERS (MM) Director Dick Huemer. Like a modern day Jonah, Goofy is swallowed by a whale, Donald is almost eaten and their tramp steamer is smashed into a thousand pieces. Mickey saves the day.

MICKEY'S PARROT (MM) Director Bill Roberts. Mickey and Pluto are frightened by a radio report of a killer's escape. Fortunately, it's only an escaped parrot that breaks into their house, although the film is full of some very atmospheric moments and delightful gags.

☆BRAVE LITTLE TAILOR (MM) Director Bill Roberts. Mickey's killing of seven pesky flies in his workshop is misinterpreted by the townsfolk who think he has killed seven giants, and the King sends him out to kill a huge giant who is terrorizing the neighbourhood. Mickey uses his ingenuity to capture the giant and, in reward, is given Princess Minnie's hand in marriage.

of Ferdinand, a peace-loving bull who prefers to sit all day smelling flowers instead of bullfighting (below). Vibrant colour styling captures the atmosphere of the Spanish countryside and, as an example of Disney animation at its peak, it rates alongside other Academy Award winners such as *The Old Mill* and *The Ugly Duckling*.

WYNKEN, BLYNKEN AND NOD (SS) Director Graham Heid. Based on the poem by Eugene

Field, this enchanting cartoon follows the adventures of three babies who fish for stars while travelling across the night sky in a giant shoe. Stunning animation and special effects enhance the film's dreamlike quality (above). The short was included in the 16mm release *Creative Film Adventures Reel 2* in 1976.

POLAR TRAPPERS (DD) Director Ben Sharpsteen. Donald and Goofy are at the South Pole. Goofy is

FARMYARD SYMPHONY (SS) Director Jack Cutting. The strains of Franz Liszt's second

THE STANDARD PARADE (Com) Produced for the Standard Oil Company, this is a 237-foot film featuring Mickey, Donald, Goofy, the Seven Dwarfs and countless other Disney characters in a parade proclaiming the wonders of the Standard Oil Company.

THE PRACTICAL PIG (SS) Director Dick Rickard. In another sequel to the popular *Three Little Pigs*, the two foolish pigs are captured by the Big Bad Wolf and his nephews. Their brother (below) rescues them, however, with the aid of his latest invention, a lie detector.

GOOFY AND WILBUR (G) Director Dick Huemer. Goofy and his pet grasshopper have an enjoyable time fishing. Some marvellous gags involve Wilbur with some of the underwater creatures and a frog, until Goofy finally rescues him.

HOCKEY CHAMP (DD) Director Jack King. Forever trying to impress his nephews, Huey, Dewey and Louie, Donald shows off his sporting prowess, but his scheme backfires as his nephews skate circles around him and win the game.

'Hungarian Rhapsody' provide part of a classic medley in this short, which follows the exploits of a tiny piglet as he scours the farm in search of breakfast.

DONALD'S GOLF GAME (DD) Director Jack King. Donald should have known better than to play golf with his nephews, Huey, Dewey and Louie. They constantly plague him with loud noises, trick clubs and a grasshopper trapped inside one of the golf balls.

MERBABIES (SS) Director Rudy Ising for Harman-Ising Studios; supervised for Disney by Ben Sharpsteen, Dave Hand, Otto Englander and Walt Disney. Often mistaken for the Silly Symphony *Water Babies*, this short continues the undersea adventures of Charles Kingsley's aquatic infants (above) as they put on a submarine circus.

☆MOTHER GOOSE GOES HOLLYWOOD (SS) Director Wilfred Jackson. The Disney artists illustrate classic nursery-rhymes with guest appearances by caricatured stars of the silver screen. But these aren't the crudely drawn fans of *Mickey's Gala Premiere*. The Studio's ability for spoofing Hollywood stars was now unrivalled: Katharine Hepburn is Little Bo Peep, W. C. Fields is Humpty Dumpty, Stan Laurel and Oliver Hardy are Simple Simon and the Pieman. The film is one of the Studio's finest examples of visual gags, gentle black comedy and technical expertise, all combined in one engaging short.

1939

DONALD'S LUCKY DAY (DD) Director Jack King. Donald's superstitious nature doesn't help when he has to collect a parcel from a shady-looking character living at Number 13. The parcel contains a bomb, but, after a number of mishaps, Donald successfully throws it into the river – the resulting explosion burying him in tons of fish which attract every single black cat in the neighbourhood.

★THE UGLY DUCKLING (SS) Director Jack Cutting. The Technicolor remake of Hans Christian

Andersen's story adds a great deal of charm to the tale of the cygnet who believes it's a duckling (below). Some amusing gags – the anxious father pacing up and down before the eggs hatch and the playful antics of the baby swans – helped to win the film, the last Silly Symphony, an Academy Award for 1939.

SOCIETY DOG SHOW (MM) Director Bill Roberts. Mickey Mouse is ridiculed by the other competitors when he enters Pluto in the local dog show. When a fire breaks out, however, Pluto becomes a hero by rescuing a prize Pekinese called Fifi.

1940

MICKEY'S SURPRISE PARTY (Com) Commissioned by the National Biscuit Company, the film took the form of a short advertisement relating how Minnie's cooking is spoilt by the antics of her pomeranian dog, Fifi. Mickey saves the situation by purchasing a box of Nabisco cookies and showing Minnie the company's extensive range of biscuits (above).

DONALD'S COUSIN GUS (DD) Director Jack King. Gus only came visiting once, which was lucky for Donald, as this gluttonous goose proceeds to eat him out of house and home. This was Gus's only screen appearance, although he dined on in a number of Carl Barks' comic stories.

BEACH PICNIC (DD) Director Clyde (Gerry) Geronimi. A day out provides plenty of mayhem for the hapless Donald and Pluto. Throughout his screen career Donald constantly fell victim to rodents and insects, and this particular short is no exception when a colony of ants swarms all over the food.

SEA SCOUTS (DD) Director Dick Lundy. After their 'successful' camping expedition in *Good Scouts*, Huey, Dewey and Louie return to plague their uncle, 'Admiral' Donald Duck. The nephews' navigational skills bring Donald into a direct confrontation with a large duck-eating shark.

☆THE POINTER (MM) Director Clyde Geronimi. While hunting quail, Mickey tries to teach Pluto how to be a pointer (below). An escapade with a large bear soon changes his mind and the two friends settle down instead to a supper of beans. Although the technique was used only occasionally in the short subjects, in this short cels of Pluto were airbrushed to give the character a more rounded, three-dimensional appearance.

DONALD'S PENGUIN (DD) Director Jack King. An unusual pet drives Donald to despair. After it has eaten his pet fish and wrecked his home, Donald decides to shoot the baby penguin ... but can't bring himself to do it. Eventually they are reunited as friends.

THE AUTOGRAPH HOUND (DD) Director Jack King. The irascible Donald sneaks into a famous Hollywood movie studio to meet the stars. Riding past the guard on the wing of Greta Garbo's car, he encounters Mickey Rooney and the Ritz Brothers and collides with Shirley Temple.

OFFICER DUCK (DD) Director Clyde Geronimi. Donald, a radio cop, serves eviction papers on the villainous Pete and succeeds in arresting him by posing as a baby. Although he only occasionally represented the law, Donald always carried out his missions with a ruthless dedication to justice.

★PINOCCHIO (F) Directors Ben Sharpsteen and Hamilton Luske. 'Rollicking fun, glowing warmth, thrilling spectacle and tingling excitement,' is how the publicity department announced the 1954 re-issue of Disney's second animated feature. If made today, this amazing and stunning technical achievement would cost in excess of $50 million. Looking at the tremendous amount of work involved in the production it's easy to see why, even in 1940, the film cost a staggering $2·5 million – a figure that had exceeded the amount spent on the highly budgeted *Snow White and the Seven Dwarfs*. Adapted from Collodi's book by Ted Sears, Otto Englander, Webb Smith, William Cottrell, Joseph Sabo, Erdman Penner and Aurelius Battaglia, the story concerns a puppet, Pinocchio, which is lovingly fashioned from wood by an old toymaker, Geppetto. Brought to life by the Blue Fairy, the marionette is befriended by Jiminy Cricket (opposite above), a wonderful creation in spats and waistcoat, who acts as his conscience. This proves to be quite a responsibility, however, for the innocent Pinocchio is lured from school by a pair of greedy villains – a fox called J. Worthington Foulfellow and Gideon, his feline accomplice – kidnapped by puppet impressario Stromboli, fooled into taking a one-way trip to Pleasure Island (a fantasy kingdom where small boys are transformed into donkeys) and finally swallowed by a terrifying leviathan called Monstro the Whale.

Although it has an episodic storyline, the film is nicely paced and neatly edited, and it is a visual *tour de force*, a great deal of the budget having been spent on refining some of the more splendid moments. Yet not long after production commenced, Walt still felt it necessary to discard months of work that didn't meet with his approval. The phenomenal artistic and financial success of *Snow White* (1937) probably increased the pressure on him to make *Pinocchio* the Studio's best film. Although it was well received in the USA, the film fared badly in Europe, as overseas markets dwindled with the outbreak of World War II. If any critics considered the poor box-office a sign of the film's shortcomings, Walt later commented in its defence that: 'technically and artistically it was superior. It indicated that we had grown considerably as craftsmen.'

Characterization, always a vital part of Disney's philosophy in his earlier films, was also one of the story's strongest points. Apart from the scene-stealing performance by Jiminy Cricket (voiced by Cliff Edwards) – who not only sings the Academy Award-winning song 'When You Wish Upon A Star' (now a Disney signature tune) but made quite a career for himself in later educational shorts and on television – the film's other personalities were as vivid and believable as the Seven Dwarfs had been. The unscrupulous

showman Stromboli (Charles Judels) who plans to tour the world with Pinocchio as his theatrical star and 'prisoner'; kindly Geppetto (Christian Rub), who risks his life to find his kidnapped son; Cleo the goldfish and Figaro the cat, who later starred in a number of animated films; Lampwick (Frankie Darro), the young tough from the wrong side of the tracks who, in one of the screen's most horrific moments, becomes a sorry victim of the more sinister side of Pleasure Island; Pinocchio (Dickie Jones), a character with whom young audiences could easily identify; and lastly, the despicable but likable rogues, Foulfellow and his mute partner Gideon, a cross between Stan Laurel and Harpo Marx.

Animation directors Fred Moore, Frank Thomas, Milt Kahl, Vladimir Tytla, Ward Kimball, Art Babbitt, Eric Larson and Wolfgang Reitherman had their work cut out with the film's more challenging aspects, including the impressive multiplane camera sequence of Pinocchio's village and the colossal size and energy expended by Monstro. Leigh Harline, Ned Washington and Paul J. Smith's musical score won an Academy Award and again demonstrated Disney's unique ability successfully to integrate music and songs into a story without slowing up the pace of the film. The script also contains some marvellous one-liners, gags and contemporary jokes that owe a lot to the best of the Hollywood comedy classics.

Although by 1985 the film had earned an incredible $25 million on re-issue, the new Studio management decided to release it on video shortly afterwards. Much to the surprise of countless Disney fans, it was shown on The

Disney Channel in 1986. But in whatever medium 'the adventures of a toy that becomes a boy' finds itself, audiences will continue to be delighted by one of the all-time movie greats. In 1978, a 16 mm extract *Pinocchio: A Lesson in Honesty*, was released for schools.

LA GRANDE PARADE DE WALT DISNEY Some of the cartoon compilations released theatrically in Europe have been changed and updated over the years. This programme of six shorts was first shown in France in 1940. A new version appeared in 1952, three more cartoons were added in 1963,

and in 1969 a completely revised version featuring 12 shorts was released.

TUGBOAT MICKEY (MM) Director Clyde Geronimi. Captain Mickey Mouse orders his crew, Donald and Goofy, to emergency stations when they pick up an SOS call over the radio. Unfortunately, Donald gets entangled with the engine and Goofy stokes up the boiler with so much coal that the ship finally explodes. Luckily, Mickey (below) discovers that their attempt at a rescue was actually in response to a play on the radio and not a real call for help.

THE RIVETER (DD) Director Dick Lundy. Donald happily sings 'Heigh Ho' on his way to find work. A vacancy on a construction site proves hazardous when Donald engages in some Harold Lloyd-style antics with a riveting hammer, much to the chagrin of Pete the foreman.

DONALD'S DOG LAUNDRY (DD) Director Jack King. Animators love to create fantastic inventions, and the canine washing device in this short is pure genius. However, persuading Pluto to take a bath is not so easy.

BILLPOSTERS (DD) Director Clyde Geronimi. Donald and Goofy team up together, but unfortunately little work gets done when Goofy gets entangled in the sails of a windmill and Donald meets a stubborn goat.

MR DUCK STEPS OUT (DD) Director Jack King. A marvellous musical score and expert dance routines are the highlights of this short. Donald visits Daisy but is embarrassed by the behaviour of his nephews, Huey, Dewey and Louie.

BONE TROUBLE (P) Director Jack Kinney. Pluto's flexible body is distorted when, in order to avoid a bulldog, he hides inside a Hall of Mirrors.

PUT-PUT TROUBLES (DD) Director Riley Thomson. Donald and Pluto go boating. 'Am I a surprised Duck,' comments Donald when the outboard motor unwinds the sides of his boat like a can-opener. Pluto, meanwhile, becomes hopelessly entangled with a washed-up bed spring.

DONALD'S VACATION (DD) Director Jack King. Donald is defeated in his attempts to construct collapsible camping equipment. Completely entangled in a folding chair, he watches helplessly as some chipmunks steal his food. A bear appears on the scene, and Donald is forced to beat a hasty retreat in his canoe.

PLUTO'S DREAM HOUSE (MM) Director Clyde Geronimi. Mickey, à la Aladdin, is wishing on a magic lamp and building a wonderful new kennel. Unfortunately, garbled radio announcements interfere with his instructions to bathe Pluto and cause all kinds of mayhem.

THE VOLUNTEER WORKER (Com) Director Riley Thomson. The demand on Disney from private companies and non-profit-making organizations to produce industrial films resulted from the popularity of the government-sponsored releases. In this short, commissioned by Community Chests and Councils, Incorporated, Donald Duck is turned down by the public in his charity campaign, but he finally meets a ditch-digger who proudly gives money to his good cause.

WINDOW CLEANERS (DD) Director Jack King. Donald Duck has his usual problems with a small bee while he is scaling the side of a skyscraper. His assistant Pluto is too sleepy to care, so the irascible duck is left to his own devices as the bee causes all kinds of high-flying disasters.

MR MOUSE TAKES A TRIP (MM) Director Clyde Geronimi. Pete, who starred opposite Mickey and the gang in a number of films, usually broke all the rules in order to play the villain. But, as conductor of a railroad train, he is a stickler for regulations regarding 'no dogs without a ticket', and he tries to stop Mickey Mouse smuggling Pluto aboard in a suitcase.

★FANTASIA (F) Directors Samuel Armstrong, James Algar, Bill Roberts, Paul Scatterfield, Hamilton Luske, Jim Handley, Ford Beebe, T. Hee, Norm Ferguson and Wilfred Jackson. Intended as an experiment, Fantasia is, perhaps, the

Studio's most successful film, both artistically and critically. On its initial release, however, it fared badly at the box-office, largely because it was shown in only a few cinemas. A feature-length Silly Symphony, it has the ability to infuriate, impress and astound its audience. Composed of eight animated sequences, each depicting a popular piece of classical music, the film is far from being a carelessly constructed mismatch of ideas. A chance meeting between Walt Disney and conductor Leopold Stokowski formed the basis of the film. Stokowski had heard that Disney planned to animate Paul Dukas' The Sorcerer's Apprentice and was eager to conduct it for him. It was during production of the short, which, against Stokowski's wishes, was to star Mickey Mouse, that an idea for a series of specials accompanied by classical music was suggested. From numerous possibilities, Disney decided on just seven other pieces, each of which was to carry the conductor's indelible mark. Musicologist Deems Taylor was chosen to host the film, introducing audiences to this 'new' kind of entertainment. The first sequence was a surrealistic journey through expressionism and colour to Bach's Toccata and Fugue in D Minor, orchestrated by Stokowski. This was followed by the film's most stunning technical sequence featuring shimmering spiders' webs, falling snowflakes and dancing mushrooms to the strains of Tchaikovsky's The Nutcracker Suite.

Mickey's adventures conjuring up brooms with the aid of his master's magic hat in The Sorcerer's Apprentice followed (above). To round off the first half of the programme, Igor Stravinsky's The Rite of Spring accompanied brilliant animation of the first stirrings of life on Earth, as volcanoes and earthquakes shape the continents, and prehistoric animals battle for supremacy in a primeval world (opposite above). Unlike the other composers whose music was used, Stravinsky was still alive and later expressed mixed feelings over the treatment of his work, notably Stokowski's tampering with his original score. Beethoven's Sixth Symphony, 'The Pastoral', follows the interlude with a fascinating, if crudely drawn, interpretation of the revelry that supposedly took place on the slopes of Mount Olympus (left). The film's most accessible sequence, a wickedly clever ballet performed by elephants, hippos and alligators to Ponchielli's Dance of the Hours (right), offers some light relief before the tremendous finale, in which the triumph over the powers of evil is magnificently brought to life in the film's last two sequences, a combination of Moussorgsky's Night on Bald Mountain and Schubert's Ave Maria.

The film explores a variety of themes and ideas, technical and artistic, many of which appear in the Toccata and Fugue sequence. Presented in a unique stereo called Fantasound, the technique, cleverly designed to enhance the experience, proved too expensive to be used for the film's general release; it did however, win special certificates for Walt Disney, technicians William Garity and John N. A. Hawkins and the RCA Company at the 1941 Academy Awards ceremony. RKO Radio Pictures, which later distributed the film, edited the picture beyond recognition until Disney had the opportunity of restoring it to its full length in the late 1940s.

In 1955, a SuperScope version was released, which, like the modern screen ratios, had catastrophic effect on the film's animated sequences. After a renewed appreciation by the drug cult in the 1970s, the film was re-released in 1982 with a re-orchestrated soundtrack in digital stereo conducted by Irwin Kostal. The Deems Taylor portions were removed and replaced with

THE LITTLE WHIRLWIND (MM) Director Riley Thomson. Mickey's efforts to clear Minnie's backyard of fallen leaves are frustrated by a baby tornado, which seeks the help of its monstrous parent when Mickey appears to be getting the upper hand (below).

GOLDEN EGGS (DD) Director Wilfred Jackson. To retrieve a basketful of eggs, Donald disguises himself as a chicken, but he reckons without the watchful rooster, who sees through his charade.

A GENTLEMAN'S GENTLEMAN (P) Director Clyde Geronimi. Pluto is sent to collect Mickey's Sunday newspaper, but the wind scatters it in different directions. He eventually returns with it covered in mud. In these later shorts Mickey's appearance became more stylized as his familiar circular ears actually moved in perspective to his head, although the result isn't as fascinating or satisfactory.

BAGGAGE BUSTER (G) Director Jack Kinney. Stationmaster Goofy has a difficult time coping with the weird contents of a magician's trunk, which include a kangaroo, a ferocious bull, a skeleton and even a dinosaur.

A GOOD TIME FOR A DIME (DD) Director Dick Lundy. After Donald Duck's frustrating time in a

trying to steal the Sunday roast, an incident with an ironing board causes him to swallow some soap flakes, and a bout of sneezing totally devastates the kitchen.

1941

TIMBER (DD) Directed Jack King. Pete, alias Pierre, forces Donald to chop down trees when he's caught stealing food. After numerous close shaves involving axes and saws, the cartoon ends with a furious chase on railroad handcars.

PLUTO'S PLAYMATE (P) Director Norm Ferguson. Pluto's ball is stolen by a baby seal. When, in his attempts to retrieve the ball, Pluto is almost drowned, the seal comes to his rescue.

a modern narration by Hugh Douglas. Even the voices of Stokowski and Mickey Mouse, heard briefly after *The Sorcerer's Apprentice*, were redubbed. But whatever the criticisms levelled at the Studio for tampering with such a classic, it does prove that, like all the Disney features, the film could arouse interest and controversy more than 40 years after it was made. 'Nothing like it in Heaven or on Earth,' claimed the Disney publicity in 1946, and it's true to say there probably never will be. As a sign of the film's continued popularity, sequences from it appeared on the *Disneyland* television series, and 16mm extracts were distributed for schools in 1955 (*A World is Born*), in 1974 (*Milestones for Mickey*) and in 1981 (*The Sorcerer's Apprentice*).

GOOFY'S GLIDER (G) Director Jack Kinney. With flying becoming increasingly popular in the early 1940s, Goofy demonstrates the right and wrong way of taking to the air (right). Unfortunately he has a great deal of trouble getting airborne in the first place, finally resorting to a cannon. The witty narration is provided by John McLeish.

FIRE CHIEF (DD) Director Jack King. Unfortunately for Donald, it's his own fire station that's burnt to the ground when, hindered by his nephews, he mistakenly connects the water hose to a gasoline supply.

PANTRY PIRATE (P) Director Clyde Geronimi. Here is Pluto at his most confused. While he is

museum of *Modern Inventions* (1937) he visits the local penny arcade. Thwarted in his efforts to win money in a claw-machine game, he rides a mechanical aircraft, which although bolted to the floor, spins out of control.

CANINE CADDY (P) Director Clyde Geronimi. Geronimi's style of dealing with Pluto's character is very apparent as Pluto caddies for Mickey. In the ensuing mayhem, the golf course is completely wrecked by a mischievous gopher.

THE RELUCTANT DRAGON (F) Director Alfred L. Werker. Disney's first semi-live action release was storyboarded like the more conventional animated films, yet its appeal is not stilted by the technique or by the fact that this type of film-making was new to Walt Disney. The movie relates how humorist Robert Benchley is persuaded by his wife (Nana Bryant) to take a children's book she is reading, *The Reluctant Dragon* by Kenneth Grahame, to show to Walt Disney. The film picks up momentum as Benchley absent-mindedly tours the Studio in Burbank visiting the various departments involved in producing animated films. When he enters the multiplane camera department, the film switches from black and white to colour, as Benchley is shown around by actress Frances Gifford (doubling as an attractive member of the Studio personnel). A number of animators, including Norm Ferguson, Woolie Reitherman and Ward Kimball, play themselves, and the film offers a fascinating insight into the operations of the Studio during its heyday. The sequence also includes a Goofy short, *How to Ride a Horse* (narrated by John McLeish); animation from *Bambi*; a circus train called Casey Jr (but not actually from *Dumbo*); Donald exploring the art of animation on the 'set' of his short *Old MacDonald Duck*; a non-technical bird's-eye view of the multiplane camera; and (long before UPA claimed credit for this style of animation) a brilliant storyboard session telling the story of the miraculous infant *Baby Weems*, introduced by Alan Ladd. When Benchley finally meets up with Walt in the projection room, he still doesn't get the chance to discuss the book because Walt is viewing a new cartoon featurette entitled *The Reluctant Dragon*. Caricatures by storyman T. Hee of Studio staff on the credits make up for

the criticism levelled at *Fantasia*, when no one was credited. Co-stars include Florence Gill and Clarence Nash, and among the voice talents for the final animation sequence are Barnett Parker (the Dragon, above) and Claud Allister (Sir Giles). With amusing songs by Frank Churchill, Larry Morey, Charles Wolcott, T. Hee and Ed Penner, and animation direction by Hamilton Luske (assisted by Jim Handley, Ford Beebe and Erwin Verity), the film is one of the Studio's more unusual excursions. Although it was never re-issued, some of the animated sequences have appeared as separate shorts, and an edited version of Benchley's tour, *Behind the Scenes of Walt Disney Studio*, turned up on 16mm in 1952.

THE NIFTY NINETIES (MM) Director Riley Thomson. Although Mickey Mouse's career began to wane in the 1940s, his spasmodic

appearances were still welcome. Here, with Minnie (below), he visits a turn-of-the-century vaudeville show, and caricatures of some of the Disney animators, including Fred Moore and Ward Kimball, appear on stage. The film also uses staff names on advertising (an idea later reused on the shop windows above Main Street, U.S.A. in Disneyland). After the show and to the tune of 'In the Good Ol' Summertime', Mickey and Minnie drive out to the country in the latest design of horseless carriage.

EARLY TO BED (DD) Director Jack King. King directed other tales of Donald's insomnia – *Wide Open Spaces* (1947) and *Drip Dippy Donald* (1948) – but this time it's the ticking of his own alarm clock that stops him getting a good night's sleep.

☆TRUANT OFFICER DONALD (DD) Director Jack King. The ill-tempered Duck forces his three nephews, Huey, Dewey and Louie, into attending school. He's embarrassed to learn that his efforts have been in vain – the schoolhouse is closed for the summer vacation.

ORPHAN'S BENEFIT (MM) Director Riley Thomson. In the Technicolor remake of the 1934 short, Mickey accompanies Clara Cluck (opposite above) on the piano, Goofy dances with Horace and Clarabelle, and Donald has a difficult time controlling an unruly audience of orphans. The film is a landmark in Mickey's illustrious career, and, combined with black and white footage from the first film, it has appeared in several Disney retrospectives.

OLD MACDONALD DUCK (DD) Director Jack King. Donald Duck busies himself about the farmyard, feeding the chickens and pigs to the accompaniment of the song 'Old MacDonald Had a Farm'. This short was the basis of a discussion on the technique of the animated film when Robert Benchley visited the Studio in the feature-length *The Reluctant Dragon*.

★LEND A PAW (P) Director Clyde Geronimi. This remake of the black and white short *Mickey's Pal*

Pluto relates what happens when Pluto saves a little kitten from drowning at the bottom of a deep well. A favourite gag in several classic shorts, Pluto's conscience wrestles with good and evil to decide the kitten's fate. The film was dedicated to 'The Tailwagger Foundation'.

★ DUMBO (F) Director Ben Sharpsteen. Produced during World War II when Disney was busy with *Bambi* and overseas markets were dwindling, *Dumbo* nevertheless rises above the Hollywood turmoil. Adapted by Joe Grant and Dick Huemer from a short story by Helen Aberson and Harold Pearl, the hero is a baby elephant with enormous ears (below), who is ridiculed by the other circus elephants. An outcast, he is befriended by Timothy, a small mouse with a large ego. Together they turn Dumbo's handicap into a profitable concern as he becomes the world's only 'flying elephant'.

The story is simply told, and therein lies its charm. Dumbo doesn't speak one word of dialogue throughout the entire film, relying instead on Timothy (voiced by Edward Brophy) to tell him the difference between right and wrong (a role not unlike Jiminy Cricket's in *Pinocchio* or Thumper's in *Bambi*). Timothy also helps Dumbo to overcome the humiliation heaped upon him by, for example, some black crows, who perform the show-stopping 'When I See an Elephant Fly'. And it's Timothy who takes the baby elephant to see his mother who has been locked up for defending Dumbo from some cruel children. Dumbo gets his own back on everyone who's treated him unfairly by spreading his 'ears' and flying, while Timothy, now his manager, handles his Hollywood contract. Other voices are provided by Sterling Holloway, as the stork who delivers Dumbo, and Cliff Edwards as Jim Crow.

The animation is among the Studio's best, particularly in the scenes of the circus train, Casey Jr, moving from town to town and of an ingenious sequence in which Dumbo and Timothy get drunk and see amazing Technicolored pink elephants. Later shown on the *Disneyland* television series in 1955, an educational extract entitled *Dumbo: A Lesson in Being Prepared* was released on 16mm in 1981.

DONALD'S CAMERA (DD) Director Dick Lundy. Seeing the notice 'Shoot nature with a camera, not a gun', Donald sets off to capture the forest wild life on film. Frustrated at every turn by chipmunks, skunks and woodpeckers, the angry duck returns, armed to the teeth with pistols, machine-guns and grenades.

THE ART OF SKIING (G) Director Jack Kinney. Goofy demonstrates the finer points of skiing to the narration of John McLeish, a resident Disney sketch artist.

THRIFTY PIG (Com) Featuring new lyrics, the song sensation of the Depression 'Who's Afraid of the Big Bad Wolf?' was re-used in Disney's first propaganda cartoon for John Grierson of the National Film Board of Canada. *Thrifty Pig* uses recycled animation from *Three Little Pigs* (1933); but this time the wolf is portrayed as a Nazi, while the Practical Pig's brick house turns out to be built of Canadian War Savings Certificates.

CHEF DONALD (DD) Director Jack King. In a cookery sequence reminiscent of a scene from *The Plastics Inventor* (1944), Donald accidentally mixes rubber cement with waffle batter. The short expertly illustrates Donald's growing anger and frustration as the gooey mixture finally wins.

THE SEVEN WISE DWARFS (Com) Directors Fred Beebe and Dick Lyford. After the success of *Thrifty Pig*, which encouraged the buying of Canadian War Savings Certificates, the National Film Board of Canada sponsored a second short starring the cast from *Snow White*. As with *Thrifty Pig*, the film uses recycled animation over new backgrounds and some stock footage showing how the dwarfs take their diamonds to town and buy War Savings Certificates. The film contains new lyrics to the song 'Heigh Ho!'

THE ART OF SELF DEFENSE (G) Director Jack Kinney. In one of his finest films, Goofy tells the story of boxing through the ages. In one hilarious sequence narrated by John McLeish and involving shadow boxing, Goofy is knocked out by his own shadow, proving he hasn't learnt a thing.

1942

During 1942 the Studio produced the following public service films for the US armed forces: *Aircraft Carrier Landing Signals* (US Navy); *Aircraft Carrier Mat Approaches and Landings* (US Navy); *Aircraft Riveting* (US Navy); *Approaches and Landings* (US Navy); *Battle of Britain* (part – US Army); *Bending and Curving* (US Navy); *Blanking and Punching* (US Navy); *Forming Methods* (US Navy); *Icing Conditions* (US Navy); *Know Your Enemy, Germany* (part – US Army); *The Nazi's Strike* [*Campaign in Poland*] (part – US Army); *Prelude to War* (part – US Army); *Protection Against Chemical Warfare* (US Navy); *US Army Identification Series — WEFT* (US Army); *US Navy Identification Series — WEFT and Warships* (US Navy).

The Studio also made *Boys Anti-Tank Rifle* [*Stop That Tank*] (National Film Board of Canada) directed by Ub Iwerks.

DONALD'S DECISION (Com) Using animation from *Donald's Better Self* (1938), in which an angel and a devil argue over whose advice Donald should take, *Donald's Decision* was the third in a series of four shorts produced for the National Film Board of Canada to stress the value of purchasing War Savings Certificates. The film was made in the early 1940s, and the devil is linked to the swastika, so it becomes doubly important that Donald follows the good advice of his angelic *alter ego*.

ALL TOGETHER (Com) The fourth film in the series produced to sell Canadian War Bonds uses recycled animation to illustrate Disney characters marching past the Canadian Parliament Building. In addition to Mickey and the gang, there's a rare appearance by Pinocchio and Geppetto.

THE VILLAGE SMITHY (DD) Director Dick Lundy. An arrogant Donald Duck boasts about his trade, but the metal rim on a cartwheel proves too much for him to master. Finally Donald attempts unsuccessfully to shoe Jenny the donkey.

☆THE NEW SPIRIT (Com) Directors Wilfred Jackson and Ben Sharpsteen. When Walt Disney was asked by John L. Sullivan of the Treasury Department to produce a film on income tax, Secretary Henry Morganthau was disappointed that Donald Duck had been picked to star. Walt successfully argued, however, that using Donald was like MGM assigning Clark Gable. 'Taxes to beat the Axis', was the film's message, as Donald speeds on foot, from Hollywood to Washington, to deliver his taxes in person. Cliff Edwards (the voice of Jiminy Cricket), sings the theme song 'Yankee Doodle Spirit'. Distributed by the War Activities Committee of the Motion Picture Industry, the film won much praise and some notoriety because of its reputed budget of $80,000.

MICKEY'S BIRTHDAY PARTY (MM) Director Riley Thomson. In 1931 Mickey Mouse celebrated his birthday at Minnie's house. In the Technicolor remake Minnie again plays host (below), but this time Mickey takes something of a back seat as Donald Duck and Clara Cluck perform an

amazing dance routine, and Goofy feverishly tries to bake a surprise birthday cake.

PLUTO, JUNIOR (P) Director Clyde Geronimi. Pluto's sleep is disturbed when a mischievous puppy (right) gets involved with a balloon, a ball, a worm and a troublesome bird.

SYMPHONY HOUR (MM) Director Riley Thomson. Mickey has an opportunity to conduct a full orchestra for a radio broadcast sponsored by Mr Macaroni, played by Peg Leg Pete. When Goofy crushes the instruments in an elevator shaft, Mickey has to force his anxious musicians to make the best of what they've got (above). Fortunately, Macaroni is delighted by the results, and Mickey is once again the hero of the day.

DONALD'S SNOW FIGHT (DD) Director Jack King. An elaborate battle ensues when Donald smashes his nephews' snowman. Finally Huey, Dewey

and Louie resort to using catapults to fire hot coals at Donald's ice fortress.

DONALD GETS DRAFTED (DD) Director Jack King. Donald's failure to stand to attention when ordered to do so by drill sergeant Pete leads to a number of hilarious gags, with some ants, a rifle and a complete lack of discipline. When last seen, Donald is peeling potatoes.

THE ARMY MASCOT (P) Director Clyde Geronimi. 'No admittance' warns the sign on the barbed wire, but hungry Pluto is so keen to become an army mascot because of the free meals he will get that he takes on a belligerent goat called Gunther and an army ammunitions dump.

DONALD'S GARDEN (DD) Director Dick Lundy. Lundy uses his expert understanding of Donald Duck's temperament to illustrate a battle between Donald and a gopher that is trying to eat his entire vegetable patch. Donald's efforts to fill a watering can rank among the highlights of his illustrious career.

THE SLEEPWALKER (P) Director Clyde Geronimi. A somnambulant Pluto gives a large bone to a small female dachshund. When he wakes up, he wants it back, which causes a few problems (opposite above).

FOUR METHODS OF FLUSH RIVETING (Com) In 1941 the National Film Board of Canada pur-

chased the rights to this ingenious animated short made by Disney in conjunction with the Lockheed Aircraft Corporation. Its success prompted the National Film Board to commission Disney to make further titles.

FOOD WILL WIN THE WAR (Com) Director Ben Sharpsteen. In 1942 the Donovan Committee and the Agriculture Department decided that the slogan 'Food will win the war and write the peace' would be a good subject for a Disney film. Costing $20,000, the short used gags to illustrate the size of the US food supplies and included an appearance by the Three Little Pigs.

DONALD'S GOLD MINE (DD) Director Dick Lundy. Donald is seeking his fortune by excavating for gold. Unfortunately, the antics of an irritable burro put Donald at the mercy of his own gold-cleaning machinery and turn him into a 'gold brick duck'.

OUT OF THE FRYING PAN INTO THE FIRING LINE (Com) Director Jack King. Made for the Conservation Division of the War Production Board, this film shows the importance of saving kitchen fats and greases for the war effort. Minnie Mouse and Pluto star in the short, which makes effective use of animated fat drippings turning into vital munitions to defeat the enemy.

☆ BAMBI (F) Supervising director David Hand. Felix Salten's story about forest animals was the subject of Walt Disney's fifth full-length animated feature, which was in production for over five years. The film contains some of the most naturalistic animation ever seen in a Disney film, for within a relatively short space of time the artists' realization of the anatomical structure of animals had progressed from the simplicity of Snow White's forest friends to drawings with a remarkable fluidity of movement. The facial

expressions of the deer, while remaining true to the animals themselves, convey an amazing sense of understanding and character. The film relates what happens to Bambi, a young deer growing up in the forest (below), who makes friends with Thumper the rabbit and Flower the skunk and finally faces up to his most dangerous enemy – man. It's a pity that, unlike Dumbo who never said a word, Bambi and his companions have to communicate with each other. However, Peter Behn is highly amusing as the voice of the mischievous Thumper, and Paula Winslowe is perfect as Bambi's Mother. Fortunately the script is kept to a minimum, and the film's lush visuals are accompanied instead by some delightful songs, including 'Little April Shower' and 'Looking for Romance', with choral arrangements by Charles Henderson and music by Frank Churchill and Edward H. Plumb. Animators Frank Thomas, Milt Kahl, Ollie Johnston and Eric Larson kept the film alive throughout its formative period while the Studio was working on a growing number of shorts and full-length features. Through the use of atmospheric backgrounds and highly effective set pieces – swirling autumn leaves, falling snow and the exquisite April shower sequence, which is as breathtaking as anything that *Fantasia's Nutcracker Suite* had to offer – the film successfully plays on the sympathies of its audience. When Bambi's Mother is shot by hunters the young fawn's loneliness and anguish are powerfully conveyed, and the scenes of panic as animals of every species flee the hunter's gun are brilliantly staged. Any criticism of artiness in Bambi can be dismissed, its amazing track record proving its lasting appeal to cinema-goers. By 1987, in America alone, the film had grossed a total box-office of $28 million. A 16mm extract, *Bambi – A Lesson in Perseverance*, was released for schools in 1978.

T-BONE FOR TWO (P) Director Clyde Geronimi. Pluto manages to steal a juicy bone from Butch the bulldog, but keeping the food proves more difficult – especially when it gets sucked inside a disused motor-horn.

HOW TO PLAY BASEBALL (G) Director Jack Kinney. A complicated game like baseball doesn't need Goofy to expound its finer points, but Goofy, cast as all the members of both teams and accompanied by an off-screen narration, demonstrates different ways of pitching .

THE VANISHING PRIVATE (DD) Director Jack King. Ordered by Sergeant Pete to camouflage a cannon, Donald coats it with a top-secret paint that makes it invisible. When Pete tries to punish Donald, he paints himself and escapes capture.

THE OLYMPIC CHAMP (G) Director Jack Kinney. Narrator John McLeish's dry intonation adds great humour to this delightful short. As the history of the Olympic Games is explained, Goofy demonstrates the not-so-delicate art of walking, running, pole vaulting, and discus and javelin throwing. Since Goofy has achieved fame as a sportsman in recent years, footage from this and other shorts have been constantly re-issued both theatrically and on television.

HOW TO SWIM (G) Director Jack Kinney. Goofy finds he can successfully imitate swimming techniques on an ordinary kitchen stool. But undressing in a beach hut, swimming in the sea and diving from a springboard are a different matter. Fortunately, narrator John McLeish is on hand to explain, and the more balletic of Goofy's movements are captured forever by 'the miracle of the slow-motion camera'.

SKY TROOPER (DD) Director Jack King. Although Private Donald Duck yearns to fly, parachuting is a different matter altogether. He loses his parachute and clings to Sergeant Pete; together they plummet to the ground, holding onto a bomb.

PLUTO AT THE ZOO (P) Director Clyde Geronimi. In his attempts to steal a large bone from a lion, Pluto has uncomfortable encounters with a kangaroo, an enormous gorilla and a pool full of alligators.

SOUTH OF THE BORDER WITH DISNEY (Com) Director Norm Ferguson. Invited by the Coordinator of Inter-American Affairs to make a goodwill tour of South America, Walt Disney and a group of his artists took a two-month working vacation visiting Rio de Janeiro, Buenos Aires, Bolivia and Mendoza. The trip resulted in two feature films (Saludos Amigos and The Three Caballeros) and a number of short subjects. The live-action part of the tour was released as South of the Border with Disney, and although this 16mm release was not intended for wide distribution, it did help to promote a feeling of unity between the US and its neighbours.

HOW TO FISH (G) Director Jack Kinney. Goofy spent nearly his entire screen career demonstrating various professions, hobbies and sporting activities. He again plays fall guy to John McLeish's deadpan narration as he attempts to demonstrate this tranquil sport.

BELLBOY DONALD (DD) Director Jack King. 'The guest is always right,' says the badge pinned to Donald Duck's red tunic. Told by the hotel manager that he will be fired if he upsets any of the guests, Donald's temper is stretched to its limits by socialite Pete and his obnoxious brat.

1943

During 1943 the Studio made the following shorts for the US armed services: Aeronca Project [Basic Maintenance of Primary Training Airplanes] (US Army and Aeronca); Air Masses and Fronts (US Navy); Air Transport Command (US Navy); Aircraft Carrier Landing Qualifications (US Navy); Aircraft Welding (US Navy); The Aleutian Islands [A.D.C. Project] (US Army); Battle of China (part – US Army); Battle of Russia (part – US Army); Beechcraft Maintenance and Repair (Beech Aircraft Corp. and US Army); British Torpedo Plane Tactics (US Navy); Carrier Rendezvous and Breakup (US Navy); The Cold Front (US Navy); Divide and Conquer (part – US Army); Fast Company (US Army); Fixed Gunnery and Fighter Tactics (US Navy); Fog (US Navy); Glider Training (US Army); Heat Treating (US Navy); High Level Precision Bombing (US Army); Know Your Enemy – Japan (part – US Army); Lofting and Layouts (US Navy); The Mark 13–Modification 1 Aerial Torpedo (US Navy); Minneapolis Honeywell Project [Auto Pilot] (US Army); Mock-Up and Tooling (US Navy); The Occluded Front (US Navy); Rules of the Nautical Road (US Navy); Substitution and Conversion (US Army); Template Reproduction (US Navy); Thunderstorms (US Navy); V.T.B. Pilot Training (US Navy) and The Warm Front (US Navy).

☆THE GRAIN THAT BUILT A HEMISPHERE (Com) Director Bill Roberts. In 1943 the Coordinator of Inter-American Affairs commissioned Disney to produce a number of films on health and agriculture for Latin America. At a CIAA seminar on visual education, members agreed that this short fared better than the others and referred to it in their summing up as 'a satisfying, historically accurate, and beautiful dramatization'. Like a number of the Studio's wartime propaganda pictures, the film borrowed footage from earlier movies, this time of grazing deer from Bambi and a piglet sequence from a 1938 short, Farmyard Symphony, to help to explain the importance of corn for feeding livestock, providing starches, alcohol, plastics and explosives.

★DER FUEHRER'S FACE (DD) Director Jack Kinney. In his most important contribution to World War II propaganda, Donald dreams he is living in Nazi Germany (below). The outrageous extremes of the totalitarian state are shown as Hitler's face glares down on the innocent Donald as he struggles in a munitions factory (a surreal sequence, animated by Les Clark, which owes a great deal to the 'pink elephants' nightmare in Dumbo) and tries to survive in an economy

ruined by all the restrictions imposed by the need to toe the party line. Everything – including houses, hedges and landscapes – is shaped like the swastika symbol. Just when life seems absolutely unbearable, Donald awakes in his Stars and Stripes decorated bedroom to the sight of a model of the Statue of Liberty standing on the window sill. The film is Disney at his most ingenious, and although it made audiences laugh, it was as powerful a graphic statement on world affairs as the Studio's *Education For Death* (1943). The film was originally referred to as *Donald Duck in Nutziland*, but the success of the song 'Der Fuehrer's Face' by Oliver Wallace persuaded Disney to change the title before release.

THE SPIRIT OF '43 (Com) Director Jack King. Disney's second film for the US Treasury Department featured Donald Duck (above) in a sequel to *The New Spirit*. Even though a number of wartime shorts used the same footage, Disney insisted that this film should be totally different. Torn between right and wrong, Donald finally decides to pay his dues to the Internal Revenue.

THE WINGED SCOURGE (Com) Director Bill Roberts. The first health film produced for the Coordinator of Inter-American Affairs marked one of the few occasions on which the Seven Dwarfs from *Snow White* appeared in another film. The narrator asks if anyone in the audience will help the Public Health Service defeat the malaria-spreading mosquito, and the dwarfs offer their services as they had in the Canadian Bond short, *The Seven Wise Dwarfs* (1941). The film shows the precautions needed to control the spread of malaria. After safeguarding their home, the dwarfs sleep soundly beneath their mosquito nets. Although it was intended for South American audiences, the film was well received abroad, and several prints were ordered by the British government for use in India. To heighten attitudes against the mosquito, the insect was referred to as 'public enemy number one' and shown as a gigantic blood-sucking monster.

EDUCATION FOR DEATH (Sp) Director Clyde Geronimi. Having succeeded in making audiences laugh at the stupidity of the Nazi military in *Der Fuehrer's Face*, Disney turned to frightening documentary with his next animated film. Based on Gregor Ziemer's book, *Education for Death: The Making of a Nazi*, the film opens with a satire on the Sleeping Beauty story: Prince Hitler arrives to awaken his true love, Princess Germania, an overweight Valkyrie who resembles Herman Goering (below). But with the comic touches out of the way, the film's mood changes completely, as it depicts how a little boy called Hans grows up indoctrinated with Nazi philosophy. At school Hans' teacher scolds him for showing sympathy with a rabbit that is eaten by the fox. As Hans reaches manhood, he becomes part of the German Army and, in the final scene, marches to his death along with other young soldiers, their helmets forming crosses in a cemetery. Clever use of shadow, perspectives and colour makes the film even more stark and terrifying, while animators Bill Tytla and Ward Kimball give the towering Nazi figure, whose eyes burn like coals within his darkened featureless visage, a horrifying aspect. But what shocked audiences most was the idea that from the day he was born Hans belonged not to his parents but to the state – that he was nothing more than an innocent victim of a society rushing headlong to destruction.

DONALD'S TIRE TROUBLE (DD) Director Dick Lundy. Donald is eventually forced to drive home on four flat tyres after a trip to the country during which the jack breaks, the radiator explodes and, one by one, the tyres burst.

☆ SALUDOS AMIGOS (F) Animated sequences directed by Bill Roberts, Jack Kinney, Hamilton Luske and Wilfred Jackson. Walt Disney and members of his staff had already made a goodwill tour to South America at the request of Nelson Rockefeller and John Hay Whitney, and the record of their trip was released in 1942 as a featurette entitled *South of the Border with Disney*. However, the trip was important for several reasons, one of the most important being that it gave the artists and storymen an opportunity to gather together ideas for a series of short subjects which turned into two feature-length 'package' films, the first of which was *Saludos Amigos*. The film opens with stock footage showing Walt and his animators arriving in South

America. Four separate cartoon shorts from various countries are then linked by animation sequences of maps and a small plane flying from city to city. Donald Duck stars as an American tourist in the hilarious *Lake Titicaca* sequence, which uses work by artists Herb Ryman, Lee and Mary Blair and Jim Bodrero. The story of Pedro the mail plane features some inspired animation from Bill Tytla, Fred Moore, Ward Kimball and Josh Meador, while Goofy (above) demonstrates the similarities between the Texas cowboy and the Argentine gaucho in *El Gaucho Goofy*, a version of the 'How To' series directed by Jack Kinney. Finally, Donald Duck is joined for a carnival in Rio by the parrot Joe Carioca, voiced by José Oliveira. Fast-paced, with some amazing set pieces and a tremendous musical score, the film, although relatively short (at 42 minutes) in terms of the usual Disney features, is a delightful potpourri, which must have seemed like propaganda at its most entertaining in the 1940s but is now appreciated as a slice of sheer invention. It has been rereleased on a number of occasions when its soft-sell politics didn't matter, but the four animated sequences have all been released as separate shorts. The entire film was shown on the *Disneyland* television show in 1958.

PLUTO AND THE ARMADILLO (P) Director Clyde Geronimi. Originally intended to be part of *The Three Caballeros*, the short, which is set in Brazil, features Mickey and Pluto. Pluto chases his rubber ball into the forest where he comes across a curled-up armadillo, which he mistakes for his ball. The two soon become firm friends and join Mickey on the aircraft to return home. It is impossible to distinguish feature film rejects from other Disney shorts made at the time, because the Studio lavished great care and attention on all its commercial releases.

FLYING JALOPY (DD) Director Dick Lundy. Used aircraft dealer Ben Buzzard tricks Donald Duck

into making him a beneficiary of a $10,000 insurance policy, and then attempts to sabotage his plane. Donald finally outwits the evil bird.

PRIVATE PLUTO (P) Director Clyde Geronimi. Chip an' Dale, as yet unnamed, make their debut in this short in which Pluto (below), ordered by the drill sergeant to guard a pillbox, is dismayed to find that the chipmunks are using it to store nuts.

FALL OUT – FALL IN (DD) Director Jack King. In the same year that Donald Duck was having nightmares about the Nazi regime in *Der Fuehrer's Face*, he was experiencing the drudgery that sometimes accompanies the life of a soldier. He marches through sun, wind and rain, until, managing to pitch his tent, he falls to sleep exhausted as the command comes to 'fall-in'.

WATER, FRIEND OR ENEMY (Com) This short, sponsored by the Coordinator of Inter-American

Affairs, uses clever animation effects such as sliding cels, dissolves and wash-offs (a technique in which parts of an illustration are erased during filming and then the footage is run in reverse to give the effect of construction). A narrator explains how to prevent the pollution of drinking water and its contamination by diseases such as cholera, typhoid and dysentery.

☆VICTORY THROUGH AIR POWER (F) Sequence directors Clyde Geronimi, Jack Kinney and James Algar; animation supervisor David Hand. The outbreak of World War II led to a number of changes at the Studio. Perhaps the most important of these was the formation of a department producing propaganda films for the armed forces and government-sponsored educational films, but even the conventional adventures of Donald, Goofy and Pluto took on a wartime flavour. The features, however, were exempt, with the exception of Walt's personal triumph, *Victory Through Air Power*. This controversial and

fascinating study in wartime propaganda was based on a book by Major Alexander P. de Seversky, who was invited to appear in the film, which explained, with the aid of highly imaginative, yet limited animated sequences, the importance of strategic bombing to defeat the Germans and to counter the growing Japanese threat. The Major, although a little awkward on screen, plays the part of a lecturer with total conviction, and Disney's numerous animators provide some intriguing effects animation of battles, aircraft and detailed maps. The film begins with a humorous look at the history of aviation, concentrating on the scientific advances made during wartime. The mood of the picture then changes as de Seversky discusses the various types of airpower needed to defeat the enemy. Perce Pearce, who worked on Disney's live-action adventures during the 1950s, keeps the story

direction taut and entertaining, while Technicolor adds to the film's stark realism. In the finale, powerful graphics show an American eagle (left) dive bombing a Japanese octopus until its tentacles lose their grip on the South Pacific atolls. Although the film's commercial life was short, the *History of Aviation* sequence was re-issued on 16mm in 1952 and appeared as part of the *Fly with Von Drake* segment of *The Wonderful World of Color* tv series in 1963, where its limited animation style suited the 1950s and 1960s approach. At the time of the film's release, *Picturegoer Magazine* called Walt Disney 'one of the brightest stones in the film world's crown'. The movie was certainly another example of his pioneering spirit and determination.

VICTORY VEHICLES (G) Director Jack Kinney. Goofy demonstrates various forms of transportation that require no gasoline or rubber, materials vital to the war effort. He manages to survive by bouncing along on a pogo stick, while the film drops all kinds of subtle hints in support of numerous wartime institutions.

DEFENSE AGAINST INVASION (Com) Director Jack King. Produced to underline the public's awareness of the importance of vaccination, the film, which combines animation and live action, was sponsored by the Coordinator of Inter-American Affairs. The human body is seen fighting off artificially induced vaccines, as a military approach is taken, with animated red blood corpuscles building tanks and ammunition to ward off invading germs. Using the letter V as the symbol of victory, the narrator concludes this stylish picture by stating: 'V for Vaccination and Victory, Victory over Invasion.'

☆ REASON AND EMOTION (Sp) Director Bill Roberts. A wartime propaganda film that studies, through ingenious animation, the conflict within the human mind. Reason is pictured as being sen-

sible (below left); Emotion is shown to be rather primitive. The action takes place inside the heads of John Doakes and a pretty girl, and the two forces – reason and emotion – are shown making decisions. Extracts from the film were later released on a Ludwig Von Drake television segment of *The Wonderful World of Color* in 1962 and as a 16mm educational release under the title *Man is His Own Worst Enemy* (1975).

FIGARO AND CLEO (Fi) Director Jack Kinney. Figaro, the feline star of *Pinocchio*, appeared in three shorts with his own title card. In the first he is re-united with Cleo the goldfish, whom he tries to eat for dinner.

THE OLD ARMY GAME (DD) Director Jack King. Private Donald Duck sneaks into barracks after lights out, but is spotted by the formidable Sergeant Pete. In the frantic chase that follows, Donald mistakenly believes he has seriously injured himself and uses the situation to great advantage.

HOME DEFENSE (DD) Director Jack King. Donald Duck is a trained aircraft spotter, but when he falls asleep at his post, his nephews trick him by launching a toy plane and model parachutists. Donald is angry at them for playing such practical jokes during wartime. But the real moral of this wartime propaganda is that Donald should have been alert at his post at all times.

CHICKEN LITTLE (Sp) Director Clyde Geronimi. Rereleased as an educational short to help teach students the importance of thinking for themselves, this wartime propaganda short relates the classic story of how wily old Foxey Loxey dupes Chicken Little into thinking he can save his friends (left) when the sky falls down. Unlike other Disney shorts, in which the villain usually loses, this sad little tale ends with the chickens trapped in the fox's cave.

1944

During 1944 the Studio produced the following films for the US armed services: *Air Brakes, Principles of Operation* (US Army); *Attack in the Pacific* (OWI); *Automotive Electricity for Military Vehicles* (US Army); *Basic Map Reading* (US Army); *Battle of Cape Gloucester* (US Army); *Carburetion, Basic Principles* (US Army); *The Case of the Tremendous Trifle* (US Army); *Electric Brakes, Principles of Operation* (US Army); *The Equatorial Front* (US Navy); *A Few Quick Facts #7[Venereal Disease]* (US Army); *Flying the Weather Map* (US Navy); *Fundamentals of Artillery Weapons* (US Army); *The Howgozit Chart* (US Navy); *Howitzer, 105mm M2A1 and Carriage M2, Principles of Operation* (US Army); *It's Your War, Too* (US Army); *Operation and Maintenance of the Electronic Turbo Supercharger* (US Army); *Theory of Simplex and Phantom Circuits* (US Army); *Tuning Transmitters* (US Army); *Two Down and One to Go* (US Army); *Ward Care of Psychotic Patients* (US Army); *Weather at War* (US Navy); *Weather for the Navigator* (US Navy); and *Your Job in Germany* (US Army).

HOW TO BE A SAILOR (G) Director Jack Kinney. Goofy takes an historical voyage through nautical navigation. However, two-thirds into the story the film takes a sharp turn, departing from the casual instructional formula of the usual Goofy shorts and ending with a display of heroism as Goofy smashes into Japanese boats and shatters the symbol of the Rising Sun.

COMMANDO DUCK (DD) Director Jack King. Although the Studio had already embarked on a number of successful wartime propaganda shorts, some military influences crept into its generally released entertainment films. This time Donald Duck finds himself in direct confrontation with the Japanese army, which is swiftly dispatched when his life-raft explodes, releasing a torrent of water that washes away an enemy airbase.

SPRINGTIME FOR PLUTO (P) Director Charles Nichols. Pan (below), one of the stars of the 'Pastoral' sequence in *Fantasia*, awakens Pluto. After being mesmerized by a dancing butterfly, Pluto has a close shave with a hive of bees, some poison ivy, goldenrod seeds and a ferocious thunderstorm. Set against some impressive backgrounds by artist Lenard Kester, the film concludes with Pluto angrily chasing away the harbinger of spring.

THE PLASTICS INVENTOR (DD) Director Jack King. Do-it-yourself fanatic Donald Duck makes a plastic aircraft from instructions given over the radio. After a successful take-off, a cloudburst melts the plane. An angry Donald pours water over the radio, which also melts. The short makes gentle fun of the 'plastic mania' that was then taking America by storm.

☆ HOW TO PLAY FOOTBALL (G) Director Jack Kinney. Yet another short in Goofy's highly popular 'How To' series. There is a great deal of misunderstanding, and it's not clear who is the more confused about the rules of the game – Goofy or the audience.

FIRST AIDERS (P) Director Charles Nichols. Minnie Mouse and Figaro the cat guest-star with Pluto. Minnie needs someone on whom to practise her nursing skills, and Pluto is the unlucky patient, much to Figaro's delight.

DONALD'S OFF DAY (DD) Director Jack Hannah. Huey, Dewey and Louie (opposite above) trick their Uncle Donald into believing that he is too ill to go out. When he does go out, he returns almost immediately, soaked in a downpour.

☆ THE THREE CABALLEROS (F) Production supervisor and director Norm Ferguson. In the 1934 MGM musical *Hollywood Party*, Mickey Mouse

THE PELICAN AND THE SNIPE (Sp) Director Hamilton Luske. Sterling Holloway narrates how Vidi the snipe spends his nights ensuring that his 'sleep-flying' friend Monte the pelican comes to no harm (above). The short had originally been proposed for inclusion in *The Three Caballeros*, but it was decided that its wartime references might seem more appropriate if released immediately, especially as it was supposedly set in Uruguay, one of the countries unfortunately overlooked in the lengthy travelogue *Saludos Amigos*.

TROMBONE TROUBLE (DD) Director Jack King. When Pete upsets the slumbers of Jupiter and Vulcan with his trombone-playing, they endow neighbour Donald Duck with the power to stop him. Unfortunately Donald discovers that he likes playing the trombone as well, and the gods' attempts at getting to sleep are again thwarted.

HOW TO PLAY GOLF (G) Director Jack Kinney. Goofy has the advantage of being joined by a diagrammatical figure to teach him golf (below), but their game is ruined by a bull, which chases them back to the clubhouse.

DONALD DUCK AND THE GORILLA (DD) Director Jack King. A radio announcement about the escape of a gorilla called Ajax frightens Huey, Dewey and Louie, much to Donald's amusement. When the gorilla breaks into their house, however, Donald isn't so brave, and it's up to his nephews to save the day.

CONTRARY CONDOR (DD) Director Jack King. Donald is caught stealing a condor egg by the mother bird. He hides inside one of the eggshells and finds himself adopted by the huge bird, who attempts to teach him how to fly. Like other cartoon shorts of the 1940s, this film has a distinctively South American flavour.

THE AMAZON AWAKENS (Com) When the Coordinator of Inter-American Affairs asked Walt Disney to make a film about the Amazon basin it proved more economical to use photographers Herbert and Trudy Knapp, who were already at work in Lima, Peru. The completed film was released as a Good Neighbor travelogue. One of the film's highlights is a visit to Henry Ford's rubber plantation 'Fordlandia', which was situated in 17,000 acres of cleared jungle.

appeared alongside comedian Jimmy Durante in a short sequence prepared especially for the film by Disney. The effect, which involved a technique pioneered in the early Alice shorts by which cartoon characters were combined with a live actress against a white background, was quite ingenious. However, by the time *The Three Caballeros* was released, Disney's technicians had achieved an almost flawless combination of media and in Technicolor. As part of the Studio's goodwill message for South America and as a sequel to the highly successful *Saludos Amigos*, the film again starred Donald Duck, who receives a parcel of gifts from his Latin American friends. The gifts include a movie projector and a film about the bird life of the southern hemisphere, which begins with the story of Pablo the cold-blooded penguin, which was narrated by Sterling Holloway. Pablo leaves the South Pole in search

of warmer climes, sailing up the west coast of the South American continent *en route* to a sun-drenched island paradise. Then follows the tale of Gauchito and the flying donkey. Donald's next present is a pop-up book about Brazil. Accompanied by his old friend Joe Carioca, the cigar-smoking parrot from *Saludos Amigos*, Donald visits the coastal town of Baia, where he meets the irritating Aracuan Bird (who returned to plague Donald in *Melody Time* and *Clown of the Jungle*). In Baia Donald falls in love with singer Aurora Miranda, who dances her way through the animated streets with her musical friends. A lengthy production number, it's a perfect example of the successful wedding of live action and animation. Donald and Joe next tour Mexico with the help of a new friend, a rooster called Panchito (below), and Donald encounters an exploding piñata (Mexican jar), a magic sarape

(flying carpet), a beach of bathing beauties, singer Dora Luz, dancer Carmen Molina and some enormous choreographed cacti. The whole extravaganza is brought to a swift end with a wild bull-fight and a fireworks display. A bewildering and fast-paced entertainment, the film doesn't contain the more obvious propaganda elements so apparent in *Saludos Amigos*. The story boasted 10 writers, including Bill Peet, Ted Sears and Ralph Wright, and the colourful and dynamic animation was provided by, among others, Ward Kimball, Eric Larson and Fred Moore, with process photography by Ub Iwerks. Songs from the film, such as 'You Belong to My Heart', 'Baia' and 'The Three Caballeros' by Manuel Esperon, Ray Gilbert, Ernesto Cortezar, Ary Barroso and Agustin Lara, became popular hit tunes during the 1940s. However, because the Studio felt that it was rather dated, the film had to wait a number of years before it was re-issued. Animated sequences such as *The Flying Gauchito*, *The Cold-Blooded Penguin* and *Feliz Navidad* (*Christmas in Mexico*) were later released on 16mm for schools, while extracts appeared in *Creative Film Adventures Reel 1* in 1976. A featurette version of the film also appeared as part of the 1984 compilation, *Donald Duck The Movie*, celebrating the star's 50th birthday.

1945

In 1945 the Studio produced the following shorts for the US armed services: *Another Chance* [*UN Peace Charter*] (US Army); *Burma Campaign* [*The Stilwell Road*] (US Army); *Dental Health* (US Army); *On to Tokyo* (US Army); and *War Comes to America* (part – US Army).

THE CLOCK WATCHER (DD) Director Jack King. The bad-tempered Donald puts his department-store job at risk by being very lazy and fooling around with the stock.

THE RIGHT SPARK PLUG IN THE RIGHT PLACE (Com) Commissioned by the Electric Auto-Lite Company, the short stresses the importance of checking and installing spark plugs in the engine to ensure 'harmony' with the ignition system.

PORTUGUESE READING FILMS 1 AND 2 (Com) Prepared by the Studio during the war in conjunction with the Coordinator of Inter-American Affairs, the shorts were made to assist Brazilian illiterates to read. Subtitled *A Historia de José* and *José Com Bien*, the films were adapted from the health films *The Human Body* and *What is Disease?* (*The Unseen Enemy*).

DOG WATCH (P) Director Charles Nichols. While keeping guard on a naval vessel, Pluto experiences some difficulties with an aggressive wharf rat when the rodent tries to steal the captain's dinner.

THE EYES HAVE IT (D) Director Jack Hannah. Donald hypnotizes Pluto and persuades him to behave like a mouse. But when Pluto assumes the character of a lion, a chase ensues that wrecks the house.

PREVENTION AND CONTROL OF DISTORTION IN ARC WELDING (Com) Sponsored by the Lincoln Electrical Company, the Studio produced a serious training film that made use of some fascinating animation to illustrate the precautions required to prevent metal shrinking as it cools.

AFRICAN DIARY (G) Director Jack Kinney. 24 November – Goofy's ship lands on the Ivory Coast, according to the narration by Frank

CANINE CASANOVA (P) Director Charles Nichols. Pluto falls helplessly in love with a female dachshund, but when he rescues her from the confines of the Municipal Dog Pound, he is surprised to find that his new sweetheart is the mother of several puppies.

INFANT CARE (Com) This film in the series on health, produced by the Studio for the Coordinator of Inter-American Affairs explains a mother's preparation for her new baby. After the birth, lessons in baby care stress the importance of vaccination, etc. to ensure the child's health.

HOLD YOUR HORSEPOWER (Com) Director Hamilton Luske. This educational film for The Texas Company examines new and improved farm machinery and how it replaces the cruder hand methods. As well as stressing the importance of machine care, the short illustrates the machinery's capability to produce more crops.

DUCK PIMPLES (DD) Director Jack Kinney. The title card reads 'Goose Pimples', with 'goose' crossed out and 'duck' written in. Directed by Kinney in a style very like a Tex Avery short, Donald's imagination runs riot as he listens to the radio and then reads a crime book from which the characters come to life. As an in-joke, the detective is named after Hugh Hennesy, a Studio art director, layout and background artist.

WHAT IS DISEASE? (Com) Also known under its alternative title *El Enemigo Invisible* or *The Unseen Enemy*, this animated film, made for the Coordinator of Inter-American Affairs, discusses the dangers of microbe invasion. Warning against the diseases carried by flies and mosquitoes, the picture stresses that the insects must be destroyed to maintain health.

THE HUMAN BODY (Com) During the war one of the most successful of the Disney health films commissioned by the Coordinator of Inter-American Affairs shows an artist drawing an animated man and demonstrating that his own body is man's most valuable possession. This use of an animated human body to demonstrate the importance of good health has been seen in a number of Disney educational films, particularly in the space films *Man in Space* (1955) and *Mars and Beyond* (1957), which showed a human figure at the mercy of extra-terrestrial forces.

TUBERCULOSIS (Com) Produced for the Coordinator of Inter-American Affairs, the short depicts the disease as man's deadliest enemy. Using animation to dissect lungs and show the symptoms, the film draws an interesting comparison between two lungs that are infected by germs and two 'lung-shaped' leaves that are being devoured by insects.

HOW DISEASE TRAVELS (Com) Another of the health films sponsored by the Coordinator of Inter-American Affairs uses animation to show how, through carelessness, a sick man's disease can easily be carried in waste water to infect others.

THE LEGEND OF COYOTE ROCK (P) Director Charles Nichols. Pluto saves some lambs from the ever-hungry coyote (left), and in the ensuing chase, the coyote falls off a cliff, the rocks settling on top of him in the shape of a giant statue, known thereafter as Coyote Rock.

NO SAIL (DD) Director Jack Hannah. Donald and Goofy go sailing in a rented boat, but unfortunately they run out of money to feed the 5¢ coin box and are marooned in the middle of the ocean. Donald has some scrapes with some

---

Graham. By Friday, 13 December, the little safari is chased back to the safety of its ship by a rather belligerent black rhino.

TIGER TROUBLE (G) Director Jack Kinney. Fred Shields narrates in a sort of pseudo-version of John McLeish's pompous narration style, used to such brilliant effect in Goofy's 'How To' series. *Tiger Trouble* follows Goofy as he sets out on the back of a wonderfully manic elephant (above) to capture a ferocious tiger. After a certain amount of confusion they return, the elephant wearing the tiger's stripes.

THE DAWN OF BETTER LIVING (Com) Westinghouse Electric sponsored an educational film to show the development of the home from log cabin era to the 1940s, with each decade illustrating an improved lighting system.

SOMETHING YOU DIDN'T EAT (Com) Sponsored by the Cereal Institute (Office of War Information, War Food Administration), the short sets out to explain, with the aid of clever animation, early experiments with vitamins and the need for a good nutritional diet. With the end of the war in sight, the film was deliberately intended to have some influence on the inhabitants of a more prosperous post-war America.

☆ DONALD'S CRIME (DD) Director Jack King. Audiences expected to see Donald being disagreeable towards Chip an' Dale, Humphrey the bear or even the occasional little bee. But when he steals money from his nephews' piggy bank, even Donald sinks to an all-time low. But his conscience finally gets the better of him, and he repays every cent.

INSECTS AS CARRIERS OF DISEASE (Com) When it was suggested to the Coordinator of Inter-American Affairs that an 'everyman' character might be better for their propaganda shorts on health than Donald Duck, the Studio created 'Careless Charlie', who is shrunk to the size of a fly and watches with horror as, what he assumed were just household pests, are revealed as monstrous carriers of germs and disease.

CLEANLINESS BRINGS HEALTH (Com) This was one of 13 educational shorts made for the Coordinator of Inter-American Affairs and

---

designed to illustrate the risks of disease. Two fictional families, the Clean Family and the Careless Family, are compared to see which is the healthier.

HOOKWORM (Com) Part of the series on prevention of disease in Latin American countries, sponsored by the Coordinator of Inter-American Affairs, the short tells the animated story of Careless Charlie and the tragedy that befell him and his family when their insanitary living conditions causes them to become inflicted by hookworm.

CALIFORNY 'ER BUST (G) Director Jack Kinney. American Indians attack a wagon train full of Goofy look-a-likes. 'They threw everything at us *but* the kitchen sink,' explains the narrator, moments before a kitchen sink hits Goofy on the head.

sharks, while Goofy, calm as ever, takes the situation in hand.

HOCKEY HOMICIDE (G) Director Jack Kinney. Depicting another round of sporting activities, this fast and furiously paced cartoon encapsulates all the worst aspects of bad sportsmanship, with Goofy playing *all* the parts (above).

CURED DUCK (DD) Director Jack King. Disgusted by Donald's constant bad temper, Daisy forces him to purchase an 'insult machine', and, for a while, he is a reformed duck (below). But when Daisy buys a new hat, Donald finds it impossible not to laugh. Daisy loses her temper.

LIGHT IS WHAT YOU MAKE IT (Com) An organization with the unusual name of the National Better Light Better Sight Bureau commissioned the Studio to produce an educational film in which the human eye is compared to a camera,

and the effects of light and dark are shown on the eye muscles.

OLD SEQUOIA (DD) Director Jack King. Forest Ranger Donald Duck is ordered by his superiors to guard an ancient tree. When some beavers decide it would make a suitable addition to their dam, Donald tries to stop them – without success.

1946

THE ABC OF HAND TOOLS (Com) Director Bill Roberts. A sequence director on a number of Disney animated features, Roberts was given the task of directing a training film for General Motors. The short illustrates various types of files, saws, chisels and so forth and the ways to prevent their misuse.

A KNIGHT FOR A DAY (G) Director Jack Hannah. Resembling one of his 'How To' films, the short

shows Goofy as a knight in not-so-shining armour attempting to win the joust and the hand of Princess Penelope. The narration is similar to that of a boxing match commentary.

THE BUILDING OF A TIRE (Com) Director Lou Debney. Using animation, the film, which was sponsored by the Firestone Tire and Rubber Company, traces the tyre from rubber plantation to factory floor.

BATHING TIME FOR BABY (Com) Director James Algar. Johnson and Johnson sponsored this amusing animated educational film, in which a stork conducts a class in the correct method of baby bathing.

ENVIRONMENTAL SANITATION (Com) Made for the Coordinator of Inter-American Affairs, the film shows the growth of a centre of urban population. Stagnant pools of water become clean living environments, and overcrowding leads to more widespread and better sanitation.

PLANNING FOR GOOD EATING (Com) Referred to in some languages as Ramon or José, Careless Charlie, who first appeared in *Insects as Carriers of Disease*, became the star of a number of animated health films, produced by Disney for the Coordinator of Inter-American Affairs. Here Charlie explains to a family portrayed as having poor health the importance of proper diet in maintaining long life.

JET PROPULSION (Com) In a purely technical exercise, the General Electric Company sponsored the Studio to produce an educational film to show the brief history of aircraft, using animated cutaways of the aerodynamics of jet engines, and to compare the plane's characteristics with those of conventional aircraft.

PLUTO'S KID BROTHER (P) Director Charles Nichols. Pluto banishes a troublesome puppy to the dog house, but an encounter with a vicious alley cat, a bulldog, the dog-catcher and a row of sausages proves to Pluto that his relation is just a chip off the old block.

IN DUTCH (P) Director Charles Nichols. Pluto and his sweetheart Dinah find themselves on location abroad, but they get into trouble for accidentally ringing the dyke alarm. When they find a real leak in one of the dykes, Dinah plugs it with her paw, while Pluto returns for help. At first, no one will believe him, but he tricks the townspeople into chasing after him, the town is saved, and the two dogs are heroes.

☆ SQUATTER'S RIGHTS (P) Director Jack Hannah. Although they are not referred to by name, Chip an' Dale appeared in this short. So that they can continue to live undisturbed inside an old stove, the chipmunks trick Mickey Mouse into thinking that Pluto has accidentally been shot.

THE PURLOINED PUP (P) Director Charles Nichols. When Butch kidnaps the puppy Ronnie, Pluto goes to the rescue. Butch gives chase but is outsmarted by Pluto who captures him and takes him to jail.

A FEATHER IN HIS COLLAR (Com) In this short sponsored by the Community Chest of America, Pluto donates his life savings (an assortment of bones) to Chest Campaign Headquarters and is awarded a red feather to wear in his collar.

DONALD'S DOUBLE TROUBLE (DD) Director Jack King. Daisy rejects Donald, and so, when he meets his double, he decides to trick her to win back her love. Unfortunately, Daisy falls for this

animation anticipates the UPA Studio's experimental styles by some five or six years, even though critics in the 1950s were slow to realize this. 'Blue Bayou' and 'Without You' (performed by Andy Russell) are among the film's most technically interesting sequences, while *Peter and the Wolf*, accompanied by Prokofiev's music and narrated by Sterling Holloway, and *Opera Pathetique*, featuring 'The Whale Who Wanted to Sing at the Met', narrated and sung by Nelson Eddy, are two of the film's finer sequences. The most disappointing, artistically and creatively, are *The Martins and the Coys*, a hillbilly tale sung by The King's Men, and *Two Silhouettes*, performed by Tatiana Riabouchinska and David Lichine and sung by Dinah Shore. There is, however, a certain amount of entertainment value in *Casey at the Bat* (imaginatively told by Jerry Colonna) and *Johnny Fedora and Alice Blue Bonnet*, sung by the Andrews Sisters. Although the film's premiere in New York was well received, the film was not a box-office success and, like its 'sequel' *Melody Time* (1948), has never been re-issued in its complete form. The more popular sequences from each film were, in fact, combined by RKO in a 1955 feature entitled *Music Land*, and they have turned up on the Disney television shows or as separate 16mm releases. *Blue Bayou* for instance appeared with its original score, 'Clair de Lune', on *The Wonderful World of Color* in 1966 and as part of *Creative Film Adventures Reel 2* in 1976.

DUMB BELL OF THE YUKON (DD) Director Jack King. Donald becomes entangled with a bear cub and an angry mother bear when he travels to the Arctic to get Daisy a new fur coat (opposite above left).

LIGHTHOUSE KEEPING (DD) Director Jack Hannah. Although Donald Duck often lost a job because of his bad temper and inability to keep discipline, he occasionally encountered an adversary who seemed determined to stop him working. In this short the irascible Duck has to contend with the antics of a large pelican, Marble-head, who will stop at nothing to keep the lighthouse beam off (opposite above right).

new, suave Donald (above), and the rivals find themselves fighting for her affections in the Tunnel of Love.

WET PAINT (DD) Director Jack King. Donald Duck, whose experience with automobiles has never been altogether harmonious, finds his attempts to paint his car frustrated by a tiny bird, which not only walks across the newly painted surface but then somehow manages to pull the upholstery apart.

MAKE MINE MUSIC (F) Directors Jack Kinney, Clyde Geronimi, Hamilton Luske, Bob Cormack and Josh Meador. Although the highly innovative *Song of the South* wasn't due to be released until November, Disney based his first 'package'

film on the ideas represented in *Fantasia* and prepared it for a summer release. Instead of using classical music, Disney turned to popular music, and the film boasted such performers as Nelson Eddy, Dinah Shore, Benny Goodman and the Andrews Sisters. Plans to use Stokowski were shelved, although the *Clair de Lune* sequence, prepared for *Fantasia*, cropped up in the film as 'Blue Bayou', sung by the Ken Darby Chorus. The film is composed of 10 musical sequences, but it has none of the recurring motifs so carefully worked out in the planning stages of *Fantasia*. Rather, it is a curious mixture of tastes and styles. Among the best sequences are the Benny Goodman jazz shorts *All the Cats Join In* (below left) and *After You've Gone* (below), in which the

TREASURE FROM THE SEA (Com) Commissioned by the Dow Chemical Company, the short demonstrates that magnesium is valuable because its 'lightness saves energy'. Its uses in locomotives, aircraft and household appliances are cited as examples of the metal's energy-saving capabilities.

BATH DAY (Fi) Director Charles Nichols. One of the three films produced featuring Figaro, the feline star of *Pinocchio*, this short shows a remarkable understanding of a cat's behaviour. A gang of alley cats gets the newly bathed Figaro dirty. Minnie is only too happy to bathe him again (below left).

THE STORY OF MENSTRUATION (Com) Sponsored by the International Cellu-Cotton Company, the short uses a combination of animation and live action to illustrate the development of a young girl's body. The film demonstrates the Studio's ability to handle any health subject in a revealing and expert way.

FRANK DUCK BRINGS 'EM BACK ALIVE (DD) Director Jack Hannah. The famous 'great white hunter' Donald meets a crazy 'wild man of the jungle', otherwise known as Goofy, who refuses to be 'discovered', whatever the cost to Donald's sanity.

★SONG OF THE SOUTH (F) Cartoon director Wilfred Jackson. This curious film is undeniably one of the Studio's best, as well as being one of Walt's personal favourites. In the original American souvenir book, Disney said of the film: 'If, now, in *Song of the South*, we have succeeded in a measure to help perpetuate a priceless literary treasure – my co-workers and I shall, indeed, be very happy.' Adapted by Dalton Reymond, Morton Grant and Maurice Rapf from the books by Joel Chandler Harris, this charming film was further enhanced by a brilliant performance by black actor James Baskett as the famous storyteller, Uncle Remus, a performance for which he won a special award at the 1947 Academy Awards, while the film's most popular song, 'Zip-A-Dee-Doo-Dah', by Ray Gilbert and Allie Wrubel also won an Oscar.

In the story, young Johnny (Bobby Driscoll) is brought to live with his mother (Ruth Warrick) and grandmother (Lucile Watson) on a plantation in the Old South. When he learns of his parents' (temporary) separation, Johnny is determined to run away but is lured back by the stories of Uncle Remus. Helped by his apocryphal tales about three wonderful characters, Brer Rabbit, Brer Fox and Brer Bear, Johnny learns how to overcome his problems. But there is still a great deal of human conflict before Johnny's family is happily reunited. Co-stars include Luana Patten, as Johnny's young friend Ginny, and Hattie McDaniel as Aunt Tempy. In addition to playing the lead, Baskett voiced Brer Fox, while Nicodemus Stewart was Brer Bear and Johnny

Lee was Brer Rabbit. Compared favourably to David O. Selznick's classic *Gone With the Wind*, the film was a departure for the Studio in that it concentrated more on the live-action story (directed by Harve Foster) than on the vivid animated sequences. Gregg Toland, who had worked on Orson Welles' *Citizen Kane*, captures the period setting with his remarkable cinematography. At the time, the posters publicized the image of the Old South and made only passing reference to the animated sequences, but for later re-issues more advertising was given to the cartoon characters (above), partly because the film had attracted critical comments from US civil rights groups.

DOUBLE DRIBBLE (G) Director Jack Hannah. Two basketball teams of Goofy lookalikes play a game to an off-screen narration in the style of a television sports match.

1947

PLUTO'S HOUSEWARMING (P) Director Charles Nichols. When Pluto is driven out of his new home by Butch the bulldog, a small turtle proves an unusual ally in helping Pluto get rid of his unwelcome guest (right).

RESCUE DOG (P) Director Charles Nichols. When a baby seal steals Pluto's keg of brandy, Pluto gives chase but falls into the icy water. The seal rescues him (opposite above left) and they become firm friends.

STRAIGHT SHOOTERS (DD) Director Jack Hannah. Donald Duck sabotages his nephews' chances of winning prizes at his carnival stall. In retaliation, Huey, Dewey and Louie disguise themselves as a glamorous 'mystic medium' and trick Donald out of his supply of free candy.

SLEEPY TIME DONALD (DD) Director Jack King. Donald sleepwalks to Daisy's house, but when she manages to get Donald back home, he wakes up and, much to her annoyance, accuses Daisy of sleepwalking.

FIGARO AND FRANKIE (Fi) Director Charles Nichols. Frankie the singing canary gets on Figaro's nerves, and Figaro decides to quieten the bird once and for all. The intervention of Butch, who would also like to eat Frankie, adds marginally to the mayhem, which ends with Frankie and Figaro as firm friends.

CLOWN OF THE JUNGLE (DD) Director Jack Hannah. An ornithological expedition brings Donald Duck face to face with the crazy Aracuan Bird (opposite above right), which also starred in *The Three Caballeros* (1945) and *Melody Time* (1948). Donald eventually goes crazy!

DONALD'S DILEMMA (DD) Director Jack King. A precursor to what was to become of Donald in shorts such as *Donald's Diary* (1954), we see here the problems confronting Daisy when a flower

pot falls on Donald's head and gives him a magnificent singing voice. (What Donald's real-life voice, Clarence Nash, thought of all this no one knows.) Fortunately for all concerned, Donald's career at Radio City is short-lived, for another flower pot restores him to his cacophonous self and to Daisy's arms (below).

CRAZY WITH THE HEAT (DD & G) Director Bob Carlson. When their car runs out of petrol in the middle of the desert, Donald and Goofy decide to walk. Goofy sees a mirage of a soda fountain, and Donald imagines that he sees huge ice mountains. Finally the imagined owner of Goofy's mirage chases them away on a real camel.

BOOTLE BEETLE (DD) Director Jack Hannah. Bootle Beetle's problem is how to escape being captured by Donald. The film uses some marvellous perspectives as seen through the beetle's eyes.

WIDE OPEN SPACES (DD) Director Jack King. Donald Duck desperately tries to get to sleep under the stars after he has complained about the price of motel beds. After some hair-raising experiences with an inflatable mattress and a tree branch, he ends up sleeping on the motel porch before being ejected by the owner into the spiny arms of a waiting cactus.

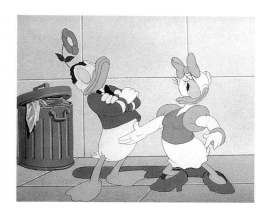

FUN AND FANCY FREE (F) Animation directors Jack Kinney, Bill Roberts and Hamilton Luske with live-action sequences directed by William Horgan. Combining live action and animation, *Fun and Fancy Free* seems to fit the mould of *The Reluctant Dragon* more than it does that of *Song of the South*. Instead of a straightforward story, it is a series of gags hosted by Jiminy Cricket, who introduces the audience to the story of *Bongo* (from a story by Sinclair Lewis), in which a small circus bear manages to escape captivity and find true happiness in the country. Containing three charming songs by Bobby Worth, Eliot Daniel and Buddy Kaye, it is narrated and sung by Dinah Shore. Spotting an invitation to a party, Jiminy

then hops over to ventriloquist Edgar Bergen's house where he meets Bergen, dummies Charlie McCarthy and Mortimer Snerd, and actress Luana Patten, fresh from her role as Ginny in *Song of the South*. Aided by occasional and often hilarious interruptions from Charlie, Bergen relates the story of three starving farmers – Mickey, Donald and Goofy (below) – and their adventures with Willie the Giant, voiced by Billy

Gilbert (Sneezy in *Snow White and the Seven Dwarfs*) in the animated special *Mickey and the Beanstalk*. The sequence contains some catchy songs by Paul J. Smith, Arthur Quenzer, William (Bill) Walsh, Ray Noble and Oliver Wallace. (At the beginning of the film Jiminy Cricket even gets to sing 'I'm a Happy-Go-Lucky Fellow' by Leigh Harline and Ned Washington, which had been written for *Pinocchio*.) At the film's climax,

Willie the Giant pops in to say hello to Bergen and his guests. *Bongo* was shown on the *Disneyland* tv series in 1955 (16mm release in 1971), and *Mickey and the Beanstalk*, narrated by Ludwig Von Drake, was shown in the 1960s.

MICKEY'S DELAYED DATE (MM) Director Charles Nichols. After Pluto has been 'lending a paw', Mickey needs all the help he can get, especially when Minnie phones to complain that he's late for their evening out. Mickey changes into his top hat and tails to take Minnie to the dance, only to encounter a runaway dustbin. Fortunately it's a costume ball, and Minnie compliments Mickey on his now tattered suit.

FOUL HUNTING (G) Director Jack Hannah. When a small duck imitates a decoy's actions, Goofy falls into the lake and his gun fills with water (above). Having failed to shoot any real ducks, he is forced to eat the decoy.

MAIL DOG (P) Director Charles Nichols. When the pilot turns back, it's up to Pluto to get the mail through on time. Against the odds – and abetted by a new friend, Flutter Foot the snowshoe rabbit – Pluto delivers on time.

☆ CHIP AN' DALE (DD) Director Jack Hannah. The chipmunks give an Oscar-worthy performance (they lost to Warner Brothers' *Tweetie Pie*) as they try to save their home, which had been chopped up for firewood by Donald Duck.

☆ PLUTO'S BLUE NOTE (P) Director Charles Nichols. The song 'You Belong To My Heart' from *The Three Caballeros* crops up again. In order to charm the female dogs in the neighbourhood, Pluto serenades them by miming to a record.

1948

THEY'RE OFF (G) Director Jack Hannah. With a humorous narration provided by Harlow Wilcox, Goofy explores the highly complex world of horse racing. Wonderfully confusing instructions mean that Goofy is no wiser about the characteristics of horses, jockeys, racing bets or the track itself at the end of the film than he was at the beginning. As usual, the film's style parodies a newsreel.

THE BIG WASH (G) Director Clyde Geronimi. Goofy has a difficult time trying to bathe Dolores the elephant. Dolores gives Goofy the slip by disguising herself as a clown, but is eventually caught and bathed.

DRIP DIPPY DONALD (DD) Director Jack King. Donald's attempts to sleep are constantly disturbed by a dripping tap. To accentuate the awakening effects of the leaking tap, King adopted surreal perspectives that turn each splash into a resounding explosion.

MICKEY DOWN UNDER (MM) Director Charles Nichols. Pluto becomes entangled with a very independent-minded boomerang, while Mickey finds an emu egg protected by an over-zealous parent.

DADDY DUCK (DD) Director Jack Hannah. Donald is guardian to a nervous kangaroo which is frightened of a bear rug. Trying to show who's boss, Donald is swallowed by the bear and has to be rescued by the kangaroo.

BONE BANDIT (P) Director Charles Nichols. Pluto attempts to retrieve his bones from a gopher who has used them in the construction of his underground home. The ensuing battle of wits involves flower pollen and an uncontrollable bout of hayfever.

DONALD'S DREAM VOICE (DD) Director Jack King. A box of pills miraculously improves the harsh tone of Donald's speech but unfortunately, he loses both the pills and the vocal range of actors like George Sanders and Basil Rathbone and is left with the sound of his own adorable quacking.

MELODY TIME (F) Directors Clyde Geronimi, Hamilton Luske, Jack Kinney and Wilfred Jackson. Like *Make Mine Music* (1946), Disney's second potpourri of popular musical extracts accompanied by animation was years ahead of the experiments in animation styles developed in the 1950s. As with the first film, Disney gathered together such noted performers as Roy Rogers, Luana Patten, Bobby Driscoll and Ethel Smith, while vocals were supplied by the Andrews Sisters, Fred Waring and his Pennsylvanians, Frances Langford and Dennis Day. In some respects it is infinitely better than *Make Mine Music*: there is far less concentration on diverse subject matter; *Bumble Boogie* a jazz interpretation of 'Flight of the Bumble Bee', in which a small insect encounters some unpredictable flora and fauna, is fast paced and highly inventive; and *Once Upon a Wintertime* (centre), *Johnny Appleseed* and *Little Toot* tell fascinating stories with great humour, and some good songs and clever gags. Indeed, *Little Toot*, sung by the Andrews Sisters, is perhaps the most ingenious of all in its retelling of Hardie Gramatky's story about a baby tugboat. The film's most ambitious

sequence, however, sung by Fred Waring and his Pennsylvanians from the poem by Joyce Kilmer, uses stunning animation effects by Ub Iwerks to illustrate the different forms of line and colour in various types of *Trees*. *Blame it on the Samba* features Ethel Smith at the organ, accompanied by Donald Duck, Joe Carioca (opposite below) and the Aracuan Bird (last seen in *Clown of the Jungle*), who perform a South American number by Ernesto Nazareth and Ray Gilbert. The film ends with Roy Rogers relating the legend of *Pecos Bill* to young Bobby Driscoll and Luana Patten, after singing, with the Sons of the Pioneers, one of the film's most delightful songs 'Blue Shadows on the Trail' by Eliot Daniel and Johnny Lange. The film was never rereleased in its complete form, but sequences were re-issued in the compilation feature *Music Land*, which was distributed by RKO Radio Pictures in 1955. Extracts have also appeared regularly on the Disney television shows and as separate theatrical and 16mm short subjects.

PLUTO'S PURCHASE (P) Director Charles Nichols. While returning home from the shops with a salami for Mickey Mouse, Pluto has to use all his ingenuity to outwit Butch the bulldog. Unbeknown to Pluto, however, Mickey plans to give the sausage to Butch as a present (above left).

THE TRIAL OF DONALD DUCK (DD) Director Jack King. Donald is accused of dining in an expensive restaurant and leaving without paying the $35 bill. Pierre the waiter wins his case and Donald is sentenced to wash up for 10 days. In revenge, he smashes all the crockery.

CAT NAP PLUTO (P) Director Charles Nichols. In addition to starring in his own series of shorts, Figaro, the feline star of *Pinocchio*, appeared in a number of Pluto cartoons. In *Cat Nap Pluto* the two tire themselves out playing games, but need help from the Sandman to get to sleep.

INFERIOR DECORATOR (DD) Director Jack Hannah. Donald Duck's attempts at being pract-ical usually end in disaster, yet he starts his day successfully hanging wallpaper – successfully, that is, until his arch-enemy the bee thinks the flowers on the wallpaper are real. Donald tries to rid himself of the pest by sticking him in the glue, but, alas for Donald, the bee escapes and summons a swarm of colleagues who take it in turns to sting Donald where it hurts most.

PLUTO'S FLEDGLING (P) Director Charles Nichols. Orville the baby bird tries to fly. In order to help him, Pluto, on whose nose Orville has landed, attempts some amazing high-flying stunts of his own (below).

SOUP'S ON (DD) Director Jack Hannah. Singing 'Zip-A-Dee-Doo-Dah' from *Song of the South*, Donald prepares lunch. When Huey, Dewey and Louie steal the food, Donald chases after them, and when he accidentally falls over a cliff, the nephews trick Donald into thinking he is now an angel (above). They have cause to regret the joke when Donald learns the truth.

THREE FOR BREAKFAST (DD) Director Jack Hannah. Donald Duck substitutes rubber pancakes for real ones, and, momentarily, Chip an' Dale are fooled – yet still manage to trick Donald out of his meal.

☆MICKEY AND THE SEAL (MM) Director Charles Nichols. A baby seal hides inside Mickey's picnic basket. Pluto tries to tell his master what has happened, but the seal remains unnoticed until he joins Mickey in the bathtub.

☆ TEA FOR TWO HUNDRED (DD) Director Jack Hannah. An army of hungry ants is after Donald's picnic lunch, and there's nothing he can do to stop them (above left).

1949

PUEBLO PLUTO (P) Director Charles Nichols. Pluto gets into some near scrapes with rolling pots, spiny cacti and a small puppy called Ronnie. Set in Mexico and co-starring Mickey Mouse, the short could well have been included in either *Saludos Amigos* or *The Three Caballeros*.

☆ SO DEAR TO MY HEART (F) Director Harold Schuster. A film that has all the charm of Disney's previous live-action release, *Song of the South*, So

Dear to My Heart has a gentle story that revolves around an excellent performance by child star Bobby Driscoll. Driscoll plays Jeremiah Kincaid, a young boy who adopts a black sheep that has been shunned by its mother. Set in 1903, the film is rich in detail and is competently adapted by John Ewing from Sterling North's book *Midnight and Jeremiah*. The film, which co-stars Burl Ives (Uncle Hiram), Beulah Bondi (Granny), Harry Carey (the judge) and Luana Patten (Tildy), uses animated sequences to highlight events in Jeremiah's life, including a scene in which, accompanied by the song 'Stick-to-it-ivity', a wise owl (above right) relates the stories of Christopher Columbus and Robert Bruce. (The latter sequence found its way into the

prologue of the televised version of *Rob Roy*.) Filmed in the lush surroundings of Sequoia National Park and the San Joaquin Valley, the movie has a wonderful period charm. The song 'Lavender Blue', adapted from a folk song by Larry Morey and Eliot Daniel, was nominated for an Academy Award, and the film remained one of Disney's personal favourites. It was screened on the *Disneyland* television series in 1954.

DONALD'S HAPPY BIRTHDAY (DD) Director Jack Hannah. Donald punishes Huey, Dewey and Louie (below) for buying cigars before discovering they have bought them for his birthday.

SEA SALTS (DD) Director Jack Hannah. Bootle Beetle returns to relate the story of how he and Captain Donald Duck survived after being shipwrecked on a desert island (opposite above).

PLUTO'S SURPRISE PACKAGE (P) Director Charles Nichols. Sent to collect the mail, Pluto is intrigued to discover that one of the packages has legs and can move on its own accord. He discovers it is a gift-wrapped turtle (opposite centre).

PLUTO'S SWEATER (P) Director Charles Nichols. Minnie knits Pluto a sweater, which he tries hard not to wear. Figaro is bemused by the situation, until the sweater gets wet and shrinks. Pluto has the last laugh when Minnie makes Figaro wear it instead (opposite below).

★ SEAL ISLAND (TLA) Director James Algar. Disney was fascinated by the footage Alfred and Elma Milotte shot of the seals of the Pribilof Islands, and he decided to put the material together into the first in a series of True-Life Adventure films. RKO, Disney's distributor, complained that 27 minutes running time was too short, but ironically, RKO later criticized Disney when he announced his intention to make feature-length documentaries, saying that featurettes were preferable. *Seal Island* covers the life-cycle of the seal, and it is more informative and serious than some of the later films in the series. It was shown in 1954 on the *Disneyland* television series.

WINTER STORAGE (DD) Director Jack Hannah. Ranger Donald Duck, busily planting acorns, is unknowingly raiding Chip an' Dale's food supply. The chipmunks seek revenge by challenging Donald to a hockey game with thousands of acorns used instead of a ball.

BUBBLE BEE (P) Director Charles Nichols. For a change, Pluto is the one to come unstuck or rather stuck when he messes with Donald's old enemy, the Bee, as they battle over a hive full of gum.

HONEY HARVESTER (DD) Director Jack Hannah. Humming 'Whistle While You Work', a little bee happily helps himself to the flower pollen in Donald's greenhouse. When Donald tries to steal the honey, the outraged insect attacks him with a cactus spine attached to his sting.

TENNIS RACQUET (G) Director Jack Kinney. Goofy stars as *both* competitors as their unique form of tennis tears up the court, much to the surprise of the spectators and the announcer.

ALL IN A NUTSHELL (DD) Director Jack Hannah. Donald runs a nut-butter store which resembles a giant walnut. Chip an' Dale, however, think they have stumbled across the world's largest food supply and set about thwarting Donald's attempts to prevent them stealing it.

GOOFY GYMNASTICS (G) Director Jack Kinney. Goofy demonstrates how *not* to exercise: he crashes out of the window, gets hopelessly tangled up in some of the body-building apparatus and bounces back to pose before a strong-man chart. (When Goofy falls out of the window, a vocal ya-hoo scream, created by Pinto Colvig, can be heard which has been used in countless other Disney shorts.) The deadpan narration was beautifully given by John McLeish.

THE GREENER YARD (DD) Director Jack Hannah. Bootle Beetle, who originally starred alongside Donald Duck in 1947, makes an anonymous re-appearance as he looks forward to all the food in Donald's garden. The young beetle is chased away by the irate Duck and decides to be content with his bean dinner.

SHEEP DOG (P) Director Charles Nichols. Those wily coyotes, Bent-Tail and Bent-Tail Junior, plague Pluto yet again. This time they try to steal lambs from the corral, but Pluto tricks Bent-Tail by disguising Junior as one of the lambs.

SLIDE, DONALD, SLIDE (DD) Director Jack Hannah. Donald wants to listen to the baseball game on the radio; the bee would prefer to listen to the music being played on another station.

☆TOY TINKERS (DD) Director Jack Hannah. Donald tries all kinds of ways to rid himself of those pesky chipmunks, which have sneaked into the house to play with the Christmas presents and to eat the nuts and sweets. In 1961 it was released on 16mm as *Christmas Capers*.

THE ADVENTURES OF ICHABOD AND MR TOAD (F) Directors Jack Kinney, Clyde Geronimi and James Algar. The Studio had a great deal of mileage out of its 11th animated feature. It started life as a full-length version of Kenneth Grahame's book *The Wind in the Willows*, but the need to produce a series of films that would bring in a quick revenue combined with the trend already set by the compilation pictures *Make Mine Music*, *Melody Time* and *Fun and Fancy Free* persuaded Disney that the time wasn't right for a complete feature. The Studio employed Basil Rathbone to narrate this shorter version, which is only loosely based on Grahame's story. Rathbone's rather dry, English accent brilliantly complements the lives of the residents of Toad Hall. Stunning animation, backgrounds and editing set *Mr Toad* apart from the majority of the Studio's late 1940s' films as Mole, Ratty and MacBadger spend a great deal of their energy chasing after Toad, whose passion for horses, cars, trains and aeroplanes constantly lands him in serious trouble.

When the film was released, Rathbone had a relatively small billing because of the inclusion of Washington Irving's story *The Legend of Sleepy Hollow*, narrated by Bing Crosby. Crosby narrates *Ichabod* and sings the film's three songs by Don Raye and Gene DePaul – 'Ichabod', 'Katrina' and 'The Headless Horseman'. The film of Ichabod, the itinerant schoolmaster, and of the problems he encountered at Sleepy Hollow has a

1950

PLUTO'S HEART THROB (P) Director Charles Nichols. Butch the bulldog tried to use his brute strength to outwit Pluto on numerous occasions, but here he proves too cowardly to rescue Pluto's sweetheart Dinah from the swimming pool, so Mickey's pet has to save the day and win her affection (right).

LION AROUND (DD) Director Jack Hannah. Huey, Dewey and Louie frighten their Uncle Donald into giving them a pie by dressing up as a lion. When Donald realizes he's been tricked, he chases after his nephews – only to be confronted by a real lion. To appease the angry beast, Donald gives up the rest of his precious pies.

PLUTO AND THE GOPHER (P) Director Charles Nichols. Pluto digs up Minnie's garden in search of a flower thief. When the gopher is trapped inside the house, it burrows into the carpet thinking it's a lawn, further frustrating Pluto's attempts to capture it.

☆CINDERELLA (F) Directors Wilfred Jackson, Hamilton Luske and Clyde Geronimi. Early in 1950 the Studio was preparing for the release of its new full-length animated feature. Live-action films such as Song of the South and So Dear to My Heart had included only a modicum of animation, while Make Mine Music and Melody Time had been released solely to improve the Studio's war-affected economy, but, as re-issues of Snow White and the Seven Dwarfs were proving highly successful at the box-office, it seemed logical to return to fairy-tales. Taking the most famous 'rags to riches' story of them all, Disney imbued the film with a host of delightful characters while at the same time retaining all the classic ingredients. Despised by her evil Stepmother and two ugly Stepsisters, Cinderella, with the help of her Fairy Godmother and the little birds and mice whom she has befriended, attends the royal ball (right). She falls in love with the Prince but has to return home before the spell breaks at midnight. She hides from the palace guard as the pumpkin, which only seconds before had been a glistening coach, is shattered into a thousand pieces beneath their horses' hooves. As in all happy endings though, Cinderella and her Prince are eventually re-united.

Apart from the highly successful addition of tiny animals to fill out the story, the human characters are expertly handled. Cinderella is wonderfully sympathetic, while her Stepmother is delightfully callous without having to resort to black magic to achieve her ends. Her two daughters are equally repulsive, with their large feet and Olive Oyl-type arms and legs. The film's musical score, although not as effective as that of Snow White, includes some catchy songs – 'Bibbidi-Bobbidi-Boo' and 'The Work Song', for example. The rest are romantic ballads, with the exception

style of animation more in keeping with the 1950s shorts. The colour and styling by Mary Blair and others were also far more surreal than the ornate furnishings and thick forests of Mr Toad's very English settings. It is also possible to detect where corners were cut in Ichabod – the use of animation cycles from the 1937 Silly Symphony The Old Mill and the fact that Ichabod's true love, Katrina, is an almost exact copy of a character from Make Mine Music. But the chase through Sleepy Hollow, animated by Wolfgang Reitherman and John Sibley, when Ichabod is pursued by the terrifying Headless Horseman

(above), is the Studio at its best. Of the other voice talents, Eric Blore is perfect as the hysterical Toad and Pat O'Malley highly amusing as the cockney horse Cyril (below). Two Fabulous Characters, as the film was going to be called, appeared in two episodes on the Disneyland television series in 1955, The Legend of Sleepy Hollow was re-released theatrically in 1958 and Mr Toad, under the title The Wind in the Willows in the UK in 1967 and in the US in 1975 as The Madcap Adventures of Mr Toad. Finally, in 1980, The Adventures of J. Thaddeus Toad was distributed on 16mm for schools.

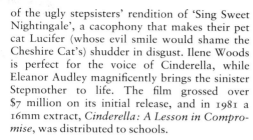

of the ugly stepsisters' rendition of 'Sing Sweet Nightingale', a cacophony that makes their pet cat Lucifer (whose evil smile would shame the Cheshire Cat's) shudder in disgust. Ilene Woods is perfect for the voice of Cinderella, while Eleanor Audley magnificently brings the sinister Stepmother to life. The film grossed over $7 million on its initial release, and in 1981 a 16mm extract, *Cinderella: A Lesson in Compromise*, was distributed to schools.

THE BRAVE ENGINEER (Sp) Director Jack Kinney. Racing against time to reach his destination, Casey Jones (below), narrated by Jerry Colonna, pulls into the station – almost on time – in a completely wrecked railway engine. The film reflects a style that was to be followed throughout the decade.

CRAZY OVER DAISY (DD) Director Jack Hannah. Chip an' Dale sabotage Donald's attempts to visit his sweetheart Daisy. Guest stars in this short, which is very reminiscent of *The Nifty Nineties* (1941), include Mickey, Minnie and Goofy.

WONDER DOG (P) Director Charles Nichols. Pluto is jealous when he sees Dinah admiring a poster of Prince, a super canine, in this short film, which also features Butch the bulldog, who ridicules Pluto's attempts to impress his sweetheart. During the ensuing chase and in a gag-filled climax, Pluto accomplishes all the circus stunts.

TRAILER HORN (DD) Director Jack Hannah. Chip an' Dale look forward to some fun when they spot Donald's camp site. Fooling the excitable duck with a trick diving-board, the chipmunks not only sabotage Donald's vacation but also manage to catapult his car into a cliff.

PRIMITIVE PLUTO (P) Director Charles Nichols. Pluto is rudely awakened from his slumbers at Mickey's Wildlife Retreat by his 'primitive instinct' in the guise of a small wolf, Primo. The little creature insists that the lazy dog should be out hunting for food in the wild like his ancestors. A too-close encounter with a grizzly bear soon changes their minds.

PUSS-CAFÉ (P) Director Charles Nichols. Melvin, a Siamese cat, and friend enter Pluto's backyard intent on stealing milk from the doorstep and fish from the pond. For once, Pluto wins.

163

MOTOR MANIA (G) Director Jack Kinney. Goofy illustrates the hazards of driving as he reverts from a mild-mannered individual into a monster when he gets behind the wheel of his car. This 'Mr Hyde' betrays all the aggressive and impatient tendencies of the bad driver. But it's a different story when Goofy becomes a pedestrian once more. A number of Disney shorts during the 1950s underlined in a humorous way the dangers of driving, making them suitable for school use. Among the other titles were *The Story of Anyburg, U.S.A.* (1957), *Freewayphobia No. 1* (1965) and *Goofy's Freeway Trouble* (1965).

TREASURE ISLAND (F) Director Byron Haskin. This swashbuckling adventure was the first in a series of British-made live-action films, produced with the Studio's overseas revenue, which was still 'frozen' after the war. It was also the first feature-length film to be made without a single animated sequence. Based on Robert Louis Stevenson's novel, the film stars Bobby Driscoll as young Jim Hawkins, who finds himself lured into the evil machinations of Long John Silver, a part performed with great relish by Robert Newton. Perce Pearce (a sequence director on *Snow White*) was producer, while special-effects-ace-turned-director Haskin was put in charge of the project. With a screenplay by Lawrence Watkin, the film is considered, along with *20,000 Leagues Under the Sea*, to be one of the Studio's finest live-action dramas. Filmed at Denham Studios, England, scenes of the rocky, windswept English coast and lush island exteriors were greatly enhanced by artist Peter Ellenshaw's magnificent glass mattes. All the excitement of the original story was brilliantly captured through the stunning photography of Academy-Award-winning cinematographer Freddie Young. A competent supporting cast included Basil Sydney, Walter Fitzgerald and Finlay Currie, as the race to claim a buried treasure is brought vividly to life. Although the film didn't fare well at the box-office, Phil Reisman, the head of RKO Radio Pictures, was convinced that it was one of the company's best. Shown on the *Disneyland* television series in 1955, a 16mm extract in the Films As Literature series was released in 1978. The film itself, unfortunately trimmed because of the censor's concern over 'violent scenes', was rereleased in 1975.

★ IN BEAVER VALLEY (TLA) Director James Algar. The winner of the 1950 Academy Award for Best Two-Reel Subject, *In Beaver Valley* portrays the beaver as the 'leading citizen' of the woodland community. But its relationship with the other animals of the forest – moose, deer, crayfish, raccoons, owls and coyote – is also explored in photography by Alfred Milotte and narration by Winston Hibler. Paul Smith, whose music 'A Symphony of Spring' was such a success in *Nature's Half Acre* (1951), used the same formula for 'A Symphony of the Night'. While Jimmy Macdonald, who supplied a variety of animal sounds for the True-Life Adventure films, scratches a bow across a piece of string to create a frog's croak, Smith accompanies the effect with a straight rendition of the sextet from *Lucia*. The Studio was never willing to let a good gag die – the jokes gradually faded away instead – and the amphibian night song is almost a direct steal from a sequence with some denizens of the lily pad in *The Old Mill* (1937). Written by Lawrence Edward Watkin and Ted Sears, *In Beaver Valley* is one of the most charming of the whole True-Life Adventure series. It was later shown on the *Disneyland* television series in 1954.

PESTS OF THE WEST (P) Director Charles Nichols. The two mischievous coyotes, Bent-Tail and Junior, who guest-starred in a number of cartoons, plague Pluto. They try to steal some hens, but Pluto is soon hot on their trail.

FOOD FOR FEUDIN' (P) Director Charles Nichols. Pluto and Chip an' Dale fight over some nuts that roll down a hill into Pluto's kennel.

HOOK, LION AND SINKER (DD) Director Jack Hannah. A sinewy-looking mountain lion guest-starred in a number of the shorts. This time, the lion and its cub try various ways of stealing fish from Donald Duck (above).

CAMP DOG (P) Director Charles Nichols. Coyotes Bent-Tail and Bent-Tail Junior return to harrass Pluto. When Pluto is left on guard, they try to steal food, Pluto's problem being that Junior thinks he's on the menu.

BEE AT THE BEACH (DD) Director Jack Hannah. In a short that makes *Jaws* pale in comparison, Donald finds that he has become shark bait when he upsets a tiny insect's day out.

HOLD THAT POSE (G) Director Jack Kinney. Donald Duck's attempts at photography ended in disaster in *Donald's Camera* (1941), and Goofy fares no better when he tries to capture a bear on film. The flash-powder angers the grizzly, which chases Goofy back to his apartment.

MORRIS, THE MIDGET MOOSE (Sp) Director Jack Hannah. Like the diminutive star of *Goliath II*, Morris is so small that he becomes an object of fun among the other members of the herd. His small body and large antlers may be a problem, but Morris is able to turn the tables on his antagonists when he teams up with Balsam, an enormous moose with tiny antlers (above right). This engaging animated film was rereleased for educational purposes in 1967.

OUT ON A LIMB (DD) Director Jack Hannah. Donald Duck convinces Chip an' Dale that his tree pruner is a sharp-beaked monster. As with his various attempts to trick the chipmunks in the

short *Dragon Around* (1954), in which his steam shovel is mistaken by the Chipmunks for a mythological creature, Donald is soon found out and, as always, loses his temper and the battle.

1951

LION DOWN (G) Director Jack Kinney. The mountain lion, first seen in *Lion Around* (1950), follows Goofy home (opposite above). In a war of nerves both try to claim the hammock in Goofy's roof garden – and the lion loses.

CHICKEN IN THE ROUGH (CD) Director Jack Hannah. In their first solo cartoon Chip an' Dale get involved with a chick and an angry rooster.

COLD STORAGE (P) Director Jack Kinney. Harsh winter weather causes Pluto to fight with a stork over possession of his kennel.

DUDE DUCK (DD) Director Jack Hannah. Donald's attempts to saddle a horse end with him strapped to the back of an angry bull. The film stars a number of animated girls who bear a striking resemblance to the bobby-soxers in *Make Mine Music*.

HOME MADE HOME (G) Director Jack Kinney. Goofy has a number of problems when he tries to construct his own house. He invites his friends over for a housewarming party, but as they celebrate, the building collapses around them.

growing, insects awakening and butterflies pumping blood into their delicate wings by John Nash Ott Jr that makes this film so fascinating. It has been shown twice on the Disney television series (1955 and 1961) and was originally released in America with *Alice In Wonderland*.

HOW TO CATCH A COLD (Com) Director Hamilton Luske. Explaining how mankind falls victim to this most prevalent of diseases, the film takes a humorous look at the problems surrounding the common cold and shows how man can do something about it. The film was sponsored by International Cellucotton Productions.

TEST PILOT DONALD (DD) Director Jack Hannah. Donald's rivals Chip an' Dale again prove a hazard to the irascible duck. This time they seriously endanger Donald's chances of survival at the controls of a runaway model aircraft.

TOMORROW WE DIET (G) Director Jack Kinney. Goofy, who proudly took part in numerous sporting activities throughout his illustrious film career, decides that it is time he loses some weight. However, he decides to 'eat, drink and be merry' and to leave the dieting until later.

LUCKY NUMBER (DD) Director Jack Hannah. Donald's suspicious nature has led to his own downfall on a number of occasions, but when his nephews decide to deliver a new car he has won, Donald, thinking it's a trick, deliberately wrecks the car before realizing, too late, the truth.

☆ ALICE IN WONDERLAND (F) Directors Clyde Geronimi, Hamilton Luske and Wilfred Jackson. A feature-length animated version of Lewis Carroll's classic was originally suggested as a possible film subject as far back as 1933. A difficult book to adapt to the screen, as was proved by the early story conferences, the idea was eventually shelved until the late 1940s. Walt wasn't all that happy at the prospect of turning Lewis Carroll's surreal and often frightening fairy-tale into an animated film, and he knew that tampering with such a literary classic as well as with the highly regarded illustrations by Sir John Tenniel would leave him wide open to criticism.

However, it is one of the best versions of the book to have been transferred to the screen, and, like *Fantasia*, the film has stood the test of time and is now greatly admired as an example of the Studio's technical ability in the early 1950s. (Disney's concern over future audience reaction meant that the Studio promoted the film heavily in its first tv special *One Hour in Wonderland*.) Alice's adventures among the strangely bizarre characters of the Disney artists' imaginations owe little to Carroll's original text, but the use of a number of veteran Disney voice talents – Verna Felton (Queen of Hearts), Bill Thompson (White Rabbit), Sterling Holloway (Cheshire Cat), Jerry Colonna (March Hare), Ed Wynn (Mad Hatter) and Kathryn Beaumont as Alice (left) – successfully breathed life into the weird residents of Wonderland. The film also features a selection of enchanting songs including 'The Walrus and the Carpenter', 'I'm Late' and 'The Unbirthday Song'.

The world premiere was, appropriately, held in Britain on 26 July 1951, but only three years later the film was relegated to an exclusive screening on the *Disneyland* television show. Criticized for lacking warmth and humour, like Disney's 1959 release *Sleeping Beauty*, *Alice* has had to wait for a more broadminded public to accept what is, at times, a rather garish extravaganza down a rabbit hole. The story was adapted

CORN CHIPS (DD) Director Jack Hannah. Chip an' Dale steal a box of popcorn. Unfortunately for Donald, when he attempts to get it back, it explodes all over his front garden.

COLD WAR (G) Director Jack Kinney. Goofy, in his role as a canine Everyman, is plagued by a cold virus, which quickly assumes a menacing character of its own.

PLUTOPIA (P) Director Charles Nichols. While vacationing at a mountain resort with Mickey, Pluto falls asleep and dreams of the high life. He even imagines that his butler is a cat and enjoys ordering him about.

★ NATURE'S HALF ACRE (TLA) Director James Algar. Another Academy Award winner, the film features some remarkable macro-photography of insects and birds. Narrator Winston Hibler explains: 'We've come upon a fantastic book of wonders, and when we get close enough to read between the leaves we may discover there's more than at first meets the eye.' As usual, some wildlife is referred to anthropomorphically: 'Mrs Robin', for example, tends her nest to the accompaniment of Paul Smith's orchestral score 'A Symphony of Spring'. Superbly filmed by Murl Deusing and eight other naturalist photographers, it is the time-lapse footage of plants

for the screen by no fewer than 13 writers – Winston Hibler, Bill Peet, Joe Rinaldi, Bill Cottrell, Joe Grant, Del Connell, Ted Sears, Erdman Penner, Milt Banta, Dick Kelsey, Dick Huemer, Tom Oreb and John Walbridge.

R'COON DAWG (MM) Director Charles Nichols. Mickey (right) and Pluto are night hunting, but the raccoon outsmarts them by throwing Pluto off the scent. When the raccoon steals Mickey's coonskin cap and pretends it's her baby, the hunters apologize for disturbing her and beat a hasty retreat.

GET RICH QUICK (G) Director Jack Kinney. It's still difficult to accept the portrayal of Goofy as the suburbanite that was depicted in the earlier Disney shorts, but, apart from rare excursions and more recent attempts to restore his hayseed persona, Goofy was saddled with that role throughout the 1950s. In the marvellously witty *Get Rich Quick*, Goofy wins at poker and tries to creep into the house without waking his wife, but when she discovers what he's been up to, she keeps all the money for herself.

COLD TURKEY (P) Director Charles Nichols. Pluto and Milton the cat go searching for food after being brainwashed by a commercial for Lurkey's Turkey, in this short that takes a gentle dig at the persuasive power of television. Ironically, Nichols later moved to television, where he was animation supervisor of, among others, *The Flintstones*.

FATHERS ARE PEOPLE (G) Director Jack Kinney. Goofy is becoming the ultimate suburbanite: he experiences the trials and tribulations of fatherhood, but finds that Junior comes out on top every time.

OUT OF SCALE (DD) Director Jack Hannah. Engineer of a miniature railway, Donald upsets Chip an' Dale by replacing their tree with a model one. When the chipmunks seek refuge from Donald's wrath by hiding in a miniature village, the irascible Duck simulates all kinds of weather conditions to flush them out. Walt, who had a passion for model trains, had only recently constructed a railroad in the garden of his home – much to the chagrin of his wife, Lilly.

NO SMOKING (G) Director Jack Kinney. Goofy demonstrates the problems of temptation. Made in the early 1950s as a rather humorous jibe at the plight of the smoker, the film has greater relevance in the health-conscious 1980s.

BEE ON GUARD (DD) Director Jack Hannah. In an interview with journalist Jim Korkis, Hannah described Donald Duck as 'a lovable twerp who could never stay out of trouble'. Here Donald disguises himself as an enormous insect and attempts to outwit some bees and steal their honey (below).

1952

FATHER'S LION (G) Director Jack Kinney. Goofy and his son go on a camping trip. Unfortunately, Goofy's tall stories lead to an encounter with a mountain lion.

☆ LAMBERT, THE SHEEPISH LION (Sp) Director Jack Hannah. Sterling Holloway, the voice of, among others, the stork in *Dumbo* and Kaa the snake in *The Jungle Book*, was also called upon to narrate the occasional Disney short. In *Lambert the Sheepish Lion*, Holloway relates the story of a small lion cub, which grows up with a flock of sheep (below) and fails to realize his potential, until the flock is threatened by a wolf.

THE OLYMPIC ELK (TLA) Director James Algar. Filmed in an almost inaccessible part of the 500 square miles of the Olympic Peninsula of Western Washington, *The Olympic Elk* features the life-cycle of this majestic animal and its battle for survival. Photographed by Herb and Lois Crisler and with music by Paul Smith, the film won an award at the Edinburgh International Film Festival and was shown on the Disney television series (1955 and 1961).

HELLO ALOHA (G) Director Jack Kinney. After his *Hawaiian Holiday* (1937), Goofy returns to the sun-drenched beaches of Hawaii. Unfortunately various unpleasant experiences leave him disillusioned with the islands.

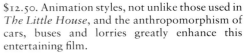

DONALD APPLECORE (DD) Director Jack Hannah. Donald Duck is the proud owner (above) of an impressively large orchard; Chip an' Dale are determined to eat his entire fruit crop. Through his own short-sightedness, Donald, as usual, loses to his tiny rivals.

TWO CHIPS AND A MISS (CD) Director Jack Hannah. Chip an' Dale fight over the affections of a glamorous chipmunk nightclub singer (below).

MAN'S BEST FRIEND (G) Director Jack Kinney. Goofy's pet dog not only upsets the neighbours and allows a burglar into the house but it also attacks Goofy when he tries to enter his own house.

LET'S STICK TOGETHER (DD) Director Jack Hannah. Donald Duck and his constant enemy, the Bee, team up to manufacture clothes, but when the Bee meets a girlfriend, Donald loses his industrious little partner. Years later, Donald and the Bee reminisce about their past adventures.

TWO GUN GOOFY (G) Director Jack Kinney. In no way a hero, Goofy unwittingly captures the villainous Pete. As a reward for such bravery, the townspeople make Goofy their sheriff.

SUSIE, THE LITTLE BLUE COUPE (Sp) Director Clyde Geronimi. An engaging story of how a young man rescues a once-proud automobile (above) from the junkyard for the princely sum of $12.50. Animation styles, not unlike those used in *The Little House*, and the anthropomorphism of cars, buses and lorries greatly enhance this entertaining film.

★ WATER BIRDS (TLA) Director Ben Sharpsteen. A publicity campaign for the True-Life Adventure series stated: 'These films are photographed in their natural settings and are completely authentic, unstaged and unrehearsed.' Not quite, for a great deal of this film is edited to music. Nevertheless, it is one of the most enjoyable of the entire series. Photographed by a team of naturalists, including Alfred Milotte, the birds, particularly the water fowl, enthrall and entertain. Winston Hibler's narration is rather pedestrian, but Paul Smith's musical score is a marvellous complement to the visuals. The film's climax, in which multitudes of birds swim, dive and migrate to the 'Friska' from Franz Liszt's *Hungarian Rhapsody No. 2*, owes not a single note to Smith's musical abilities. The sight of gannets and pelicans diving into the sea to the thunderous crashes of Hungarian gypsy music must have excited the judges of the 1952 Academy Awards, for the film won the Oscar for Best Two-Reel Short Subject. Made in cooperation with the National Audubon Society and the Denver Museum of Natural History, the film was released in America with *The Story of Robin Hood* and was shown twice on the Disney television series (1956 and 1960).

TEACHERS ARE PEOPLE (G) Director Jack Kinney. Goofy discovers that a schoolroom full of children is something of a challenge; he emerges beaten, bedraggled and a great deal wiser.

UNCLE DONALD'S ANTS (DD) Director Jack Hannah. Having been plagued by ants in *Tea for Two Hundred* (1948), Donald Duck again encounters insects when he unknowingly leaves a sugar trail on the sidewalk. The ants eventually take over his entire house.

THE LITTLE HOUSE (Sp) Director Wilfred Jackson. The Studio produced a number of animated specials during the late 1940s and early

Mickey, Chip an' Dale are living in the Christmas tree, which Pluto wrecks in order to expose them. The final tableau sees the Spirit of Christmas uniting the friends as they watch Minnie, Donald and Goofy singing carols in the snow.

HOW TO BE A DETECTIVE (G) Director Jack Kinney. This brilliantly surreal cartoon stars Goofy as Johnny Eyeball, Private Eye. There is intrigue and danger at every turn, and the film ends in classic 'whodunnit' style.

1953

A number of cartoon compilations were released theatrically by RKO Radio Pictures in 1953. Among the titles were the following: *Christmas Jollities, New Year's Jamboree, 4th of July Firecrackers, Mickey's Birthday Party, Halloween Hilarities* and *Thanksgiving Day Mirthquakes*.

PETER PAN (F) Directors Hamilton Luske, Clyde Geronimi and Wilfred Jackson. Whatever reservations Walt may have had over *Alice in Wonderland*, they were quickly dispelled with the release of this film, based on J.M. Barrie's tale of the little boy who refused to grow up, which is full of delightful songs and some wonderful characters. Disney child-star Bobby Driscoll provides the voice of Peter, while Kathryn Beaumont voices Wendy. Hans Conried speaks for the infamous Captain Hook (right) and Wendy's father, Mr Darling, while Disney voice Bill Thompson plays the bumbling Mr Smee. Publicized in 1953 as 'Walt Disney's greatest animated feature', the story had, in fact, been in preparation throughout the 1940s and was certainly one of Disney's most charming post-war movies. Of the songs by Sammy Cahn and Sammy Fain, 'You Can Fly, You Can Fly, You Can Fly', which was accompanied by beautifully executed aerial sequences of London at night, and the lilting ballad 'The Second Star to the Right', are among the film's many highlights. One character who never speaks in the film, although she steals most of the scenes she appears in, is the fairy Tinker Bell. Resembling a 1950s Hollywood nymphet, she is

1950s, and in this example a small cottage finds itself overshadowed by progress when giant city skyscrapers flatten the surrounding countryside. Fortunately, the house (above) is rescued in the nick of time by a young married couple who restore it to a tranquil setting in the country. The highly detailed animation – with the patchwork fields and ugly skyscrapers – is expertly based on a number of inspirational sketches by colour stylist Mary Blair and taken from the popular children's book by Virginia Lee Burton.

THE STORY OF ROBIN HOOD (F) Director Ken Annakin. The success of *Treasure Island* encouraged Disney to set up a permanent production company at Denham Studios, England, to shoot more live-action features. The first of these, starring Richard Todd as the legendary outlaw of Sherwood Forest, is a robust adventure in sparkling Technicolor, with admirable performances from the supporting cast: Joan Rice as Maid Marian, Peter Finch as the Sheriff of Nottingham, James Hayter as Friar Tuck, James Robertson Justice as Little John, Martita Hunt as Queen Eleanor and Hubert Gregg as Prince John. Unlike previous Hollywood versions of the story, the film avoids the over-glorification of the central character. Todd plays it very straight but obviously enjoys the part. Incorporating all the right ingredients – the meeting of the lead characters for the first time, the famous archery tournament and the overthrow of the villainous Sheriff – the film was well liked by theatre audiences. Although it was screened in two parts on the *Disneyland* television series in 1955, it has been re-issued successfully in Europe.

PLUTO'S PARTY (MM) Director Milt Schaffer. Pluto gets left out of the fun at his own party when the neighbourhood children push him around. Fortunately, Mickey saves him a slice of cake. Although the gags are amusing, the animation is disappointing.

TRICK OR TREAT (DD) Director Jack Hannah. Donald thinks he has had the last laugh on his three nephews: he douses them with water when

they knock on his door dressed in Halloween costumes (below). But Huey, Dewey and Louie are befriended by Witch Hazel, who uses her magic powers to help them get their own back on 'Unca Donald'.

TWO WEEKS VACATION (G) Director Jack Kinney. Goofy's attempts to enjoy a well-earned rest meet with difficulties. His encounters with a railroad and a runaway trailer land him in jail, where, at last, he gets to relax.

PLUTO'S CHRISTMAS TREE (MM) Director Jack Hannah. This short is perhaps one of the Studio's best-known films, having been screened over the holiday season year after year. Unknown to

shown running the gamut of emotions from being jealous of Wendy to joining forces with the evil Captain Hook to teach Pan a lesson. In a less passionate guise, Tinker Bell has featured regularly introducing the Disney television shows as well as at the theme parks. Rereleased on a number of occasions, the film has so far garnered $24 million at box-office in the US alone.

★ THE LIVING DESERT (TLA) Director James Algar. The success of the True-Life Adventure featurettes prompted Walt to propose a feature film about animal life in the American deserts (right). His distributor, RKO, didn't like the idea of a feature-length documentary, and this dispute finally led Disney to form its own distribution company, Buena Vista. The company's first release was also the first of many feature-length nature films. *The Living Desert* cost under $300,000 to make but grossed nearly $7 million on its initial release. Narrated by Winston Hibler, who co-wrote the script with Algar and Ted Sears, the film was shot on 16mm in such locations as Death Valley, the Yuma Sand Dunes and the Salton Sea mud pots. After the familiar and impressive series logo – a gleaming Earth spinning within a frame set against a sky-blue background – the film opens with the animated paintbrush colouring the North American continent. In the stunning desert footage, the film-

makers capture the lives of the animals, reptiles and birds as they struggle to survive in a harsh landscape of scorched earth and sudden flash floods. In an amusing sequence in which two scorpions perform a mating ritual, Hibler adds narration for a typical square dance: 'Stingers up for the Stingaree, but watch out gal you don't sting me.' In another scene a bobcat escapes from some wild pigs by climbing to the top of a Saguaro cactus, a sequence achieved by filming the cat in a controlled compound. It was this kind of trickery that the critics objected to, but in *The Best of Walt Disney's True-Life Adventures* (1975), Hibler made no excuses for Disney: 'He set the rhythms of nature to music and had fun in doing it.'

The film won numerous awards, including an Oscar for Best Feature-Length Documentary of the Year, and it has been successfully rereleased on a number of occasions. Animated effects were provided by John Hench, Josh Meador and Art Riley, and the magnificent musical score was by Paul J. Smith. Extracts from the film were issued for educational use in 1974 under the titles *Predators of the Desert, What is a Desert?* and *Animals at Home in the Desert.*

★ BEAR COUNTRY (TLA) Director James Algar. The publicity claimed that no camera trickery had been used: 'In the making of these films, Nature is the dramatist. There are no fictitious situations or characters.' After the familiar animated paintbrush has pictured the forests of North America, the film is full to overflowing with a number of endearing personalities, especially two mischievous bear cubs, which have various encounters with other woodland creatures. Selected for the Royal Film Performance in London, this entertaining featurette, which was written by Algar, has been screened twice on the Disney television series (1957 and 1960).

★ THE ALASKAN ESKIMO (P & P) Director James Algar. Having grown tired of educational films

and concerned that the Studio's main aim should be to entertain, Walt assigned travelogue filmmakers Alfred and Elma Milotte to record all aspects of life in Alaska. The resulting footage was condensed into the first of the new series of documentaries, People and Places. Using stunning photography, *The Alaskan Eskimo* relates how Eskimos live by hunting for food in the summer and sheltering underground in the winter. It won the 1953 Academy Award for Best Short Subject (Documentary) and in 1956 appeared on the *Disneyland* television series.

FATHER'S DAY OFF (G) Director Jack Kinney. Goofy's problems continue: when his wife goes out, he is left in charge of the household chores. Catastrophe strikes when he leaves the iron on and has to summon the fire department.

THE SIMPLE THINGS (MM) Director Charles Nichols. Unbeknown by the cinema-going public at the time, this was to be Mickey's last theatrical appearance until *Mickey's Christmas Carol* (1983). Mickey and Pluto set off for a quiet day's fishing but are plagued by a flock of noisy seagulls (below), which tries to steal their catch. Largely because of a change in theatre owners' attitudes toward cartoon shorts in the 1950s and the increasing popularity of Donald and Goofy, Mickey was from now on assigned instead to hosting television's *The Mickey Mouse Club* and to putting in 'personal' appearances at Disneyland.

FOR WHOM THE BULLS TOIL (G) Director Jack Kinney. Goofy, mistaken for a matador while visiting Mexico, is pitted against a crazy bull.

ADVENTURES IN MUSIC: MELODY (Sp) Directors Charles Nichols and Ward Kimball. 'The screen's first animated cartoon in 3-D,' was how the Studio publicity announced the first of its shortlived Adventures in Music series. (In fact, although this was the first 3-D animated short in the US, it was beaten by Halas and Batchelor's

British stereo-scope cartoon *The Owl and the Pussycat*, 1952.) Released on the same programme as Columbia Pictures' *Fort Ti*, the film was presented in a simplified but gimmicky animation style. Professor Owl, voiced by Bill Thompson, introduces the pupils in his music class; in turn, they recite a story to music. Among the highlights is a stylish rendition of 'The Bird and the Cricket and the Willow Tree', which is reminiscent of the work of Paul Klee. When enthusiasm for 3-D fizzled out in the late 1950s, the film appeared on the Disney tv series.

DON'S FOUNTAIN OF YOUTH (DD) Director Jack Hannah. Donald Duck always took great delight in playing practical jokes. Here he tricks Huey, Dewey and Louie into believing that he has reverted to his childhood. Some unfriendly alligators, however, quickly put paid to his charade.

FATHER'S WEEK-END (G) Director Jack Kinney. After a busy week at work Goofy discovers that a restful Sunday with the family can sometimes be even more hectic.

HOW TO DANCE (G) Director Jack Kinney. After a brief look at the history of dance, Goofy tries to teach himself with the aid of a dummy. Thrown out of a real dance school, he ends up at a casino dancing to a lively jazz beat. The dancing looks rather primitive, and the narrator, likening it to the dance rituals of early man, questions our progress.

THE SWORD AND THE ROSE (F) Director Ken Annakin. In this lavishly mounted costume drama, Richard Todd, fresh from his role in *Robin Hood*, stars as Charles Brandon, a young man on his way to America. Glynis Johns, who later starred in *Rob Roy* (1954) and *Mary Poppins* (1964), plays Mary Tudor, who falls in love with him. Her brother, Henry VIII, played with rascally good nature by James Robertson Justice, is determined that Mary shall marry the aging King of France (Jean Mercure). However, to further complicate matters, the evil Duke of Buckingham (Michael Gough) has some ideas of his own about young Mary's future. The film is every bit as enjoyable as *Robin Hood* and, with its competent screenplay by Lawrence E. Watkin, decidedly wittier. Peter Ellenshaw's impressive matte paintings, over 60 of them, add to the film's overall splendour, and although the story is in no way historically accurate, it made for a very unusual Disney picture and a true delight. In 1956 it was edited into two parts for the *Disneyland* television show and retitled *When Knighthood was in Flower*.

PROWLERS OF THE EVERGLADES (TLA) Director James Algar. The last of the True-Life Adventure series to be released by RKO Radio Pictures, the film highlights the problems facing alligators living in the Florida swamps in protecting their young from all kinds of predators – raccoons, skunks and herons. A recipient of an award at the Edinburgh International Film Festival and by the Southern California Motion Picture Council, this fascinating documentary was released in the US with *The Sword and the Rose*. It was shown on the *Disneyland* television series in 1957.

THE NEW NEIGHBOR (DD) Director Jack Hannah. Whenever he appeared, Pete meant trouble for Mickey and the gang. Here, thinly disguised as Mr Suburbia, Pete throws rubbish into Donald Duck's backyard. The ensuing battle is eagerly captured on film by television cameras. Although Walt's own relationship with the small screen was a good one, his Studio couldn't help

poking fun at the lengths to which television reporters went to get a story.

FOOTBALL NOW AND THEN (Sp) Director Jack Kinney. In this unusual short a young boy and his grandfather argue whether football was better in the past than it is in the present.

☆ RUGGED BEAR (DD) Director Jack Hannah. Although produced in a very simple style, shorts such as this have a charm of their own, and

Rugged Bear is just one example of the Studio's diverse approach to animation. The story concerns a bear (above), which hides in Donald's cabin during the hunting season only to find that the cabin is more hazardous than the wild. The bear's grunts and groans were supplied by Pinto Colvig, the voice of Goofy.

☆ BEN AND ME (Sp) Director Hamilton Luske. Based on Robert Lawson's book, this excellent featurette relates the story of a little mouse called

Amos. Born into a family of 26 church mice, he decides to set out on his own. 'We were a downtrodden race,' he tells us, as he is rejected wherever he goes. Finally he arrives at the home of Benjamin Franklin and helps with the invention of the famous Franklin stove and the first newspaper, *The Pennsylvania Gazette*. Kite-flying in a thunderstorm almost electrocutes Amos, who severs his friendship with Ben, but they are reunited – on 4 July 1776 – when Amos accidentally comes up with the classic opening lines of the Declaration of Independence. Narrated by Sterling Holloway, from a story by Bill Peet, *Ben and Me* was shown as part of *The Liberty Story* on the *Disneyland* television series in 1957 and in *The Wonderful World of Color* in 1964.

★ TOOT, WHISTLE, PLUNK, AND BOOM (Sp) Directors Charles Nichols and Ward Kimball. Of the early 1950s Adventures in Music shorts, this CinemaScope presentation was the most successful. Professor Owl (below), again voiced by Bill Thompson, returns in this sequel to *Melody* to teach his students about the origins of musical instruments. Animated in a clear and colourful style, the film features some innovative backgrounds by Eyvind Earle, who had worked on *Sleeping Beauty*. Witty gags and a catchy theme-song have ensured that this particular film is constantly re-issued, although, sadly, not for the widescreen. In 1959 it was combined with a number of other musical shorts in an episode of the *Disneyland* television show.

WORKING FOR PEANUTS (DD) Director Jack Hannah. In one of the few commercially released shorts to be presented in 3-D, Chip an' Dale steal peanuts from Dolores the elephant (Dolores' first appearance since the 1948 short *The Big Wash*). Zoo-keeper Donald uses her trunk like a machine-gun to fire peanuts at the tiny thieves. In 1956 a special featurette entitled *3-D Jamboree*, including this cartoon as part of its programme, was released in Disneyland.

HOW TO SLEEP (G) Director Jack Kinney. In his suburbanite persona, Goofy explores the various positions in which a man relaxes. The short shows that, when it comes to sleeping at night, Goofy has the worst case of insomnia his doctor has ever seen.

CANVAS BACK DUCK, (DD) Director Jack Hannah. Donald Duck's constant bragging to Huey, Dewey and Louie is put to the test when he finds himself up against a vicious fighter called Peewee Pete at the local carnival. Fortunately for Donald, he wins and is hero-worshipped by his nephews.

1954

SPARE THE ROD (DD) Director Jack Hannah. Huey, Dewey and Louie prefer to play instead of helping their Uncle Donald with boring household chores like chopping wood. An unusual cartoon – the story is split into sections, each of which is introduced by a title card – it also stars Donald's conscience (voiced by Bill Thompson) and a trio of 'duck-eating' cannibals.

DONALD'S DIARY (DD) Director Jack Kinney. In a style reminiscent of the later Goofy shorts and against a backdrop of towering San Francisco skylines, a suave, sophisticated Donald Duck recalls his lucky escape from marrying his sweetheart Daisy. In films such as this Donald, like Goofy, has become a suburbanite who parodies modern man.

ROB ROY – THE HIGHLAND ROGUE (F) Director Harold French. Richard Todd's third Disney movie was another swashbuckling adventure filmed entirely on location in England. This 'highland rogue' was not, however, as successful or as entertaining as *Robin Hood* or *The Sword and the Rose*, and most of the blame for that has been levelled at the rather dull direction. Heavily weighed down by its emphasis on historical 'accuracy' instead of on the drama and romance of Sir Walter Scott's novel, the all-British cast, which included Glynis Johns, James Robertson Justice, Michael Gough and Finlay Currie, battles with Lawrence E. Watkin's unimaginative script as the legendary Rob Roy MacGregor and his fellow Scots oppose the dictatorial rule of English King George. Unbeknown to the rebels, it's the evil Secretary of State, not the King, who is causing all the trouble. Peter Ellenshaw fills in the scenery with some marvellous matte paintings. Disney's last British production until *Kidnapped* (1960), the film, which was chosen for the Royal Film Performance in the UK, was shown on the *Disneyland* television series in 1956, when it was spruced up with host Walt Disney introducing sequences from the People and Places short *Scotland* and animation from *So Dear to My Heart*.

STORMY – THE THOROUGHBRED WITH AN INFERIORITY COMPLEX (F) Director Larry Lansburgh. Neatly told through the horse's eyes, this is a touching story of how a handsome colt, born on a breeding farm in the Blue Grass region of Kentucky, is too young to become a thoroughbred race horse. Becoming a polo pony instead, he shows his innate good manners and expertise by winning the game. The film was later shown on the *Disneyland* television series in 1956, while Lansburgh went on to helm a number of excellent animal featurettes for the Studio.

THE LONE CHIPMUNKS (D) Director Jack Kinney. It was the turn of Chip an' Dale to star in one of the Studio's more streamlined animated films. Pete is a notorious bank robber, who hides his stolen money in their tree. Chip an' Dale manage

to apprehend the crook before the cavalry arrives. Directed with Kinney's usual flair for the ridiculous, the film spoofed *The Lone Ranger* tv series, which ran from 1949 until 1961.

☆ PIGS IS PIGS (Sp) Director Jack Kinney. The hilarious story by Leo Salkin, based on the book by Ellis Parker Butler, tells how bureaucratic red tape slows up a simple decision about whether guinea pigs are pets or pigs. While head office pontificates over the problem, station-master Flannery (below) has trouble dealing with thousands of multiplying guinea pigs. In this, one of Kinney's finest shorts, brilliant backgrounds by Eyvind Earle and clever animation show that

Disney was capable of beating UPA (the so-called king of limited animation styles) at its own game, even if the Studio did lose the Oscar to UPA's *Mr Magoo Flew*.

DRAGON AROUND (DD) Director Jack Hannah. The Disney animators have always excelled at drawing dragons, but here Donald's anthropomorphic steam shovel resembles a menacing dragon to Chip an' Dale, who fight to stop it tearing down their home. Donald is beaten when his hydraulic monster falls to pieces, and, as far as the chipmunks (above) are concerned, the mighty beast is slain.

CASEY BATS AGAIN (Sp) Director Jack Kinney. Having found the inimitable baseball player Casey too good a character to waste after his whirlwind performance in *Make Mine Music* (1946), Disney brought him back for a sequel. Casey, hoping to restore the family name, is disappointed when his wife presents him with nine daughters. Fortunately, the girls are brilliant baseball players, and Casey once again sees his name in the Baseball Hall of Fame.

the melodious strains of 'The Anvil Chorus' and the humorous antics of the prairie chickens add greatly to the overall entertainment. In a visually stunning climax, a prairie fire is started by a bolt of lightning, the flames eventually being doused by a flash flood. In 1962 four 16mm extracts were released – *Pioneer Trails: Indian Lore and Bird Life of the Plains, Small Animals of the Plains, Large Animals That Once Roamed the Plains* and *The Buffalo – Majestic Symbol of the Plains*. A lengthy sequence appeared on the Disney tv show *Nature's Better Built Homes*, and a diorama, loosely based on the film, appears in 'The Land' at EPCOT Center. The film was originally re-leased in the US with Disney's ultimate anthro-pomorphic cartoon, *The Whale Who Wanted to Sing at the Met* from *Make Mine Music*.

SOCIAL LION (Sp) Director Jack Kinney. A ma-jestic King of the beasts, tired of life in the jungle, allows himself to be captured so that he can experience life in the big city. He soon discovers that civilization isn't for him.

THE FLYING SQUIRREL (DD) Director Jack Hannah. Annoyed at Donald for tricking him, the squirrel challenges the irate Duck to a fight. Needless to say, the squirrel wins.

★20,000 LEAGUES UNDER THE SEA (F) Director Richard Fleischer. One of the Studio's most exciting live-action adventures was also one of its most successful films. Handled with enormous flair by Fleischer (son of independent animator Max Fleischer), the film, which was made in CinemaScope, is thrilling entertainment. James Mason stars as Jules Verne's infamous hero Captain Nemo, who uses his atomic-powered submarine *The Nautilus* to sink ships. In one such incident, the survivors – harpoonist Ned Land (Kirk Douglas), scientist Professor Aronnax (Paul Lucas) and his assistant Conseil (Peter Lorre) – find themselves unwanted guests of the mysterious captain when they inadvert-ently make their way aboard the submarine. Compelled to show them the wonders of the ocean floor and reveal some of its secrets, Nemo befriends the two scientists, but Ned wins the captain's friendship only after rescuing him from the grip of a giant squid. This amazing sequence, in which a hydraulically controlled full-size sea monster is shown battling with the crew (left), is one of the film's many highlights. It was originally shot in calm waters, but Disney, dissatisfied with the results, ordered the entire sequence to be refilmed with a ferocious man-made storm added to complement the special effects. Careful story-boarding (a technique used in animated films) ensured that the director got the best possible footage of the fight, while Ralph Hammeras' special effects photography, Till Gabbani's stunning underwater camera work and Peter Ellenshaw's impressive matte paintings greatly add to the film's visual impact. Effects veterans Ub Iwerks, John Hench and Joshua Meador were called in to assist the production, and, as a result of their labours, the Studio won the Academy Award for Best Special Effects. A catchy song, 'A Whale of a Tale', by Al Hoffman and Norman Gimbel was sung, in the film, by Kirk Douglas, and prior to release, Walt hosted a television first – a programme about the making of the film entitled *Operation Undersea*. (This fascinating documentary was awarded an Emmy for 1954.) The lavish interior of *The Nautilus*, designed by John Meehan, was displayed for a period in Disneyland from 1955, and extracts from the film were used in the prologue to the educational

GRIN AND BEAR IT (DD) Director Jack Hannah. Humphrey the Bear tries to trick tourist Donald Duck out of his picnic lunch in Brownstone National Park. Making his screen debut, the Ranger, J. Audubon Woodlore (opposite above), is on hand to smooth over the difficulties.

★THE VANISHING PRAIRIE (TLA) Director James Algar. The second feature-length True-Life Adventure contains the work of 12 photo-graphers, led by Tom McHugh, who were assigned to film life on the vast expanse of wilderness from the Mississippi to the Rockies and from the Gulf of Mexico to the plains of Canada. The film underlined the point that, unlike in *The Living Desert*, when the burning sands are too hostile an environment for man, wildlife on the prairie (above) is constantly endangered by man's presence. Included in the magnificent photography is a sequence in which a buffalo gives birth to a calf, a scene that outraged the New York censors, who decided to ban the film. Ridiculed by the press and after pressure from the American Civil Liberties Union, they were forced to withdraw, but the film was criticized for scenes of animals synchronized to Paul Smith's majestic score. Even if the critics did carp, the sight of bighorn rams crossing horns to

special *Our Friend the Atom*. Rereleased on a number of occasions to excellent box-office returns, an excerpt was later distributed to schools in 1978 in the Films As Literature series.

GRAND CANYONSCOPE (DD) Director Charles Nichols. Years before naturalist-cameraman Ernst A. Heiniger invaded the Grand Canyon for a breathtaking Disney-eye-view of life in this most splendid of natural wonders, Donald Duck (above) was on hand to spread a little mayhem along the rocky paths of this national monument. Ignoring the Ranger's good advice, Donald, his burro and a mountain lion manage, between them, to fill the entire canyon with rubble. This CinemaScope-sized disaster scares away the canyon's inhabitants including one or two dinosaurs. The Ranger gives the guilty parties a shovel and tells them to dig the debris out of the Colorado River or else . . .

☆ SIAM (P & P) With photography by veteran film-makers Herb and Trudy Knapp, the second movie in the People and Places series presents a fascinating insight into the lives of Siam's people. Also included is a visit to Bangkok and a trip in a teak sampan with a Siamese family. The film has been retitled *Thailand*.

1955

☆ No HUNTING (DD) Director Jack Hannah. Donald and his great Grandpappy join forces to hunt game. Unfortunately, the forest is already alive with hunters in this CinemaScope cartoon, and they only just escape being shot at themselves.

ARIZONA SHEEPDOG (Sp) Director Larry Lansburgh. While herding sheep for the Navajos, a sheepdog called Nick has to rescue strays from fast-flowing rapids, aggressive skunks and the occasional mountain lion in this live-action short.

DAVY CROCKETT, KING OF THE WILD FRONTIER (F) Director Norman Foster. Of the Studio's feature films released theatrically outside America, some were adapted from segments of the

Disneyland television series. One of these was *Davy Crockett, King of the Wild Frontier*, which started life in 1954 as *Davy Crockett*. A whole year before Mickey Mouse Club ears were in fashion, kids wore coonskin caps and sang Tom Blackburn and George Bruns' overnight hit 'The Ballad of Davy Crockett'. Although the tv show was screened in black and white, Disney was intuitive enough to shoot the series in colour, and when Davy Crockett became an enormous success, the Studio spliced three one-hour programmes into a 93-minute feature film. Fess Parker stars as Davy (below), while Buddy Ebsen

plays his sidekick George Russel. They encounter all kinds of adventures involving thieves and American Indians, and, of course, the Battle of the Alamo. Scenes were linked by artists Joshua Meador, Art Riley and Ken Anderson.

LADY AND THE TRAMP (F) Directors Hamilton Luske, Clyde Geronimi and Wilfred Jackson. The Studio's return to feature-length films such as *Cinderella* and *Peter Pan* in the early 1950s misled theatre audiences into thinking that the fairy-tale formula was definitely a part of the company's future plans. But, after a post-war period of diversification and experimentation, a number of animated films were made that moved in an entirely different direction. Presented in widescreen, as were many 1950s movies in order to compete with television, *Lady and the Tramp* is considered by many to be one of the Studio's most delightful films. The idea originated with storyman Joe Grant and was expanded into a full-length treatment by author Ward Greene. Lady, a small pedigree cocker spaniel, lives with her owners Jim Dear and Darling in a small American town in the early 1900s. Her social life is threatened, however, by the amorous attentions of a roguish mongrel called Tramp. Together (right) they share dangerous and exciting adventures and meet a marvellous assortment of characters. There's Trusty, a bloodhound who has lost his sense of smell, Jock, a Scotty with a fiery temperament, two Siamese cats, a gang of dog-pound residents called Bull, Toughy, Pedro and Boris, and an ex-show dog known as Peg. It's Peg who sings one of the film's most endearing songs, 'He's a Tramp'. Peggy Lee, who composed the songs for the picture in collaboration with Sonny Burke, voices Peg, Darling and the Siamese cats. Barbara Luddy speaks for Lady, while Larry Roberts supplies the voice of Tramp, and George Givot steals the scene as Tony the sympathetic restaurateur, who sings the romantic ballad 'Bella Notte'. Some of the film's animation doesn't seem as effective in CinemaScope. A large part of the budget was spent on altering appara-

BEARLY ASLEEP (DD) Director Jack Hannah. In this CinemaScope release forest ranger Donald Duck is pestered by Humphrey the Bear, who is looking for somewhere to hibernate.

BEEZY BEAR (DD) Director Jack Hannah. Humphrey the Bear is the star of another CinemaScope short when he attempts to steal honey from Donald Duck's beehives.

tus for the new ratio – drawing-boards, for example, had to be adjusted to accommodate widescreen – yet, apart from some highly atmospheric and beautifully rendered backgrounds by, among others, Claude Coats, Al Dempster, Thelma Witmer and Eyvind Earle, the scenery at times seems empty and lifeless. Nevertheless, the movie has, on subsequent re-issues, grossed over $36 million at the US box-office. In 1978, an educational extract was released on 16mm entitled *A Lesson in Sharing Attention*.

☆ SWITZERLAND (P & P) Director Ben Sharpsteen. This People and Places featurette travels across the Swiss Alps by aircraft and then tours the

cities, lakes and countryside of this scenic country (below). Filmed in CinemaScope, the movie accompanies three young Swiss mountaineers as they scale the slopes of the Matterhorn. Disney was so inspired by films such as this and by the feature-length production *The Third Man on the Mountain* that in 1959 he constructed a scale version of the famous mountain incorporating an exciting bobsled ride at Disneyland.

CIRCARAMA U.S.A. (A Tour of the West) (TP) This was the original 360° film to be screened in Tomorrowland when Disneyland opened in 1955. The film was replaced by the *Circle-Vision* production *America the Beautiful* (1958).

THE LITTLEST OUTLAW (F) Director Roberto Galvadon. 'Watch out! He'll steal the hearts of all!' claimed the extravagant publicity that was used to describe 'the boy wonder of the screen', Mexican actor Andres Velasquez. Velasquez is certainly a competent actor. He plays the part of Pablito (above), a small boy who steals a magnificent horse, Conquistador, which has accidentally thrown General Torres' daughter. Torres (Pedro Armendariz) demands that his groom, Chato (Rodolfo Acosta), have the animal destroyed. Pablito and the horse have all manner of adventures, including a confrontation with bandits, a meeting with a sympathetic padré (Joseph Calleia) and rescue from certain death in the bullring. Shot entirely on location in Mexico, the film is entertaining and has a good strong cast. Unfortunately, the 'boy wonder of the screen' soon faded into obscurity, and the movie was relegated to a showing on the *Disneyland* television series in 1958.

UP A TREE (DD) Director Jack Hannah. Having attempted to pull down their tree home in the short *Dragon Around* (1954), Donald Duck threatens to chop down Chip an' Dale's house. As usual, the chipmunks win, managing to steer the felled tree into Donald's jeep and, ultimately, into his house, with destructive results.

THE EMPEROR PENGUINS (Sp) Director Mario Marret. This black and white French film was acquired by the Studio because of the public's growing interest in animal documentaries. The film, which was made in 1953, traces the life story of the penguin, and it was photographed during an Antarctic Expedition led by Paul Emile Victor.

★ MEN AGAINST THE ARCTIC (P & P) Director Winston Hibler. The Studio's documentary cameramen have frequented the frozen wastes of the North and South Poles for a number of film specials including the *Disneyland* television programme *To the South Pole for Science* and the True-Life Adventure *White Wilderness*. *Men Against the Arctic* records the arduous work of those specially designed ships that break through

the massive ice-flows around Thule in Greenland. Breathtaking photography captures the indomitable spirit of the men who navigate these heavy-duty icebreakers of the US Coast Guard's Arctic patrol.

THE AFRICAN LION (TLA) Director James Algar. 'I'm still telling the boys,' Walt Disney once remarked about the photographers on his True-Life Adventures, 'don't get too inventive, just watch the animals and record what they do.' So the Milottes lived with lions night and day in a specially equipped truck, which was their home and laboratory, for the third feature-length True-Life Adventure. *The New York Times* was so impressed with the realism of the film that it advised movie-goers to 'wear helmets and take a firm hold on their nerves'. The location footage is indeed spectacular, with a snow-capped Kilimanjaro providing a breathtaking backdrop for the life story of the lion. There is a stirring musical score by Paul Smith, and Winston Hibler's narration puts the social side of the beast neatly into perspective: he is generally lazy, while the lioness catches the meals, wards off intruders and looks after the cubs (right). Excerpts were shown on the *Disneyland* television series in 1958 under the title *His Majesty - The King of Beasts*, and in 1969 16mm extracts, including *African Lion and his Realm, Elephants and Hippos in Africa* and *Birds, Baboons and other Animals – Their Struggle for Survival*, were released.

1956

SARDINIA (P & P) Director Ben Sharpsteen. This, the sixth film in the People and Places series, was one of the only two films in the series to be re-issued. It takes us on a railway journey through the rugged countryside, and we visit some of the stone structures of early history and see the lives and customs of the Sardinian people.

CHIPS AHOY (DD) Director Jack Kinney. The chipmunks set sail in Donald's model ship, which they 'borrow' so that they can get to an acorn-laden tree on the opposite bank of the river. Needless to say, after a little mayhem, Chip an' Dale get their acorns.

I'M NO FOOL WITH A BICYLCE (Ed) A series of six highly popular 16mm educational shorts was aimed at instructing youngsters in lessons of safety. Hosted by Pinocchio's conscience Jiminy Cricket (who became so well known through these films that a number of educational comic books about his teachings were merchandised), this particular film gave an animated history of the bicycle while emphasizing basic rules and regulations. The shorts were originally made for *The Mickey Mouse Club* tv series.

3-D JAMBOREE (TP) Released at Disneyland a year after the park opened, the short features a selection of live-action musical numbers with the Mouseketeers in addition to two theatrically released 3-D animated cartoons – *Adventures in Music: Melody* and *Working for Peanuts* (both 1953).

I'M NO FOOL WITH FIRE (Ed) The second title in the Studio's first-ever educational series, was revised in 1986. Jiminy Cricket demonstrates man's use of an important, but sometimes hazardous, element.

HOOKED BEAR (Sp) Director Jack Hannah. Humphrey the Bear comes unstuck again. Forced by the Ranger to catch fish the natural way (below), he attempts instead to steal from the fish tank in the Ranger's helicopter.

YOU – AND YOUR FIVE SENSES (Ed) Launching a highly successful series on the human body, Jiminy Circket, star of *Pinocchio*, explains that although man has the same number of senses as animals, his ability to reason causes him to respond differently.

YOU – THE HUMAN ANIMAL (Ed) Director Les Clark. Again hosted by Jiminy Cricket, this film, which looks at intelligence, language skills and the ability to adapt, was originally shown on *The Mickey Mouse Club* television series.

THE NATURE OF THINGS (Ed) *The Mickey Mouse Club* television shows featured a variety of educational series among its entertainment line-up. *The Nature of Things* looks at the lives of various animals, and two of these shorts were eventually released on 16mm for schools. Hosted by Jiminy Cricket, *The Nature of Things: The Camel*, discusses the physical characteristics of the 'ship of the desert' and reveals some fascinating facts about this remarkable animal. Also introduced by Jiminy Cricket, who was by now achieving worldwide fame for his various educational series, *The Nature of Things: The Elephant* explains about the evolution of this incredibly strong but gentle animal. The series formed the basis of a Dell comic book spin-off in 1957.

THE GREAT LOCOMOTIVE CHASE (F) Director Frances D. Lyon. In 1927, Buster Keaton – whose film *Steamboat Bill Jr* had influenced Disney's first Mickey Mouse adventure – starred in *The General*, a spoof on the story of Andrews' Raiders and their escapades during the American Civil War. In Disney's more straight-laced ver-

series would follow. In *Davy Crockett and the River Pirates*, compiled from *Davy Crockett's Keelboat Race* and *Davy Crockett and the River Pirates*, Davy (Fess Parker) and George Russel (Buddy Ebsen) thwart a group of pirates on the Mississippi, after befriending the notorious King of the River, Mike Fink (Jeff York). Their popularity encouraged the Studio to contract Parker and York to star in a number of other films.

☆ MAN IN SPACE (Sp) Director Ward Kimball. 'First get the material straight, then find the way you can tell it in an entertaining fashion,' Walt Disney told his artists in 1954 when they started to produce the first science-fact programme for the *Disneyland* television series. As the show's host, Disney introduces Kimball, who, in turn, hands the programme over to scientist Wernher von Braun. Braun, who came to live in America at the end of World War II, looks a little awkward on screen as he explains about his four-stage rocket ship and, anticipating the Space Shuttle, the nose cone that will return to Earth like a conventional aircraft. His colleague Dr Heinz Haber explains the problems of living in space and the effects of zero-gravity on the human body (below). The film was originally aired on 9 March 1955 and was repeated three times before being released theatrically in 1956. Narrated by Dick Tufeld, the atmospheric animation was supervised by Ken O'Connor, whose experience in colour styling went back to *Snow White and the Seven Dwarfs*. In 1964 a 16mm extract, *All About Weightlessness*, was released.

IN THE BAG (Sp) Director Jack Hannah. Having made successful guest appearances in a number of Donald Duck shorts, Ranger J. Audubon Woodlore and Humphrey the Bear appeared together in a story of their own. Filmed in CinemaScope, the short reveals the rivalry that exists between the pair as Humphrey tries to clean up the park litter by throwing it all in a geyser.

I'M NO FOOL AS A PEDESTRIAN (Ed) Jiminy Cricket, who was also hosting an educational series on the human body, takes a look at the importance of road safety in this 16mm film. He also offers a history of reckless driving from 3000 BC to the present day.

sion, Fess Parker stars as James J. Andrews (above), who, with a group of 22 Union spies, captures a passenger train from under the noses of 4,000 Confederate troops near Atlanta, Georgia. Unfortunately, his plans are dashed by the persistent young conductor William A. Fuller (Jeffrey Hunter). The action never lets up, as the determined Southerner pursues the thieves across country. Jeff York and Kenneth Tobey co-star in this above-average historical drama, and the Baltimore and Ohio Railroad Museum receives special thanks. The film crew was lucky enough to have Walt's own personal interest in the project because of his fascination for railroads. The film was publicized in a television special, *Behind the Scenes with Fess Parker*, and it was eventually shown on *Walt Disney Presents* in 1961 under the title *Andrews' Raiders*.

HOW TO HAVE AN ACCIDENT IN THE HOME (DD) Director Charles Nichols. In the first of Donald Duck's two lessons on safety through common sense, a small bearded duck called J.J. Fate provides the narrative as Donald demonstrates domestic disasters by standing on a rocking chair, lighting his pipe in a gas-filled room and being careless with electricity. J.J Fate's moral – 'Average people have accidents because they don't use average intelligence' – concludes this cleverly animated film.

JACK AND OLD MAC (Sp) Director Bill Justice. 'If that's what they're buying, now let's try it,' Walt told composer George Bruns when he was scoring this bizarre cartoon short, which features two jazz sequences in limited animation. During a rendition of 'The House that Jack Built', characters (centre) are formed out of the words of the song, and during 'Old MacDonald Had a Farm', Old Mac plays the piano while the farmyard animals jive to a jam session.

DAVY CROCKETT AND THE RIVER PIRATES (F) Director Norman Foster. Westerns were proving popular with television audiences, so it seemed inevitable that, hot on the heels of the first Davy Crockett feature, a second adaptation of the tv

☆ COW DOG (Sp) Director Larry Lansburgh. A California rancher and his daughter enlist the aid of a farmer and his three Australian herding dogs to help capture a wild Brahma bull, which has been upsetting their prize herds. The film was released with *Secrets of Life*.

A COWBOY NEEDS A HORSE (Sp) Director Bill Justice. Looking as if they were made for television, shorts such as this, which fitted neatly into programme compilations, showed that the Disney animators were more than a match for their rivals at UPA. A little boy dreams of being a wild west hero (above) to the ballad 'A Cowboy Needs a Horse'. Footage of an Indian attack is recycled from the Goofy short, *Californy 'er Bust*.

SECRETS OF LIFE (TLA) Director James Algar. 'Here are the fiercest, strangest, most gorgeous and yet most delightfully humorous beings in our universe,' claims the publicity for the fourth feature-length True-Life Adventure, which was written by Algar and narrated by Winston Hibler. John Nash Ott Jr again leads a team of specialists in time-lapse photography to show scenes of plant seeds blowing in the wind and fruits ripening. Unlike the other True-Life Adventures, this film has no central theme; instead it begins with breathtaking views of the universe, clouds, sea and land before the camera zooms in to scrutinize the pollination of flowers (below), tiny creatures on the floor of the forest and the microscopic inhabitants of a single drop of water. The film ends with spectacular footage

of lava flows from volcanic eruptions, artwork of which adorned the European film posters. The Studio saw the value of supplying extracts from such films to schools and colleges, and Walt Disney was becoming well established as an educator as well as an entertainer. Extracts entitled *Secrets of the Bee World*, ... *Ant World*, ... *Plant World* and ... *Underwater World* were released on 16mm in 1960.

WESTWARD HO. THE WAGONS! (F) Director William Beaudine. Filmed in CinemaScope, this was more of a curiosity than a box-office success. The film, which is composed of a number of segments, relates the adventures that befall a wagon train of settlers heading west. Their scout is John 'Doc' Grayson (Fess Parker, fresh from his success as Davy Crockett on the *Disneyland* tv series), while romantic interest is provided by Kathleen Crowley as Laura Thompson. With co-stars Jeff York, David Stollery, Sebastian Cabot, George Reeves (television's Superman) and child stars from *The Mickey Mouse Club*, the pioneers encounter numerous American Indians, including Hollywood veteran Iron Eyes Cody. Filmed on the Conejo Ranch at Thousand Oaks, California, the film made use of some impressive matte paintings by Peter Ellenshaw and his assistant Albert Whitlock. One of the film's songs, 'Wringle Wrangle' by Stan Jones, was heavily promoted and even appeared as the title of a special comic-book version of the film. A teaser, *Along the Oregon Trail*, appeared on the *Disneyland* television series in 1956, although the film itself had to wait five years before being screened on *Walt Disney Presents* in 1961.

DISNEYLAND, U.S.A. (P & P) Director Hamilton Luske. After successfully promoting Disneyland on his weekly tv series, Walt saw the potential in a theatrical release. Thinly disguised as part of the People and Places series, *Disneyland U.S.A.* is a CinemaScope tour of the Magic Kingdom. After looking at each of the lands, the film finishes with the flag-lowering ceremony and scenes of the park at night. The Studio has given regular television updates on the theme parks, but this early film offers a fascinating insight into the early Disneyland, and it is a valuable historical document of one man's dream. It was originally released with *Westward Ho. The Wagons!*

☆ SAMOA (P & P) Director Ben Sharpsteen. Photographed by, among others, travelogue filmmakers Herb and Trudy Knapp, this People and

Places featurette tells the story of village life in the island paradise. There is a modicum of drama to heighten the events depicted, and the film ends with a look at traditional evening festivities.

1957

THE BLUE MEN OF MOROCCO (P & P) Director Ralph Wright. 'Mysteries of a forgotten race from beyond the burning sands,' read the poster by-line for the eighth film in the People and Places series. The approach was to show that the way of life of the Blue Men of the Sahara Desert has changed little since Biblical times. In true dramatic style, the film shows how these desert nomads protect themselves from a fierce dust storm.

I'M NO FOOL HAVING FUN (Ed) Jiminy Cricket continues to show youngsters how to enjoy themselves while observing a number of safety rules and regulations in this 16mm short.

I'M NO FOOL IN WATER (Ed) Jiminy Cricket underlines the safety aspects of swimming and when the rules should be observed in this short, which was revised in 1986.

IF ALL THE GUYS IN THE WORLD (F) Director Christian Jaque. Buena Vista's only non-Disney release during 1957 was a rather obscure French film, which relates how a group of radio hams from around the world work together to save a disease-stricken crew on a lone trawler in the North Sea. J.L. Trintignant plays the 'ham' who first picks up the SOS in Togoland, and André Valmy plays the captain of the ship. Quickly forgotten, this masculine little tale might have worked 'if all the guys in the world' had gone to see it.

YOU – AND YOUR EARS (Ed) Host Jiminy Cricket explains the anatomical structure of the inner ear and how care should be taken of these vital organs.

YOU – AND YOUR EYES (Ed) Simple animation techniques are used to explain all aspects of eye care and safety and the basic functions of the optic nerve.

JOHNNY TREMAIN (F) Director Robert Stevenson. Originally intended for a screening on the *Disneyland* television series, *Johnny Tremain* proved so costly to make that it was released theatrically in the U.S. Based on a novel by Esther Forbes, the story relates how Johnny (played by Disney discovery Hal Stalmaster, opposite above), an apprentice silversmith, finds himself caught up in the American Revolution in 1773. Studio protégée Luana Patten, who starred in *Song of the South* and *Fun and Fancy Free*, plays his sweetheart Cilla Lapham. Stevenson, who was making his directorial debut for Disney before going on to helm a number of important films for the Studio including *Mary Poppins*, was criticized for his handling of the drama, which was seen as too light-hearted, and some thought the Boston Tea Party sequence was too comic. Co-starring Dick Beymer, Jeff York, Whit Bissell and Sebastian Cabot (the voice of Bagheera in *The Jungle Book*), the film's expensive production costs couldn't save it from a television screening for long, and in 1958 it was shown on *Walt Disney Presents* in two parts, *The Boston Tea Party* and *The Shot That Was Heard 'Round the World*. Under these titles, 16mm educational versions were released in 1966.

★ THE WETBACK HOUND (Sp) Director Larry Lansburgh. In addition to its Academy Award for

Best Live-Action Short Subject, this short received awards from the Berlin International Film Festival and the Southern California Motion Picture Council. The story concerns a hound called Paco, which has more fun chasing deer than tracking mountain lions. Escaping from his master, he swims across a border river between Mexico and the United States, thus earning the title of a true 'wetback'. First shown on the *Disneyland* television series in 1959, it was later repeated on *The Wonderful World of Color* in 1962.

THE STORY OF ANYBURG, U.S.A. (Sp) Director Clyde Geronimi. This appealing animated film relates how man continually blames his own stupidity on others. In this case it's the automobile, as accidents in Anyburg reach an all-time high. In a courtroom scene, reminiscent of Toad's judicial problems in the feature *Ichabod and Mr Toad*, the innocent car is questioned and cross-questioned by an aggressive prosecuting council.

LAPLAND (P & P) Producer Ben Sharpsteen. Although not as successful as the True-Life Adventure films, the People and Places series continued throughout the 1950s and proved popular enough for educational use on 16mm. *Lapland* shows just how harsh life can be for the people living where the Arctic Circle crosses the northernmost parts of Norway, Sweden, Finland and Russia. With no allegiance to any one nation, the Lapps are free to move across these frontiers searching for the herds of migrating reindeer.

ALASKAN SLED DOG (Sp) Director Ben Sharpsteen. Charles Shows narrates this epic tale of bravery. When Eskimo Ki-Buk is stranded on an ice flow, his son takes a young dog sled team to rescue him. Although a documentary, the film provides a fictional scenario to illustrate the abilities of these well-trained animals (centre). Produced by Bill Walsh, this CinemaScope release was shown on *The Mickey Mouse Club*.

NIOK (Sp) Director Edmond Séchan. This French film was picked up by Disney for distribution. It relates what happens to a baby elephant that is separated from its mother and cared for by a gang of Cambodian children. When the elephant is bought by a wealthy hunter, one of the boys risks his life to save it. Winner of the Southern California Motion Picture Council Award, this engaging story was aired on the *Disneyland* television series in 1959.

☆ THE TRUTH ABOUT MOTHER GOOSE (Sp) Directors Wolfgang Reitherman and Bill Justice. An entertaining short that explores the history behind three classic nursery rhymes: 'Jack Horner' (below), 'Mary, Mary, Quite Contrary' and 'London Bridge'. Ingenious gags, effective set pieces and a catchy jazz score add to the appeal. It was screened on *The Wonderful World of Color* in 1963 and hosted by Ludwig Von Drake.

NAVAJO ADVENTURE (Sp) Producer Ben Sharpsteen. Released theatrically in Europe and looking as if it belonged in the People and Places

series, the film tells the remarkable story of the Indians living in Monument Valley. In 1967 it was released on 16mm under the title *The Navajos – Children of the Gods*.

☆ PORTUGAL (P & P) Producer Ben Sharpsteen. The tenth film in the People and Places series opens with the animated story of brave Portuguese explorers. Lengthy live-action sequences then illustrate the colour and excitement of the country and its people, concluding with a look at the bull-fighting rituals that begin in the countryside and end in the city arenas.

☆ PERRI (F) Directors N. Paul Kenworthy Jr and Ralph Wright. Filmed amid the impressive scenery of the Uintah National Forest, Utah, and Jackson Hole, Wyoming, this was the first – and only – 'True-Life Fantasy'. Disney approached the subject in much the same way his animators had brought *Bambi* to the screen – indeed, it was, like *Bambi*, based on a book by Felix Salten – letting the animals tell their story before a backdrop of changing seasons, a story-telling

device used in all the True-Life Adventures. Perri is a young female squirrel (above) who learns about survival in the wilderness through some hair-raising adventures. In a marvellous dream sequence, she imagines a winter wonderland inhabited by rabbits, a weasel and an owl. The movements of the creatures are highlighted by some stunning animated effects by Ub Iwerks, Peter Ellenshaw and Joshua Meador. Paul Smith provides his usual atmospheric musical score, and among the film's photographers was Walt's nephew Roy E. Disney. A 16mm extract was released to schools in *Creative Film Adventures Reel 2* in 1976.

OLD YELLER (F) Director Robert Stevenson. Based on a novel by Fred Gipson, who co-wrote the screenplay with William Tunberg, this is one of Disney's finest animal films, and it started a spate of boy-and-his-dog adventures, including a sequel of sorts entitled *Savage Sam*. *Old Yeller* stars Dorothy McGuire as Katie Coates, who is left with her two sons – Travis (Tommy Kirk) and Arliss (Kevin Corcoran) – to look after the farm when her husband Jim (Fess Parker) joins a cattle drive. A stray dog, which Travis calls Old Yeller (below), joins the family and proves a worthy member of the household, coming to the rescue on a number of occasions. Sadly, however, after Old Yeller fights with a rabid wolf, Travis is forced to shoot the infected dog. 'Everyone will love "Old Yeller",' claimed the publicity, and everyone did. It grossed a remarkable $10 million at the US box-office and is a lasting tribute to one of Disney's most talented directors, Robert Stevenson. For educational use, two extracts

were later released on 16mm. The first, in 1975, was entitled *Love and Duty: Which Comes First?*, and the second, in 1979, was an instalment in the Films As Literature series. Spike, the dog who played Old Yeller, featured in a teaser called *The Best Doggoned Dog in the World* on the *Disneyland* tv show.

MARS AND BEYOND (Sp) Director Ward Kimball. Accompanied by a giant mechanical robot, Walt Disney briefly introduces the costliest and most ambitious of the three space-fact shows devised by Ward Kimball, Wernher von Braun, Heinz Haber and Willy Ley for the Tomorrowland segment of the *Disneyland* television show. *Mars and Beyond*, which was narrated by Paul Frees, explores the mysteries surrounding the planet Mars. Although publicized as an accurate account of a future trip to the planet, the programme is a highly entertaining, imaginatively conceived fantasy, with special effects by Eustace Lycett. Stirring music by George Bruns highlights a pioneering journey to Mars that would last 13 months and 6 days, in 500-foot wide parasol-shaped spaceships designed by scientist Dr Ernst Stuhlinger. The most interesting section of the film, however, is Kimball's idea of life on Mars – weird plants and creatures that were bizarre enough in 1957 for Disney to ask Kimball, 'How do you guys think up all that crazy stuff?' Proving that such films are still entertaining when viewed today, extracts appeared in a 1979 cartoon short *Cosmic Capers*.

1958

STAGE STRUCK (F) Director Sidney Lumet. Although Disney had severed his relationship with RKO Radio Pictures, this RKO film was distributed by Buena Vista. Based on Zoë Akins' play *Morning Glory* and with a screenplay by Ruth and Augustus Goetz, the film relates the story of Eva Lovelace (Susan Strasberg), a determined young actress who, against the glittering backdrop of New York theatrical life, transfers her adoration of producer Lewis Easton (Henry Fonda) into a deeply committed love of the theatre. Touching, poignant performances are expertly handled by co-stars Joan Greenwood (who later starred in *The Moon-Spinners*), Herbert Marshall and Christopher Plummer (in his first screen role).

AMERICA THE BEAUTIFUL (TP) This new version of Disneyland's *Circarama U.S.A.* was premiered at the Brussels World's Fair in 1958. A 16-minute tour of America, the 360° film was re-shot in *Circle-Vision* for the new Tomorrowland in 1967. When Disneyland celebrated its 20th birthday in 1975, a revised version was produced, which included new scenes of Philadelphia. Touring the world in the early 1970s in the USA Traveldome, *America the Beautiful* was replaced at Disneyland in 1984 by a brand new film, *American Journeys*. A 16mm release in normal ratio was distributed for educational use in 1980.

THE MISSOURI TRAVELLER (F) Director Jerry Hopper. In a movie that could easily have been made by Walt Disney and not just distributed by Buena Vista, Brandon de Wilde stars as Biarn Turner, a 14-year-old runaway orphan who is helped by a curious cross-section of people. These include Lee Marvin as bullying farmer Tobias Brown, Gary Merrill as newspaperman Doyle Magee and Paul Ford (who achieved great acclaim in the Phil Silvers television series) as café proprietor Finas Daugherty. With stunning

Technicolor photography by Winton C. Hoch, the film proved popular with young audiences.

THE STORY OF VICKIE (F) Director Ernst Marischka. Based on Queen Victoria's letters and diaries, the film stars international starlet Romy Schneider as the young Victoria and relates how the teenage Princess becomes engaged to Prince Albert of Saxe-Coburg (Adrian Hoven). Filmed at the Sie-Vering Studios in Vienna in beautifully simulated settings of Kensington Palace, the film, originally entitled *Maedchenjahre einer Koenigin* (*Girlhood of a Queen*), was picked up for distribution through Buena Vista because of Disney's success with foreign-based historical dramas. Known in the UK as *Dover Interlude*, the film was a moderate success, probably because of Schneider's personal appearances in connection with the US release.

FROM AESOP TO HANS CHRISTIAN ANDERSEN (Sp) Director Clyde Geronimi. This cartoon compilation was first shown on the *Disneyland* television series in 1955. Walt Disney introduces classic fairy tales as illustrated in some of the Disney films. In addition to an excerpt from *Snow White and the Seven Dwarfs*, the film features four cartoon shorts: *The Tortoise and the Hare* (1935), *The Country Cousin* (1936), *Brave Little Tailor* (1938) and *The Ugly Duckling* (1939).

MAN IN FLIGHT (Sp) Director Hamilton Luske. Produced with the cooperation of the Armed Forces of the United States and the American aviation industry and written by Heinz Haber and Milt Banta, *Man in Flight* was originally screened on the *Disneyland* television series in 1957. Walt Disney hosts a look at man's various attempts to fly. A lengthy animated sequence traces the origins of flying, from the first Chinese experiments with paper kites and fireworks, through the inventions of Leonardo da Vinci, the Montgolfier brothers of France (who built the first passenger-carrying balloon), the father of aeronautics, Sir George Cayley, and Orville and Wilbur Wright's first man-powered flight, to the giant leaps made in aviation during the two world wars. The film ends with modern jets trail-blazing across the skies – 'a vast arena for a symphony of wings,' explains the narrator – as a simulated space flight is shown. In fact little of the film's 34 minutes is made up of original footage, most of the aviation sequences being lifted out of Disney's little-seen feature *Victory Through Air Power* (1943).

MAGIC HIGHWAY U.S.A. (Sp) Walt Disney hosts this film that was shown on the *Disneyland* television series in 1958 and released on 16mm in the same year. Rare archive footage captures the pioneering spirit of the first highway travellers, while the movie contemplates the modern (1950s) roads of America and looks ahead, by means of clever limited animation, to a future of coloured traffic lanes, heated pavements, air-conditioned tubular highways and computer-programmed cars. Extracts from this fascinating document on how post-war America looked into the future appear on a display screen in 'Horizons' at EPCOT Center.

WALES (P & P) Director Geoffrey Foot. Continuing the series' tradition of illustrating a country and its customs, the film explores the Welsh coastline (which makes up three-fourths of its boundary) and the important use of the Welsh language in revivals of ancient ceremonies.

☆ PAUL BUNYAN (Sp) Director Les Clark. Bunyan is '10 axe handles' high, and his height enables him

to clear vast tracks of woodland for new farming communities. He befriends a blue ox, called Babe, an animal as large as himself, and the two are admired across the length and breadth of the country (left), until, that is, industry encroaches on their lives and the mighty lumberjack loses a contest with a new steam saw. Vividly animated in a simple, clear style, the film, released only a year before *Sleeping Beauty*, was another fine example of Disney's experimentation with the art of animation.

★ WHITE WILDERNESS (TLA) Director James Algar. The work of 11 film-makers, this is among the most visually attractive of all the True-Life Adventure films, covering, as it does, the lives of polar bears (below), ermines, musk oxen, ring seals, migrant caribou, eider ducks, wolves and lemmings from the Canadian and Alaskan timber lines to the very edge of the polar ice cap. Amazingly, all footage was shot on 16mm and exploded to 35mm for theatrical release, and the spectacular results are a tribute to the hard-working talents that put it together. There is little of the camera trickery usually associated with the True-Life Adventure series. Disney and his photographers never tried to hide the fact that nature can be savage and brutal, yet, discordantly, the film's publicity campaign had a by-line that read: 'Whoops! How long has it been since you've had this much fun?' *White Wilderness* won the 1958 Academy Award for Best Documentary Feature. A number of educational extracts, including *Arctic Region and its Polar Bears*, *Lemmings and Arctic Bird Life* and *Large Animals of the Arctic*, were released in 1964.

THE PROUD REBEL (F) Director Michael Curtiz. Another 1950s film to be distributed by Buena

Vista worldwide stars Alan Ladd (who had guest-starred in the *The Reluctant Dragon*) as John Chandler, a rebel from the American South who tries to find a doctor to cure his mute son, David (David Ladd). Befriended by Miss Linnett Moore (Olivia de Havilland), Chandler helps save her farm from the vicious Burleigh gang. In a show-down, the boy regains his voice and, by shouting a warning, saves his father from being shot. This light-weight western has some fine moments and co-stars Dean Jagger, Cecil Kellaway, Henry Hull and John Carradine.

SCOTLAND (P & P) Director Geoffrey Foot. Foot had worked on the feature-length *Rob Roy* and was available to direct this People and Places featurette. The film examines the three distinct regions of the country – the Highlands, the islands and the Lowlands – while vivid Technicolor photography highlights the traditions of the Scottish people. Special mention is made of the national instrument, the bagpipes.

THE LIGHT IN THE FOREST (F) Director Herschel Daugherty. Daugherty took time off from working on such long-running tv series as *Alfred Hitchcock Presents* and *Wagon Train* to make his feature film debut. Based on Conrad Richter's novel, the film stars James MacArthur as Johnny Butler, a white boy who had been captured by Indians and spent much of his childhood living with them. When, in 1764, a peace treaty between the British and the Delaware Indians demands that all white prisoners be returned to their people, Butler, christened True Son by the Indians, is released. Wendell Corey stars as Wilse Owens, a white man who hates the Indians, and Carol Lynley provides the romantic interest as Wilse's servant, Shenandoe, with whom Butler falls in love. With technical advice supplied by Hollywood veteran Iron Eyes Cody, the film was shot in some picturesque locations in Tennessee. In 1961, the film was shown on *The Wonderful World of Color* television series under the titles *Return of True Son* and *True Son's Revenge*. In 1976 a 16mm educational extract was released entitled *Prejudice: Hatred or Ignorance?*

★THE AMA GIRLS (P & P) Director Ben Sharpsteen. This, the eleventh in the People and Places series, won the 1958 Academy Award for Best Short Subject (documentary). The setting is Japan, and the film records a typical working day of an Ama, or diving girl, whose arduous task it is to collect a variety of seaweed called Heaven's Grass. Released with *White Wilderness*, the film was distributed on 16mm in 1961 under the title *Japan Harvests the Sea*.

OUR FRIEND THE ATOM (Sp) Director Hamilton Luske. 'Fiction often has a way of becoming fact,' claims Walt Disney in his introduction. To illustrate his point, this featurette on the future of atomic energy begins with extracts from the film *20,000 Leagues Under the Sea*, in which 'Jules Verne' tells how Captain Nemo discovered a terrible power that could either benefit mankind or destroy the world. The rest of the film, which was written by Milt Banta, is hosted by Heinz Haber – a doctor of space medicine who, with Wernher von Braun and Willy Ley, devised the successful series of space films for the Studio.

The film charts the important breakthroughs in atomic research and a further understanding of the atom itself. All this is brilliantly staged in animated sequences lifted from the pages of Haber's book, *Our Friend the Atom*. Among the touches of pure invention are the idea that Einstein's formula $E = mc^2$ can be compared to

the fable of the 'Fisherman and the Genie' and that a tabletop full of mousetraps and ping-pong balls could be a simplified version of an atomic chain reaction. The threat of nuclear weapons is quickly dismissed, the film favouring the positive uses of the atomic reactor and its potential in providing the Earth with power, radioactive isotopes to benefit medical science and the promise of world peace. With an atmospheric musical score by Oliver Wallace, the animation techniques employed to illustrate the scientific processes of the atom are highly imaginative, and Haber's delivery helps to keep a serious subject firmly tongue in cheek yet informative. It was first shown on the *Disneyland* tv series in 1957.

THE SIGN OF ZORRO (F) Directors Norman Foster and Lewis R. Foster. Pleased with the success of the Davy Crockett tv shows when they were released as two theatrical films, Disney decided to exploit the potential of his popular ABC tv series *Zorro*. This black and white film stars Guy Williams as Don Diego (alias Zorro), who returns from his schooling in Spain to challenge the evil tyranny of Monastario (Britt Lomond), commandante of the pueblo of Los Angeles. Henry Calvin co-stars as the blundering Sergeant Garcia, and Gene Sheldon is Diego's servant Bernardo. The masked avenger, whose calling card was a letter Z carved with his foil on walls and objects, became an instant hit with audiences, although the sequel, *Zorro the Avenger*, failed to receive an American theatrical release because of the continuing tv repeats.

MAN AND THE MOON (Sp) Director Ward Kimball. The second science film to be presented on the *Disneyland* television series is narrated by Wernher von Braun, fresh from his success in *Man in Space*. Concentrating on a manned spaceflight to the moon, the film illustrates the importance of building a space station in orbit around the Earth. This would be easy to achieve, claimed the film, with solar-powered 'bottle suits', also designed by Braun. Instead of using animated sequences for the rocket flight to the lunar surface, the voyage was filmed with real actors on studio sets. 'We just rented a lot of hokey instruments from a guy in Hollywood and did our best, all with Braun's approval of course,' recalled Kimball. In the best Disney tradition the flight is made more exciting by the inclusion of a space walk, *à la* George Pal's 1950 *Destination Moon*, with astronauts in spacesuits designed by Braun, layout man Ken O'Connor and writer Bill Bosche. It was first shown on television in 1955.

YOU – AND YOUR FOOD (Ed) Host Jiminy Cricket explains the dietary needs of humans and of animals.

YOU – THE LIVING MACHINE (Ed) Jiminy Cricket demonstrates how the body converts food into energy and transports it to all areas of the 'human machine'.

TONKA (F) Director Lewis R. Foster. Set at the time of the Battle of the Little Big Horn, *Tonka* is based on David Appel's novel about a magnificent wild stallion called Comanche. Sal Mineo stars as the Indian White Bull, whose love for the horse is shared by cavalry captain Miles Keogh (Philip Carey). Against the backdrop of the hatred of the Army and Indians for each other, the two become friends. But Keogh, along with his entire regiment, is slaughtered at Custer's Last Stand. Tonka/Comanche is honoured by the 7th Cavalry for bravery and presented to White Bull. Co-stars include Jerome Courtland and Rafael

Campos, with H.M. Wynant as the evil Yellow Bull. The rousing theme song was written by Gil George and George Bruns. The film was shown on *The Wonderful World of Color* in 1962.

SEVEN CITIES OF ANTARCTICA (P & P) Director Winston Hibler. Disney dispatched veteran film reporters Lloyd Beebe and Elmo Jones with navy photographers to Antarctica to record all phases of the ambitious US expedition 'Operation Deepfreeze'. Although footage was used in later television shows, the Studio also released a film in the People and Places series. The featurette, which won awards from the British Film Academy and the Southern California Motion Picture Council, looks back at the early explorers – Wilkes, Palmer and Admiral Byrd – and shows how the modern icebreakers cope with the towering glaciers and mountains of snow.

1959

★GRAND CANYON (Sp) Director James Algar. Although not part of the True-Life Adventure series, this short combines dramatic and awe–inspiring scenes with brilliant photography and captures the very essence of life amid the precipitous cliffs of red rock, towering above the fast flowing Colorado River in Northern Arizona. Winner of the 1958 Academy Award for Best Live-Action Short Subject, the film was shot in breathtaking CinemaScope by Ernst A. Heiniger, who had to synchronize the visuals to the stirring 'Grand Canyon Suite', composed in 1929 by Ferde Grofe. There is no narrative, the music alone accompanying the many and ever-changing moods of the Canyon – sunrise, sunset, thunderstorms – and the many species of wild life that inhabit the rock face. Heiniger worked with a portable record player to choose the best camera angles, and the film took up to a year to complete. The 'On the Trail' section of Grofe's score also accompanies the lavish diorama of the Grand Canyon's South Rim, which is simulated on the Disneyland Railroad attraction.

NATURE'S STRANGEST CREATURES (Sp) Producer Ben Sharpsteen. Filmed in the style of a True-Life Adventure, the short examines the peculiar wildlife of Australia and Tasmania, including giant bats, kangaroos and the duck-billed platypus.

CRUISE OF THE EAGLE (P & P) Producer Ben Sharpsteen. In this dramatic documentary about the men of the Sea and Air Rescue Services, the crew of a lightship keeps a lonely vigil to warn ships of hidden dangers; a cutter races to the scene of an air-liner's emergency landing; and an ice-breaker traverses the frozen wastes of the Arctic circle warning of gale-force winds.

THE SHAGGY DOG (F) Director Charles Barton. This huge success – over $12 million to date in America alone – proved to Disney that bizarre teenage comedies were just what audiences craved in the late 1950s. (His last animated feature *Sleeping Beauty* had been a financial disaster.) Tommy Kirk stars as Wilby Daniels, a misfit youngster who loves inventing things. When a mysterious ring transforms him into a large, shaggy dog, he is mistaken for the nextdoor neighbour's pet. Having discovered a plot to steal government missile plans, the 'dog' and his brother Moochie (Kevin Corcoran) decide to trap the spies themselves. Based on Felix Salten's novel *The Hound of Florence*, the film was originally intended as a pilot for a tv series. The Studio capitalized on some of the low-budget horror pictures circulating at the time by sub-titling the movie 'I Was a Teenage Boy!' In 1976, Disney made a sequel, *The Shaggy D.A.*, with Dean Jones in the role of Wilby Daniels, and *The Return of the Shaggy Dog* was made for tele-vision screening in the autumn of 1987.

GOOFY SUCCESS STORY (Sp) Jack Kinney's classic short *Motor Mania* (1950) becomes a vital ingredient of this compilation, which also fea-tures the shorts *Moving Day* (1936), *Moose Hunters* (1937) and *How To Ride a Horse* (1941). This filmic biography of one of the Studio's most enduring stars was first shown on the *Disneyland* television series in 1955.

EYES IN OUTER SPACE (Sp) Director Ward Kimball. This winner of the 1960 Thomas Edison Foundation Award continues along the lines of science-fact of the Wernher von Braun space films. This time the Disney animators demon-strate man's future ability to control the weather and, in a combined live-action and animated climax, use huge weather towers (above) to drive

a dangerous tropical hurricane out to sea. Because of the information contained in the film and the importance of satellites, the short was shown on *The Wonderful World of Color* in 1962 as part of the programme *Spy in the Sky*.

☆ DONALD IN MATHMAGIC LAND (DD) Director Hamilton Luske. Heinz Haber, one of the scient-ists who had worked on the Disney space films, collaborated on this story. Donald stars as a kind of modern 'Alice in Wonderland' as he explores the mysterious world of maths with the help of the Spirit of Adventure (voiced by Paul Frees). Mathmagic Land is a fascinating place, com-posed of square root trees (below), set square birds and streams full of numbers. Excellent colour styling by John Hench and Art Riley adds

to this educational title's entertainment value. The film also looks at the history of mathematics and its relationship with art, architecture and nature. In one sequence with a game of chess, Donald actually becomes Lewis Carroll's heroine. He then explores the use of mathematics in sports. Overlong by about 5 minutes, the movie has received a number of film festival awards in America, Scotland and Italy and is the most popular educational film ever released by Disney. In 1961 it was screened on *The Wonder-ful World of Color* television series.

HOW TO HAVE AN ACCIDENT AT WORK (DD) Director Charles Nichols. Donald Duck, like Goofy, spent a great deal of his later film career instructing audiences in the right and wrong ways of going about things. Here, after having already shown the dangers lurking in domesticity in *How To Have An Accident in the Home* (1956), Donald proceeds to demonstrate a total disregard for personal safety by operating machinery and forgetting to wear his safety helmet (opposite below). The narrator, the small bearded duck called J.J. Fate, talks Donald through this series of mishaps. Cleverly written and animated, the short is an excellent educational primer on the importance of safety regulations.

THE BIG FISHERMAN (F) Director Frank Borzage. Disney always gave careful consideration to the subject matter of the non-Disney feature films released by Buena Vista and tried to ensure that the contents were always suitable for family audiences. Even when a Disney film was released in Europe, any supporting film from another studio would be carefully vetted by the Studio beforehand. This Buena Vista release, which was based on the novel by Lloyd C. Douglas, stars Howard Keel as the 'fisher of men' and co-stars John Saxon, Martha Hyer, Herbert Lom and Beulah Bondi. This Biblical epic was filmed in Panavision 70mm.

ZORRO THE AVENGER (F) Director Charles Barton. After the theatrical success in Europe of *The Sign of Zorro* (1958), which had been been

woodcutter's cottage deep in the forest. But, on her 16th birthday, Maleficent's evil raven discovers the whereabouts of the Princess, thus ensuring that the dreadful prophecy comes true. Gallantly, Prince Phillip, the neighbouring King Hubert's handsome son, rescues the Princess and defeats Maleficent in a heart-stopping finale, in which the Studio's effects animators excel themselves with a forest of thorns created by lightning bolts and the evil fairy's transformation into a towering, fire-breathing dragon (left). This overly technical style, the almost real-life movement of the main characters (achieved through rotoscoping live-action footage) and Eyvind Earle's extensively detailed backgrounds gave the critics plenty of ammunition with which to criticize the film. Mary Costa voices the young Princess (centre), although her mature operatic singing of songs such as 'I Wonder' and 'Once Upon a Dream' (by Sammy Fain, Jack Lawrence, Winston Hibler, Ted Sears and George Bruns) tends to clash with her more delicate cartoon appearance. Bill Shirley voices Prince Phillip, while Eleanor Audley supplies Maleficent's deep and demonic voice, which adds great depth to the on-screen presence of Marc Davis's animation. Studio veterans Verna Felton, Barbara Luddy, Bill Thompson and Candy Candido are responsible for the other characters, while the whole affair is directed without a single frame being wasted by Clyde Geronimi and sequence directors Eric Larson, Wolfgang Reitherman and Les Clark. George Bruns' orchestral score, based on Tchaikovsky's ballet *The Sleeping Beauty* and nominated for an Academy Award, adds to the film's better moments, especially the powerful imagery apparent in Prince Phillip's fight with the dragon. Sadly neglected by film students, the movie is a worthy addition to the Studio's more accomplished works. A visual *tour de force*, the film is a lasting tribute to Walt Disney's dream to have the animated film recognized as an art form in its own right.

DARBY O' GILL AND THE LITTLE PEOPLE (F) Director Robert Stevenson. 'My thanks to King Brian of Knocknasheega and his leprechauns, whose gracious cooperation made this picture

Unfortunately, lack of audience appreciation at such a daring undertaking meant that it marked instead the end of an era at the Studio. Throughout the 1950s Disney had turned more and more to live action: animation techniques were being simplified for television use, while the ornate animated film was becoming a thing of the past.

In this classic retelling of Charles Perrault's *La Belle au Bois Dormant*, adapted for the screen by Ted Sears, Winston Hibler, Bill Peet, Ralph Wright and, later, Erdman Penner and Joe Rinaldi, the evil fairy Maleficent places a curse on the infant Princess Aurora, claiming that before her 16th birthday she will prick her finger on the spindle of a spinning-wheel and die. To protect their child, King Stefan and his Queen reluctantly agree to allow the three good fairies, Flora, Fauna and Merryweather, to bring up the child at the

edited from some of the 78 episodes of Disney's highly popular tv series starring Guy Williams, the Studio released a sequel outside the US. In this entertaining adventure yarn about deception, fraud and impersonation, the villains are finally brought to justice by the infamous swordsman. Co-stars included Henry Calvin and Gene Sheldon. Although it was filmed in black and white, the original tv series was a great success in syndication throughout the 1960s and is now (1987) on The Disney Channel.

☆ SLEEPING BEAUTY (F) Supervising director Clyde Geronimi. Costing over $6 million and taking seven years to produce, Walt Disney's most ambitious feature-length animated film was a financial disaster at the box-office. Presented in Technirama 70mm and supported by a full stereophonic soundtrack, the film was intended to herald in a new age in animated movies.

possible,' commented Walt Disney at the time of the film's release. Walt even went to the trouble of being photographed with the fabled King Brian, who so kindly lent his permission for this entertaining fantasy adventure. The film was inspired by H. T. Kavanagh's Darby O'Gill stories and stars veteran actor Albert Sharpe as Darby (opposite below), an inveterate old storyteller, who finally meets up with King Brian of the leprechauns (Jimmy O'Dea). Darby tricks the tiny King into arranging for his daughter Katie (Janet Munro) to fall in love with Michael McBride (Sean Connery). Unfortunately, Katie is injured chasing after her horse, and the dreaded Costa Bower (Death Coach) comes to fetch her. Darby goes in her place, but, with one final wish from King Brian, he manages to escape his fate and everybody lives happily ever after. Pre-007 Connery is a little wooden, but his rendition of Oliver Wallace's song 'Pretty Irish Girl' is highly competent. Both he and Albert Sharpe are overshadowed, however, by the film's stunning effects by Peter Ellenshaw, Eustace Lycett and Joshua Meador. In one highly complex matte shot, Darby, having stumbled on the underground kingdom of the little people, plays his fiddle while tiny leprechauns on horseback gallop around his feet. Scenes like these were achieved through the use of 'forced perspective', a cinematic device whereby actors who are to appear normal size are placed in the foreground while the 'miniature' people are in the distance. Careful colour grading ensures a realistic blend of the two images. The appearance of the banshee and the terrifying Death Coach provide genuine moments of horror and underline Disney's ability to scare audiences as well as entertain them. Amazingly the film didn't win even a nomination for Best Special Effects at the 1959 Academy Awards, yet it is as visually staggering as *Ben Hur* or *Journey to the Centre of the Earth*. Ironically, although Walt Disney visited Ireland in his search for authenticity, the entire film was shot in California with the assistance of Peter Ellenshaw's matte paintings. Not a huge success at the box-office, parts of the film were re-dubbed to make the Irish accent easier on American ears.

THE PETER TCHAIKOVSKY STORY (F) Director Charles Barton. Without involving itself in the composer's more controversial lifestyle, the featurette concentrated on the turbulent musical career of one of Russia's finest composers. Grant Williams, a popular actor in the 1950s, takes the title role, while Lilyan Chauvin and Rex Hill co-star. First shown on the *Disneyland* series, it marked a television first for Disney in that the musical passages were played in stereo simultaneously on AM and FM radio stations.

THE THIRD MAN ON THE MOUNTAIN (F) Director Ken Annakin. Based on James Ramsey Ullman's book *Banner in the Sky*, this is a rousing, action-packed adventure that puts movies like *Ten Who Dared* (1960) completely in the shade. James MacArthur, fresh from his role in *A Light in the Forest*, stars as Rudi Matt, a young man who dreams of conquering the Matterhorn (referred to as the Citadel in the story) after his father has been killed on a similar expedition. Rudi is accompanied by Captain John Winter (Michael Rennie) and Emil Saxo (Herbert Lom). Outstanding location work in Switzerland and excellent matte photography by Peter Ellenshaw, add to the film's tremendous impact. Annakin spent hours pouring over the details for the film at the Studio in Burbank and handles the whole affair expertly. Walt, who loved holidaying in Switzerland and had already sent a People and Places crew over in 1955, took great delight in constructing a scale model of the real Matterhorn at Disneyland. The film was not a huge financial success, however, and it was shown on *The Wonderful World of Color* in 1963, while extracts were released for educational use in 1976, *Ambition: What Price Fulfilment?*, and in 1979 in the Films As Literature series.

☆ NOAH'S ARK (Sp) Director Bill Justice. Because of its involvement in television, the Studio was producing as much film in a week as it had previously produced in a year, and animator Bill Justice recalled that this led to short cuts in the animation process. Assisted by Xavier Atencio, he directed a bizarre little stop-motion film, which told the Biblical story with characters made of objects bought in a hardware store. The results (left) are inventive if a little tiresome. A similar idea was used on the musical sequences of Bill Justice's *A Symposium on Popular Songs* (1962).

☆ MYSTERIES OF THE DEEP (Sp) Production associate Ben Sharpsteen. Walt Disney's nephew, Roy E. Disney, wrote the narration for a number of the Studio's films during the late 1950s, and one of these, *Mysteries of the Deep*, was nominated for an Academy Award for Best Short Subject. Although it lost to another underwater documentary (by the legendary oceanographer Jacques-Yves Cousteau), the Disney film, photographed by, among others, naturalist H. Pederson, is still a fascinating insight into the lives of the sea creatures living in the giant coral reefs.

THE NINE LIVES OF ELFEGO BACA (F) Director Norman Foster. Starting life as six episodes on the *Walt Disney Presents* television show in 1958, this complex story was edited for theatrical release in Europe. Robert Loggia stars as a gun-toting lawman who cleans up the city of Socorro and pursues a criminal across the Mexican border. When his girlfriend Anita (Lisa Montell) rejects his offer of marriage, Baca hangs up his six-shooters and sheriff's badge and sets off for Santa Fé to study law. Both the series and film release proved the growing popularity of the western as entertainment.

1960

☆ GOLIATH II (Sp) Director Wolfgang Reitherman. In this charming tale, advertised as 'tiny but mighty, small but wonderful', a minute elephant (below) proves his bravery to a herd of enormous elephants by defeating their dreaded enemy – a mouse. Apart from being one of the few occasions on which a mouse has been the 'baddie' in a Disney film, this short looks at times like an early test for Col Hathi's Elephant Brigade in *The Jungle Book* (1967). The story was written by Bill Peet, storyman on numerous Disney features, and the miniature hero was voiced by Disney child star Kevin Corcoran.

GALA DAY AT DISNEYLAND (Sp) Producer Hamilton Luske. It seemed that cinema audiences could never tire of seeing the visual splendours of Disneyland, but this film is particularly important because it underlines the ever-changing face of the park by celebrating the opening of three new attractions: an underwater submarine voyage, a bobsled ride down the Matterhorn and a glimpse into the future aboard the sleek monorail trains. Walt and Roy, accompanied by numerous guests and VIPs, participate in a parade through Main Street.

TOBY TYLER OR TEN WEEKS WITH A CIRCUS (F) Director Charles Barton. Young Toby (Kevin Corcoran) runs away from his aunt and uncle (Edith Evanson and Tom Fadden) to join a circus,

where he is befriended by Mr Stubbs, a mischievous monkey and a variety of circus personnel – concessionaire Harry Tupper (Bob Sweeney), strongman Ben Cotter (Henry Calvin) and the glamorous Mademoiselle Jeanette (Barbara Beaird). Corcoran, well known to audiences as Moochie in the Disney tv series and a star of countless Disney films, is perfect in the lead, while Bill Walsh and Lillie Hayward's screenplay, based on a novel by James Otis Kaler, gives a wonderfully impressionistic view of circus life. The film was shown on *The Wonderful World of Color* tv series in 1964.

KIDNAPPED (F) Director Robert Stevenson. Disney returned to the swashbuckling adventure yarn with this colourful version of Robert Louis Stevenson's classic story. James MacArthur, in his third film for the Studio, plays David Balfour (above), a young man who is shanghaied at the request of his cunning Uncle Ebenezer (John Laurie). He befriends Alan Breck Stewart (Peter Finch), who helps David return to Scotland so that he may claim his rightful inheritance. Also starring Niall MacGinnis, Bernard Lee, Finlay Currie, Miles Malleson and Peter O'Toole, the film lacks the excitement of *Treasure Island*, and the broad Scottish accents seriously affected box-office receipts. It was screened on *The Wonderful World of Color* in 1963, and an educational sequence in the Films As Literature series was released in 1978.

☆ ISLANDS OF THE SEA (Sp) Producer Ben Sharpsteen. A number of Disney nature 'specials' were produced alongside the True-Life Adventure series. Among these was *Islands of the Sea*, which was narrated by Winston Hibler. Remarkable photography by Conrad Hall captures the inhabitants of the Galapagos, the Falklands and the tiny atolls of the Midway group.

TEXAS JOHN SLAUGHTER (F) Director Harry Keller. From the *Walt Disney Presents* television series, episodes of this popular western series starring Tom Tryon as Texas John were edited together into a feature-length release in Europe and the Far East. The film follows the fortunes of

a cattle rancher who is driven to joining the rangers in order to uphold law and order in the untamed west of 1870. Robert Middleton and Norma Moore co-star in this competent drama, which spawned four sequels.

MICKEY MOUSE FESTIVAL. Premiered in Germany, this feature-length compilation includes 11 shorts.

JAPAN (P & P) Producer Ben Sharpsteen. The penultimate film in the People and Places series makes careful use of cross-screen filters to give the photography a softness that suggests oriental paintings. In contrast, its exploration of the country's colourful customs, ceremonies and sporting activities gives it a vibrant energy that places it high on the list of the Studio's successful documentary excursions.

THE DANUBE (P & P) Director Ben Sharpsteen. Known as the 'River Highway of Central Europe', the Danube passes through some of the world's most beautiful scenery, and this, the last in the People and Places series follows the river through the Black Forest, Bavaria and Austria. Photographed by Herb and Trudy Knapp, the film concludes with a spectacular tour of Vienna, described in the narration as the 'Queen of the Danube'.

★ POLLYANNA (F) Director David Swift. Hayley Mills' first film for Walt Disney earned her an Honorary Oscar statuette at the 1960 Academy Awards – a well-deserved tribute to a splendid performance. David Swift, who not only wrote the screenplay from the novel by Eleanor H. Porter but made his directorial debut, handles the whole affair in a competent and entertaining fashion. The story is set in about 1912, and Pollyanna goes to live with her rich Aunt Polly (Jane Wyman, right). A happy-go-lucky child, she befriends Jimmy Bean (Kevin Corcoran), and together they change the lives of those around them – miserable Mr Pendergast (Adolphe Menjou), crotchety Mrs Snow (Agnes Moorehead) and the misunderstood Reverend Paul Ford (Karl Malden). When Pollyanna is hurt in an

accident, the whole town join forces to wish her a speedy recovery under the guidance of Dr Edmund Chilton (Richard Egan). Making use of a great deal of outside production talent, Disney turned this charming film into one of his best live-action features, although it was not an enormous success at the box-office. Of the cast, Wyman and Malden each returned in another Disney film, while Hayley Mills, whom Disney had picked after seeing her in the British film *Tiger Bay*, signed a contract with the Studio and went on to star in five other films during the early 1960s. The film was shown on *The Wonderful World of Color* in 1963, and in 1975 an educational extract, *Optimist/Pessimist: Which Are You?*, was released on 16mm.

THE HOUND THAT THOUGHT HE WAS A RACCOON (F) Director Tom McGowan. In a story not too dissimilar to Disney's later animated feature *The Fox and the Hound*, a dog called Nubbin befriends a raccoon – the very animal he is trained to kill. This successful featurette, which received an Award from the Southern California Motion Picture Council, was adapted by Rutherford Montgomery from his original story *Weecha the Raccoon*. Eventually shown on *The Wonderful World of Color* television series in 1964, the film is nicely photographed and captures the unique companionship of two natural enemies.

JUNGLE CAT (TLA) Director James Algar. Putting the jaguar into a proper perspective and justifying its title as the 'greatest hunter of them all', Winston Hibler explains about the cat family, from domestic varieties to their cousins on the African plains. From then on *Jungle Cat* concentrates on the jaguar itself (opposite above) and its life in the jungles of South America. No creature, it seems, is safe from this vicious predator, whether it is a peccary, jacare or a fully grown boa constrictor. Photographed by, among others, James R. Simon, it was the last film made under the banner of True-Life Adventure. Subsequent films, *The Legend of Lobo* and *Nikki, Wild Dog of the North*, for example, were fictionalized animal adventures, and only recently, with the need for documentary-style film-making at some of the science pavilions in EPCOT Center, has the

1961

ITALIA '61 – CIRCLING ITALY WITH CIRCARAMA (Sp) The success of *Circarama U.S.A.* in Disneyland led Fiat to sponsor a 16mm *Circle-Vision* film for the 1961 Exposition in Turin. Later blown up to 35 mm, the film traces the history of the Italian nation. The Italian crew, headed by Elio Piccon, was instructed in the use of the cameras by Don Iwerks (the son of Walt and Roy's first partner Ub). Among the visual highlights are the harbour at Genoa, an off-shore oil rig in the Adriatic, Fiat-built jet fighters in aerial acrobatics and a flight over Mount Vesuvius.

THE MAGNIFICENT REBEL (F) Director Georg Tressler. The star of the sinister British horror film *Peeping Tom*, Carl Boehm, was cast as the fiery young Ludwig van Beethoven, in a story depicting the composer's love for music. Filmed on location in Europe, the screenplay was written by Joanne Court. As in all Disney historical dramas, there's a lot of excitement, particularly when Beethoven is captured and thrown into prison by Napoleon's army. Co-starring Giulia Rubini (in her American debut) as the Countess Giulietta, to whom the composer dedicated his 'Moonlight' Sonata, the film makes extensive use of Beethoven's music, which is performed by the Berlin Symphony Orchestra. Released theatrically in Europe and described in the publicity as a film about 'a man alone – daring to fight destiny to thrust his greatness on the world!', it was actually thrust straight onto *The Wonderful World of Color* tv series in 1962.

DONALD AND THE WHEEL (DD) Director Hamilton Luske. As educator, Donald Duck was called upon to impart knowledge to cinema audiences in the same way that Jiminy Cricket was teaching students in schools. After exploring the complicated world of mathematics in 1959, Donald found himself an inventor. With the assistance of the Spirits of Progress he discovers that the wheel is the basic concept of the whole universe.

Studio returned to producing this kind of film. Shown in part on *The Wonderful World of Color* in 1964 and spawning two 16mm extracts – *Jungle Cat of the Amazon* and *Animals of the South American Jungle* – the film is a stunning tribute to a series that spanned a dozen years.

TEN WHO DARED (F) Director William Beaudine. This mediocre drama was based on the journal of Major John Wesley Powell, who, in 1869, led an expedition down the fast-flowing Colorado River in the depths of the Grand Canyon. John Beal, who provided one of the voices for the animated sequences in *So Dear to My Heart*, plays the one-armed explorer Powell, who recruits nine other men to accompany him. Matte artist Albert Whitlock created some spectacular paintings of the Canyon for sequences shot in the Studio. The film co-stars Brian Keith, James Drury and Ben Johnson.

★THE HORSE WITH THE FLYING TAIL (F) Director Larry Lansburgh. Narrators George Fenneman and Dorian Williams relate the true story of a proud palomino called Nautical, who goes on to win the King George V Cup. Filmed over two years in five countries, it won the 1960 Academy Award for Best Documentary Feature and was shown on *The Wonderful World of Color* in 1963.

SWISS FAMILY ROBINSON (F) Director Ken Annakin. British star John Mills plays father to a family, shipwrecked on an unexplored island, which has to learn how to survive the elements, wild animals and bloodthirsty pirates. Dorothy McGuire plays his wife, while James MacArthur (fresh from his role in *Kidnapped*), Tommy Kirk and Kevin Corcoran (right, with MacArthur) play his sons, Fritz, Ernst and Francis, even if their accents do seem more international than the author intended. Befriending another shipwrecked victim, Roberta (Janet Munro), the family domesticates its island paradise through sheer hard work and determination. The battle with the pirates, led by Sessue Hayakawa, is a visual delight, although the Studio underplayed any evidence of the villainous hordes actually

being killed off. Adapted for the screen by Lowell S. Hawley from the novel by Johann Wyss, the film has proved to be among the Studio's most popular cinematic endeavours, and, although it is slightly long-winded, it is on a par, for sheer thrills and excitement, with *20,000 Leagues Under the Sea*. The movie was filmed in Panavision amid the lush surroundings of the island of Tobago, and what add to the film's charm are the tremendous attention to detail and preplanning by the production team, including a most elaborate tree house, which was later simulated in the Disney theme parks and has proved a popular attraction. In 1978, a 16mm extract was released for schools in the Films As Literature series.

ONE HUNDRED AND ONE DALMATIANS (F) Directors Wolfgang Reitherman, Hamilton Luske and Clyde Geronimi. One of the Studio's most popular re-issues, it has earned over $37 million to date at the US box-office. The film's appeal lies in the uncluttered storyline, which was adapted from Dodie Smith's book by Bill Peet. When 15 Dalmatian puppies are stolen from the London home of Roger and Anita Radcliff (above) and all human attempts to trace the pups fail, their Dalmatian pets, Pongo and Perdita, begin their own search with the help of the 'Twilight Bark', a unique, canine 'telephone' network. Anita's old schoolfriend, the villainous Cruella De Vil, is responsible for the theft, and she has imprisoned the puppies, together with 84 other Dalmatians, in her sinister mansion Hell Hall. (During this sequence the puppies are seen watching an extract from the Silly Symphony *Flowers and Trees* on tv.) Her henchmen, Jasper and Horace Badun, who have orders to turn the dogs into fur coats for their boss, reckon without the unexpected arrival of Pongo, Perdita, a wily cat called Sergeant Tibs and a pompous old sheep dog called the Colonel. But Cruella doesn't give up that easily, and the story culminates in a hairraising chase through the wintry English countryside. It's here that the film excels, not only because the characters are a delight to watch, but also because the backgrounds by Al Dempster, Ralph Hulett, Anthony Rizzo and Bill Layne, using designs by Ken Anderson, are brilliantly executed. The evil Cruella De Vil, voiced by Betty Lou Gerson and delightfully brought to the screen by animator Marc Davis, ranks alongside the best of the Disney villains, including even the Queen in *Snow White*, Captain Hook in *Peter Pan* and Maleficent in *Sleeping Beauty*. Other voices were provided by Rod Taylor (Pongo), Lisa Davis (Anita), Cate Bauer (Perdita), Ben Wright (Roger) and J. Pat O'Malley (the Colonel,

Jasper Badun *inter alia*). In 1981 a 16mm extract was released called *A Lesson in Self-Assertion*.

THE SAGA OF WINDWAGON SMITH (Sp) Director Charles Nichols. During the late 1950s and early 1960s, the Studio produced a number of animated specials, and these gradually came to replace the shorts starring Mickey and the gang. Although they were expensive to make, they did have a future on the Disney television shows and on

16mm for schools. *The Saga of Windwagon Smith* was very popular in compilations of old American legends. Ingenious editing and impressive use of limited animation styles are used to retell the story of how Windwagon Smith, navigator of the seven seas (below), 'sails' across the American prairies in his impressive invention, the 'windwagon'. Interestingly, the film marked the reappearance, albeit anonymous, of Jasper and Horace Badun from *One Hundred and One Dalmatians*.

☆ THE ABSENT MINDED PROFESSOR (F) Director Robert Stevenson. The highly complex nature of the special effects that were used led the Studio to shoot the picture in black and white, but an excellent script and hilarious performances by Fred MacMurray and Keenan Wynn elevated the film above the status of 'supporting feature' and guaranteed its success. Having created a 'gooey' substance called 'Flubber', which negates gravity and allows people and objects to fly, Professor Brainard (MacMurray) has a difficult time convincing his fiancée (Nancy Olson) of the importance of his discovery. Not until he uses it in the engine of his Model T Ford and flies to Washington, does she fully appreciate its potential. When Brainard irons 'Flubber' (which, according to the film's publicity, was 'the funniest discovery since laughter') onto the shoes of his college's basketball team, they successfully win the game by leaping and bounding over the opposing side. The intricate special effects consisted of a combination of sodium screen matte work, miniatures and wire supported mock-ups. Robert A. Mattey and Eustace Lycett were nominated for an Academy Award for Best Special Effects, and Edward Colman was nominated for Best Achievement in Black and White Cinematography. Co-stars Forrest Lewis and James Westerfield play two very inept and 'flubbergasted' policemen, repeating their roles in *The Shaggy Dog*.

THE LITTERBUG (DD) Director Hamilton Luske. Donald Duck's general carelessness in shorts such as *How To Have An Accident At Work*

made him the perfect choice to portray the 'sports bug', the 'sneak bug', the 'highway bug', the 'beach bug' and the 'mountain bug' as he journeys around the country, filling it up with litter. The forest animals perform a catchy theme-song, deploring the pollution caused by such a pest.

☆ THE PARENT TRAP (F) Director David Swift. Hayley Mills, who had already won an Honorary Academy Award for her performance as *Pollyanna*, made an even greater impact when she played opposite *herself*. In this rather convoluted story, which is based on *Das doppelte Lottchen* (*Lottie and Lisa*) by Erich Kästner, Sharon McKendrick (Hayley Mills) meets her twin sister, Susan Evers (Hayley Mills), at a girls' summer camp, thanks to coincidence and some remarkable trick photography by Ub Iwerks. The girls plot to bring their divorced parents (Brian Keith and Maureen O'Hara, below) back together, but this proves difficult, especially as Mr Evers has fallen in love with money-grabbing Vicky Robinson (Joanna Barnes). Undaunted, the girls change places and spend the majority of the film's 129 minutes setting up a meeting for their estranged parents. Hayley Mills gives two excellent performances and scene-stealing cameos are provided by guest stars Charlie Ruggles as Grandfather and Leo G. Carroll as Reverend Dr Mosby, who is bemused by the whole affair. The film contains an inventive title sequence (which was itself the subject of an episode of the *Walt Disney Presents* television series) by stop-motion experts T. Hee, Bill Justice and Xavier Atencio, and some delightful songs by Richard and Robert Sherman are performed by Miss Mills, Annette Funicello and Tommy Sands. Oscar nominations were awarded for Sound and Film Editing. An abridged version was later released, and in 1986 a much older Hayley Mills recreated her dual roles in the imaginatively entitled sequel *Parent Trap II*, which was directed for The Disney Channel by Ronald F. Maxwell.

NIKKI, WILD DOG OF THE NORTH (F) Directors Jack Couffer and Dan Haldane. In this film,

which underlined the Studio's ability to combine a fictional animal story with the tried and trusted formula of a True-Life Adventure, Jean Coutu plays André Dupas, a trapper whose wolf-dog Nikki befriends a bear cub (above). When the animals are accidentally separated from Dupas, they team up in order to survive. Unfortunately, Nikki is captured by an evil trapper, Jacques Le Beau (Emile Genest, who later starred in *The Incredible Journey*). Training Nikki to kill for

sport, he meets his comeuppance when the dog turns on him in the savage climax. Based on a novel by James Oliver Curwood and narrated by Jacques Fauteux, the film proved that the Studio was not afraid to make some of its animal stories real and devoid of over-sentimentality. It was shown on *The Wonderful World of Color* television series in 1964.

THE HORSEMASTERS (F) Director William Fairchild. Not so much a story about young people training to become top horse instructors, but a vehicle to promote the up-and-coming talents of ex-*Mickey Mouse Club* star Annette, a shapely young lady in high heels and sheath dresses, who was by this time receiving more fan mail than most adult movie stars in Hollywood. Her trip to England, where *The Horsemasters* was filmed, created a great deal of press coverage. In the story, which was based on Don Stanford's book and heralded by publicity as 'a refreshing new experience in movie-going', Dinah Wilcox (Annette) and Danny Grant (Tommy Kirk) join other youngsters at a tranquil Surrey training school to earn their Horsemaster's Certificate. Short on thrills but full of romance, the film co-starred Tony Britton, John Fraser, Janet Munro and Britain's own singing star Millicent Martin. It was shown on *The Wonderful World of Color* in October 1961.

MICKEY MOUSE CARTOON FESTIVAL. This cartoon compilation, which was first released in Panama, contains eight separate shorts, which varied from country to country.

GUNFIGHT AT SANDOVAL (F) Director Harry Keller. Tom Tryon's success as Wild West hero Texas John Slaughter on the *Walt Disney Presents* tv series from 1958 to 1961 paved the way for a number of successful feature-film adaptations. Released in Europe and one of five theatrical spin-offs, *Gunfight at Sandoval* finds

Slaughter on the trail of the infamous Barko gang. He succeeds in hunting them down by impersonating a desperado. Co-stars are Dan Duryea and Beverly Garland.

☆ BABES IN TOYLAND (F) Director Jack Donohue. The Studio's first live-action musical, which is based on the original operetta by Victor Herbert, opens like a stage play. The action takes place in Mother Goose Village, where evil Barnaby (Ray Bolger), wishing to marry attractive Mary Contrary (Annette Funicello), kidnaps her sweetheart Tom Piper (Tommy Sands, below, with Ed Wynne, Annette, Kevin and Brian Corcoran, Marilee and Melanie Arnold, and Ann Jillian). Tom's rescue eventually leads through the Forest of No Return to Toyland. Barnaby steals a ray gun, which reduces objects in size, from the bumbling toymaker (Ed Wynn) and miniaturizes his opponents. But, leading an army of toy soldiers, Tom comes to the rescue and defeats the villain. The film contains some brilliant special effects sequences written by Ward Kimball, who co-wrote the screenplay, and designed by effects experts Eustace Lycett, Robert Mattey, Joshua Meador, Bill Justice and Xavier Atencio. But unfortunately for Disney, the more mature members of the cinema audience could probably remember having had more fun watching Laurel and Hardy's 1934 version of the story.

GREYFRIARS BOBBY (F) Director Don Chaffey. 'It was photographed where it happened! You'll have to see it to believe it!', claimed the earth-shattering announcements for what was, in fact, a sentimental picture relating the true story of how an entire city took pity on the plight of a small Skye terrier. Based on the book by Eleanor Atkinson, this competent film was shot on location in Scotland. Set in Edinburgh in 1865, it relates how Bobby became the first and only dog in history to be given the freedom of the city thanks to the intervention of the Lord Provost (Andrew Cruickshank) and to the devoted attention of restaurant owner Mr Traill (Laurence Naismith) and the churchyard caretaker James Brown (Donald Crisp, above). Bobby himself is as endearing as any Disney dog, and there are appealing performances from the poor children who befriend Bobby, while the rural Scottish settings add to the film's considerable charm. In fact, the film's only fault lies in its Scottish accents, some of which totally mystified American audiences, and it was not long before it was relegated to an early television screening on The Wonderful World of Color (1964).

☆ AQUAMANIA (G) Director Wolfgang Reitherman. Goofy has serious problems with his water-skiing and a rather irate octopus in this short, which tries desperately to capture the spirit of Jack Kinney's earlier Goofy movies.

1962

MOON PILOT (F) Director James Neilson. It's interesting that Disney, in its first feature-length film about the space age, should take a humorous swipe at the red tape surrounding America's space programme. Tom Tryon stars as Captain Richmond Talbot, who is volunteered to be the first American in space by veteran astronaut Charlie the chimpanzee. But he meets the attractive Lyrae (Dany Saval), an alien from the planet Beta Lyrae. Although she wishes only to impart vital scientific information to Talbot, Lyrae falls hopelessly in love with him, and, as the rocket blasts off, they sing of their future together beneath the 'Seven Moons of Beta Lyrae', much to the consternation of Major General John Vanneman (Brian Keith). This mildly amusing film was shown on The Wonderful World of Color television series in 1966.

CHICO, THE MISUNDERSTOOD COYOTE (Sp) Director Walter Perkins. When his mother is killed by hunters, Chico grows up with a hatred for man. Actually made for The Wonderful World of Color television series in 1961, the film, which is similar in style to the True-Life Adventures, underlines the animal's vulnerability at the hands of man and won audience sympathy for the coyote's struggle to survive and escape the restraints of captivity.

A STORM CALLED MARIA (Ed) Director Ken Nelson. Released on 16mm in 1962 but originally shown on the Walt Disney Presents tv series in 1959, the film, with a screenplay by James Algar and Larry Clemmons, from George R. Stewart's book Storm, is narrated by Don Holt. It follows the devastating effect of hurricanes on land and at sea, and, using newsreel footage, explains man's attempts to survive these terrifying events.

THE PRINCE AND THE PAUPER (F) Director Don Chaffey. First shown on The Wonderful World of Color television series in March 1962, the film was released theatrically abroad. Based on the book by Mark Twain, the film stars Guy Williams (star of the tv series Zorro), Laurence Naismith, Donald Houston, Sean Scully and Niall MacGinnis. Prince Edward, son of Henry VIII, meets pauper Tom Canty. They change places with each other and have many exciting adventures. An extract in the Films As Literature series was released on 16mm in 1978.

LITTLE LEAGUE MOOCHIE (F) Child star Kevin Corcoran, who appeared in a number of Disney feature films including Swiss Family Robinson, became the star of his own tv serial on Walt Disney Presents in 1959. Two of the episodes were edited into a 16mm release co-starring James Brown, Frances Rafferty, Reginald Owen and Stuart Erwin. Montgomery Morgan Jr, Moochie to his friends, is a 10-year-old baseball fanatic determined to make the Little League team.

☆ BON VOYAGE (F) Director James Neilson. In one of the few Hollywood films to poke fun at an American family's visit to Europe, Fred MacMurray, popular tv star of My Three Sons, plays Harry Willard, who, together with his long-suffering wife (Jane Wyman), daughter (Deborah Walley) and two sons (Tommy Kirk and Kevin Corcoran), finds himself encountering all sorts of problems in Paris. Willard gets lost in the city sewers (a scene witnessed by 16 million people on Disney's Christmas television show in 1961 as a teaser for the film's spring release) and is propositioned by a street-walker in a scene that, like a bar-room sequence in Popeye (1981), seems strangely out of place in a Disney film. Based on the book by Marrijane and Joseph Hayes and with a screenplay adapted by Bill Walsh, the film was shot entirely on location. The catchy theme-song was written by Richard and Robert Sherman. Walt Disney and his family often visited Europe, which was why he was particularly fond of this film.

BIG RED (F) Director Norman Tokar. Dogs, whether of the animated variety as in One Hundred and One Dalmatians or, as here, a real-life Irish Setter, mean good box-office. Walter

Pidgeon stars as James Haggin, who is jealous of the bond between his dog and a young orphan, Rene Dumont (Gilles Payant, below with Walter Pidgeon). When Red and his mate escape from a train, Rene goes into the wilderness to look for them. Now concerned for the boy's safety, Haggin sets off after him but is trapped by a mountain lion. In the nick of time, however, he is rescued by Dumont and Big Red, and the three are reunited. The story was based on the novels of Jim Kjelgaard and filmed in La Malbaie, a small French-Canadian town on the shores of the St Lawrence River. It was shown on the television series *Wonderful World of Color* in 1964.

A FIRE CALLED JEREMIAH (Sp) Director James Algar. First shown on *The Wonderful World of Color* in 1961 but released theatrically outside the US, the film tells the true story of the 'Smoke Jumpers', the men and women trained by the Forestry Department to alert the authorities to the whereabouts of potential forest fires and to fight those fires.

DISNEYLAND AFTER DARK (Sp) Directors William Beaudine and Hamilton Luske. Featuring highlights of the theme park's many stage shows throughout the year, the special was first screened on *The Wonderful World of Color* in 1962 and includes as guests Louis Armstrong, Annette Funicello, Bobby Burgess and the Osmond Brothers.

YOU – AND YOUR SENSE OF SMELL AND TASTE (Ed) The seventh film in the popular This Is You series hosted by Jiminy Cricket shows students the relationship between aromas and their influence on the taste buds.

YOU – AND YOUR SENSE OF TOUCH (Ed). The last film in this excellent series explores in simple animation the sensations of cold, heat, pressure and pain as perceived by the brain.

ALMOST ANGELS (UK: BORN TO SING) (F) Director Steve Previn. The location Austria – three years before American audiences 'discovered' the country in *The Sound of Music* – but instead of singing nuns, there was the Vienna Boys' Choir.

Unfortunately the film is rather mediocre and succeeds only in its appraisal of the Choir's virtuoso performances, but Disney was encouraged by its box-office performance to continue shooting films in Europe. The film was released as the support feature to a re-issue of *Lady and the Tramp*, and its publicity read 'BOYSTEROUS DOGS and the DOG-GONDEST BOYS!' It was shown on the *Wonderful World of Color* series in 1965.

THE HUNTING INSTINCT (F) Director Hamilton Luske. Professor Ludwig Von Drake, one of Donald's relations and a star after frequent tv appearances on *The Wonderful World of Color*, subjects host Walt Disney to a lecture on the topic of hunting. The film, first shown on American television in 1961, contains the following shorts, interspersed with footage of Von Drake and his little buddy, a beetle called Herman: *Bootle Beetle, The Pointer, Clown of the Jungle, The Lone Chipmunks, R'Coon Dawg, Tiger Trouble, The Plastics Inventor, Contrary Condor, The Fox Hunt* and *Rugged Bear*.

THE LEGEND OF LOBO (F) Co-producer James Algar. 'His name became a legend cross the great

southwest,' is how narrator Rex Allen and the Sons of the Pioneers begin their stirring ballad. The film, based on a story by Ernest Thompson Seton and photographed by True-Life Adventure veteran Jack Couffer, tells how Lobo, king of the wolfpack, is feared by the cattle herders. When the herders capture his mate, Lobo leads the pack in an attack on the farm, and, together once more, the animals head into the northern wilderness to escape re-capture. Not as attractive visually as *Perri* (1957) nor as entertaining as *The Incredible Journey* (1963), the film is still an example of how expert film-making can be combined with technical ability to produce a convincing animal story.

STAMPEDE AT BITTER CREEK (F) Director Henry Keller. Released theatrically outside America, this is the third film to be made up from episodes of *Texas John Slaughter* shown on the *Walt Disney Presents* television series in 1958 and 1959. Tom Tryon stars as Slaughter, who resigns from the Texas Rangers and sets up home on a cattle ranch. Co-stars in this below-average western adventure are Stephen McNally, Grant Williams, Sidney Blackmer and Bill Williams.

THE PIGEON THAT WORKED A MIRACLE (Sp) Director Walter Perkins. First shown on the *Disneyland* television series in 1958, this featurette tells how Chad Smith (Brad Payne), a young crippled boy, finds the strength to walk again when he cares for a neglected pigeon he calls 'Pidge'. Winston Hibler was Associate Producer and the script was written by Otto Englander.

IN SEARCH OF THE CASTAWAYS (F) Director Robert Stevenson. 'A thousand thrills and Hayley Mills!' – the sort of advertising to set the pulses of many a red-blooded male racing, although it must be admitted that the 'thrills' when Disney met Jules Verne for the second time somewhat detract from Miss Mills, who, together with the rest of the cast – Maurice Chevalier, Wilfrid Hyde-White and George Sanders – has to take second place to the special effects. Based on *Among the Cannibals* (an adaptation of Jules Verne's *Les Enfants du Capitaine Grant*), the film tells how teenager Mary Grant (Hayley Mills, above with Maurice Chevalier), her brother Robert (Keith Hampshire) and Jacques Paganel (Maurice Chevalier) persuade a wealthy shipping magnate (Wilfrid Hyde-White) to journey to South America in search of the children's father. Their adventures take them to Australia and then to New Zealand, but not before special effects expert Syd Pearson has thrown an earthquake, avalanche, flash flood, waterspout, giant condor

and erupting volcano at them. Almost as entertaining as Henry Levin's *Journey to the Centre of the Earth* and far superior to Disney's *Island At the Top of the World*, the film was promoted as being more exciting than *Swiss Family Robinson*. Capitalizing on Levin's approach to Verne, Disney includes some songs by Richard and Robert Sherman, including the catchy 'Enjoy It', which is sung by Chevalier and Mills. Rereleased on a number of occasions worldwide and billed as 'An earthquake of entertainment', the film has taken over $10 million at the US box-office since its initial release.

☆ A SYMPOSIUM ON POPULAR SONGS (Sp) Director Bill Justice. Described by the Studio as 'a new twist on the old *ragtime*', this entertaining look at several famous songs is illustrated by stop-motion figures made up from kitchen utensils and pieces of fabric (above), and is hosted by Ludwig Von Drake. An educational version was released on 16mm in 1980.

SIX GUN LAW (F). The second feature film compiled from episodes of the *Walt Disney Presents* tv series *The Nine Lives of Elfego Baca* stars Robert Loggia as Baca. Released in the UK, the film relates what happens when the lawyer saves an old friend from being wrongly accused of robbing a bank and wins an important case against his former law partner, J. Henry Newman. Co-stars in this western adventure were Annette Funicello and James Dunn.

1963

SON OF FLUBBER (F) Director Robert Stevenson. With the exception of television episodes strung together into features and released abroad, this was the first-ever sequel to a major theatrical release. Continuing his adventures begun in *The Absent Minded Professor* (1961), Ned Brainard (Fred MacMurray), experiments with 'Dry Rain', a special kind of gun that creates artificial clouds when fired at the sky. His student Biff Hawk (Tommy Kirk) has meanwhile created a variation of 'Flubber' called 'Flubbergas', which enables

the college football team to win an important game (below). Made in black and white, with some highly inventive special effects, the film features amusing performances from co-stars Nancy Olson, Keenan Wynn, Charlie Ruggles and Paul Lynde, and it even marks the acting debut of Walt's grandson, Walter Elias Disney Miller.

THE HORSE WITHOUT A HEAD (F) Director Don Chaffey. 'The most daring crime since the dawn of time,' claimed the publicity, although it isn't as gruesome as the title suggests, because the horse isn't real. It belongs to a gang of French children, and stashed inside it is the key to some money stolen by crooks Schiapa (Herbert Lom) and Roublot (Leo McKern), while hot on *their* heels is

Inspector Sinet (Jean-Pierre Aumont). The film's catchy theme-song, 'Knights of the Headless Horse', was composed by the Sherman brothers. Based on Paul Berna's *A Hundred Million Francs*, this French production was not a runaway success at the European box-office. Originally made for showing on the *Wonderful World of Color* television series, it was shown on tv in late 1963.

MIRACLE OF THE WHITE STALLIONS (F) Director Arthur Hiller. 'The day a war stood still ... One of the great untold stories of World War II.' Robert Taylor gives a rather dull performance as Colonel Alois Podhajsky, the man responsible for rescuing the famous Lipizzan horses of the Spanish Riding School in Vienna during World War II. Lilli Palmer co-stars as his wife Verena, while Curt Jurgens plays General Tellheim, who is sympathetic with the Colonel's plans. Eventually, with the help of the US 20th Army Corps, the horses are evacuated to safety under the leadership of General Patton (John Larch). Based on Colonel Podhajsky's book *The Dancing White Horses of Vienna*, the film features a catchy song 'Just Say Auf Wiedersehen' by Richard and Robert Sherman but suffers from a pedestrian script. Shown on American television and sold in Europe as 'primarily adult entertainment' with the word 'Flight' used instead of 'Miracle', it's a neatly structured film but of definitely limited appeal to non-horse-lovers.

SAMMY, THE WAY-OUT SEAL (F) Director Norman Tokar. Originally made for *The Wonderful World of Color* television series in 1962 and released theatrically in the UK, the film stars Billy Mumy and Michael McGreevey as two small boys who nurse a baby seal back to health and, unbeknown to their parents, smuggle it home. As usual in films of this type, Sammy escapes and causes a considerable amount of havoc around town. Sammy steals every scene, while co-stars Robert Culp, Patricia Barry and Jack Carson do their best. ...

ESCAPADE IN FLORENCE (F) Director Steve Previn. 'It's a wow ... and how!' claimed the publicity.

Starring Annette Funicello and Tommy Kirk (above), the film relates how two students thwart a gang of art thieves when they attempt to pirate the art treasures of Florence. It was the first major film to be shot by Disney in Italy and was originally made for *The Wonderful World of Color* tv series in 1962. Not a particularly memorable movie, it was released theatrically only outside the US as a supporting feature to *Son of Flubber*.

SAVAGE SAM (F) Director Norman Tokar. 'How long is it,' asked the promotional material, 'since you've played a picture with guts – a picture that publicity-wise you can really get your teeth into, fully confident that you will not be misleading the public in your efforts to try and get them in?' Those exhibitors who followed the syntax were probably lost for an answer, but certainly this sequel to the Studio's successful *Old Yeller* (1957) was sufficiently action packed to sell itself. Based on the book by Fred Gipson, the film stars Tommy Kirk and Kevin Corcoran as the two brothers, Travis and Arliss, who are left to fend for themselves while their parents are in San Antonio. When they and a visiting neighbour, Lisbeth Searcy (Marta Kristen), are kidnapped by Indians, Travis' dog, Savage Sam, leads Uncle Beck (Brian Keith) and a rescue party to save them. Although Tokar handled the drama and action scenes, culminating in a furious battle between the rescuers and the Indians, competently, the film lacks the warmth and sentiment so apparent in *Old Yeller* and it failed at the box-office. As usual in these cases, it was quickly snapped up for a screening on *The Wonderful World of Color* (1966).

YELLOWSTONE CUBS (F) Producer Charles Draper. Bear cubs Tuffy and Tubby hide inside a motorist's trailer at Yellowstone National Park. Their mother Nokomis causes an uproar when she sets out to find them. Eventually shown on *The Wonderful World of Color* in 1965.

MICKEY MOUSE PARADE This cartoon compilation featuring 11 shorts was premiered in Germany.

SUMMER MAGIC (F) Director James Neilson. Large posters emblazoned with the words 'Hayley's here!' and featuring a smiling portrait of the Studio's most bankable star heralded the arrival of this feature, which was based on Kate Douglas Wiggin's *Mother Carey's Chickens*. Cinema audiences began to believe that they were sharing in the growing up of one of the screen's most popular teenagers, as Miss Mills celebrates her 17th birthday and another whirlwind romance, this time with co-star Peter Brown. Hayley plays Nancy Carey, who, together with her recently widowed mother Margaret (Dorothy McGuire) and her two brothers, sets up home in a dilapidated house in Maine. Burl Ives is on hand as town postmaster Osh Popham, and there's plenty of opportunity for the cast to sing a selection of catchy songs by Richard and Robert Sherman, most notably Ives' rendition of 'The Ugly Bug Ball'. Although it was not a huge success artistically, the movie did quite well at the box-office, due, no doubt, largely to the popularity of its English star. It was shown on *The Wonderful World of Color* in 1965.

GOLDEN HORSESHOE REVUE (Sp) Director Ron Miller. In 1962 Walt Disney's son-in-law, Ron Miller, was assigned the job of directing a tv tribute to the 10,000th performance of Disneyland's longest running stage show at the Golden Horseshoe. Little did anybody realize at the time that this humorous slice of Wild-West-saloon-style entertainment would still be running two decades later, nor that it would be listed in the *Guinness Book of Records* as the world's most enduring stage show, with over 40,000 performances. Although a number of film and television personalities appeared on stage during the revue, the real star was comedian Wally Boag, whose name was immortalized on a window above Main Street U.S.A.'s Ice Cream Parlor, when he retired after 28 years in 1982. In this early film tribute, Boag is joined by Walt Disney, Annette Funicello, Gene Sheldon, Ed Wynn and Betty Taylor, who regularly played the character 'Slue Foot Sue'. Originally shown on *The Wonderful World of Color* in 1962.

THE INCREDIBLE JOURNEY (F) Director Fletcher Markle. Although the acting leaves a lot to be desired, the sheer visual entertainment more than compensates – but then the real stars of this story are three scene-stealing animals: Bodger, a bull terrier, Tao, a Siamese cat, and Luath, a Labrador retriever (below). Together they survive the hazards of a 250-mile journey across mountainous Canadian wilderness to reach their home. Emile Genest and John Drainie are among the human cast, and the film is narrated by Rex Allen (who provided a whimsical voice-over on a number of Disney animal pictures). The Canadian backwoods are remarkably captured on film by True-Life Adventure photographers

Jack Couffer and Lloyd Beebe, and watching the three animals defend themselves against fast-flowing rivers, angry grizzly bears, a porcupine and a mountain lion makes one appreciate the technical expertise involved in this type of film. Disney's second co-production with Cangary Ltd, the film was based on a book by Sheila Burnford. A 16mm extract in the Films As Literature series was released in 1979.

DR SYN, ALIAS THE SCARECROW (F) Director James Neilson. In 1937 George Arliss starred in a film based on Russell Thorndyke's novels about the adventures of Dr Syn, an 18th-century vicar in Dymchurch, England, who acted like a latter-day Robin Hood. In 1962 Hammer Films twisted the plot and cast Peter Cushing as Captain Clegg. A year later Walt Disney brought the mysterious Dr Syn to the screen once more. The Disney version was released theatrically in Europe and was shown in three parts on The Wonderful World of Color tv series in 1964 under the title The Scarecrow of Romney Marsh. Patrick McGoohan stars as the seemingly innocent vicar of Dymchurch who transforms his saintly attire into the tattered rags of the smuggler known as The Scarecrow. Unlike the Hammer version, Disney keeps The Scarecrow's identity secret from the authorities and makes him a thoroughly likable rogue. In his second picture for Disney – he had just completed The Three Lives of Thomasina (see below) – Patrick McGoohan is perfect, playing the dual roles of Dr Syn and the Scarecrow with total conviction. A fine British supporting cast includes George Cole, Tony Britton, Michael Hordern and Patrick Wymark, and the film features some stunning location shots of the sweeping marshlands of the Kent-Sussex coast of England. Terry Gilkyson wrote a 'Scarecrow' song. Usually shown as a supporting feature, the 98-minute film was subsequently re-issued in an abridged version lasting only 75 minutes.

THE THREE LIVES OF THOMASINA (F) Director Don Chaffey. Before Karen Dotrice and Matthew Garber met up with their wonderful nanny Mary Poppins, they starred together in a heart-warming story based on a book by Paul Gallico.

It is as charming a picture as Greyfriars Bobby and, thanks to a strong cast led by Patrick McGoohan and Susan Hampshire, infinitely more enjoyable. The film tells the story of Scottish veterinarian Andrew MacDhui and his daughter Mary, whose affection for a beautiful cat called Thomasina comes between them. When the cat is seriously injured, Mary's father 'puts the cat to sleep', but Thomasina is discovered by Lori MacGregor, who nurses the cat back to health. Her love and understanding finally reunite father and daughter in a touching climax. Co-stars include Laurence Naismith and Finlay Currie, and although the film was not a huge box-office success, it is considered one of the best of the foreign productions released by the Studio during the early 1960s. In 1965 it was screened on The Wonderful World of Color in three parts.

☆ THE SWORD IN THE STONE (F) Director Wolfgang Reitherman. Described on the original poster as a 'whiz-bang Whizard of whimsy!' the feature-length animated film was greeted with a mixed reaction by audiences and critics alike. It was animator Reitherman's first solo directorial credit on a full-length picture, but it was another example of the Studio's cost-cutting approach towards animation (the first being One Hundred and One Dalmatians). Based on the book by T.H. White, the story, adapted for the screen by Bill Peet, relates the legend of young King Arthur, who is befriended by Merlin, 'the world's most powerful magician', and his talking owl Archimedes (above). Arthur, nicknamed Wart by his guardian Sir Ector, learns through a series of magical adventures some very valuable lessons, although even Merlin fails to realize that the boy is on his way to greater fame, for only he will be able to pull the mystical sword from the stone and take his rightful place as King of all England. Apart from the bumbling Merlin, voiced by Karl Swenson, the plucky Wart (Ricky Sorenson) and the scene-stealing Archimedes (Junius Matthews), the other characters lack depth. Fortunately, the film makes good use of its limited animation techniques, especially in the marvellous wizards' duel, in which Merlin and the evil

Madame Mim (voiced by Martha Wentworth) transform themselves into a variety of animals, and the beautifully rendered backgrounds by Walt Peregoy, Bill Layne, Al Dempster, Anthony Rizzo, Ralph Hulett and Fil Mottola more than make up for any shortcomings in the draughtsmanship of the characters. Lack-lustre songs by the Sherman brothers, which are seldom heard outside the film, help to keep the story moving. Not a great success financially, even on re-issue, the film did eventually inspire the inclusion of a Sword in the Stone ceremony at Disneyland in 1984.

1964

THE MISADVENTURES OF MERLIN JONES (F) Director Robert Stevenson. The publicity campaign in Europe went to great pains to explain to the obviously 'square' exhibitors what the word 'kook' means: 'a scrambled egg-head, way-out and wacky,' it told them. 'A gink with a kink living on cloud 9, the campus crackpot who's flipped his lid! Got it?' Fortunately for the now more than ever confused theatre-owners, the kids did, and this weird tale of how oddball inventor Merlin Jones (Tommy Kirk) and his girlfriend Jennifer (Annette Funicello) get mixed up reading people's minds by means of a strange contraption and then get involved with hypnotism and a stolen chimpanzee is both fast paced and amusing. The film's episodic nature looks as if it was originally intended as a television show, but it was successful enough to warrant a sequel, The Monkey's Uncle (1965). The film's title song was written by the Sherman Brothers and sung by Annette.

★ MARY POPPINS (F) Director Robert Stevenson. By the end of the 1950s musicals were becoming something of a rarity in Hollywood. Walt had, in fact, largely avoided any large-scale live-action musical because his animated films with their memorable songs continued to sweep the board. Finally, in the early 1960s, a story about a magical nanny by English writer P.L. Travers persuaded Disney that the time was right for a lavish musical spectacular, quite unlike anything he had done before. Adapted for the screen by veteran writers

Bill Walsh and Don Da Gradi, *Mary Poppins* was an overnight sensation. Although some members of the Studio staff couldn't understand why Disney was spending so much money on what other film companies now considered to be 'old hat', Walt's instinct was, as usual, right. Audiences flocked to the film, and the sale of merchandise added daily to the phenomenal box-office takings, which are to date (1987) over $45 million in the US alone. After a glittering London premiere, the film was nominated for no fewer than 13 Academy Awards (it won in five categories – Best Actress, Film Editing, Original Score, Song and Special Visual Effects). The story concerns the arrival of Mary Poppins as the new nanny to children Jane and Michael Banks. Much to the youngsters' delight, she turns out to be a wonderful person who takes them on all kinds of marvellous magical adventures accompanied by their friend Bert (opposite right and above). Mary even manages to break down the barriers that had existed between the children and their authoritarian father. The star of the film is undoubtedly Julie Andrews, who, like the character she plays, is 'practically perfect in every way', whether it's floating gently down to Earth, umbrella in one hand and carpet-bag clutched firmly in the other, or singing and dancing to one of the film's numerous production numbers. She was ably supported by Dick Van Dyke as Bert, who, cockney accent aside, gives a *tour de force*. Anyone less talented might have been completely upstaged by Miss Andrews' screen presence, but his musical routines with her are captivating and thoroughly delightful. Excellent performances

are also provided by David Tomlinson and Glynis Johns as Mr and Mrs Banks, Matthew Garber and Karen Dotrice as the children, Ed Wynn as Uncle Albert and Hermione Baddeley as Ellen the maid. The film's unforgettable songs, including 'Supercalifragilisticexpialidocious', 'Chim-Chim-Cheree', 'A Spoonful of Sugar', 'Jolly Holiday' and the haunting 'Feed the Birds', are among the best that the Sherman Brothers ever penned for a Disney film. Set in Edwardian London, the film's impressive sets were constructed within the confines of the Studio and their story-book appearance adds an amazing air of fantasy to the whole proceedings. This is particularly apparent in the highly energetic and furious chimney-sweep dance number. One of the film's highlights is the 'Jolly Holiday' sequence which combines live-action with some amusing animated characters, although the inclusion of dancing 'penguins' seems out of place in the English countryside. The animated sequence was directed by Hamilton Luske, with special effects by Eustace Lycett and Robert A. Mattey.

In the short time between the film's release and his death in 1966, Walt discarded any plans for a sequel, while Julie Andrews went on to star in one of 20th Century-Fox's most successful films, *The Sound of Music*. In later years, however, the Studio attempted to recapture the spirit of 'Poppins' in a number of big screen musicals – *Bedknobs and Broomsticks* and *Pete's Dragon*, for example – but their failure, both artistic and financial, helped to underline the fact that there could be only one *Mary Poppins*, a screen great and a personal triumph for Walt Disney.

GOOFY SPORTS STORY (Sp) Goofy, the Studio's most lovable character, appeared in a number of shorts depicting various sporting activities over the years. Most were directed by Jack Kinney, whose combined work appeared in this compilation, which was first shown on the *Disneyland* television series in 1956. In this film, which is, according to a Studio document, 'dedicated to sports and good sportsmanship', Goofy explores the athletic origins of the Olympic Games.

GERONIMO'S REVENGE (F) Directors James Neilson and Harry Keller. Author Tom Tryon began his career as an actor and was a great success on the tv series *Walt Disney Presents* playing cowboy hero Texas John Slaughter. In the feature-length movie, adapted from episodes shown on tv in 1960 and released theatrically in Europe, Slaughter desperately tries to prevent Geronimo from ending the peace that has been established with the Apaches. Darryl Hickman co-stars.

HANS BRINKER, OR THE SILVER SKATES (F) Director Norman Foster. Of the Disney feature films produced in Europe, a number were made specifically for screening on the Disney television shows. The film, which was based on Mary Mapes Dodge's book, relates how the young Hans Brinker, played by Rony Zeander, loses an important skating competition but turns his disappointment into a true victory by bringing much needed finance to his family. Shot on 16mm amid the beautiful scenery of Zuider Zee in Holland, the film was shown on *The Wonderful World of Color* in 1962.

THE SILVER FOX AND SAM DAVENPORT (F) Director Henry Schloss. With narration written by Winston Hibler and Roy E. Disney, the featurette was first shown on *The Wonderful World of Color* television series in 1962. Domino, a silver fox with a pelt worth $1,000 is chased onto Sam Davenport's farm. The wily animal manages to elude the farmer and his dog and escape into the safety of a neighbouring valley. Gordon L. Perry stars as Sam Davenport in this engaging little drama, which was released on a double bill in the UK with a John Wayne western.

DONALD DUCK GOES WEST First released in Sweden in 1964, this compilation of 10 shorts with a distinctly Wild West flavour was eventually released in the UK in 1975.

FESTIVAL DE DIBUJOS ANIMADOS A compilation of 10 animated shorts released theatrically in Argentina.

THE TATTOOED POLICE HORSE (Sp) Director Larry Lansburgh. Jolly Roger, a registered trotting horse, is officially banned from racing for continuously breaking from a trot into a gallop. Purchased for use by a Boston police captain (below), the horse eventually proves himself a champion back on the racetrack. Jolly Roger's co-stars are Sandy Saunders, Charles Seel and Shirley Skiles.

THE WALTZ KING (F) Director Steve Previn. First shown in 1963 on *The Wonderful World of Color* television series in two parts, the film was released in Europe early the following year. It stars Kerwin Mathews in the title role of Johann Strauss Jr (above). Although it was not the first time the Strauss family was immortalized on celluloid, the role made a change for Mathews, who had spent a great deal of his career fighting mythical creatures in the fantasy films of Ray Harryhausen. Co-stars Senta Berger, as opera singer and sweetheart Yetty Treffz, and Brian Aherne, as Strauss Sr, help explore the tempestuous life and loves of the Viennese composer. Filmed at the Rosenhügel Studios in Austria, the dazzling musical sequences are splendidly captured by Gunther Anders' photography.

THE MERRY TROUPE This cartoon compilation featuring eight individual shorts was premiered in Italy.

A TIGER WALKS (F) Director Norman Tokar. Brian Keith found himself in a variety of roles in five Disney films during the 1960s. As sheriff Pete Williams he is shamed by his daughter Julie (Pamela Franklin) into rescuing an escaped circus tiger (right) which is terrorizing a small American town. Co-stars Vera Miles and Kevin Corcoran lend admirable support in this exposé of small-town politics, which also features veteran film star Sabu. A moderate success at the box-office, it was shown on *The Wonderful World of Color* television series in 1966.

FLASH, THE TEENAGE OTTER (Sp) Director Hank Schloss. As movies about teenagers became more successful in the early 1960s, Disney incorporated the idea into a featurette about a family of otters. The film was first screened on the television series *Walt Disney Presents* in 1961. An adaptation of the screenplay by Rutherford Montgomery was published soon after and relates the adventures of the otter, Flash, and his family.

SANCHO, THE HOMING STEER (F) Director Tom McGowan. First shown on *The Wonderful World of Color* tv series in 1962 and released on 16mm in 1964, this is the story of a longhorn steer, whose instinct drives him home across 1,500 miles of hazardous terrain from Montana to Texas. It stars Bill Shurley, Rosita Fernandez, Arthur Custis and is narrated by Rex Allen.

FOUR ARTISTS PAINT ONE TREE (Ed) A short made to demonstrate the various styles that can be adopted, by four Disney artists, to paint one subject – a stately old oak tree. It was screened on the Disney television show in 1958 and released on 16mm as an educational film.

GRAND PARADE OF WALT DISNEY Released in Germany under the title *Lustige Micky Maus Revue*, this compilation features 10 classic shorts.

EMIL AND THE DETECTIVES (F) Director Peter Tewksbury. Erich Kästner's book had already been filmed on numerous occasions before the Disney version was released in 1964. The plot relates what happens when Emil (Bryan Russell) and a group of young detectives uncover a plot by The Baron (Walter Slezak) to rob the Berlin Bank. The film, the first Disney movie to be shot at the UFA Studios in West Germany, was warmly received by the critics, but, unfortunately, although the Studio tried to generate publicity by encouraging youngsters to partake in Sherlock Holmes-type adventures, the film failed to do much business at the box-office. It was shown on *The Wonderful World of Color* in 1966.

THE MOON-SPINNERS (F) Director James Neilson. Still a highly bankable star, Hayley Mills appears in her fifth Disney film. Arriving in Greece with her aunt (Joan Greenwood), Nikky Ferris (Hayley Mills) meets handsome Englishman, Mark Camford (Peter McEnery, opposite above). Camford, who has been framed for a robbery by hotelier Stratos (Eli Wallach) finds an ally in Nikky, and together they work on a plan to clear his name. Although the Studio publicity hinted that this was the film in which teenage Hayley 'gets her man', she is strangely ignored by the over-melodramatic Camford, who spins out his explanation for being after Stratos, thus causing the film to move at a snail's pace. Pola Negri co-

196

stars in her first screen role for 20 years, although her commitment to the film meant that only interiors could be shot at Pinewood Studios, England, and it remains something of a mystery why the Studio was so keen to cast her in the first place. Despite the stunningly photographed Greek countryside and a catchy musical score by Ron Grainer, with songs by Terry Gilkyson, *The Moon-Spinners* was a moderate box-office success. It was shown in three instalments on *The Wonderful World of Color* in 1966.

1965

MAGIC OF THE RAILS (Sp) Having successfully produced a 360° film for the Italia '61 Exposition in Turin, Disney was hired by the Swiss Federal Railways to make a *Circle-Vision* special of a train tour through Europe. It was shown at an exposition in Lucerne and later in Germany.

STEEL AND AMERICA (Ed) Produced for the American Iron and Steel Institute, the 16mm release stars Donald Duck and combines live-action footage with animation to tell the story of steel from ore to finished product. In 1974 a revised and updated version was released.

THOSE CALLOWAYS (F) Director Norman Tokar. Based on Paul Annixter's *Swiftwater*, this touching and moving story tells of burly forester Cam Calloway (Brian Keith) and his desire to construct a wildlife sanctuary outside the New England town of Swiftwater. The crux of the tale is whether the townspeople will give him their support or sell out to a wealthy businessman, and there are plenty of exciting subplots to keep the film moving along. Vera Miles and Brandon de Wilde co-star as Cam's long suffering wife and son, and Ed Wynn and Walter Brennan turn in two excellent performances in supporting roles. Lloyd Beebe, who worked on numerous animal pictures for Disney, handled the wildlife sequences, and the songs were written by Richard and Robert Sherman, while veteran Hollywood composer Max Steiner was commissioned to write the film's lush score. An extract was

released on 16mm in 1975 entitled *Responsibility: What Are Its Limits?*

THE MONKEY'S UNCLE (F) Director Robert Stevenson. In this sequel to *The Misadventures of Merlin Jones*, Tommy Kirk and Annette Funicello (below) were teamed up to continue the adventures of 'crackpot' scientist Merlin Jones and his long-suffering girlfriend Jennifer. Accompanying them in this episodic story, which features a chimpanzee called Stanley and an experimental man-powered flying machine, are co-stars Leon Ames, Frank Faylen and Arthur O'Connell. The theme-song, written by the Shermans, was sung by Annette and the Beach Boys. The

exhibitors were rather condescendingly told: 'Don't be an old grouch! Life's too short to take seriously – get out and sell [the film] for laughs – and have laughs doing it.'

THAT DARN CAT! (F) Director Robert Stevenson. Hayley Mills' last theatrical film for Disney was based on the book *Undercover Cat* by Mildred and Gordon Gordon. A pet Siamese (above), referred to by his mistress, Patti Randall (Hayley Mills'), as D.C. (Darn Cat), stumbles on a kidnapping when he follows the purchaser of some appetizing salmon back to a strange apartment. Patti is suspicious of some scratches on D.C.'s collar and, against her sister's wishes, calls in the

Federal Security Agency. Enter Zeke Kelso, an enthusiastic, but feline-allergic investigator, played by Dean Jones. With D.C.'s help they track down the villains, Iggy (Frank Gorshin) and his accomplice Dan (Neville Brand), and rescue hostage Margaret Miller (Grayson Hall). A catchy title song by the Sherman brothers and sung by Bobby Darin adds to the film's appeal, as does an amusing cameo performance from Roddy McDowall as next-door neighbour Gregory Benson. Dorothy Provine stands around looking pretty, but the film's 116 minutes tend to drag in places. As usual in films of this nature, the cat (who also played Tao in *The Incredible Journey*) steals most of the scenes.

A COUNTRY COYOTE GOES HOLLYWOOD (F) Director Winston Hibler. The film opens with its title imprinted in cement outside Grauman's Chinese Theater in Hollywood. Chico the Coyote hitches a lift on a truck bound for Los Angeles, but when he causes problems among the residents near Griffith Park, he and other coyotes are rounded up and put back in the wild. But starved of city life, Chico hitches another ride, this time on a truck headed for New York. It was later shown on *The Wonderful World of Color* television series.

FREEWAYPHOBIA No. 1 (G) Director Les Clark. In a film geared toward a more adult audience, Goofy introduces students to the rules of safe driving, reliving his role of the motorist from *Motor Mania* (1950), as well as Motoramus Fidgitus, Driverius Timidicus, Stupidicus Ultimus and Neglecterus Maximus. Goofy illustrates the regulations governing driving on and off the freeway. *Freewayphobia No. 2* was released as *Goofy's Freeway Trouble* (see below).

THE LEGEND OF YOUNG DICK TURPIN (F) Director James Neilson. This re-telling of the classic tale of the most famous highwayman of them all omits Turpin's last ride to York, which resulted in the death of his horse Black Bess, by restricting its story to the rogue's earlier adventures. It was one of Disney's last films to be made in Europe in the 1960s. Made in England with an all-British cast, which includes David Weston, Bernard Lee (in his second film for Disney), George Cole and Maurice Denham, the film was shown on *The Wonderful World of Color* tv series in 1966.

WALT DISNEY'S FUN PARADE Featuring eight individual shorts and an extract from *Snow White and the Seven Dwarfs*, the feature-length compilation was premiered in Italy.

KIDS IS KIDS (Sp) Director Hamilton Luske. This package of five Donald Duck cartoons includes linking footage starring child psychologist Ludwig Von Drake. First shown on *The Wonderful World of Color* in 1961, it was repeated years later under its alternative titles *Donald Duck Quacks Up* and *Mickey and Donald Kidding Around*. It contains a series of classic encounters between Donald and his nephews.

SQUARE PEG IN A ROUND HOLE (Sp) Director Hamilton Luske. First shown on *The Wonderful World of Color* tv series in 1963, this combination of live action and animation features Professor Ludwig Von Drake, who calls upon his nephew, Donald, to explain man's foibles and human behaviour in general. Also known as *Goofing Around with Donald Duck*, the film features, among others, the short *Beezy Bear*.

THE WAHOO BOBCAT (Sp) Producer Hank Schloss. First shown on *The Wonderful World of Color* tv series in 1963, the film tells the story of Tiger, an aging Florida bobcat, who is unjustly accused of raiding the chicken house. In a happy ending, the bobcat is taken to a small island where he will be free for the rest of his days.

VON DRAKE IN SPAIN (Sp) Director Norman Foster; associate producer Hamilton Luske. First shown on *The Wonderful World of Color* television series in 1962, the featurette stars the eccentric professor as he presents the country's most renowned dancers. There are live-action sequences of José Greco and Rafael de Cordova.

PILE OU FARCES DE WALT DISNEY Premiered in France, the feature-length compilation contains 11 shorts featuring Mickey and the gang.

GOOFY'S FREEWAY TROUBLE (G) Director Les Clark. Having expounded the problems of bad driving in *Freewayphobia No. 1* Goofy again assumes the role of Stupidicus Ultimus. As a careless motorist, he ignores the state of his tyres and the mechanical condition of his vehicle.

JOHNNY SHILOH (F) Director James Neilson. This drama of the American Civil War was released theatrically in Japan but had been first screened on *The Wonderful World of Color* in 1963. Kevin Corcoran plays the role of drummer boy John Lincoln Clem, who inspires the Union forces to a victory at the Battle of Shiloh in Tennessee on 6 April 1862. Brian Keith (who went on to star in a number of Disney films) co-stars as Clem's friend, Sergeant Gabe.

CARNAVAL DE WALT DISNEY Released in Argentina, the feature-length compilation contains 10 classic shorts, the contents varying in other countries. A new version was released in December 1966.

1966

WINNIE THE POOH AND THE HONEY TREE (F) Director Wolfgang Reitherman. Although there was considerable controversy about the Studio's 'tampering' with A.A. Milne's classics – not least about the inclusion of an 'American' Gopher, voiced by Howard Morris – Pooh's 'Disney debut' is, on the whole, competently handled. Narrated by Sebastian Cabot (the voice of Bagheera in *The Jungle Book*), the story tells how Pooh borrows a balloon from Christopher Robin so that he can reach a bees' nest high in a tree. When this ends in disaster, Pooh invites himself round to Rabbit's house (below), where he eats so much honey that he becomes stuck in the doorway. Sterling Holloway, who was responsible for countless voices in previous Disney films, is perfect as the voice of Winnie the Pooh, and he gives a wonderful rendition of the delightful songs by Richard and Robert Sherman. Extremely popular with audiences, Pooh became a regular member of the Disney line-up of characters. Frequently re-issued, *Winnie the Pooh and the Honey Tree*, combined with two sequels, was made into a feature-length film in 1977.

THE UGLY DACHSHUND (F) Director Norman Tokar. Dean Jones and Suzanne Pleshette team up in this mediocre comedy, which was optimistically described in the publicity as 'hilarious havoc'. A young commercial artist, Mark Garrison, and his wife, Fran, adopt a Great Dane puppy and allow it to grow up with their family of dachshunds (right). A dog show and the usual animal antics add to the fun. Co-stars include Charlie Ruggles, Kelly Thordsen and Parley Baer.

BALLERINA (F) Director Norman Campbell. After the success of a story set among the choristers of The Vienna Boys' Choir, it was the turn of the Royal Danish Ballet. Mette Sorenson (Mette Honnigen) wants to become a ballerina but finds her parents are against the idea. An opportunity to dance professional ballet finally convinces Mette's family of her abilities. First shown on the television series *The Wonderful World of Color* in 1966, the film was released theatrically in Europe. In 1976 an educational extract appeared under the title *Your Career: Your Decision?*

THE TENDERFOOT (F) Director Byron Paul. First shown on *The Wonderful World of Color* tv series in 1964 and released theatrically in Europe as a supporting feature to *The Ugly Dachshund*, this above-average western stars Brandon de Wilde as Jim Tevis, who is tutored in the ways of the old west by experienced scout (and older brother of Kit Carson), Moses Carson (Brian Keith). After numerous encounters with Apaches, Tevis helps Carson to capture an army deserter who has escaped across the Mexican border. James Whitmore co-stars.

GRETA, THE MISFIT GREYHOUND (F) Director Larry Lansburgh. First screened on *The Wonderful World of Color* in 1963, this is a story of a racing greyhound, which, abandoned by her owner, is forced to try to survive in the wild. Fortunately, Greta befriends a collie named Chip and finds a secure home with his owner, Domingo, who teaches Greta how to be a sheepdog. The film's catchy theme-song by Richard and Robert Sherman was sung by Rex Allen, who also provided the narration.

ONE DAY AT TETON MARSH (Ed) Based on a book by Sally Carrighar, the 16mm film was first screened on *The Wonderful World of Color* tv series in 1964. A nature study, it describes the wildlife that lives in the swamps of Wyoming.

DONALD'S FIRE SURVIVAL PLAN (Ed) Revised in 1984 with new updated live-action footage and improved fire regulations, the 16mm film, which demonstrates the importance of fire prevention in the home, has been the recipient of a number of educational awards.

RUN, APPALOOSA, RUN! (F) Director Larry Lansburgh. Narrator Rex Allen tells the engaging story of one of the rare spotted Appaloosa horses named Sky Dancer by his Nez Perce Indian owner. Looking at times like a documentary, and eventually released on 16mm for educational purposes, the film follows the horse's adventures when, parted from its rider, it ends up in a rodeo. Sky Dancer eventually wins the dangerous Hell's Mountain Suicide Relay Race and is reunited with his owner. The cast includes Adele Palacios, Wilbur Plaugher and Jerry Gatlin.

A HOLSTER FULL OF LAW (F) Director James Neilson. Further television adventures of Texas John Slaughter (Tom Tryon) as he tries to clean up crime in the town of Tombstone. Originally shown on *Walt Disney Presents* in 1961 and released theatrically in Europe.

THE ADVENTURES OF DONALD DUCK Premiered in Germany, this compilation of 10 shorts features the irascible Duck.

FOLLOW ME BOYS (F) Director Norman Tokar. Not hugely successful with critics and cut on re-issue from 131 to 107 minutes, *Follow Me Boys*, was popular with audiences, who enjoyed shedding tears over this sentimental tale of saxophone player Clem Siddons (Fred MacMurray). Siddons decides to set up home in a small Illinois town, where he falls in love, marries Vida Downey (Vera Miles) and starts a Boy Scout troop that touches the hearts of the entire community. Based on Mackinlay Kantor's book *God and My Country*, this folksy tale co-stars Lillian Gish, Charlie Ruggles, Elliot Reid, Luana Patten and a very young Kurt Russell. Advance announcements for the film declared: 'Out of the ordinary things in life Walt Disney has fashioned an *extraordinary* motion picture.' This was backed up with what the campaign called 'a three-prong' plan of action: 'This is a family picture, this is an adult picture and this is a children's picture.' Obviously the Studio wanted to please everyone. To date, in the US, the film has grossed in excess of $7 million, and as recently as 1975 an educational extract was released entitled *Alcoholism: Who Gets Hurt?*

WINNIE THE POOH SHORTS PROGRAM The adventures of A.A. Milne's delightful bear headlined the six films featured in a compilation originally released in Sweden.

THE FIGHTING PRINCE OF DONEGAL (F) Director Michael O'Herlihy. 'A reckless young rebel rocks an empire,' boasted the publicity campaign. Disney's first British adventure film since the early 1950s is set in 16th-century Ireland and concerns Red Hugh (Peter McEnery), who prefers to make a treaty with the English instead of fighting. The evil Captain Leeds (Gordon Jackson) imprisons Hugh in Dublin, and captures Donegal castle. The Prince escapes and gathers the northern clans together to recapture his home and turn the tables on the villainous Leeds. Based on Robert T. Reilly's book *Red Hugh, Prince of Donegal*, the film is action packed and well photographed. Peter McEnery, perfect as the gallant young Irish hero, is supported by a fine British cast, which includes Susan Hampshire, Tom Adams and Andrew Keir (below). Gordon Jackson, who had a minor role in *Greyfriars Bobby*, makes a wonderful villain.

tion. It seemed inevitable, therefore, that the Studio should cast him in yet another film. This tells the tedious story of how Crusoe (Van Dyke), forced to bail out of his plane onto a tropical island, befriends a chimpanzee (who was thought lost by scientists working on the space programme, left) and a native girl called Wednesday (Nancy Kwan). There are problems when Wednesday's chieftain father believes that Crusoe wants to marry his daughter. It was all extremely silly but did well at the box-office, largely because of the unfailing support for Dick Van Dyke's multitudinous talents. The screenplay was based on a story by 'Retlaw Yensid', which is Walter Disney spelt backwards.

1967

EPCOT (Sp). As early as 1967 a film featuring Walt Disney appeared on Florida television stations to inform audiences about his future Florida project, EPCOT (Experimental Prototype Community of Tomorrow). A City of the Future, it didn't turn out quite how Disney had originally imagined it, but this film is a fascinating document on what had been planned when compared to the reality.

CANADA '67 (Sp) Long before the Studio produced a special 360° motion picture on the wonders of Canada for World Showcase at EPCOT Center, a specially filmed Circle-Vision 'tour of the Country' was produced for Expo '67 in Montreal.

THE ADVENTURES OF BULLWHIP GRIFFIN (F) Director James Neilson. Sid Fleischman's novel of the great California gold rush, By the Great Horn Spoon, provided the inspiration for a comical outing in which Boston butler, Griffin (Roddy McDowall, below with Bryan Russell and Karl Malden), is an unwilling travelling

RUSTY AND THE FALCON (F) Director N. Paul Kenworthy, Jr. First shown on the Disneyland television series in 1958, the film is based on Charlton Ogburn's The White Falcon and stars Jerome Courtland, who directed a number of Disney films. Rusty is a 12-year-old boy who captures a wounded falcon and nurses it back to health. When the bird grows over confident, it upsets some of the trigger-happy residents of the Rocky Mountain mining town. The film also stars Rudy Lee.

DONALD DUCK GOES CAMPING Sweden was the first country to witness Donald's outdoor adventures, which feature a programme of nine shorts.

THE MOONCUSSERS (F) Director James Neilson. Although it was originally screened on The Wonderful World of Color in 1962, The Mooncussers had to wait a few years before receiving a theatrical release outside the US. The story concerns Jonathan Feather (Kevin Corcoran), who learns that ex-pirates are luring sailing ships onto the perilous reefs of the American East Coast. Oscar Homolka co-stars in this exciting adventure yarn.

LT ROBIN CRUSOE U.S.N. (F) Director Byron Paul. One of the brightest comedy stars of the 1960s was Dick Van Dyke. He had already starred in Disney's most successful musical, Mary Poppins, and he was hugely popular in his own tv series with Mary Tyler Moore, which was, by the late 1960s, enjoying constant re-runs in syndica-

companion when his young master Jack Flagg (Russell) sets off to join the hunt for gold. They team up with an actor (Richard Haydn), whose map of buried treasure has been stolen by the evil Judge Higgins (Malden). A boxing match against a saloon bouncer called Mountain Ox and the rescue of Jack's sister Arabella (Suzanne Pleshette) finally bring 'Bullwhip', as he is now nicknamed, face to face with the dastardly Judge in a confrontation from which Bullwhip emerges a hero. An enjoyable farce, the film is unfortunately, at 110 minutes, overlong, and the songs, while not intrusive, are unmemorable. Some lively touches of animation between episodes in the plot were provided by Ward Kimball. Co-starring Harry Guardino, the film made little impact at the box-office and was quickly added to the Disney television schedules.

MONKEYS GO HOME (F) Director Andrew McLaglen. McLaglen had the unenviable task of dealing with a group of chimps who successfully steal the limelight from American olive-farm owner Hank Dussard (Dean Jones) and girlfriend Maria Riserau (Yvette Mimieux). Even Maurice Chevalier, who plays Father Sylvain, fails to upstage the monkeying around of the animal cast. Based on G.K. Wilkinson's book *The Monkeys*, the film, supposedly set in France, was shot entirely on the Studio back lot.

☆ THE JUNGLE BOOK (F) Director Wolfgang Reitherman. 'Now for a new generation . . . a new swinging kind of Disney!' trumpeted the publicity for the last feature-length animated film personally supervised by Walt Disney. Loosely based on Rudyard Kipling's books, *The Jungle Book* is one of the Studio's most successful films, grossing nearly $40 million at the US box-office since its release. The purists were, of course, rather shocked at the sight of Kipling's jungle boy singing and dancing to a jazz beat with bears and apes. The film relates how Mowgli grows up in the Indian jungle until it's time for Bagheera the panther to return him to the Man-Village. Determined to stay, however, Mowgli runs away and meets Baloo the bear, a happy-go-lucky 'jungle bum', who prefers a life of leisure (left). When he is kidnapped by the cunning King Louie, Bagheera and Baloo join forces to rescue the boy. Feeling betrayed, Mowgli once again runs away, only to be confronted by the tiger Shere Khan. The animation isn't as smooth as in Disney's earlier classics, but the colour styling and highly detailed backgrounds by Albert Dempster, Bill Layne, Art Riley, Ralph Hulett, Thelma Witmer and Frank Armitage are excellent, and the film is tightly edited to ensure maximum audience involvement. There is also a lushness that was sadly missing in *One Hundred and One Dalmatians* and in *The Sword in the Stone* (due, in part, to the Studio's turnaround policy after the box-office failure of *Sleeping Beauty*). But it's the wonderful array of characters that brings this film to life. Phil Harris (terribly miscast in later Disney films) is perfect as the voice of the lazy-good-for-nothing Baloo, Sebastian Cabot is just right as the pompous Bagheera, and the snake, the slithery Kaa (voiced by Sterling Holloway), comes over as one of the most engaging villains. The scene in which Kaa and Shere Khan (voiced by George Sanders) discuss poor Mowgli's future is one of the film's finest moments (below left). Colonel Hathi (J. Pat O'Malley) and his 'dawn patrol' of the elephants crash aimlessly around the jungle, and even Mowgli's native girlfriend, who finally lures him back to civilization, manages to rise above the mundane. Mowgli (voiced by the director's son Bruce) works well as a character, even if he does resemble Wart from *The Sword in the Stone*. The Sherman brothers wrote some of their best songs for the film – 'Trust in Me', 'That's What Friends Are For', 'My Own Home', 'Colonel Hathi's March' and the hit song 'I Wanna Be Like You', which is sung by the devious King Louie (Louis Prima). However, it was Terry Gilkyson's song 'The Bare Necessities', sung by Baloo, that won a nomination for the 1967 Academy Awards. Such was the film's success that the Studio attempted to repeat its popularity by injecting into its next two feature-length cartoons – *The Aristocats* and *Robin Hood* – similar music and voice talents. Both were, however, inferior copies and looked as much. In 1981, a 16mm educational extract was released, entitled *Jungle Book: A Lesson in Accepting Change*.

MOSBY'S MARAUDERS (F) Director Michael O' Herlihy. Made for *The Wonderful World of Color* television series, *Willie and the Yank*, a three-part adventure serial about the American Civil War, was released theatrically in the UK under the title *Mosby's Marauders*. Kurt Russell stars as Willie Prentiss, a 15-year-old who becomes a scout for John Singleton Mosby, the Grey Fox of the Confederacy. Co-stars in this minor adventure include James MacArthur and Nick Adams.

THE ACADEMY AWARD SHORTS PROGRAM A revised version of the compilation of 1937 Oscar-winning shorts was released in France; it included nine films, from *Flowers and Trees* to *Lend a Paw*.

SCROOGE MCDUCK AND MONEY (Sp) Director Hamilton Luske. 'The tale of a penny pinching billion-buck Duck,' was how the by-line described Donald's relation, Scrooge McDuck, originally created as a comic-strip character by Carl Barks, in his first theatrical appearance. The musical special takes the form of a lecture, as Scrooge explains to Huey, Dewey and Louie the history of money and the importance of sound investment (above). The nephews are charged for the good advice, for, as Scrooge points out, 'nothing good is ever free'.

THE LEGEND OF THE BOY AND THE EAGLE (F) Director Jack Couffer. The sensitively told story of Tutuvina, a Hopi Indian boy, who defied the gods by saving his pet eagle from being sacrificed. To this day, the Hopi Indians perform a traditional eagle dance in honour of his memory.

☆ **THE HAPPIEST MILLIONAIRE** (F) Director Norman Tokar. Considered by many at the Studio to be the last live-action film to carry Walt's personal imprint, this large-scale musical is a disappointing affair. Tokar had directed a number of Disney comedies, and it was hoped that the talents that had made *Mary Poppins* such a success would produce another winner. But even with 12 songs from the Oscar-winning Richard and Robert Sherman and choreography by Marc Breaux and Dee Dee Wood, the film lacked *Poppins'* magical whimsy. Based on the book by Kyle Crichton and Cordelia Drexel Biddle, the story concerns a modern-day Romeo and Juliet. One of the rival families is led by eccentric millionaire Anthony J. Drexel Biddle (Fred MacMurray), who threatens the budding romance between his daughter Cordelia (Lesley Ann Warren) and Angie Duke (John Davidson). Fortunately, the Irish butler, John Lawless (Tommy Steele), is on hand to help bring the two families together. There are some nice performances from co-stars Greer Garson, Geraldine Page and Gladys Cooper, but the film is too long-winded to hold an audience's attention – even with the addition of some independently motivated alligators. Like its next (fantasy) musical *Bedknobs and Broomsticks*, the Studio seemed to lose faith in the product, and after its world premiere in Los Angeles in June 1967 it was edited from its original 164 minutes to 141 minutes for all pre-release engagements. It was trimmed even further to 118 minutes for general release in 1968 . The full version with its stereophonic soundtrack was rediscovered in the early 1980s and screened on The Disney Channel.

CHARLIE THE LONESOME COUGAR (F) Field producers Lloyd Beebe, Charles L. Draper and Ford Beebe. Following in the footprints – or rather the pawprints – of such popular animal stories as *Born Free*, in which a wild animal is befriended and then released into the wild, this was a reasonable success at the box-office. Shot in the northwest of the United States, the film relates how a young forester adopts Charlie (below) as a kitten and then lets him go. Unable to fend for himself, he is recaptured and released into an animal sanctuary where he finally settles down. Starring Ron Brown, Bryan Russell and Linda Wallace, the film was co-produced by True-Life Adventure consultant Winston Hibler. Hibler declined the opportunity to narrate the film, giving the job instead to Rex Allen, who, together with the Sons of the Pioneers, had worked on the soundtrack of *The Legend of Lobo* (1962).

SU CARROUSEL DE ALEGRIA A programme of 10 shorts featuring Mickey Mouse and the gang was premiered in Argentina.

FAMILY PLANNING (Ed) Produced in association with the Population Council, this animated film teaches students about the enrichment, rather than the restriction, of life.

THE MILLION DOLLAR COLLAR (F) Director Vincent McEveety. Guy Stockwell makes his screen debut and Craig Hill co-stars in this story about a sea-going Airedale called Hector. Circus owner Hugo Danzer (Eric Pohlmann) is so impressed by the dog's intelligence that he plots to 'dognap' him when the ship reaches Lisbon. Problems occur, however, when jewel thieves attempt to smuggle stolen diamonds to Barcelona in Hector's collar. Based on a book by Homer Brightman, the film was first shown on *The Wonderful World of Color* television series in 1964 under the title *The Ballad of Hector the Stowaway Dog*.

GOOFY ADVENTURES Having guest-starred in a number of other cartoon compilations, Goofy now appears in one of his own, which was released first in Germany and featured 10 shorts, although the contents varied in some other countries.

THE GNOME-MOBILE (F) Director Robert Stevenson. After an enjoyable outing with the leprechauns of Ireland in *Darby O'Gill and the Little People*, it was the turn of the American tree gnomes. 'Take off your brakes and laugh!' urged the publicity, as D.J. Mulrooney (Walter Brennan) drives his 1930s Rolls-Royce through California redwood country, accompanied by his grandchildren Rodney and Elizabeth Winthrop (Matthew Garber and Karen Dotrice). They meet a 2-foot-high gnome called Jasper (Tom Lowell) and his grandfather (also played by Walter

Brennan), who are alarmed that Mulrooney's lumber men are cutting down their forest. Fortunately, the children are on hand to save the day. Based on the book by Upton Sinclair, the film contains some excellent special effects by Eustace Lycett and Robert A. Mattey. In one sequence 12 'mini-skirted' pixyish girls chase after Jasper, perhaps reflecting the more liberated attitude of the 1960s gnome. The title song was written by Richard and Robert Sherman.

THE CERAMIC MURAL (Ed) The 16mm educational release gives step-by-step instructions on the design and construction of a ceramic mural.

KEEP TO THE RIGHT Premiered in Sweden, the cartoon compilation features six animated shorts.

DISNEYLAND AROUND THE SEASONS (Sp) Director Hamilton Luske. This highly entertaining tour around the Magic Kingdom was first shown on *The Wonderful World of Color* in 1966. It includes popular attractions such as It's A Small World and the train ride through the Grand Canyon and Primeval World.

1968

BLACKBEARD'S GHOST (F) Director Robert Stevenson. It seemed that a good way to promote this supernatural comedy was to announce that, due to popular demand, Dean Jones was once again co-starring with Susanne Pleshette – the successful comedy team from *The Ugly Dachshund*. Jones was a very bankable star as far as Disney was concerned, and over the years his eight motion pictures for the Studio had a national box-office return exceeding $60 million, while Pleshette was proving herself an amiable comedienne after a number of dramatic portrayals. Jones plays Steve Walker, a college track coach who inadvertently conjures up the spirit of Blackbeard the Pirate (brilliantly played by Peter Ustinov, below) who is invisible to everyone except Walker. The pirate prevents his old home, now a hotel, from being demolished by an unscrupulous businessman and helps Walker's athletics team to win the local track meet. Through these good deeds, Blackbeard earns the eternal rest he so desires. Elsa Lanchester plays

Emily Stowecroft, one of the pirate's descendants, and Joby Baker portrays the villainous Silky Seymour.

THE COYOTE'S LAMENT (Sp) First shown on the tv series *Walt Disney Presents* in 1961, this animated tale of the plight of the coyote (above) stars Pluto and is narrated by the Sons of the Pioneers.

THE ONE AND ONLY, GENUINE, ORIGINAL FAMILY BAND (F) Director Michael O'Herlihy. Based on Laura Bower Van Nuys' autobiographical novel, the film stars Walter Brennan as Grandpa Bower who, with his talented musical family (below), overcomes a number of personal and political difficulties in order to perform. Co-stars include Buddy Ebsen, Lesley Ann Warren, John Davidson, Janet Blair and Wally Cox, and the Sherman brothers wrote a number of songs for the film, which failed to receive a theatrical release in Europe.

OF CATS AND MEN (Ed) The history of the domestic cat is traced in a 16mm release which was originally shown on television. This entertaining history of the feline species explains how the Egyptians revered the animal as a god, while the people of the Dark Ages feared it with superstitious fervour.

THE WILD CAT FAMILY – THE COUGAR (Ed) Stock footage from the Disney nature films supplied material for a 16mm featurette illustrating the family life and hunting habits of the mountain lion. The film compares its lifestyle with that of other cats.

THE WILD DOG FAMILY – THE COYOTE (Ed) Stock 16mm footage is used to tell the story of the intelligent wild dogs which survive on the desolate plains of western America.

THE WEASEL FAMILY (Ed) Another 16mm documentary for schools in Disney's widely acclaimed animal series studies the lives of the otter, mink, marten, skunk and wolverine. Explaining the characteristics of each, the film also highlights their struggle for survival.

TRIANGLE OF HEALTH (Ed) The 16mm animated educational film *Steps Toward Maturity and Health*, produced for Upjohn's Triangle of Health, explores the process of life from birth through adolescence. Numerous citations from international film festivals were awarded to *Understanding Stresses and Strains*, the second 16mm film produced for the series. It explains what can be done to minimize illness brought about through excessive anxiety.

OUTDOOR FOR LAUGHS Although the contents varied in other countries, this cartoon compilation premiered in Germany contained 10 shorts.

NEVER A DULL MOMENT (F) Director Jerry Paris. 'They're having such a wonderful crime. . . . It's a shame to call the police,' is how Disney promoted Dick Van Dyke's third film for the Studio. Based on a book by John Godey, the film tells how tv actor Jack Albany (Van Dyke) is mistaken for hired killer Ace Williams (Jack Elam). This puts him into a spot of bother with wealthy gangster Joseph Smooth (Edward G. Robinson in his 85th film) and attractive Sally Inwood (Dorothy Provine). Fortunately for Albany, he manages to turn the tables on the hoodlums and prevent Smooth from stealing a 42-foot-long painting, 'A Field of Sunflowers', from the Manhattan Museum of Art. Despite the title, the film *does* contain some dull moments, but it is a better vehicle for Mr Van Dyke's talents than the vapid *Lt Robin Crusoe U.S.N.*

THE DEER FAMILY (Ed) Stunning slow-motion photography combined with the expertise of some outstanding nature film-makers provide an excellent tribute to the horned and antlered animals of North America – the elk, caribou, moose and many others.

★ WINNIE THE POOH AND THE BLUSTERY DAY (F) Director Wolfgang Reitherman. Pooh's second screen adventure proved even more successful than the first. It again combined the voice talents of Sterling Holloway as Pooh, Sebastian Cabot as the narrator and Jon Walmsley as Christopher Robin, in the story in which Tigger (voiced by Paul Winchell) arrives in the Hundred Acre Wood one dark and stormy night. The next morning Pooh has to rescue Piglet when the rain causes a flood and all the animals seek refuge at Christopher Robin's house. In a wonderfully surreal dream sequence (below), which borrows unashamedly from the 'pink elephants' scene in *Dumbo*, Pooh has a nightmare that mythical creatures called 'heffalumps' and 'woozles' are trying to steal his honey.

OF HORSES AND MEN (Ed) Exploring the history of this most graceful of animals and demonstrating their usefulness to man throughout the ages, this 16mm film was originally screened on American television.

THE HORSE IN THE GRAY FLANNEL SUIT (F) Director Norman Tokar. With a dearth of films for the whole family to enjoy, Disney set about promoting its movies as being the only exception to the new Hollywood trend of sex and violence. Publicized as 'suitable for all', and with ad-lines in the UK such as 'all's fair in love and woah', this feature stars Dean Jones (left), Diane Baker, Lloyd Bochner and Kurt Russell. Fred Bolton (Jones) is a young widower who uses his daughter's grey horse to promote his company's best-selling stomach pill, Aspercel. But things, as in all Disney comedies, don't work out the way he'd hoped!

1969

GALLEGHER (F) The success of *Emil and the Detectives* led the Studio to make *Gallegher*, a story set in 1899 about a newspaper copy boy who imagines himself to be a detective. Starring Roger Mobley as the boy reporter and Edmond O'Brien as the editor-in-chief, the film was originally shown in three parts on the *Wonderful World of Color* in 1965. Such was its success, that three tv sequels have followed – *Further Adventures of Gallegher* (1965), *Gallegher Goes West* (1966–7) and *The Mystery of Edward Sims* (1968).

THE LOVE BUG (F) Director Robert Stevenson. Herbie the Volkswagen's screen debut was released just as San Francisco was recovering from flower power, and it seemed inevitable that Disney would use this to publicize its 'wackiest' film to date in the US. In Europe, however, where Volkswagens were widely known as 'Beetles', the Studio was determined to put anxious British distributors' minds at rest: 'There'd be nothing clever about re-titling the movie *The Love Beetle*,' the film's campaign book reassured them. 'So all you Union Jack wavers are stuck to a label that's arguably not exactly hunky-100-per-cent-dorey. Fret thee not, for as the Big Bard once questioned, "What's in a name?"' Fortunately this campaign was dropped for re-issues of a film that, over the years, has proved to be a huge box-office success. Originally referred to in pre-production as 'Boy-Car-Girl', the film stars Dean Jones as Jim Douglas, who believes he's the world's greatest racing driver. Although he'd love to be able to afford Peter Thorndyke's (David Tomlinson) sports car, he settles for a little Volkswagen with a mind of its own. Accompanied by his sidekick Tennessee Steinmetz (Buddy Hackett) and Carole Bennett (Michele Lee), Douglas finally wins the most important racing event of his life, even though the villainous Thorndyke uses every dirty trick in the book to stop him. As Herbie was called upon to perform some amazing driving stunts, even for a dependable Volkswagen, second unit director Art Vitarelli and his 127-man crew fitted the car with a bus engine for some scenes and a Porsche engine for others. With a screenplay by Bill Walsh and Don Da Gradi, the film is hugely enjoyable from start to finish and has earned the Studio a staggering $23 million at the box-office as well as launching Herbie into a successful series of sequels over the next decade.

SMITH (F) Director Michael O'Herlihy. Described by the Studio as 'a warm love story with a message', this gentle drama stars Glenn Ford in the title role. Smith irritates his family by befriending the Nez Perce Indians, led by Canadian actor Chief Dan George, and when one of the Indians is falsely accused of murder, Smith exonerates him and wins the affection of all. Nancy Olson, in her first Disney film since *Son of Flubber*, co-stars as his wife Norah, and the film also stars Dean Jagger, Keenan Wynn and Warren Oates. It is based on Paul St Pierre's book *Breaking Smith's Quarter Horse*.

WALT DISNEY WORLD – PHASE 1 (Sp) With growing media interest in the opening of a Disney theme park in Florida, the Studio prepared a press conference that would feature a specially produced film. This 16mm release included background information on the project, together with artwork, models and aerial photography of the 45-square-mile site.

HANG YOUR HAT ON THE WIND (F) Director Larry Lansburgh. Starring Ric Natoli and Judson Pratt, it's a story about a small Mexican boy who befriends a handsome thoroughbred yearling and who, after a series of adventures, is justly rewarded for his kindness.

RASCAL (F) Director Norman Tokar. Billy Mumy (right) returned to the Studio after a successful career in the tv series *Lost in Space* to play opposite a wily raccoon called Rascal. The film explores the special friendship between the boy, his dog and the raccoon, until, after many adventures, the boy releases his pet into the wild. The screenplay was based on an autobiographical story by Sterling North, whose material the Studio had used in *So Dear To My Heart*. Balmy summer days are expertly captured by William Snyder's cinematography, and Bobby Russell's song 'Summer Sweet' rounds off a most engaging film. Co-stars include Steve Forrest, Pamela Toll, Elsa Lanchester and Henry Jones.

GUNS IN THE HEATHER (F) Director Robert Butler. 'An international spy thriller ... *adult*-ivated!' announced the publicity. Filmed entirely

on location in Ireland and with a screenplay by Herman Groves, the film is a fast-moving drama starring Kurt Russell, Glenn Corbett and Alfred Burke. The story concerns two boys who accidentally become involved in a sinister plot to kidnap a scientist, and it culminates in a dramatic boat chase and a daring rescue by glider. Although tightly edited from the three-part television serial *The Secret of Boyne Castle*, shown earlier in the year on *The Wonderful World of Color*, it ended up in the UK as a support feature to Disney's box-office blockbuster *The Love Bug*, proving that a Volkswagen called 'Herbie' with a mind of its own, was now more popular than a contemporary version of a Hardy Boys mystery.

ADVENTURE IN MUSIC A compilation of Disney shorts featuring music was premiered in Germany; it contains nine films, including some Silly Symphonies.

PABLO AND THE DANCING CHIHUAHUA (F) Director Walter Perkins. Pablo, a young Mexican boy (Armando Islas), slips across the border into the United States in search of his uncle. He is followed by a small chihuahua, which belongs to American tourist Helen Gordon (Francesca Jarvis), and together the two friends have many exciting adventures. Narrated by Winston Hibler and nicely photographed, with much location footage shot in the Arizona desert, this rather mediocre affair was originally made for American tv in 1968.

DONALD DUCK AND HIS COMPANIONS Although the contents of this compilation varied from country to country, its Portuguese premiere included 12 shorts.

★ IT'S TOUGH TO BE A BIRD (Sp) Director Ward Kimball. Animator Kimball's zany humour was allowed free reign on a number of occasions, particularly in the more humorous sections of the 1950s space films. But he surpasses even himself with this hectic look at the plight of our feathered friends. Animated host M.C. Bird (above, voiced

by Richard Bakalyan) explores the contribution of birds to mankind's development with the aid of some bizarre cut-out animation techniques (long before this type of animation became vogue with animators like *Monty Python's* Terry Gilliam). In an amusing live-action sequence, the townsfolk of Hinckley, Ohio, are shown honouring the turkey vulture as Ruth Buzzi sings in an off-key soprano 'When the Buzzards Return to

Hinckley Ridge'. For some European audiences, unexposed to Disney's 1950 style of animation, films such as this were quite a surprise after continued re-issues of *Pinocchio*, *Fantasia* or *Dumbo*.

TRIANGLE OF HEALTH (Ed) The third 16mm animated film in Upjohn's Triangle of Health series, *Physical Fitness and Good Health* examines the need for exercise and a proper diet. *The Social Side of Health*, produced on 16mm for the series, focuses attention on learning to live with others while retaining one's individuality.

WHAT SHOULD I DO ? (Ed) In the 16mm animated short *The Flight*, the first film in this series, students are encouraged to resolve their difficulties peaceably. In the second film, *The Game*, animated characters learn to play by the rules.

WALT DISNEY WORLD – VACATION KINGDOM (Sp) The Studio publicity machine worked at full capacity to make the public aware of the new theme park project in Florida. This 16mm release gave a preview of the new amusement areas considered for the park; as the complex took shape, a new film, *Project Florida*, was made (1971).

THE MAGIC OF DISNEYLAND (Sp) With the opening of Walt Disney World in Florida only two years away, the Studio produced an updated tour of its first theme park in Anaheim, California. This 16mm release takes in the spectacular Pirates of the Caribbean attraction, the Enchanted Tiki Room, It's A Small World and the new Tomorrowland exhibits – the PeopleMover and the Carousel of Progress.

RIDE A NORTHBOUND HORSE (F) Director Robert Totten. All the right ingredients for a 'schoolboy western' are included as Michael Shea stars as Cav Rand, a 15-year-old orphan who outbids a villainous peddler called Shawnee (Carroll O'Connor) to buy a fast black horse called Coal.

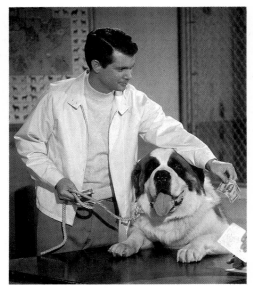

1970

Refusing to be outdone, Shawnee forces Cav (above) at gunpoint to destroy the bill of sale and then has him thrown in jail. Ben Johnson and Andy Devine co-star in this above-average story based on the book by Richard Wormser.

THE COMPUTER WORE TENNIS SHOES (F) Director Robert Butler. Described in the publicity as 'The only man in the world who can *really* turn himself on,' Kurt Russell stars as student Dexter Riley (below), who gets his wires crossed with an electronic brain. With the machine's entire memory and calculating capabilities inside his head, Dexter becomes an instant genius. His adventures involve appearances on tv game shows like *College Knowledge*, dealing with a gang of crooks and getting involved in a crazy car chase. Medfield College, which had put in a winning appearance in *The Absent Minded Professor* (1961), is seen again as super-student Riley's campus, and Cesar Romero plays an engaging villain.

FIESTA MAGICA Although the contents varied in some countries, this cartoon compilation of 10 shorts was first released in Argentina.

KING OF THE GRIZZLIES (F) Director Ron Kelly. 'Half a ton and ten feet tall . . . Ruler of the Rockies!' ran the Studio's publicity. John Yesno stars as Moki, a Cree Indian who obtains the job of foreman on a ranch belonging to Colonel Pierson (Chris Wiggins). When a bear and her cubs invade the Colonel's land, he shoots them, although one of the cubs called Wahb escapes. Moki tracks and captures the animal, then sets it free. Years later Wahb, now an enormous grizzly, comes back to the ranch. In a dramatic confrontation Moki saves the Colonel and the bear returns to the wilderness. Based on Ernest Thompson Seton's *The Biography of A Grizzly*, the film is narrated by True-Life Adventure veteran Winston Hibler, while Lloyd Beebe, also responsible for a number of the Disney nature films, acts as field producer. But, as always in films of this type, it's the bear that steals every scene, towering – literally – above the rest of the cast.

MY DOG, THE THIEF (F) Director Robert Stevenson. Dwayne Hickman (above right) plays a helicopter traffic reporter with an unusual

mascot, a huge St Bernard called Barabbas. The screenplay by William Raynor and Myles Wilder of this above-average Disney comedy relates the story of a series of adventures involving a million-dollar necklace and a gang of jewel thieves. Co-starring Elsa Lanchester, in her third film for the Studio, it was originally shown on the Disney tv series and released theatrically in Europe.

WHAT SHOULD I DO? (Ed) The third 16mm film in the series, *The New Girl* helps students to understand the importance of accepting others. *Lunch Money* continues the series, this time teaching students all about the need for honesty and integrity when dealing with others. *The Project*, which concludes the series, shows youngsters how to develop positive attitudes when helping others.

THE BEAR FAMILY (Ed) Released on 16mm, live-action stock footage from the True-Life Adventure films *Bear Country* and *White Wilderness* are featured in this film.

THE BEASTS OF BURDEN FAMILY (Ed) A 16mm release to illustrate the usefulness of working animals around the world from Tibetan yaks to Alaskan huskies.

THE MICKEY MOUSE ANNIVERSARY SHOW Written and produced by animator Ward Kimball, this isn't just the usual feature-length compilation. Although it does contain a number of Mickey's most popular adventures, the film, originally shown on US television in 1968, was released to celebrate the Mouse's 40th birthday and includes archive footage depicting the creation of Mickey and the gang.

THE BOATNIKS (F) Director Norman Tokar. Robert Morse plays ensign Thomas Garland, appointed to the Coast Guard at Newport Beach, California. With his girlfriend Kate (Stefanie Powers), he thwarts a gang of jewel thieves led by Harry Simmons (Phil Silvers, still reliving the wise-cracking Sergeant Bilko character, opposite above). One of the film's unlikely by-lines read: 'The Boatniks say: Save water . . . shower with a friend!', while an interesting item of tie-in merchandise were the 'porthole peepers', cardboard spectacles with lifebelt-shaped rims.

SMOKE (F) Director Vincent McEveety. Teenager Ronny Howard (right) stars in this UK release originally shown on US television. The boy befriends a German shepherd dog named Smoke and runs away with him when the real owner

turns up. An interesting drama, which captures the spirit of adolescence, the film co-stars Earl Holliman and Jacqueline Scott. An educational extract entitled *Step-Parents: Where is the Love?* was released in 1975.

DAD, CAN I BORROW THE CAR? (Sp) A bizarre little tale from the vivid imagination of animator Ward Kimball. The short, narrated by Kurt Russell, follows a young man's fascination for cars throughout his life from birth to courtship, with some of the vehicles taking on lives of their own (centre).

DONALD DUCK PARADE Another programme of Disney shorts featuring Donald and his duckling gang. The eight classic films varied in countries outside Denmark where it was first released.

THE ARISTOCATS (F) Director Wolfgang Reitherman. When *The Jungle Book* opened to a domestic box-office of $13 million in 1967, Disney quickly saw the advantage of adding a jazz soundtrack to this story of a kidnapped aristocratic feline and her kittens in order to cash in on the success of the animated Kipling stories. The results had none of the appeal of the previous film, even though the Studio re-used the voice talents of Phil Harris and commissioned some catchy songs by the Sherman Brothers and Terry Gilkyson. In the story, Duchess (below with O'Malley) and her kittens – the heirs to Madame Bonfamille's fortune – are kidnapped by Edgar the butler so that he may claim their inheritance for himself. His dastardly scheme backfires when the Aristocats are rescued by Thomas O'Malley (Phil Harris), a large ginger tom with a heart as big as his ego; a little mouse called Roquefort (voiced by Sterling Holloway) and a band of alley cats led by Scat Cat (Scatman Crothers), who provided the jazz interlude. As the story is set in France, Harris' rather throaty American accent seems out of place, especially when the Studio cast Eva Gabor to voice Duchess and Maurice Chevalier came out of retirement to sing the title

song out of 'respect for Walt Disney'. Although the film has some good characterization, the animation, supervised by Disney veterans Milt Kahl, Ollie Johnston, Frank Thomas and John Lounsbery, is surprisingly lacklustre. All in all, the film is a rather unmemorable affair, although it did well at the box-office, particularly in Europe where the French adored it.

1971

PROJECT FLORIDA (Sp) Director James Algar. Released in the year that Walt Disney World opened and beginning with Herb Ryman's impressive painting of the Cinderella Castle, the film features scale models of the park, the preview centre in Florida, exclusive behind-the-scenes footage of WED (the company responsible for designing the parks) and shots of the building work during 1970. Animators, including Marc Davis, are shown preparing preliminary sketches of the Country Bear Jamboree, and the 16mm featurette includes historic sequences from a 1966 tv film in which Walt himself discusses the exciting future of the project.

THE WILD COUNTRY (F) Director Robert Totten. This impressive drama could easily have fitted into the release schedule of Touchstone Pictures, had it existed in 1971. Steve Forrest stars as Jim Tanner who, together with his wife Kate (Vera Miles) and two sons Virgil (Ronny Howard) and Andrew (Clint Howard, above), sets up a farm in the Wyoming of the 1880s. A villainous cattle rancher, Ab Cross (Morgan Woodward), tries to sabotage the Tanners' efforts by refusing to allow water for their ranch to cross his land. At the climax of the film, young Virgil faces the evil Cross in a life or death gunfight. Based on Ralph Moody's book *Little Britches*, the film is entertaining, gritty and well above average.

LITTLE DOG LOST (F) Director Walter Perkins. Candy, a small Welsh corgi, becomes separated from his master and is forced to brave the wilderness. Released on 16mm, this engaging tale was based on a book by Meindert De Jong, and was first shown on *The Wonderful World of Color* in 1963.

BRISTLE FACE (F) Director Bob Sweeney. The title refers to a 'fun-loving but trouble-prone mongrel', which a small orphan boy trains to become a respectable hunting dog. The film stars Brian Keith, Phillip Alford, Jeff Donnell and Wallace Ford, and it was premiered on *The Wonderful World of Color* tv series in 1964.

WILD GEESE CALLING (Sp) Producer James Algar. In this entertaining featurette, a young boy, horrified to see a gander winged by a hunter, takes the bird home and nurses it back to health. He is further saddened when the wild creature has to be set free to join the flocks of geese flying south for the winter.

THE BAREFOOT EXECUTIVE (F) Director Robert Butler. The Southern California Motion Picture Council gave an award to this comedy, probably because it relished the idea of a pet chimpanzee,

called Raffles, being capable of picking out top television programmes and catapulting a network television company to the top of the ratings. Kurt Russell, who was 19 years old, stars as an employee who makes a monkey out of his colleagues by exploiting the ape's ability. Costars veteran comedy actors Wally Cox, Joe Flynn and Harry Morgan appear to be enjoying themselves immensely in this story, which, according to the press release, was based on fact.

TEETH ARE FOR CHEWING (Ed) In this short, which combines animation and live action, students are made aware of how important it is to care for their teeth. The film also compares the different types of teeth of a variety of animals.

THE HALL OF PRESIDENTS (TP) Liberty Square, one of the six themed lands of Walt Disney World in Florida, houses an impressive theatre

presentation illustrating the history of America. A roll-call of 39 American Presidents concludes the show. A sweeping 70mm film, composed of 85 paintings, tells the dramatic and sometimes moving story of the American people before Abraham Lincoln, voiced by actor Royal Dano (who starred in *Something Wicked This Way Comes*), addresses the audience by means of 'Audio-Animatronics'.

THE ADVENTURES OF CHIP AN' DALE. This compilation of 10 shorts relating the adventures of the two chipmunks was first released in Denmark.

GET THE MESSAGE This early 16mm film explains the development of communication techniques.

FESTIVAL OF FOLK HEROES Animated shorts depicting tales of American heroes were combined into a 16mm feature-length release. Among the famous characters included were *Pecos Bill* (from *Make Mine Music*), *Johnny Appleseed* (from *Melody Time*), *The Saga of Windwagon Smith*, *Paul Bunyan* and 'Casey of the Mudville Nine'. Other variations of this programme appeared regularly on the Disney tv shows.

SCANDALOUS JOHN (F) Director Robert Butler. 'He's the kind of guy who throws a candlestick through the window when he wants fresh air and shoots out the light when he goes to bed,' is how the Studio publicized this Don Quixote-type fantasy. Based on a book by Richard Gardner, the film is set in modern times and concerns an 80-year-old rancher and his Mexican handyman who go on a cattle drive to do battle against a wealthy industrialist. It is an entertaining comedy western, which has some poignant touches that put it in league with box-office successes such as

Cat Ballou. Brian Keith has a wonderful time with the lead role (opposite above right) and is ably supported by co-stars Alfonso Arau as Paco, Michele Carey as Amanda and Harry Morgan as Sheriff Pippin. The catchy musical score is provided by Rod McKuen.

THE MILLION DOLLAR DUCK (F) Director Vincent McEveety. Dean Jones stars as university professor Albert Dooley (opposite below), whose behavioural-test duck, Charley, is accidentally exposed to radiation while nibbling a strange form of apple sauce. Miraculously, Charley begins to lay solid gold eggs. Sandy Duncan, Joe Flynn and Tony Roberts co-star in this tale in which, as always, the animals steal the show.

★BEDKNOBS AND BROOMSTICKS (F) Director Robert Stevenson. Rarely seen in its original format, the musical had been heavily cut even before its premiere in London in October 1971. Since then, the film's 117 minutes' running time has been edited down to 98 minutes. Most of the songs are missing in the shorter version, even though the Studio was certain that this film would be as successful as *Mary Poppins*. Based on two books by Mary Norton, *Bedknobs* tells how, in 1940, amateur witch Eglantine Price (Angela Lansbury) – with the help of bogus magician Emelius Browne (David Tomlinson, above), a sinister book of spells and three cockney children evacuated from London – repels a German invasion of England. Their adventures take them on a magical brass bed to the mysterious Lost Isle of Naboombu, where they witness a bizarre football match between two rival teams of animals. They have a close encounter with an unscrupulous book dealer (Sam Jaffe) and watch a battle between medieval suits of armour and

Nazi soldiers. Angela Lansbury is perfect as the mid-20th-century witch who wishes only to do good, and the songs – 'The Old Home Guard', 'Eglantine', 'The Beautiful Briny', 'The Age of Not Believing', 'Substitutiary Locomotion' and 'Portobello Road' – are worthy of the talents of award-winning songwriters Richard and Robert Sherman. But some unlikely cameo performances from Roddy McDowall and Tessie O'Shea only add to the episodic nature of the film. The animation sequence directed by Ward Kimball is, however, reminiscent of the splendid 'Jolly Holiday' routine in *Mary Poppins*. Unfortunately, this particular sequence is one of the few highlights of what is a dull musical comedy. Even the film's climax, in which, with the aid of a magical incantation, Eglantine leads an army of museum relics against the Germans, simply becomes a series of unrelated gags. Stevenson had 14 major Disney screen credits to his name; producer and co-author Bill Walsh was responsible for the Studio's 1969 blockbuster *The Love Bug* – nevertheless, the box-office returns were rather disappointing, and the Studio was persuaded that large-scale musicals were a risky business. The film did, however, win an Academy Award for Best Visual Effects over Jim Danforth's *When Dinosaurs Ruled the Earth*, and when re-issued in 1979, the advertising cashed in on Warner Brothers' *Superman* with posters that read: 'You'll believe a woman can fly.'

1972

LEONARDO DA VINCI - FIRST MAN OF THE RENAISSANCE (Ed) Producer Anthony Corso. Beginning with a look at the artist's childhood, this 16mm educational film traces the remarkable achievements and talents of this 15th-century genius.

THE MAGIC WHISTLE (Ed) Producer Dave Bell. This 16mm release is a touching story of how a boy's imagination finds magic in a broken whistle.

MRS PEABODY'S BEACH (Ed) Producer Dave Bell. A teenager learns about basic economics when he uses his enthusiasm for surfing to create a highly profitable business.

HISTORY ALIVE! (Ed) Producer Turnley Walker. Five 16mm films were made for educational use. *Democracy – Equality or Privilege?* considers the political disagreements between Thomas Jefferson and Alexander Hamilton in the 1790s. *Impeachment of a President* illustrates Thaddeus Stevens's attempts to incriminate Andrew Jackson in 1868. *The Right of Dissent* discusses the private citizen's rights in governmental matters. *The Right of Petition* concerns the arguments over anti-slavery laws between John Quincy Adams and Thomas Marshall, and *States' Rights* covers the fight over the 1832 tariff law.

THE BOY WHO STOLE THE ELEPHANT (F) Director Michael Caffey. Originally made for tv in 1970, the movie stars British actor Mark Lester as a boy whose love for a circus elephant saves it from death. Co-stars in this non-theatrical 16mm release are David Wayne and June Havoc.

TRACK OF THE GIANT SNOW BEAR (F) Originally shown on television, this remarkably photographed featurette is the story of a young Eskimo boy who befriends a gigantic polar bear but soon realizes that he can't make a pet out of such a wild animal. It was later released on 16mm.

THE BISCUIT EATER (F) Director Vincent McEveety. The title refers to a young hunting dog (below, with Johnny Whitaker), which is trained to be a champion by two young boys in the

swamplands of Tennessee. An earlier film, also based on the book by James Street, was produced in 1940 by Paramount Pictures. The Disney version stars Earl Holliman and Lew Ayres.

SUPERSTAR GOOFY A compilation featuring 11 shorts was premiered in Denmark.

MENACE ON THE MOUNTAIN (F) Director Vincent McEveety. Originally shown on US television, the film was released theatrically in the UK and stars Mitch Vogel and Charles Aidman. It relates the harrowing task that befalls Jamie, a 14-year-old boy who has to protect his family from a gang of raiders while his father is fighting in the Confederate Army.

JUSTIN MORGAN HAD A HORSE (F) Based on the book by Marguerite Henry, this feature-length film was originally made for the Disney television series and eventually released on 16mm. The story, starring Don Murray, Lana Wood and Gary Crosby, is set in post-Revolutionary Vermont, where, against seemingly insurmountable odds, school-teacher Morgan trains a young colt into a championship racer.

THE GREAT SEARCH – MAN'S NEED FOR POWER AND ENERGY (Ed) So that students will appreciate the importance of safer energy resources, this 16mm educational title uses live action and animation to trace the discovery, development and application of those resources. It also illustrates the dangers inherent in upsetting the Earth's ecological balance.

☆ NAPOLEON AND SAMANTHA (F) Director Bernard McEveety. Actor Michael Douglas makes his Disney debut in this film, but his four-footed co-star, Major McTavish, a retired circus lion, was already a movie veteran – 16 years old and weighing 500 pounds, he had guest-starred on the *Tarzan* films and tv series with Mike Henry and Ron Ely as well as appearing on *The Wonderful World of Color*. Johnny Whitaker and Jodie Foster play Napoleon and Samantha (above), two children who, fearful of losing their pet lion when Napoleon's grandfather dies, run away in search of their friend Danny (Michael Douglas). Nicely photographed by Monroe P. Askins, the children's adventures in the wilderness are nevertheless reminiscent of the dangers encountered by

the stars of *The Incredible Journey*. In 1976 an educational extract entitled *Death: How Can You Live With It?* was released to schools.

SNOWBALL EXPRESS (F) Director Norman Tokar. Dean Jones (left, with Nancy Olson) stars as Johnny Baxter, an insurance company accountant, who inherits the Grand Imperial Hotel, which is some 10,000 feet up the Rocky Mountains. Based on Frankie and John O'Rear's book *Château Bon Vivant*, the film follows Baxter's various mishaps with a shady banker (Keenan Wynn) and a snowmobile race. This above-average comedy has some excellent photography of snow-capped mountains by Frank Phillips and special effects by Eustace Lycett, Art Cruickshank and Danny Lee. Nancy Olson, Harry Morgan and Disney discovery Kathleen Cody co-star in this entertaining outing.

WALT DISNEY'S CARNIVAL OF HITS Featuring 10 animated shorts, the compilation was premiered in Denmark; the contents varied in Sweden.

NOW YOU SEE HIM, NOW YOU DON'T (F) Director Robert Butler. Ever since H.G. Wells' *The Invisible Man* was first filmed by Hollywood, the secret of invisibility has thrilled audiences in countless films and television series. A weird substance created in a college laboratory makes student Dexter Riley (Kurt Russell, above with Joyce Menges) disappear. This enables him both to save the college from closure and to capture the villainous A. J. Arno (played with delightful relish by Cesar Romero). Clever special effects by

Studio veterans Eustace Lycett and Danny Lee add to the fun, which culminates in an invisible car chase. Co-stars include Joe Flynn, William Windom and Jim Backus.

RUN, COUGAR, RUN (F) Director Jerome Courtland. Later shown on *The Wonderful World of Color* tv series, the film is based on Robert Murphy's book *The Mountain Lion*. Living in the red-rock mesa area of Utah, Seeta the mountain lion and her three kittens find friendship with a shepherd, Etio (Alfonso Arau). Stuart Whitman plays a professional lion-hunter who threatens the animals' survival.

THE MAGIC OF WALT DISNEY WORLD (Sp) Director Tom Leetch. An affectionate look at the gigantic Florida project – 43 square miles of entertainment, sporting activities, exciting night life and resort facilities are explored. Doing double duty as a public relations tool, and with a varied and stirring musical score by Buddy Baker, it is a tremendous tribute to the sheer ingenuity of such a vast undertaking, but does now appear dated because of the total lack of any mention of Walt's real dream for Florida – EPCOT Center, which opened 10 years later.

1973

VD ATTACK PLAN (Ed) Director Les Clark. An educational short, written by Bill Bosché, which uses simple graphics and an amusing array of characters to teach students about the dangers of sexual diseases. Made before AIDS became such a

threat, the film stresses the medical help that is available. Narrator Keenan Wynn recounts how the leader of the VD viruses marshals his gruesome troops to the attack. The style of the film recalls the methods used by the storymen on the Disney health films made during the war. Two versions of the film exist, running for 14 or 16 minutes depending on the age group watching.

THE WORLD'S GREATEST ATHLETE (F) Director Robert Scheerer. Star of numerous television series and Charles Bronson's companion in *The Mechanic*, actor Jan-Michael Vincent found himself in a very different type of film when he undertook this title role. The film relates how Sam Archer (John Amos), the coach of Merrivale College, and his assistant Milo (Tim Conway) trick jungle-boy Nanu (Vincent, above with Amos and Conway) and his pet tiger, Harri into going to America to become a star athlete. After numerous adventures, in which Archer gets his just desserts by being shrunk to a height of three inches by the witch-doctor Gazenga (Roscoe Lee Brown), Nanu wins the trophies for Merrivale but decides to return to Africa, this time accompanied by his girlfriend Jane Douglas (Dayle Haddon). Vincent is excellent as a kind of naïve Tarzan, although the film's highlights are the sequences, by effects veterans Eustace Lycett, Art Cruickshank and Danny Lee, involving giant telephones and everyday objects when Archer is miniaturized.

THE WALT DISNEY STORY (TP) Housed in an attractive building in Town Square at the entrance to the Magic Kingdom in Walt Disney World in Florida is an exhibition of memorabilia on the life of Walt Disney. A complement to this collection of rare Disneyana is this 23-minute featurette, which uses rare footage of Walt and narration from interviews with him to tell the story of this great entrepreneur and his motion-picture achievements. The film was released on 16mm in 1987, and an edited and revised version is shown in Disneyland as part of the Great Moments with Mr. Lincoln exhibit. Only 7 minutes long, it concentrates on how the 'Audio-Animatronics' figure of Lincoln was constructed.

A DISNEY CARTOON JUBILEE A compilation, premiered in Denmark (although its contents varied in other European countries), including among the 11 titles *Cold Turkey*, *Three Blind Mouseketeers* and *Morris, the Midget Moose*.

HOW ALASKA JOINED THE WORLD (Ed) Clever animation is used to trace the history of Alaska in this 16mm release, which goes on to explain how,

after its discovery, the land was purchased by the United States. It was edited from a tv show.

ALASKA'S BUSH PILOT HERITAGE (Ed) Released in 16mm, this is the story of the men who are trained to fly safely through the perilous Alaskan landscape.

CHARLEY AND THE ANGEL (F) Director Vincent McEveety. Based on *The Golden Evenings of Summer* by Will Stanton, this humorous little film recounts how an angel (Harry Morgan) visits Earth to warn Charley (Fred MacMurray), a small-town businessman, of the dangers he faces if he neglects his family (including Vince Van Patten, above) and ambitions. Hollywood has

always enjoyed stories about celestial messengers, and although this is not as thought-provoking as the classic *It's a Wonderful Life* starring James Stewart, MacMurray is nevertheless excellent as the endearing character in need of some spiritual guidance.

THE ALASKAN GOLD RUSH (Ed) Released in 16mm for schools, this film relates the story of the hardy pioneers using historical photographs from a family album.

ONE LITTLE INDIAN (F) Director Bernard McEveety. Two obstreperous camels provide the laughs as James Garner, in his first film for Disney, plays Clint Keyes, a prisoner of the US

Cavalry. Managing to escape from the army on the back of Rosie the camel, he is accompanied by his mount's offspring, Thirsty, and a young runaway Indian boy (Clay O'Brien). Jodie Foster and Vera Miles co-star in this comedy adventure, which has a complicated plot and some endearing animal stars.

DIAMONDS ON WHEELS (F) Director Jerome Courtland. This mediocre film, made for American television, has very little to recommend it. English actor Peter Firth plays Robert Stewart, who restores a wrecked MG sports car without realizing that hidden in the driver's seat is a fortune in stolen diamonds. It's a race against time when Stewart discovers how important the car is to a gang of crooks who will stop at nothing to reclaim it. Patrick Allen co-stars as Chief Inspector Cook. The film at times resembles some of the weaker efforts of the Children's Film Foundation.

HENRY O. TANNER: PIONEER AMERICAN BLACK ARTIST (Ed) Producer Anthony Corso. This sensitive educational short explores the world-wide recognition afforded the first black artist whose paintings of America and Europe have inspired art lovers everywhere.

JOHN MUIR: FATHER OF OUR NATIONAL PARKS (Ed) Producer Anthony Corso. A dramatization of one man's struggle to preserve America's scenic wonders; Muir has since been immortalized as an 'Audio-Animatronics' figure in EPCOT Center's The American Adventure.

I'M NO FOOL WITH ELECTRICITY (Ed) Produced more than 15 years later than the rest of the titles, this completes the *I'm No Fool* series of educational films hosted by Jiminy Cricket. Lessons in electrical safety are easily explained with the aid of games and cheerful songs.

DONALD'S CARTOON REVUE Although the contents varied depending on the country of release, this compilation contains 10 classic shorts.

VARDA, THE PEREGRINE FALCON (F) This superbly photographed wildlife adventure was originally shown on the Disney television series. It shows how the falcon, once the ally of the huntsman, is now an endangered species.

NATURE'S WILD HEART (F) In this 16mm film, originally shown on the Disney tv series, two children spend a summer in the Canadian wilderness. They encounter all kinds of animals and learn to appreciate the rhythm of nature.

☆ ROBIN HOOD (F) Producer and director Wolfgang Reitherman. Having already capitalized on the success of *The Jungle Book* with its 1970 production *The Aristocats*, Disney was not about to turn its back on a winning streak: the full-length animated version of the story of Robin Hood contained all the popular ingredients of those earlier films. The characters were animals: Robin Hood (a fox) and Little John (a bear) combine cunning and ingenuity to defeat the villainous Prince John (a lion, left) and the slimy Sir Hiss (a snake). The animation, directed by Milt Kahl, Ollie Johnston, Frank Thomas and John Lounsbery, was above average. Among the stars chosen to voice the characters were Brian Bedford (Robin), Roger Miller (a country-and-western version of the minstrel Allan-a-Dale), Andy Devine (Friar Tuck), Monica Evans (Maid Marian), Pat Buttram (the Sheriff of Nottingham) and Carole Shelley (Lady Kluck). In keeping with tradition, Phil Harris was cast as Little John. The most humorous performances, however, fell to

Peter Ustinov as the voice of the cowardly Prince John and to Terry Thomas as Sir Hiss. The story was written for the screen by Larry Clemmons, but the songs – with the exception of 'The Phoney King of England' by Johnny Mercer and sung by Phil Harris – are instantly forgettable. 'Meet Robin Hood and his Merry *Men*agerie,' exhorted the publicity, and, to date, the film has earned over $17 million at the American box-office, yet it pales in comparison with the Studio's animation output of the 1960s.

1974

SUPERDAD (F) Director Vincent McEveety. Pre-released in December 1973 so that it might qualify for the Academy Award nominations, this comedy failed to make an impact on either critics or cinema audiences. Bob Crane (star of the tv series *Hogan's Heroes*) plays successful lawyer Charlie McCready, whose attempts to bridge the generation gap with his daughter's friends provide the laughs. Kathleen Cody, Barbara Rush and Kurt Russell co-star in this mediocre affair, which is based on a story by Harlan Ware.

HERBIE RIDES AGAIN (F) Director Robert Stevenson. The popularity of Herbie, the Love Bug, a Volkswagen with a mind of its own, made the car a regular member of the cast in the *Disney On Parade* shows during the 1970s and led to three film sequels, of which this was the first. It relates how Herbie helps Mrs Steinmetz (Helen Hayes) to save her home from evil property tycoon Alonzo Hawk (Keenan Wynn). Co-stars Ken Berry and Stefanie Powers (below) add a light romantic touch to this entertaining story, although, as always, Herbie steals the show.

MAGIC CARPET 'ROUND THE WORLD (TP) When the 360° *Circle-Vision* film was premiered at Walt Disney World in 1974, it concentrated on scenes of the Middle East. But when, in 1983, it opened at Tokyo Disneyland, the Japanese requested more footage of America and Europe, and the

new version features Tower Bridge and the Statue of Liberty. The film has since been replaced at Walt Disney World by another *Circle-Vision* presentation, *American Journeys*.

☆ WINNIE THE POOH AND TIGGER TOO (F) Director John Lounsbery. Pooh's third escapade in the Hundred Acre Wood relates how Pooh, Rabbit and Piglet decide it's time to teach the 'bouncy, flouncy, pouncy' Tigger a lesson, because he's always bouncing into people. When Tigger gets stuck up a tree, he promises never to bounce again. But, being of a forgiving nature, the animals have to admit that they preferred Tigger the way he was before. As in all the Pooh shorts, clever use is made of the storybook techniques by

which characters jump from page to page and lines of text become a ladder so that a frightened Tigger (below) can climb safely down to the ground. Songs by Richard and Robert Sherman enhance this delightful featurette.

THE BEARS AND I (F) Director Bernard McEveety. Set in the Canadian Rockies, the film stars Patrick Wayne as ex-soldier Bob Leslie (above), who finds himself caught in the conflict between the Taklute Indians and the Parks Commission. To further complicate matters, Leslie 'adopts' three bear cubs, which the Indians revere and believe should be freed. Magnificently photographed, the film was produced by Winston Hibler, narrator of the True-Life Adventure series.

occasion he teamed up with Vera Miles. Robert Culp and Eric Shea co-star.

SEQUOYAH (Ed) Producer Anthony Corso. The 16mm featurette relates the moving story of how a Cherokee silversmith dreams of unifying his people through the creation of a written language that will be accepted by all.

THE DONALD DUCK STORY A compilation of 11 shorts, including *Rugged Bear*, *Orphan's Benefit* (colour remake) and *The New Neighbor*, was first seen in Sweden.

MAN, MONSTERS AND MYSTERIES (Sp) Veteran Disney voice talent Sterling Holloway had the opportunity to speak for a new character – Nessie (below). Produced in a style similar to *It's Tough To Be a Bird*, the film, which was narrated by Sebastian Cabot, explores the legend of the Loch Ness monster. The audience's scepticism about the monster's existence is challenged by an indignant Nessie, who asks us to remember how other legends were at first ignored by science – the gorilla, the komodo dragon and so on. Filmed entirely on location in Scotland, this European theatrical release was far superior to the feature it supported – *One of Our Dinosaurs Is Missing*.

☆ THE ISLAND AT THE TOP OF THE WORLD (F) Director Robert Stevenson. Pleased with the success of previous fantasy blockbusters in the mould of Jules Verne – *20,000 Leagues Under the Sea* (1954) and *In Search of the Castaways* (1962) – Disney embarked on a new adventure film incorporating bits of *Around the World in 80 Days*, *The Lost World* and *Five Weeks in a Balloon*. The result is a curious mis-match of boys'-own thrills and spills and good old pioneering derring-do. Based on Ian Cameron's book *The Lost Ones*, the film miscast British comedy actor Donald Sinden as the explorer Sir Anthony Ross, who sets off with Captain Brieux (Jacques Marin), Professor John Ivarsson (David Hartman) and Oomiak (Mako) in a giant airship called *The Hyperion* to search for his lost son. Their adventures take them deep within the Arctic circle to a mysterious cloud-enshrouded land populated by Viking warriors. Sentenced to death by the high priest Godi, they escape being

engulfed by a lava flow by crossing the perilous Bay of Whales. Alas, excellent effects by Peter Ellenshaw, Art Cruickshank and Danny Lee fail to rescue this tedious and overlong film, which was premiered in England in December 1974.

1975

CARTOON CAROUSEL Featuring 13 classic short cartoons, including *Window Cleaners*, *Father's Lion* and *Bee at the Beach*, the compilation was released in Denmark in 1975.

THE STRONGEST MAN IN THE WORLD (F) Director Vincent McEveety. Kurt Russell returns as troublesome Medfield College student Dexter Riley (below). This time Riley attains superman strength when he eats a cereal containing a strange chemical. He tries to find out what's responsible for his new powers, which he uses to help Medfield win a weight-lifting contest with another college. Co-stars include Joe Flynn as Dean Higgins, Eve Arden as Harriet, the head of a company that buys the secret formula, Cesar Romero as the villainous A. J. Arno and Phil Silvers as Harriet's competitor, the wily Krinkle.

LET'S RELAX Originally released in Denmark, this cartoon compilation features 10 individual cartoons.

MAGIC AND MUSIC (Ed) Hans Conried, the voice of Captain Hook in *Peter Pan*, guest-starred on the Disney television special *One Hour in Wonderland* in 1950 disguised as the Magic Mirror from *Snow White*. In 1958 he re-appeared in the role in the *Disneyland* show *Magic and Music*. In the 16mm release of the same title, he introduces students to Rimsky-Korsakoff's 'Flight of the Bumblebee' and Beethoven's Sixth symphony with extracts from *Bumble Boogie* (from *Melody Time*) and *Fantasia*.

THE CASTAWAY COWBOY (F) Director Vincent McEveety. Using some stunning location shots, the film is set on the island of Kauai in the 1850s. Vera Miles plays Henrietta MacAvoy. Together with her son Booten she rescues Lincoln Costain (James Garner, above), a Texas cowboy who has been shanghaied. MacAvoy persuades Costain to stay and teach the Hawaiian farm-hands how to profit from their herds of wild cattle. Garner's second film for Disney was also the second

If The Fergi Fits, Wear It (Or Turning T-Shirts into Profit) (Ed) Producer Dave Bell. The first in a series of four 16mm educational titles explains how a small business can be run successfully.

Barbara: Inside Out (Ed) Producer Sandy Whiteside. The 16mm short uses fantasy to show how mental health can be improved and inter-personal conflicts resolved.

The Apple Dumpling Gang (F) Director Norman Tokar. A comedy western, in the wake of Mel Brooks' immensely successful *Blazing Saddles*, starring Bill Bixby, Slim Pickens and Don Knotts, and Tim Conway (opposite above with Knotts) as the bungling Hash Knife Outfit, *The Apple Dumpling Gang* had all the right ingredients to make it a modest success. Donavan (Bixby), a professional gambler, inherits a fortune when he becomes the unwilling guardian of three orphaned youngsters who are co-owners of a recently discovered gold mine. Two of the children form the Apple Dumpling Gang and plot to steal their own gold so that they can stay with Donavan instead of their real guardian, the greedy Wintle. Based on a book by Jack M. Bickham, the film proved popular enough with audiences for a sequel, *The Apple Dumpling Gang Rides Again*, in 1979 and a spin-off tv series.

Escape To Witch Mountain (F) Director John Hough. Based on the book by Alexander Key, the film tells how bizarre psychic powers draw two unusual children (Kim Richards and Ike Eisenmann) to a mysterious alien encounter, one that will they hope bring them a safe haven from the evil billionaire Aristotle Bolt (Ray Milland), who wants to use their incredible powers of levitation, precognition and telepathy for his own sinister use. But the children have one secret that even Bolt is unaware of – they are extra-terrestrials and must reach Witch Mountain to rendezvous with their spaceship. This highly entertaining science-fiction film has some interesting special effects, including a scene in which a flying mobile-home is pursued by an upside-down helicopter. The cast includes Donald Pleasence and Eddie Albert, and such was the film's popularity that it was followed by a sequel, *Return From Witch Mountain* (1978). In 1982 a 16mm extract was released in the Films As Literature series.

History of Animation (Ed) On the *Disneyland* television series in 1955, Walt Disney hosted a special on the technique of film animation entitled *The Story of the Animated Drawing*. In 1975 a 16mm educational version was released which incorporated a great deal of original footage with new colour animated sequences. Exploring the pioneering efforts of the early animators, it features scenes of Winsor McCay's Gertie the Dinosaur, Pat Sullivan's Felix the Cat and Disney's own star, Mickey Mouse.

A Day in Nature's Community (Ed) Adapted from *One Day on Beetle Rock*, this 16mm film offers a fascinating insight into the survival and ecological relationships of the animals living in the mountainous region of the Sierra Nevada.

Donald Duck's Frantic Antics Released in Finland, this cartoon compilation includes among its 12 titles *Pluto's Housewarming*, *Pluto's Christmas Tree* and *Crazy With the Heat*.

Return of the Big Cat (F) Director Tom Leetch. This fascinating story of a wild dog called Boomer was first shown on the Disney television series in 1974. Tamed by a pioneering family living in northern California in 1890, the dog rescues the youngest member of the family from an attack by a man-eating cougar. Among the stars of this neatly photographed film are Jeremy Slate, Pat Crowley, Jeff East and David Wayne.

Fantasy on Skis (F) Director Fred Iselin. First shown on *The Wonderful World of Color* tv series in 1962, the featurette, which was released theatrically in 1975, concerns 9-year-old Susie, who lives in her father's ski-lodge in Aspen, Colorado. When she is trapped in an avalanche her St Bernard dog, Bruno, comes to the rescue.

One of Our Dinosaurs is Missing (F) Director Robert Stevenson. Peter Ustinov, no stranger to Disney films after starring in *Blackbeard's Ghost* and voicing Prince John and King Richard in the animated *Robin Hood*, returns as Hnup Wan of the Chinese London Intelligence Office. Microfilm of the mysterious and top secret Lotus X formula has been hidden inside a dinosaur skeleton at the Natural History Museum by Lord Southmere (Derek Nimmo). Hnup Wan, his replacement from Peking, Quon (Clive Revill), and a band of English nannies become involved in a race against time to retrieve it. Based on *The Great Dinosaur Robbery* by David Forrest, the film has crazy car chases (left), melodramatic performances, brilliant miniature special effects and some appalling kung fu battles (a martial art popular with the teen audience at the time) between Chinese heavies and umbrella-wielding nannies. The cast includes Helen Hayes, Joan Sims, Roy Kinnear, Bernard Bresslaw, Joss Ackland and a host of British stars, yet neither they nor Peter Ustinov, who plays Hnup as a cross between J. Carroll Naish and Fu Manchu, can elevate the film much above the level of slapstick. Successful in Europe, it didn't do so well at the US box-office.

The Best of Walt Disney's True-Life Adventures (F) Director James Algar. Winston Hibler narrates this feature-length tribute to Walt Disney's pioneering nature films (below). Using sequences from *The Living Desert*, *The Vanishing Prairie*, *White Wilderness* and so on, the film also includes scenes of Walt introducing various types of animals from the prologues to his television shows. At the end is the entertaining climax to the featurette *Water Birds* (1953).

1976

NO DEPOSIT, NO RETURN (F) Director Norman Tokar. The stars are outsmarted by Duster the skunk, an appealing little character who adds to the mayhem when 11-year old Tracy Osborne (Kim Richards) and her 8-year-old brother Jay (Brad Savage) find themselves sharing accommodation in California with two inept safe-crackers, Duke Mayfield (Darren McGavin) and Bert Delaney (Don Knotts (right)). Hoping to raise money so that they can spend their holidays in Hong Kong with their mother (Barbara Feldon), the children pretend to be kidnapped and ask their rich uncle, J. W. Osborne (David Niven), for a ransom of $100,000. A thrilling climax, in which the children are trapped in a giant safe, adds to the excitement of this above-average comedy.

RIDE A WILD PONY (F) Director Don Chaffey. A moralistic tale of love and jealousy, which was adapted from James Aldridge's novel *A Sporting Proposition* by Rosemary Anne Sisson, the film relates what happens when a poor Australian boy, Scotty Pirie (Robert Bettles), loses his pony to a crippled rich girl, Josie Eyre (Eva Griffith). Co-stars in this touching drama include Michael Craig and John Meillon. In 1976, an educational extract, *Being Right: Can You Still Lose?*, was released. The Studio hoped that the moral story would earn the film a nomination for an Academy Award, so it was pre-released in December 1975.

GUS (F) Director Vincent McEveety. This little-known feature relates the unlikely story of how the California Atoms football team wins a place in the Super Bowl thanks to an extraordinary team member – a Yugoslav mule called Gus (below). Don Knotts stars as the team's long-suffering coach, while Ed Asner (who later sacrificed comedy roles for a more serious television career) portrays the team's owner. Co-stars Tim Conway and Tom Bosley appear as two con-men determined to sabotage the game.

DONALD AND MICKEY Most compilations featuring classic Disney shorts have been released in feature-length format, but on this occasion, the film contained only four cartoons and was a programme filler for Japanese distribution.

FILMING NATURE'S MYSTERIES (Ed) A behind-the-scenes look at how some of the spectacular wildlife footage in Disney's nature classics was filmed. Among the techniques highlighted in the 16mm film are micro-photography, time-lapse photography and the use of the strobe light.

TREASURE OF MATECUMBE (F) Director Vincent McEveety. The Studio hoped to recapture some of the spirit of such films as *In Search of the Castaways* and *Island at the Top of the World* with this adventure yarn set in post-Civil War America, but it failed miserably. Peter Ustinov stars as medicine man Dr Snodgrass (below with Attmore), who is befriended by Davie (Johnny Doran) and Thad (Billy Attmore) in a search for buried treasure off the Florida Keys. Indians, alligators and a hurricane beset the group on their quest, not to mention the villainous Spangler (Vic Morrow) and his henchmen, who want the treasure for themselves. The storm scenes were impressively staged on a Florida beach under the watchful eye of Walt Disney World ecologist

Wynn). Unfortunately, his past catches up with him when the strange ring that had transformed him into a dog some years before falls into the hands of ice-cream salesman Tim (Tim Conway). A series of adventures follows in which Wilby is involved in a custard-pie routine, an escape from a dog pound and a bizarre car chase. In the climax, the villainous Slade is turned into a bulldog. The film was based on a book by Felix Salten, the author of *Bambi* and the screenplay was by Don Tait. Suzanne Pleshette co-stars.

1977

EPCOT '77 (Sp) A 16mm presentation gives an update on the progress of EPCOT's two future lands, Future World and World Showcase. As the Studio had suppressed, as far as the public was concerned, film of Disney's original ideas for EPCOT as a living blueprint of a future city, the film is free to express the entertainment possibilities that lie in the new-look EPCOT.

☆ THE RESCUERS (F) Directors Wolfgang Reitherman, John Lounsbery and Art Stevens. Although this may not be the best feature-length animated film to be produced by the Studio since Walt's death in 1966, it was a welcome return to a style of animation and storytelling sadly missing since the early 1960s. Based on books by Margery Sharp and adapted for the screen by Larry Clemmons and Ken Anderson, the film relates the adventures of two mice, Bernard and Bianca (voiced by Bob Newhart and Eva Gabor), who rescue a small orphan called Penny (Michelle Stacy) from the evil clutches of the greedy Madame Medusa (below, brilliantly brought to life in animation by Milt Kahl and voiced by Geraldine Page), her sinister sidekick Mr Snoops (Joe Flynn) and her alligator bodyguards, Brutus and Nero. The mice are ably assisted by Orville the albatross (Jim Jordan), Rufus the cat (John McIntire), a whole army of swamp folk and a brave little dragonfly, who doubles as an outboard motor, called Evinrude (James Macdon-

Kathy Shannon, who, as well as being responsible for looking after the actors' wellbeing, was also there to ensure that the environment wasn't damaged by the artificially produced gale-force winds. Based on a book by Robert Lewis Taylor, the film co-stars Robert Foxworth and Joan Hackett.

THE REUNION (Ed) Producer Glenn Johnson Productions. A look at the career awareness of 6th-graders, showing the implications of their individual choices 10 years on.

DONALD DUCK FUN FESTIVAL Originally released in Denmark, the compilation contains 10 shorts featuring Donald and the gang.

THE SHAGGY D.A. (F) Director Robert Stevenson. Loosely based on the Studio's classic hit *The Shaggy Dog* (1959) the sequel couldn't live up to the original's box-office performance. Dean Jones (above) takes the part (originally played by Tommy Kirk) of young lawyer Wilby Daniels, who decides to run for office against the resident District Attorney, 'Honest' John Slade (Keenan

mine, Lord Harrogate (Alastair Sim, in his last film, left, with Maurice Colbourne). The story, expertly photographed by Paul Beeson, takes place in the Yorkshire mining village of Emsdale in 1909, and the film successfully captures the volatile situation within the mining community. Co-starring Peter Barkworth, Susan Tebbs and Geraldine McEwan, the film is a perfect example of how well the European Disney product could compare with its US counterpart.

THE MANY ADVENTURES OF WINNIE THE POOH (F) Directors Wolfgang Reitherman and John Lounsbery. Although this full-length animated feature (below left) is a compilation of three theatrical featurettes – *Winnie the Pooh and the Honey Tree*, *Winnie the Pooh and the Blustery Day* and *Winnie the Pooh and Tigger Too* – three new linking animated sequences were added. The last was based on the final chapter of A. A. Milne's *The House At Pooh Corner*, in which Pooh and Christopher Robin say goodbye. Despite this sad parting, a new film was released in 1983 entitled *Winnie the Pooh and A Day for Eeyore*, and an educational film, *Winnie the Pooh Discovers the Seasons*, was released in 1981.

ald). After many exciting adventures, the little animals turn the tables on the evil Madame Medusa and thwart her search for the Devil's Eye diamond. There are some engaging songs by Carol Conners, Ayn Robbins and Sammy Fain. The animation was supervised by Studio veterans Ollie Johnston, Milt Kahl, Frank Thomas and Don Bluth, and although it used some footage from *Bambi*, the film proved a huge success in Europe and has prompted the Studio to consider a sequel.

FREAKY FRIDAY (F) Director Gary Nelson. Jodie Foster gives a remarkable performance as a 13-year-old schoolgirl with the mind of her 35-year-old mother. Based on the book by Mary Rodgers, the film tells how a mother and daughter, who never see eye to eye, change places with

one another, and it describes the problems they encounter before they realize that they both preferred things the way they were. Co-stars were Barbara Harris, who received a Best Actress nomination at the annual Golden Globe Awards, and John Astin as the confused husband and father. In 1979 a 16mm extract was released in the Films As Literature series.

THE LITTLEST HORSE THIEVES (released in Britain in May 1976 as ESCAPE FROM THE DARK) (F) Director Charles Jarrott. An emotional tale of three children, Alice (Chloe Franks), Dave (Andrew Harrison) and Tommy (Benjie Bolgar), who rescue some pit ponies from being slaughtered when their usefulness in the coalmines is at an end. Their daring act leads the miners into industrial confrontation with the owner of the

DONALD DUCK'S SUMMER MAGIC More feature-length specials were made of Donald Duck films than of any other Disney character, mostly because all his solo films, unlike Mickey's, were colour. The 11 cartoons featuring in this compilation, include *Trailer Horn*, *Out On a Limb* and *Pluto's Party*.

HERBIE GOES TO MONTE·CARLO (F) Director Vincent McEveety. 'The Love Bug falls "hood-over-wheels" for a classy chassis!' in the third Volkswagen adventure, which was filmed on location in Paris and Monaco. Herbie teams up with his old friend Jim Douglas (Dean Jones), who, together with his mechanic Wheely (Don Knotts), arrives in France to enter the first annual road race from Paris to Monte Carlo. Herbie's petrol tank becomes the hiding place for the

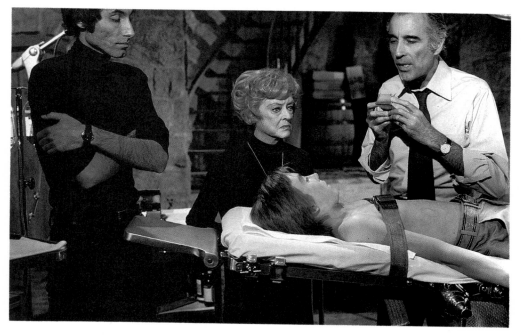

Etoile de Joie diamond, which was stolen by two jewel thieves (Bernard Fox and Roy Kinnear). In the meantime Douglas has fallen in love with one of the other contestants, Diane Darcy (Julie Sommars), and Herbie is totally besotted with her attractive car, a Lancia Scorpion. A predictable tale, but with some hilarious performances, as Herbie defeats yet another gang of crooks.

FERGI GOES INC (Ed) Producer Dave Bell. Winner of the American Film Festival Red Ribbon Award, this 16mm film examines how capital is acquired and how advertising increases business.

FERGI DIVERSIFIES (Ed) Producer Dave Bell. Students are taught how a company grows, sells stock, takes on loans and merges to increase business and profits.

THE PEOPLE ON MARKET STREET (Ed) Producer Terry Kahn Organization. Seven 16mm educational films were made with the cooperation of the University of California. Each invites students to meet the ordinary people of Market Street and learn about important economic concepts. *Cost* illustrates how the activities involved in throwing a party can be used to underline the saving of money, time and resources. *Demand* teaches students the fundamental laws of demand and how they affect wealth and occupation. *Market Clearing Price* offers an easy-to-understand guide to the inventory and competitive market prices. *Property Rights and Pollution* uses basic examples to focus on the use and misuse of property rights in the exchange economy. *Scarcity and Planning* discusses organizing and coordinating production to achieve the right amount of goods. *Supply* explains how it affects production costs and eventual unit cost, and finally *Wages and Production* shows how such subjects can influence the number of workers an employer chooses to hire.

BORN TO RUN (F) Director Don Chaffey. A young Australian boy and his grandfather train a colt to win a harness race and save their farm from bankruptcy. The film stars Tom Farley, Robert Bettles (above) and Andrew McFarlane.

☆ PETE'S DRAGON (F) Director Don Chaffey. Dragons have featured prominently in a number of Disney films, but in *Pete's Dragon*, the Studio's first musical since *Bedknobs and Broomsticks*, the fire-breathing star saves what is, in many

respects, a lacklustre affair. Sean Marshall stars as Pete, a 9-year-old orphan who is befriended by Elliott, a 30-foot dragon with green scales, purple wings (opposite below) and the ability to become invisible. Elliott helps Pete to escape from his wicked foster parents, Lena Gogan (Shelley Winters) and her husband Merle (Charles Tyner), and their two oafish sons (Gary Morgan and Jeff Conaway) to the nearby town of Passamaquoddy, where Pete finds companionship with the lighthouse-keeper Lampie (Mickey Rooney) and his daughter Nora (Helen Reddy). After many adventures and a number of tiresome songs, Pete finds a permanent home with Nora, her sweetheart Paul (Cal Bartlett) and Lampie, thanks to the help and support of his amazing friend Elliott. Unfortunately the human cast, with the exception of young Sean Marshall, is disappointing. Elliott, however, created by Ken Anderson and directed by animator Don Bluth, is a wonderful scene-stealer. Effects animation by Dorse A. Lanpher flawlessly combines the fiery star with the humans in numerous sequences. Based on a story by Seton I. Miller and S.S. Field, the film was launched with an advertising campaign that rivalled that accorded to *Mary Poppins*, and, perhaps as a result, the US box-office took $18 million. Although Helen Reddy is a competent singer, her acting leaves a lot to be desired; Miss Winters, on the other hand, scales new heights in the art of over-acting. Even the slapstick routines of co-stars Jim Dale and Red Buttons fail to save the day. The songs by Al Kasha and Joel Hirschhorn are, with the exception of 'Candle on the Water', forgettable, and many were the first casualties when the Studio, disappointed by the audience's reaction at premiere engagements, edited the film for general release – a fate that befell many of the post-*Poppins* musicals.

1978

CANDLESHOE (F) Director Norman Tokar. Based on the book *Christmas at Candleshoe* by Michael Innes, the film stars Jodie Foster as Casey, a Los Angeles tomboy who pretends to be the heiress of a stately English manor called Candleshoe. Assisted by the butler, Priory (David Niven), and the real owner, Lady Gwendolyn (Helen Hayes), Casey turns the tables on a sinister Englishman

called Bundage (Leo McKern) and uncovers the buried treasure of the late Captain St Edmund. Foster plays her fifth role in a Disney film convincingly, but David Niven, who plays a number of different parts in the film, steals the show. Shot on location in Los Angeles, southern England and at Pinewood Studios, the film was pre-released in December 1977 for possible inclusion in the nominations for the 1978 Academy Awards.

RETURN FROM WITCH MOUNTAIN (F) Director John Hough. The more contemporary threat of radioactive fallout becomes the central theme of the sequel to 1975's *Escape to Witch Mountain*. Extra-terrestrial children Tia (Kim Richards) and Tony Malone (Ike Eisenmann) are kidnapped by evil scientist Dr Victor Gannon (Christopher Lee) and his scheming partner Letha Wedge (Bette Davis, above with Ike Eisenmann). Brainwashed by the scientist, Tony uses his supernatural powers to attack his sister, in a taunt finale in which the countdown to a nuclear explosion has already begun. Set in and around Los Angeles, this entertaining saga has interesting special effects by Eustace Lycett, Art Cruickshank and Danny Lee, which help to make this adventure yarn better than the original film.

DONALD DUCK'S CARTOON MANIA Released in Denmark, this programme of 11 shorts includes *Little Hiawatha*, *Don's Fountain of Youth* and *Bootle Beetle*.

MICKEY MOUSE GOLDEN JUBILEE SHORTS PROGRAM Mickey Mouse celebrates his 50th birthday in a feature-length compilation containing 12 separate cartoons released in Germany.

HOT LEAD AND COLD FEET (F) Director Robert Butler. Kevin Corcoran, who as a child actor had starred in a number of Disney features (including *Toby Tyler*, *Old Yeller* and *Swiss Family Robinson*), turned associate producer on this Jim Dale vehicle, a western parody in the *Apple Dumpling Gang* vein. Co-stars include Karen Valentine, Don Knotts and Jack Elam, as Dale (who plays three parts in the film) tries to take possession of a rickety old cow-town called Bloodshy.

TRICKS OF OUR TRADE (Ed) Hosted by Walt Disney, this edited 16mm release originally appeared on the *Disneyland* television series in

1979

TAKE DOWN (F) Director Kieth Merrill. The first non-Disney film to be picked up for distribution by Buena Vista since Walt's death in 1966 concerns an English teacher who finds himself in the unlikely position of coach to a high school wrestling team. The Studio's first PG (Parental Guidance) rated release, it stars Edward Herrmann, Kathleen Lloyd, Lorenzo Lamas, Maureen McCormick and Stephen Furst (who went on to star in another Buena Vista release, *Midnight Madness*).

THE NORTH AVENUE IRREGULARS (F) Director Bruce Bilson. 'The FBI couldn't do it ... the CIA couldn't do it ... so they sent for ...' The film (entitled *Hill's Angels* in Europe after a well-

1957. It is infinitely more entertaining than *The Story of the Animated Drawing* (the 16mm *History of Animation*) because it concentrates on principles of film-making at the Studio. The film also uses sequences from *Snow White* and *Bambi* and contains the first tv screening of *The Dance of the Hours* sequence from *Fantasia*. An added bonus is archive footage of effects animators at work, including a drawing class with a live model.

FERGI MEETS THE CHALLENGE (Ed) Producer Dave Bell. The fourth 16mm film in the *Fergi Builds A Business* series teaches students how businesses cope with success and failure.

THE CAT FROM OUTER SPACE (F) Director Norman Tokar. Although the cast includes Roddy McDowall, Ken Berry (above), Sandy Duncan, McLean Stevenson and Harry Morgan (in his sixth film for Disney), the real star is 'Zunar 5J/90 Doric 47', or, in Earth-talk, 'Jake the cat', an Abyssinian extraterrestrial, which speaks English, levitates his friends and pilots a beetle-shaped spacecraft in what the film's advertising referred to as 'A Close Encounter of the "Furred" Kind!' Alan Young, the voice of Scrooge McDuck in *Mickey's Christmas Carol*, makes a guest appearance as Dr Wenger, a well-intentioned veterinarian. As in Steven Spielberg's *E.T.*, the extraterrestrial, Jake, is trying to get home before being captured by the military; unlike *E.T.*, however, Jake falls for an earthly feline called Lucy Belle and accepts citizenship of the United States instead.

EYEWITNESS TO HISTORY (Ed) Producer Christian Blackwood Productions. Three black and white films were made on 16mm. *The Events* uses newsreel footage to show Lindbergh's famous flight, Hitler's invasion of Poland and Martin Luther King's fight for equality. *The Lifestyles* highlights sporting events as seen through the lens of the newsreel cameras, including a visit to the Olympics. *The People* looks at personalities like Albert Einstein, Teddy Roosevelt and Al Capone through newsreel recordings.

THE SMALL ONE (F) Director Don Bluth. A poignant story of how Small One, a donkey, is taken by his reluctant owner, a Hebrew boy, to be sold at a Jerusalem market (below). The boy eventually finally sells his donkey to a kindly man named Joseph, who uses it to take his pregnant wife Mary to Bethlehem. This gentle story, which was based on the book by Charles Tazewell, was sympathetically transferred to the screen by Vance Gerry and Pete Young, and it includes some delightful songs by Don Bluth and Richard Rich.

known television series), which is set in the small town of New Campton, stars Edward Herrmann as the Reverend Mike Hill (left, with Virginia Capers), who is disappointed to find that his congregation is uninterested in church affairs. When a syndicate threatens to close down the church, he enlists the aid of his female parishioners – Susan Clark, Barbara Harris, Karen Valentine and Cloris Leachman. Bilson, who won an Emmy for directing episodes of *Get Smart*, manages to inject comic timing into the story, which was a book by the Reverend Albert Fay Hill.

FOOTLOOSE FOX (F) In this featurette, one of a series of popular animal films, a young fox and an 'apartment-hunting' badger build up a unique relationship while sharing a den together.

THE APPLE DUMPLING GANG RIDES AGAIN (F) Director Vincent McEveety. A cliché-ridden title that did nothing to guarantee the box-office receipts of the first film. Tim Conway and Don Knotts again star as the inept Hash Knife Gang but finally manage to bring some real villains to justice.

UNIDENTIFIED FLYING ODDBALL (F) Director Russ Mayberry. Disney was at the forefront of the early-1980s revival in time-travel films. In ths adaptation of Mark Twain's *A Connecticut Yankee in King Arthur's Court*, Dennis Dugan stars as astronaut Tom Trimble, who unwillingly launches himself into space and, more importantly, back in time to England A.D. 508 and the reign of King Arthur, who is played by Kenneth More (below with Rodney Bewes and Dennis Dugan). The treacherous Sir Mordred (Jim Dale) is plotting with Merlin the Magician (Ron Moody) to overthrow the King, while co-stars John le Mesurier and Sheila White add to the mayhem. Cliff Culley's photographic effects, including the magnificent spacecraft *Stardust One*, are most convincing. Known in Europe as *The Spaceman and King Arthur*, the film, which was shot on location in England, proved reasonably successful at the box-office.

THE TRULY EXCEPTIONAL . . . (Ed) Producer Dave Bell and Associates for the Walt Disney Educational Media Company. Three short films were included in the series. *The Truly Exceptional: Carol Johnston*, which won the CINE Golden Eagle Award, highlights the bravery and dedication of one-armed champion gymnast Carol Johnston. This film was eventually expanded into a television special and released in 1981 as a 48-minute featurette retitled *Lefty*. *The Truly Exceptional: Dan Haley* helps students to be more aware of their potential by exploring the

fulfilled life of a 16-year-old blind boy, who refuses to allow his handicap to prevent him from achieving success. *The Truly Exceptional: Tom and Virl Osmond* looks at the remarkable achievements of the two eldest Osmond Brothers, who, although deaf since birth, have been able to help their talented brothers and sister in show business.

THE RESTLESS SEA (Ed) Revised and updated from a 1964 television programme on oceanography, this 16mm educational release uses animation and live action to illustrate some fascinating facts about oceans of the world.

☆ THE BLACK HOLE (F) Director Gary Nelson. 'A journey that begins where everything ends,' seemed slightly inappropriate publicity for Disney's first science-fiction epic. From the audience's point of view, the film seemed to end where everything should have begun. Maximilian Schell stars as Dr Hans Reinhardt, an eccentric megalomaniac who is attempting to voyage through the heart of a black hole, a mysterious whirlpool in which the gravitational pull of a collapsed star absorbs all matter including light. His impressive spacecraft, *The Cygnus*, becomes a prison for Earth travellers Dr Alex Durant (Anthony Perkins), Captain Dan Holland (Robert Forster), Lieutenant Charles Pizer (Joseph Bottoms), Dr Kate McCrae (Yvette Mimieux, above), Harry Booth (Ernest Borgnine) and a cute robot called V.I.N.Cent (voiced by Roddy McDowall). They discover that the sinister Reinhardt has robotized the original crew, while his bodyguard, a formidable robot called (curiously enough) Maximilian, shoots lasers and has spinning can-openers for hands. In an effects-laden climax, when science fact is thrown out of the spaceship, the three surviving Earth people try to escape being crushed to death as the ship plunges into the all-enveloping black hole. Unfortunately these pyrotechnics mean very little: the action is hindered by a pedestrian script by Jeb Rosebrook and Gerry Day, and the film appears, on the surface at least, to be *20,000 Leagues*

Under the Sea in space. The film is reported to have cost $20 million. Special effects veterans Peter Ellenshaw, Art Cruickshank and Eustace Lycett have a wonderful time with the spiralling black hole, the highly detailed miniatures and impressive sets – the laser battles are so well executed that they put the random firing of weapons in *Star Wars* to shame – and animator Joe Hale was among those nominated for an Academy Award for his work on the film. Originally announced under the title *Space Probe One* as early as 1977, it's obvious that the Studio embarked on the project only because of the popularity of George Lucas' film. The promotional campaign consisted of an incredible array of media advertising – 'If this doesn't pull them in – nothing will!' claimed the Studio. Sadly, nothing did, not even a black hole, and although it earned $25 million at the US box-office, the film was quickly swallowed up in a plethora of science-fiction rip-offs that appeared in the early 1980s.

INCIDENT AT HAWK'S HILL (Ed) Based on the book by Allen Eckert, this film was adapted from the 1975 television show *The Boy Who Talked To Badgers* for 16mm educational use. As part of Disney's Films As Literature series, it relates how a lonely boy finds companionship in the wild animals he befriends.

UNDERSTANDING ALCOHOL USE AND ABUSE (Ed) Producers Reynolds Film Export and John Ewing. This 16mm animated educational release explains to youngsters in an imaginative way the dangers of alcohol.

THE NATIONAL STUDENT SAFETY TEST Five 16mm films were hosted by various television celebrities to help educate children in the importance of everyday safety. *The National Student First Aid Test* features Ruth Buzzi, star of the *Laugh-In* tv series and the voice in a number of Disney films, who teaches children the rules of first aid. In *The National Student Fire Safety Test* Ernest Lee Thomas reinforces student awareness of fire prevention. *The National Student Recreational Safety Test* stars Jimmie Walker of *Good Times*, who demonstrates how to prevent playground mishaps caused through carelessness. *The National Student School Safety Test*, hosted by Susan Richardson, shows youngsters the importance of safety at school. *The National Student Traffic Safety Test*, with actor Kent McCord of the *Adam-12* tv series, explains the correct procedures when crossing the road or riding a bike.

DONALD DUCK'S CARNIVAL OF LAUGHS Released in Denmark, this compilation of 11 shorts includes *Father's Lion*, *Susie the Little Blue Coupe* and *Chicken in the Rough*.

THE LONDON CONNECTION (filmed under the title *The London Affair*) (F) Director Robert Clouse. 'A spiralling web of mystery and intrigue,' claimed the posters. Luther Sterling (Jeffrey Byron) and his fellow American, Roger Pike (Larry Cedar), witness the kidnapping of an East European scientist by the sinister organization, OMEGA. A spectacular climax rounds off this James Bond-style adventure, which co-stars Roy Kinnear, Mona Washbourne, David Kossoff, Frank Windsor and Nigel Davenport. The film which was first shown on television in the US as *The Omega Connection*, was shot entirely on location in London, with British film veteran Jack Shampan as art director and Hugh Attwooll, one of the Founder Members of the Guild of Film Production Executives, as associate producer.

1980

MIDNIGHT MADNESS (F) Directors David Wechter and Michael Nankin. Rated PG (Parental Guidance) in the US, this film comedy was one of a small number of movies released without the Disney name (later titles, with the exception of *Trenchcoat* were marketed under the Touchstone banner). The story takes place in and around Los Angeles, where an eccentric student devises a weird game called the Great All Nighter. Five teams set off to uncover the clues on foot, while Harold (Stephen Furst) uses his computer to help solve the mystery. The co-stars are David Naughton, Debra Clinger, Eddie Deezen, Brad Wilkin and Maggie Roswell. Fast-paced and highly amusing, the film was marketed for a teenage audience and dictated the Studio's future policy regarding films for PG13 audiences. It was not released theatrically in Europe.

MICKEY MOUSE DISCO (Sp) In order to update the adventures of Mickey and the gang, the Studio hit on the idea of rereleasing extracts from some of the classic cartoons synchronized to a modern 'pop music' soundtrack, already released on a

Disneyland album in 1975. *Mickey Mouse Disco* (below) was the result, and it proved very popular with theatre audiences. The idea eventually grew into a successful series on The Disney Channel called *DTV*, in which songs by other artists were also synchronized to animation. The advertising for the album and film version showed Mickey spoofing John Travolta's classic dance pose from *Saturday Night Fever*.

THE LAST FLIGHT OF NOAH'S ARK (F) Director Charles Jarrott. Starring Elliott Gould, Genevieve Bujold, Ricky Schroder and Vincent Gardenia, the comedy drama is based on a story by Ernest K. Gann and relates what happens to a high-living pilot, Noah Dugan (Gould), and a straight-laced evangelist, Bernadette Lafleur (Bujold), when their transport, a dilapidated B-29 bomber, crash-lands with two young stowaways and some farm animals on an uncharted island. Here they encounter two Japanese soldiers who are unaware that World War II is over. Hostility turns to friendship as the group devises a way of converting their stricken plane into a floating 'Noah's Ark'. It's undemanding entertainment, even if the ad line 'On a wing and a prayer . . . they built a legend,' seems a bit over the top.

HERBIE GOES BANANAS! (F) Director Vincent McEveety. 'Olé! It's south of the border disorder,' hooted the publicity for the Love Bug's last adventure. Comedienne Cloris Leachman stars as Aunt Louise, who is thwarted in her attempts to sponsor the car in the Grande Premio de Brasil race by eccentric Captain Blythe, who dumps Herbie overboard on their way to South America (right). Befriended by a young boy called Paco (Joaquin Garay III), the Volkswagen survives its watery ordeal and takes on the roles of taxi, toreador, detective and hi-jacker and finally goes bananas in its attempt to capture a gang of smugglers. During a 10-year film career, the little

CALL IT COURAGE (Ed) Director Roy E. Disney. Based on Armstrong Sperry's award-winning novel, this abridged version of a 1973 television show is about a South Seas youth who overcomes his fear of the ocean by sailing beyond the safety of the island's barrier reef.

POPEYE (F) Director Robert Altman. It seems somehow ironic that Disney should be involved in co-financing and promoting a live-action version of an animated character who was at one time a rival to Mickey and the gang. The result was a disappointment, however. Starring television personality Robin Williams in the title role, the film relates the bizarre adventures of the spinach-eating sailor who is capable of great feats of strength. Accompanied by his girlfriend Olive Oyl (superbly played by Shelley Duvall) and hamburger fan Wimpy (Paul Dooley), Popeye stops his enemy Bluto (Paul L. Smith, below, with Williams) from stealing buried treasure on Scab Island. Having first appeared in the Thimble Theatre comic strip by E.C. Segar in 1929, Popeye's illustrious film career began at the Max Fleischer Studios in 1932. This Paramount/ Disney co-production, despite its large cast, some spectacular effects and an expensive set built in Malta, pales in comparison with some of the earlier animated adventures of the 1930s and '40s. The prostitutes of Hotcash Harry's betting parlour seem slightly out of place in a Disney film, and the songs by Harry Nilsson are instantly forgettable. Written for the screen by Jules Feiffer, the film has not damaged the enduring appeal of the original cartoon version of the character. Disney handled the distribution outside America, where the film was edited from 114 to 97 minutes.

1981

☆ DRAGONSLAYER (F) Director Matthew Robbins. 'Its talons tear, its breath burns, it is terror,' claimed the publicity for Disney's second co-production with Paramount Pictures. The film is a medieval fantasy with all manner of magic and

car had also made history: it was the first car to be issued an American passport in which it was described as: '5 feet tall with sealed beam eyes and a sunroof in place of hair.' It was also the first car to leave tyre marks outside Grauman's Chinese Theater and to 'drive' through the locks of the Panama Canal. In short, Herbie had become as endearing and enduring a Disney character as any of the animal stars and proved that anthropomorphism worked just as well in live action as in animation.

THE SKY TRAP (Ed) Director Jerome Courtland. A 16mm release that relates what happens when a young sailplane pilot is blackmailed into smuggling a cargo of heroin into the United States across the Mexican border. It was first seen on tv in 1979.

FOODS AND FUN: A NUTRITION ADVENTURE (Ed) Director Rick Reinert. In 1971 a new Disney animated character, the Orange Bird, appeared at the Florida Citrus Sunshine pavilion in Walt Disney World. Some years later he became the star of a short in which he teaches students the importance of sensible eating, rest and proper exercise. There were songs by the Sherman brothers.

RICK, YOU'RE IN: A STORY ABOUT MAIN-STREAMING (Ed) Producer Dave Bell & Associates. A 16mm educational film underlining the difficulties confronting a handicapped student confined to a wheelchair and showing how such a person can be readily accepted at high school.

FIT TO BE YOU (Ed) Three 16mm films were included in the series. Flexibility and Body Composition, which explains the relationship of mass to fat in maintaining proper body composition, includes a humorous animated sequence. Heart and Lungs teaches students how these vital organs work and how daily exercise helps to improve their efficiency. Muscles uses animation to explore the inside of the human body and stresses the importance of physical fitness.

THE ATOM: A CLOSER LOOK (Ed) Producer Corporate Productions. The need to revise the

Studio's thinking about the morality of atomic energy led to a revised version of 1958's Our Friend the Atom. The new film discusses the public's concern over the dangers of radioactivity and the recycling of atomic waste, although it still promotes a positive attitude to nuclear power. The future of the atom is covered by new animated sequences, and the ingenious idea that an atomic chain reaction can be compared to a table of ping-pong balls catapulted out of mouse-traps survives intact from 1958. The film's presenters offer a more lucid approach to the subject than Heinz Haber did, but the film fails to entertain as the original had done so successfully.

mayhem, co-starring Sir Ralph Richardson, Caitlin Clarke, Emrys James and Albert Salmi. Peter MacNicol plays Galen, a young man who dreams of becoming a dragonslayer. When homes and families in faraway Urland are ravaged by a terrifying flying dragon called Vermithrax Pejorative, Galen sets out to do battle with the hideous creature. Unusually for Disney, even in a co-production, the Middle Ages are not represented by the sunlit English hills of *The Unidentified Flying Oddball* or the wholesomeness of *The Sword in the Stone*. Urland in the 6th century is a dark and pitiful place where young maidens are sacrificed to the mighty dragon. The film is visually staggering; the dazzling effects, nominated for an Academy Award (but losing to *Raiders of the Lost Ark*), were produced at George Lucas' Industrial Light and Magic in California under the watchful eye of Brian Johnson (who began his career working on *2001 A Space Odyssey*). The dragon (above) is exceptionally realistic, and its first appearance, towering above Galen on the lake of fire, is reminiscent of Maleficent's monstrous form in *Sleeping Beauty*. There is a pounding musical score by Alex North, but unfortunately the film is terribly slow and the wait for the final confrontation between good and evil a long one. Only a moderate success at the box-office, *Dragonslayer* convinced Disney that joint-studio ventures were not a good idea. So the Studio set about launching its own subsidiary film unit to make and release films not usually associated with the Disney name.

THE NICK PRICE STORY OF NON-MANIPULATIVE SELLING (Ed) Three educational films form this series. *A Better Way to Go: An Introduction to Non-Manipulative Selling* encourages salesmen to be not only persuasive but skilled in problem solving as well. *The Danbury Secret of Flexible Behaviour* teaches students how to use a relaxed and varied attitude toward customers. *The Voice: Questions That Help You Sell* explains the importance of communication at work and how customer relations can be improved.

AMY (F) Director Vincent McEveety. Jenny Agutter (below) stars as a young women who, in 1913, left home on a personal crusade to teach the deaf. Although it was made for television, this heartwarming story was released to theatres, and a 16 mm extract for schools, *Amy On the Lips*, was issued the same year.

THE DEVIL AND MAX DEVLIN (F) Director Steven Hilliard Stern. 'Not since *Dante's Inferno* has Hollywood seen anything to rival the elaborate sets created for *The Devil and Max Devlin*,' claimed the publicity handout, as Stage 3 at the

Studio was transformed into a 'living hell'. Twenty butane furnaces and 36,000 pounds of dry ice provide the backdrop for a humorous story in which a crooked apartment manager, Max Devlin (Elliott Gould), finds himself in Hell. The Devil's left-hand man, Barney Satin (Bill Cosby), offers him a reprieve from eternal damnation if Devlin brings him the souls of three innocent people. But, once he's back on Earth, Devlin acts in such a 'disgustingly nice way' that the occupants of Hell decide to let him live, as his changed character could set a bad example and contaminate their fiery environment.

THE DREAM CALLED EPCOT (TP) In the same way that a promotional film was presented to visitors in a special exhibition building before the opening of Walt Disney World in 1971, a similar motion picture was used to tell audiences about the new EPCOT complex, due to open in 1982, at the EPCOT Preview Center in the Magic Kingdom.

THE FOX AND THE HOUND (F) Directors Art Stevens, Ted Berman and Richard Rich. With the success of the animated feature *The Rescuers* (1977), the Studio had high hopes for its next animated film, which was based on the book by Daniel P. Mannix. It was well-hyped prior to release, the Studio even referring to it as its 20th full-length animated feature – which is rather odd, as *The Black Cauldron*, which followed in 1985, was advertised as Disney's 25th animated film. (Obviously the Disney publicists had been involved in a little skulduggery to come up with this jump in numbers.) Briefly, the film relates the story of an unusual friendship between a young fox, Tod, and a hunting dog, Copper (above), whose owner, Amos Slade, believes it's against the law of nature for a fox and a hound to get

along. As they grow up they learn about fear and to hate each other, but in a heart-rending climax, when Tod lies helpless in front of Slade's gun, it's Copper who breaks the rules and comes to the rescue. Unfortunately there are few highlights, although a fight between Copper and a ferocious bear is a sequence worthy of Disney's earlier

animated classics. Tod and Copper are voiced by Mickey Rooney and Kurt Russell, while Pearl Bailey lends her singing talents to the wise old owl, Big Mama. Other voices include Pat Buttram, Paul Winchell, Jack Albertson and Jeannette Nolan. What is particularly interesting about the film is that it's the first major effort by a whole new generation of Disney artists, although animators Ollie Johnston, Frank Thomas and Cliff Nordberg were involved in a supervisory capacity. Animators Wolfgang Reitherman and Art Stevens acted as co-producers, with Walt's son-in-law Ron Miller as Executive Producer. A satisfactory film, if not in the classic mould, it was well publicized and grossed more than any other animated feature at the American box-office. The same year a 16mm extract was released for schools entitled *The Fox and the Hound: A Lesson in Being Careful.*

ONCE UPON A MOUSE (Sp) Producer Kramer/ Rocklin Studios in association with Walt Disney Productions. There have been several retrospectives exploring the magic of the Disney product. None has been quite as effective, however, as this whirlwind tour of the Disney worlds of entertainment. The life of Mickey Mouse is combined with footage of Walt Disney and special photographic techniques from films such as *The Black Hole*. An inspired climax sees a 'march past' of some of the Studio's finest creations.

CONDORMAN (F) Director Charles Jarrott. 'Take a pinch of James Bond, a small sprinkling of Superman, mix lightly together and the result might well be *Condorman*!' Or so the Studio wanted audiences to believe. Woody, a comic-strip artist played by Michael Crawford (below) gets involved with the CIA; a KGB villain, Krokov (Oliver Reed); and a beautiful Russian agent, Natalia (Barbara Carrera). Unfortunately the ingredients didn't really mix at all, and the film comes across as a strange mis-match of ideas, with Crawford especially seeming out of place in

this silly film. The stunt work is remarkable, however, and there are some frantic car and boat chases, supervised by effects expert Colin Chilvers. The screenplay by Marc Stirdivant, from Robert Sheckley's book *The Game of X*, raised few eyebrows.

WINNIE THE POOH DISCOVERS THE SEASONS (Ed) Director Rick Reinert. Helped by his friends, Pooh learns about hibernation, temperature and weather conditions. The film's lively and amusing format earned it an Honorable Mention at the 1982 American Film Festival.

REACHING OUT: A STORY ABOUT MAIN-STREAMING (Ed) Producer Dave Bell & Associates. The touching story of a multiply-handicapped girl called Mary, who joins a regular class. The film explores the special relationships between Mary and her colleagues as she 'reaches out' to win new friends.

SMOKING: THE CHOICE IS YOURS (Ed) Director John Ewing. A Blue Ribbon winner at the American Film Festival, the animated short effectively debunks the often glamorous image associated with tobacco. Narrated by Jack Angel, the film relates what happens when sports fanatic Edgar has to decide which is more important – smoking or his health.

THE COOKIE KID (Ed) Producer The Glynn Group. The 16mm film tells the extraordinary story of Markita, the holder of the world record for selling Girl Scout Cookies, and shows how the right sales techniques and the setting of personal goals lead to success.

COMETS: TIME CAPSULES OF THE SOLAR SYSTEM (Ed) This winner of the American Film Festival Red Ribbon features a combination of live action and animation to explain how our solar system was formed and the important role played by comets in unravelling the mysteries of space.

THE WATCHER IN THE WOODS (F) Director John Hough. This ill-fated ghost story should have been a success, but sadly the Studio lost faith in the production before its general release when, at special preview screenings in April 1980, audiences ridiculed the film's supposedly terrifying dénouement. The film was hastily withdrawn in the US, and the gap filled with a re-issue of *Mary Poppins*. The pedestrian script by Brian Clemens, Harry Spalding and Rosemary Anne Sisson (from the novel by Florence Engel Randall) and the below-average acting from Lynn-Holly Johnson

and Ian Bannen sealed its fate. Lynn-Holly plays teenager Jan, who is haunted by a mysterious force that lurks in the woods outside the rented English house where she is staying with her mother (Carroll Baker), father (David McCallum), sister Ellie (Kyle Richards) and mysterious recluse (Bette Davis, of course). The sinister spook turns out to be a creature from another dimension, and the original special effects ending in which the alien appears was so disappointing that the footage was cut from the final prints and a new ending was filmed. Even with some atmospheric direction and Alan Hume's 'roller coaster' photography, the film is boring. However, Bette Davis is wonderful in the melodramatic role of the secretive Mrs Aylwood (left), although there are some irrelevant cameo performances from co-stars Richard Pasco and Benedict Taylor. In 1983, a 25-minute extract was released on 16mm for schools.

DONALD DUCK'S CARTOON MEDLEY Released in Denmark in 1981, the compilation consists of seven classic shorts.

1982

NIGHT CROSSING (F) Director Delbert Mann. On 15 September 1979 two desperate families escaped across the East–West German border (below) at 1,500 feet in a home-made hot-air balloon. Disney wasted no time in bringing this incredible story to the screen and shot it entirely on location at the Bavaria Studios in Munich. Unfortunately, the film is a curious hodge-podge of missed opportunities, and there is some leaden acting from John Hurt as Peter Strelzyk and Beau Bridges as Gunter Wetzel. Although the balloon flight sequences generate some interest, the film suffers from bland characterization, and only Jane Alexander is convincing as Strelzyk's wife Doris. Even the music by Jerry Goldsmith fails to save this unmemorable PG-rated effort.

TEX (F) Director Tim Hunter. This is a strangely controversial film for Disney. In one sense it is a reworking of a number of the Studio's basic plots about a child or orphan who finds love and

understanding after a life of loneliness. But it is decidedly more adult in its approach than earlier pictures. Based on a modern tale of misguided youth by S.E. Hinton, the film stars Matt Dillon as Tex McCormick (above), a trouble-making adolescent who lives on a farm in Oklahoma with his rodeo-rider father (Bill McKinney) and 17-year-old brother Mason (Jim Metzler). Tex's future happiness is jeopardized by his involvement with the police, drugs and teenage violence, but finally the family is reunited and Tex is accepted for the individual that he is. Although it was released before the creation of Touchstone Films, the publicity still underplayed the Disney name. A critical success as a study of the American dream gone sour, a disappointing reception at the box-office meant its European release was cancelled. Meg Tilly, Frances Lee McCain and Ben Johnson guest-star in this early attempt at coming to terms with the cinema audiences of the 1980s. An extract on 16mm was later released for discussion in schools.

FITNESS FOR LIVING (Ed) Three films, endorsed by the President's Council on Physical Fitness, make up the series. *How To Get Fit* gives students a practical guide to developing their own fitness by bicycling or jogging to develop the heart and lungs. *Measuring Up* shows the importance of fitness tests by allowing them to measure their own achievements against those of athletes at the National Athletic Health Institute. *What Is Physical Fitness?* demonstrates how lack of exercise causes lethargy, inattentiveness and a host of other ills.

GET IT RIGHT: FOLLOWING DIRECTIONS WITH GOOFY (Ed) Mickey's pal has good reason to look concerned as he comes to realize the importance of understanding instructions – visual, spoken and written – to avoid making mistakes.

AMERICA WORKS ... AMERICA SINGS (Ed) Producer Bill Shippey for Cornerstone Productions. The origins of American folk songs are explored in this 16mm song-and-dance extravaganza.

CLOSE UP ON THE PLANETS (Ed) Director Charles L. Finance. This 16mm film uses stunning JPL/NASA computer-generated graphics to show how a satellite can circle the solar system picking up vital information and returning it to Earth. Hosted by scientists Eugene Shoemaker, Harold Masursky and Richard Terrile, the film, though not as much fun as Disney's 1950s space films *Man in Space* and *Mars and Beyond*, is a coldly accurate account of our neighbouring planets. It is narrated by Greg Heimer.

SPEAKING OF WEATHER (Ed) Producer Bill Shippey for Cornerstone Productions. A 16mm educational release explaining to students the basic concepts of weather and climate. How climate affects our lives is demonstrated through the use of clever animation and impressive live-action footage.

BUYER BE WISE (Ed) Goofy shows how the consumer can make mistakes in this 16mm film. Fortunately, Mickey and Donald are on hand to help him get the best value for money.

THE EPCOT EARTH STATION FILM (TP) A unique film informs visitors to EPCOT Center about the many places to visit. The film is shown on giant screens within Earth Station, the information centre at the foot of AT&T's Spaceship Earth and uses animation projected onto pixilated screens above the heads of the audience. This type of special screen breaks up the line and not only gives the impression of digitized animation, but also resembles a video format.

THE ENERGY SAVERS (Ed) In this 16mm animated film Mickey, Donald and Goofy illustrate to students the importance of energy conservation.

COMPUTERS: THE FRIENDLY INVASION (Ed) Originally part of a 1982 television special called *Computers Are People Too!* featuring scenes from *Tron*, this short explains the background technology and how computers work.

THE WATER ENGINE (TP) Producer Bob Rogers for Transcenter Films. Sponsored by General Motors for its World of Motion exhibit at Walt Disney World's EPCOT Center, the film is shown on nine unique screens, resembling piston rods, via three synchronized 35mm projectors. In the story nine animated characters are seen debating the future of the engine and its possible power sources.

VINCENT (Sp) Director Tim Burton. Made for as little as $60,000, the short tells the macabre story of 7-year-old Vincent Malloy, who idolizes horror star Vincent Price. Instead of pursuing normal, healthy interests, Vincent prefers to experiment on his pet dog, read Edgar Allen Poe stories and dream about dipping his aunt in boiling wax. With the backing of Disney's Vice-President Tom Wilhite, the film was made in black and white using three-dimensional models and animated by Stephen Chiodo, a technique unused since *A Symposium on Popular Songs* (1962) and later taken to fascinating extremes in the climax of *Return to Oz*. Narrated by Vincent Price, it at times resembles a surrealist nightmare and encouraged Disney to finance Burton's equally spooky *Frankenweenie* (1984).

SPEED ROOMS (TP) If You Had Wings, which is located in Tomorrowland at Walt Disney World, is an attraction that features a unique film system where sequences of moving vehicles are projected onto giant screens that totally envelop the guest. (A greatly enlarged version may be found in EPCOT Center's impressive World of Motion feature.) The illusion of travelling at great velocity is created by projecting 70mm film shot from speeding trains, bobsleds and other modes of transport onto tunnel-shaped screens. Effects footage from *Tron* has recently been incorporated into this attraction.

ENERGY: YOU MAKE THE WORLD GO ROUND (TP) A kinetic, multi-image pre-show for the Universe of Energy at EPCOT Center was designed by Emil Radok. A scope screen, 90 foot by 14 foot, with 100 three-sided rotating segments, is keyed by micro-processors to turn independently, coordinating itself to synchronize sequences of spinning crystal formations, bolts of lightning and other forms of energy, which are shown on five 35mm projectors.

ENERGY CREATION STORY (TP) Director Jack Boyd. Although only five minutes long, the film which introduces visitors to the Universe of Energy at EPCOT Center is considered to be the largest single piece of multiplane animation ever done for a motion picture. Three 70mm projectors are used to throw an image onto a screen 155 feet wide and 22 feet high, and the film explores the origins of fossil fuels and traces the beginning of life on Earth. It includes a recycled sequence of the dinosaurs from *The Rite of Spring* sequence in *Fantasia*.

UNIVERSE OF ENERGY (TP) Directors Norman Gerald and Jerry Sims. Scriptwriter Randy Bright went through 40 re-writes for the central film of the Universe of Energy at EPCOT Center. 'Energy is an industrial subject,' he remarked. 'It's big and ugly. But we have to tell the story and entertain the public at the same time.' The film is shown on a curved screen, 210 feet by 30 feet, from three 70mm projectors. Impressive photography captures some of the world's most dramatic sources of energy. Niagara Falls, the Alaska pipeline and an oil rig in the North Sea. Sponsored by one of America's giant oil corporations, Exxon, the film features atomic energy and solar power, and climaxes with the launch of the Space Shuttle, footage considered so unusual that NASA asked for a copy of it.

MIRRORED THEATER (TP) Director David Moore for Moore Graphics and Film (a company responsible for a number of tv commercials and animated logos). At the conclusion of EPCOT Center's Universe of Energy feature, the audience witnesses a remarkable computer light show. The images of trees, cityscapes and human figures, presented in the show's triangular theatre are projected by one 35mm and three 70mm projectors onto a variety of mirrors and screens, all of which results in one of the most spectacular film presentations to be seen at Walt Disney World.

SYMBIOSIS (TP) Director Paul Gerber. 'Nothing in the Universe exists alone,' explains the narrator. 'Every drop of water, every human being, all creatures in the web of life and all ideas in the web of knowledge are part of an immense evolving, dynamic whole as old – and as young – as the Universe itself.' Stirring words for an inspired motion picture event, which is shown at the Harvest Theater in The Land at EPCOT Center. A blend of science and entertainment, this film's breathtaking photography makes it the most outstanding of all the film presentations at Walt Disney World.

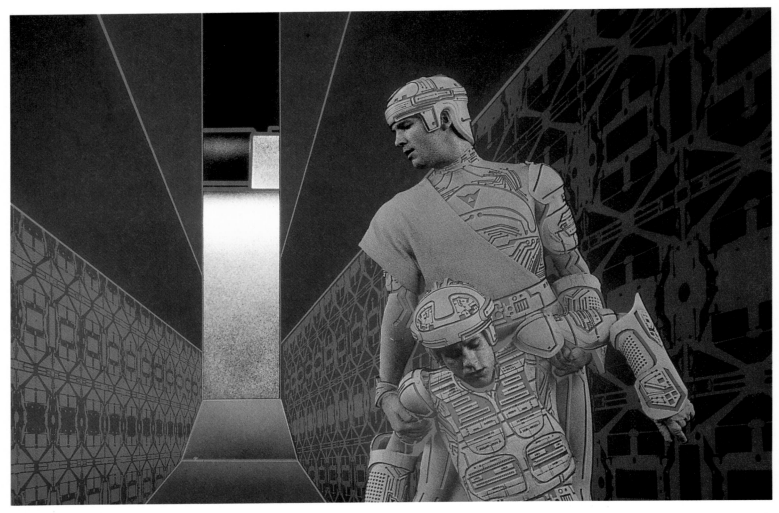

O CANADA! (TP) Directors Bill Bosché and Randy Bright. Presented in *Circle-Vision* at the Canada pavilion at EPCOT Center, this is not as entertaining as some of the park's other 360° films, but it does contain some startling footage of the Calgary Stampede rodeo and the snow-capped Canadian Rockies.

☆ TRON (F) Director Steven Lisberger. Presented in the impressive dimension of Super Panavision 70mm, the science-fiction adventure was considered by the Studio to be ahead of its time. Certainly this is true of the remarkable visuals, which, incorporating an incredible array of computer graphics and simulated animation techniques, explore the sinister world within the electronic brain of an evil computer, MCP (Master Control Program). The story, however, of how computer genius Flynn (Jeff Bridges, above) travels into this strange new world to defeat the machine is, in comparison, rather dull. Flynn is befriended in this surreal electronic dimension by Tron (Bruce Boxleitner), and the two make use of sophisticated light cycles, tanks and flying machines to defeat the powerful computer core. David Warner co-stars as ENCOM director Dillinger, the man who created the MCP by devious and underhand methods. Illustrator Syd Mead, who designed such films as *Bladerunner*, worked on the film's spectacular visuals together with comic artist Jean Moebius Giraud and commercial artist Peter Lloyd. Matte painter Harrison Ellenshaw, whose father had worked on numerous Disney pictures, acted as associate producer. The idea, originally sold to Disney in 1980 by Lisberger and Donald Kushner, contains highly innovative sequences and a superb musical score by Wendy Carlos, and the film

was nominated for the Academy Award for Best Costuming. Unfortunately, it did little business at the box-office. In 1983, however, a 16mm extract was released to schools and sequences of the lavish special effects have been incorporated into The World of Motion at Walt Disney World's EPCOT Center.

WONDERS OF CHINA (TP) Director Jeff Blyth. The 360° *Circle-Vision* presentation in World Showcase at EPCOT Center is unique because it shows parts of the country rarely seen by outsiders, like the palace of Lhasa in Tibet. Poetry by the 8th-century Chinese philosopher Li-Po is used on the soundtrack of this fascinating record of an ancient civilization. Blyth, who worked on the impressive IMAX movie *To Fly*, found working with the nine cameras required for photography quite a challenge. The most satisfying of all the 360° motion pictures shown in the park, the film was later seen in 1984 at Disneyland where it alternated with *American Journeys*.

DREAMFINDER'S SCHOOL OF DRAMA (TP) A video presentation, not a film, which is shown in Imagination at EPCOT Center, uses chroma-key effects to combine members of the public and exotic backgrounds in a number of different adventures.

MAGIC JOURNEYS (TP) Director Murray Lerner. *Sea Dream* in 1983 was the first 3-D film to be officially included in the Cannes Film Festival, and its director, Lerner, had just finished producing a unique polarized 3-D colour film for Kodak's Magic Eye Theater at EPCOT Center. It was photographed with twin 65mm cameras, especially designed and built by Art Cruickshank and Don Iwerks, both Disney special effects

experts. The film, which has music by the Sherman brothers, goes on a voyage of discovery through a child's imagination by means of stunning optical effects and the latest in 3-D techniques. It was replaced in 1986 by Francis Coppola's 3-D film *Captain EO*.

IMPRESSIONS DE FRANCE (TP) Director Rick Harper. 'Scheduled to be shown 30 times a day, 7 days a week for the next 10 years,' is how the publicity campaign announced this EPCOT film, which was shot with five cameras. Although it is not a *Circle-Vision* presentation, its impressive 200° screen is 150 feet across by 51 feet high. During production it was referred to by Studio personnel as a 'live-action' *Fantasia*, because stunning visuals of the Loire Valley, Cheverny Forest, Versailles, Paris and the French Alps are accompanied by the music of Offenbach, Debussy, Satie and Saint-Saëns.

FUN WITH MR FUTURE (Sp) Using an 'Audio-Animatronics' talking head, this short combines new animated sequences and live-action stock footage to show what family life in the future will be like.

1983

WINNIE THE POOH AND A DAY FOR EEYORE (F) Director Rick Reinert. The characters created by A.A. Milne have proved highly profitable for the Studio in terms of film releases and merchandise. After three successful featurettes, a popular children's series on The Disney Channel and the appeal of life-size three-dimensional characters in the theme parks, a fourth film was commissioned from sources outside the Studio. *Winnie the Pooh and a Day for Eeyore* tells how everyone clubs together to give the melancholy Eeyore a magnificent birthday party. Written by Studio veterans Steve Hulett, Tony L. Marino and Peter Young, the film compares badly with Pooh's previous adventures. Paul Winchell again provides the voice of Tigger, while John Fiedler speaks for Piglet. Laurie Main narrates the story, while Hal Smith has a stab at imitating the great Sterling Holloway as the voice of Pooh himself. A recipient of a number of educational awards, the film was eventually rereleased on 16mm and on video in 1985.

THE MISADVENTURES OF CHIP AN' DALE Premiered in Denmark, the feature-length cartoon compilation contains eight shorts featuring the chipmunks.

FUN TO BE FIT (Ed) Three educational films introduce students to physical fitness in a fresh, imaginative style. *Getting Physically Fit* shows youngsters how to achieve physical fitness through a carefully planned programme. *Physical Fitness* stresses the importance of developing body strength, and how it helps to improve the quality of studying, working and playing. *Why Be Physically Fit?* is the question put before students in this film on how to feel better and cope with stress.

TRENCHCOAT (F) Director Michael Tuchner. Margot Kidder stars in this PG (Parental Guidance) rated film. Mystery writer Mickey Raymond (Kidder) visits Malta to research her next book. A map leading to buried plutonium involves her with Arab kidnappers, German and Irish terrorists, and a transvestite stripper. Robert Hays, David Suchet, Gila Von Wertershausen and Ronald Lacey (below, with Kidder) co-star in this above-average entertainment, although its box-office performance in the US failed to guarantee the movie a theatrical release in Europe.

☆ MICKEY'S CHRISTMAS CAROL (F) Director Burny Mattinson. The welcome return to the cinema screen of Mickey after an absence of 30 years cost

over $3 million and unfortunately meant the postponement of any further projects featuring the gang. After *The Simple Things* (1953), Disney had decided to make Mickey the host on his own tv series and feature him as a 'real' character in the Disneyland theme park. Mickey's new film, which was, in fact, inspired by a record album released in 1974, was based on Charles Dickens' story and was adapted for the screen by Mattinson. In the lead as the miserly Ebenezer Scrooge is Donald's uncle, Scrooge McDuck (above). Animated guest stars from previous Disney films play the other characters – Jiminy Cricket is the Ghost of Christmas Past; Willie the Giant from *Fun and Fancy Free* plays an overweight Ghost of Christmas Present; and villainous Pete portrays the shrouded figure of Christmas Yet To Come. Mickey is cast in the role of Scrooge's humble book-keeper, Bob Cratchit, and although his name is featured in the title, he takes rather a back seat to the antics of his money-grabbing employer. Donald Duck, voiced by Clarence Nash, plays Scrooge's nephew, while Daisy Duck and the cast of *The Wind in the Willows* (from *Ichabod and Mr Toad*) star in cameo roles. Newcomer Wayne Allwine recreates Mickey's famous falsetto. This tightly scripted film was the first Disney animated featurette since 1974 to be nominated for an Academy Award. Goofy's 'spirited' appearance as the ghost of Scrooge's

partner Jacob Marley steals the film and successfully makes up for any faults in characterization.

SOMETHING WICKED THIS WAY COMES (F) Director Jack Clayton. Clayton seemed the perfect choice for this megabuck screen version of Ray Bradbury's classic tale, but unfortunately the film was both a financial and an artistic failure. Rumours hinted at Clayton's inability to transfer the more subtle and thought-provoking ideas contained in Bradbury's screenplay successfully to film, but the author, a self-confessed Disneyphile, denies these accusations. The story concerns a group of bizarre visitors who arrive in a turn-of-the-century Mid-West town one windy night calling themselves Dark's Pandemonium Carnival and presided over by the sardonic Mr Dark (Jonathan Pryce, above). Their sinister influence begins to take a hold on the town's inhabitants, in particular on two young boys, Will Halloway (Vidal Peterson), who is having problems relating to his father, town librarian Charles Halloway (Jason Robards), and Jim Nightshade (Shawn Carson), who feels neglected by his mother. In one nightmarish scene, Dark's accomplice, the Dust Witch (Pam Grier), unleashes a horde of hairy tarantulas that trap the boys in their room, while in the terribly contrived climax the boys find themselves face to face with the forces of evil. Atmospheric music by James Horner helps to heighten the tension, and the beautifully constructed sets (on the Disney backlot) are nicely photographed by Stephen Burum. The special effects include some amazing miniatures, a tornado and some reasonably effective matte paintings, but a computer-generated sequence at the fairground was edited from the film as the Studio wrestled with Clayton for control of the project. The result was a film that was too juvenile for adults and too wordy for kids. Co-stars included Diane Ladd and Royal Dano. In 1983, a 16mm extract was released for schools.

KINGDOM OF DREAMS AND MAGIC – TOKYO DISNEYLAND (TP) After a series of successful documentaries on the wonders of the Disney theme parks in California and Florida, the Studio released a new film to tell visitors of the splendid

facilities now available in the third major park, which had opened in spring 1983.

THE TIME TRAVELERS' GUIDE TO ENERGY (Ed) A boy from the future finds himself in trouble after erasing vital historical data in this 16mm release. Combining live action and animation, the film, which won second place in the National Educational Film Festival, investigates the ingenuity man has shown in the 20th century in harnessing all forms of energy.

RUNNING BRAVE (F) Director Ira Englander. One of the Studio's outside acquisitions, released through Buena Vista, was this Canadian film starring Robby Benson. It is the true story of Sioux Indian Billy Mills who became an Olympic gold medallist.

A VISIT TO EPCOT CENTER (Sp) Released on 16mm and then video, this was the first film produced after the billion-dollar complex was opened in 1982. Although it is somewhat dated, the film, which includes footage of the opening of Disneyland in 1955, is still a fascinating exploration of the 260-acre theme park.

JIMINY CRICKET, P.S. (PROBLEM SOLVER) (Ed) Jiminy Cricket returns to help Goofy make up his mind about when to go on vacation. Introducing highlights from classic Disney shorts, Donald Duck and tv star Ludwig Von Drake take time off to share some insights into problem solving.

FUTUREWORK (Ed) Interspersing humorous dialogue, catchy songs and some dance routines, the 16mm educational film makes students aware of the world of tomorrow and suggests how they might expand their work options.

A GOOFY LOOK AT VALENTINE'S DAY (Ed) Vintage Disney footage is used to explain the importance of Cupid's arrows. Goofy learns to appreciate the significance of the day and how people have expressed their love for each other at this most romantic of times in this 16mm film.

SKILLS FOR A NEW TECHNOLOGY: WHAT A KID NEEDS TO KNOW TODAY (Ed) Three 16mm films comprise an educational series presented by EPCOT Educational Media. Elmer, a cheerful

school custodian, demonstrates in Basic Communication Skills that reading, writing, listening and speaking are as important as ever in the age of technology. In Living With Change Elmer discovers that technological advances benefit society and that he need not fear the future. The computer's many applications are introduced to Elmer on a magical cross-country tour in Living With Computers.

DISNEY'S HAUNTED HALLOWEEN (Ed) Incorporating classic film sequences from the earlier shorts, the 16mm explores the world of bats, ghosts and witches, as a spooky, animated Jack O'Lantern teaches Goofy about the holiday traditions linked with Halloween.

DISNEY'S WONDERFUL WORLD OF WINTER (Ed) In this 16mm film, Stanley the snowman, a professor of 'winterology', explains to Goofy about the traditions behind Thanksgiving, Christmas and New Year.

DECISION MAKING: CRITICAL THOUGHT IN ACTION (Ed) A 16mm film presented by EPCOT Educational Media takes students through problem-solving, using everyday situations as the basis of research.

CHOOSE YOUR TOMORROW (TP) At the conclusion of Horizons at EPCOT Center, the visitor is requested to pick one of three return trips to Earth via the 'Horizons 1 Space Shuttle' – 'Space', 'Desert' or 'Undersea'. Supervised by Dave Jones, a unique system of mechanics isolates each individual passenger vehicle for the 'flight plan back to the future port'. Although presented on a continuous video format, models and special effects were filmed in a rented hangar at Burbank Airport.

COMPUTERS: THE TRUTH OF THE MATTER (Ed) A winner of the CINE Golden Eagle Award, this film shows the importance of computer technology and its variety of services.

OMNISPHERE (TP) During Horizons, one of EPCOT Center's most impressive rides, audiences are treated to film sequences depicting the blast off of a Space Shuttle, an aerial flight over Manhattan and a computer-generated trip across the Earth's surface. The film incorporates twin hemispherical screens, 80 feet in diameter, on to which an Omnimax 70mm projection system presents the first-ever microphotography, super macro-photography and underwater footage.

☆ NEVER CRY WOLF (F) Director Carroll Ballard. A remarkable Disney film in that it is the personal achievement of documentary film-maker Ballard. The PG (Parental Guidance) rated movie concerns a young government biologist, Tyler (Charles Martin Smith, opposite), who is working on the Lupus Project to study Alaskan wolves living in the Arctic wilderness of northern Canada. Befriending an Eskimo called Ootek (Zachary Ittimangnaq) and his English-speaking accomplice Mike (Samson Jorah), Tyler learns all about wolves and their relationship with the vanishing herds of caribou; more importantly, he learns about himself. Based on Farley Mowat's autobiographical writings, the film is a stunning example of how loneliness and despair can turn to warmth and understanding. It's an unusual picture for Disney yet, in a sense, it is the epitome of all the positive thinking that went into the highly successful True-Life Adventure series. Co-starring Brian Dennehy as aircraft pilot Rosey, who represents the 'nastier' side of civilization, the film was co-produced by Jack Couffer who

had worked on *Nikki, Wild Dog of the North* and *The Incredible Journey*. A brave experiment by executive producer Ron Miller, the film is a tribute to the Studio's daring and expertise, and it justified the Studio's faith in the project by earning $15 million at the US box-office. A 16mm extract was released in 1984.

DONALD DUCK'S CARTOON JAMBOREE Nine classic shorts are included in this compilation, originally released in Denmark.

1984

FITNESS AND ME (Ed) Producer Sun West Productions. Three 16mm films make up a series that won the Gold Award at the Houston International Film Festival. *How To Exercise* features the story of Knight Light and his preparation to fight a dragon, only to discover that neither of them is fit enough to do battle. *What Is Fitness Exercise?* shows youngsters the importance of good health through the story of the scrawny Knight Light and his travels. In *Why Exercise?* Knight Light, who is by now well on his way to being in top shape, helps a paunchy friend when they are sent to recover the king's stolen crown.

TIGER TOWN (F) Director Alan Shapiro. Relegated to video release in Europe, the film was based on actual events surrounding the 1968 baseball season. Roy Scheider stars as Billy Young, a member of the Detroit Tigers, who is convinced that winning a pennant in his last season will be impossible. A young boy called Alex teaches him otherwise, however, in this engaging story co-starring Justin Henry, Ron McLarty and Bethany Carpenter, which was originally made for The Disney Channel.

AMERICAN JOURNEYS (TP) Notable for containing the first ever underwater *Circle-Vision* sequences, this short opened in both the Disney theme parks in 1984, replacing *Magic Carpet 'Round the World* and *America the Beautiful*. Highlights include the eruption of Mount St Helens, Cape Canaveral and spectacular fireworks over the Statue of Liberty. Although 360° photography can be unsatisfying, *Circle-Vision*

presentations have proved a constant attraction to audiences.

ALL BECAUSE MAN WANTED TO FLY (TP) The pre-show to Disneyland's *Circle-Vision* presentation *American Journeys* is hosted by *The Rescuers* star Orville the albatross, who explains mankind's often dangerous but always humorous attempts to rise above the ground.

NOW I CAN TELL YOU MY SECRET (Ed) Producer Hallman Plus Productions. As part of the Disney educational programme dealing with controversial topics, the 16mm release explains to youngsters their right to protect themselves from sexual advances by adults.

HAROLD AND HIS AMAZING GREEN PLANTS (Ed) Producer Kurtz and Friends. This animated tale stars a small boy and characters from the Kitchen Kabaret at EPCOT Center and teaches students the importance of green plants as a food source. It was a finalist in the Birmingham International Film Festival and a winner of the Blue Ribbon at the American Film and Video Festival.

LIGHTS! CAMERA! FRACTIONS! (Ed) Producer Grey Havens Productions. The Disney educationalists used all the methods of film-making available to them to teach youngsters the basics of fractions. A combination of live action, 'clay animation' and stop-action animation is used to make this difficult subject easier to understand.

ETHICS IN THE COMPUTER AGE (Ed) The EPCOT Educational Media film contains two mini-dramas dealing with the issues of software piracy and computer 'hacking'. Winner of numerous awards, the short teaches students about the importance of honesty in computer use.

EPCOT ADVANCED INFORMATION SYSTEM (Ed) Making information available to even greater numbers of people is a problem, but the designers of EPCOT knew that the size of Walt Disney World would require a system that could cope with the questions likely to be asked by over 23 million visitors a year. The World Key Information Service is explained in detail, and the film shows how such an idea could be expanded for future use.

ENERGY IN PHYSICS (Ed) Students are introduced to the fundamental laws of physics and of the conservation of energy, by drawing parallels with their use in everyday life.

CHILD MOLESTATION: BREAKING THE SILENCE (Ed) Producer Hallman Plus Productions. The Walt Disney Educational Media Company is more than capable of presenting the important issues of the day. The film not only offers guidelines on how to identify children who suffer sexual abuse but also shows how youngsters can protect themselves.

THE CHALLENGE OF SURVIVAL (Ed) Producer Dick Young Productions. Three films in the EPCOT Educational Media programme look at environmental issues. *Chemicals*, a National Educational Film Festival winner, underlines the problems caused by the use of chemicals in pest control. *Land* discusses the causes of soil erosion. *Water* concentrates on the proper methods of irrigation.

DONALD DUCK THE MOVIE To celebrate Donald's 50th birthday, a feature-length compilation was released in Britain. In addition to seven shorts, it includes the tv version of *The Three Caballeros*.

DESTINATION (Ed) Donald Duck is the host in a series of four films in the EPCOT Educational Media programme. *Careers* introduces the concept that the future lies not in 'getting a job', but in 'building a career'. *Communications* opens with cavemen's primitive sketches and concludes with today's technological explosion. *Excellence* shows Donald demonstrating that hard work, determination and perseverance are necessary for success, while *Science* explains how technological developments help further scientific research.

☆ COUNTRY (F) Director Richard Pearce. The second Touchstone film stars Jessica Lange (who co-produced the picture) and Sam Shepard. It promised much but delivered little. Set on a farm in the American heartland at harvest time, the film relates how Jewell (Lange) and Gilbert Ivy (Shepard) strive to keep their family going even though the government is threatening to foreclose the family farm. Personal turmoil divides the pair, and while Gilbert drinks away his problems, Jewell works hard to protect her future. Miss Lange's performance is a *tour de force*, but unfortunately this bleak example of a family's struggle to survive natural disasters, politics and internal pressures appeared at the same time as two similar productions – *The River* and *Places in the Heart*. The problem with *Country* is that its personal statement is rather heavy-handed.

DONALD DUCK'S BIRTHDAY PARTY Showing excerpts from over 20 individual cartoons, the feature-length compilation was originally released in Brazil.

FRANKENWEENIE (Sp) Director Tim Burton. Although most of the major Hollywood studios avoid featurettes because of the poor rentals, Disney kept its hand in throughout the early 1980s with *Once Upon A Mouse*, *Fun With Mr Future* and *Vincent*, the last being a horror story for children, on the strength of which Burton was given the go-ahead to make this black and white film. It stars Shelley Duvall, Paul Bartel and Barret Oliver in a homage to the Universal *Frankenstein* films. Victor Frankenstein is a young boy and his creation is his pet dog called Sparky, brought miraculously back to life, complete with neck electrodes, after an automobile

accident. Fans of the 1930s films were pleased to see that Burton used the original electrical equipment that brought Boris Karloff to life!

☆ SPLASH! (F) Director Ron Howard. The slightly suggestive by-line of the Studio's most successful film since *Mary Poppins* went as follows: 'She was the woman of Allen's dreams. She had large dark eyes, a beautiful smile and a great pair of fins.' The 'woman' is, in fact, a very attractive blonde mermaid played by Daryl Hannah; her terrestrial lover Allen (Tom Hanks, above) is very much a human being. The first film to be released under the new Touchstone banner was a chance for Production Executive Ron Miller to change the direction of film-making at Disney and at the same time to rescue an ailing section of the company. Still the best of all the Touchstone releases, the film is an amusing – if not often riotous – teenage/adult comedy of how a confused New York bachelor falls in love with a mysterious mermaid. Written for the screen by Bruce Jay Friedman, the film is the most risqué yet to come from the Studio and has some very un-Disneyesque dialogue. There are excellent performances from co-stars Eugene Levy, as crazy scientist Walter Kornbluth, and John Candy, as Allen's brother 'fat' Freddie. A climactic car chase and a poignant ending guaranteed a healthy US box-office gross of $35 million.

1985

BABY ... SECRET OF THE LOST LEGEND (F) Director B.W.L. Norton. Touchstone's third film is a strange mixture of Disney cuteness and the 1980s demand for more screen violence. Patrick McGoohan plays Dr Kiviat, a scientist searching the dense African jungle for a dinosaur – to be precise a family of brontosauri. He is beaten to his goal by a young zoologist Susan Matthews-Loomis (Sean Young) and her husband George Loomis (William Katt), who are alarmed at Kiviat's mercenary attitude toward the lumbering sauropods (below) – in particular a specimen

of baby dinosaur (hence the film's title). After numerous adventures, the animals escape, but not before Kiviat is chewed to death. With the exception of Kiviat's gruesome demise, this sounds like a charming Disney film, but the script contains lines like 'I'd whip the bitch!', and the story is not short on blood and gore. Moreover,

the men-in-suit dinosaurs, designed by Isodoro Raponi and Roland Tantin, look more alive on screen than their human co-stars. Unable to cope with McGoohan's outrageous performance as the mad scientist, Norton makes this film as uninteresting as his efforts with *More American Graffiti* in 1979.

THE BLACK CAULDRON (F) Directors Ted Berman and Richard Rich. Disney's 25th full-length animated film should have been the Studio's crowning achievement. Instead it comes across as just another cartoon. It was rumoured that it had been in production for up to 10 years. Costing $25 million, it is one of Disney's most expensive films, and it was certainly in some stages of preparation throughout the filming of *The Rescuers* (1977) and *The Fox and the Hound* (1981). Animators strikes, management takeovers and the retirement of some of the Studio's veteran animators all added to the delay in finishing the picture. The story is based on the series 'The Chronicles of Prydain' by Lloyd Alexander. Taran, a young pig keeper (above right), sets off to find and destroy the Black Cauldron before it falls into the clutches of the evil Horned King. *En route*, Taran meets Princess Eilonwy, a musician called Fflewddur Fflam and a weird creature called Gurgi, but they are captured by the Horned King and his sidekick Creeper. An army of dead warriors comes forth from the Black Cauldron to take over the world, and, in a desperate struggle, Taran and his friends escape, leaving the evil monarch at the mercy of the all-enveloping power of the cauldron. The first Disney feature in 70mm since *Sleeping Beauty*, the film suffers (as did the earlier one) from wide static backgrounds and empty-looking scenery, and the story is episodic and unsatisfying as characters are introduced and quickly forgotten. On the credit side, however, the effects are stunning, and the film has one of the best uses of light and shadow since the dwarfs tiptoed through their cottage in *Snow White*. But that's the problem – it's all been done before. Although the Horned King – a skull-faced abomination (above) – should be the ultimate Disney villain, his evil cannot match the towering magnificence of Chernabog in *Fantasia*, and the distant shots of the Horned King's castle, surrounded by lightning bolts, pales in comparison to a similar sequence of Maleficent's stronghold, the Forbidden Mountains, in *Sleeping Beauty*. An impressive array of voice talents includes John Hurt, Freddie Jones and Nigel Hawthorne, and among the nine screenwriters was Walt's nephew Roy E. Disney, who re-joined the studio as Head of the Animation Department in 1984, while Rosemary Anne Sisson supplied additional dialogue. Produced by Disney veteran Joe Hale, the film was executive produced by former chairman Ron Miller with additional financial backing from Silver Screen Partners II.

MY SCIENCE PROJECT (F) Director Jonathan Betuel. Touchstone's third attempt to exploit the fantasy movie genre (after *Splash!* and *Baby ... Secret of the Lost Legend*) is a time-travel adventure yarn. Michael Harlan (John Stockwell), Ellie Sawyer (Danielle Von Zerneck), Vince Latello (Fisher Stevens) and Sherman (Raphael Sbarge) are four obnoxious kids who, with some assistance from their high school teacher Bob Roberts (Dennis Hopper), tamper with a component from a flying saucer and unwittingly punch a hole into the fourth dimension. As the time warp expands and threatens to engulf the whole world, the teenagers, armed to the teeth like teeny-bopper Rambos, set out to destroy the alien machine. This gives them an opportunity to flatten their school as they tackle apemen, future-space travellers and a fully grown *Tyrannosaurus rex*. Effects supervisor John Scheele brings the dinosaur to life through a complicated form of puppetry, but its screen appearance is short – it's blown to bits by some of the time warp's less desirable inhabitants. Produced by Jonathan Taplin, the film is a mish-mash of half-baked ideas and scientific inaccuracy. The brash American characterization persuaded Disney to abandon any plans to release it theatrically in Europe, and Touchstone decided in future to rely on the box-office popularity of its adult comedies.

ON YOUR OWN (Ed) Children are taught certain safety measures and self-care skills for times when they are left alone in a film that stresses the need for parents and children to communicate with each other.

ECONOMICS BY CHOICE (Ed) Produced in conjunction with the National Center of Economic Education for Children, the 16mm release illustrates a number of situations to which children can relate.

EXPECTATIONS - A STORY ABOUT STRESS (Ed) The sad fact that the underlying cause of 75 per cent of all illness and disease among children is stress is explored in this winner of the American Film and Video Festival Blue Ribbon. The 16mm film highlights the problems and shows how to overcome them.

FLIGHT! (Ed) Presented by EPCOT Educational Media, this live-action 16mm film teaches stu-

BEFORE IT'S TOO LATE – A FILM ON TEENAGE
SUICIDE (Ed) A dramatic approach underlines the
causes behind suicidal tendencies and the problems of rejection.

A TIME TO TELL: TEEN SEXUAL ABUSE (Ed)
Winner of the CINE Golden Eagle Award, this
sensitive film encourages students to discuss their
fears of sexual molestation.

ADVICE ON LICE (Ed) Producer Playing With
Time, Inc. A girl is embarrassed when she
contracts head lice, but the school nurse comes to
the rescue and dispatches the parasites, ugly
animated characters belonging to the League to
Infect Children Everywhere, by applying the
correct medical treatment.

☆ THE JOURNEY OF NATTY GANN (F) Director
Jeremy Kagan. By the mid-1980s Walt Disney
Pictures and its subsidiary production company
Touchstone were finally achieving separate identities, but it hadn't always been so. Titles like *Baby*
and *My Science Project* could, with judicious
editing, have fitted into the Disney mould, while
Disney's *The Journey of Natty Gann* in its
complete form seems better suited to Touchstone. The film is set in Chicago in the depression
of 1935. Natalie Gann, expertly played by 15-
year-old Meredith Salenger (below), sets off
across 2,000 miles of American wilderness in

dents the principles of physical science including
aerodynamics. It won an award at the National
Educational Film Festival.

DECIMALS: WHAT'S THE POINT? (Ed) A short
made to illustrate the importance of decimals as
fractional equivalents and their use in the world
around us. Presented in the style of a 'music
video', the 16mm film features songs by the aptly
named The Tenths.

☆ RETURN TO OZ (F) Director Walter Murch. Gary
Kurtz joined forces with Disney in 1984 to
produce a film sequel that had for long fascinated
him. *The Wizard of Oz*, originally made by
MGM in 1939 and starring Judy Garland, was
based on just one of a number of books by L.
Frank Baum, and Walt had owned the rights to
the novels for a number of years, even embarking
in the late 1950s on an aborted feature starring
members of The Mickey Mouse Club. In *Return
to Oz*, which was shot on location at Elstree
Studios in England, young Fairuza Balk plays
Dorothy, who returns to Oz after being washed
away in a fast-flowing river with a talking hen
called Billina. Heading for the Emerald City,
Dorothy finds that the Yellow Brick Road is in
ruins and that the city itself is in decay. But she
meets a wonderful clockwork robot, Tik Tok,
encounters the menacing Wheelers (above), is
captured by the evil Princess Mombi (Jean
Marsh) and escapes on the flying 'Gump' with
Tik Tok and Jack Pumpkinhead. She confronts
the evil Nome King, brilliantly portrayed by
Nicol Williamson, and, with her friends, defeats
the villain and restores the land of Oz to normal.
Co-stars include Piper Laurie as Aunt Em and
Emma Ridley as Ozma, the Princess of Oz.

Impressive technical effects by Lyle Conway,
terrifying 'claymation' creatures by Will Vinton
and impressive studio sets by Norman Reynolds
add to the entertaining spectacle. Budgeted at
$25 million, the film had a disappointing
performance at the box-office, mainly because its
approach to the story falls between two areas of
audience interest. Overlong at 110 minutes and
sacrificing musical numbers for a more sombre
storyline, the film has now faded into obscurity.

search of her father. The journey is a hazardous one, but fortunately she is befriended by a wild wolf who becomes her travelling companion and protector. John Cusack plays a young drifter called Harry who also befriends Natty on her travels. Ray Wise, Barry Miller, Lainie Kazan and Scatman Crothers co-star. Kagan gives the picture an overall grittiness, and this general unpleasantness slightly undermines its Disney image (although the film does include a snippet of a Mickey Mouse cartoon thrown in for good measure). The title must have confused most cinemagoers, and in Europe it was decided to play down the role of the wolf as there was concern that audiences still remembered a previous Disney film, *Never Cry Wolf*. In 1987, the film won the Gold Prize at the Moscow International Film Festival.

ONE MAGIC CHRISTMAS (F) Director Phillip Borsos. The screenplay was written by Thomas Meehan, and the film, which took a leaf out of successful film scenarios like *Miracle on 34th Street* and *It's A Wonderful Life*, was co-financed by Walt Disney Pictures in association with Telefilm Canada. Mary Steenburgen stars as Ginnie, a woman who is disillusioned by the Christmas spirit when her husband is killed in a bank raid and her two children are kidnapped. Gideon, a Christmas angel (brilliantly played by Harry Dean Stanton), appears on the scene and uses his supernatural powers to restore everything to normal, including Ginnie's faith. In a remarkable sequence set at the North Pole, production designer Bill Brodie constructed Santa's Workshop and included a unique collection of antique toys insured for $1 million. Achieving its aims without having to resort to over-sentimentality, and skilfully combining dreams, time travel and gritty reality, the film deserved more attention, but with its European release delayed because of the similarity of its original title (*Father Christmas*) with Ilya Salkind's *Santa Claus*, this emotional film finally surfaced as a video release only after fading into obscurity with a disappointing box-office of less than $6 million.

1986

AIDS (Ed) Director Joanne Parrent. After the success of the educational film on the dangers of venereal disease, the new documentary on the facts behind the deadly virus was welcomed by both parents and teaching organizations. Hosted by popular film personality Ally Sheedy and written and produced as well as directed by Parrent, the film asks many of the questions that concern teenagers about the risks of the disease and uses computer-animated graphics and information from doctors and health educators to help answer them.

SEA WATCH (TP) The Living Seas at EPCOT Center at Walt Disney World in Florida contains an impressive underwater laboratory called Seabase Alpha, where a number of exhibits incorporate motion pictures of the ocean depths. Although it is a rear screen video display as opposed to film, *Sea Watch* gives a continuous newsreel update on all subjects relating to the world's oceans.

AN ANIMATED ATLAS OF THE WORLD (TP) Director Mike West. West voices a muscular strongman who complains about having to carry the Earth on his shoulders. Sharing some of the burden with the film's narrator, Bernard Fox, West explains about earthquakes, volcanoes,

tidal waves, the climate and '4.5 billion years of Earth's history' in this entertaining 7½ minute addition to Seabase Alpha at EPCOT Center's the Living Seas.

THE SEAS (TP) Director Paul Gerber. Inspired narration, atmospheric music and remarkable photography enhance this most impressive film on show at EPCOT Center. Sponsored by United Technologies and lasting for only 7 minutes, this picture charts the origins of the world's oceans and attempts to explain man's fascination for them.

SUITED FOR THE SEA (TP) One of the animated shorts running continuously at Seabase Alpha in the Living Seas at EPCOT Center is a history of the diving suit, illustrated by two fish who explain the obstacles to deep-water exploration and the ways in which humans have learnt to defeat them.

DOWN AND OUT IN BEVERLY HILLS (F) Director Paul Mazursky. After the indifferent dinosaur epic *Baby* and the time-travelling tedium of *My Science Project*, Disney bounced back from the primeval swamps of prehistory with a movie about the more primeval attitudes of 20th-century man in a new Touchstone release. Mazursky manages to push Mickey's moral code as far as it will go and then beyond, and this is the Studio's first film to include four-letter words (and they're not 'Walt') and sweaty bodies locked in poses of sexual abandon. Loosely based on Jean Renoir's 1932 French comedy *Boudu Saved From Drowning*, the film stars Nick Nolte as 'down and out' Jeremy Baskin, who tries to commit suicide in the swimming pool of millionaire 'coathanger king' Dave Whiteman (Richard Dreyfuss) and his crazy wife Barbara (Bette Midler). Rescued by Whiteman, Baskin stays on and changes the family's lifestyle, values and attitudes.

The treatment of confused sexual relationships is a speciality of Mazursky's (as we saw in his previous endeavours such as *Bob and Carol and Ted and Alice* or *An Unmarried Woman*), while the film offers some delightful cameo performances, including that of a crazy canine who tries to outdo *The Ugly Dachshund*. Unlike *My Science Project*, which, because of its poor performance at the American box-office, was not released theatrically in Europe, Mazursky's social satire opened very strongly worldwide, grossing $62 million in the US alone.

SIMPLE MACHINES: A MOVING EXPERIENCE (Ed) Producer Sun West Productions. The educational film gives a basic introduction to the concepts of mechanical physics through the use of simple machines.

THE WUZZLES, BULLS OF A FEATHER (Sp) In 1985, in association with the toy manufacturer Hasbro, Disney launched a new group of characters, the Wuzzles, in their own tv series. They live in the wonderful Land of Wuz, and each creature combines the physical appearance of two others: Bumblelion, for example, is a cross between a bee and a lion; Eleroo is part elephant and part kangaroo. The first screen adventure of these curious but curiously lovable characters (above) was released theatrically in Britain in March 1986. The Wuzzles find a mysterious egg and set out to return it to its mother. The limited drawing techniques utilized for the film were produced by the Walt Disney Pictures Television Animation Group.

PORTRAITS OF CANADA (Com) The popularity of the *Circle-Vision* films used in the Disney theme parks continued to encourage a number of outside commissions. For Expo '86 in Vancouver, Telecom Canada co-financed a 360° film to reveal the splendours of the country.

OFF BEAT (F) Director Michael Dinner. Judge Reinhold made his Disney debut in this Touchstone release. Written by Mark Medoff, the story concerns Joe Gower, a young library assistant who impersonates a New York cop and falls hopelessly in love with a beautiful young policewoman played by Meg Tilly. Rated PG (Parental Guidance), the film's approach is different from Touchstone's usual hard-boiled comedy, and it was a moderate box-office success. It was released in Europe on video only.

RUTHLESS PEOPLE (F) Directors Jim Abrahams, David Zucker and Jerry Zucker. The most unattractive aspect of Touchstone Pictures is that a majority of its so-called American comedies are full of totally unlikable characters. In *Baby ... Secret of the Lost Legend*, they're over-melodramatic; In *Down and Out in Beverly Hills* they're obnoxious; and in *Ruthless People* they're just despicable. The film stars Bette Midler as Barbara, the foul-mouthed wife of loathsome businessman Sam Stone, played by Danny DeVito. Stone plans to have his wife murdered, but she falls instead into the hands of amateur kidnappers Ken and Sandy (Judge Reinhold and Helen Slater). Stone is delighted and refuses to pay the ransom. When Barbara learns of his reaction, she joins forces with the kidnappers to take her revenge. Brilliant casting puts Bette Midler in the sort of raucous part at which she excels; DeVito is able to curl his top lip nastily as much as he likes; the supporting cast looks on in horror. A sad statement on human relationships, the movie nevertheless did good business at the box-office ($31 million in America). It is difficult to believe that the Studio that gave life to *Snow White* was also responsible for this sleazy farrago.

THE GUMMI BEARS, A NEW BEGINNING (Sp) While it seems unlikely at present that there will be more tv adventures for the Wuzzles (see above), the Gummi Bears are (in 1987) in their third season on US tv. Created from an original idea by Company Chairman and Chief Executive Officer, Michael Eisner, the Gummi Bears appeared in a theatrical version of their adventures, which was released in Britain. Among the characters is Sunni Gummi, an energetic teenager; Gruffi Gummi, the group's leader; Zummi Gummi, a magician; Tummi Gummi, a kind-hearted glutton; Cubbi Gummi, the youngest member of the family; and Grammi Gummi, the official taste mistress of Gummiberry Juice. Together (below) they battle to keep the medieval kingdom of Dunwyn free from the evil Duke Igthorn and his legion of ogres.

THE GREAT MOUSE DETECTIVE (UK: BASIL: THE GREAT MOUSE DETECTIVE) (F) Directors John Musker, Ron Clements and Dave Michener. In early 1984 Disney decided to move the animation department to a new address across the street from WDI (Walt Disney Imagineering – the company responsible for the three-dimensional attractions at Disneyland and Walt Disney World), and the Studio's 26th full-length animated feature was the second Disney animated film to be made entirely outside the Burbank Studio lot. What is good news, however, is that this particular film is a welcome return to a style that had been missing since *The Jungle Book* (1967). Based on the book by Eve Titus, the film follows the exploits of a supersleuth mouse called Basil (opposite), who lives below the damp course in the basement of 221B Baker Street, the residence of the famous Sherlock Holmes. Accompanied by a portly mouse called Dr Dawson, Basil sets off to rescue Flaversham, a toymaker who has been kidnapped by the evil Professor Ratigan as part of a plot to overthrow Queen Moustoria. Basil is a more sinewy mouse than Mickey, but he's just as brave, as he attempts to thwart the dastardly Ratigan's sinister plans. Veteran Disney animator Eric Larson schooled the talent required to produce an entertaining array of Disney characters: Basil, voiced by Barrie Ingham, is a quick-witted fellow with indomitable courage; his companion Dr Dawson (Val Bettin), is a respectable upholder of law and order; Ratigan (opposite below), voiced with affectionate villainy by Vincent Price, is a thorough rogue; and he has the unquestioning assistance of two ruthless characters – Fidgit, a peg-leg bat and an enormous 'mouser' called Felicia. The film was four years in development, with animation, which began in 1984, under the guidance of Roy E. Disney, son of Walt's brother and company co-founder. It was released only a year after *The Black Cauldron*, underlining the Studio's desire to increase its animation output. Burny Mattinson produced the film, and some stunning computer animation at the picture's climax, depicting the interior of Big Ben, was supplied by Phil Nibbelink and Ted Gielow. The score by Henry Mancini, which includes three delightful songs, in no way intrudes into the story. The whole is skilfully edited and is a true delight.

FLIGHT OF THE NAVIGATOR (F) Director Randal Kleiser. Joey Cramer stars as David Freeman, a 12-year-old boy who becomes hopelessly mixed up with NASA and a flying saucer. Accidentally knocked unconscious, David is taken aboard an alien spacecraft that has been sent to study life on Earth. Unfortunately, when he awakens from the trip, he discovers to his horror that in reality eight years have passed. His parents (Veronica Cartwright and Cliff De Young) were convinced he was dead and are shocked to find him still only 12 years old. The mystery behind his disappearance involves him with the authorities, who have captured the spacecraft (a fascinating interstellar vehicle designed by Steve Austin), some extra-terrestrial life forms and a robot called Max. In a gripping climax, David manages to return to his own time and so destroy his alternative future. The film's screenplay, by Michael Burton and Matt MacManus, owes a lot to films like *E.T.*, *The Last Starfighter*, *Explorers* and *Back To The Future*, but it is an engaging little story.

TOUGH GUYS (F) Director Jeff Kanew. What could have been a rather bland Touchstone comedy, benefited enormously from the inclusion of Hollywood veterans Kirk Douglas and Burt Lancaster. The story, written by James Orr and Jim Cruickshank, concerns the adventures of two ex-convicts, Harry Doyle (Lancaster) and Archie Long (Douglas), who are released from jail after 30 years. They were originally imprisoned for attempting to rob The Gold Coast Flyer, and they discover that the same train is due for one last historic run. Helped by probation officer Richie Evans (Dana Carvey), they steal, for old time's sake, the entire train and are hotly pursued by police sergeant Deke Yablonski (Charles Durning) and assassin Leon B. Little (Eli Wallach). The film works on a number of levels, largely because of the excellent rapport that exists between the two leads. Although some of the jokes misfire – notably a token encounter with a street gang and a visit to a local discotheque – this is, with the exception of Splash!, one of the Studio's most satisfying adult comedies, and the tremendous climax, filmed on the Eagle Mountain railroad south of Palm Springs, is highly entertaining.

★THE COLOR OF MONEY (F) Director Martin Scorsese. With the change in management in 1984, Touchstone shied away from the 'adult fantasy' of Splash! and re-surfaced with a number of slightly bizarre comedies – Down and Out in Beverly Hills and Ruthless People; for example. The Color of Money is, however, far from amusing, even though Paul Newman, as pool player Eddie Felson, delivers his lines with a wry smile and a twinkle in his eye. Felson, who was last seen in the 1961 movie The Hustler, is promoting a new young pool player called Vincent (Tom Cruise). Richard Price's screenplay, based on the novel by Walter Tevis, follows this unlikely pair as Vincent becomes more self-reliant and Felson comes to terms with his own inadequacies and missed opportunities. It's inevitable that the two should end up challenging each other in the ultimate pool game, paving the way, it seems, for a possible sequel. Slow paced, the film is exceptionally well directed by Scorsese, an unusual name to find on the Disney payroll after movies like Taxi Driver and Mean Streets. Scorsese had a great deal of influence in the filming of the pool sequences, and he collaborated with Michael Ballhaus on some remarkable cinematography.

CAPTAIN EO (TP) Director Francis Coppola. Walt Disney Imagineering (formerly WED) joined forces with Star Wars producer George Lucas to produce this 3-D space spectacular, which stars Michael Jackson as a futuristic space pilot who, with the help of a bizarre rock band, brings harmony to a troubled universe. The film lasts just 17 minutes and is rumoured to have cost more than $20 million. Premiering simultaneously at Disneyland and EPCOT Center, *EO* features 'state of the art' polarized 3–D on two synchronized 70mm strips of film, in-house effects that involve the audience (below) and full stereo sound. Energetic and fast-paced, it's a very different type of entertainment from the relative peace and quiet of Lerner's *Magic Journeys*, which had been presented at EPCOT Center since 1982.

1987

OUTRAGEOUS FORTUNE (F) Director Arthur Hiller. Bette Midler signed a three-picture deal with Touchstone Films in 1985, and after the amusing *Down and Out in Beverly Hills* and the terrible *Ruthless People*, she finds a perfect role as bit actress Sandy Brozinsky in *Outrageous Fortune*. With co-star Shelley Long, as Lauren Ames, she chases across the country after their mutual lover Michael (Peter Coyote). Unfortunately, he turns out to be engaged in a plot to hold the US government to ransom. Robert Prosky plays KGB man Stanislav Korzenowski, and John Schuck

shuffles around in the background as CIA agent Atkins. Although it has a smattering of indecent behaviour and bad language, the only real fault in this engaging comedy lies in its overlong dénouement in New Mexico.

STAR TOURS (TP) Director George Lucas. It seemed inevitable that a maker of fantasy films like Lucas would one day find himself at the home of fantastic films – The Walt Disney Studios and Walt Disney Imagineering. The results were a new 3-D film, *Captain EO* (1986) and a sophisticated 'film ride' at Disneyland in California. Visitors to this impressive attraction are seated in spacecraft-shaped flight simulators called Starspeeders, which synchronize the feeling of movement with a series of images projected onto a view screen in front of them. A 4-minute flight through space takes visitors to the moon of Endor, via a meteor storm and the Death Star. Lucas film 'droids', R2-D2 and C-3PO, welcome guests to this rollercoaster ride that, physically, goes nowhere, and a crazy robot pilot, RX-24 (Rex), is the host as incredible effects footage by

Industrial Light and Magic is transferred to the screen by a sophisticated audio/video system to greatly enhance this tremendous 70mm entertainment.

TIN MEN (F) Director Barry Levinson. Richard Dreyfuss and Danny DeVito team up in a comedy for Touchstone Pictures. Set in Baltimore in 1963, the story revolves around two aluminium-siding salesmen, Tilly (DeVito) and BB (Dreyfuss). When they're not hoodwinking the gullible public into buying yards of shiny weatherproof metal for their house exteriors, the two find time to feud over what had begun as a trivial automobile accident. In the style of all Touchstone productions, the film sets out to shock its audience with hard-hitting black comedy. In one sequence, for example, BB sleeps with Tilly's wife Nora (Barbara Hershey) purely as a means of getting revenge against his adversary. The mood of the time is brilliantly captured, however, by Levinson's script and Peter Sova's photography. John Mahoney, Jackie Gayle and Stanley Brook co-star in this above-average comedy.

ERNEST GOES TO CAMP (F) Director John R. Cherry III. Actor Jim Varney, who portrays know-all Ernest P. Worrell in countless American tv advertisements, makes his feature film debut in this Touchstone comedy. Filmed in Nashville, Tennessee, the movie tells how Ernest wreaks havoc as the handyman at a boy's summer camp, and its screenplay by Cherry and Coke Sams, successfully exploits Ernest's zany slapstick humour. Unlike the comedian's popular, but brief, television appearances, the film proved too long for most audiences.

BENJI THE HUNTED (F) Director Joe Camp. Made by Mulberry Square Productions, the film, a highly successful sequel to *Benji*, was picked up by Buena Vista and Walt Disney Pictures for a US theatrical release. Shipwrecked after a storm, Benji, who reacts with human intelligence, leads some orphaned cougars to safety in this tale of animal endurance. Among the human cast are Red Steagall, Nancy and Mike Francis, and Frank Inn.

ADVENTURES IN BABYSITTING (F) Director Chris Columbus. Written by David Simkins, this Touchstone comedy stars Elizabeth Shue as a 17-year-old suburban babysitter who, accompanied by co-stars Keith Coogan and Maia Brewton, is chased across downtown Chicago by some very unsavoury characters including gangsters and thieves. Fraternity boys and blues musicians also appear in this film, which, although not a runaway success at the box-office, more than makes up for a dull storyline with some sharp humour.

STAKEOUT (F) Director John Badham. Richard Dreyfuss, appearing in his third Touchstone picture, stars alongside Emilio Estevez. Together they play inept Seattle policemen who are assigned to staking out the house occupied by a psychopathic killer's girlfriend (Madeleine Stowe). The film's R (restricted) rating means that, true to the Touchstone formula, the story contains a heady mixture of soft sex and bad language, trademarks for The Walt Disney Company in the 1980s, it seems. However, Badham paces the storyline well from a screenplay by Jim Kouf, and the film has provided a healthy return at the US box-office.

SELECT
BIBLIOGRAPHY

Books

Bailey, Adrian, *Walt Disney's World of Fantasy*, Everest House, New York/Paper Tiger, London, 1982

Bain, David and Harris, Bruce, *Mickey Mouse: Fifty Happy Years*, Harmony Books, New York/New English Library, London, 1977

Barks, Carl, *Walt Disney – Donald Duck 'Best Comics'* (Introduction), Abbeville Press Inc, New York, 1978

Barrier, Mike, *Building a Better Mouse*, Library of Congress, Washington, 1978

Beard, Richard R., *Walt Disney's EPCOT*, Harry N. Abrams Inc, New York, 1982

Behlmer, Rudy, 'They Called it "Disney's Folly"' in *America's Favorite Movies: Behind the Scenes*, Frederick Ungar, New York, 1982

Blitz, Marcia, *Donald Duck*, Harmony Books, New York/New English Library, London, 1980

Bowles, Jerry, *Forever Hold Your Banner High: The Story of the Mickey Mouse Club and What Happened to the Mouseketeers*, Doubleday & Co Inc, New York, 1976

Brosnan, John, *Movie Magic: The Story of Special Effects in the Cinema*, McDonald & Janes, London, 1974

Canemaker, John, *Treasures of Disney Animation Art* (Introduction), Abbeville Press, New York, 1982

Charlot, Jean, *Art from the Mayans to Disney*, Sheed & Ward, New York/London, 1939

Culhane, John, *Walt Disney's 'Fantasia'*, Harry N. Abrams Inc, New York, 1983

Culhane, Shamus, *Talking Animals and Other People*, St Martin's Press, New York, 1986

Disney, Walt, 'Mickey Mouse Presents' in *We Make the Movies* (ed Nancy Naumberg), Norton, New York, 1937

Eisenstein, Sergei, 'On Disney' in *Walt Disney*, La Biennale di Venezia, Italy, 1985

Eyles, Allen, *Walt Disney's 'Three Little Pigs'* (Afterword), Simon & Schuster, New York/Collins, London, 1987

Feild, Robert Durant, *The Art of Walt Disney*, Macmillan, New York, 1942; Collins, London 1944

Finch, Christopher, *The Art of Walt Disney: From Mickey Mouse to the Magic Kingdoms* with a special essay by Peter Blake, Harry N. Abrams Inc, New York 1973

——, ——, *Walt Disney's America*, Abbeville Press Inc, New York, 1978

Fleming, Alice, *The Movie Makers: A History of American Movies Through the Lives of 10 Great Directors*, St Martin's Press, New York, 1973

Foster, Alan Dean, *Walt Disney - Animated Features and Silly Symphonies 'Best Comics'* (Introduction), Abbeville Press Inc, New York, 1980

Geis, Darlene (ed), *Walt Disney's Treasury of Children's Classics*, Harry N. Abrams Inc, New York, 1978; Hamlyn Books, Feltham, 1979

Goldstein, Fred and Goldstein, Stan, *Prime-Time Television: A Pictorial History from Milton Berle to FALCON CREST*, Crown Publications Inc, New York, 1983

Goldstein, Ruth and Zornow, Edith, *Movies for Kids*, Frederick Ungar, New York, 1973 (revised edition 1980)

Gottfredson, Floyd, *Walt Disney - Mickey Mouse 'Best Comics'* (Introduction), Abbeville Press, New York, 1978

Haden-Guest, Anthony, *Down the Programmed Rabbit-Hole: Travels through Muzak, Hilton, Coca-Cola, Walt Disney and other World Empires*, Hart-Davis MacGibbon, London, 1972; William Morrow & Co, New York (as *The Paradise Program*), 1973

Halas, John and Manvell, Roger, *The Technique of Film Animation*, Focal Press, London, 1968

Harman, Kenny, *Comic Strip Toys*, Wallace-Homestead Book Co, Iowa, 1975

Heide, Robert and Gilman, John, *Cartoon Collectibles: 50 Years of Dime Store Memorabilia*, Doubleday & Co Inc, New York, 1983

Hillier, Bevis, *Walt Disney's Mickey Mouse Memorabilia* (Introduction), Harry N. Abrams, New York/Octopus Books, London, 1986

Holliss, Richard and Sibley, Brian, *Walt Disney's Mickey Mouse: His Life and Times*, Harper & Row, New York/Fleetway Books, London, 1986

——, ——, and ——, ——, *Walt Disney's 'Snow White and the Seven Dwarfs' and the Making of the Classic Film*, Simon & Schuster, New York/André Deutsch, London, 1987

Jacobs, Lewis, *The Rise of the American Film: A Critical History*, Harcourt, Brace & Co, New York, 1939 (revised 1948 and 1967); reprinted by Teachers College Press, Columbia, 1968

Jones, Tom, *Walt Disney's Christmas Treasury* (Introduction), Abbeville Press, New York, 1978

Keller, Keith (compiler), *The Mickey Mouse Club Scrapbook*, Grosset & Dunlap, New York, 1975

Koehler, William R., *Wonderful World of Disney Animals*, Howell Book House, New York, 1979

Leebron, Elizabeth and Gartley, Lynn, *Walt Disney: A Guide to References and Resources*, G. K. Hall & Co, Boston, 1979

Le Farge, 'Walt Disney and the Art Form' in *Theater Arts Anthology* (ed Rosamond Gilder), Theater Arts Books/Robert M. MacGregor, New York, 1950

Lejeune, C. A., *Cinema*, Alexander Maclehose, London, 1931

Lenberg, Jeff, *Encyclopedia of Animated Cartoon Series*, Arlington House, New York, 1981

McVay, Douglas, *The Film Musical*, Zwemmer, London, 1967

Maltin, Leonard, *The Disney Films*, Crown, New York/Thomas Nelson, London, 1973 (revised edition 1985)

——, ——, *Of Mice and Magic: A History of American Animated Cartoons*, New American Library, New York/London, 1980

Miller, Diane Disney (as told to Pete Martin), *The Story of Walt Disney*, Holt, New York, 1957; Odhams, London (as *Walt Disney*), 1958

Montgomery, John, *Comedy Films 1894–1954*, George Allen & Unwin, London, 1954 (revised edition 1968)

Munsey, Cecil, *Disneyana: Walt Disney Collectibles*, Hawthorn Books Inc, New York, 1974

O'Brien, Flora, *Walt Disney's Donald Duck: 50 Years of Happy Frustration*, HP Books, Tucson, Arizona/Three Duck Editions, London, 1984

——, ——, *Walt Disney's Goofy: The Good Sport* HP Books, Tucson, Arizona/Ebury Press, London, 1985

Peary, Gerald and Peary, Danny, *The American Animated Cartoon*, E.P. Dutton, New York, 1980

Perine, Robert, *Chouinard: An Art Vision Betrayed*, Artra Publishing Inc, Encinitas, 1985

Platt, Rutherford, *Walt Disney's Worlds of Nature*, Simon & Schuster, New York/Purnell, London, 1957

Powell, Dilys, 'Disney Profiles' in *The Saturday Book*, Hutchinson, London, 1943

Rotha, Paul and Griffiths, Richard, *The Film Till Now*, Vision Mayflower, New York, 1949

Schickel, Richard, *The Disney Version: The Life, Times, Art and Commerce of Walt Disney*, Simon & Schuster, New York/Weidenfeld & Nicolson, London (as *Walt Disney*), 1968; revised edition Simon & Schuster, New York/Pavilion Books, London, 1986

Schroeder, Horst, *Walt Disney – Goofy 'Best Comics'* (Introduction), Abbeville Press Inc, New York, 1979

Shale, Richard, *Donald Duck Joins Up – The Walt Disney Studio During World War II*, UMI Research Press, Michigan, 1982

Sibley, Brian, 'The Enchanted Realms of Walt Disney' in *Movies of the Forties* (ed Ann Lloyd and David Robinson), Orbis, London, 1982

——, ——, *Alice's Adventures in Wonderland* by Lewis Carroll with David

Hall's previously unpublished illustrations for Walt Disney Productions (Afterword) Simon & Schuster, New York, /Methuen, London, 1986

Sklar, Martin A., *Walt Disney's Disneyland*, Walt Disney Productions, 1964

Solomon, Jack (ed), *Walt Disney's 'Snow White and the Seven Dwarfs'* (Postscript Steve Hulett), Circle Fine Art Press, New York, 1978

Stephenson, Ralph, *Animation in the Cinema*, Zwemmer, London, 1967

Taylor, Deems, *Walt Disney's 'Fantasia'* (Foreword by Leopold Stokowski), Simon & Schuster, New York, 1940

Taylor, John, *Storming the Magic Kingdom: Wall Street, the Raiders, and the Battle for Disney*, Alfred Knopf, New York, 1987

Thomas, Bob, *The Art of Animation: The Story of the Disney Studio Contribution to a New Art* (with research by Don Graham), Golden Press, New York, 1958

———, ———, *Walt Disney: An American Original*, Simon & Schuster, New York, 1976; New English Library, London (as *The Walt Disney Biography*), 1977

Thomas, Frank and Johnston, Ollie, *Disney Animation: The Illusion of Life*, Abbeville Press Inc, New York, 1981

Thompson, Don and Lupoff, Dick, *The Comic-Book Book*, Arlington House, New York, 1973

Tumbusch, Tom, *Tomart's Illustrated Disneyana Catalog and Price Guide* (3 vols), Tomart Publications, Dayton, Ohio, 1975

Wicking, Christopher and Vahimagi, Tise, *The American Vein: Directors and Directions in Television*, Talisman Books, London, 1979

Wiley, Mason and Bona, Damien, *Inside Oscar: The Unofficial History of the Academy Awards* (ed Gail MacColl), Columbus Books, New York, 1986

Willis, Donald (ed), *Variety's Complete Science Fiction Reviews*, Garland Publishing Inc, New York/London, 1985

Woolery, George W., *Children's Television: The First Thirty-Five Years 1946–1981 Part II Live, Film and Tape Series*, The Scarecrow Press, New York/London, 1985

Zanotto, Piero, *Walt Disney – Uncle Scrooge 'Best Comics'* (Introduction), (Foreword Carl Barks), Abbeville Press, New York, 1979

Newspaper and Magazine Articles

(Unless otherwise indicated, all publications are American)

Adamson, Joe, 'Crabquacks', *Take One*, January 1978

Allan, Robin, 'Alice in Disneyland', *Sight & Sound* (UK), Spring 1985

———, ———, 'Make Mine Disney', *Animator* (UK), April-June 1987

———, ———, 'The Fairest Film of All: *Snow White* Reassessed', *Animator* (UK), October/December 1987

Alpert, Hollis, 'The Wonderful World of Walt Disney', *Woman's Day*, October 1962

Andrae, Tom, 'Floyd Gottfredson: The Mouse's Other Master', *Nemo*, April 1984

———, ———, 'Animation Vs. Comic Book Creation in Barks' Work', *Nemo*, June 1984

Apple, Max, 'Uncle Walt' (part of 'A Celebration of Fifty American Originals'), *Esquire*, December 1983

Babbitt, Art and Williams, Richard, 'Goofy and Babbitt', *Sight & Sound* (UK), Spring 1974

Barrier, Mike, 'Father to the Man', *Funnyworld*, 11, 1969

———, ———, 'Screenwriter for a Duck: Carl Barks at the Disney Studio', *Funnyworld*, 21, Fall 1979

———, ———, 'Starting Out in the Comics: Carl Barks becomes "The Duck Man"', *Funnyworld*, 22, 1980

Barrier, Mike and Gray, Milton, 'An Interview with Carl Stalling', *Funnyworld*, 13, Spring 1971

Barks, Carl and Gottfredson, Floyd, 'Two Disney Legends Share Their Memories', *Nemo*, June 1984

Bart, Peter and Bart, Dorothy, 'As Told and Sold by Disney', *The New York Times Book Review*, 9 May 1965

Bates, David, 'Triumph of a Dreamsmith (Walt Disney's *Fantasia*)' *The Rocket's Blast Comicollector*, September 1979

Benson, John, 'Mickey Mouse', *Funnyworld*, 11, 1969

Birmingham, Stephen, 'Once Upon a Time in the Magic Land of Hollywood there lived the Greatest One-Man Show on Earth', *McCall's*, July 1964

Blake, Peter, 'Mickey Mouse for Mayor', *New York*, 7 February 1972

———, ———, 'Walt Disney World', *The Architectural Forum*, June 1972

Blyth, H.E., 'Small Town Man: Walt Disney's Rise to Fame', *World Film News*, July 1938

Boone, Andrew R., 'When Mickey Mouse Speaks', *Scientific American*, March 1983

Borsock, William, 'What Can You Learn from Disney's Work?', *SM/Sales Meetings Magazine*, July 1969

Bradbury, Ray, 'The Machine-Tooled Happy-land', *Holiday*, October 1965

———, ———, 'The Man With the Mickey Mouse Obsession', *The Observer Magazine* (UK), 13 January 1980

Bragdon, Claude, 'Mickey Mouse and What He Means', *Scribner's Magazine*, July 1934

Bright, John, 'Disney's Fantasy Empire', *The Nation*, 6 March 1967

Brittain, Juliet, 'Walt Disney: business man and magic maker', *Time and Tide* (UK), 26 November 1964

Brody, Howard T., 'Building the Greatest Dream', *Starlog*, August 1982

Business Week, 'Disney's live action profits', 24 July 1965

———, 'Riding the coat-tails of Mickey Mouse', 11 September 1971

———, 'Disney's Magic', 9 March 1987

Butcher, Harold, 'An International Mouse', *The New York Times*, 28 October 1934

Canemaker, John, 'Sincerely Yours . . . Frank Thomas', *Storyboard*, January 1975

———, ———, 'Grim Natwick', *Film Comment*, January/February 1975

Care, Ross, 'Cinesymphony: Music and Animation at the Disney Studio 1928–42' *Sight & Sound* (UK), Winter 1976–77

———, ———, 'Symphonists for the Sillies: The Composers for Disney's Shorts', *Funnyworld*, 18, Summer 1978

Caselotti, Adriana, 'Snow White Speaks', *People Weekly*, 18 May 1987

Chamberlain, Michael, 'How the World of Disney is Building for the Future', *Marketing Week* (UK), 11 December 1981

Charlot, Jean, 'But is it Art? A Disney Disquistion', *The American Scholar*, Summer 1939

Churchill, Douglas W., 'Now Mickey Mouse Enters Art's Temple', *The New York Times Magazine*, 3 June 1934

———, ———, 'Disney's Philosophy', *The New York Times Magazine*, 6 March 1938

Collier, Richard, 'Wish Upon a Star: The Magical Kingdoms of Walt Disney', *Reader's Digest*, October 1971

Crowther, Bosley, 'The Dream Merchant', *The New York Times*, 16 December 1966

Culhane, John, 'The Last of the "Nine Old Men"', *American Film*, June 1977

———, ———, 'A Mouse for All Seasons', *Saturday Review*, 11 November 1978

———, ———, 'The Remarkable Visions of Peter Ellenshaw', *American Film*, September 1979

Curtis, John Parke, 'Oasis in Burbank', *Antiquarian Book Monthly Review* (UK), December 1979

Davidson, Bill, 'The Fantastic Walt Disney', *Saturday Evening Post*, 7 November 1964

Davis, Douglas, 'The World that Disney Built', *Newsweek*, 15 October 1973

Decker, Dwight R., 'Carl Barks: The Good Duck Artist', *The Comic's Journal*, July 1982

Delehanty, Thornton, 'Disney Studio at War', *Theatre Arts* (UK), January 1943

De Roos, Robert, 'The Magic Worlds of Walt Disney', *National Geographic*, August 1963

Derrick, Norman, 'The Train Standing in Your Hotel is for "Magic Kingdom"', *Daily Telegraph* (UK), 6 November 1971

Disney, Lillian (as told to Isabella Taves), 'I Live With a Genius', *McCall's*, February 1953

Disney, Roy, 'My Unforgettable Brother', *The Reader's Digest*, March 1969

Disney, Walt, 'Mickey Mouse: How He Was Born', *Windsor* (UK), October 1931

———, ———, 'The Cartoon's Contribution to Children', *Overland Monthly*, October 1933

———, ———, 'The Life Story of Mickey Mouse', *Windsor* (UK), January 1934

———, ———, 'The Inside Story of the Filming of *Pinocchio*', *The News of the World* (UK), 17 March 1940

———, ———, 'The Years Before I Met Mickey Mouse', *The News of the World* (UK), 24 March 1940

———, ———, 'I Dreamt of Stardom and Got "The Hook" Instead', *The News of the World* (UK), 31 March 1940

———, ———, 'Mickey was a Real Mouse in the Long Ago', *The News of the World* (UK), 7 April 1940

———, ———, 'How We Made Mickey "OK for Sound"', *The News of the World* (UK), 14 April 1940

———, ———, 'Mickey as Professor', *Public Opinion Quarterly*, Summer 1945

———, ———, 'What Mickey Means to Me', *Who's Who in Hollywood*, 1948

———, ———, 'There's Always a Solution', *Guideposts*, June 1949

Dougherty, Margot, 'The Lost Snow White', *Life*, April 1987

The Economist (UK), 'Mickey Mouse is 50', 7 July 1973

Eglin, Roger, 'Disney's Magic Money Machine', *Observer* (UK), 10 October 1971

Ehrlich, Henry, 'What Hath Disney Wrought?', *Look*, 6 April 1971

Eisen, A., 'Two Disney Artists' [John Hench and Marc Davis], *Crimmer's: The Harvard Journal of Pictorial Fiction*, Winter 1975

English, Horace B., '*Fantasia* and the Psychology of Music', *Journal of Aesthetics and Art Criticism*, Winter 1942

Ericsson, Peter, 'Walt Disney', *Sequence Film Quarterly*, 10 (UK), New Year 1950

Feaver, William, 'Disney's Dreams Come to Life', *The Observer Magazine* (UK), 19 December 1976

Fidler, James M., 'A Mouse in a Million', *Screenland*, February 1935

Film Dope (UK), 'Walt Disney' (Postscript by Richard Williams), June 1977

Finch, Christopher, 'Walt Disney: Master of Moving Pictures', *The Walt Disney Fiftieth Anniversary Film Retrospective Program*, Lincoln Center, July-August 1973

Fisher, David, 'Disney and UPA', *Sight & Sound* (UK), July-September 1953

Fishwick, Marshall, 'Aesop in Hollywood', *The Saturday Review*, 10 July 1954

Forbes, 'Disney Without Walt', 1 July 1967

——, 'Disney Dollars', 1 May 1971

——, 'Yes, Virginia, there is a Walt Disney', 15 February 1974

Forster, E.M., 'Mickey and Minnie', *The Spectator* (UK), 19 January 1934

Fortune, 'The Big, Bad Wolf . . . and why it may never huff nor puff again at Walt Disney's door', November 1934

Foster, Frederick, 'Walt Disney's Naturalist Cinematographers', *American Cinematographer*, February 1954

Frazier, Joe and Hathorne, Harry, '*20,000 Leagues Under the Sea*: The Filming of Jules Verne's Science Fiction Novel', *Cinefantastique*, May 1984

Friendly, David T., 'Team Disney – Flying High in Burbank', *Los Angeles Times Calendar*, 28 July 1985

Gabor, Andrea and Hawkins, Steve L., 'Of Mice and Money in The Magic Kingdom', *US News and World Report*, 22 December 1986

Garity, William E., 'The Production of Animated Cartoons', *Journal of the Society of Motion Picture Engineers*, April 1933

Garity, William E. and Ledeen, J. L., 'The New Walt Disney Studio', *Journal of the Society of Motion Picture Engineers*, January 1941

Gilbert, Nick, 'Fat Cat Chasing Mickey Mouse', *Sunday Times* (UK), 3 June 1984

Goldberger, Paul, 'Mickey Mouse Teaches the Architects', *The New York Times Magazine*, 22 October 1972

Gordon, Arthur, 'Walt Disney', *Look*, 26 July 1955

Gordon, Bruce and Mumford, David, 'Tomorrowland 1986: The Comet Returns', *Starlog*, September 1985

——, ——, 'Tomorrowland 1986: Yesterday's Futures' *Starlog*, October 1985

Gordon, Bruce, Mumford, David and Tietz, Chris, 'Star Wars: The Disneyland Journey', *Starlog*, May 1987

Grosvenor, Melville Bell, 'Walt Disney: Genius of Laughter and Learning', *National Geographic*, August 1963

Haden-Guest, Anthony, 'An Instant Promised Land', *Daily Telegraph Magazine*, 18 April 1973

Halevy, Julian, 'Disneyland and Las Vegas . . .', *The Nation*, 7 June 1958

Hamilton, Sara, 'The Dramatic Life and Death of Dopey', *Movie Mirror*, May 1938

Hanson, Steve, 'The Mouse that Roared', *Stills* (UK), 13 October 1984

Harmetz, Aljean, 'The Man Reanimating Disney', *The New York Times Magazine*, 29 December 1985

Hayes, Thomas C., 'Trouble Stalks the Magic Kingdom', *The New York Times*, 17 June 1984

Hinxman, Margaret, 'Cinderella Man', *Picturegoer* (UK), 24 June 1950

——, ——, 'Mickey's Brave New World', *Sunday Telegraph* (UK), 7 November 1971

Holliday, Kate, 'Donald Duck Goes to War', *Coronet*, September 1942

Holliss, Richard, 'Starburst Fantasy Classic: *Fantasia*', *Starburst* (UK), 26, 1980

——, ——, 'Starburst Fantasy Classic: *Snow White and the Seven Dwarfs*', *Starburst* (UK), 33, 1981

——, ——, *Sleeping Beauty*, *Starburst* (UK), November 1981

——, ——, 'Interview with Wolfgang Reitherman', *Starburst* (UK), February 1982

——, ——, 'The Walt Disney Story', *Starburst* (UK), December 1983

——, ——, 'The New Worlds of Disney', *Starburst* (UK), October 1986

——, ——, 'Behind the Magic Mirror', *Animator* (UK), July/September 1987

Hollister, Paul, 'Walt Disney: Genius at Work', *Atlantic*, December 1940

Houston, David, 'A Black Hole at the Crossroads', *Starlog*, February 1980

Huemer, Dick, 'Huemeresque: Thumbnail Sketches', *Funnyworld*, 21, Fall 1979

——, ——, 'Huemeresque: The Battle of Washington', *Funnyworld*, 22, 1980

Hutchinson, David, 'Undersea with Harper Goff', *Starlog*, February 1980

Isaacs, Hermine Rich, 'New Horizons: *Fantasia* and Fantasound', *Theatre Arts* (UK), January 1941

Iwerks, Ub, 'Movie Cartoons Come to Life', *Popular Mechanics*, January 1942

Johnston, Alva, 'Mickey Mouse', *Woman's Home Companion*, July 1934

Kimball, Ward, 'Cartooning in Cinemascope', *Films in Review*, March 1954

——, ——, 'Disney Animator – Ward Kimball', *The Illustrator*, Winter 1977

Kinney, Jack, 'Bambi and the Goof', *Funnyworld*, 21, Fall 1979

Klein, I., 'Some Close-Up Shots of Walt Disney During the "Golden Years"', *Funnyworld*, 23, Spring 1983

Knight, Frances J., 'Disney Joins In', *Chamber's Journal* (UK), April 1944

Kozlenko, William, 'The Animated Cartoon and Walt Disney', *New Theater*, August 1936

Landau, Roy, 'Mickey Mouse The Great Dictator (The Disney game as a control system)', *Architectural Design* (UK), September 1973

Lee, Rohama, 'Mickey is the Symbol', *Film News*, 8, 1953

Life, 'A Silver Anniversary for Walt and Mickey', 2 November 1953

——, 'Mickey Opens in Florida – Disney Moves East', 15 October 1971

Lofficer, Randy and Lofficer Jean-Marc, 'Ringmaster to a Dark Carnival: Jack Clayton directing *Something Wicked This Way Comes*', *Starlog*, June 1983

Look, 'Walt Disney: Teacher of Tomorrow', 17 April 1945

——, 'Florida: Boom! Boom! Boom?', 6 April 1971

Low, David, 'Leonardo da Disney', *The New Republic*, 5 January 1942

Lowry, Brian, 'Animating *The Black Cauldron*', *Starlog*, August 1985

McDonald, John, 'Now the Bankers Come to Disney', *Fortune*, May 1966

McDonald, George, 'The Mickey Mouse Legacy', *International Management*, July 1970

McEvoy, J. P., 'McEvoy in Disneyland', *The Readers' Digest*, February 1955

Mann, Arthur, 'Mickey Mouse's Financial Career', *Harper's*, May 1934

Maltin, Leonard, 'Walt Disney Films', *Film Fan Monthly*, February 1967

——, ——, 'Walt Disney's Films Constitute the Most Creative Body of Work of any Producer to Date', *Films in Review*, October 1967

Marsh, Peter, 'Science Meets Mickey Mouse', *New Scientist* (UK), 18 March 1982

Mayersberg, Paul, 'The American Nightmare', *New Society* (UK), 11 April 1968

Menan, Aubrey, 'Dazzled in Disneyland', *Holiday*, July 1963

Mills, Bart, 'Disney Looks for a Happy Ending to its Grim Fairy Tale', *American Film*, July-August 1982

Mooring, W. H., 'The Daring of Disney', *Picturegoer* (UK), 31 August 1946

——, ——, 'Disney in Wonderland', *Picturegoer* (UK), 24 June 1950

Morgenstern, Joseph, 'Walt Disney (1901–1966): Imagineer of Fun', *Newsweek*, 26 December 1966

——, ——, 'What Hath Disney Wrought!', *Newsweek*, 18 October 1971

Motion Picture Herald, 'The Disney Story: From Mickey Mouse to Buena Vista', 20 November 1954

Munson, Brad, '*Something Wicked This Way Comes*: Adding the Magic', *Cinefex*, April 1983

——, ——, '*Return to Oz*', *Cinefex*, June 1985

Murray, Douglas, 'The Science Fiction World of Walt Disney', *Space Wars*, December 1978

Nater, Carl, 'Walt Disney – as I know him . . .', *Film News*, 8, 1953

Newsweek, 'A Wonderful World: Growing Impact of the Disney Art', 18 April 1955

——, 'The Wide World of Walt Disney', 31 December 1962

——, 'Tinker Bell, Mary Poppins, Cold Cash', 12 July 1965

Nugent, Frank S., 'Disney is now Art – but he Wonders', *The New York Times Magazine*, 26 February 1939

Parker, S. R., 'Make-Believe World', *New Society* (UK), 8 April 1971

Peck, A. P., 'What Makes *Fantasia* Click', *Scientific American*, January 1941

Peri, Don, 'Roy Williams – An Interview', *Funnyworld*, 17, Fall 1977

Popular Science Monthly, 'How Disney Combines Living Actors with his Cartoon Characters', September 1944

Potter, William E., 'Walt Disney World: A Venture in Community Planning and Development', *ASHRAE Journal*, March 1972

Powell, Dilys, 'Walt Disney', *Sunday Times* (UK), 18 December 1966

Prizer, Edward L., 'Inside EPCOT', *Orlando-Land Magazine*, June 1980

Rafferty, Max, 'The Greatest Pedagogue of All', *Los Angeles Times*, 18 April 1967

Reddy, John, 'The Living Legacy of Walt Disney', *The Reader's Digest*, June 1967

——, ——, 'Roll Up for Disney World!', *The Reader's Digest*, January 1974

Robinson, David, 'The Beginning of Disney's Wonderful World' *The Movie* (UK), 15, 1980

Robley, Les Paul, 'Computer Graphics Aid Animation Rebirth', *American Cinematographer*, October 1986

Rogers, Peter, 'Money-spinning monument to the American Dream', *Guardian* (UK), 12 October 1972

Rosenbaum, Jonathan, 'Walt Disney', *Film Comment*, January-February 1975

Russell, Herbert, 'L'affaire Mickey Mouse', *The New York Times Magazine*, 26 December 1937

Santora, Phil, 'Disney: Modern Merlin', *Daily News*, 29 and 30 September, 1 and 2 October 1964

Sayers, Frances Clarke and Weisenberg, Charles M., 'Walt Disney Accused', *The Horn Book Magazine*, December 1965

Schickel, Richard, 'Bringing Forth the Mouse', *American Heritage*, April 1968

Scobie, William, 'Disney's Magic Kingdom Under Seige', *Observer* (UK), 8 April 1984

Screen Ads Monthly, 'Screen Ads Tribute to Walt Disney', December 1967

Seldes, Gilbert, 'Mickey Mouse Maker', *The New Yorker*, 19 December 1931

——, ——, Disney and Others', *The New Republic*, 8 June 1932

——, ——, 'No Art Mr Disney?', *Esquire*, September 1937

Sibley, Brian, 'A Californian Yankee at the Court of Queen Alice', *Jabberwocky: The Journal of the Lewis Carroll Society* (UK), Summer 1973

——, ——, 'Disney's World', *Third Way* (UK), November 1985

——, ——, 'Reitherman Remembered', *Animator* (UK), Autumn/Winter 1985/6

——, ——, 'Disneyland: The Greatest Walk-Thru Cartoon Ever Drawn', *Animator* (UK), Spring 1986

——, ——, 'Walt Disney's *Pinocchio*: Animation Master Work', *Animator* (UK), Summer 1986

——, ——, 'Disney's Fabulous Folly', *Animator* (UK), July/September 1987

——, ——, 'With a Smile and a Song', *Animator* (UK), October/December 1987

Sight & Sound, 'Walt Disney and Mickey Mouse', Summer 1935

Smith, David R., 'It all Started with a Mouse: The Walt Disney Archives', *California Librarian*, January 1972

——, ——, 'Ub Iwerks, 1901–1971', *Funnyworld*, 14, Spring 1972

——, ——, 'Ben Sharpsteen … 33 Years with Disney', *Millimeter*, April 1975

——, ——, 'The Sorcerer's Apprentice: Birthplace of *Fantasia*', *Millimeter*, February 1976

——, ——, 'They're Following Our Script: Walt Disney's Trip to Tomorrowland', *Future*, May 1978

——, ——, 'Walt Disney's Conquest of Space', *Starlog*, 13 May 1978

——, ——, 'Up to Date in Kansas City', *Funnyworld*, 19, Fall 1978

——, ——, 'Disney Before Burbank: The Kingswell and Hyperion Studios', *Funnyworld*, 20, Summer 1979

——, ——, 'Donald Duck: This is Your Life', *Starlog*, July 1981

——, ——, 'Fifty Years of Mickey Mouse Time', *Starlog*, January 1984

Sorensen, Peter, 'Tronic Imagery', *Cinefex*, April 1982

Stuart, Alexander, 'Decay of an American Dream', *Films and Filming* (UK), November 1973

Summer, Edward, 'Of Ducks and Men', *Panels*, Spring 1981

——, ——, 'Walt Disney's *Pinocchio*: An Appreciation', *Starlog*, January 1985

Sunday Times (UK), 'Mickey Mouse to Rob Roy', 25 October 1953

Theisen, Earl, 'Sound Tricks of Mickey Mouse', *Modern Mechanix*, January 1937

Tibbets, John, 'Of Mouse and Man', *American Classic Screen*, May-June 1978

Time, 'Mouse and Man', 27 December 1937

——, 'Father Goose', 27 December 1954

——, 'Walt Disney: Images of Innocence', 23 December 1966

——, 'Disney World: Pixie Dust Over Florida', 18 October 1971

Today's Cinema, 'The Versatile Genius Walt Disney', 27 October 1953

Tucker, Nicholas, 'Who's Afraid of Walt Disney?', *New Society* (UK), 4 April 1968

Vauncez, Sidney, 'Alice Through the Disney-glass', *Picturing Today* (UK), August-September 1951

Wallace, Irving, 'Mickey Mouse and How He Grew', *Collier's*, 9 April 1949

Wallace, Kevin, 'Onward and Upward with the Arts: The Engineering of Ease', *The New Yorker*, 7 September 1963

The Wall Street Journal, 'Disney's Land: dream, diversify – and never miss an angle', 4 February 1958

Wansell, Geoffrey, 'Fifty Years of Mice and Men', *The Times* (UK), 10 March 1973

Whicker, Alan, 'The House the Mouse Built', *Punch* (UK), 21 July 1971

Whitaker, Frederick, 'A Day with Disney', *American Artist*, September 1965

Williams, Richard, 'The Disney Legend', *The Movie* (UK), 15, 1980

Wilson, S.S., '*Dragonslayer*', *Cinefex*, October 1981

Wolfert, Ira, 'Walt Disney's Magic Kingdom', *The Reader's Digest*, April 1960

Wolters, Larry, 'The Wonderful World of Walt Disney', *Today's Health*, April 1962

Zimmerman, Gereon, 'Walt Disney: Giant at the Fair', *Look*, 11 February 1964

Zinser, William, 'Walt Disney's Secret Freakout', *Life*, 27 April 1970

Zolotow, Maurice, 'Happy Birthday, Donald Duck', *The Reader's Digest*, June 1984

In addition to these and many other books and periodicals, the authors have referred to the Annual Reports of Walt Disney Productions/The Walt Disney Company 1940–86 and various other company documents, as well as the following publicity and staff publications: *The Disney World, Disney News, The Disney Channel Magazine, Walt Disney World Vacationland, Castle View, Disney Newsreel, Disneyland Line* and *Walt Disney World Eyes and Ears*.

INDEX OF DISNEY FILM TITLES

X

Y

Z

ACKNOWLEDGEMENTS

This book could not have been written without the very considerable help of many individuals who, over several years of research, have shared their knowledge, opinions and memories and to whom the authors express their grateful thanks. Present and former employees of The Walt Disney Company, authors, performers, critics and independent observers, some now deceased, they are (in alphabetical order):

Bill Anderson, Art Babbitt, Felix Barker, Tony Baxter, Don Bluth, Wally Boag, Ray Bradbury, Randy Bright, Pat Buttram, Candy Candido, Adriana Caselotti, Bill Cottrell, John Culhane, Jack and Camille Cutting, Roald Dahl, Marc and Alice Davis, Roy E. Disney, Norm Doerges, John Dreyer, Peter Ellenshaw, Morgan Evans, John Halas, John Hench, Margaret Hinxman, Dick Huemer, Bill Justice, Ward and Betty Kimball, Jack Kinney, Irwin Kostal, Jack Lindquist, Fred MacMurray, Leonard Maltin, Bill Martin, Junius C. Matthews, Bob Mervine, Hayley Mills, Clarence Nash, Grim Natwick, Mary Norton, Dick Nunis, Dilys Powell, Wolfgang Reitherman, Betsy Richman, Charles Ridgway, Herbert Ryman, Wallace Sears, Pat Scanlon, Russell Schroeder, Bill Schultz, Charles Schulz, Ben Sharpsteen, Richard M. and Robert B. Sherman, Donald Sinden, Dodie Smith, Andrew Thewlis, Frank Thomas, P. L. Travers, Tom Tumbusch, Barbara U'ren, Don Williams, Richard Williams, Card Walker and Ralph Wright.

Thanks are also due, for providing various research material, to Robin Allan, Ron Aubry, Brian Beacock, Michael Goldstein, Peter Halsey, Muir Hewitt, Philip Jenkinson, Linda Russell, Kathy Smith, Richard Stratford, Graham Webb and the staff of the British Library, and the British Film Institute Library.

A particular debt of gratitude is owing to Walt Disney archivists David R. Smith and Paula Sigman and their colleagues Karen Brower and Rose Motzko for their diligent research assistance and checking of the manuscript; to Keith Bales, Bo Boyd, David Cleghorn, Greg Crosby, Wayne Morris, Wendall Mohler and Bruce Portman for their unstinting support and cooperation; to Joe and Jennie Grant, for their special help and friendship; and, finally, to Christine Holliss and Alex Platt, for their hours of labour at the typewriter.